BIG IDEAS MATH®
Modeling Real Life

Grade 7
Advanced

TEACHING EDITION

Ron Larson
Laurie Boswell

Erie, Pennsylvania
BigIdeasLearning.com

Big Ideas Learning, LLC
1762 Norcross Road
Erie, PA 16510-3838
USA

For product information and customer support, contact Big Ideas Learning at **1-877-552-7766** or visit us at *BigIdeasLearning.com*.

Cover Image:
Valdis Torms, cobalt88/Shutterstock.com

Front Matter:
xxxiii Heyourelax/iStock/Getty Images Plus; **xxxiv** Valengilda/iStock/Getty Images Plus; **xxxv** Juanmonino/E+/Getty Images; **xxxvi** stockcam/iStock/Getty Images Plus; **xxxvii** supergenijalac/iStock/Getty Images Plus; **xxxix** tawan/Shutterstock.com; **xl** uatp2/ iStock/Getty Images Plus; **xli** carlosgaw/E+/Getty Images; **xlii** Georgethefourth/iStock/Getty Images Plus; **xliii** ©iStockphoto.com/ryasick; **xliv** ©iStockphoto.com/Eric Isselée; **xlv** peepo/E+/Getty Images; **xlvi** tropper2000/iStock/Getty Images Plus

Copyright © 2022 by Big Ideas Learning, LLC. All rights reserved.

No part of this work may be reproduced or transmitted in any form or by any means, electronic or mechanical, including, but not limited to, photocopying and recording, or by any information storage or retrieval system, without prior written permission of Big Ideas Learning, LLC, unless such copying is expressly permitted by copyright law. Address inquiries to Permissions, Big Ideas Learning, LLC, 1762 Norcross Road, Erie, PA 16510.

Big Ideas Learning and *Big Ideas Math* are registered trademarks of Larson Texts, Inc.

Printed in Mexico

IBSN 13: 978-1-63708-402-1

Print Number: 04   Print Year: 2022

One Voice from Kindergarten Through Algebra 2

Written by renowned authors, Dr. Ron Larson and Dr. Laurie Boswell, *Big Ideas Math* offers a seamless math pedagogy from elementary through high school. Together, Ron and Laurie provide a consistent voice that encourages students to make connections through cohesive progressions and clear instruction. Since 1992, Ron and Laurie have authored over 50 mathematics programs.

Each time Laurie and I start working on a new program, we spend time putting ourselves in the position of the reader. How old is the reader? What is the reader's experience with mathematics? The answers to these questions become our writing guides. Our goal is to make the learning targets understandable and to develop these targets in a clear path that leads to student success.

— Ron Larson

Ron Larson, Ph.D., is well known as lead author of a comprehensive and widely used mathematics program that ranges from elementary school through college. He holds the distinction of Professor Emeritus from Penn State Erie, The Behrend College, where he taught for nearly 40 years. He received his Ph.D. in mathematics from the University of Colorado. Dr. Larson engages in the latest research and advancements in mathematics education and consistently incorporates key pedagogical elements to ensure focus, coherence, rigor, and student self-reflection.

My passion and goal in writing is to provide an essential resource for exploring and making sense of mathematics. Our program is guided by research around the learning and teaching of mathematics in the hopes of improving the achievement of all students. May this be a successful year for you!

— Laurie Boswell

Laurie Boswell, Ed.D., is the former Head of School at Riverside School in Lyndonville, Vermont. In addition to authoring textbooks, she provides mathematics consulting and embedded coaching sessions. Dr. Boswell received her Ed.D. from the University of Vermont in 2010. She is a recipient of the Presidential Award for Excellence in Mathematics Teaching and later served as president of CPAM. Laurie has taught math to students at all levels, elementary through college. In addition, Laurie has served on the NCTM Board of Directors and as a Regional Director for NCSM. Along with Ron, Laurie has co-authored numerous math programs and has become a popular national speaker.

Contributors, Reviewers

Big Ideas Learning would like to express our gratitude to the mathematics education and instruction experts who served as our advisory panel, contributing specialists, and reviewers during the writing of *Big Ideas Math: Modeling Real Life*. Their input was an invaluable asset during the development of this program.

Contributing Specialists and Reviewers

- **Sophie Murphy**, Ph.D. Candidate, Melbourne School of Education, Melbourne, Australia
  Learning Targets and Success Criteria Specialist and Visible Learning Reviewer

- **Linda Hall**, Mathematics Educational Consultant, Edmond, OK
  Advisory Panel and Teaching Edition Contributor

- **Michael McDowell**, Ed.D., Superintendent, Ross, CA
  Project-Based Learning Specialist

- **Kelly Byrne**, Math Supervisor and Coordinator of Data Analysis, Downingtown, PA
  Advisory Panel and Content Reviewer

- **Jean Carwin**, Math Specialist/TOSA, Snohomish, WA
  Advisory Panel and Content Reviewer

- **Nancy Siddens**, Independent Language Teaching Consultant, Las Cruces, NM
  English Language Learner Specialist

- **Nancy Thiele**, Mathematics Consultant, Mesa, AZ
  Teaching Edition Contributor

- **Kristen Karbon**, Curriculum and Assessment Coordinator, Troy, MI
  Advisory Panel and Content Reviewer

- **Kery Obradovich**, K–8 Math/Science Coordinator, Northbrook, IL
  Advisory Panel and Content Reviewer

- **Jennifer Rollins**, Math Curriculum Content Specialist, Golden, CO
  Advisory Panel

- **Becky Walker**, Ph.D., School Improvement Services Director, Green Bay, WI
  Advisory Panel

- **Anthony Smith**, Ph.D., Associate Professor, Associate Dean, University of Washington Bothell, Seattle, WA
  Reading/Writing Reviewer

- **Nicole Dimich Vagle**, Educator, Author, and Consultant, Hopkins, MN
  Assessment Reviewer

- **Jill Kalb**, Secondary Math Content Specialist, Arvada, CO
  Content Reviewer

- **Janet Graham**, District Math Specialist, Manassas, VA
  Response to Intervention and Differentiated Instruction Reviewer

- **Sharon Huber**, Director of Elementary Mathematics, Chesapeake, VA
  Universal Design for Learning Reviewer

Student Reviewers

- Jackson Currier
- Mason Currier
- Taylor DeLuca
- Ajalae Evans
- Malik Goodwine
- Majesty Hamilton
- Reilly Koch
- Kyla Kramer
- Matthew Lindemuth
- Greer Lippert
- Zane Lippert
- Jeffrey Lobaugh
- Riley Moran
- Zoe Morin
- Deke Patton
- Brooke Smith
- Dylan Throop
- Jenna Urso
- Madison Whitford
- Jenna Wigham

and Research

Research

Ron Larson and Laurie Boswell used the latest in educational research, along with the body of knowledge collected from expert mathematics instructors, to develop the *Modeling Real Life* series. By implementing the work of renowned researchers from across the world, *Big Ideas Math* offers at least a full year's growth within a full year's learning while also encouraging a growth mindset in students and teachers. Students take their learning from surface-level to deep-level, then transfer that learning by modeling real-life situations. For more information on how this program uses learning targets and success criteria to enhance teacher clarity, see pages xiv–xv.

The pedagogical approach used in this program follows the best practices outlined in the most prominent and widely accepted educational research, including:

- *Visible Learning*
  John Hattie © 2009

- *Visible Learning for Teachers*
  John Hattie © 2012

- *Visible Learning for Mathematics*
  John Hattie © 2017

- *Principles to Actions: Ensuring Mathematical Success for All*
  NCTM © 2014

- *Adding It Up: Helping Children Learn Mathematics*
  National Research Council © 2001

- *Mathematical Mindsets: Unleashing Students' Potential through Creative Math, Inspiring Messages and Innovative Teaching*
  Jo Boaler © 2015

- *What Works in Schools: Translating Research into Action*
  Robert Marzano © 2003

- *Classroom Instruction That Works: Research-Based Strategies for Increasing Student Achievement*
  Marzano, Pickering, and Pollock © 2001

- *Principles and Standards for School Mathematics*
  NCTM © 2000

- *Rigorous PBL by Design: Three Shifts for Developing Confident and Competent Learners*
  Michael McDowell © 2017

- *Universal Design for Learning Guidelines*
  CAST © 2011

- *Rigor/Relevance Framework®*
  International Center for Leadership in Education

- *Understanding by Design*
  Grant Wiggins and Jay McTighe © 2005

- Achieve, ACT, and The College Board

- *Elementary and Middle School Mathematics: Teaching Developmentally*
  John A. Van de Walle and Karen S. Karp © 2015

- *Evaluating the Quality of Learning: The SOLO Taxonomy*
  John B. Biggs & Kevin F. Collis © 1982

- *Unlocking Formative Assessment: Practical Strategies for Enhancing Students' Learning in the Primary and Intermediate Classroom*
  Shirley Clarke, Helen Timperley, and John Hattie © 2004

- *Formative Assessment in the Secondary Classroom*
  Shirley Clarke © 2005

- *Improving Student Achievement: A Practical Guide to Assessment for Learning*
  Toni Glasson © 2009

Focus and Coherence from

Instructional Design

A single authorship team from Kindergarten through Algebra 2 results in a logical progression of focused topics with meaningful coherence from course to course.

FOCUS
A focused program reflects the balance in grade-level standards while simultaneously supporting and engaging students to develop conceptual understanding of the major work of the grade.

The **Learning Target** and **Success Criteria** for each section focus the learning into manageable chunks, using clear teaching text and Key Ideas within the Student Edition.

2.1 Multiplying Integers

Learning Target: Find products of integers.
Success Criteria:
- I can explain the rules for multiplying integers.
- I can find products of integers with the same sign.
- I can find products of integers with different signs.

Key Idea

Ratios

Words A **ratio** is a comparison of two quantities. The **value of the ratio** a to b is the number $\frac{a}{b}$, which describes the multiplicative relationship between the quantities in the ratio.

Examples 2 snails *to* 6 fish

$\frac{1}{2}$ cup of milk *for every* $\frac{1}{4}$ cup of cream

Algebra The ratio of a to b can be written as $a : b$.

Laurie's Notes

Laurie's Notes prepare you for the math concepts in each chapter and section and make connections to the threads of major topics for the course.

Chapter 5 Overview

The study of ratios and proportions in this chapter builds upon and connects to prior work with rates and ratios in the previous course. Students should have an understanding of how ratios are represented and how ratio tables are used to find equivalent ratios. Tape diagrams and double number lines were also used to represent and solve problems involving equivalent ratios.

a Single Authorship Team

COHERENCE

A single authorship team built a coherent program that has intentional progression of content within each grade and between grade levels. Your students will build new understanding on foundations from prior grades and connect concepts throughout the course.

The authors developed content that progresses from prior chapters and grades to future ones. In addition to charts like this one, Laurie's Notes provide point of use insights about where your students have come from and where they are going in their learning progression.

Through the Grades

Grade 7	Grade 8	High School
• Use samples to draw inferences about populations. • Compare two populations from random samples using measures of center and variability. • Approximate the probability of a chance event and predict the approximate relative frequency given the probability.	• Construct and interpret scatter plots. • Find and assess lines of fit for scatter plots. • Use equations of lines to solve problems and interpret the slope and the y-intercept. • Construct and interpret a two-way table summarizing data. Use relative frequencies to describe possible association between the two variables.	• Classify data as quantitative or qualitative, choose and create appropriate data displays, and analyze misleading graphs. • Make and use two-way tables to recognize associations in data by finding marginal, relative, and conditional relative frequencies. • Interpret scatter plots, determine how well lines of fit model data, and distinguish between correlation and causation.

One author team thoughtfully wrote each course, creating a seamless progression of content from Kindergarten to Algebra 2.

See pages xxviii and xxix for the K–8 Progressions chart.

	Grade 4	Grade 5	Grade 6	Grade 7	Grade 8
	Operations and Algebraic Thinking		**Expressions and Equations**		
lems involving nd subtraction	Solve problems involving addition and subtraction within 20. Work with equal groups of objects. Chapters 1–6, 15	Solve problems involving multiplication and division within 100. Apply properties of multiplication. Solve problems involving the four operations, and identify and explain patterns in arithmetic. Chapters 1–5, 8, 9, and 14	Use the four operations with whole numbers to solve problems. Understand factors and multiples. Generate and analyze patterns. Chapters 2–6, 12	Write and interpret numerical expressions. Analyze patterns and relationships. Chapters 2, 12	Perform arithmetic with algebraic expressions. Chapter 5 Solve one-variable equations and inequalities. Chapters 6, 8 Analyze relationships between dependent and independent variables. Chapter 6	Write equivalent expressions. Chapter 3 Use numerical and algebraic expressions, equations, and inequalities to solve problems. Chapters 3, 4, 6	Understand the connections between proportional relationships, lines, and linear equations. Chapter 4 Solve linear equations and systems of linear equations. Chapters 1, 5 Work with radicals and integer exponents. Chapters 8, 9
							Functions
							Define, evaluate, and compare functions, and use functions to model relationships between quantities.

You have used number lines to find sums of positive numbers, which involve movement to the right. Now you will find sums with negative numbers, which involve movement to the left.

Throughout each course, lessons build on prior learning as new concepts are introduced. Here the students are reminded of the use of number lines with positive numbers.

Using Number Lines to Find Sums

a. Find $4 + (-4)$.

Draw an arrow from 0 to 4 to represent 4. Then draw an arrow 4 units to the left to represent adding -4.

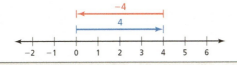

Rigor in Math: A Balanced Approach

Instructional Design
The authors wrote every chapter and every section to give you a meaningful balance of rigorous instruction.

RIGOR
A rigorous program provides a balance of three important building blocks.
- **Conceptual Understanding** Discovering why
- **Procedural Fluency** Learning how
- **Application** Knowing when to apply

Conceptual Understanding
Students have the opportunity to develop foundational concepts central to the *Learning Target* in each *Exploration* by experimenting with new concepts, talking with peers, and asking questions.

EXPLORATION 1 Understanding Quotients Involving N

Work with a partner.
a. Discuss the relationship between multiplication your partner.
b. **INDUCTIVE REASONING** Complete the table. Th for dividing (i) two integers with the same sign a different signs.

Expression	Type of Quotient	Quoti
$-15 \div 3$	Integers	
$12 \div (-6)$		
$10 \div (-2)$		

Conceptual Thinking
Ask students to think deeply with conceptual questions.

29. MP NUMBER SENSE Without solving, determine whether $\frac{x}{4} = \frac{15}{3}$ and $\frac{x}{15} = \frac{4}{3}$ have the same solution. Explain your reasoning.

EXAMPLE 1 Graphing a Linear Equation in Standard Form

Graph $-2x + 3y = -6$.

Step 1: Write the equation in slope-intercept form.

$-2x + 3y = -6$ Write the equation.
$3y = 2x - 6$ Add $2x$ to each side.
$y = \frac{2}{3}x - 2$ Divide each side by 3.

Step 2: Use the slope and the y-intercept to graph the equation.

The y-intercept is -2. So, plot $(0, -2)$.

Use the slope to plot another point, $(3, 0)$.

Procedural Fluency
Solidify learning with clear, stepped-out teaching and examples.

Then shift conceptual understanding into procedural fluency with *Try Its*, *Self-Assessments*, *Practice*, and *Review & Refresh*.

STEAM Applications
Students begin every chapter with a fun, engaging STEAM video to see how math applies to everyday life. Students apply what they learn in the chapter with a related *Performance Task*.

STEAM Video: "Trophic Status"

Chapter 3 Performance Task

Chlorophyll in Plants

What is needed for photosynthesis? How can you use the amount of chlorophyll in a lake to determine the level of biological productivity?

Photosynthesis is the process by which plants acquire energy from the sun. Sunlight, carbon dioxide, and water are used by a plant to produce glucose and dioxygen.

Before: 6 Carbon Dioxide + 6 Water → After: Glucose + 6 Dioxygen

1. You want to make models of the molecules involved in photosynthesis for a science fair project. The table shows the number of each element used for each molecule. Let x, y, and z represent the costs of a model carbon atom, model hydrogen atom, and

Molecule	Number of Atoms		
	Carbon	Hydrogen	Oxygen
Carbon Dioxide	1	0	2
Water	0	2	1

Daily Application Practice
Modeling Real Life, *Dig Deeper*, *Problem Solving*, and other non-routine problems help students apply surface-level skills to gain a deeper understanding. These problems lead students to independent problem-solving.

36. **DIG DEEPER!** The *girth* of a package is the distance around the perimeter of a face that does not include the length as a side. A postal service says that a rectangular package can have a maximum combined length and girth of 108 inches.

    a. Write an inequality that represents the allowable dimensions for the package.

    b. Find three different sets of allowable dimensions that are reasonable for the package. Find the volume of each package.

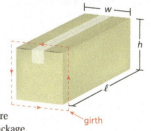

Problem-Solving Plan
Walk students through the Problem-Solving Plan, featured in many examples, to help students make sense of problems with confidence.

THE PROBLEM-SOLVING PLAN

1. **Understand the Problem**
   Think about what the problem is asking, what information you know, and how you might begin to solve.

2. **Make a Plan**
   Plan your solution pathway before jumping in to solve. Identify any relationships and decide on a problem-solving strategy.

3. **Solve and Check**
   As you solve the problem, be sure to evaluate your progress and check your answers. Throughout the problem-solving process, you must continually ask, "Does this make sense?" and be willing to change course if necessary.

Embedded Mathematical Practices

Encouraging Mathematical Mindsets

Developing proficiency in the **Mathematical Practices** is about becoming a mathematical thinker. Students learn to ask why, and to reason and communicate with others as they learn. Use this guide to communicate opportunities in your classroom for students to develop proficiency with the mathematical practices.

1 One way to **Make Sense of Problems and Persevere in Solving Them** is to use the Problem-Solving Plan. Students should take time to analyze the given information and what the problem is asking to help them plan a solution pathway.

Look for labels such as:
- Explain the Meaning
- Find Entry Points
- Analyze Givens
- Make a Plan
- Interpret a Solution
- Consider Similar Problems
- Consider Simpler Forms
- Check Progress
- Problem Solving

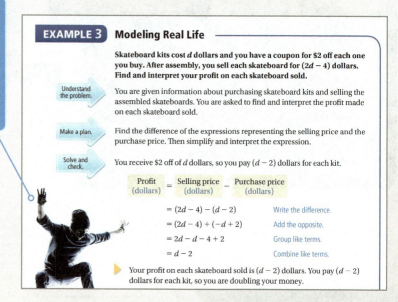

EXAMPLE 3 Modeling Real Life

Skateboard kits cost d dollars and you have a coupon for \$2 off each one you buy. After assembly, you sell each skateboard for $(2d - 4)$ dollars. Find and interpret your profit on each skateboard sold.

Understand the problem. You are given information about purchasing skateboard kits and selling the assembled skateboards. You are asked to find and interpret the profit made on each skateboard sold.

Make a plan. Find the difference of the expressions representing the selling price and the purchase price. Then simplify and interpret the expression.

Solve and check. You receive \$2 off of d dollars, so you pay $(d - 2)$ dollars for each kit.

$$\text{Profit (dollars)} = \text{Selling price (dollars)} - \text{Purchase price (dollars)}$$

$= (2d - 4) - (d - 2)$ Write the difference.
$= (2d - 4) + (-d + 2)$ Add the opposite.
$= 2d - d - 4 + 2$ Group like terms.
$= d - 2$ Combine like terms.

▶ Your profit on each skateboard sold is $(d - 2)$ dollars. You pay $(d - 2)$ dollars for each kit, so you are doubling your money.

2 Students **Reason Abstractly** when they explore a concrete example and represent it symbolically. Other times, students **Reason Quantitatively** when they see relationships in numbers or symbols and draw conclusions about a concrete example.

a. Represent each table in the same coordinate plane. Which graph represents a proportional relationship? How do you know?

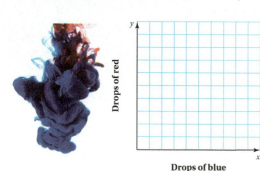

Look for labels such as:
- Make Sense of Quantities
- Use Equations
- Use Expressions
- Understand Quantities
- Use Operations
- Number Sense
- Reasoning

Math Practice

Reasoning
How is the graph of the proportional relationship different from the other graph?

b. Which property can you use to solve each of the equations modeled by the algebra tiles? Solve each equation and explain your method.

46. **MP LOGIC** When you multiply or divide each side of an inequality by the same negative number, you must reverse the direction of the inequality symbol. Explain why.

Math Practice

Make Conjectures
Can you use algebra tiles to solve any equation? Explain your reasoning.

3
When students **Construct Viable Arguments and Critique the Reasoning of Others**, they make and justify conclusions and decide whether others' arguments are correct or flawed.

Look for labels such as:
- Use Assumptions
- Use Definitions
- Use Prior Results
- Make Conjectures
- Build Arguments
- Analyze Conjectures
- Use Counterexamples
- Justify Conclusions
- Compare Arguments
- Construct Arguments
- Listen and Ask Questions
- You Be the Teacher
- Logic

36. **MP APPLY MATHEMATICS** You decide to make and sell bracelets. The cost of your materials is $84.00. You charge $3.50 for each bracelet.

   a. Write a function that represents the profit P for selling b bracelets.
   b. Which variable is independent? dependent? Explain.
   c. You will *break even* when the cost of your materials equals your income. How many bracelets must you sell to break even?

Look for labels such as:
- Apply Mathematics
- Simplify a Solution
- Use a Diagram
- Use a Table
- Use a Graph
- Use a Formula
- Analyze Relationships
- Interpret Results
- Modeling Real Life

4
To **Model with Mathematics**, students apply the math they have learned to a real-life problem, and they interpret mathematical results in the context of the situation.

BUILDING TO FULL UNDERSTANDING
Throughout each course, students have opportunities to demonstrate specific aspects of the mathematical practices. Labels throughout the book indicate gateways to those aspects. Collectively, these opportunities will lead students to a full understanding of each mathematical practice. Developing these mindsets and habits will give meaning to the mathematics they learn.

Embedded Mathematical Practices (continu

5 To **Use Appropriate Tools Strategically**, students need to know what tools are available and think about how each tool might help them solve a mathematical problem. When students choose a tool to use, remind them that it may have limitations.

Look for labels such as:
- Choose Tools
- Recognize Usefulness of Tools
- Use Other Resources
- Use Technology to Explore
- Using Tools

d. Enter the function $y = \left(\dfrac{1}{10}\right)^x$ into your graphing calculator. Use the *table* feature to evaluate the function for positive integer values of x until the calculator displays a y-value that is not in standard form. Do the results support your answer in part (c)? Explain.

 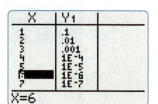

Math Practice

Use Technology to Explore
How can writing $\dfrac{1}{10}$ as a power of 10 help you understand the calculator display?

6 When students **Attend to Precision**, they are developing a habit of being careful in how they talk about concepts, label their work, and write their answers.

Add 1.459 + 23.7.

```
    1
   1.459
 + 23.700
 --------
   25.159
```

Insert zeros so that both numbers have the same number of decimal places.

Look for labels such as:
- Communicate Precisely
- Use Clear Definitions
- State the Meaning of Symbols
- Specify Units
- Label Axes
- Calculate Accurately
- Precision

Math Practice

Calculate Accurately
Why is it important to line up the decimal points when adding or subtracting decimals?

49. **MP PRECISION** Consider the equation $c = ax - bx$, where a, b, and c are whole numbers. Which of the following result in values of a, b, and c so that the original equation has exactly one solution? Justify your answer.

$a - b = 1, c = 0$ $a = b, c \neq 0$ $a = b, c = 0$ $a \neq b, c = 0$

MP STRUCTURE Tell whether the triangles are similar. Explain.

14.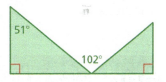

15.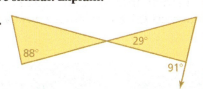

Students Look For and Make Use of Structure by looking closely to see structure within a mathematical statement, or stepping back for an overview to see how individual parts make one single object.

Find the sum of the areas of the faces.

Surface Area = Area of bottom + Area of a side + Area of a side + Area of a side + Area of a side

S = 49 + 35 + 35 + 35 + 35 = 189

Look for labels such as:
- Look for Structure
- Look for Patterns
- View as Components
- Structure
- Patterns

Math Practice

Look for Patterns
How can you find the surface area of a square pyramid by calculating the area of only two of the faces?

35. **MP REPEATED REASONING** You have been assigned a nine-digit identification number.

   a. Should you use the Fundamental Counting Principle or a tree diagram to find the total number of possible identification numbers? Explain.

   b. How many identification numbers are possible?

When students **Look For and Express Regularity in Repeated Reasoning**, they can notice patterns and make generalizations. Remind students to keep in mind the goal of a problem, which will help them evaluate reasonableness of answers along the way.

Look for labels such as:
- Repeat Calculations
- Find General Methods
- Maintain Oversight
- Evaluate Results
- Repeated Reasoning

Visible Learning Through Learning Targets

Making Learning Visible

Knowing the learning intention of a chapter or section helps learners focus on the purpose of an activity, rather than simply completing it in isolation. This program supports visible learning through the consistent use of Learning Targets and Success Criteria to ensure positive outcomes for all students.

Every chapter and section shows a **Learning Target** and related **Success Criteria**. These are purposefully integrated into each carefully written lesson.

4.4 Writing and Graphing Inequalities

Learning Target: Write inequalities and represent solutions of inequalities on number lines.

Success Criteria:
- I can write word sentences as inequalities.
- I can determine whether a value is a solution of an inequality.
- I can graph the solutions of inequalities.

Chapter Learning Target: Understand equations and inequalities.

Chapter Success Criteria:
- I can identify key words and phrases to write equations and inequalities.
- I can write word sentences as equations and inequalities.
- I can solve equations and inequalities using properties.
- I can use equations and inequalities to model and solve real-life problems.

The **Chapter Review** reminds students to rate their understanding of the learning targets.

Chapter Self-Assessment

As you complete the exercises, use the scale below to rate your understanding of the success criteria in your journal.

1	2	3	4
I do not understand.	I can do it with help.	I can do it on my own.	I can teach someone else.

6.1 Writing Equations in One Variable (pp. 245–250)

Learning Target: Write equations in one variable and write equations that represent real-life problems.

Write the word sentence as an equation.
- The product of a number m and 2 is 8.

Students review each section with a reminder of that section's learning target.

○ Icons throughout **Laurie's Notes** suggest ways to target where students are in their learning.

QUESTIONS FOR LEARNERS

As students progress through a section, they should be able to answer the following questions.
- What are you learning?
- Why are you learning this?
- Where are you in your learning?
- How will you know when you have learned it?
- Where are you going next?

○ **Fist of Five:** Ask students to indicate their understanding of the first and second success criterion. Then select students to explain each one.

Success Criteria, and Self-Assessment

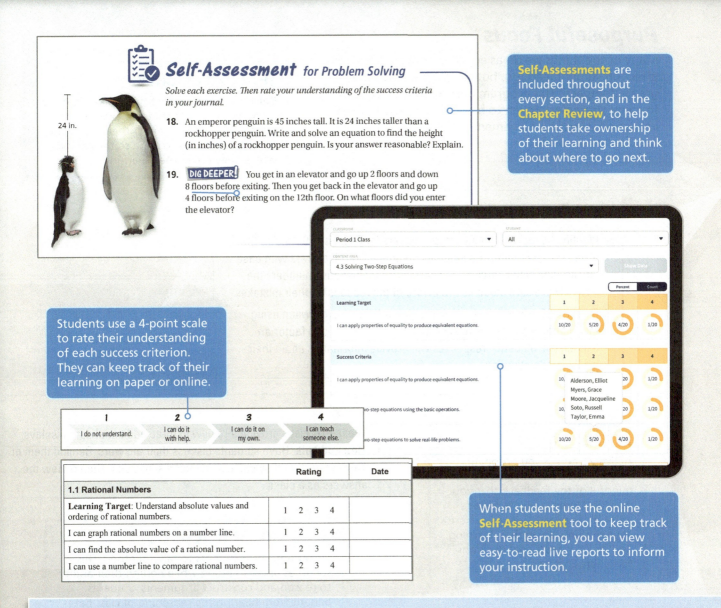

Self-Assessment for Problem Solving

Solve each exercise. Then rate your understanding of the success criteria in your journal.

18. An emperor penguin is 45 inches tall. It is 24 inches taller than a rockhopper penguin. Write and solve an equation to find the height (in inches) of a rockhopper penguin. Is your answer reasonable? Explain.

19. **DIG DEEPER!** You get in an elevator and go up 2 floors and down 8 floors before exiting. Then you get back in the elevator and go up 4 floors before exiting on the 12th floor. On what floors did you enter the elevator?

Self-Assessments are included throughout every section, and in the **Chapter Review**, to help students take ownership of their learning and think about where to go next.

Students use a 4-point scale to rate their understanding of each success criterion. They can keep track of their learning on paper or online.

1	2	3	4
I do not understand.	I can do it with help.	I can do it on my own.	I can teach someone else.

	Rating	Date
1.1 Rational Numbers		
Learning Target: Understand absolute values and ordering of rational numbers.	1 2 3 4	
I can graph rational numbers on a number line.	1 2 3 4	
I can find the absolute value of a rational number.	1 2 3 4	
I can use a number line to compare rational numbers.	1 2 3 4	

When students use the online **Self-Assessment** tool to keep track of their learning, you can view easy-to-read live reports to inform your instruction.

Ensuring Positive Outcomes

John Hattie's *Visible Learning* research consistently shows that using Learning Targets and Success Criteria can result in two years' growth in one year, ensuring positive outcomes for student learning and achievement.

Sophie Murphy, M.Ed., wrote the chapter-level learning targets and success criteria for this program. Sophie is currently completing her Ph.D. at the University of Melbourne in Australia with Professor John Hattie as her leading supervisor. Sophie completed her Master's thesis with Professor John Hattie in 2015. Sophie has over 20 years of experience as a teacher and school leader in private and public school settings in Australia.

xv

High-Impact Strategies

Purposeful Focus

Many of the things we do as educators have a positive effect on student learning, but which ones have the greatest impact? This program purposefully integrates **five key strategies** proven to have some of the highest impact on student achievement.

TEACHER CLARITY
Before starting a new topic, make clear the learning target. As students explore and learn, continue to connect their experiences back to the success criteria so they know where they are in their learning.

Self-Assessment for Concepts & Skills

- Identify the reasons for incorrect answers for Exercises 9–14. Are the errors computational? Do students complete Exercises 9–12 with ease but struggle with Exercises 13 and 14? Are the negative numbers the issue? Make sure students are aware of the reasons for their mistakes.
- Exercise 15 asks students to explain the relationship between using the Distributive Property to simplify an expression and to factor an expression. Students' responses will provide information about their level of understanding.

FEEDBACK
Actively listen as you probe for student understanding, being mindful of the feedback that you provide. When students provide you with feedback, you see where your students are in their learning and make instructional decisions for where to go next.

Try It
- These exercises provide a review of three additional data displays.
- **Turn and Talk:** Have students discuss their answers. Remind them of *Talk Moves* that they can use in their discussions. Then review the answers as a class.

CLASSROOM DISCUSSION
Encourage your students to talk together! This solidifies understanding while honing their ability to reason and construct arguments. Students benefit from hearing the reasoning of classmates and hearing peers critique their own reasoning.

Daily Support from a Master Educator

In Laurie's Notes, master educator Laurie Boswell uses her professional training and years of experience to help you guide your students to better understanding.

Laurie studied Professor John Hattie's research on *Visible Learning* and met with Hattie on multiple occasions to ensure she was interpreting his research accurately and embedding it effectively. Laurie's expertise continues with an ongoing collaboration with Sophie Murphy, who is pursuing her Ph.D. under Professor Hattie.

for Student Achievement

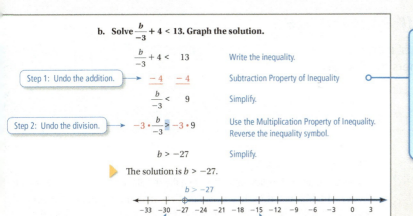

DIRECT INSTRUCTION
Follow exploration and discovery with explicit instruction to build procedural skill and fluency. Teach with clear Key Ideas and powerful stepped-out examples that have been carefully designed to meet the success criteria.

SPACED PRACTICE
Effective practice does not just focus on a single topic of new learning; students must revisit concepts over time so deeper learning occurs. This program cohesively offers multiple opportunities for students to build their conceptual understanding by intentionally revisiting and applying concepts throughout subsequent lessons and chapters. *Review & Refresh* exercises in every section also provide continual practice on the major topics.

▶ Review & Refresh

Solve the inequality. Graph the solution.

1. $-3x \geq 18$
2. $\frac{2}{3}d > 8$
3. $2 \geq \frac{g}{-4}$

Find the missing values in the ratio table. Then write the equivalent ratios.

4.
Flutes	7		28
Clarinets	4	12	

5.
Boys	6	3	
Girls	10		50

6. What is the volume of the cube?
   A. $8\,\text{ft}^3$
   B. $16\,\text{ft}^3$
   C. $24\,\text{ft}^3$
   D. $32\,\text{ft}^3$

2 ft

Five Strategies for Purposeful Focus

Professor John Hattie, in his *Visible Learning* network, identified more than 250 influences on student learning, and developed a way of ranking them. He conducted meta-analyses and compared the influences by their **effect size**—the impact the factor had on student learning.

We focus on **STRATEGIES** with some of the **HIGHEST IMPACT** on student achievement—up to 2 years of learning for a year of input.

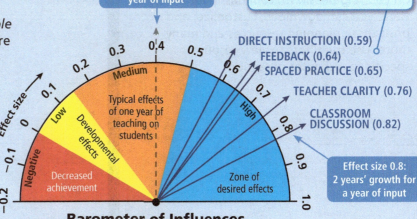

Average effect size 0.4: 1 year of growth for a year of input

DIRECT INSTRUCTION (0.59)
FEEDBACK (0.64)
SPACED PRACTICE (0.65)
TEACHER CLARITY (0.76)
CLASSROOM DISCUSSION (0.82)

Effect size 0.8: 2 years' growth for a year of input

Barometer of Influences

xvii

How to Use This Program: Plan

Taking Advantage of Your Resources

You play an indispensable role in your students' learning. This program provides rich resources for learners of all levels to help you **Plan**, **Teach**, and **Assess**.

Plan every chapter and section with tools in the Teaching Edition such as **Suggested Pacing**, **Progression Tables**, and chapter and section **Overviews** written by Laurie Boswell.

Suggested Pacing

Chapter Opener	1 Day
Section 1	2 Days
Section 2	2 Days
Section 3	2 Days
Section 4	2 Days
Section 5	

Preparing to Teach
- Students should be familiar with organizing the results of an **experiment** in a table.
- **Model with Mathematics:** In this exploration, students will gain a conceptual sense of **probability** by performing activities to determine the likelihood of an **event**. They will pursue the concept of possible **outcomes**, which leads to describing the likelihood of an event.

Through the Chapter				
Standard	7.1	7.2	7.3	7.4
Understand that a function is a rule that assigns to each input exactly one output. The graph of a function is the set of ordered pairs consisting of an input and the corresponding output.	●	★		
Compare properties of two functions each represented in a different way (algebraically, graphically, numerically in tables, or by verbal descriptions).			★	
Interpret the equation $y = mx + b$ as defining a linear function, whose graph is a straight line; give examples of functions that are not linear.			●	★

Find Your Resources Digitally

Use the resources page that is available on your *BigIdeasMath.com* dashboard. Here, you can download, customize, and print these planning resources and many more. Use the filters to view resources specific to a chapter or section.

xviii

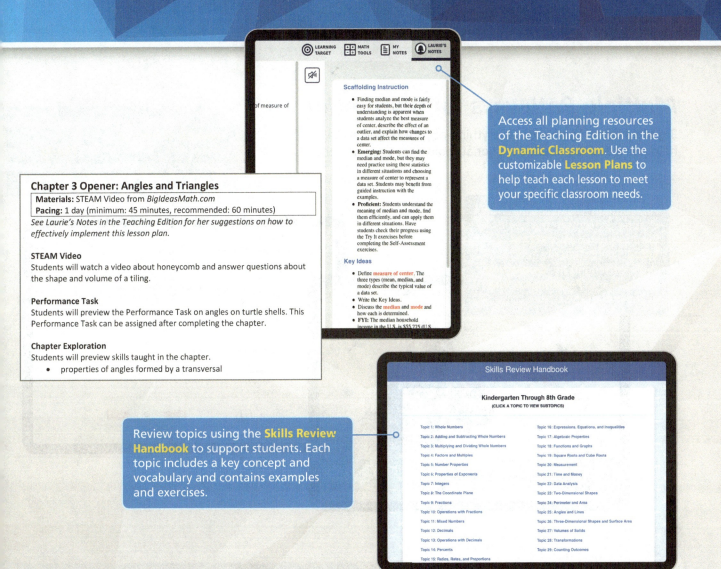

Access all planning resources of the Teaching Edition in the **Dynamic Classroom**. Use the customizable **Lesson Plans** to help teach each lesson to meet your specific classroom needs.

Review topics using the **Skills Review Handbook** to support students. Each topic includes a key concept and vocabulary and contains examples and exercises.

Plan Online

Remember as you are planning, that the *Dynamic Classroom* has the same interactive tools, such as the digital *Sketchpad,* that students will use to model concepts. Plan ahead by practicing these tools to guide students as they use these manipulatives and models.

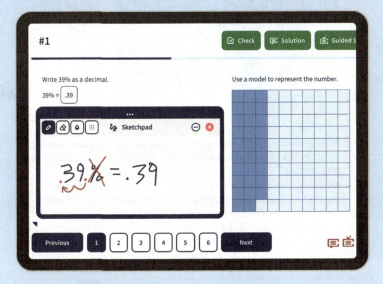

How to Use This Program: Teach

Multiple Pathways for Instruction

Big Ideas Learning provides everything at your fingertips to help you make the best instructional choices for your students.

Present all content digitally using the **Dynamic Classroom**. Send students a page link on-the-fly with **Flip-To** to direct where you want your students to go.

Have students think ahead about chapter concepts in the world around them with a **STEAM video**. Then, students transfer their learning in the **Connecting Concepts** and **Performance Task** at the end of the chapter.

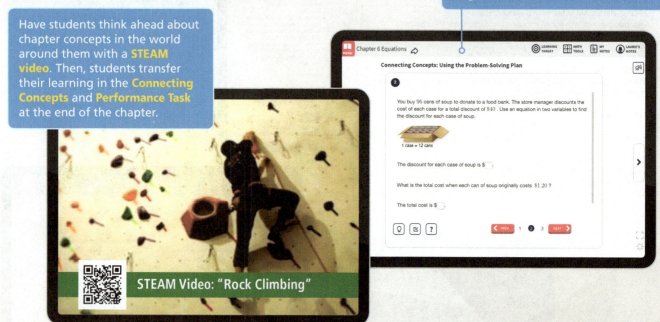

STEAM Video: "Rock Climbing"

Engage students with a creative hook at the beginning of each section with **Motivate**. This activity, written by master educator Laurie Boswell, provides a conceptual introduction for the section. Then, encourage mathematical discovery with **Exploration**.

Motivate

- ❓ Show students a collection of algebra tiles and ask, "Can the collection be simplified? Can you remove zero pairs? What is the expression represented by the collection?"
- **Model:** As a class, model the equations $x + 3 = 7$ and $x + 2 = 5$ using algebra tiles. These do not require a zero pair to solve and will help remind students how to solve equations using algebra tiles.
- Remind students that they need to think of subtracting as *adding the opposite* when using algebra tiles (i.e., $x - 3$ as $x + (-3)$).
- ❓ "What does it mean to solve an equation?" To find the value of the variable that makes the equation true.

4.1 Solving Equations Using Addition or Subtraction

Learning Target: Write and solve equations using addition or subtraction.

Success Criteria:
- I can apply the Addition and Subtraction Properties of Equality to produce equivalent equations.
- I can solve equations using addition or subtraction.
- I can apply equations involving addition or subtraction to solve real-life problems.

EXPLORATION 1 Using Algebra Tiles to Solve Equations

Work with a partner.

a. Use the examples to explain the meaning of each property.

Addition Property of Equality:
$$x + 2 = 1$$
$$x + 2 + 5 = 1 + 5$$

Subtraction Property of Equality:
$$x + 2 = 1$$
$$x + 2 - 1 = 1 - 1$$

Are these properties true for equations involving negative numbers? Explain your reasoning.

b. Write the four equations modeled by the algebra tiles. Explain how you can use algebra tiles to solve each equation. Then find the solutions.

Lead students to procedural fluency with clear **Examples** and **Self-Assessment** opportunities for students to try on their own.

EXAMPLE 1 Determining Whether Two Quantities are Proportional

Tell whether x and y are proportional. Explain your reasoning.

a.
x	1	2	3	4
y	−2	0	2	4

Plot the points. Draw a line through the points.

b.
x	0	2	4	6
y	0	2	4	6

Plot the points. Draw a line through the points.

▶ The line does *not* pass through the origin. So, x and y are not proportional.

▶ The line passes through the origin. So, x and y are proportional.

EXAMPLE 3 Modeling Real Life

The graph shows the area y (in square feet) that a robotic vacuum cleans in x minutes. Find the area cleaned in 10 minutes.

The graph is a line through the origin, so x and y are proportional. You can write an equation to represent the relationship between area and time.

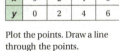

Because the graph passes through the point (1, 16), the unit rate is 16 square feet per minute and the constant of proportionality is $k = 16$. So, an equation of the line is $y = 16x$. Substitute to find the area cleaned in 10 minutes.

$y = 16x$ Write the equation.
$ = 16(10)$ Substitute 10 for x.
$ = 160$ Multiply.

▶ So, the vacuum cleans 160 square feet in 10 minutes.

Help students apply and problem solve with **Modeling Real Life** applications, **Dig Deeper** problems, and **Math Practice** conceptual problems.

Let **Laurie's Notes** guide your teaching and scaffolding decisions at every step to support and deepen all students' learning. You may want to group students differently as they move in and out of these levels with each skill and concept. Student self-assessment and feedback help guide your instructional decisions about how and when to layer support.

Scaffolding Instruction

- In the exploration, students discussed various methods of solving proportions. They will continue this work in the lesson.
- **Emerging:** Students may be able to create a ratio table but may struggle to write and/or solve the proportion. Students will benefit from close examination of the examples.
- **Proficient:** Students can write and solve proportions using a variety of methods (including tables). Students should review Examples 4 and 5 before proceeding to the Self-Assessment exercises.

Name _____ Date _____

Lesson 7.1 Extra Practice

You randomly choose one of the tiles shown.

1. How many possible outcomes are there?
2. What are the favorable outcomes of choosing a number greater than 6?
3. In how many ways can choosing a number divisible by 2 occur?

Differentiate and support your learners with **Differentiating the Lesson**, **Resources by Chapter**, **English Language Support**, and much more.

xxi

How to Use This Program: Assess

Powerful Assessment Tools

Gain insight into your students' learning with these powerful formative and summative assessment tools tailored to every learning target and standard.

Access real-time data and navigate easily through student responses with **Formative Check**.

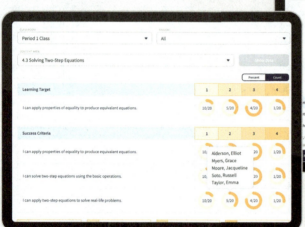

Use the **Mini-Assessment** to assess understanding of lesson concepts.

Scaffold **Practice** from the **Assignment Guide and Concept Check**. Assign print or digital versions, and project answers and solutions in class using the **Answer Presentation Tool**.

Mini-Assessment

Write the word sentence as an inequality.

1. A number a is at least 5. $a \geq 5$
2. Four times a number b is no more than -4.73. $4b \leq -4.73$
3. Tell whether -2 is a solution of $6g - 14 > -21$.   not a solution
4. A rollercoaster is at most 45 meters high. Write and graph an inequality that represents the height of the rollercoaster.
   $h \leq 45$;

Scaffold assignments to support all students in their learning progression. The suggested assignments are a starting point. Continue to assign additional exercises and revisit with spaced practice to move every student toward proficiency.

6.1 Practice

▶ Review & Refresh

Find the missing dimension. Use the scale 1 : 15.

	Item	Model	Actual
1.	Figure skater	Height: in.	Height: 67.5 in.
2.	Pipe	Length: 5 ft	Length: ft

Simplify the expression.

3. $2(3p - 6) + 4p$
4. $5n - 3(4n + 1)$

Assignment Guide and Concept Check

Level	Assignment 1	Assignment 2
Emerging	4, 8, 9, 10, 11, 14, 16, 17, 26, 27, 31	18, 19, 32, 33, 35, 36, 39, 40, 41, 42
Proficient	4, 8, 9, 10, 11, 17, 18, 19, 26, 28, 30, 32, 48	25, 33, 35, 37, 39, 40, 42, 43, 47
Advanced	4, 8, 9, 12, 13, 14, 23, 25, 26, 30, 32, 33, 48	38, 40, 45, 46, 47, 49, 50, 51

- Assignment 1 is for use after students complete the Self-Assessment for Concepts & Skills.
- Assignment 2 is for use after students complete the Self-Assessment for Problem Solving.
- The red exercises can be used as a concept check.

Assign **Quizzes** or **Chapter Tests** to assess understanding of section or chapter content or use **Alternative Assessments** and **Performance Tasks**, which include scoring rubrics.

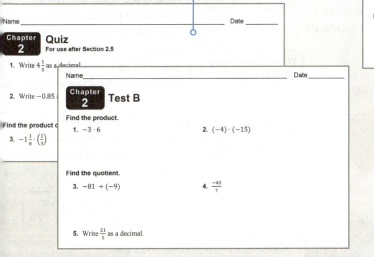

Assess student learning of standards throughout the year with cumulative **Course Benchmark Tests** to measure progress. Use the results to help plan instruction and intervention.

Measure learning across grades with adaptive **Progression Benchmark Tests**.

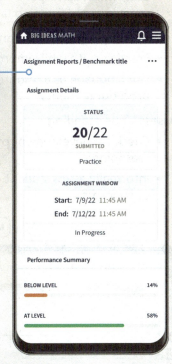

Use the **Assignment Builder** to assign digital versions of the print **Quizzes**, **Chapter Tests**, and **Course Benchmark Tests**. Receive immediate feedback through robust reporting.

Assessment item point values are weighted. You can customize an item's total point value to fit your needs.

xxiii

Strategic Support for All Learners

Support for English Language Learners

Big Ideas Learning supports English Language Learners (ELLs) with a blend of print and digital resources available in Spanish. Look to your Teaching Edition for opportunities to support all students with the language development needed for mathematical understanding.

Students' WIDA scores are a starting point. As the year progresses, students may move in and out of language levels with varying language demands of the content and as students change and grow.

Clarify, Connect, and Scaffold

- Clarify language that may be difficult or confusing for ELLs
- Connect new learning to something students already know
- Differentiate student comprehension while completing practice exercises
- Target Beginner, Intermediate, and Advanced ELLs, which correspond to **WIDA** reading, writing, speaking, and listening language mastery levels

Practice Language and Content

- Practice math while improving language skills
- Use language as a resource to develop procedural fluency

Assess Understanding

- Check for development of mathematical reasoning
- Informally assess student comprehension of concepts

WIDA 1: Entering
WIDA 2: Emerging

WIDA 3: Developing
WIDA 4: Expanding

WIDA 5: Bridging
WIDA 6: Reaching

ELL Support

After demonstrating Example 1, have students practice language by working in pairs to complete Try It Exercises 1–3. Have one student ask another, "What is the first step? Do you add or subtract? What is the solution?" Have students alternate roles.

Beginner: Write the steps and provide one-word answers.

Intermediate: Answer with phrases or simple sentences such as, "First, I add five."

Advanced: Answer with detailed sentences such as, "First, I add five to each side of the equation."

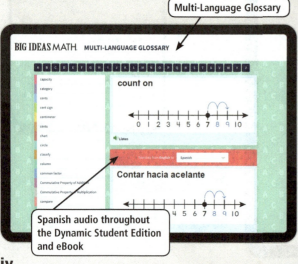

Multi-Language Glossary

Spanish audio throughout the Dynamic Student Edition and eBook

Family Letters in multiple languages

Games available in Spanish

Assess students with Spanish quizzes and chapter tests

Students Get the Support They Need, When They Need It

There will be times throughout this course when students may need help. Whether students missed a section, did not understand the content, or just want to review, take advantage of the resources provided in the *Dynamic Student Edition*.

Students use the **Self-Assessment** tool to keep track of their understanding of the section's Learning Target and Success Criteria.

Students can take notes throughout the lesson using the **My Notes** function. These notes will be organized for them by chapter and section.

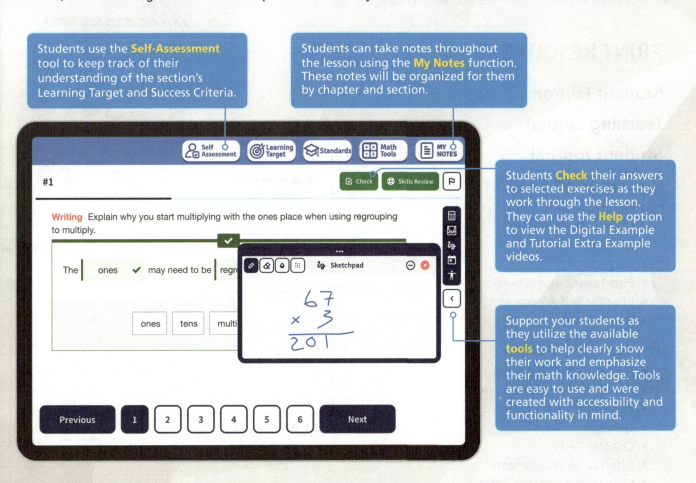

Students **Check** their answers to selected exercises as they work through the lesson. They can use the **Help** option to view the Digital Example and Tutorial Extra Example videos.

Support your students as they utilize the available **tools** to help clearly show their work and emphasize their math knowledge. Tools are easy to use and were created with accessibility and functionality in mind.

USE THESE QR CODES TO EXPLORE ADDITIONAL RESOURCES

Multi-Language Glossary
View definitions and examples of vocabulary words

Skills Trainer
Practice previously learned skills

Interactive Tools
Visualize mathematical concepts

Skills Review Handbook
A collection of review topics

Meeting the Needs of All Learners

Resources at Your Fingertips

This robust, innovative program utilizes a mixture of print and digital resources that allow for a variety of instructional approaches. The program encompasses hands-on activities, interactive explorations, videos, scaffolded instruction, learning support, and many more resources that appeal to students and teachers alike.

PRINT RESOURCES

Student Edition

Teaching Edition

Student Journal

Resources by Chapter
- Family Letter
- Warm-Ups
- Extra Practice
- Reteach
- Enrichment and Extension
- Chapter Self-Assessment
- Puzzle Time

Assessment Book
- Prerequisite Skills Practice
- Pre- and Post-Course Tests
- Course Benchmark Tests
- Quizzes
- Chapter Tests
- Alternative Assessments
- STEAM Performance Tasks

Rich Math Tasks
Skills Review Handbook

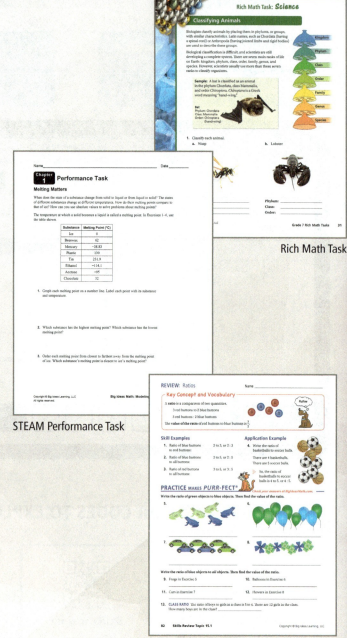

Rich Math Task

STEAM Performance Task

Skills Review Handbook

Through Program Resources

TECHNOLOGY RESOURCES

Dynamic Student Edition
- Interactive Tools
- Interactive Explorations
- Digital Examples
- Tutorial Extra Example Videos
- Self-Assessments

Dynamic Classroom
- Laurie's Notes
- Interactive Tools
- Interactive Explorations
- Digital Examples with PowerPoints
- Formative Check
- Flip-To
- Digital Warm-Ups and Closures
- Mini-Assessments

Dynamic Assessment System
- Practice
- Assessments
- Progression Benchmark Tests
- Detailed Reports

Video Support for Teachers
- Life on Earth Videos
- Professional Development Videos
- Concepts and Tools Videos

Resources
- Answer Presentation Tool
- Chapter at a Glance
- Complete Materials List
- Cross-Curricular Projects
- Skills Trainer
- Vocabulary Flash Cards
- STEAM Videos
- Game Library
- Multi-Language Glossary
- Lesson Plans
- Differentiating the Lesson
- Graphic Organizers
- Pacing Guides
- Worked-Out Solutions Key
- Math Tool Paper
- Family Letters
- Homework App
- Skills Review Handbook

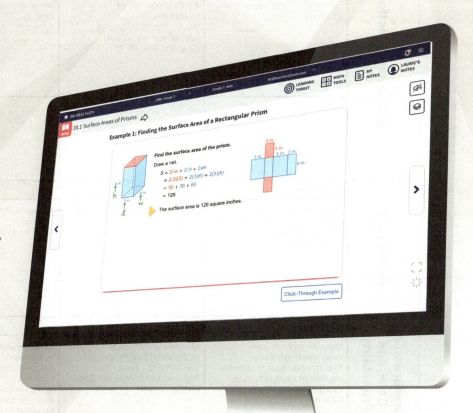

Cohesive Progressions

		Grade K	Grade 1	Grade 2	Grade 3
Number and Quantity		**Counting and Cardinality** Know number names and the count sequence. Count to tell the number of objects. Compare numbers. *Chapters 1–4, 6, 8–10*			
		Number and Operations – Base Ten Work with numbers 11–19 to gain foundations for place value. *Chapter 8*	Extend the counting sequence. Use place value and properties of operations to add and subtract. *Chapters 6–9*	Use place value and properties of operations to add and subtract. *Chapters 2–10, 14*	Use place value and properties of operations to perform multi-digit arithmetic. *Chapters 7–9, 12*
					Num. and Oper. – Fractions Understand fractions as numbers. *Chapters 10, 11, 14*
Algebra and Functions		**Operations and Algebraic Thinking** Understand addition as putting together and adding to, and understand subtraction as taking apart and taking from. *Chapters 5–7*	Solve problems involving addition and subtraction within 20. Apply properties of operations. Work with addition and subtraction equations. *Chapters 1–5, 10, 11*	Solve problems involving addition and subtraction within 20. Work with equal groups of objects. *Chapters 1–6, 15*	Solve problems involving multiplication and division within 100. Apply properties of multiplication. Solve problems involving the four operations, and identify and explain patterns in arithmetic. *Chapters 1–5, 8, 9, and 14*
Geometry		**Geometry** Identify and describe shapes. Analyze, compare, create, and compose shapes. *Chapters 11, 12*	Reason with shapes and their attributes. *Chapters 12, 14*	Reason with shapes and their attributes. *Chapter 15*	Reason with shapes and their attributes. *Chapters 10, 13*
Measurement, Data, and Probability		**Measurement and Data** Describe and compare measurable attributes. Classify objects and count the number of objects in each category. *Chapters 4, 11, 13*	Measure lengths indirectly and by iterating length units. Tell and write time. Represent and interpret data. *Chapters 10–12*	Measure and estimate lengths in standard units. Relate addition and subtraction to length. Work with time and money. Represent and interpret data. *Chapters 11–14*	Solve problems involving measurement and estimation of intervals of time, liquid volumes, and masses of objects. Represent and interpret data. Understand the concepts of area and perimeter. *Chapters 6, 12, 14, 15*

Through the Grades

Grade 4	Grade 5	Grade 6	Grade 7	Grade 8
Number and Operations – Base Ten		**The Number System**		
Generalize place value understanding for multi-digit whole numbers. Use place value and properties of operations to perform multi-digit arithmetic. *Chapters 1–5*	Understand the place value system. Perform operations with multi-digit whole numbers and with decimals to hundredths. *Chapters 1, 3–7*	Perform operations with multi-digit numbers and find common factors and multiples. *Chapter 1* Divide fractions by fractions. *Chapter 2* Extend understanding of numbers to the rational number system. *Chapter 8*	Perform operations with rational numbers. *Chapters 1, 2*	Extend understanding of numbers to the real number system. *Chapter 9*
Number and Operations – Fractions		**Ratios and Proportional Relationships**		
Extend understanding of fraction equivalence and ordering. Build fractions from unit fractions. Understand decimal notation for fractions, and compare decimal fractions. *Chapters 7–11*	Add, subtract, multiply, and divide fractions. *Chapters 6, 8–11*	Use ratios to solve problems. *Chapters 3, 4*	Use proportional relationships to solve problems. *Chapters 5, 6*	
Operations and Algebraic Thinking		**Expressions and Equations**		
Use the four operations with whole numbers to solve problems. Understand factors and multiples. Generate and analyze patterns. *Chapters 2–6, 12*	Write and interpret numerical expressions. Analyze patterns and relationships. *Chapters 2, 12*	Perform arithmetic with algebraic expressions. *Chapter 5* Solve one-variable equations and inequalities. *Chapters 6, 8* Analyze relationships between dependent and independent variables. *Chapter 6*	Write equivalent expressions. *Chapter 3* Use numerical and algebraic expressions, equations, and inequalities to solve problems. *Chapters 3, 4, 6*	Understand the connections between proportional relationships, lines, and linear equations. *Chapter 4* Solve linear equations and systems of linear equations. *Chapters 1, 5* Work with radicals and integer exponents. *Chapters 8, 9*
				Functions
				Define, evaluate, and compare functions, and use functions to model relationships between quantities. *Chapter 7*
Geometry				
Draw and identify lines and angles, and classify shapes by properties of their lines and angles. *Chapters 13, 14*	Graph points on the coordinate plane. Classify two-dimensional figures into categories based on their properties. *Chapters 12, 14*	Solve real-world and mathematical problems involving area, surface area, and volume. *Chapter 7*	Draw, construct, and describe geometrical figures and describe the relationships between them. *Chapters 5, 9, 10* Solve problems involving angle measure, area, surface area, and volume. *Chapters 9, 10*	Understand congruence and similarity. *Chapters 2, 3* Use the Pythagorean Theorem. *Chapter 9* Solve problems involving volumes of cylinders, cones, and spheres. *Chapter 10*
Measurement and Data		**Statistics and Probability**		
Solve problems involving measurement and conversion of measurements from a larger unit to a smaller unit. Represent and interpret data. Understand angles and measure angles. *Chapters 10–13*	Convert measurement units within a given measurement system. Represent and interpret data. Understand volume. *Chapters 11, 13*	Develop understanding of statistical variability and summarize and describe distributions. *Chapters 9, 10*	Make inferences about a population, compare two populations, and use probability models. *Chapters 7, 8*	Investigate patterns of association in bivariate data. *Chapter 6*

Suggested Pacing

Chapters A–10　　　　　　　　159 Days

Chapter A (14 Days)
Chapter Opener	1 Day
Section A.1	1 Day
Section A.2	1 Day
Section A.3	2 Days
Section A.4	2 Days
Section A.5	1 Day
Section A.6	1 Day
Section A.7	2 Days
Connecting Concepts	1 Day
Chapter Review	1 Day
Chapter Test	1 Day
Year-To-Date	**14 Days**

Chapter B (9 Days)
Chapter Opener	1 Day
Section B.1	1 Day
Section B.2	1 Day
Section B.3	1 Day
Section B.4	2 Days
Connecting Concepts	1 Day
Chapter Review	1 Day
Chapter Test	1 Day
Year-To-Date	**23 Days**

Chapter C (10 Days)
Chapter Opener	1 Day
Section C.1	1 Day
Section C.2	1 Day
Section C.3	2 Days
Section C.4	2 Days
Connecting Concepts	1 Day
Chapter Review	1 Day
Chapter Test	1 Day
Year-To-Date	**33 Days**

Chapter D (9 Days)
Chapter Opener	1 Day
Section D.1	1 Day
Section D.2	1 Day
Section D.3	1 Day
Section D.4	1 Day
Section D.5	1 Day
Connecting Concepts	1 Day
Chapter Review	1 Day
Chapter Test	1 Day
Year-To-Date	**42 Days**

Chapter E (10 Days)
Chapter Opener	1 Day
Section E.1	1 Day
Section E.2	1 Day
Section E.3	1 Day
Section E.4	1 Day
Section E.5	1 Day
Section E.6	1 Day
Connecting Concepts	1 Day
Chapter Review	1 Day
Chapter Test	1 Day
Year-To-Date	**52 Days**

Chapter 1 (10 Days)
Chapter Opener	1 Day
Section 1.1	1 Day
Section 1.2	1 Day
Section 1.3	2 Days
Section 1.4	2 Days
Connecting Concepts	1 Day
Chapter Review	1 Day
Chapter Test	1 Day
Year-To-Date	**62 Days**

Chapter 2 (14 Days)
Chapter Opener	1 Day
Section 2.1	1 Day
Section 2.2	2 Days
Section 2.3	2 Days
Section 2.4	1 Day
Section 2.5	2 Days
Section 2.6	1 Day
Section 2.7	1 Day
Connecting Concepts	1 Day
Chapter Review	1 Day
Chapter Test	1 Day
Year-To-Date	**76 Days**

Chapter 3 (8 Days)
Chapter Opener	1 Day
Section 3.1	1 Day
Section 3.2	1 Day
Section 3.3	1 Day
Section 3.4	1 Day
Connecting Concepts	1 Day
Chapter Review	1 Day
Chapter Test	1 Day
Year-To-Date	**84 Days**

Chapter 4 (11 Days)
Chapter Opener	1 Day
Section 4.1	1 Day
Section 4.2	1 Day
Section 4.3	1 Day
Section 4.4	1 Day
Section 4.5	1 Day
Section 4.6	1 Day
Section 4.7	1 Day
Connecting Concepts	1 Day
Chapter Review	1 Day
Chapter Test	1 Day
Year-To-Date	**95 Days**

Chapter 5 (12 Days)
Chapter Opener	1 Day
Section 5.1	2 Days
Section 5.2	2 Days
Section 5.3	2 Days
Section 5.4	2 Days
Connecting Concepts	1 Day
Chapter Review	1 Day
Chapter Test	1 Day
Year-To-Date	**107 Days**

Chapter 6 (9 Days)
Chapter Opener	1 Day
Section 6.1	1 Day
Section 6.2	2 Days
Section 6.3	1 Day
Section 6.4	1 Day
Connecting Concepts	1 Day
Chapter Review	1 Day
Chapter Test	1 Day
Year-To-Date	**116 Days**

Chapter 7 (14 Days)
Chapter Opener	1 Day
Section 7.1	2 Days
Section 7.2	2 Days
Section 7.3	2 Days
Section 7.4	2 Days
Section 7.5	2 Days
Connecting Concepts	1 Day
Chapter Review	1 Day
Chapter Test	1 Day
Year-To-Date	**130 Days**

Chapter 8 (11 Days)
Chapter Opener	1 Day
Section 8.1	1 Day
Section 8.2	1 Day
Section 8.3	1 Day
Section 8.4	1 Day
Section 8.5	1 Day
Section 8.6	1 Day
Section 8.7	1 Day
Connecting Concepts	1 Day
Chapter Review	1 Day
Chapter Test	1 Day
Year-To-Date	**141 Days**

Chapter 9 (10 Days)
Chapter Opener	1 Day
Section 9.1	1 Day
Section 9.2	1 Day
Section 9.3	1 Day
Section 9.4	1 Day
Section 9.5	1 Day
Section 9.6	1 Day
Connecting Concepts	1 Day
Chapter Review	1 Day
Chapter Test	1 Day
Year-To-Date	**151 Days**

Chapter 10 (8 Days)
Chapter Opener	1 Day
Section 10.1	1 Day
Section 10.2	1 Day
Section 10.3	1 Day
Section 10.4	1 Day
Connecting Concepts	1 Day
Chapter Review	1 Day
Chapter Test	1 Day
Year-To-Date	**159 Days**

An editable version of the Pacing Guide is available in two forms (regular and block scheduling) at *BigIdeasMath.com*.

Equations

	STEAM Video/Performance Task	1
	Getting Ready for Chapter 1	2
■ Section 1.1	**Solving Simple Equations**	
	Exploration	3
	Lesson	4
■ Section 1.2	**Solving Multi-Step Equations**	
	Exploration	11
	Lesson	12
■ Section 1.3	**Solving Equations with Variables on Both Sides**	
	Exploration	17
	Lesson	18
■ Section 1.4	**Rewriting Equations and Formulas**	
	Exploration	25
	Lesson	26
	Connecting Concepts	31
	Chapter Review	32
	Practice Test	36
	Cumulative Practice	37

■ Major Topic
■ Supporting Topic
■ Additional Topic

Transformations

	STEAM Video/Performance Task	41
	Getting Ready for Chapter 2	42
■ Section 2.1	**Translations**	
	Exploration	43
	Lesson	44
■ Section 2.2	**Reflections**	
	Exploration	49
	Lesson	50
■ Section 2.3	**Rotations**	
	Exploration	55
	Lesson	56
■ Section 2.4	**Congruent Figures**	
	Exploration	63
	Lesson	64
■ Section 2.5	**Dilations**	
	Exploration	69
	Lesson	70
■ Section 2.6	**Similar Figures**	
	Exploration	77
	Lesson	78
■ Section 2.7	**Perimeters and Areas of Similar Figures**	
	Exploration	83
	Lesson	84
	Connecting Concepts	89
	Chapter Review	90
	Practice Test	96
	Cumulative Practice	97

xxxiii

Angles and Triangles

	STEAM Video/Performance Task	101
	Getting Ready for Chapter 3	102
■ Section 3.1	**Parallel Lines and Transversals**	
	Exploration	103
	Lesson	104
■ Section 3.2	**Angles of Triangles**	
	Exploration	111
	Lesson	112
■ Section 3.3	**Angles of Polygons**	
	Exploration	117
	Lesson	118
■ Section 3.4	**Using Similar Triangles**	
	Exploration	123
	Lesson	124
	Connecting Concepts	129
	Chapter Review	130
	Practice Test	134
	Cumulative Practice	135

■ Major Topic
■ Supporting Topic
■ Additional Topic

Graphing and Writing Linear Equations

	STEAM Video/Performance Task	139
	Getting Ready for Chapter 4	140
■ Section 4.1	**Graphing Linear Equations**	
	Exploration	141
	Lesson	142
■ Section 4.2	**Slope of a Line**	
	Exploration	147
	Lesson	148
■ Section 4.3	**Graphing Proportional Relationships**	
	Exploration	155
	Lesson	156
■ Section 4.4	**Graphing Linear Equations in Slope-Intercept Form**	
	Exploration	161
	Lesson	162
■ Section 4.5	**Graphing Linear Equations in Standard Form**	
	Exploration	167
	Lesson	168
■ Section 4.6	**Writing Equations in Slope-Intercept Form**	
	Exploration	173
	Lesson	174
■ Section 4.7	**Writing Equations in Point-Slope Form**	
	Exploration	179
	Lesson	180
	Connecting Concepts	185
	Chapter Review	186
	Practice Test	192
	Cumulative Practice	193

5 Systems of Linear Equations

STEAM Video/Performance Task 197
Getting Ready for Chapter 5 198

- **Section 5.1** **Solving Systems of Linear Equations by Graphing**
  Exploration 199
  Lesson 200

- **Section 5.2** **Solving Systems of Linear Equations by Substitution**
  Exploration 205
  Lesson 206

- **Section 5.3** **Solving Systems of Linear Equations by Elimination**
  Exploration 211
  Lesson 212

- **Section 5.4** **Solving Special Systems of Linear Equations**
  Exploration 219
  Lesson 220

Connecting Concepts 225
Chapter Review 226
Practice Test 230
Cumulative Practice 231

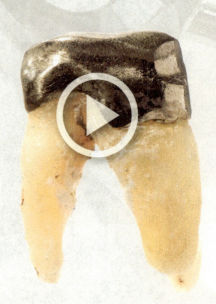

- Major Topic
- Supporting Topic
- Additional Topic

Data Analysis and Displays

	STEAM Video/Performance Task	**235**
	Getting Ready for Chapter 6	**236**
■ Section 6.1	**Scatter Plots**	
	Exploration	237
	Lesson	238
■ Section 6.2	**Lines of Fit**	
	Exploration	243
	Lesson	244
■ Section 6.3	**Two-Way Tables**	
	Exploration	249
	Lesson	250
■ Section 6.4	**Choosing a Data Display**	
	Exploration	255
	Lesson	256
	Connecting Concepts	**263**
	Chapter Review	**264**
	Practice Test	**268**
	Cumulative Practice	**269**

xxxvii

7 Functions

STEAM Video/Performance Task 273
Getting Ready for Chapter 7 274

- **Section 7.1 Relations and Functions**
  Exploration 275
  Lesson 276

- **Section 7.2 Representations of Functions**
  Exploration 281
  Lesson 282

- **Section 7.3 Linear Functions**
  Exploration 289
  Lesson 290

- **Section 7.4 Comparing Linear and Nonlinear Functions**
  Exploration 295
  Lesson 296

- **Section 7.5 Analyzing and Sketching Graphs**
  Exploration 301
  Lesson 302

Connecting Concepts 307
Chapter Review 308
Practice Test 312
Cumulative Practice 313

■ Major Topic
■ Supporting Topic
■ Additional Topic

xxxviii

Exponents and Scientific Notation

	STEAM Video/Performance Task....317
	Getting Ready for Chapter 8..........318
■ Section 8.1	**Exponents**
	Exploration 319
	Lesson 320
■ Section 8.2	**Product of Powers Property**
	Exploration 325
	Lesson 326
■ Section 8.3	**Quotient of Powers Property**
	Exploration 331
	Lesson 332
■ Section 8.4	**Zero and Negative Exponents**
	Exploration 337
	Lesson 338
■ Section 8.5	**Estimating Quantities**
	Exploration 343
	Lesson 344
■ Section 8.6	**Scientific Notation**
	Exploration 349
	Lesson 350
■ Section 8.7	**Operations in Scientific Notation**
	Exploration 355
	Lesson 356
	Connecting Concepts..................361
	Chapter Review 362
	Practice Test 366
	Cumulative Practice 367

9 Real Numbers and the Pythagorean Theorem

	STEAM Video/Performance Task....371
	Getting Ready for Chapter 9..........372
■ Section 9.1	**Finding Square Roots**
	Exploration 373
	Lesson 374
■ Section 9.2	**The Pythagorean Theorem**
	Exploration 381
	Lesson 382
■ Section 9.3	**Finding Cube Roots**
	Exploration 389
	Lesson 390
■ Section 9.4	**Rational Numbers**
	Exploration 395
	Lesson 396
■ Section 9.5	**Irrational Numbers**
	Exploration 401
	Lesson 402
■ Section 9.6	**The Converse of the Pythagorean Theorem**
	Exploration 409
	Lesson 410
	Connecting Concepts...........415
	Chapter Review......................416
	Practice Test..........................420
	Cumulative Practice..............421

■ Major Topic
■ Supporting Topic
■ Additional Topic

Volume and Similar Solids

	STEAM Video/Performance Task	425
	Getting Ready for Chapter 10	426
■ Section 10.1	**Volumes of Cylinders**	
	Exploration	427
	Lesson	428
■ Section 10.2	**Volumes of Cones**	
	Exploration	433
	Lesson	434
■ Section 10.3	**Volumes of Spheres**	
	Exploration	439
	Lesson	440
■ Section 10.4	**Surface Areas and Volumes of Similar Solids**	
	Exploration	445
	Lesson	446
	Connecting Concepts	453
	Chapter Review	454
	Practice Test	458
	Cumulative Practice	459

xli

A Equations and Inequalities

	STEAM Video/Performance Task	463
	Getting Ready for Chapter A	464
■ **Section A.1**	**Solving Equations Using Addition or Subtraction**	
	Exploration	465
	Lesson	466
■ **Section A.2**	**Solving Equations Using Multiplication or Division**	
	Exploration	471
	Lesson	472
■ **Section A.3**	**Solving Two-Step Equations**	
	Exploration	477
	Lesson	478
■ **Section A.4**	**Writing and Graphing Inequalities**	
	Exploration	483
	Lesson	484
■ **Section A.5**	**Solving Inequalities Using Addition or Subtraction**	
	Exploration	489
	Lesson	490
■ **Section A.6**	**Solving Inequalities Using Multiplication or Division**	
	Exploration	495
	Lesson	496
■ **Section A.7**	**Solving Two-Step Inequalities**	
	Exploration	503
	Lesson	504
	Connecting Concepts	509
	Chapter Review	510
	Practice Test	514
	Cumulative Practice	515

■ Major Topic
■ Supporting Topic
■ Additional Topic

Probability

	STEAM Video/Performance Task	519
	Getting Ready for Chapter B	520
■ Section B.1	**Probability**	
	Exploration	521
	Lesson	522
■ Section B.2	**Experimental and Theoretical Probability**	
	Exploration	529
	Lesson	530
■ Section B.3	**Compound Events**	
	Exploration	537
	Lesson	538
■ Section B.4	**Simulations**	
	Exploration	545
	Lesson	546
	Connecting Concepts	551
	Chapter Review	552
	Practice Test	556
	Cumulative Practice	557

xliii

C Statistics

	STEAM Video/Performance Task	561
	Getting Ready for Chapter C	562
■ Section C.1	**Samples and Populations**	
	Exploration	563
	Lesson	564
■ Section C.2	**Using Random Samples to Describe Populations**	
	Exploration	569
	Lesson	570
■ Section C.3	**Comparing Populations**	
	Exploration	575
	Lesson	576
■ Section C.4	**Using Random Samples to Compare Populations**	
	Exploration	581
	Lesson	582
	Connecting Concepts	587
	Chapter Review	588
	Practice Test	592
	Cumulative Practice	593

■ Major Topic
■ Supporting Topic
■ Additional Topic

Geometric Shapes and Angles

	STEAM Video/Performance Task	597
	Getting Ready for Chapter D	598
■ Section D.1	**Circles and Circumference**	
	Exploration	599
	Lesson	600
■ Section D.2	**Areas of Circles**	
	Exploration	607
	Lesson	608
■ Section D.3	**Perimeters and Areas of Composite Figures**	
	Exploration	613
	Lesson	614
■ Section D.4	**Constructing Polygons**	
	Exploration	619
	Lesson	620
■ Section D.5	**Finding Unknown Angle Measures**	
	Exploration	627
	Lesson	628
	Connecting Concepts	635
	Chapter Review	636
	Practice Test	640
	Cumulative Practice	641

E Surface Area and Volume

STEAM Video/Performance Task	645
Getting Ready for Chapter E	646

- **Section E.1 Surface Areas of Prisms**
  - Exploration 647
  - Lesson 648

- **Section E.2 Surface Areas of Cylinders**
  - Exploration 653
  - Lesson 654

- **Section E.3 Surface Areas of Pyramids**
  - Exploration 659
  - Lesson 660

- **Section E.4 Volumes of Prisms**
  - Exploration 665
  - Lesson 666

- **Section E.5 Volumes of Pyramids**
  - Exploration 671
  - Lesson 672

- **Section E.6 Cross Sections of Three-Dimensional Figures**
  - Exploration 677
  - Lesson 678

Connecting Concepts	683
Chapter Review	684
Practice Test	688
Cumulative Practice	689

■ Major Topic
■ Supporting Topic
■ Additional Topic

Additional Answers **A1**
English-Spanish Glossary **A9**
Index **A19**
Mathematics Reference Sheet **B1**

A. Equations and Inequalities

- **A.1** Solving Equations Using Addition or Subtraction
- **A.2** Solving Equations Using Multiplication or Division
- **A.3** Solving Two-Step Equations
- **A.4** Writing and Graphing Inequalities
- **A.5** Solving Inequalities Using Addition or Subtraction
- **A.6** Solving Inequalities Using Multiplication or Division
- **A.7** Solving Two-Step Inequalities

Chapter Learning Target:
Understand equations and inequalities.

Chapter Success Criteria:
- I can identify key words and phrases to write equations and inequalities.
- I can write word sentences as equations and inequalities.
- I can solve equations and inequalities using properties.
- I can use equations and inequalities to model and solve real-life problems.

STEAM Video: "Space Cadets"

Laurie's Notes

Chapter A Overview

From the first day, you want to establish a norm in your classroom that each student will discuss mathematical problems with a partner or group. Explorations at the beginning of each lesson, and Formative Assessment Tips such as *Turn and Talk*, are explicit opportunities for student engagement. I hope you find the suggestions in Laurie's Notes to be helpful in promoting student dialogue and engagement.

In previous grades, students solved one-step equations and one-step inequalities using positive rational numbers only. There were no computations involving negative integers. In graphing $x < 3$, the graph extended to values less than 0, as students had learned about negative rational numbers.

The first half of the chapter extends equation solving to include negative rational numbers and two-step equations. Students' ability to use mental math decreases as they encounter problems such as $x - 4.25 = -12.5$. They should still be thinking, "What number can I subtract 4.25 from to get -12.5?" Visualizing a number line, students should be thinking that the answer is around -8.5. Encourage students to estimate the answer before they begin solving an equation and check answers when they finish.

Students who are not proficient in rational-number operations will be challenged to solve equations without making errors. Technology can support these students and they generally need instruction on how to enter rational numbers into a calculator correctly.

This chapter provides an opportunity for review and practice of many skills. The two equations shown are equivalent.

$$-0.6x = -14.4 \qquad -\frac{3}{5}x = -14\frac{2}{5}$$

The value of x must be positive because the product of x and the coefficient is negative. Writing $-14\frac{2}{5}$ as an improper fraction and multiplying by the reciprocal of $-\frac{3}{5}$ may result in fewer errors than dividing -14.4 by -0.6. Representation is another area of difficulty. All of the equations shown are equivalent.

$$-\frac{x}{3} + 4 = -8 \qquad 4 - \frac{1}{3}x = -8 \qquad -8 = -\frac{1}{3}x + 4$$

The underlying mathematics of why they are equivalent must be shared with students, so they become more confident in understanding which operations are being represented.

Solving one- and two-step inequalities is a natural progression in the second half of the chapter. Be sure to use precise language when discussing multiplying or dividing an inequality by a negative quantity. Use language such as, "The direction of the inequality symbol must be reversed." Simply saying, "switch the sign" is not precise.

Suggested Pacing

Chapter Opener	1 Day
Section 1	1 Day
Section 2	1 Day
Section 3	2 Days
Section 4	2 Days
Section 5	1 Day
Section 6	1 Day
Section 7	2 Days
Connecting Concepts	1 Day
Chapter Review	1 Day
Chapter Test	1 Day
Total Chapter A	**14 Days**
Year-to-Date	**14 Days**

Chapter Learning Target
Understand equations and inequalities.

Chapter Success Criteria
- Identify key words and phrases to write equations and inequalities.
- Write word sentences as equations and inequalities.
- Solve equations and inequalities using properties.
- Use equations and inequalities to model and solve real-life problems.

Chapter A Learning Targets and Success Criteria

Section	Learning Target	Success Criteria
A.1 Solving Equations Using Addition or Subtraction	Write and solve equations using addition or subtraction.	• Apply the Addition and Subtraction Properties of Equality to produce equivalent equations. • Solve equations using addition or subtraction. • Apply equations involving addition or subtraction to solve real-life problems.
A.2 Solving Equations Using Multiplication or Division	Write and solve equations using multiplication or division.	• Apply the Multiplication and Division Properties of Equality to produce equivalent equations. • Solve equations using multiplication or division. • Apply equations involving multiplication or division to solve real-life problems.
A.3 Solving Two-Step Equations	Write and solve two-step equations.	• Apply properties of equality to produce equivalent equations. • Solve two-step equations using basic operations. • Apply two-step equations to solve real-life problems.
A.4 Writing and Graphing Inequalities	Write inequalities and represent solutions of inequalities on number lines.	• Write word sentences as inequalities. • Determine whether a value is a solution of an inequality. • Graph the solutions of inequalities.
A.5 Solving Inequalities Using Addition or Subtraction	Write and solve inequalities using addition or subtraction.	• Apply the Addition and Subtraction Properties of Inequality to produce equivalent inequalities. • Solve inequalities using addition or subtraction. • Apply inequalities involving addition or subtraction to solve real-life problems.
A.6 Solving Inequalities Using Multiplication or Division	Write and solve inequalities using multiplication or division.	• Apply the Multiplication and Division Properties of Inequality to produce equivalent inequalities. • Solve inequalities using multiplication or division. • Apply inequalities involving multiplication or division to solve real-life problems.
A.7 Solving Two-Step Inequalities	Write and solve two-step inequalities.	• Apply properties of inequality to generate equivalent inequalities. • Solve two-step inequalities using the basic operations. • Apply two-step inequalities to solve real-life problems.

Progressions

Through the Grades

Grade 6	Grade 7	Grade 8
• Determine if a value is a solution. • Write and solve one-step equations and inequalities. • Represent constraints with inequalities. • Write equations in two variables.	• Solve two-step equations. Compare algebraic solutions to arithmetic solutions. • Solve two-step inequalities involving integers and rational numbers.	• Show that a linear equation in one variable has one solution, infinitely many solutions, or no solution by transforming the equation into simpler forms. • Solve multi-step equations. • Understand that the solution of a system of linear equations in two variables corresponds to the point of intersection of their graphs. • Solve systems of two linear equations in two variables graphically and algebraically. • Solve real-world and mathematical problems leading to systems of two linear equations in two variables.

Through the Chapter

Standard	A.1	A.2	A.3	A.4	A.5	A.6	A.7
Solve word problems leading to equations of the form $px + q = r$ and $p(x + q) = r$, where p, q, and r are specific rational numbers. Solve equations of these forms fluently. Compare an algebraic solution to an arithmetic solution, identifying the sequence of the operations used in each approach.	●	●	★				
Solve word problems leading to inequalities of the form $px + q > r$ or $px + q < r$, where p, q, and r are specific rational numbers. Graph the solution set of the inequality and interpret it in the context of the problem.				●	●	●	★

Key

▲ = preparing   ★ = complete

● = learning   ■ = extending

Laurie's Notes

STEAM Video

Before the Video
- To introduce the STEAM Video, read aloud the first paragraph of Space Cadets and discuss the question with your students.
- ❓ "Can you think of any other real-life situations where inequalities are useful?"

During the Video
- In the video, Robert and Tory are discussing NASA's astronaut qualifications.
- ❓ Pause the video at 1:19 and ask, "What are the requirements to be a NASA astronaut?" U.S. citizen, college degree, 3 years of experience, 20/20 vision, normal blood pressure while sitting, between 62 inches to 75 inches tall
- Watch the remainder of the video.

After the Video
- ❓ Ask, "Which requirements did Robert and Tory represent with inequalities?" height, current age (for the 3 years of experience requirement), and vision correction
- Have students work with a partner to answer Questions 1 and 2.
- As students discuss and answer the questions, listen for understanding of writing and interpreting inequalities.

Performance Task

- Use this information to spark students' interest and promote thinking about real-life problems.
- ❓ Ask, "How do you think you can use one value to describe the brightnesses of all the stars that can be seen from Earth? Explain your reasoning."
- After completing the chapter, students will have gained the knowledge needed to complete "Distance and Brightness of the Stars."

STEAM Video

1. no; *Sample answer:* Many numbers satisfy each requirement.
2. *Sample answer:* In 4 months, it will be one year since the surgery, so find the time t such that $4 + t = 12$.

Performance Task

Sample answer: Use an inequality and the least apparent magnitude.

Mathematical Practices

Students have opportunities to develop aspects of the mathematical practices throughout the chapter. Here are some examples.

1. **Make Sense of Problems and Persevere in Solving Them**
   A.3 Math Practice note, *p. 478*
2. **Reason Abstractly and Quantitatively**
   A.7 Exercise 28, *p. 508*
3. **Construct Viable Arguments and Critique the Reasoning of Others**
   A.5 Math Practice note, *p. 489*
4. **Model with Mathematics**
   A.4 Exercise 35, *p. 488*
5. **Use Appropriate Tools Strategically**
   A.1 Math Practice note, *p. 467*
6. **Attend to Precision**
   A.4 Math Practice note, *p. 483*
7. **Look for and Make Use of Structure**
   A.7 Exercise 10, *p. 505*
8. **Look for and Express Regularity in Repeated Reasoning**
   A.2 Math Practice note, *p. 471*

STEAM Video

Space Cadets

Inequalities can be used to help determine whether someone is qualified to be an astronaut. Can you think of any other real-life situations where inequalities are useful?

Watch the STEAM Video "Space Cadets." Then answer the following questions. Tori and Robert use the inequalities below to represent requirements for applying to be an astronaut, where height is measured in inches and age is measured in years.

$h \geq 62$ $h \leq 72$ $Q \geq G + 3$ $Q \geq V + 1$
h: height Q: current age G: college graduation age
V: age when vision corrected

1. Can you use equations to correctly describe the requirements? Explain your reasoning.

2. The graph shows when a person who recently had vision correction surgery can apply to be an astronaut. Explain how you can determine when they had the surgery.

Performance Task

Distance and Brightness of the Stars

After completing this chapter, you will be able to use the concepts you learned to answer the questions in the *STEAM Video Performance Task*. You will be given information about the celestial bodies below.

Sirius   **Earth**

Centauri   **Sun**

You will use inequalities to calculate the distances of stars from Earth and to calculate the brightnesses, or *apparent magnitudes*, of several stars. How do you think you can use one value to describe the brightnesses of all the stars that can be seen from Earth? Explain your reasoning.

Getting Ready for Chapter

Chapter Exploration

$+ = +1$
$- = -1$
$+ = x$

1. Work with a partner. Use algebra tiles to model and solve each equation.

   a. $x + 4 = -2$

   Model the equation $x + 4 = -2$.

   Add four -1 tiles to each side.

   Remove the zero pairs from the left side.

   Write the solution of the equation.

   b. $-3 = x - 4$

   Model the equation $-3 = x - 4$.

   Add four $+1$ tiles to each side.

   Remove the zero pairs from each side.

   Write the solution of the equation.

   c. $x - 6 = 2$
   d. $x - 7 = -3$
   e. $-15 = x - 5$
   f. $x + 3 = -5$
   g. $7 + x = -1$
   h. $-5 = x - 3$

2. **WRITE GUIDELINES** Work with a partner. Use your models in Exercise 1 to summarize the algebraic steps that you use to solve an equation.

Vocabulary

The following vocabulary terms are defined in this chapter. Think about what each term might mean and record your thoughts.

equivalent equations   inequality   solution set

Laurie's Notes

Chapter Exploration

- Students solved one-step equations in the previous course. This exploration reviews the process of solving equations using algebra tiles.
- **Reason Abstractly and Quantitatively:** Algebra tiles can help students make sense of equations. Algebra tiles are a concrete representation, deepening student understanding of what it means to solve an equation.
- Remind students of the meaning of each tile and work through Exercise 1(a) as a class.
- ❓ "What do you have to do to get the variable tile by itself?" Students may mention removing 4 yellow tiles from each side or adding 4 red tiles to each side.
- **Reason Abstractly and Quantitatively:** Subtracting 4 is equivalent to adding -4. In the solution, the approach is to add -4 to each side. Removing the yellow tiles is intuitive to students when the symbolic representation is introduced, but adding -4 (the inverse operation) will make sense in the algebraic representation. Students need to recognize the equivalence.
- After adding -4 to each side, the green variable-tile is equal to -6.
- Have students complete the remaining parts with a partner. Then have each pair compare their solutions with another pair. Discuss any discrepancies as a class.
- **Popsicle Sticks:** Solicit responses for Exercise 2. Ask several students to share with the class. Discuss similarities and differences between students' summaries.

Vocabulary

- These terms represent some of the vocabulary that students will encounter in Chapter A. Discuss the terms as a class.
- Where have students heard the term *inequality* outside of a math classroom? In what contexts? Students may not be able to write the actual definition, but they may write phrases associated with *inequality*.
- Allowing students to discuss these terms now will prepare them for understanding the terms as they are presented in the chapter.
- When students encounter a new definition, encourage them to write in their *Student Journals*. They will revisit these definitions during the Chapter Review.

ELL Support

Point out that the word *equal* means "the same." Cognates are words that sound similar in different languages and have the same meaning. Students whose first language is Spanish, Portuguese, or French will likely know the cognates *igual* or *égal*. Point out that the two root words *equi–* and *equa–* are related to *equal*. Have students guess the meanings of the terms *equivalent equations* and *inequality* based on what they know. You may want to point out that the prefix *in–* means "not."

Topics for Review

- Comparing Numbers
- Converting Between Fractions and Decimals
- Distributive Property
- Evaluating Expressions
- Graphing Inequalities
- Order of Operations
- Writing Algebraic Expressions

Chapter Exploration

1. a. $x = -6$
   b. $x = 1$
   c. $x = 8$
   d. $x = 4$
   e. $x = -10$
   f. $x = -8$
   g. $x = -8$
   h. $x = -2$

2. *Sample answer:* Add or subtract the same amount on both sides of the equation to isolate the variable.

T-464

Learning Target
Write and solve equations using addition or subtraction.

Success Criteria
- Apply the Addition and Subtraction Properties of Equality to produce equivalent equations.
- Solve equations using addition or subtraction.
- Apply equations involving addition or subtraction to solve real-life problems.

Warm Up
Cumulative, vocabulary, and prerequisite skills practice opportunities are available in the *Resources by Chapter* or at BigIdeasMath.com.

ELL Support
The Math Practice note asks students to analyze the relationship between addition and subtraction. Clarify the meaning of the word *relationship*. Explain that the mother of Sam's mother is Sam's grandmother. The word *grandmother* describes Sam's relationship to his mother's mother. If necessary, draw a family tree on the board to clarify and describe other relationships within a family. Explain that students will identify the relationship between addition and subtraction. You may want to point out that one operation is the opposite of the other. The words *positive* and *negative* may help with the analysis.

Exploration 1
a–b. See Additional Answers.

c. Use the Addition and Subtraction Properties of Equality.

Laurie's Notes

Check out the Dynamic Classroom.
BigIdeasMath.com

Preparing to Teach
- **Reason Abstractly and Quantitatively:** Algebra tiles can help students make sense of equations. Algebra tiles are a concrete representation, deepening student understanding of what it means to solve an equation.

Motivate
- ? Show students a collection of algebra tiles and ask, "Can the collection be simplified? Can you remove zero pairs? What is the expression represented by the collection?"
- **Model:** As a class, model the equations $x + 3 = 7$ and $x + 2 = 5$ using algebra tiles. These do not require a zero pair to solve and will help remind students how to solve equations using algebra tiles.
- Remind students that they need to think of subtracting as *adding the opposite* when using algebra tiles (i.e., $x - 3$ as $x + (-3)$).
- ? "What does it mean to solve an equation?" To find the value of the variable that makes the equation true.

Exploration 1
- Have students complete part (a) and then discuss their reasoning as a class.
- ? In part (b), work through the first model as a class. "What do you have to do to get the variable tile by itself?" Students may mention removing 3 red tiles from each side or adding 3 yellow tiles to each side.
- **Reason Abstractly and Quantitatively:** Subtracting −3 is equivalent to adding 3. In the exploration, the approach is to add 3 to each side. Removing the red tiles is intuitive to students when the symbolic representation is introduced, but adding 3 (the inverse operation) will make sense in the algebraic representation. Students need to recognize the equivalence.
- After adding 3 to each side, the green variable-tile is equal to −1.
- Students may say they can use mental math to solve. It is the tactile experience of adding and removing tiles that will be helpful as the equations become more complex.
- **Representation:** While the equations $-5 = x + 2$ and $x + 2 = -5$ are the same to mathematics teachers, students may see these as very different equations. Students even see $2 + x = -5$ as a different equation. Take time to discuss the equivalence of all three.
- ? When students finish solving the second equation, ask, "What did you do to both sides of the equation to solve it?" Added 2 red tiles. "Adding −2 is equivalent to what operation?" subtracting 2
- For part (c), you may want to introduce using a number line to find the solution of an equation. For example, the number line below represents solving the equation $x + (-3) = -4$. Because the second arrow is 1 unit to the left of the end of the first arrow, the solution is $x = -1$.

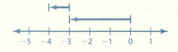

A.1 Solving Equations Using Addition or Subtraction

Learning Target: Write and solve equations using addition or subtraction.

Success Criteria:
- I can apply the Addition and Subtraction Properties of Equality to produce equivalent equations.
- I can solve equations using addition or subtraction.
- I can apply equations involving addition or subtraction to solve real-life problems.

EXPLORATION 1 Using Algebra Tiles to Solve Equations

Work with a partner.

a. Use the examples to explain the meaning of each property.

Addition Property of Equality: $x + 2 = 1$
$x + 2 + 5 = 1 + 5$

Subtraction Property of Equality: $x + 2 = 1$
$x + 2 - 1 = 1 - 1$

Are these properties true for equations involving negative numbers? Explain your reasoning.

b. Write the four equations modeled by the algebra tiles. Explain how you can use algebra tiles to solve each equation. Then find the solutions.

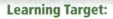

Math Practice

Analyze Relationships
How can you use the relationship between addition and subtraction to solve $x + 3 = -5$?

c. How can you solve each equation in part (b) without using algebra tiles?

A.1 Lesson

Key Vocabulary 🔊
equivalent equations, p. 466

Two equations are **equivalent equations** when they have the same solutions. The Addition and Subtraction Properties of Equality can be used to produce equivalent equations.

Key Ideas

Addition Property of Equality

Words Adding the same number to each side of an equation produces an equivalent equation.

Algebra If $a = b$, then $a + c = b + c$.

Subtraction Property of Equality

Words Subtracting the same number from each side of an equation produces an equivalent equation.

Algebra If $a = b$, then $a - c = b - c$.

Remember
Addition and subtraction are inverse operations.

EXAMPLE 1 Solving Equations

a. Solve $x - 5 = -1$.

$$x - 5 = -1 \quad \text{Write the equation.}$$

Undo the subtraction. ⟶ $\underline{+5 \quad +5}$ Addition Property of Equality

$$x = 4 \quad \text{Simplify.}$$

▶ The solution is $x = 4$.

Check
$x - 5 = -1$
$4 - 5 \stackrel{?}{=} -1$
$-1 = -1$ ✓

b. Solve $z + \dfrac{3}{2} = \dfrac{1}{2}$.

$$z + \dfrac{3}{2} = \dfrac{1}{2} \quad \text{Write the equation.}$$

Undo the addition. ⟶ $\underline{-\dfrac{3}{2} \quad -\dfrac{3}{2}}$ Subtraction Property of Equality

$$z = -1 \quad \text{Simplify.}$$

▶ The solution is $z = -1$.

Check
$z + \dfrac{3}{2} = \dfrac{1}{2}$
$-1 + \dfrac{3}{2} \stackrel{?}{=} \dfrac{1}{2}$
$\dfrac{1}{2} = \dfrac{1}{2}$ ✓

Try It Solve the equation. Check your solution.

1. $p - 5 = -2$ **2.** $w + 13.2 = 10.4$ **3.** $x - \dfrac{5}{6} = -\dfrac{1}{6}$

Laurie's Notes

Scaffolding Instruction
- Students explored the first two success criteria using algebra tiles. Now they will solve equations using properties of equality.
- **Emerging:** Students may struggle when using algebra tiles to solve equations. They will benefit from guided instruction for the examples.
- **Proficient:** Students can solve equations with or without algebra tiles. They should review the Key Ideas to solidify the properties and then complete Try It Exercises 1–3 before moving on to Example 2. Remind students to check their solutions.

Key Ideas
❓ "What are inverse operations?" Operations that undo one another.
- Ask students to give examples of inverse operations. They may say addition and subtraction or multiplication and division. They may even offer actions, such as opening and closing a door.

EXAMPLE 1
- Work through each part as a class.
- ❓ **Discuss:** In both equations, the variable is on the left. "Would part (a) have the same solution if it was written as $-1 = x - 5$?" yes "Would part (b) have the same solution if it was written as $\frac{1}{2} = z + \frac{3}{2}$?" yes
- Remind students to always check their solutions. This will help them find their own errors.
- Notice that a vertical format is used in both solutions, but you can show the process horizontally as well. Use color to show the quantity being added to or subtracted from each side.

$x - 5 = -1$ Write the equation.
$x - 5 + 5 = -1 + 5$ Addition Property of Equality
$x = 4$ Simplify.

Try It
- Students should work independently, supplying the appropriate properties and checking their solutions. Then have students *Turn and Talk* with a neighbor to resolve any discrepancies.

Scaffold instruction to support all students in their learning. Learning is individualized and you may want to group students differently as they move in and out of these levels with each skill and concept. Student self-assessment and feedback help guide your instructional decisions about how and when to layer support for all students to become proficient learners.

Extra Example 1
a. Solve $t + 6 = -5$. $t = -11$
b. Solve $y - \frac{4}{5} = -\frac{2}{5}$. $y = \frac{2}{5}$

ELL Support
After demonstrating Example 1, have students practice language by working in pairs to complete Try It Exercises 1–3. Have one student ask another, "What is the first step? Do you add or subtract? What is the solution?" Have students alternate roles.
Beginner: Write the steps and provide one-word answers.
Intermediate: Answer with phrases or simple sentences such as, "First, I add five."
Advanced: Answer with detailed sentences such as, "First, I add five to each side of the equation."

Try It
1. $p = 3$
2. $w = -2.8$
3. $w = \frac{2}{3}$

Extra Example 2

You spend $7.25 this week. This is $3.65 less than the amount s you spent last week. Which equation can be used to find s?

A. $3.65 = s - 7.25$

B. $3.65 = s + 7.25$

C. $7.25 = s - 3.65$

D. $7.25 = s + 3.65$

C

Try It

4. $P - 145.25 = 120.50$

Self-Assessment
for Concepts & Skills

5. $c = 8$

6. $k = -14.7$

7. $w = 1\frac{2}{3}$

8. yes; Both solutions are $m = -8$.

9. $x + 1 = -5$; The other equations are equivalent to $x = -4$.

Laurie's Notes

EXAMPLE 2

- **Financial Literacy:** Discuss the word *profit* and how it is computed: profit = income − expenses.
- The second sentence contains key information. When translated into symbols, students can tell that "this profit" refers to "the profit this week."
- Color-coding is very helpful in assisting students as they translate from words to symbols. Students may not recognize that "is" translates to "equals," so give a quick example.

"Three plus four is seven," translates to $3 + 4 = 7$.

Formative Assessment Tip

Think-Alouds

This technique is used when you want to hear how well partners comprehend a process involved with solving a problem. It is important to model the process first so that students have a sense of what is expected.

Think-Alouds give students the opportunity to hear the metacognitive processes used by someone who is a proficient problem solver. Hearing someone else describe a process using mathematical language will improve all students' problem-solving abilities.

Use this technique with a multi-step problem. Model using a starter sentence such as: "The problem is asking …," "I can use the strategy of …," "The steps I will use in solving this problem are …," "This problem is similar to …,"or "I can check my answer by …."

You can use *Think-Alouds* for a variety of problem types. Listen for comprehension of skills, concepts, procedures, and precision of language.

Try It

- **Think-Alouds:** Pose Exercise 4 and say, "The problem is asking…" Ask Partner A to think aloud for Partner B to hear what the problem is asking for and how to write a verbal model to represent the situation.

Self-Assessment for Concepts & Skills

Have students complete the exercises independently. Then have students use *Thumbs Up* to indicate their understanding of the success criteria.

ELL Support

Allow students to work in pairs for extra support and to practice language. Ask each pair to display their answers to Exercises 5–7 on a whiteboard for your review. Have pairs do the same for the equations they choose as answers to Exercise 9. Have two pairs form a group to discuss explanations for Exercises 8 and 9. Monitor discussions and provide support as needed.

The Success Criteria Self-Assessment chart can be found in the *Student Journal* or online at *BigIdeasMath.com*.

EXAMPLE 2 Writing an Equation

A skydiving company has a profit of $750 this week. This profit is $900 more than the profit P last week. Which equation can be used to find P?

- **A.** $750 = 900 - P$
- **B.** $750 = P + 900$
- **C.** $900 = P - 750$
- **D.** $900 = P + 750$

Math Practice

Recognize Usefulness of Tools

Would it be efficient to use algebra tiles to solve the equations in Example 2? What other tools could you use?

Write an equation by rewriting the given information.

Words	The profit this week	is	$900 more than	the profit last week.
Equation	750	=	P +	900

▶ The equation is $750 = P + 900$. The correct answer is **B**.

Try It

4. A bakery has a profit of $120.50 today. This profit is $145.25 less than the profit P yesterday. Write an equation that can be used to find P.

Self-Assessment for Concepts & Skills

Solve each exercise. Then rate your understanding of the success criteria in your journal.

SOLVING AN EQUATION Solve the equation. Check your solution.

5. $c - 12 = -4$
6. $k + 8.4 = -6.3$
7. $-\dfrac{2}{3} = w - \dfrac{7}{3}$

8. **WRITING** Are the equations $m + 3 = -5$ and $m - 4 = -12$ equivalent? Explain.

9. **WHICH ONE DOESN'T BELONG?** Which equation does *not* belong with the other three? Explain your reasoning.

$x + 3 = -1$ $x + 1 = -5$

$x - 2 = -6$ $x - 9 = -13$

Section A.1 Solving Equations Using Addition or Subtraction

EXAMPLE 3 Modeling Real Life

You and your friend play a video game. The line graph shows both of your scores after each level. What is your score after Level 4?

Understand the problem.

You are given a line graph that shows that after Level 4, your friend's score of −8 is 33 points less than your score. You are asked to find your score after Level 4.

Make a plan.

Use the information to write and solve an equation to find your score after Level 4.

Solve and check.

Words	Your friend's score **is** 33 points **less than** your score.
Variable	Let s be your score after Level 4.
Equation	$-8 = s - 33$

$$-8 = s - 33 \qquad \text{Write equation.}$$
$$\underline{+\,33 \qquad +\,33} \qquad \text{Addition Property of Equality}$$
$$25 = s \qquad \text{Simplify.}$$

▸ Your score after Level 4 is 25 points.

> **Another Method** After Level 4, your score is 33 points greater than your friend's score. So, your score is $-8 + 33 = 25$. ✓

Self-Assessment for Problem Solving

Solve each exercise. Then rate your understanding of the success criteria in your journal.

10. You have $512.50. You earn additional money by shoveling snow. Then you purchase a new cell phone for $249.95 and have $482.55 left. How much money do you earn shoveling snow?

11. **DIG DEEPER!** You swim 4 lengths of a pool and break a record by 0.72 second. The table shows your time for each length compared to the previous record holder. How much faster or slower is your third length than the previous record holder?

Length	Time (seconds)
1	−0.23
2	0.11
3	?
4	−0.42

Laurie's Notes

EXAMPLE 3

- **Teaching Tip:** The problems on the last page of each lesson can involve much of a class period. Having students work on the problems in class where you and other students can support their learning is more productive than solving application problems for homework and having little support.
- This example includes a line graph as a way to present information about the problem. Take time to have students *read and interpret* the information in the line graph.
- ❓ Here are some questions to ask about the graph.
  - "What information is displayed on each axis of the line graph?" The horizontal axis shows the level of a video game, and the vertical axis shows the number of points scored.
  - "Were the scores ever tied?" Yes, at the very start and at some point in Level 3.
  - "Who was ahead after Level 2?" your friend
  - "What does the *33 points* on the line graph mean?" The difference between your score and your friend's score after Level 4.
  - "Describe each player's performance from start to finish." *Sample answer:* Your friend did better than you at the beginning, but after Level 2 your score increased and your friend's score decreased. You ended Level 4 with 33 more points than your friend.
- **Model with Mathematics:** Take time to discuss the verbal model and how it translates information from the line graph. Mathematically proficient students are able to identify important quantities in a graph and make use of them to solve problems.
- Discuss the Another Method note, which is an arithmetic solution. It is important to compare arithmetic and algebraic solutions as you progress through this chapter. Continuously making these comparisons will strengthen students' understanding of the reasoning behind the procedures of solving equations.
- **Check Reasonableness:** From the graph, your score after Level 4 is between 20 points and 30 points. So, 25 points is a reasonable answer.

✓ Self-Assessment for Problem Solving

- The goal for all students is to feel comfortable with the problem solving plan. It is important for students to problem-solve in class, where they may receive support from you and their peers. Keep in mind, some students may only be ready for the first step.
- Encourage students to write the key words and phrases using colored pencils before translating the verbal model into symbols.
- Remind students to check their answers for reasonableness.

The Success Criteria Self-Assessment chart can be found in the *Student Journal* or online at *BigIdeasMath.com*.

Closure

- **Exit Ticket:** Solve each equation. Check your solution.
  a. $p - 3.5 = -1.3$ $p = 2.2$
  b. $-4.2 + m = 8.6$ $m = 12.8$

Extra Example 3
Your score is –1 point after Level 2 of a video game. Your score is 24 points less than your friend's score. What is your friend's score after Level 2?
$-1 = f - 24$; 23 points

Self-Assessment for Problem Solving

10. $220

11. -0.18 sec

Learning Target
Write and solve equations using addition or subtraction.

Success Criteria
- Apply the Addition and Subtraction Properties of Equality to produce equivalent equations.
- Solve equations using addition or subtraction.
- Apply equations involving addition or subtraction to solve real-life problems.

Review & Refresh

1. $4(x-5)$
2. $-6(y+3)$
3. $-\frac{2}{5}(w-2)$
4. $0.75(z-9)$
5. -56
6. -72
7. -9
8. -6.5
9. B

Concepts, Skills, & Problem Solving

10. $x = -2$; Add six -1 tiles to each side of the equation.
11. $x = -2$; Add three $+1$ tiles to each side of the equation.
12. $x = -2$; Add seven $+1$ tiles to each side of the equation.
13. $a = 19$
14. $z = 5$
15. $k = -20$
16. $x = -18$
17. $g = -10$
18. $c = 3.6$
19. $w = -15.4$
20. $q = -\frac{1}{6}$
21. $p = \frac{2}{3}$
22. $d = -5.9$
23. $y = -2.08$
24. $x = -13.53$
25. $q = \frac{5}{18}$
26. $r = -1\frac{9}{20}$
27. $w = -1\frac{13}{24}$
28. yes; The solution is correct.
29. $n - 4 = -15$; $n = -11$
30. $c + 10 = 3$; $c = -7$
31. $y + (-3) = -8$; $y = -5$
32. $p - 6 = -14$; $p = -8$

T-469

Assignment Guide and Concept Check

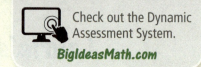

Scaffold assignments to support all students in their learning progression. The suggested assignments are a starting point. Continue to assign additional exercises and revisit with spaced practice to move every student toward proficiency.

Level	Assignment 1	Assignment 2
Emerging	3, 4, 6, 8, 9, 10, 13, 15, 17, 19, 29, 30	20, 22, 24, 28, 31, 32, 33, 34, 36, 44
Proficient	3, 4, 6, 8, 9, 11, 16, 18, 20, 22, 29, 30	24, 27, 28, 31, 34, 35, 37, 39, 42, 44, 45
Advanced	3, 4, 6, 8, 9, 12, 22, 26, 27, 28, 29, 31	34, 35, 38, 39, 40, 41, 42, 43, 44, 46, 47

- Assignment 1 is for use after students complete the Self-Assessment for Concepts & Skills.
- Assignment 2 is for use after students complete the Self-Assessment for Problem Solving.
- The red exercises can be used as a concept check.

Review & Refresh Prior Skills

Exercises 1–4 Factoring Out the Coefficient of the Variable Term
Exercises 5 and 6 Multiplying Integers
Exercises 7 and 8 Dividing Integers
Exercise 9 Multiplying Rational Numbers

Common Errors

- **Exercises 13–27** Students may use the same operation instead of the inverse operation to solve. Simplify the equation on the board to demonstrate that this will not work. Students may have ignored the side with the variable when they made this mistake. Remind them to check their answers in the original equation.
- **Exercises 13–27** Students may add or subtract the number on the side of the equation without the variable. For example, $-14 + 14 = k + 6 + 14$ instead of $-14 - 6 = k + 6 - 6$. Remind students that they are trying to get the variable by itself, so they should start on the side with the variable and use the inverse of that operation.

A.1 Practice

Review & Refresh

Factor out the coefficient of the variable term.

1. $4x - 20$ 2. $6y - 18$ 3. $\frac{w}{5} + \frac{4}{5}$ 4. $0.132 - 0.15$

Multiply or divide.

5. -7×8 6. $6 \times (-12)$ 7. $18 \div (-2)$ 8. $-26 \div 4$

9. A class of 144 students voted for a class president. Three-fourths of the students voted for you. Of the students who voted for you, $\frac{5}{3}$ are female. How many female students voted for you?

Concepts, Skills, & Problem Solving

USING ALGEBRA TILES Solve the equation using algebra tiles. Explain your reasoning. (See Exploration 1, p. 465.)

SOLVING AN EQUATION Solve the equation. Check your solution.

16. $x + 4 = -14$

19. $-10.1 = w + 5.3$ 20. $\frac{1}{2} = a + \frac{2}{3}$ 21. $p - 3\frac{1}{6} = -2\frac{1}{2}$

22. $-9.3 = d - 3.4$ 23. $4.58 + y = 2.5$ 24. $x - 5.2 = -18.73$

25. $q + \frac{5}{9} = \frac{5}{6}$ 26. $-2\frac{1}{4} = r - \frac{4}{5}$ 27. $w + 3\frac{3}{8} = 1\frac{5}{6}$

28. **YOU BE THE TEACHER** Your friend solves the equation $x + 8 = -10$. Is your friend correct? Explain your reasoning.

WRITING AND SOLVING AN EQUATION Write the word sentence as an equation. Then solve the equation.

29. 4 less than a number n is -15.   30. 10 more than a number c is 3.

31. The sum of a number y and -3 is -8.

32. The difference of a number p and 6 is -14.

Common Errors

- **Exercises 36–38** Students may try to use inverse operations to combine like terms on the same side of the equation. Remind students that inverse operations are used on both sides of the equation, not just one side.

Mini-Assessment
Solve the equation. Check your solution.
1. $x + 3.6 = -4.75$ $x = -8.35$
2. $-15.8 = y - 24.3$ $y = 8.5$
3. $t - 2\frac{2}{3} = -\frac{5}{2}$ $t = \frac{1}{6}$
4. $-\frac{5}{6} = z + \frac{1}{8}$ $z = -\frac{23}{24}$
5. You withdrew $47.25 from your checking account. Now your balance is −$23.75. Write and solve an equation to find the amount of money in your account before you withdrew the money. $x - 47.25 = -23.75$; $23.50

Concepts, Skills, & Problem Solving

33. $t - 184.9 = -109.3$; 75.6°F
34. −$1.16 million; The solution of $p + 2.54 = 1.38$ is $p = -1.16$.
35. $10\frac{3}{4}$ m; The solution of $h - \left(-7\frac{3}{4}\right) = 18\frac{1}{2}$ is $h = 10\frac{3}{4}$.
36. 4 cm
37. 3.8 in.
38. 11.9 ft
39. 152 ft; The solution of $305 = h + 153$ is $152 = h$.
40. $-250\frac{5}{6}$ ft
41. $41\frac{4}{15}$ km; The solution of $65\frac{3}{5} = d + 24\frac{1}{3}$ is $41\frac{4}{15} = d$.
42. 108.9°
43. 74.36
44. −17
45. 2, −2
46. 0
47. 13, −13

Section Resources

Surface Level	Deep Level
Resources by Chapter • Extra Practice • Reteach • Puzzle Time Student Journal • Self-Assessment • Practice Differentiating the Lesson Tutorial Videos Skills Review Handbook Skills Trainer	Resources by Chapter • Enrichment and Extension Graphic Organizers Dynamic Assessment System • Section Practice

Learning Target
Write and solve equations using multiplication or division.

Success Criteria
- Apply the Multiplication and Division Properties of Equality to produce equivalent equations.
- Solve equations using multiplication or division.
- Apply equations involving multiplication or division to solve real-life problems.

Warm Up
Cumulative, vocabulary, and prerequisite skills practice opportunities are available in the *Resources by Chapter* or at *BigIdeasMath.com*.

ELL Support
Review the meaning of the word *relationship*. Remind students that the relationship of the operations of addition and subtraction might be described as opposites. Discuss the relationship of multiplication and division.

Exploration 1
a. *Sample answer:* Multiplying or dividing by the same number on both sides of the equation produces equivalent expressions; yes; Multiplying or dividing by any nonzero value on both sides of the equation produces equivalent expressions.

b. See Additional Answers.

c. Use the Multiplication and Division Properties of Equality.

Laurie's Notes

Check out the Dynamic Classroom.
BigIdeasMath.com

Preparing to Teach
- Students have used algebra tiles to model solving equations involving addition and subtraction. Now they will use algebra tiles to solve equations involving multiplication and division.
- **Reason Abstractly and Quantitatively:** Algebra tiles can help students make sense of equations. Algebra tiles are a concrete representation, deepening student understanding of what it means to solve an equation.

Motivate
- **Model:** Display 2 green variable-tiles and 4 yellow integer-tiles to the class.
- ? "If 2 green tiles equal 4 yellow tiles, what does one green tile equal?" 2 yellow tiles
- ? "How did you decide that 1 green tile equals 2 yellow tiles?" Divide each side into groups. The number of groups is the number of variable tiles.

Exploration 1
- Give students time to read and consider part (a). Then ask volunteers to explain each of the properties.
- For part (b), model the first equation as students model the equation at their desks. Write the corresponding algebraic equation represented by the tiles. Encourage students to do the same.
- ? "What does it mean to solve an equation using algebra tiles?" To get one variable tile by itself. Tell students that this is called "isolating the variable."
- ? "If 8 yellow tiles equal 4 green tiles, what is the value of each green tile?" 2 "How did you find your answer?" To get 1 green tile, you need 4 groups. So, divide the 8 yellow tiles into 4 equal groups.
- Remind students that variables can be on either side of the equation. If students are more comfortable with variables on the left, they can write $4x = 8$ instead of $8 = 4x$.
- After students work on the problems in pairs, ask volunteers to demonstrate to the class. Listen for how students describe the solutions.
- The third equation will be more difficult to solve using algebra tiles than the others. Students should find $-x = -3$. Then they will need to use what they know about zero pairs to add x and 3 to each side. At this point, students should see the importance of the Multiplication Property of Equality.
- ? **Extension:** "Why is it difficult to model the equation $\frac{1}{3}x = 6$ with algebra tiles? You cannot show $\frac{1}{3}$ of a green variable-tile, but you can talk about the meaning. If $\frac{1}{3}$ of a green variable-tile is 6, then $\frac{2}{3}$ would be 12, and $\frac{3}{3}$ (or a whole green variable-tile) would be 18.
- **Use Appropriate Tools Strategically:** Ask students what kind of eq.0uations lend themselves to being solved using algebra tiles or number lines and which do not.
- Have students use *Paired Verbal Fluency* to discuss part (c).

A.2 Solving Equations Using Multiplication or Division

Learning Target: Write and solve equations using multiplication or division.

Success Criteria:
- I can apply the Multiplication and Division Properties of Equality to produce equivalent equations.
- I can solve equations using multiplication or division.
- I can apply equations involving multiplication or division to solve real-life problems.

EXPLORATION 1   Using Algebra Tiles to Solve Equations

Work with a partner.

a. Use the examples to explain the meaning of each property.

Multiplication Property of Equality:
$$3x = 1$$
$$2 \cdot 3x = 2 \cdot 1$$

Division Property of Equality:
$$3x = 1$$
$$\frac{3x}{4} = \frac{1}{4}$$

Are these properties true for equations involving negative numbers? Explain your reasoning.

b. Write the three equations modeled by the algebra tiles. Explain how you can use algebra tiles to solve each equation. Then find the solutions.

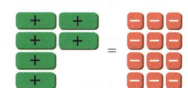

Math Practice

Find General Methods

How can you use properties of equality to solve equations of the form $ax = b$?

c. How can you solve each equation in part (b) without using algebra tiles?

A.2 Lesson

Key Ideas

Multiplication Property of Equality

Words Multiplying each side of an equation by the same number produces an equivalent equation.

Algebra If $a = b$, then $a \cdot c = b \cdot c$.

Division Property of Equality

Words Dividing each side of an equation by the same number produces an equivalent equation.

Algebra If $a = b$, then $a \div c = b \div c$, $c \neq 0$.

Remember
Multiplication and division are inverse operations.

EXAMPLE 1 Solving Equations

a. Solve $\dfrac{x}{3} = -6$.

$\dfrac{x}{3} = -6$ Write the equation.

Undo the division. → $3 \cdot \dfrac{x}{3} = 3 \cdot (-6)$ Multiplication Property of Equality

$x = -18$ Simplify.

▶ The solution is $x = -18$.

Check
$\dfrac{x}{3} = -6$
$\dfrac{-18}{3} \stackrel{?}{=} -6$
$-6 = -6$ ✓

b. Solve $18 = -4y$.

$18 = -4y$ Write the equation.

Undo the multiplication. → $\dfrac{18}{-4} = \dfrac{-4y}{-4}$ Division Property of Equality

$-4.5 = y$ Simplify.

▶ The solution is $y = -4.5$.

Check
$18 = -4y$
$18 \stackrel{?}{=} -4(-4.5)$
$18 = 18$ ✓

Try It Solve the equation. Check your solution.

1. $\dfrac{x}{5} = -2$ 2. $-a = -24$ 3. $3 = -1.5n$

Laurie's Notes

Scaffolding Instruction
- Students explored the first two success criteria using algebra tiles. Now they will formalize the process of solving equations using the Multiplication and Division Properties of Equality.
- **Emerging:** Students may be able to identify the properties but struggle when using them to solve algebraic equations. Examples 1 and 2 provide practice using properties to solve equations.
- **Proficient:** Students use precise mathematical language and solve algebraic equations with ease. Have them self-assess using the Try It exercises before completing the Self-Assessment exercises.

Key Ideas
- Write the properties on the board. Ask students to explain the properties in their own words. Students will likely say, "You can multiply or divide both sides of an equation by the same number and the solution will be the same," but encourage students to use precise vocabulary, *equivalent equations*.
- Remind students that although you can multiply by zero, you cannot divide by zero, which is why $c \neq 0$ is in the Division Property of Equality.
- Remind students of how multiplication and division are typically represented with a variable, such as $4x$ and $\frac{x}{4}$.

Formative Assessment Tip

No-Hands Questioning

Typically when you ask a question there are hands that immediately go up, often the same hands each time. Some students need a longer time to process a question and think through their responses. This technique instructs students not to put their hands in the air when the question is posed. You can then use *Popsicle Sticks* to call on students, or purposely call on those students whose voices you do not hear enough. The questions posed during *No-Hands Questioning* should require more than simple responses.

EXAMPLE 1
- Explain that you will be utilizing *No-Hands Questioning* during this lesson.
- Work through each problem. If possible, use colors to show the multiplication or division on each side of the equation.
- **FYI:** Note that the -6 is written in parentheses in the solution of part (a). In class, you may want to write both numbers in parentheses $(3)(-6)$ to avoid students thinking that the multiplication dot is a decimal point.
- ❓ "Can the problem be represented as $(-6) \cdot 3$ instead of $3 \cdot (-6)$? Why or why not?" Yes, because multiplication is commutative.

Try It
- If students have difficulty as they work through these problems, assess whether it is algebraic (how to solve the equation) or computational (how to multiply or divide rational numbers).

Scaffold instruction to support all students in their learning. Learning is individualized and you may want to group students differently as they move in and out of these levels with each skill and concept. Student self-assessment and feedback help guide your instructional decisions about how and when to layer support for all students to become proficient learners.

Extra Example 1
a. Solve $\frac{c}{8} = -7$. $c = -56$
b. Solve $-32 = -5p$. $p = 6.4$

ELL Support

After demonstrating Example 1, have students practice language by working in pairs to complete Try It Exercises 1–3. Have one student ask another, "What is the first step? Do you multiply or divide? What is the solution?" Have students alternate roles.
Beginner: Write the steps and provide one-word answers.
Intermediate: Answer with phrases or simple sentences such as, "First, I multiply by five."
Advanced: Answer with detailed sentences such as, "First, I multiply both sides of the equation by five."

Try It
1. $x = -10$
2. $a = 24$
3. $n = -2$

Extra Example 2

a. Solve $-\frac{5}{9}m = 25$. $m = -45$

b. Solve $-3 = -\frac{6}{7}d$. $d = 3\frac{1}{2}$

Try It

4. $b = -3\frac{1}{8}$
5. $h = -24$
6. $x = -21$

ELL Support

Allow students to work in pairs for extra support. Ask each pair to display their answers for Self-Assessment for Concepts & Skills Exercises 7–9 on a whiteboard for your review. Have two pairs form a group to discuss and form answers for Exercises 10–14. After groups have completed their answers and explanations, have each group present their answers to another group. The two groups must reach an agreement if their ideas differ. Monitor discussions and provide support.

Self-Assessment
for Concepts & Skills

7. $d = 4$
8. $t = -12$
9. $p = 15$
10. Multiplication is the inverse operation of division, so it can undo division.
11. yes; Both solutions are $m = -6$.
12. adding 12
13. dividing by $-\frac{1}{8}$
14. subtracting -6

Laurie's Notes

EXAMPLE 2

- Remind students that the goal for solving an equation is to get x or $1x$ alone on one side of the equation, or isolate the variable.
- Write the problem on the board. Remind students that you are still using *No-Hands Questioning*.
- ? "What is x being multiplied by?" $-\frac{4}{5}$
- ? "What do you need to do to get x by itself?" Divide both sides by $-\frac{4}{5}$. "Is there another option?" Multiply both sides by $-\frac{5}{4}$.
- Remind students that the product of a number and its reciprocal is 1 (Multiplicative Inverse Property).
- Tell students that dividing by $-\frac{4}{5}$ in part (a) leads to the same result as multiplying by $-\frac{5}{4}$. This is how you would solve the equation if the coefficient was written as -0.8. Both of these processes are equivalent.
- **Look for and Make Use of Structure:** Dividing by a fraction is equivalent to multiplying by its reciprocal.
- Students may need a quick review of multiplying fractions. You may need to write out an extra step or point out that you can use the properties to group the fractions and multiply them first.
- In part (a), $-\frac{5}{4} \cdot (-8) = -\frac{5}{4} \cdot \left(-\frac{8}{1}\right) = \frac{40}{4} = 10$
- Remind students that $\frac{x}{3}$ and $\frac{1}{3}x$ are equivalent. Discuss how to multiply a fraction and a whole number: $\frac{1}{3}x = \frac{1}{3} \cdot \frac{x}{1} = \frac{x}{3}$.

Try It

- **Think-Pair-Share:** Students should read each exercise independently and then work in pairs to complete the exercises. Then have each pair compare their answers with another pair and discuss any discrepancies.

✓ Self-Assessment for Concepts & Skills

- Students are continuing to work on the first two success criteria. After completing the exercises independently, have students work with partners. Each partner should select a problem and explain how to solve it.

The Success Criteria Self-Assessment chart can be found in the *Student Journal* or online at *BigIdeasMath.com*.

EXAMPLE 2 Solving Equations Using Reciprocals

a. Solve $-\frac{4}{5}x = -8$.

$-\frac{4}{5}x = -8$ Write the equation.

Multiply each side by $-\frac{5}{4}$, the reciprocal of $-\frac{4}{5}$.

$-\frac{5}{4} \cdot \left(-\frac{4}{5}x\right) = -\frac{5}{4} \cdot (-8)$ Multiplication Property of Equality

$x = 10$ Simplify.

▸ The solution is $x = 10$.

b. Solve $-6 = \frac{3}{2}z$.

$-6 = \frac{3}{2}z$ Write the equation.

Multiply each side by $\frac{2}{3}$, the reciprocal of $\frac{3}{2}$.

$\frac{2}{3} \cdot (-6) = \frac{2}{3} \cdot \frac{3}{2}z$ Multiplication Property of Equality

$-4 = z$ Simplify.

▸ The solution is $z = -4$.

Try It Solve the equation. Check your solution.

4. $-\frac{8}{5}b = 5$ **5.** $\frac{3}{8}h = -9$ **6.** $-14 = \frac{2}{3}x$

Self-Assessment for Concepts & Skills

Solve each exercise. Then rate your understanding of the success criteria in your journal.

SOLVING AN EQUATION Solve the equation. Check your solution.

7. $6d = 24$ **8.** $\frac{t}{3} = -4$ **9.** $-\frac{2}{5}p = -6$

10. WRITING Explain why you can use multiplication to solve equations involving division.

11. MP STRUCTURE Are the equations $\frac{2}{3}m = -4$ and $-4m = 24$ equivalent? Explain.

MP REASONING Describe the inverse operation that will undo the given operation.

12. subtracting 12   **13.** multiplying by $-\frac{1}{8}$ **14.** adding -6

Section A.2 Solving Equations Using Multiplication or Division

EXAMPLE 3 Modeling Real Life

The temperature at midnight is shown at the left. The temperature decreases 4.5°F each hour. When will the temperature be 32°F?

The temperature at midnight is 56°F. To determine when the temperature will reach 32°F, find how long it will take the temperature to decrease 56°F − 32°F = 24°F. Write and solve an equation to find the time.

Verbal Model Change in temperature (°F) = Hourly change in temperature (°F per hour) · Time (hours)

Variable Let t be the time for the temperature to decrease 24°F.

> The changes in temperature are negative because they are decreasing.

Equation $-24 = -4.5 \cdot t$

$$-24 = -4.5t \quad \text{Write equation.}$$

$$\frac{-24}{-4.5} = \frac{-4.5t}{-4.5} \quad \text{Division Property of Equality}$$

$$5.\overline{3} = t \quad \text{Simplify.}$$

The temperature will be 32°F at $5\frac{1}{3}$ hours after midnight, or 5 hours and 20 minutes after midnight.

▶ So, the temperature will be 32°F at 5:20 A.M.

Math Practice

Understand Quantities
Describe a procedure you can use to find the number of minutes in $\frac{1}{3}$ hour.

Self-Assessment for Problem Solving

Solve each exercise. Then rate your understanding of the success criteria in your journal.

15. The elevation of the surface of a lake is 315 feet. During a drought, the water level of the lake changes $-3\frac{1}{5}$ feet per week. Find how long it takes for the surface of the lake to reach an elevation of 299 feet. Justify your answer.

16. **DIG DEEPER!** The patio shown has an area of 116 square feet. What is the value of h? Justify your answer.

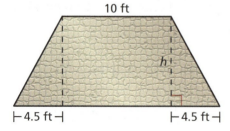

474 Chapter A Equations and Inequalities

Laurie's Notes

EXAMPLE 3

- Ask a volunteer to read the problem. Then ask another student to put the problem in his or her own words. If the student cannot, ask him or her to re-read the problem. Students need to understand that they may need to read the problem multiple times before they are able to interpret it.
- Ask another volunteer to explain the verbal model. Students often try to write an equation before writing a verbal model. Encourage them to always write the verbal model first and then use it to write the equation.
- ❓ "Why are the negative signs used?" Because the changes in temperature are negative.
- Have students solve the equation on whiteboards.
- Select students to share different methods. Students may use fractions or long division.
- ❓ "What does the $5.\overline{3}$ or $5\frac{1}{3}$ represent?" The time it takes for the temperature to reach 32°F. "Is that the answer to the question? Explain." No, the question asks when the temperature will reach 32°F, not how long it will take.
- Remind students to always check that they have answered the question and that the answer is reasonable. For this problem, you can check for reasonableness by using a table to find the temperature each hour.

Time	12 A.M.	1 A.M.	2 A.M.	3 A.M.	4 A.M.	5 A.M.	6 A.M.
Temperature	56°F	51.5°F	47°F	42.5°F	38°F	33.5°F	29°F

−4.5   −4.5   −4.5   −4.5   −4.5   −4.5

So, the temperature is 32°F between 5 A.M. and 6 A.M.

✓ Self-Assessment for Problem Solving

- Allow time in class for students to practice using the problem-solving plan. Remember, some students may only be able to complete the first step.
- **Think-Pair-Share:** Students should read the problems independently and write a verbal model for each problem. Then have each student discuss his or her verbal model with a partner. After agreeing on the verbal models, students should solve the problems independently and then compare their solutions.

The Success Criteria Self-Assessment chart can be found in the *Student Journal* or online at *BigIdeasMath.com*.

Closure

- ⊙ **Writing:** The variable in a one-step equation is being multiplied by $-\frac{3}{4}$. Describe how to solve the equation for *x*. *Sample answer:* Multiply both sides of the equation by $-\frac{4}{3}$ and simplify.

Extra Example 3

The record low temperature in Montana is −70°F. The record low temperature in Montana is 1.4 times the record low temperature in Nevada. What is the record low temperature in Nevada? $-70 = 1.4n$; −50°F

Self-Assessment for Problem Solving

15. 5 days; The solution of $-3\frac{1}{5}x = -16$ is $x = 5$.

16. 8 ft; The solution of $116 = \frac{29}{2}h$ is $8 = h$.

Learning Target
Write and solve equations using multiplication or division.

Success Criteria
- Apply the Multiplication and Division Properties of Equality to produce equivalent equations.
- Solve equations using multiplication or division.
- Apply equations involving multiplication or division to solve real-life problems.

Review & Refresh

1. $n = -3$
2. $m = 1\frac{1}{4}$
3. $h = -15.1$
4. -7
5. -9
6. 12
7. -9
8. B

Concepts, Skills, & Problem Solving

9. $x = -4$; Divide each side into 4 equal groups.
10. $x = -3$; Divide each side into 2 equal groups.
11. $x = 4$; Divide each side into 5 equal groups, then add a $+$ variable and four $+1$ tiles to each side of the equation.
12. $h = 5$
13. $t = 9$
14. $n = -14$
15. $k = -27$
16. $m = -2$
17. $t = -4$
18. $x = -8$
19. $b = 40$
20. $p = -8$
21. $d = -9$
22. $n = 8$
23. $p = 24$
24. $g = -16$
25. $c = -20$
26. $f = 6\frac{3}{4}$
27. $y = -16\frac{1}{4}$
28. no; Divide each side by -4.2.
29. $\frac{x}{-9} = -16$; $x = 144$
30. $\frac{2}{5}x = \frac{3}{20}$; $x = \frac{3}{8}$
31. $15x = -75$; $x = -5$
32. $\frac{x}{-1.5} = 21$; $x = -31.5$

Assignment Guide and Concept Check

Scaffold assignments to support all students in their learning progression. The suggested assignments are a starting point. Continue to assign additional exercises and revisit with spaced practice to move every student toward proficiency.

Level	Assignment 1	Assignment 2
Emerging	2, 7, 8, 9, 12, 13, 14, 15, 28, 29, 30	18, 22, 24, 31, 32, 33, 34, 35, 39, 43
Proficient	2, 7, 8, 10, 16, 18, 22, 24, 28, 29, 30	26, 31, 32, 33, 34, 36, 39, 40, 41, 43
Advanced	2, 7, 8, 11, 20, 22, 24, 26, 28, 31, 32	36, 38, 39, 40, 41, 42, 43, 44, 45

- Assignment 1 is for use after students complete the Self-Assessment for Concepts & Skills.
- Assignment 2 is for use after students complete the Self-Assessment for Problem Solving.
- The red exercises can be used as a concept check.

Review & Refresh Prior Skills

Exercises 1–3 Solving an Equation
Exercises 4–7 Subtracting Integers
Exercise 8 Finding Percents

Common Errors

- **Exercises 13, 18–20, 23, and 25–27** When the variable is multiplied by a negative number, students may not remember to keep the negative with the number and will really solve for $-x$ instead of x. Demonstrate an example of one of these problems on the board. Solve for $-x$ and ask students if x is by itself. If they do not realize it, remind them that there is a -1 in front of the variable and that they must divide by -1 to isolate the variable.
- **Exercises 24–27** Students may not understand why they should multiply by the reciprocal and may try to divide by the reciprocal. Ask students how they would solve the problem without using the reciprocal (divide by the fractional coefficient). Then ask how to divide a number by a fraction (multiply by the reciprocal). It is a shortcut to multiply by the reciprocal from the beginning.

T-475

A.2 Practice

Go to BigIdeasMath.com to get HELP with solving the exercises.

▶ Review & Refresh

Solve the equation. Check your solution.

1. $n - 9 = -12$
2. $-\dfrac{1}{2} = m - \dfrac{7}{4}$
3. $-6.4 = h + 8.7$

Find the difference.

4. $5 - 12$
5. $-7 - 2$
6. $4 - (-8)$
7. $-14 - (-5)$

8. Of the 120 apartments in a building, 75 have been scheduled to receive new carpet. What percent of the apartments have not been scheduled to receive new carpet?

   A. 25%   **B.** 37.5%   **C.** 62.5%   **D.** 75%

▶ Concepts, Skills, & Problem Solving

USING ALGEBRA TILES Solve the equation using algebra tiles. Explain your reasoning. (See Exploration 1, p. 471.)

9. $4x = -16$
10. $2x = -6$
11. $-5x = -20$

SOLVING AN EQUATION Solve the equation. Check your solution.

12. $3h = 15$
13. $-5t = -45$
14. $\dfrac{n}{2} = -7$
15. $\dfrac{k}{-3} = 9$

16. $5m = -10$
17. $8t = -32$
18. $-0.2x = 1.6$
19. $-10 = -\dfrac{b}{4}$

20. $-6p = 48$
21. $-72 = 8d$
22. $\dfrac{n}{1.6} = 5$
23. $-14.4 = -0.6p$

24. $\dfrac{3}{4}g = -12$
25. $8 = -\dfrac{2}{5}c$
26. $-\dfrac{4}{9}f = -3$
27. $26 = -\dfrac{8}{5}y$

28. **YOU BE THE TEACHER** Your friend solves the equation $-4.2x = 21$. Is your friend correct? Explain your reasoning.

    $-4.2x = 21$
    $\dfrac{-4.2x}{4.2} = \dfrac{21}{4.2}$
    $x = 5$

WRITING AND SOLVING AN EQUATION Write the word sentence as an equation. Then solve the equation.

29. A number divided by -9 is -16.
30. A number multiplied by $\dfrac{2}{5}$ is $\dfrac{3}{20}$.

31. The product of 15 and a number is -75.

32. The quotient of a number and -1.5 is 21.

Section A.2 Solving Equations Using Multiplication or Division

33. **MP MODELING REAL LIFE** You make a profit of $0.75 for every bracelet you sell. Write and solve an equation to determine how many bracelets you must sell to earn enough money to buy the soccer cleats shown.

34. **MP MODELING REAL LIFE** A rock climber averages $12\frac{3}{5}$ feet climbed per minute. How many feet does the rock climber climb in 30 minutes? Justify your answer.

OPEN-ENDED Write (a) a multiplication equation and (b) a division equation that has the given solution.

35. -3 36. -2.2 37. $-\frac{1}{2}$ 38. $-1\frac{1}{4}$

39. **MP REASONING** Which method(s) can you use to solve $-\frac{2}{3}c = 16$?

   - Multiply each side by $-\frac{2}{3}$.
   - Multiply each side by $-\frac{3}{2}$.
   - Divide each side by $-\frac{2}{3}$.
   - Multiply each side by 3, then divide each side by -2.

40. **MP MODELING REAL LIFE** A stock has a return of $-\$1.26$ per day. Find the number of days until the total return is $-\$10.08$. Justify your answer.

41. **MP PROBLEM SOLVING** In a school election, $\frac{3}{4}$ of the students vote. There are 1464 votes. Find the number of students. Justify your answer.

42. **DIG DEEPER!** The diagram shows Aquarius, an underwater ocean laboratory located in the Florida Keys National Marine Sanctuary. The equation $\frac{31}{25}x = -62$ can be used to calculate the depth of Aquarius. Interpret the equation. Then find the depth of Aquarius. Justify your answer.

43. **MP PROBLEM SOLVING** The price of a bike at Store A is $\frac{5}{6}$ the price at Store B. The price at Store A is $150.60. Find how much you save by buying the bike at Store A. Justify your answer.

44. **CRITICAL THINKING** Solve $-2|m| = -10$.

45. **MP NUMBER SENSE** In 4 days, your family drives $\frac{5}{7}$ of the total distance of a trip. The total distance is 1250 miles. At this rate, how many more days will it take to reach your destination? Justify your answer.

Mini-Assessment

Solve the equation. Check your solution.

1. $7x = -84$ $x = -12$
2. $-0.3y = 2.4$ $y = -8$
3. $\dfrac{m}{-2} = -\dfrac{6}{7}$ $m = 1\dfrac{5}{7}$
4. $4\dfrac{1}{2} = -\dfrac{8}{9}k$ $k = -5\dfrac{1}{16}$
5. A stock has a return of −$1.40 per day. Write and solve an equation to find the number of days until the total return is −$12.60. $-1.4d = -12.6$; 9 days

Section Resources

Surface Level	Deep Level
Resources by Chapter • Extra Practice • Reteach • Puzzle Time Student Journal • Self-Assessment • Practice Differentiating the Lesson Tutorial Videos Skills Review Handbook Skills Trainer	Resources by Chapter • Enrichment and Extension Graphic Organizers Dynamic Assessment System • Section Practice

Concepts, Skills, & Problem Solving

33. $0.75n = 36$; 48 bracelets
34. 378 ft; The solution of $\dfrac{x}{30} = 12\dfrac{3}{5}$ is $x = 378$.
35–38. Sample answers are given.
35. a. $3x = -9$
    b. $\dfrac{x}{2} = -1.5$
36. a. $-2x = 4.4$
    b. $\dfrac{x}{1.1} = -2$
37. a. $5x = -\dfrac{5}{2}$
    b. $\dfrac{x}{2} = -\dfrac{1}{4}$
38. a. $4x = -5$
    b. $\dfrac{x}{5} = -\dfrac{1}{4}$
39. All of them except "multiply each side by $-\dfrac{2}{3}$."
40. 8 days; The solution of $-1.26n = -10.08$ is $n = 8$.
41. 1952 students; The solution of $\dfrac{3}{4}s = 1464$ is $s = 1952$.
42. Sample answer: $\dfrac{31}{25}$ of the depth of Aquarius is −62 feet; −50 feet; The solution of the equation is $x = -50$.
43. $30.12; The solution of $150.60 = \dfrac{5}{6}x$ is $180.72 = x$ and $180.72 - 150.60 = \$30.12$.
44. $-5, 5$
45. $1\dfrac{3}{5}$ days; The solution of $\dfrac{5}{7}d = 4$ is $d = 5\dfrac{3}{5}$ and $5\dfrac{3}{5} - 4 = 1\dfrac{3}{5}$.

Learning Target
Write and solve two-step equations.

Success Criteria
- Apply properties of equality to produce equivalent equations.
- Solve two-step equations using the basic operations.
- Apply two-step equations to solve real-life problems.

Warm Up
Cumulative, vocabulary, and prerequisite skills practice opportunities are available in the *Resources by Chapter* or at BigIdeasMath.com.

ELL Support
Students may be familiar with the word *step* as it applies to walking or climbing stairs. Explain that a step is also one action taken when using a process that has more than one action. A two-step equation is an equation that requires two actions (or operations) to solve it. You may want to mention that the two-step is also a type of dance.

Exploration 1
a. $2x - 3 = -5; x = -1$
b. *Sample answer:* The steps are similar.
c. $2x + 2 = -6, x = -4;$
   $-13 = 3x - 4, -3 = x;$
   $-2x + 4 = -2, x = 3$
d. Subtract b from both sides of the equation and divide both sides of the equation by a.

Laurie's Notes

Preparing to Teach
- Students have used algebra tiles to solve one-step equations. Now they will use algebra tiles to explore solving two-step equations.
- **Reason Abstractly and Quantitatively:** Algebra tiles can help students make sense of equations. Algebra tiles are a concrete representation, deepening student understanding of what it means to solve an equation.

Motivate
- "Four friends each purchase a large beverage and share a $9 pizza. The total bill before tax is $16. What is the cost of each beverage?" $1.75
- Ask students to explain how they solved this problem. Listen for students to mention subtracting the cost of the pizza from the total before dividing by 4.
- "Why didn't you divide by 4 and then subtract 9?" *Sample answer:* You need to do the steps in the reverse of the order of operations to undo the calculations.
- Explain that today you will investigate how to solve equations with two operations, like the number problem. These are called two-step equations.

Exploration 1
- For part (a), have students write an equation corresponding to each step so that they connect the model to the algebraic representation.
- **Discuss:** When students have finished, summarize by saying, "The goal is to find the value of just one green variable-tile, so it should seem reasonable to 'get rid of' the red integer-tiles on the left side." Encourage students to use the proper terminology, isolating the variable.
- "How do you get the 2 green variable-tiles by themselves?" Add 3 yellow integer-tiles to each side or remove 3 red integer-tiles from each side.
- Adding 3 yellow tiles to each side is represented by $2x - 3 + 3 = -5 + 3$, which results in $2x = -2$. Removing 3 red tiles from each side is represented by $2x - 3 - (-3) = -5 - (-3)$, which also results in $2x = -2$.
- **Reason Abstractly and Quantitatively:** Mathematically proficient students recognize the equivalence of adding 3 and subtracting -3.
- For parts (b) and (c), ask volunteers to show their work and discuss different methods.
- **Attend to Precision:** Listen to the language that students use when they explain their solutions for part(c). If they say, "I'll put 2 red tiles on each side," ask them to express their steps mathematically. They *should* say, "Add 2 red tiles to each side." You want students to be able to connect their manipulations of the tiles with the operations they will record symbolically.
- Students may use different methods to solve the second equation. Some students may add 4 yellow tiles to each side (add the opposite), and others may remove 4 red tiles from each side (subtract -4).
- After one method is described, ask if anyone approached the problem in another way so students don't think their method is wrong.
- For part (d), select a student to share his or her explanation. Be sure to choose a student that you know has a correct answer.

A.3 Solving Two-Step Equations

Learning Target: Write and solve two-step equations.

Success Criteria:
- I can apply properties of equality to produce equivalent equations.
- I can solve two-step equations using the basic operations.
- I can apply two-step equations to solve real-life problems.

EXPLORATION 1 Using Algebra Tiles to Solve Equations

Work with a partner.

a. What is being modeled by the algebra tiles below? What is the solution?

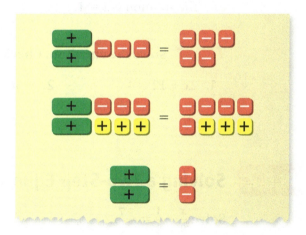

b. Use properties of equality to solve the original equation in part (a). How do your steps compare to the steps performed with algebra tiles?

c. Write the three equations modeled by the algebra tiles below. Then solve each equation using algebra tiles. Check your answers using properties of equality.

Math Practice

Use Operations
In part (c), what operations are you performing first? Why?

d. Explain how to solve an equation of the form $ax + b = c$ for x.

Section A.3   Solving Two-Step Equations   477

A.3 Lesson

EXAMPLE 1 Solving a Two-Step Equation

Solve $-3x + 5 = 2$.

	$-3x + 5 = 2$	Write the equation.
Undo the addition. →	$\;\;-5\;\;-5$	Subtraction Property of Equality
	$-3x = -3$	Simplify.
Undo the multiplication. →	$\dfrac{-3x}{-3} = \dfrac{-3}{-3}$	Division Property of Equality
	$x = 1$	Simplify.

Check
$-3x + 5 = 2$
$-3(1) + 5 \stackrel{?}{=} 2$
$-3 + 5 \stackrel{?}{=} 2$
$2 = 2$ ✓

▶ The solution is $x = 1$.

Try It Solve the equation. Check your solution.

1. $2x + 12 = 4$ **2.** $-5c + 9 = -16$ **3.** $9 = 3x - 12$

EXAMPLE 2 Solving a Two-Step Equation

Solve $\dfrac{x}{8} - \dfrac{1}{2} = -\dfrac{7}{2}$.

$\dfrac{x}{8} - \dfrac{1}{2} = -\dfrac{7}{2}$	Write the equation.
$\phantom{\dfrac{x}{8}}\;+\dfrac{1}{2}\;\;\;+\dfrac{1}{2}$	Addition Property of Equality
$\dfrac{x}{8} = -3$	Simplify.
$8 \cdot \dfrac{x}{8} = 8 \cdot (-3)$	Multiplication Property of Equality
$x = -24$	Simplify.

Math Practice

Consider Simpler Forms
Can you solve the original equation by first multiplying each side by 8? Explain your reasoning.

Check
$\dfrac{x}{8} - \dfrac{1}{2} = -\dfrac{7}{2}$
$\dfrac{-24}{8} - \dfrac{1}{2} \stackrel{?}{=} -\dfrac{7}{2}$
$-3 - \dfrac{1}{2} \stackrel{?}{=} -\dfrac{7}{2}$
$-\dfrac{7}{2} = -\dfrac{7}{2}$ ✓

▶ The solution is $x = -24$.

Try It Solve the equation. Check your solution.

4. $\dfrac{m}{2} + 6 = 10$ **5.** $-\dfrac{z}{3} + 5 = 9$ **6.** $\dfrac{2}{5} + 4a = -\dfrac{6}{5}$

Laurie's Notes

Scaffolding Instruction

- Students have explored the first two success criteria using algebra tiles. Now they will formalize their understanding and use properties of equality to solve two-step equations.
- **Emerging:** Students may struggle to solve two-step equations without using algebra tiles. These students will benefit from guided instruction of the examples.
- **Proficient:** Students can explain how to solve a two-step equation algebraically. They should complete Try It Exercises 1–6 before moving on to Example 3.

EXAMPLE 1

- **Vocabulary Review:** "In the expression $-3x + 5$, what is -3 called?" the coefficient
- Work through the example. Before doing each step, ask students what the next step should be.
- Take the time to check the solution so that students see this as important.

Try It

- Review the methods students used to solve each problem. In Exercise 3, for example, some students may subtract 12 from both sides and some may realize they can divide both sides of the equation by 2.
- Remind students to always check their work.

EXAMPLE 2

- "If you knew the value of x, how would you evaluate the expression $\frac{x}{8} - \frac{1}{2}$?"
  Sample answer: Divide the number by 8 and then subtract $\frac{1}{2}$.
- "What is the first step to solve this equation?" Add $\frac{1}{2}$ to each side.
- "What is the second step?" Multiply each side by 8.
- Point out the Math Practice note and ask, "Why was 8 chosen?" Because it is the LCD of the fractions in the equation.
- "Could 16 have been used?" yes "Does this make the problem easier? Explain." No, because then the coefficient of the variable would be 2.

Try It

- **Think-Pair-Share:** Students should read each exercise independently and then work in pairs to solve the equations. Have each pair compare their answers with another pair and discuss any discrepancies.

Scaffold instruction to support all students in their learning. Learning is individualized and you may want to group students differently as they move in and out of these levels with each skill and concept. Student self-assessment and feedback help guide your instructional decisions about how and when to layer support for all students to become proficient learners.

Extra Example 1
Solve $4t - 7 = -15$. Check your solution. $t = -2$

Extra Example 2
Solve $\frac{n}{9} + \frac{2}{3} = -\frac{2}{3}$. Check your solution. $n = -12$

ELL Support

After demonstrating Examples 1 and 2, have students practice language by working in groups to complete Try It Exercises 4–6. Provide these questions to guide discussion: "Which operations do you need to use? What is the first step? Why? What is the solution?" Have students alternate roles.
Beginner: Write the steps and provide one-word answers.
Intermediate: Answer with phrases or simple sentences such as, "subtraction and multiplication."
Advanced: Answer with detailed sentences such as, "You need to use subtraction and multiplication to solve the equation."

Try It

1. $x = -4$
2. $c = 5$
3. $x = 7$
4. $m = 8$
5. $z = -12$
6. $a = -\frac{2}{5}$

Extra Example 3

Solve $12.5 = 0.3m - 2.8m$. $m = -5$

Try It

7. $y = 8$
8. $x = -5$
9. $m = 10$

ELL Support

Allow students to work in pairs to complete Self-Assessment for Concepts & Skills Exercises 10–16. To check comprehension of Exercises 10–13, have pairs create four cards with A, B, C, and D written on them. As you ask for the answer to each exercise, have pairs hold up the appropriate card. Check comprehension of Exercises 14–16 by having each pair display their answers on a whiteboard for your review. Discuss Exercise 17 as a class.

Self-Assessment
for Concepts & Skills

10. B
11. D
12. C
13. A
14. $p = -\frac{1}{2}$
15. $d = 25$
16. $g = 6$
17. no; *Sample answer:* The solution of $3x + 12 = 6$ is $x = -2$ and the solution of $-2 = 4 - 3x$ is $x = 2$.

Laurie's Notes

EXAMPLE 3

- This problem requires students to combine like terms as the first step.
- ❓ "What do you call $3y$ and $-8y$?" like terms
- Work through each problem as shown. Then have students check the solutions.

Formative Assessment Tip

Pass the Problem

This technique provides students the opportunity to work with others to solve a problem that requires more than a few steps. One way to use *Pass the Problem* is to begin by placing students in groups. Pose a problem that one student from each group begins to work on. After the completion of the first step, the problem is passed to the student seated to the right. The recipient completes the next step, or makes corrections to the problem. If changes are made, they must explain why there was an error. This continues until all steps are complete. *Pass the Problem* gives all students the opportunity to participate in the lesson and receive feedback on their work. When students have finished the problem, they will confer with one another to discuss the problem and offer additional feedback. One thing you hope to hear is positive feedback on the clarity of thinking that was recorded, allowing students to make sense of the work.

Try It

- **Think-Pair-Share:** Students should read each exercise independently and then work in pairs to solve the equations. Have each pair compare their answers with another pair and discuss any discrepancies.
- After completing the exercises, have students work in groups of four to *Pass the Problem*. Have each student write an equation similar to the ones in Exercises 7–9. Then have students pass their problems to the right. The recipient completes the first step of solving the equation and then passes to the right. That recipient completes the last step and then passes to the right. The last recipient checks the solution.

✓ Self-Assessment for Concepts & Skills

- **Neighbor Check:** Have students complete the exercises independently and then have their neighbors check their work. Have students discuss any discrepancies.

The Success Criteria Self-Assessment chart can be found in the *Student Journal* or online at *BigIdeasMath.com*.

EXAMPLE 3 **Combining Like Terms Before Solving**

a. Solve $3y - 8y = 25$.

$3y - 8y = 25$ Write the equation.

$-5y = 25$ Combine like terms.

$y = -5$ Divide each side by -5.

 The solution is $y = -5$.

b. Solve $-6 = \dfrac{1}{4}w - \dfrac{1}{2}w$.

$-6 = \dfrac{1}{4}w - \dfrac{1}{2}w$ Write the equation.

$-6 = -\dfrac{1}{4}w$ Combine like terms.

$24 = w$ Multiply each side by -4.

 The solution is $w = 24$.

Try It Solve the equation. Check your solution.

7. $4 - 2y + 3 = -9$ **8.** $7x - 10x = 15$ **9.** $-8 = 1.3m - 2.1m$

Self-Assessment for Concepts & Skills

Solve each exercise. Then rate your understanding of the success criteria in your journal.

MATCHING Match the equation with the step(s) to solve it.

10. $4 + 4n = 12$ **11.** $4n = 12$ **12.** $\dfrac{n}{4} = 12$ **13.** $\dfrac{n}{4} - 4 = 12$

    A. Add 4 to each side. Then multiply each side by 4.

    B. Subtract 4 from each side. Then divide each side by 4.

    C. Multiply each side by 4.

    D. Divide each side by 4.

SOLVING AN EQUATION Solve the equation. Check your solution.

14. $4p + 5 = 3$ **15.** $-\dfrac{d}{5} - 1 = -6$ **16.** $3.6g = 21.6$

17. WRITING Are the equations $3x + 12 = 6$ and $-2 = 4 - 3x$ equivalent? Explain.

EXAMPLE 4 Modeling Real Life

You install 500 feet of invisible fencing along the perimeter of a rectangular yard. The width of the yard is 100 feet. What is the length of the yard?

Understand the problem. You are given that the perimeter of a rectangular yard is 500 feet and the width is 100 feet. You are asked to find the length of the yard.

Make a plan. Draw a diagram of the yard. Then use the formula for the perimeter of a rectangle to write and solve an equation to find the length of the yard.

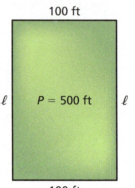

Solve and check.

$P = 2\ell + 2w$	Perimeter of a rectangle
$500 = 2\ell + 2(100)$	Substitute for P and w.
$500 = 2\ell + 200$	Multiply.
$300 = 2\ell$	Subtract 200 from each side.
$150 = \ell$	Divide each side by 2.

So, the length of the yard is 150 feet.

> **Another Method** Use a different form of the formula for the perimeter of a rectangle, $P = 2(\ell + w)$.
>
> | | |
> |---|---|
> | $500 = 2(\ell + 100)$ | Substitute for P and w. |
> | $250 = \ell + 100$ | Divide each side by 2. |
> | $150 = \ell$ | Subtract 100 from each side. |
>
> So, the length of the yard is 150 feet. ✓

Self-Assessment for Problem Solving

Solve each exercise. Then rate your understanding of the success criteria in your journal.

18. You must scuba dive to the entrance of your room at Jules' Undersea Lodge in Key Largo, Florida. The diver is 1 foot deeper than $\frac{2}{3}$ of the elevation of the entrance. What is the elevation of the entrance?

19. **DIG DEEPER!** A car drives east along a road at a constant speed of 46 miles per hour. At 4:00 P.M., a truck is 264 miles away, driving west along the same road at a constant speed. The vehicles pass each other at 7:00 P.M. What is the speed of the truck?

Laurie's Notes

EXAMPLE 4

- Ask a volunteer to read the problem. Then ask another student to explain the problem in their own words. Make sure that students understand that invisible fencing is an electronic system that often uses buried wires and an electronic collar to contain a pet. As a pet approaches the boundary of the fence, a warning sound and/or mild shock are emitted.
- **Make Sense of Problems and Persevere in Solving Them:** As the equations and real-life problems get more complex, students can become overwhelmed and may want to give up. Remind them to ask themselves, "What *can* I do? What is the problem asking?"
- Diagrams play an important part in problem solving. Remind students that they should draw and label a diagram whenever possible.
- Students may not remember the formula for the perimeter of a rectangle, $P = 2\ell + 2w$. Remind students that they can use the Distributive Property to factor out the 2 in the formula to get $P = 2(\ell + w)$. After working through the example as shown, work through the Another Method note.
- ? "How are the two methods similar?" They both use the perimeter formula, subtraction, and division. "How are the two methods different?" In the first method, you subtract before dividing. In the second method, you divide before subtracting. "Which do you prefer?" Answers will vary.
- ? "Can you solve this problem without using an equation? Explain." Yes, subtract the lengths from the perimeter to find the sum of the widths: $500 - 2 \cdot 100 = 500 - 200 = 300$. Then divide the sum of the widths by 2. Have students compare this arithmetic solution to the algebraic solution.

✓ Self-Assessment for Problem Solving

- Students may benefit from trying the exercises independently and then working with peers to refine their work. It is important to provide time in class for problem solving, so that students become comfortable with the problem-solving plan.
- Ask volunteers to share their strategies for each problem and allow others to ask questions for clarification.
- **Look for and Make Use of Structure:** Students can use two different methods for Exercise 19.
    Method 1: The car travels $3(46) = 138$ miles. The truck travels $264 - 138 = 126$ miles, so it travels $126 \div 3 = 42$ miles per hour. Equation: $3s + 3(46) = 264$, where s is the speed of the truck.
    Method 2: The rate at which the vehicles approach each other is $264 \div 3 = 88$ miles per hour, so the truck is traveling at $88 - 46 = 42$ miles per hour. Equation: $264 \div 3 = 46 + s$.

The Success Criteria Self-Assessment chart can be found in the *Student Journal* or online at *BigIdeasMath.com*.

Closure

- Explain how the solutions of the two equations are similar.

    $$4x - 5 = 7 \qquad \frac{4}{3}x - \frac{5}{3} = \frac{7}{3}$$

    Sample answer: You can multiply each term in the second equation by 3 and then the two equations will be the same. The solution is the same.

Extra Example 4
A taxi charges $2.50 plus $2 for every mile traveled. Find the number of miles traveled for a fare of $10.50.
$2.5 + 2m = 10.5$; 4 miles

Self-Assessment
for Problem Solving

18. -21 ft
19. 42 mi/h

Learning Target
Write and solve two-step equations.

Success Criteria
- Apply properties of equality to produce equivalent equations.
- Solve two-step equations using the basic operations.
- Apply two-step equations to solve real-life problems.

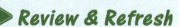

Review & Refresh

1. $z = 6$
2. $p = -5$
3. $m = -20$
4. $k = -12$
5. -34.72
6. $-6\frac{2}{3}$
7. $-3\frac{1}{8}$
8. 6.2
9. C

10. $2x + 6 = -4; x = -5$
11. $-3x + 4 = -11; x = 5$
12. $v = -2$
13. $b = -3$
14. $k = 3\frac{4}{5}$
15. $t = -4$
16. $n = -1.825$
17. $g = 4.22$
18. $t = -9$
19. $p = 3\frac{1}{2}$
20. $x = -1$
21. $h = -8.5$
22. $f = 3.1$
23. $y = -6.4$
24. no; *Sample answer:* Add 6 to each side of the equation before dividing by 2.
25. no; *Sample answer:* Use the Distributive Property first.
26. $g = -5$
27. $a = 1\frac{1}{3}$
28. $z = -1\frac{1}{2}$
29. $b = 13\frac{1}{2}$
30. $x = -1\frac{7}{20}$
31. $v = -\frac{1}{30}$

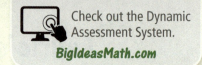

Assignment Guide and Concept Check

Scaffold assignments to support all students in their learning progression. The suggested assignments are a starting point. Continue to assign additional exercises and revisit with spaced practice to move every student toward proficiency.

Level	Assignment 1	Assignment 2
Emerging	2, 4, 6, 8, 9, 10, 13, 15, 17, 24, 26, 27, 33	18, 20, 22, 25, 28, 29, 32, 34, 35, 37, 38, 42
Proficient	2, 4, 6, 8, 9, 10, 14, 16, 18, 24, 27, 28, 34	20, 22, 25, 29, 30, 32, 35, 36, 37, 39, 42
Advanced	2, 4, 6, 8, 9, 11, 18, 20, 23, 24, 28, 29, 34	25, 30, 31, 35, 36, 38, 39, 40, 41, 42

- Assignment 1 is for use after students complete the Self-Assessment for Concepts & Skills.
- Assignment 2 is for use after students complete the Self-Assessment for Problem Solving.
- The red exercises can be used as a concept check.

Review & Refresh Prior Skills

Exercises 1–4 Solving an Equation
Exercises 5 and 6 Multiplying Rational Numbers
Exercises 7 and 8 Dividing Rational Numbers
Exercise 9 Writing a Decimal as a Fraction

Common Errors

- **Exercises 12–23** Students may divide the coefficient first instead of adding or subtracting first. Tell students that while this is a valid method, they must remember to divide each part of the equation by the coefficient.
- **Exercises 26–31** Students may immediately multiply each term by one of the denominators without thinking if it will help them solve for the variable. Ask students to check if all the denominators would be eliminated.
- **Exercises 28 and 30** Students may try to add or subtract without distributing. Remind students that when parentheses are present, they either need to use the Distributive Property or undo the multiplication first.

A.3 Practice

> Go to *BigIdeasMath.com* to get HELP with solving the exercises.

▶ Review & Refresh

Solve the equation.

1. $3z = 18$
2. $-8p = 40$
3. $-\dfrac{m}{4} = 5$
4. $\dfrac{5}{6}k = -10$

Multiply or divide.

5. -6.2×5.6
6. $\dfrac{8}{3} \times \left(-2\dfrac{1}{2}\right)$
7. $\dfrac{5}{2} \div \left(-\dfrac{4}{5}\right)$
8. $-18.6 \div (-3)$

9. Which fraction is *not* equivalent to 0.75?

   A. $\dfrac{15}{20}$ **B.** $\dfrac{9}{12}$ **C.** $\dfrac{6}{9}$ **D.** $\dfrac{3}{4}$

▶ Concepts, Skills, & Problem Solving

USING ALGEBRA TILES Write the equation modeled by the algebra tiles. Then solve the equation using algebra tiles. Check your answer using properties of equality. (See Exploration 1, p. 477.)

10.

11.

SOLVING AN EQUATION Solve the equation. Check your solution.

12. $2v + 7 = 3$
13. $4b + 3 = -9$
14. $17 = 5k - 2$
15. $-6t - 7 = 17$
16. $8n + 16.2 = 1.6$
17. $-5g + 2.3 = -18.8$
18. $2t + 8 = -10$
19. $-4p + 9 = -5$
20. $15 = -5x + 10$
21. $10.35 + 2.3h = -9.2$
22. $-4.8f + 6.4 = -8.48$
23. $7.3y - 5.18 = -51.9$

MP YOU BE THE TEACHER Your friend solves the equation. Is your friend correct? Explain your reasoning.

24.
$$-6 + 2x = -10$$
$$-6 + \dfrac{2x}{2} = -\dfrac{10}{2}$$
$$-6 + x = -5$$
$$x = 1$$

25.
$$-3(x + 6) = 12$$
$$-3x = 6$$
$$\dfrac{-3x}{-3} = \dfrac{6}{-3}$$
$$x = -2$$

SOLVING AN EQUATION Solve the equation. Check your solution.

26. $\dfrac{3}{5}g - \dfrac{1}{3} = -\dfrac{10}{3}$
27. $\dfrac{a}{4} - \dfrac{5}{6} = -\dfrac{1}{2}$
28. $-\dfrac{1}{3}(4 + z) = -\dfrac{5}{6}$
29. $2 - \dfrac{b}{3} = -\dfrac{5}{2}$
30. $-\dfrac{2}{3}\left(x + \dfrac{3}{5}\right) = \dfrac{1}{2}$
31. $-\dfrac{9}{4}v + \dfrac{4}{5} = \dfrac{7}{8}$

Temperature at 1:00 P.M.

32. PRECISION Starting at 1:00 P.M., the temperature changes −4°F per hour. Write and solve an equation to determine how long it will take for the temperature to reach −1°F.

COMBINING LIKE TERMS Solve the equation. Check your solution.

33. $3v - 9v = 30$

34. $12t - 8t = -52$

35. $-8d - 5d + 7d = 72$

36. $-3.8g + 5 + 2.7g = 12.7$

37. MODELING REAL LIFE You have $9.25. How many games can you bowl if you rent bowling shoes? Justify your answer.

38. MODELING REAL LIFE A cell phone company charges a monthly fee plus $0.25 for each text message you send. The monthly fee is $30.00. You owe $59.50. How many text messages did you send? Justify your answer.

39. PROBLEM SOLVING The height at the top of a roller coaster hill is 10 times the height h of the starting point. The height decreases 100 feet from the top to the bottom of the hill. The height at the bottom of the hill is −10 feet. Find h.

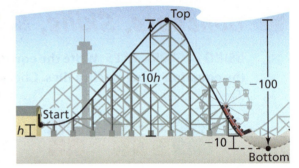

40. MODELING REAL LIFE On a given day, the coldest surface temperature on the Moon, −280°F, is 53.6°F colder than twice the coldest surface temperature on Earth. What is the coldest surface temperature on Earth that day? Justify your answer.

41. DIG DEEPER! On Saturday, you catch insects for your science class. Five of the insects escape. The remaining insects are divided into three groups to share in class. Each group has nine insects.

   a. Write and solve an equation to find the number of insects you catch on Saturday.

   b. Find the number of insects you catch on Saturday without using an equation. Compare the steps used to solve the equation in part (a) with the steps used to solve the problem in part (b).

   c. Describe a problem that is more convenient to solve using an equation. Then describe a problem that is more convenient to solve without using an equation.

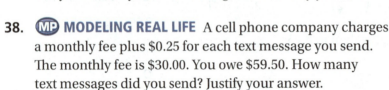

42. GEOMETRY How can you change the dimensions of the rectangle so that the ratio of the length to the width stays the same, but the perimeter is 185 centimeters? Write an equation that shows how you found your answer.

Mini-Assessment

Solve the equation. Check your solution.

1. $4x + 16.4 = -3.6$ $\quad x = -5$
2. $-12.78 = -2.1n - 2.16n$ $\quad n = 3$
3. $-\dfrac{4}{5} + \dfrac{1}{2}m = -\dfrac{1}{5}$ $\quad m = 1\dfrac{1}{5}$
4. $-\dfrac{5}{9} = \dfrac{2}{3}b - \dfrac{1}{3}$ $\quad b = -\dfrac{1}{3}$
5. A gym charges $8.75 for each swimming class and a one-time registration fee of $12.50. A student paid a total of $56.25. How many swim classes did the student take? $8.75x + 12.5 = 56.25$; 5 classes

Section Resources

Surface Level	Deep Level
Resources by Chapter • Extra Practice • Reteach • Puzzle Time Student Journal • Self-Assessment • Practice Differentiating the Lesson Tutorial Videos Skills Review Handbook Skills Trainer	Resources by Chapter • Enrichment and Extension Graphic Organizers Dynamic Assessment System • Section Practice
Transfer Level	
Dynamic Assessment System • Mid-Chapter Quiz	Assessment Book • Mid-Chapter Quiz

Concepts, Skills, & Problem Solving

32. $-4x + 35 = -1$; 9 hours (10:00 P.M.)
33. $v = -5$
34. $t = -13$
35. $d = -12$
36. $g = -7$
37. 3 games; The solution of $2.5 + 2.25x = 9.25$ is $x = 3$.
38. 118 text messages; The solution of $0.25x + 30 = 59.5$ is $x = 118$.
39. $h = 9$
40. $-113.2°F$; The solution of $-280 = 2x - 53.6$ is $-113.2 = x$.
41. a. $\dfrac{x-5}{3} = 9$; 32 insects
    b. 32 insects; Sample answer: $3 \cdot 9 + 5 = 32$
    c. Sample answers: The length of a rectangle is 3 inches more than 2 times the width. The perimeter is 52 inches. Find the length; You currently have 13 coins after a classmate gave you 5 coins. How many coins did you start with?
42. Sample answer: Multiply by 2.5; $2(12x + 25x) = 185$

T-482

Learning Target
Write inequalities and represent solutions of inequalities on number lines.

Success Criteria
- Write word sentences as inequalities.
- Determine whether a value is a solution of an inequality.
- Graph the solutions of inequalities.

Warm Up
Cumulative, vocabulary, and prerequisite skills practice opportunities are available in the *Resources by Chapter* or at *BigIdeasMath.com*.

ELL Support
Write the symbols > and < and the phrases *greater than* and *less than* below each. Then explain comparatives. *Greater* means "larger" and *less* means "smaller." To compare, you usually add the ending *–er* to an adjective, as in *greater* and *smaller*. Some words have irregular forms which must be memorized. For example, the comparative of *little* is *less*. *Greater* and *less* are the terms used in math. Explain the difference between "5 less than a number" and "5 is less than a number." Caution students to read or listen carefully for all words, so they understand the statement correctly.

Exploration 1
a. *Sample answer:* any integer 3 or greater; any positive number less than 7.5; any number −1 or less; any number greater than $-8\frac{1}{2}$

b. *Sample answer:* plot the points

Laurie's Notes

Check out the Dynamic Classroom.
BigIdeasMath.com

Preparing to Teach
- Students should know how to graph numbers on a number line and how to solve one-variable inequalities using whole numbers. In the exploration, students will be translating inequalities from verbal statements to graphical representations and symbolic sentences.
- **Attend to Precision:** Mathematically proficient students communicate precisely to others. This is done orally, in writing, and in the graphs they construct.

Motivate
- Ask students to write down their heights in two ways: in feet and inches and just in inches.
- For instance, my height is 5 feet 7 inches or 67 inches. Tell students you are going to ask questions about their heights in both forms.
- ❓ Read each statement below. Have students stand up (or raise their hands) when the statement is true for their heights. Discuss each statement before going on to the next one. For instance, for the first statement ask, "Should someone who is 72 inches tall stand?" yes "Should someone who is 64 inches tall stand?" no
  - Your height is greater than 64 inches ($h > 64$ inches).
  - Your height is at most 5 feet 2 inches ($h \leq 5$ feet 2 inches).
  - Your height is at least 63 inches ($h \geq 63$ inches).

Exploration 1
- If possible, create a large number line on the floor. Have each student stand at a different location to represent an integer on the number line. Students can hold index cards with their numbers written on them. As you read each statement in part (a), have students raise their hands if their numbers could represent the situation. If this is not practical, students can make number lines on whiteboards.
- **Big Idea:** You want students to recognize that there are an infinite number of solutions to each statement (although some solutions may not make sense in the context of the problem). Students may say that −3 is a solution to the second statement, but you cannot have a ring size of −3.
- Students should also recognize that there is a boundary point for the set of solutions and they need to pay attention to the words to understand that boundary point. *At least 3* will include the student at 3 on the number line. *Less than 7* will not include the student at 7.
- Although students only represent integers on the number line, they should recognize that the solutions for the third and fourth statements include values that are not integers. For example, the third statement includes −8.3°F.
- Remind students of the meanings of inequality symbols in the Math Practice note.
- For part (b), have students represent the solutions on whiteboards.

T-483

A.4 Writing and Graphing Inequalities

Learning Target: Write inequalities and represent solutions of inequalities on number lines.

Success Criteria:
- I can write word sentences as inequalities.
- I can determine whether a value is a solution of an inequality.
- I can graph the solutions of inequalities.

EXPLORATION 1

Understanding Inequality Statements

Work with a partner. Create a number line on the floor with both positive and negative numbers.

a. For each statement, stand at a number on your number line that could represent the situation. On what other numbers can you stand?

- At least 3 students from our school are in a chess tournament.

- Your ring size is less than 7.5.

- The temperature is no more than -1 degree Fahrenheit.

- The elevation of a frogfish is greater than $-8\frac{1}{2}$ meters.

> **Math Practice**
>
> **State the Meaning of Symbols**
>
> What do the symbols $<, >, \leq,$ and $\geq$ mean?

b. How can you represent all of the solutions for each statement in part (a) on a number line?

A.4 Lesson

Key Vocabulary
inequality, p. 484
solution of an inequality, p. 484
solution set, p. 484
graph of an inequality, p. 486

An **inequality** is a mathematical sentence that compares expressions. It contains the symbols <, >, ≤, or ≥. To write a word sentence as an inequality, look for the following phrases to determine where to place the inequality symbol.

	Inequality Symbols			
Symbol	<	>	≤	≥
Key Phrases	• is less than • is fewer than	• is greater than • is more than	• is less than or equal to • is at most • is no more than	• is greater than or equal to • is at least • is no less than

EXAMPLE 1 Writing an Inequality

A number q plus 5 is less than or equal to -7.9. Write this word sentence as an inequality.

A $\underbrace{\text{number } q \text{ plus 5}}_{q+5}$ $\underbrace{\text{is less than or equal to}}_{\leq}$ $\underbrace{-7.9}_{-7.9}$.

▶ An inequality is $q + 5 \leq -7.9$.

Try It Write the word sentence as an inequality.

1. A number x is at least -10.
2. Twice a number y is more than $-\dfrac{5}{2}$.

A **solution of an inequality** is a value that makes the inequality true. An inequality can have more than one solution. The set of all solutions of an inequality is called the **solution set**.

Reading
The symbol means is not less than or equal to.

Value of x	$x + 2 \leq -1$	Is the inequality true?
-2	$-2 + 2 \stackrel{?}{\leq} -1$ $0 \not\leq -1$ ✗	no
-3	$-3 + 2 \stackrel{?}{\leq} -1$ $-1 \leq -1$ ✓	yes
-4	$-4 + 2 \stackrel{?}{\leq} -1$ $-2 \leq -1$ ✓	yes

484 Chapter A Equations and Inequalities Multi-Language Glossary at BigIdeasMath.com

Laurie's Notes

Scaffolding Instruction
- In the exploration, students were introduced to all of the success criteria. Now they will formalize their understanding of inequalities.
- **Emerging:** Students may struggle with the idea that there is more than one solution to a problem or with the inequality symbols. These students will benefit from guided instruction of the vocabulary and examples.
- **Proficient:** Students can translate word sentences into inequalities. These students should review the vocabulary after Example 1 and then self-assess using the Try It and Self-Assessment exercises.

Discuss
- Check students' progress with the success criteria by asking them to use a number line to compare $x = 2$ and $x > 2$. Students should say that $x = 2$ will have a closed circle at 2, while $x > 2$ will include all the numbers to the right of 2 (2 is not included).
- "Is $x \geq -4$ the same as $-4 \leq x$?" yes
- Write the definition of an **inequality**.
- Review the four inequality symbols and key phrases that suggest each inequality.

EXAMPLE 1
- Write the word sentence on the board and ask, "How do you write *a number q plus 5* in symbols?" $q + 5$
- Have students write the mathematical sentence using the appropriate symbol.
- Notice the use of color to help students translate each portion of the inequality.

Try It
- **Think-Pair-Share:** Students should read each word sentence independently and then work in pairs to write the inequalities. Have each pair compare their answers with another pair and discuss any discrepancies.

Discuss
- Discuss what is meant by a **solution of an inequality**. Inequalities can, and generally do, have more than one solution. All of the solutions are collectively referred to as the **solution set**.
- It is helpful to write the inequality and substitute the value you are checking, as shown in the table. Make sure students understand that the last column indicates whether or not the value of *x* is a solution to the inequality.
- **Common Error:** Students will often make the mistake of thinking $-2 \geq -1$ forgetting that relationships are reversed on the negative side of 0; $-2 \leq -1$. Remind students to think of the locations on a number line.

Scaffold instruction to support all students in their learning. Learning is individualized and you may want to group students differently as they move in and out of these levels with each skill and concept. Student self-assessment and feedback help guide your instructional decisions about how and when to layer support for all students to become proficient learners.

Extra Example 1
A number *y* minus 3 is greater than −15.3. Write this word sentence as an inequality. $y - 3 > -15.3$

ELL Support
After demonstrating Example 1, have students practice language by working in pairs to complete Try It Exercises 1 and 2. Have a student with more advanced language proficiency read the exercise aloud while his or her partner writes the inequality. Then have both partners state the inequality as written.
Beginner: Write the inequality and read it aloud.
Intermediate: Read or write, depending on the language levels of their partners.
Advanced: Read the exercise and the inequality aloud.

Try It
1. $x \geq -10$
2. $2y > -\dfrac{5}{2}$

Extra Example 2

a. Tell whether -3 is a solution of $y + 6 < 4$. solution

b. Tell whether -3 is a solution of $\frac{y}{-4} > 4$. not a solution

Try It

3. not a solution
4. not a solution
5. solution

Self-Assessment
for Concepts & Skills

6. no; $x < 5$ is all values of x less than 5 and $5 < x$ is all values of x greater than 5.

7. k is at least -3; $k \geq -3$; $k \leq -3$

8. solution
9. not a solution
10. not a solution

Laurie's Notes

EXAMPLE 2

- "How do you determine whether -2 is a solution of an inequality?" Substitute -2 for the variable, simplify, and decide whether the resulting inequality is true.
- Work through each part as shown.
- In part (b), students must recall that the product of two negatives is positive.

Try It

- **Common Error:** In Exercise 3, when students substitute -5 for x, they may incorrectly see the result $7 > 7$ as a true inequality. Remind students to pay close attention to the inequality symbol.
- Ask volunteers to share their work at the board.

✓ Self-Assessment for Concepts & Skills

- **Neighbor Check:** Have students complete the exercises independently and then have their neighbors check their work. Have students discuss any discrepancies.
- Listen carefully to students' discussions about Exercise 7 to assess their understanding of the terminology used for inequalities.

> **ELL Support**
>
> Allow students to work in pairs to write their answers to Exercises 6 and 7. After pairs complete their explanations, have them present their ideas to another pair. Have pairs compare their explanations and reach an agreement. Check comprehension of Exercises 8–10 by having students use a thumbs up to answer *yes* and a thumbs down to answer *no*.

The Success Criteria Self-Assessment chart can be found in the *Student Journal* or online at *BigIdeasMath.com*.

EXAMPLE 2 **Checking Solutions**

a. Tell whether −2 is a solution of $y − 5 \geq −6$.

$y − 5 \geq −6$ Write the inequality.

$-2 − 5 \stackrel{?}{\geq} −6$ Substitute −2 for y.

$−7 \not\geq −6$ ✗   Simplify.

▶ So, −2 is *not* a solution of the inequality.

Math Practice

Consider Similar Problems
Compare the solutions of $y − 5 = −6$ to the solutions of $y − 5 \geq −6$.

b. Tell whether −2 is a solution of $−5.5y < 14$.

$−5.5y < 14$ Write the inequality.

$−5.5(−2) \stackrel{?}{<} 14$ Substitute −2 for y.

$11 < 14$ ✓   Simplify.

▶ So, −2 is a solution of the inequality.

Try It Tell whether −5 is a solution of the inequality.

3. $x + 12 > 7$ **4.** $1 − 2p \leq −9$ **5.** $n \div 2.5 \geq −3$

Self-Assessment for Concepts & Skills

Solve each exercise. Then rate your understanding of the success criteria in your journal.

6. **MP REASONING** Do $x < 5$ and $5 < x$ represent the same inequality? Explain.

7. **DIFFERENT WORDS, SAME QUESTION** Which is different? Write "both" inequalities.

A number k is less than or equal to −3.

A number k is at least −3.   A number k is at most −3.

A number k is no more than −3.

CHECKING SOLUTIONS Tell whether −4 is a solution of the inequality.

8. $c + 6 \leq 3$ **9.** $6 > p \div (−0.5)$ **10.** $−7 < 2g + 1$

Section A.4   Writing and Graphing Inequalities   485

The **graph of an inequality** shows all the solutions of the inequality on a number line. An open circle ○ is used when a number is *not* a solution. A closed circle ● is used when a number is a solution. An arrow to the left or right shows that the graph continues in that direction.

EXAMPLE 3 Modeling Real Life

A rock climber's sleeping bag is recommended for temperatures no less than −15°C. Write and graph an inequality that represents the recommended temperatures for the sleeping bag.

Words	temperatures	no less than	−15°C
Variable	Let t be the recommended temperatures.		
Inequality	t	$\geq$	-15

An inequality is $t \geq -15$. Graph the inequality.

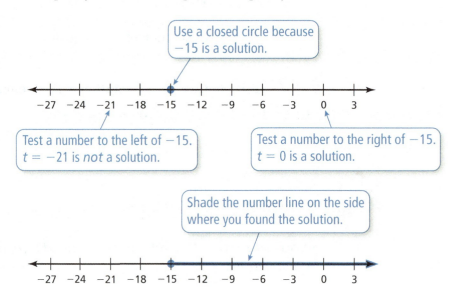

Use a closed circle because −15 is a solution.

Test a number to the left of −15. $t = -21$ is *not* a solution.

Test a number to the right of −15. $t = 0$ is a solution.

Shade the number line on the side where you found the solution.

> The graph in Example 3 shows that the inequality has *infinitely many* solutions.

 Self-Assessment for Problem Solving

Solve each exercise. Then rate your understanding of the success criteria in your journal.

Fitness Test
- Jog at least 2 kilometers
- Perform 25 or more push-ups
- Perform at least 10 pull-ups

11. The three requirements to pass a fitness test are shown. Write and graph three inequalities that represent the requirements. Then give a set of possible values for a person who passes the test.

12. To set a depth record, a submersible vehicle must reach a water depth less than −715 feet. A vehicle breaks the record by more than 10 feet. Write and graph an inequality that represents the possible depths reached by the vehicle.

Laurie's Notes

Discuss
- Discuss what is meant by the **graph of an inequality**.
- Remind students of the difference between open and closed circles. Have students use their hands to represent each type of circle. Students should make a closed fist for a closed circle. For an open circle, they can press the tips of their forefingers to the tips of their thumbs. Read the following phrases and ask students to identify the type of circle using these gestures. You could also ask students to represent the direction of the arrows with their arms.
  - at least closed
  - is fewer than open
  - is more than open
  - is no less than closed
  - at most closed

EXAMPLE 3
- Have students read the problem. Then ask a volunteer to explain the problem.
- Work through the problem as shown and encourage students to pay close attention to the graph. Students need to understand that the arrow indicates that the problem has infinitely many solutions. The direction of the arrow indicates whether the inequality is *greater than* or *less than*.
- Help students understand how to check the answer using the graph.

✓ Self-Assessment for Problem Solving

- Encourage students to use a Four Square to complete these exercises. Until students become comfortable with the problem-solving plan, they may only be ready to complete the first square.

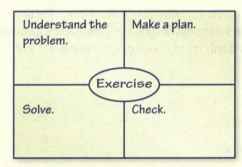

- ⊙ Have students use *Fist of Five* to indicate their understanding of each success criterion.

The Success Criteria Self-Assessment chart can be found in the *Student Journal* or online at *BigIdeasMath.com*.

Closure
- **Writing:** Write an inequality for each graph. Describe all the values of *x* that make the inequality true.

  a. 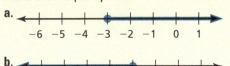 $x \geq -3$; all values of x greater than or equal to -3

  b. $x \leq 4.5$; all values of x less than or equal to 4.5

Extra Example 3
A fish is more than -3 meters below sea level. Write and graph an inequality that represents the location of the fish.
$f < -3$;

Formative Assessment Tip

Fist of Five
This technique asks students to indicate the extent to which they understand a concept or procedure. Students hold 1 to 5 fingers in front of their chests, where 5 fingers represent mastery and 1 finger signifies uncertainty. This strategy can be a quick way for students to communicate where their learning is with respect to a specific success criterion.

Self-Assessment
for Problem Solving

11. See Additional Answers.

12. $d < -725$ feet

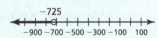

Learning Target
Write inequalities and represent solutions of inequalities on number lines.

Success Criteria
- Write word sentences as inequalities.
- Determine whether a value is a solution of an inequality.
- Graph the solutions of inequalities.

▶ Review & Refresh

1. $p = 11$
2. $w = -3.6$
3. $x = -7$
4. $v = -\dfrac{1}{2}$
5. $n = 5$
6. $h = -3$
7. C

▶ Concepts, Skills, & Problem Solving

8. *Sample answer:* 8; all values greater than 6.5
9. *Sample answer:* 21; all integers greater than or equal to 20
10. *Sample answer:* 1700; all nonnegative values less than or equal to 1800
11. *Sample answer:* -600; all values less than -400
12. $y \leq -8$
13. $w + 2.3 > 18$
14. $-4t \geq -\dfrac{2}{5}$
15. $b - 4.2 < -7.5$
16. $5k \leq -\dfrac{5}{9}$
17. yes; The inequality is correct.
18. yes
19. no
20. no
21. yes
22. yes
23. no

Assignment Guide and Concept Check

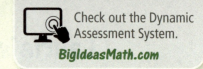

Scaffold assignments to support all students in their learning progression. The suggested assignments are a starting point. Continue to assign additional exercises and revisit with spaced practice to move every student toward proficiency.

Level	Assignment 1	Assignment 2
Emerging	2, 5, 6, 7, 8, 9, 12, 13, 17, 18, 19, 29	14, 15, 20, 22, 24, 25, 26, 28, 30, 31, 33, 34
Proficient	2, 5, 6, 7, 9, 11, 13, 14, 17, 20, 22, 29, 30	15, 16, 23, 24, 25, 26, 28, 31, 32, 33, 34
Advanced	2, 5, 6, 7, 10, 11, 14, 16, 17, 22, 23, 29, 30	25, 26, 27, 31, 32, 33, 34, 35, 36

- Assignment 1 is for use after students complete the Self-Assessment for Concepts & Skills.
- Assignment 2 is for use after students complete the Self-Assessment for Problem Solving.
- The red exercises can be used as a concept check.

Review & Refresh Prior Skills

Exercises 1–6 Solving an Equation
Exercise 7 Adding Integers

Common Errors

- **Exercise 22** Students may not understand when the boundary point is a solution of the inequality. Remind students that the inequality is true for the boundary point only when the inequality symbol is $\leq$ or $\geq$.

T-487

A.4 Practice

 Go to *BigIdeasMath.com* to get HELP with solving the exercises.

► Review & Refresh

Solve the equation. Check your solution.

1. $p - 8 = 3$
2. $8.7 + w = 5.1$
3. $x - 2 = -9$
4. $8v + 5 = 1$
5. $\frac{7}{8} - \frac{1}{4}n = -\frac{3}{8}$
6. $1.8 = 2.1h - 5.7 - 4.6h$

7. Which expression has a value less than -5?

    A. $5 + 8$ **B.** $-9 + 5$ **C.** $1 + (-8)$ **D.** $7 + (-2)$

► Concepts, Skills, & Problem Solving

UNDERSTANDING INEQUALITY STATEMENTS Choose a number that could represent the situation. What other numbers could represent the situation? (See Exploration 1, p. 483.)

8. Visibility in an airplane is greater than 6.5 miles.

9. You must sell no fewer than 20 raffle tickets for a fundraiser.

10. You consume at most 1800 calories per day.

11. The elevation of the Dead Sea is less than -400 meters.

WRITING AN INEQUALITY Write the word sentence as an inequality.

12. A number y is no more than -8.

13. A number w added to 2.3 is more than 18.

14. A number t multiplied by -4 is at least $-\frac{2}{5}$.

15. A number b minus 4.2 is less than -7.5.

16. $-\frac{5}{9}$ is no less than 5 times a number k.

17. **YOU BE THE TEACHER** Your friend writes the word sentence as an inequality. Is your friend correct? Explain your reasoning.

    > Twice a number x is at most -24.
    > $2x \leq -24$

CHECKING SOLUTIONS Tell whether the given value is a solution of the inequality.

18. $n + 8 \leq 13$; $n = 4$
19. $-15 < 5h$; $h = -5$
20. $p + 1.4 \leq 0.5$; $p = 0.1$
21. $\frac{a}{6} > -4$; $a = -18$
22. $6 \geq -\frac{2}{3}s$; $s = -9$
23. $\frac{7}{8} - 3k < -\frac{1}{2}$; $k = \frac{1}{4}$

Section A.4 Writing and Graphing Inequalities 487

GRAPHING AN INEQUALITY Graph the inequality on a number line.

24. $r \leq -9$
25. $g > 2.75$
26. $x \geq -3\frac{1}{2}$
27. $1\frac{1}{4} > z$

28. **MP MODELING REAL LIFE** Each day at lunchtime, at least 53 people buy food from a food truck. Write and graph an inequality that represents this situation.

CHECKING SOLUTIONS Tell whether the given value is a solution of the inequality.

29. $4k < k + 8;\ k = 3$
30. $\frac{w}{3} \geq w - 12;\ w = 15$
31. $7 - 2y > 3y + 13;\ y = -1$
32. $\frac{3}{4}b - 2 \leq 2b + 8;\ b = -4$

33. **MP PROBLEM SOLVING** A single subway ride for a student costs $1.25. A monthly pass costs $35.

   a. Write an inequality that represents the numbers of times you can ride the subway each month for the monthly pass to be a better deal.

   b. You ride the subway about 45 times per month. Should you buy the monthly pass? Explain.

34. **MP LOGIC** Consider the inequality $b > -2$.

   a. Describe the values of b that are solutions of the inequality.

   b. Describe the values of b that are *not* solutions of the inequality. Write an inequality that represents these values.

   c. What do all the values in parts (a) and (b) represent? Is this true for any similar pair of inequalities? Explain your reasoning.

Habitable Zone

35. **MP MODELING REAL LIFE** A planet orbiting a star at a distance such that its temperatures are right for liquid water is said to be in the star's *habitable zone*. The habitable zone of a particular star is at least 0.023 AU and at most 0.054 AU from the star (1 AU is equal to the distance between Earth and the Sun). Draw a graph that represents the habitable zone.

36. **DIG DEEPER!** The *girth* of a package is the distance around the perimeter of a face that does not include the length as a side. A postal service says that a rectangular package can have a maximum combined length and girth of 108 inches.

   a. Write an inequality that represents the allowable dimensions for the package.

   b. Find three different sets of allowable dimensions that are reasonable for the package. Find the volume of each package.

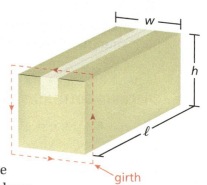

Common Errors
- **Exercises 24–27** Students may shade the number line in the wrong direction. This often happens when the variable is on the right side of the inequality. Remind students to use test points to the left and right of the boundary point to determine which direction to shade the number line.
- **Exercises 24–27** Students may draw a closed circle instead of an open circle and vice versa. Remind students that an open circle means the number is not included and a closed circle means the number is included.

Mini-Assessment
Write the word sentence as an inequality.
1. A number a is at least 5. $a \geq 5$
2. Four times a number b is no more than -4.73. $4b \leq -4.73$
3. Tell whether -2 is a solution of $6g - 14 > -21$.   not a solution
4. A rollercoaster is at most 45 meters high. Write and graph an inequality that represents the height of the rollercoaster.

   $h \leq 45$;

Section Resources

Surface Level	Deep Level
Resources by Chapter • Extra Practice • Reteach • Puzzle Time Student Journal • Self-Assessment • Practice Differentiating the Lesson Tutorial Videos Skills Review Handbook Skills Trainer	Resources by Chapter • Enrichment and Extension Graphic Organizers Dynamic Assessment System • Section Practice

Concepts, Skills, & Problem Solving

24. number line with closed circle at -9, shaded left; marks $-12, -11, -10, -9, -8, -7, -6$

25. number line with open circle at 2.75, shaded right; marks $-1, 0, 1, 2, 3, 4, 5$

26. number line with closed circle at $-3\frac{1}{2}$, shaded left; marks $-6, -5, -4, -3, -2, -1, 0$

27. number line with open circle at $1\frac{1}{4}$, shaded right; marks $-2, -1, 0, 1, 2, 3, 4$

28. $p \geq 53$; number line with closed circle at 53, shaded right; marks $51, 52, 53, 54, 55, 56, 57$

29. no   30. yes   31. no   32. yes

33. **a.** $1.25x > 35$
    b. yes; It cost \$56.25 for 45 trips, which is more than the \$35 monthly pass.

34. **a.** any value that is greater than -2
    b. any value that is less than or equal to -2; $b \leq -2$
    c. They represent the entire set of real numbers; yes; *Sample answer:* Any number either is a solution or is not a solution of an inequality.

35. number line with closed circle at 0.023 and open circle at 0.054; marks 0.01 through 0.07

36. **a.** $\ell + 2w + 2h \leq 108$
    b. *Sample answer:* $\ell = 12$, $w = 5$, $h = 5$, $V = 300$; $\ell = 20$, $w = 8$, $h = 12$, $V = 1920$; $\ell = 30$, $w = 20$, $h = 19$, $V = 11{,}400$

Learning Target
Write and solve inequalities using addition or subtraction.

Success Criteria
- Apply the Addition and Subtraction Properties of Inequality to produce equivalent inequalities.
- Solve inequalities using addition or subtraction.
- Apply inequalities involving addition or subtraction to solve real-life problems.

Warm Up
Cumulative, vocabulary, and prerequisite skills practice opportunities are available in the *Resources by Chapter* or at *BigIdeasMath.com*.

ELL Support
Explain that students will roll number cubes in the exploration. Point out that the word *roll* may mean different things. Students may be familiar with the type of roll that is eaten. Explain that when you push or toss something along the ground, you roll it. The word roll describes and names the action taken. It functions as both a verb and a noun. You roll the number cube. When you have rolled it once, you have completed one roll. A homophone is the word *role*, which describes a part that a person has in a play.

Exploration 1
a. yes; *Sample answer:* The relationship between the sides holds true.

b. yes; *Sample answer:*
$$-2 < -1$$
$$-2 + (-3) < -1 + (-3)$$
$$-5 < -4$$

c. Subtract a from both sides of the inequality.

Laurie's Notes

Preparing to Teach
- In this lesson, students will use addition and subtraction to solve one-step inequalities.
- **Look for and Make Use of Structure:** Students have solved equations using addition and subtraction. Structurally, inequalities involving these operations are solved in the same fashion. Mathematically proficient students recognize the similarity between solving $x + 9 = 17$ and $x + 9 < 17$.

Motivate
- Tell students that airlines have guidelines for the maximum weight of a checked bag. The maximum weight for one airline is 50 pounds.
- ❓ "What inequality represents this situation?" $w \leq 50$
- Ask students to write inequalities to represent other scenarios.
  - ❓ "If my bag weighs 41.5 pounds, how much more weight can I add?" $w + 41.5 \leq 50$; 8.5 pounds
  - ❓ "How much weight will I have to remove if I pack 57.5 pounds?" $w + 57.5 \leq 50$; 7.5 pounds
- Tell students that today's lesson involves these types of inequalities.

Exploration 1
- **Teaching Tip:** For this exploration, students will be rolling number cubes. Electronic number cubes are available at *BigIdeasMath.com*. If students do not have access to these number cubes, then the exploration can be completed as a whole-class activity with the teacher using the electronic number cubes.
  - If you prefer to use real number cubes, it would be best to use two different colors so that one color represents the cube with negative odd numbers and the other color represents the cube with negative even numbers. The number cubes should be marked with negative signs as described in the directions.
- Have students read the exploration and clarify any questions they may have about the directions. Discuss how students will organize their work (a table might be best).
- Have students complete all three parts.
- **Popsicle Sticks:** Solicit responses to part (c) and discuss the conjectures as a class.

A.5 Solving Inequalities Using Addition or Subtraction

Learning Target: Write and solve inequalities using addition or subtraction.

Success Criteria:
- I can apply the Addition and Subtraction Properties of Inequality to produce equivalent inequalities.
- I can solve inequalities using addition or subtraction.
- I can apply inequalities involving addition or subtraction to solve real-life problems.

EXPLORATION 1   Writing Inequalities

Work with a partner. Use two number cubes on which the odd numbers are negative on one of the number cubes and the even numbers are negative on the other number cube.

- Roll the number cubes. Write an inequality that compares the numbers.
- Roll one of the number cubes. Add the number to each side of the inequality and record your result.
- Repeat the previous two steps five more times.

a. When you add the same number to each side of an inequality, does the inequality remain true? Explain your reasoning.

b. When you subtract the same number from each side of an inequality, does the inequality remain true? Use inequalities generated by number cubes to justify your answer.

c. Use your results in parts (a) and (b) to make a conjecture about how to solve an inequality of the form $x + a < b$ for x.

Math Practice

Analyze Conjectures

Use your conjecture to solve $x + 3 < 1$. Does the solution make sense?

Section A.5   Solving Inequalities Using Addition or Subtraction   489

A.5 Lesson

> You can solve inequalities in the same way you solve equations. Use inverse operations to get the variable by itself.

Key Ideas

Addition Property of Inequality

Words When you add the same number to each side of an inequality, the inequality remains true.

Numbers
$$-4 < 3$$
$$\underline{+2 \quad +2}$$
$$-2 < 5$$

Algebra If $a < b$, then $a + c < b + c$.
If $a > b$, then $a + c > b + c$.

Subtraction Property of Inequality

Words When you subtract the same number from each side of an inequality, the inequality remains true.

Numbers
$$-2 < 2$$
$$\underline{-3 \quad -3}$$
$$-5 < -1$$

Algebra If $a < b$, then $a - c < b - c$.
If $a > b$, then $a - c > b - c$.

These properties are also true for $\leq$ and $\geq$.

EXAMPLE 1 Solving an Inequality Using Addition

Solve $x - 5 < -3$. Graph the solution.

$$x - 5 < -3 \qquad \text{Write the inequality.}$$

Undo the subtraction. $\longrightarrow$

$$\underline{+5 \quad +5} \qquad \text{Addition Property of Inequality}$$
$$x < 2 \qquad \text{Simplify.}$$

The solution is $x < 2$.

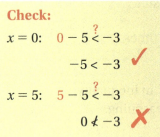

Check:
$x = 0$: $0 - 5 \stackrel{?}{<} -3$
$-5 < -3$ ✓

$x = 5$: $5 - 5 \stackrel{?}{<} -3$
$0 \not< -3$ ✗

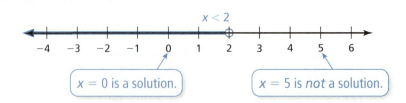

Try It Solve the inequality. Graph the solution.

1. $y - 6 > -7$ **2.** $b - 3.8 \leq 1.7$ **3.** $-\dfrac{1}{2} > z - \dfrac{1}{4}$

Laurie's Notes

Scaffolding Instruction
- Students have explored solving addition and subtraction inequalities. Now they will use properties of inequality to solve addition and subtraction inequalities.
- **Emerging:** Students may see the connection between equations and inequalities but struggle to find solutions. They will benefit from guided instruction of the examples.
- **Proficient:** Students made the transfer from equations to inequalities with ease. They should review the Key Ideas before proceeding to the Self-Assessment exercises.

Key Ideas
- Write the Key Ideas. These properties should look familiar, as they are similar to the Addition and Subtraction Properties of Equality that students have used in solving equations.
- Have students compare solving addition and subtraction inequalities to solving the same types of equations.
- **Teaching Tip:** Summarize these two properties in the following way: George is older than Martha. In two years, George will still be older than Martha.

  George's age > Martha's age   If $a > b$,
  George's age + 2 > Martha's age + 2   then $a + c > b + c$.

  Two years ago, George was older than Martha.

  George's age > Martha's age   If $a > b$,
  George's age -2 > Martha's age -2 then $a - c > b - c$.

EXAMPLE 1
- ❓ Write the problem and ask, "How do you isolate the variable, meaning get x by itself?" Add 5 to each side of the inequality.
- Adding 5 is the inverse operation of subtracting 5.
- Solve, graph, and check.
- Take time to check test points to the left and right of the boundary point. 0 is generally an easy value to work with.

Try It
- These problems integrate fraction and decimal operations.

Scaffold instruction to support all students in their learning. Learning is individualized and you may want to group students differently as they move in and out of these levels with each skill and concept. Student self-assessment and feedback help guide your instructional decisions about how and when to layer support for all students to become proficient learners.

Extra Example 1
Solve $x - 2 \geq -4$. Graph the solution.
$x \geq -2$;

ELL Support
After demonstrating Example 1, have students practice language by working in pairs to complete Try It Exercises 1–3. Have one student ask another, "What is the first step? Which operation do you need to perform? What is the solution? How do you graph the solution?" Have students alternate roles.
Beginner: Write out the problem and provide one-word answers.
Intermediate: Use phrases or simple sentences such as, "First, I add six."
Advanced: Answer with detailed sentences such as, "I add six to both sides of the inequality."

Try It

1. $y > -1$

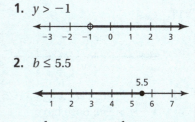

2. $b \leq 5.5$

3. $-\dfrac{1}{4} > z$ or $z < -\dfrac{1}{4}$

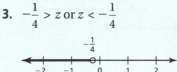

Extra Example 2

Solve $14 > x + 8$. Graph the solution.

$x < 6$;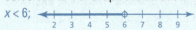

Try It

4. $w \leq -4$

5. $d \leq -1.5$

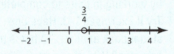

6. $x > \frac{3}{4}$

Self-Assessment
for Concepts & Skills

7. yes; Both solutions are $c > 2$.

8. $w + \frac{7}{4} < \frac{3}{4}$; The others are equivalent to $w > -1$.

9. $x > -2$

10. $z \leq 1.25$

11. $g < -\frac{1}{10}$

12. Sample answer: $x + 3 > -2$; $x - 4 > -9$; Both have solutions of $x > -5$.

Laurie's Notes

EXAMPLE 2

- Write the inequality and ask, "How do you isolate the variable?" Subtract 14 from each side of the inequality.
- **Common Error:** When students graph the solution, they may look at the inequality symbol $\leq$ and shade to the left of -1. It helps to rewrite the solution $-1 \leq x$ as $x \geq -1$.

Try It

- **Think-Pair-Share:** Students should read each exercise independently and then work in pairs to solve and graph the inequalities. Have each pair compare their answers with another pair and discuss any discrepancies.

Self-Assessment for Concepts & Skills

- Have students complete the exercises independently and then share their work with the class.
- Exercises 9–11 provide information on students' procedural understanding. If mistakes are made, have students determine whether they made a computational or procedural error.
- Students need to understand that the graph in Exercise 12 represents the solution to an inequality. They are looking for equivalent inequalities. As students complete this problem, have them write their inequalities on the board. When all students are finished, have them work with a partner to determine if their inequalities are equivalent. Have students use *Thumbs Up* to show agreement and then discuss any discrepancies.

ELL Support

Allow students to work in pairs. Check understanding of Exercise 7 by having students indicate *yes* or *no* using a thumbs up or down signal. For Exercise 8, have students hold up 1, 2, 3, or 4 fingers to indicate which of the four inequalities shown does not belong. Have pairs display their solutions to Exercises 9–11 on whiteboards. Have two pairs form a group to discuss explanations and justifications for Exercises 7, 8, and 12. Provide support as needed.

The Success Criteria Self-Assessment chart can be found in the *Student Journal* or online at *BigIdeasMath.com*.

EXAMPLE 2 **Solving an Inequality Using Subtraction**

Solve $13 \leq x + 14$. Graph the solution.

	$13 \leq x + 14$	Write the inequality.
Undo the addition. →	$-14 \quad\quad -14$	Subtraction Property of Inequality
	$-1 \leq x$	Simplify.

▶ The solution is $x \geq -1$.

Reading
The inequality $-1 \leq x$ is the same as $x \geq -1$.

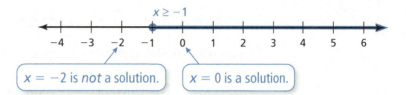

$x = -2$ is *not* a solution. $x = 0$ is a solution.

Try It Solve the inequality. Graph the solution.

4. $w + 3 \leq -1$ **5.** $8.5 \geq d + 10$ **6.** $x + \dfrac{3}{4} > 1\dfrac{1}{2}$

Self-Assessment for Concepts & Skills

Solve each exercise. Then rate your understanding of the success criteria in your journal.

7. WRITING Are the inequalities $c + 3 > 5$ and $c - 1 > 1$ equivalent? Explain.

8. WHICH ONE DOESN'T BELONG? Which inequality does *not* belong with the other three? Explain your reasoning.

$$w + \dfrac{7}{4} < \dfrac{3}{4} \quad\quad w - \dfrac{3}{4} > -\dfrac{7}{4}$$

$$w + \dfrac{7}{4} > \dfrac{3}{4} \quad\quad -\dfrac{7}{4} < w - \dfrac{3}{4}$$

SOLVING AN INEQUALITY Solve the inequality. Graph the solution.

9. $x - 4 > -6$ **10.** $z + 4.5 \leq 3.25$ **11.** $\dfrac{7}{10} > \dfrac{4}{5} + g$

12. OPEN-ENDED Write two different inequalities that can be represented using the graph. Justify your answers.

EXAMPLE 3 **Modeling Real Life**

To become an astronaut pilot for NASA, a person can be no taller than 6.25 feet. Your friend is 5 feet 9 inches tall. How much can your friend grow and still meet the requirement?

Because the height requirement is given in feet and your friend's height is given in feet and inches, rewrite your friend's height in feet.

$$9 \text{ in.} = 9 \text{ in.} \times \frac{1 \text{ ft}}{12 \text{ in.}} = \frac{9}{12} \text{ ft} = 0.75 \text{ ft}$$

$$5 \text{ ft } 9 \text{ in.} = 5 \text{ ft} + 0.75 \text{ ft} = 5.75 \text{ ft}$$

Use a verbal model to write an inequality that represents the situation.

Verbal Model   Current height (feet) + Amount your friend can grow (feet) ≤ Height limit (feet)

Variable Let h be the possible amounts (in feet) your friend can grow.

Inequality   5.75   + h ≤   6.25

$5.75 + h \leq 6.25$		Write the inequality.
$-\ 5.75 \qquad -\ 5.75$		Subtraction Property of Inequality
$h \leq 0.5$		Simplify.

 So, your friend can grow no more than 0.5 foot, or 6 inches.

 Self-Assessment for Problem Solving

Solve each exercise. Then rate your understanding of the success criteria in your journal.

13. **DIG DEEPER!** A volcanologist rappels 1200 feet into a volcano. He wants to climb out of the volcano in less than 4 hours. He climbs the first 535 feet in 100 minutes. Graph an inequality that represents the average rates at which he can climb the remaining distance and meet his goal. Justify your answer.

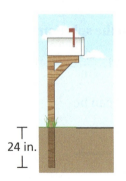

14. You install a mailbox by burying a post as shown. According to postal service guidelines, the bottom of the box must be at least 41 inches, but no more than 45 inches, above the road. Write and interpret two inequalities that describe the possible lengths of the post.

Laurie's Notes

EXAMPLE 3

- Ask a volunteer to read the problem.
- ❓ "The height limit is written as a decimal number of feet. Your friend's height is written in feet and inches. Can you work with the measurements as they are?" No, one of the forms must be changed to the other form.
- ❓ "How can you change 9 inches into feet?" Multiply by the conversion factor $\frac{1 \text{ ft}}{12 \text{ in}}$.
- ❓ "Could you have changed all the measurements to inches?" yes
- **Model with Mathematics:** Writing verbal models is an important step in helping students gain confidence in translating and setting up equations and inequalities. Color code the verbal model, if possible.
- Continue to solve the problem as shown.
- **Teaching Strategy:** Interpret the answer, $h \leq 0.5$, in terms of a decimal number of feet and in terms of inches.
- **Extension:** You can introduce the idea of a compound inequality by extending the example to include the minimum height (62 inches) for an astronaut. The compound inequality would be $62 \leq h \leq 75$, where h represents the height (in inches) of an astronaut.

✓ Self-Assessment for Problem Solving

- The goal for all students is to feel comfortable with the problem-solving plan. It is important for students to problem-solve in class, where they may receive support from you and their peers. Keep in mind that some students may only be ready for the first step.
- Remind students that they may have to read the problem several times to understand what the problem is asking.
- Students need to write a verbal model before writing the inequality. Take time to check students' verbal models.
- ⊙ Have students use *Fist of Five* to indicate their understanding of the success criteria.

The Success Criteria Self-Assessment chart can be found in the *Student Journal* or online at *BigIdeasMath.com*.

Closure

- A ride at an amusement park has a maximum height limit of 48 inches. When your sister grows 3 inches, she will still be able to go on the ride. Write, solve, and graph an inequality to describe your sister's current height. $x + 3 \leq 48$; $x \leq 45$;

Teaching Strategy

Students may forget to interpret the solution to an equation or an inequality. They get a solution, such as $h \leq 0.5$, and stop because they have found an answer. Repeatedly remind students to answer the *question*. This might include changing units of measure. Encourage students to write a sentence to answer the question. For example, "So, your friend can grow no more than 0.5 foot, or 6 inches."

Extra Example 3

A person can be no taller than $6\frac{5}{12}$ feet to become a fighter pilot for the United States Air Force. Your friend is 6 feet 3 inches tall. How much can your friend grow and still meet the requirement? $6\frac{1}{4} + h \leq 6\frac{5}{12}$; Your friend can grow at most $\frac{1}{6}$ foot, or 2 inches.

Self-Assessment for Problem Solving

13. See Additional Answers.
14. $x \geq 65$; the length of the post is at least 65 inches; $x \leq 69$; the length of the post is at most 69 inches

Learning Target

Write and solve inequalities using addition or subtraction.

Success Criteria

- Apply the Addition and Subtraction Properties of Inequality to produce equivalent inequalities.
- Solve inequalities using addition or subtraction.
- Apply inequalities involving addition or subtraction to solve real-life problems.

▶ Review & Refresh

1. $p > 5$
2. $3z \le -4.8$
3. $n + \dfrac{2}{3} \ge 5\dfrac{1}{3}$
4. $x = 9$
5. $w = -27$
6. $b = -22$
7. $h = 80$
8. A

Concepts, Skills, & Problem Solving

9. $-1 < 4$; yes; $1 < 6$
10. $-3 > -6$; yes; $-1 > -4$
11. $-4 < -1$; yes; $-2 < 1$
12. $x \ge 11$

    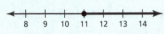

13. $a > 6$

14. $-4 \le g$

15. $k \le -11$

    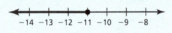

16. $-6 < y$

17. $n < 9$

18. $t \le -2$

19. $p \ge 1\dfrac{3}{4}$

20. $-\dfrac{3}{7} > b$

    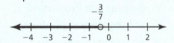

21–26. See Additional Answers.

27. no; The graph should have an open circle at 5.

28. no; The wrong side of the number line is shaded.

T-493

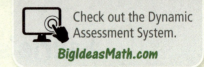

Assignment Guide and Concept Check

Scaffold assignments to support all students in their learning progression. The suggested assignments are a starting point. Continue to assign additional exercises and revisit with spaced practice to move every student toward proficiency.

Level	Assignment 1	Assignment 2
Emerging	3, 6, 7, 8, 9, 12, 13, 14, 19, 21, 27, 28	22, 24, 25, 29, 30, 32, 34
Proficient	3, 6, 7, 8, 10, 16, 18, 20, 22, 27, 28	24, 26, 29, 30, 31, 32, 33, 34
Advanced	3, 6, 7, 8, 11, 18, 20, 24, 26, 27, 28	30, 31, 32, 33, 34, 35, 36

- Assignment 1 is for use after students complete the Self-Assessment for Concepts & Skills.
- Assignment 2 is for use after students complete the Self-Assessment for Problem Solving.
- The red exercises can be used as a concept check.

Review & Refresh Prior Skills

Exercises 1–3 Writing an Inequality
Exercises 4–7 Solving an Equation
Exercise 8 Writing a Decimal as a Fraction

🮲 Common Errors

- **Exercises 12–26** Students may use the same operation instead of the inverse operation to isolate the variable. Remind students that when a number is added to the variable, they must subtract that number from each side. When a number is subtracted from the variable, they must add that number to each side. Remind students to check their answers in the original inequality.
- **Exercises 12–26** Students may shade the number line in the wrong direction. This often happens when the variable is on the right side of the inequality. Remind students to use test points to the left and right of the boundary point to determine which direction to shade the number line.

A.5 Practice

Go to BigIdeasMath.com to get HELP with solving the exercises.

▶ Review & Refresh

Write the word sentence as an inequality.

1. A number p is greater than 5.
2. A number z times 3 is at most -4.8.
3. The sum of a number n and $\frac{2}{3}$ is no less than $5\frac{1}{3}$.

Solve the equation. Check your solution.

4. $4x = 36$
5. $\frac{w}{3} = -9$
6. $-2b = 44$
7. $60 = \frac{3}{4}h$

8. Which fraction is equivalent to -2.4?

   A. $-\frac{12}{5}$ B. $-\frac{51}{25}$ C. $-\frac{8}{5}$ D. $-\frac{6}{25}$

▶ Concepts, Skills, & Problem Solving

WRITING AN INEQUALITY Write an inequality that compares the given numbers. Does the inequality remain true when you add 2 to each side? Justify your answer. (See Exploration 1, p. 489.)

9. $-1; 4$
10. $-3; -6$
11. $-4; -1$

SOLVING AN INEQUALITY Solve the inequality. Graph the solution.

12. $x + 7 \geq 18$
13. $a - 2 > 4$
14. $3 \leq 7 + g$
15. $8 + k \leq -3$
16. $-12 < y - 6$
17. $n - 4 < 5$
18. $t - 5 \leq -7$
19. $p + \frac{1}{4} \geq 2$
20. $\frac{2}{7} > b + \frac{5}{7}$
21. $z - 4.7 \geq -1.6$
22. $-9.1 < d - 6.3$
23. $\frac{8}{5} > s + \frac{12}{5}$
24. $-\frac{7}{8} \geq m - \frac{13}{8}$
25. $r + 0.2 < -0.7$
26. $h - 6 \leq -8.4$

YOU BE THE TEACHER Your friend solves the inequality and graphs the solution. Is your friend correct? Explain your reasoning.

27.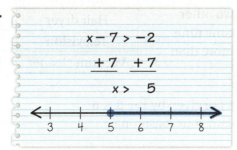

28.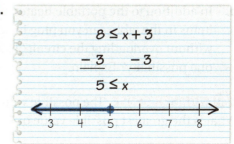

29. **MP MODELING REAL LIFE** A small airplane can hold 44 passengers. Fifteen passengers board the plane.

   a. Write and solve an inequality that represents the additional numbers of passengers that can board the plane.

   b. Can 30 more passengers board the plane? Explain.

GEOMETRY Find the possible values of x.

30. The perimeter is less than 28 feet.

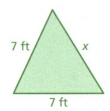

31. The base is greater than the height.

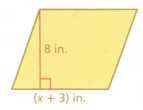

32. The perimeter is less than or equal to 51 meters.

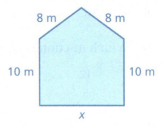

33. **MP REASONING** The inequality $d + s > -3$ is equivalent to $d > -7$. What is the value of s?

34. **MP LOGIC** You can spend up to $35 on a shopping trip.

   a. You want to buy a shirt that costs $14. Write and solve an inequality that represents the remaining amounts of money you can spend if you buy the shirt.

   b. You notice that the shirt is on sale for 30% off. How does this change your inequality in part (a)?

35. **DIG DEEPER!** If items plugged into a circuit use more than 2400 watts of electricity, the circuit overloads. A portable heater that uses 1050 watts of electricity is plugged into the circuit.

   a. Find the additional numbers of watts you can plug in without overloading the circuit.

   b. In addition to the portable heater, what two other items in the table can you plug in at the same time without overloading the circuit? Is there more than one possibility? Explain.

Item	Watts
Aquarium	200
Hair dryer	1200
Television	150
Vacuum cleaner	1100

36. **MP NUMBER SENSE** The possible values of x are given by $x + 8 \leq 6$. What is the greatest possible value of $7x$? Explain your reasoning.

Mini-Assessment
Solve the inequality. Graph the solution.

1. $x - 4 > 11$

   $x > 15$;

2. $11 \leq w + 3.4$

   $w \geq 7.6$;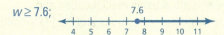

3. $k - \dfrac{2}{5} < -\dfrac{4}{5}$

   $k < -\dfrac{2}{5}$;

4. There are currently 203 students seated in the school cafeteria. The cafeteria can seat 250 students. Write and solve an inequality that represents the additional number of students that can be seated in the cafeteria.
   $203 + s \leq 250$; $s \leq 47$; At most 47 more students can be seated in the cafeteria.

Section Resources

Surface Level	Deep Level
Resources by Chapter • Extra Practice • Reteach • Puzzle Time Student Journal • Self-Assessment • Practice Differentiating the Lesson Tutorial Videos Skills Review Handbook Skills Trainer	Resources by Chapter • Enrichment and Extension Graphic Organizers Dynamic Assessment System • Section Practice

Concepts, Skills, & Problem Solving

29. **a.** $15 + p \leq 44$; $p \leq 29$ passengers

    b. no; Only 29 more passengers can board the plane.

30. $x < 14$ ft

31. $x > 5$ in.

32. $x \leq 15$ m

33. 4

34. **a.** $x + 14 \leq 35$; $x \leq \$21$

    b. $x + 9.8 \leq 35$

35. **a.** $x \leq 1350$ watts

    b. *Sample answer:* aquarium and television; yes; $200 + 150 = 350$ watts, $200 + 1100 = 1300$ watts

36. -14; *Sample answer:* $x \leq -2$ and $7(-2) = -14$.

T-494

Learning Target
Write and solve inequalities using multiplication or division.

Success Criteria
- Apply the Multiplication and Division Properties of Inequality to produce equivalent inequalities.
- Solve inequalities using multiplication or division.
- Apply inequalities involving multiplication or division to solve real-life problems.

Warm Up
Cumulative, vocabulary, and prerequisite skills practice opportunities are available in the *Resources by Chapter* or at BigIdeasMath.com.

ELL Support
The Math Practice note mentions the use of counterexamples. Students may be familiar with the word *counter* as a stand in a store or a marker for counting things. Explain that when *counter–* is used as a prefix, it means "against" or "opposite." A counterexample for an inequality is a value of the variable that shows the inequality is *not* true.

Exploration 1
a. sometimes; *Sample answer:* The inequality does not remain true when multiplying each side by a negative value.

b. sometimes; *Sample answer:*

$-4 < 5 \qquad -6 < 3$

$\dfrac{-4}{2} \stackrel{?}{<} \dfrac{5}{2} \qquad \dfrac{-6}{-2} \stackrel{?}{<} \dfrac{3}{-2}$

$-2 < \dfrac{5}{2} \qquad 3 \not< -\dfrac{3}{2}$

c. See Additional Answers.

T-495

Laurie's Notes

Preparing to Teach
- Students should know how to solve equations using multiplication and division. They should also be able to evaluate expressions and decide whether a number is a solution of an inequality.
- **Construct Viable Arguments and Critique the Reasoning of Others:** Mathematically proficient students use the results of investigations to observe patterns and make conjectures. Although student conjectures are not always correct, encourage them to try. Prior to this exploration, students tend to think that inequalities involving multiplication and division will be solved in the same fashion as the related equations. After completing the exploration, students may revise their thoughts.

Motivate
❓ Ask a series of questions and record students' solutions.
- "What integers are solutions of $x > 4$?" $5, 6, 7, \ldots$
- "What integers are solutions of $-x > 4$, meaning what numbers have an opposite that is greater than 4?" $-5, -6, -7, \ldots$
- "What integers are solutions of $x < -4$?" $-5, -6, -7, \ldots$
- Leave these three problems on the board, so you can refer to them later.

Exploration 1
- **Teaching Tip:** For this exploration, students will be rolling number cubes. Electronic number cubes are available at *BigIdeasMath.com*. If students do not have access to these number cubes, then the exploration can be completed as a whole-class activity with the teacher using the electronic number cubes.
  - If you prefer to use real number cubes, it would be best to use two different colors so that one color represents the cube with negative odd numbers and the other color represents the cube with negative even numbers. The number cubes should be marked with negative signs as described in the directions.
- Have students read the exploration and clarify any questions they may have about the directions. Discuss how students will organize their work (a table might be best).
- **Note:** Students are asked to complete more repetitions in this exploration than in the previous section, so that they are more likely to roll a good mix of positive and negative multipliers and divisors. You can reduce the number of repetitions by having groups share their results.
- Have students complete all three parts.
- **Popsicle Sticks:** Solicit responses to part (c) and discuss the conjectures as a class.
- **Look for and Express Regularity in Repeated Reasoning:** Students may expect the results of this exploration to be similar to the results in the previous section. Depending on how well students organize their information, it may or may not be easy to see what happens when multiplying or dividing both sides of an inequality by a negative number.
- Discuss the Math Practice note and have students share counterexamples.

A.6 Solving Inequalities Using Multiplication or Division

Learning Target: Write and solve inequalities using multiplication or division.

Success Criteria:
- I can apply the Multiplication and Division Properties of Inequality to produce equivalent inequalities.
- I can solve inequalities using multiplication or division.
- I can apply inequalities involving multiplication or division to solve real-life problems.

EXPLORATION 1 Writing Inequalities

Work with a partner. Use two number cubes on which the odd numbers are negative on one of the number cubes and the even numbers are negative on the other number cube.

- Roll the number cubes. Write an inequality that compares the numbers.
- Roll one of the number cubes. Multiply each side of the inequality by the number and record your result.
- Repeat the previous two steps nine more times.

a. When you multiply each side of an inequality by the same number, does the inequality remain true? Explain your reasoning.

b. When you divide each side of an inequality by the same number, does the inequality remain true? Use inequalities generated by number cubes to justify your answer.

c. Use your results in parts (a) and (b) to make a conjecture about how to solve an inequality of the form $ax < b$ for x when $a > 0$ and when $a < 0$.

Math Practice

Use Counterexamples

Use a counterexample to show that $2a \geq a$ is not true for every value of a.

Section A.6 Solving Inequalities Using Multiplication or Division 495

A.6 Lesson

🗝 Key Idea

Multiplication and Division Properties of Inequality (Case 1)

Words When you multiply or divide each side of an inequality by the same *positive* number, the inequality remains true.

Numbers $-4 < 6$ $\qquad\qquad$ $4 > -6$

$2 \cdot (-4) < 2 \cdot 6$ $\qquad$ $\dfrac{4}{2} > \dfrac{-6}{2}$

$-8 < 12$ $\qquad\qquad$ $2 > -3$

Algebra If $a < b$ and c is positive, then

$$a \cdot c < b \cdot c \qquad \text{and} \qquad \dfrac{a}{c} < \dfrac{b}{c}.$$

If $a > b$ and c is positive, then

$$a \cdot c > b \cdot c \qquad \text{and} \qquad \dfrac{a}{c} > \dfrac{b}{c}.$$

These properties are also true for $\leq$ and $\geq$.

EXAMPLE 1 Solving an Inequality Using Multiplication

Solve $\dfrac{x}{5} \leq -3$. Graph the solution.

$\dfrac{x}{5} \leq -3$ $\qquad$ Write the inequality.

[Undo the division.] → $5 \cdot \dfrac{x}{5} \leq 5 \cdot (-3)$ $\qquad$ Multiplication Property of Inequality

$x \leq -15$ $\qquad$ Simplify.

▸ The solution is $x \leq -15$.

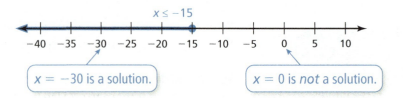

Try It Solve the inequality. Graph the solution.

1. $n \div 3 < 1$ $\qquad$ **2.** $-0.5 \leq \dfrac{m}{10}$ $\qquad$ **3.** $-3 > \dfrac{2}{3}p$

Laurie's Notes

Scaffolding Instruction

- Students have explored solving inequalities involving multiplication and division. Now they will use the Multiplication and Division Properties of Inequality to solve inequalities.
- **Emerging:** Students may see the connection between equations and inequalities but struggle to find solutions. These students will benefit from guided instruction of the examples.
- **Proficient:** Students made the transfer from equations to inequalities with ease. They should review both Key Ideas. Then have students self-assess using the Try It exercises before proceeding to the Self-Assessment exercises.

Key Idea

- These properties should look familiar, as they are similar to the Multiplication and Division Properties of Equality used in solving equations.
- Have students compare solving multiplication and division inequalities to solving the same types of equations.
- Note that the properties are restricted to multiplying and dividing by a *positive* number. This is very important.

EXAMPLE 1

- ❓ "How do you isolate the variable, meaning get *x* by itself?" Multiply each side of the inequality by 5.
- Multiplying by 5 is the inverse operation of dividing by 5.
- ❓ "Does the graph of the solution have an open or closed circle?" closed "Why is the circle closed?" Because *x* is less than or equal to −15, so −15 is included in the solution.

Try It

- **Think-Pair-Share:** Students should read each exercise independently and then work in pairs to solve and graph the inequalities. Have each pair compare their answers with another pair and discuss any discrepancies.
- Division is represented differently in Exercises 1 and 2. The second representation is more common in algebra and higher mathematics.
- After solving the inequality in Exercise 3, the result will be $-\frac{9}{2} > p$. Students can also rewrite this as $p < -\frac{9}{2}$. The direction of the inequality symbol is reversed *only* because the solution is being rewritten with the variable on the left side of the inequality symbol.

Scaffold instruction to support all students in their learning. Learning is individualized and you may want to group students differently as they move in and out of these levels with each skill and concept. Student self-assessment and feedback help guide your instructional decisions about how and when to layer support for all students to become proficient learners.

Extra Example 1

Solve $\frac{m}{4} > -4$. Graph the solution.

$m > -16$;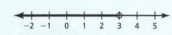

Try It

1. $n < 3$

2. $m \geq -5$

3. $p < -\frac{9}{2}$

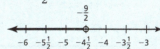

Extra Example 2

Solve $7y \leq -21$. Graph the solution.

$y \leq -3$;

ELL Support

After demonstrating Example 2, have students practice language by working in pairs to complete Try It Exercises 4–6. Have one student ask another, "What is the first step? Which operation do you need to perform? What is the solution? How do you graph the solution?" Have students alternate roles.

Beginner: Write out the problem and provide one-word answers.

Intermediate: Use phrases or simple sentences such as, "First, I divide by four."

Advanced: Answer with detailed sentences such as, "I divide both sides of the inequality by four."

Try It

4. $b \geq \dfrac{1}{2}$

5. $k \leq -2$

6. $q > -6$

Laurie's Notes

EXAMPLE 2

- **?** "What operation is being performed on x?" multiplication
- **?** "How do you undo multiplication?" division
- Solve, graph, and check.

Try It

- **Think-Pair-Share:** Students should read each exercise independently and then work in pairs to solve and graph the inequalities. Have each pair compare their answers with another pair and discuss any discrepancies.
- **Construct Viable Arguments and Critique the Reasoning of Others:** Notice that although all of the coefficients are positive, sometimes the constant is negative. This is important in helping students understand when the direction of the inequality symbol is going to be reversed. The focus is on the sign of the coefficient, not the sign of the constant.
- For Exercise 6, remind students that after solving this inequality, the result will be $-6 < q$. Students can rewrite this as $q > -6$. The direction of the inequality symbol is reversed *only* because the two sides of the inequality are being reversed. Reversing the sign has nothing to do with the negative constant (-6).
- These problems integrate decimal operations.

Key Idea

- These properties look identical to what students have been using in the lesson, *except* now the direction of the inequality symbol must be reversed for the inequality to remain true because they are multiplying or dividing by a *negative* quantity!
- The short version of the property: When you multiply or divide by a negative quantity, reverse the direction of the inequality symbol.
- **Common Error:** When students solve $2x < -4$, they sometimes reverse the inequality symbol because there is a negative number in the problem. You reverse the inequality symbol when you multiply or divide each side by a negative number to eliminate a negative coefficient. You do not reverse the inequality symbol just because there is a negative constant.
- **?** "What happens to the inequality symbol when you multiply both sides of an inequality by 0?" The inequality symbol changes to an equal sign ($0 = 0$).

EXAMPLE 2 **Solving an Inequality Using Division**

Solve $6x > -18$. Graph the solution.

$6x > -18$ Write the inequality.

Undo the multiplication. → $\dfrac{6x}{6} > \dfrac{-18}{6}$ Division Property of Inequality

$x > -3$ Simplify.

▶ The solution is $x > -3$.

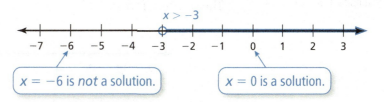

$x = -6$ is *not* a solution. $x = 0$ is a solution.

Try It Solve the inequality. Graph the solution.

4. $4b \geq 2$ **5.** $12k \leq -24$ **6.** $-15 < 2.5q$

Key Idea

Multiplication and Division Properties of Inequality (Case 2)

Words When you multiply or divide each side of an inequality by the same *negative* number, the direction of the inequality symbol must be reversed for the inequality to remain true.

Numbers
$-4 < 6$ $\qquad$ $4 > -6$

$-2 \cdot (-4) > -2 \cdot 6$ $\qquad$ $\dfrac{4}{-2} < \dfrac{-6}{-2}$

$8 > -12$ $\qquad$ $-2 < 3$

Algebra If $a < b$ and c is negative, then

$a \cdot c > b \cdot c$ and $\dfrac{a}{c} > \dfrac{b}{c}$.

If $a > b$ and c is negative, then

$a \cdot c < b \cdot c$ and $\dfrac{a}{c} < \dfrac{b}{c}$.

These properties are also true for $\leq$ and $\geq$.

Common Error

A negative sign in an inequality does not necessarily mean you must reverse the inequality symbol.

Only reverse the inequality symbol when you multiply or divide each side by a negative number.

EXAMPLE 3 Solving an Inequality Using Multiplication

Solve $-\dfrac{3}{2}n \leq 6$. Graph the solution.

$-\dfrac{3}{2}n \leq 6$ Write the inequality.

$-\dfrac{2}{3} \cdot \left(-\dfrac{3}{2}n\right) \geq -\dfrac{2}{3} \cdot 6$ Use the Multiplication Property of Inequality. Reverse the inequality symbol.

$n \geq -4$ Simplify.

▸ The solution is $n \geq -4$.

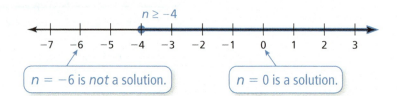

$n = -6$ is *not* a solution. $n = 0$ is a solution.

Math Practice

Look for Structure
Why do you reverse the inequality symbol when solving in Example 3, but not when solving in Examples 1 and 2?

Try It Solve the inequality. Graph the solution.

7. $\dfrac{x}{-3} > -4$

8. $0.5 \leq -\dfrac{y}{2}$

9. $-12 \geq \dfrac{6}{5}m$

10. $-\dfrac{2}{5}h \leq -8$

Self-Assessment for Concepts & Skills

Solve each exercise. Then rate your understanding of the success criteria in your journal.

11. OPEN-ENDED Write an inequality that you can solve using the Division Property of Inequality where the direction of the inequality symbol must be reversed.

12. MP PRECISION Explain how solving $4x < -16$ is different from solving $-4x < 16$.

SOLVING AN INEQUALITY Solve the inequality. Graph the solution.

13. $6n < -42$

14. $4 \geq -\dfrac{g}{8}$

15. WRITING Are the inequalities $12c > -15$ and $4c < -5$ equivalent? Explain.

Laurie's Notes

EXAMPLE 3

- Write the inequality.
- ❓ "What operation is being performed on *n*?" multiplication
- ❓ "How do you undo multiplying by $-\frac{3}{2}$?" Divide by $-\frac{3}{2}$.
- ❓ "What is equivalent to dividing by $-\frac{3}{2}$?" Multiplying by $-\frac{2}{3}$
- Solve as usual, but remember to reverse the direction of the inequality symbol when multiplying each side by $-\frac{2}{3}$.
- When graphing, remember to use a closed circle because the inequality is *greater than or equal to*.
- **Another Method:**

$$-\frac{3}{2}n \leq 6 \quad \text{Write the inequality.}$$
$$-\frac{3}{2}n + \frac{3}{2}n \leq 6 + \frac{3}{2}n \quad \text{Addition Property of Inequality}$$
$$0 \leq 6 + \frac{3}{2}n \quad \text{Simplify.}$$
$$0 - 6 \leq 6 - 6 + \frac{3}{2}n \quad \text{Subtraction Property of Inequality}$$
$$-6 \leq \frac{3}{2}n \quad \text{Simplify.}$$
$$\frac{2}{3} \cdot (-6) \leq \frac{2}{3} \cdot \frac{3}{2}n \quad \text{Multiplication Property of Inequality}$$
$$-4 \leq n \quad \text{Simplify.}$$

Students should realize that moving the variable term to the other side to make it positive has the same effect as reversing the inequality symbol. You may need to rewrite the solution as $n \geq -4$ to make this clearer.

Try It

- **Think-Pair-Share:** Students should read each exercise independently and then work in pairs to solve and graph the inequalities. Have each pair compare their answers with another pair and discuss any discrepancies.
- ⊙ Refer to the three inequalities from the Motivate: $x > 4$, $-x > 4$, and $x < -4$.
- ❓ "Which inequalities have the same solution? $-x > 4$ and $x < -4$
- ❓ "Is this consistent with what you discovered in the exploration? Explain." yes; *Sample answer:* When you divide both sides of $-x > 4$ by -1, the inequality sign is reversed, so the solution is $x < -4$.

✓ Self-Assessment for Concepts & Skills

- Students should complete the exercises independently. Have students share their answers to Exercise 11. Have students use *Thumbs Up* to show agreement that the inequality symbol must be reversed. Discuss any common errors that may arise.

The Success Criteria Self-Assessment chart can be found in the *Student Journal* or online at *BigIdeasMath.com*.

Extra Example 3
Solve $-\frac{4}{3}b > 8$. Graph the solution.

$b < -6$;

Try It

7. $x < 12$
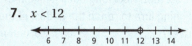

8. $y \leq -1$

9. $m \leq -10$
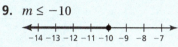

10. $h \geq 20$
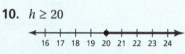

ELL Support

Allow students to work in pairs to practice language as they answer the Self-Assessment for Concepts & Skills exercises. Check comprehension of Exercises 13 and 14 by having each pair display their answers on a whiteboard for your review. Discuss their ideas about Exercises 11, 12, and 15 as a class.

Self-Assessment for Concepts & Skills

11. *Sample answer:* $-3x \leq 21$

12. The first inequality will be divided by a positive number. The second inequality will be divided by a negative number, so the direction of inequality symbol will be reversed.

13. $n < -7$
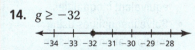

14. $g \geq -32$
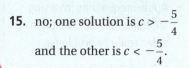

15. no; one solution is $c > -\frac{5}{4}$ and the other is $c < -\frac{5}{4}$.

T-498

Extra Example 4

A fishing lure descends 2 feet per second from the top of a river. The bottom of the river is deeper than -5.2 feet. How long does it take the fishing lure to reach the bottom of the river? $-2t < -5.2$; at least 2.6 seconds

Self-Assessment
for Problem Solving

16. $c \geq 10$

17. Sample answer: $50t < 375$; $t < 7.5$; $d = rt$, so as r increases, t decreases.

Learning Target
Write and solve inequalities using multiplication or division.

Success Criteria
- Apply the Multiplication and Division Properties of Inequality to produce equivalent inequalities.
- Solve inequalities using multiplication or division.
- Apply inequalities involving multiplication or division to solve real-life problems.

T-499

Laurie's Notes

EXAMPLE 4
- Ask a volunteer to read the problem. Select another student to explain what the problem is asking.
- Work through the problem as shown, paying close attention to the verbal model and the definition of the variable.
- Explain how to convert the minutes into hours, minutes, and seconds. 101 minutes is 1 hour, 41 minutes. 0.6 minute is 0.6 of 60 seconds, so $0.6(60) = 36$ seconds.

Teaching Strategy

Review the problem-solving plan with students. Divide the class into four groups. Assign each group a part of the problem-solving Four Square. Ask them to make a list of items that should be completed in that square. Have groups write their lists on large pieces of paper and display them in the classroom. Some possible items for each square are provided below.

Understand the problem. Read the problem, re-read the problem, explain the problem in your own words, and draw a picture or diagram.

Make a plan. Use the given information to plan how you are going to solve the problem, decide what method(s) will be useful, and how you are going to implement those methods.

Solve. Use your plan to solve the problem, write a verbal model, define a variable, translate the model into an equation or inequality, use properties to isolate the variable, and write a sentence to answer the question.

Check. Use another method, check for reasonableness, test values of the variable to check the solution, and make sure that the answer includes any appropriate units of measure.

Discuss each group's list and ideas as a class. As you discuss, add any new ideas to the lists.

✓ Self-Assessment for Problem Solving

- **Teaching Strategy:** Review the problem-solving Four Square with students.
- Encourage students to use a Four Square to complete the exercises. Until students become comfortable with the problem-solving plan, they may only be ready to complete the first square.
- Ask students to read both problems and write a verbal model for each. Have students *Turn and Talk* to verify their models.

The Success Criteria Self-Assessment chart can be found in the *Student Journal* or online at *BigIdeasMath.com*.

Closure

- **Exit Ticket:** Solve each inequality. Graph each solution.

    a. $\dfrac{x}{-3} \leq -9$ $x \geq 27$;

    b. $-8 > 4x$ $x < -2$;

EXAMPLE 4 Modeling Real Life

A submersible descends 37.5 meters per minute from sea level to explore a recent shipwreck. The shipwreck rests on the ocean floor at an elevation deeper than −3810 meters, the elevation of the Titanic shipwreck. How long does it take the submersible to reach the shipwreck?

The submersible begins at sea level, where the elevation is 0 feet. Write and solve an inequality to find how long it takes to reach elevations below −3810 meters.

Verbal Model Change in elevation (meters per minute) • Time (minutes) < Elevation of Titanic (meters)

Variable Let t be the time (in minutes) that the submersible descends.

Inequality $-37.5 \cdot t < -3810$

The change in elevation is negative because the submersible is descending.

$-37.5t < -3810$ Write the inequality.

$\dfrac{-37.5t}{-37.5} > \dfrac{-3810}{-37.5}$ Division Property of Inequality

$t > 101.6$ Simplify.

▸ So, the submersible takes more than 101.6 minutes, or 1 hour, 41 minutes, and 36 seconds, to reach the shipwreck.

Self-Assessment for Problem Solving

Solve each exercise. Then rate your understanding of the success criteria in your journal.

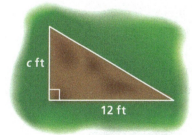

16. You want to put up a fence that encloses a triangular region with an area greater than or equal to 60 square feet. Describe the possible values of c.

17. A motorcycle rider travels at an average speed greater than 50 miles per hour. Write and solve an inequality to determine how long it will take the motorcycle rider to travel 375 miles. Explain your reasoning.

Section A.6 Solving Inequalities Using Multiplication or Division

A.6 Practice

▶ Review & Refresh

Solve the inequality. Graph the solution.

1. $h + 4 < 6$
2. $c - 5 \geq 4$
3. $\dfrac{7}{10} \leq n + \dfrac{4}{5}$

Solve the equation. Check your solution.

4. $-2w + 4 = -12$
5. $\dfrac{v}{5} - 6 = 3$
6. $3(x - 1) = 18$
7. $\dfrac{m}{4} + 50 = 51$

8. What is the value of $\dfrac{2}{3} + \left(-\dfrac{5}{7}\right)$?

   A. $-\dfrac{3}{4}$ B. $-\dfrac{1}{21}$ C. $\dfrac{7}{10}$ D. $1\dfrac{8}{21}$

▶ Concepts, Skills, & Problem Solving

WRITING AN INEQUALITY Write an inequality that compares the given numbers. Does the inequality remain true when you multiply each number in the inequality by 2? by −2? Justify your answers. (See Exploration 1, p. 495.)

9. $-2; 5$
10. $4; -1$
11. $6; -3$

SOLVING AN INEQUALITY Solve the inequality. Graph the solution.

12. $2n > 20$
13. $\dfrac{c}{9} \leq -4$
14. $2.2m < 11$
15. $-16 > x \div 2$
16. $\dfrac{1}{6}w \geq 2.5$
17. $7 < 3.5k$
18. $3x \leq -\dfrac{5}{4}$
19. $4.2y \leq -12.6$
20. $11.3 > \dfrac{b}{4.3}$

21. **MP MODELING REAL LIFE** You earn $9.20 per hour at your summer job. Write and solve an inequality that represents the numbers of hours you can work to earn enough money to buy a smart phone that costs $299.

22. **DIG DEEPER!** You have $5.60 to buy avocados for a guacamole recipe. Avocados cost $1.40 each.

    a. Write and solve an inequality that represents the numbers of avocados you can buy.

    b. Are there infinitely many solutions in this context? Explain.

500   Chapter A   Equations and Inequalities

Assignment Guide and Concept Check

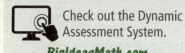

Check out the Dynamic Assessment System.
BigIdeasMath.com

Scaffold assignments to support all students in their learning progression. The suggested assignments are a starting point. Continue to assign additional exercises and revisit with spaced practice to move every student toward proficiency.

Level	Assignment 1	Assignment 2
Emerging	1, 6, 7, 8, 9, 12, 13, 14, 23, 24, 25, 32, 33	15, 16, 19, 21, 22, 26, 27, 30, 34, 36, 41, 47
Proficient	1, 6, 7, 8, 10, 15, 16, 17, 23, 28, 32, 33	20, 21, 22, 29, 30, 34, 37, 39, 40, 42, 46, 47, 48
Advanced	1, 6, 7, 8, 11, 16, 19, 20, 25, 27, 30, 32, 33	34, 36, 38, 39, 40, 42, 43, 44, 45, 46, 49, 50

- Assignment 1 is for use after students complete the Self-Assessment for Concepts & Skills.
- Assignment 2 is for use after students complete the Self-Assessment for Problem Solving.
- The red exercises can be used as a concept check.

Review & Refresh Prior Skills

Exercises 1–3 Solving an Inequality
Exercises 4–7 Solving an Equation
Exercise 8 Adding Rational Numbers

Common Errors

- **Exercises 12–20** Students may use the same operation instead of the inverse operation to isolate the variable. Remind students that when the variable is multiplied by a number, they must divide each side by that number. When the variable is divided by a number, they must multiply each side by that number. Remind students to check their answers in the original inequality.
- **Exercises 12–20** Students may shade the number line in the wrong direction. This often happens when the variable is on the right side of the inequality. Remind students to use test points to the left and right of the boundary point to determine which direction to shade the number line.
- **Exercises 13, 15, 18, and 19** When there is a negative in the inequality, students may reverse the direction of the inequality symbol. Remind students that they only reverse the direction when they are multiplying or dividing by a negative number. All of these exercises keep the same inequality symbol.

Review & Refresh

1. $h < 2$
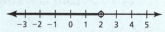

2. $c \geq 9$
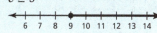

3. $n \geq -\dfrac{1}{10}$
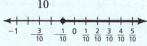

4. $w = 8$ 5. $v = 45$
6. $x = 7$ 7. $m = 4$
8. B

Concepts, Skills, & Problem Solving

9. $-2 < 5$; yes; no; $-4 < 10$, $4 \not< -10$

10. $4 > -1$; yes; no; $8 > -2$, $-8 \not> 2$

11. $6 > -3$; yes; no; $12 > -6$, $-12 \not> 6$

12. $n > 10$

13. $c \leq -36$

14. $m < 5$

15. $x < -32$

16. $w \geq 15$

17. $k > 2$

18–20. See Additional Answers.

21. $9.2x \geq 299$; $x \geq 32.5$ h

22. **a.** $1.40x \leq 5.60$; $x \leq 4$ avocados

b. no; You must buy a whole number of avocados.

T-500

Concepts, Skills, & Problem Solving

23. $n \geq -3$

24. $w > -7$

25. $h \leq -24$

26. $x < 45$

27. $y > \dfrac{14}{3}$

28. $d \leq -13$

29. $m < -27$

30. $k \geq -9$

31. $b > 6$

32. no; The inequality symbol should not have been reversed.

33. yes; The properties of inequalities were all used correctly to find the solution.

34. $\dfrac{g}{-4} \leq 5;\ g \geq -20$

35. $\dfrac{p}{7} < -3;\ p < -21$

36. $6w \geq -24;\ w \geq -4$

37. $-2x > 30;\ x < -15$

38. $\dfrac{3}{4} \geq \dfrac{k}{-8};\ -6 \leq k$

39. $-2.5s < -20;\ s > 8$ sec

40. **a.** $27x \leq 150;\ x \leq \dfrac{50}{9}$, or $5\dfrac{5}{9}$

   b. no; 6 boxes have a height of 13.5 feet.

Common Errors

- **Exercises 23, 25–28, 30, and 31** Students may forget to reverse the inequality symbol when multiplying or dividing by a negative number. Remind students of this rule. Encourage students to substitute values into the original inequality to check that the solution is correct.
- **Exercises 24 and 29** When there is a negative in the inequality, students may reverse the direction of the inequality symbol. Remind students that they only reverse the direction when they are multiplying or dividing by a negative number.

SOLVING AN INEQUALITY Solve the inequality. Graph the solution.

23. $-5n \leq 15$
24. $7w > -49$
25. $-\dfrac{1}{3}h \geq 8$
26. $-9 < -\dfrac{1}{5}x$
27. $-3y < -14$
28. $-2d \geq 26$
29. $-4.5 > \dfrac{m}{6}$
30. $\dfrac{k}{-0.25} \leq 36$
31. $-2.4 > \dfrac{b}{-2.5}$

YOU BE THE TEACHER Your friend solves the inequality. Is your friend correct? Explain your reasoning.

32.
$$\dfrac{x}{3} < -9$$
$$3 \cdot \dfrac{x}{3} > 3 \cdot (-9)$$
$$x > -27$$

33.
$$-3m \geq 9$$
$$+3m \quad +3m$$
$$0 \geq 9 + 3m$$
$$-9 \quad -9$$
$$-9 \geq 3m$$
$$\dfrac{-9}{3} \geq \dfrac{3m}{3}$$
$$-3 \geq m$$

WRITING AND SOLVING AN INEQUALITY Write the word sentence as an inequality. Then solve the inequality.

34. The quotient of a number g and -4 is at most 5.

35. A number p divided by 7 is less than -3.

36. Six times a number w is at least -24.

37. The product of -2 and a number x is greater than 30.

38. $\dfrac{3}{4}$ is greater than or equal to a number k divided by -8.

39. **MODELING REAL LIFE** A *cryotherapy* chamber uses extreme cold to reduce muscle soreness. A chamber is currently 0°F. The temperature in the chamber is dropping 2.5°F every second. Write and solve an inequality that represents the numbers of seconds that can pass for the temperature to drop below -20°F.

40. **MODELING REAL LIFE** You are moving some of your belongings into a storage facility.

   a. Write and solve an inequality that represents the numbers of boxes that you can stack vertically in the storage unit.

   b. Can you stack 6 boxes vertically in the storage unit? Explain.

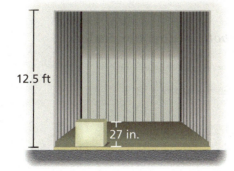

GEOMETRY Write and solve an inequality that represents *x*.

41. Area ≥ 120 cm²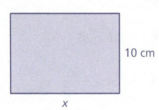

42. Area < 20 ft²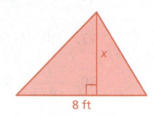

43. **MP MODELING REAL LIFE** A device extracts no more than 37 liters of water per day from the air. How long does it take to collect at least 185 liters of water? Explain your reasoning.

44. **MP REASONING** Students in a science class are divided into 6 equal groups with at least 4 students in each group for a project. Describe the possible numbers of students in the class.

45. **PROJECT** Choose two novels to research.

a. Use the Internet to complete the table below.

b. Use the table to find and compare the average number of copies sold per month for each novel. Which novel do you consider to be the most successful? Explain.

c. Assume each novel continues to sell at the average rate. For what numbers of months will the total number of copies sold exceed twice the current number sold for each novel?

	Author	Name of Novel	Release Date	Current Number of Copies Sold
1.				
2.				

46. **MP LOGIC** When you multiply or divide each side of an inequality by the same negative number, you must reverse the direction of the inequality symbol. Explain why.

MP NUMBER SENSE Describe all numbers that satisfy *both* inequalities. Include a graph with your description.

47. $4m > -4$ and $3m < 15$

48. $\dfrac{n}{3} \geq -4$ and $\dfrac{n}{-5} \geq 1$

49. $2x \geq -6$ and $2x \geq 6$

50. $-\dfrac{1}{2}s > -7$ and $\dfrac{1}{3}s < 12$

Mini-Assessment
Solve and graph the inequality.

1. $\dfrac{b}{6} > -11$

   $b > -66$;

2. $4c \leq -28$

   $c \leq -7$;

3. $-\dfrac{6}{7}k > -12$

   $k < 14$;

4. $-4b \leq 9.6$

   $b \geq -2.4$;

5. You have $6.72 to buy apples for an apple crisp recipe. Apples cost $0.96 each. Write and solve an inequality that represents the numbers of apples you can buy. $0.96a \leq 6.72$; $a \leq 7$ apples

Section Resources

Surface Level	Deep Level
Resources by Chapter • Extra Practice • Reteach • Puzzle Time Student Journal • Self-Assessment • Practice Differentiating the Lesson Tutorial Videos Skills Review Handbook Skills Trainer	Resources by Chapter • Enrichment and Extension Graphic Organizers Dynamic Assessment System • Section Practice

Concepts, Skills, & Problem Solving

41. $10x \geq 120$; $x \geq 12$ cm

42. $4x < 20$; $x < 5$ ft

43. at least 5 days; The solution of $37d \geq 185$ is $d \geq 5$.

44. $x \geq 24$

45. **a–c.** Answers will vary.

46. *Sample answer:* Consider the inequality $5 > 3$. If you multiply or divide each side by -1 without reversing the direction of the inequality symbol, you obtain $-5 > -3$, which is not true. So, whenever you multiply or divide an inequality by a negative number, you must reverse the direction of the inequality symbol to obtain a true statement.

47. $m > 1$ and $m < 5$

    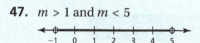

48. $n \geq -12$ and $n \leq -5$

    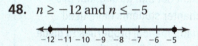

49. $x \geq 3$

50. $s < 14$

    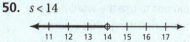

Learning Target
Write and solve two-step inequalities.

Success Criteria
- Apply properties of inequality to generate equivalent inequalities.
- Solve two-step inequalities using the basic operations.
- Apply two-step inequalities to solve real-life problems.

Warm Up
Cumulative, vocabulary, and prerequisite skills practice opportunities are available in the *Resources by Chapter* or at BigIdeasMath.com.

ELL Support
Point out that throughout this chapter students have used mathematical properties to guide their work. Explain that in the context of math, the word *property* refers to a rule. In everyday language, however, it is more common to use the word *property* to describe things that a person owns. For example, your board games are your property.

Exploration 1
a. $2x + 4 < -2; x < -3$

b. $x < -3$
   Sample answer: The steps are similar.

c. $3x - 5 \geq -2; x \geq 1$
   $9 > 4x - 5; 3\frac{1}{2} > x$
   $-2x - 6 \leq 2; x \geq -4$

d. Sample answer: Use inverse operations to isolate the variable.

Laurie's Notes

Preparing to Teach
- In this lesson, students will combine the properties of inequality from the previous two lessons to solve two-step inequalities.
- **Reason Abstractly and Quantitatively:** Algebra tiles can help students make sense of inequalities. Algebra tiles are a concrete representation, deepening student understanding of what it means to solve an inequality.

Motivate
- ❓ "Have any of you ever wondered what score you needed on a particular test to have a certain average?" Answers will vary.
- Share the following scenario with students.
  - Student A has test scores of 82, 94, 86, and 81.
  - Student B has test scores of 92, 98, 88, and 94.
- Student A wants to achieve an average of at least 85, and Student B wants to achieve an average of at least 90. What must each student score on the fifth and final test to meet their goals? Student A: $x \geq 82$; Student B: $x \geq 78$
- ❓ "Do you think it is mathematically possible for Student A and Student B to achieve their goals?" Answers will vary.

Exploration 1
- For part (a), have students write an inequality corresponding to each step so that they connect the model to the algebraic representation.
- ❓ After students finish part (a), ask, "What is the goal for solving an inequality?" to isolate the variable
- ❓ "How do you get the 2 green variable-tiles by themselves?" Add 4 red tiles to each side.
- ❓ "How do you get 1 green variable-tile by itself?" Divide both sides by 2.
- In part (b), as students are solving the inequality algebraically, ask them to justify each step. Students may need to refer to the Key Ideas in the previous two sections. Circulate and check students' work.
- **Attend to Precision:** Ask volunteers to explain their solutions for part (c). Listen to the language that students use. If they say, "I'll put 5 yellow tiles on each side," ask them to express their steps mathematically. They *should* say, "Add 5 yellow tiles to each side." You want students to be able to connect their manipulations of the tiles with the operations they will record symbolically.
- Students may use different methods to solve the inequalities in part (c). As you circulate, take note of the different methods used to either write or solve the inequalities. Have students share their methods. Be sure to select students that you know have correct answers.
- For part (d), have students use *Paired Verbal Fluency* to discuss their answers.

A.7 Solving Two-Step Inequalities

Learning Target: Write and solve two-step inequalities.

Success Criteria:
- I can apply properties of inequality to generate equivalent inequalities.
- I can solve two-step inequalities using the basic operations.
- I can apply two-step inequalities to solve real-life problems.

EXPLORATION 1

Using Algebra Tiles to Solve Inequalities

Work with a partner.

a. What is being modeled by the algebra tiles below? What is the solution?

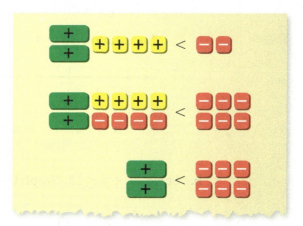

b. Use properties of inequality to solve the original inequality in part (a). How do your steps compare to the steps performed with algebra tiles?

c. Write the three inequalities modeled by the algebra tiles below. Then solve each inequality using algebra tiles. Check your answer using properties of inequality.

Math Practice

Consider Similar Problems

How is using algebra tiles to solve inequalities similar to using algebra tiles to solve equations?

d. Explain how solving a two-step inequality is similar to solving a two-step equation.

A.7 Lesson

You can solve two-step inequalities in the same way you solve two-step equations.

EXAMPLE 1 Solving Two-Step Inequalities

a. Solve $5x - 4 \geq 11$. Graph the solution.

	$5x - 4 \geq 11$	Write the inequality.
Step 1: Undo the subtraction.	$\underline{+4 \quad +4}$	Addition Property of Inequality
	$5x \geq 15$	Simplify.
Step 2: Undo the multiplication.	$\dfrac{5x}{5} \geq \dfrac{15}{5}$	Division Property of Inequality
	$x \geq 3$	Simplify.

▶ The solution is $x \geq 3$.

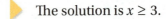

$x = 0$ is *not* a solution. $x = 4$ is a solution.

b. Solve $\dfrac{b}{-3} + 4 < 13$. Graph the solution.

	$\dfrac{b}{-3} + 4 < 13$	Write the inequality.
Step 1: Undo the addition.	$\underline{-4 \quad -4}$	Subtraction Property of Inequality
	$\dfrac{b}{-3} < 9$	Simplify.
Step 2: Undo the division.	$-3 \cdot \dfrac{b}{-3} > -3 \cdot 9$	Use the Multiplication Property of Inequality. Reverse the inequality symbol.
	$b > -27$	Simplify.

▶ The solution is $b > -27$.

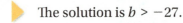

$b = -30$ is *not* a solution. $b = -15$ is a solution.

Try It Solve the inequality. Graph the solution.

1. $6y - 7 > 5$
2. $4 - 3d \geq 19$
3. $\dfrac{w}{-4} + 8 > 9$

Laurie's Notes

Scaffolding Instruction
- Students have discussed the similarities between solving two-step inequalities and two-step equations.
- **Emerging:** Students may see the connection between equations and inequalities but struggle to find solutions. These students will benefit from guided instruction of Examples 1 and 2.
- **Proficient:** Students made the transfer from equations to inequalities with ease. They should complete the Try It exercises before proceeding to the Self-Assessment exercises.

Scaffold instruction to support all students in their learning. Learning is individualized and you may want to group students differently as they move in and out of these levels with each skill and concept. Student self-assessment and feedback help guide your instructional decisions about how and when to layer support for all students to become proficient learners.

Discuss
- ❓ "Are there any differences between solving two-step inequalities and solving two-step equations? Explain." Yes, you need to reverse the inequality symbol when multiplying or dividing by a negative number.
- Remind students that the goal for solving an equation is to isolate the variable. The same is true for inequalities.

EXAMPLE 1
- ❓ "In part (a), what operations are being performed on the left side of the inequality?" multiplication and subtraction
- Notice that subtracting 4 would have been the last step in evaluating the left side, so its inverse operation is the first step in solving the inequality.
- ❓ "To solve for x, what is the last step?" Divide both sides by 5.
- Because you are dividing by a positive quantity, the inequality symbol does not change. The solution is $x \geq 3$. Graph and check.
- Part (b) is solved in a similar fashion.
- ❓ "How do you solve $\frac{b}{-3} < 9$?" Multiply both sides by -3 and change the direction of the inequality symbol.
- Graph and check. Use an open circle because the variable cannot equal -27.
- Point out to students that the number line has increments of 3 units.

Try It
- **Think-Pair-Share:** Students should read each exercise independently and then work in pairs to solve and graph the inequalities. Have each pair compare their answers with another pair and discuss any discrepancies.

ELL Support
After demonstrating Example 1, have students practice language by working in groups to complete Try It Exercises 1–3. Provide these questions to guide instruction: Which operations do you need to perform? What is the first step? What is the solution? How do you graph the solution? Have students alternate roles.
Beginner: Write the steps and provide one-word answers.
Intermediate: Use phrases or simple sentences such as, "addition and division."
Advanced: Answer with detailed sentences such as, "First, you add seven to both sides of the inequality. Then you divide both sides of the inequality by six."

Extra Example 1
a. Solve $17 \leq 3y - 4$. Graph the solution.
$y \geq 7$;

b. Solve $\frac{x}{-2} - 8 \geq -6$. Graph the solution.
$x \leq -4$;

Try It
1. $y > 2$

2. $d \leq -5$

3. $w < -4$

T-504

Extra Example 2

Which graph represents the solution of $12 < -2(y - 4)$?

A.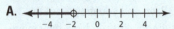

B. (number line, open circle at −2)

C. (number line, open circle at 2)

D. (number line, open circle at 2, shaded right)

A; (number line, open circle at −2, shaded right)

Try It

4. $k < 8$
   (number line, open circle at 8, shaded left)

5. $n > 2$
   (number line, open circle at 2, shaded right)

6. $y \geq -14$
   (number line, closed circle at −14, shaded right)

Self-Assessment
for Concepts & Skills

7. $d \geq 5$
   (number line, closed circle at 5, shaded right)

8. $z > 14$
   (number line, open circle at 14, shaded right)

9. $g \geq -6$
   (number line, closed circle at −6, shaded right)

10. *Sample answer:* Divide both sides by 3, then subtract 5 from both sides; Use the Distributive Property, subtract 15 from both sides, then divide both sides by 3.

11. no; *Sample answer:* The first solution is $x \geq 1$ while the second solution is $x \leq 1$.

12. *Sample answer:* $-5x - 6 < 19$; The solution is $x > -5$.

T-505

Laurie's Notes

EXAMPLE 2

- **Look for and Make Use of Structure:** There is another way to solve this example. The inequality has two factors on the left side: -7 and $(x + 3)$. Instead of distributing, divide both sides by -7. Dividing by a negative number changes the direction of the inequality symbol.

$$-7(x + 3) \leq 28 \quad \text{Write the inequality.}$$
$$\frac{-7(x+3)}{-7} \leq \frac{28}{-7} \quad \begin{array}{l}\text{Division Property of Inequality}\\ \text{Reverse the inequality symbol.}\end{array}$$
$$x + 3 \geq -4 \quad \text{Simplify.}$$
$$\underline{-3} \quad \underline{-3} \quad \text{Subtraction Property of Inequality}$$
$$x \geq -7 \quad \text{Simplify.}$$

- Discuss each method with students.

Try It

- Have students use *Think-Pair-Share* to solve these problems.

✓ Self-Assessment for Concepts & Skills

- As students complete the exercises, check that they are writing the step of reversing the inequality only when multiplying or dividing by a negative number.
- For Exercise 10, select two students that have used different methods to share with the class.
- As students review the exercises and their solutions, they will be able to evaluate their progress with the success criteria.

ELL Support

Allow students to work in pairs and have them display their solutions for Exercises 7–9 on whiteboards. After pairs have worked on their explanations for Exercises 10–12, have them present their answers to another pair. Have pairs compare their answers and refine them based on discussion. Then have each group present their final answers to the class.

The Success Criteria Self-Assessment chart can be found in the *Student Journal* or online at *BigIdeasMath.com*.

EXAMPLE 2 Graphing an Inequality

Which graph represents the solution of $-7(x+3) \leq 28$?

A. number line from −10 to −4, closed circle at −7, shaded right

B. number line from −10 to −4, closed circle at −7, shaded right

C. number line from 4 to 10, closed circle at 7, shaded left

D. number line from 4 to 10, closed circle at 7, shaded right

$$-7(x + 3) \leq 28 \qquad \text{Write the inequality.}$$
$$-7x - 21 \leq 28 \qquad \text{Distributive Property}$$

Step 1: Undo the subtraction.
$$\underline{+21 \quad +21} \qquad \text{Addition Property of Inequality}$$
$$-7x \leq 49 \qquad \text{Simplify.}$$

Step 2: Undo the multiplication.
$$\frac{-7x}{-7} \geq \frac{49}{-7} \qquad \text{Use the Division Property of Inequality.}$$
$$\text{Reverse the inequality symbol.}$$
$$x \geq -7 \qquad \text{Simplify.}$$

▶ The correct answer is **B**.

Try It Solve the inequality. Graph the solution.

4. $2(k - 5) < 6$ **5.** $-4(n - 10) < 32$ **6.** $-3 \leq 0.5(8 + y)$

Self-Assessment for Concepts & Skills

Solve each exercise. Then rate your understanding of the success criteria in your journal.

SOLVING AN INEQUALITY Solve the inequality. Graph the solution.

7. $3d - 7 \geq 8$ **8.** $-6 > \dfrac{z}{-2} + 1$ **9.** $-6(g + 4) \leq 12$

10. **MP STRUCTURE** Describe two different ways to solve the inequality $3(a + 5) < 9$.

11. **WRITING** Are the inequalities $-6x + 18 \leq 12$ and $2x - 4 \leq -2$ equivalent? Explain.

12. **OPEN-ENDED** Write a two-step inequality that can be represented by the graph. Justify your answer.

EXAMPLE 3 Modeling Real Life

A football team orders the sweatshirts shown. The price per sweatshirt decreases $0.05 for each sweatshirt that is ordered. How many sweatshirts should the team order for the price per sweatshirt to be no greater than $32.50?

Write and solve an inequality to determine how many sweatshirts the team should order for the price per sweatshirt to be no greater than $32.50.

Verbal Model	Base price (dollars)	−	Price decrease (dollars)	•	Number of sweatshirts ordered	≤	Desired price (dollars)

Variable Let n be the number of sweatshirts ordered.

Inequality $40 \;-\; 0.05 \;\cdot\; n \;\leq\; 32.50$

$$40 - 0.05n \leq 32.50 \quad \text{Write the inequality.}$$
$$\underline{-40} \qquad \underline{-40} \quad \text{Subtraction Property of Inequality}$$
$$-0.05n \leq -7.50 \quad \text{Simplify.}$$
$$\frac{-0.05n}{-0.05} \geq \frac{-7.50}{-0.05} \quad \text{Use the Division Property of Inequality. Reverse the inequality symbol.}$$
$$n \geq 150 \quad \text{Simplify.}$$

▸ So, the team should order at least 150 sweatshirts for the price per sweatshirt to be no greater than $32.50.

Self-Assessment for Problem Solving

Solve each exercise. Then rate your understanding of the success criteria in your journal.

13. A fair rents a thrill ride for $3000. It costs $4 to purchase a token for the ride. Write and solve an inequality to determine the numbers of ride tokens that can be sold for the fair to make a profit of at least $750.

14. **DIG DEEPER!** A theater manager predicts that 1000 tickets to a play will be sold if each ticket costs $60. The manager predicts that 20 less tickets will be sold for every $1 increase in price. For what prices can the manager predict that at least 800 tickets will be sold? Use an inequality to justify your answer.

Laurie's Notes

EXAMPLE 3

- Point out the steps of problem-solving plan as you solve this problem.
- Ask two different students to read the problem to the class. Use *Popsicle Sticks* to select students interpret the problem.
- Discuss the verbal model. Ask students to explain each part.
- ❓ Stop at $n \geq 150$ and ask, "Is this the answer to the question?" Remind students to answer the question with a sentence.

✓ Self-Assessment for Problem Solving

- Students may benefit from trying the exercises independently and then working with peers to refine their work. It is important to provide time in class for problem solving, so that students become comfortable with the problem-solving plan.
- Remind students to follow the steps of the problem-solving plan. Students may complain about writing the steps, but it will make solving more complicated problems easier.

The Success Criteria Self-Assessment chart can be found in the *Student Journal* or online at *BigIdeasMath.com*.

Formative Assessment Tip

Sentence Summary
This technique asks students to write a single sentence to describe what they have learned about a topic. You may ask students to summarize new information, make a comparison, or describe a problem and solution. Give students time to reflect before writing. Discourage responses like, "I learned how to subtract." *Sentence Summary* can give you a quick glimpse into each student's level of understanding of the material.

Closure

- ⦿ **Sentence Summary:** Give each student an index card. Ask students to write about what they have learned about solving two-step inequalities. Allow time for students to reflect and discourage responses like, "I learned how to find the solution." Use these responses to plan your instruction for the next day.

Extra Example 3
A cheerleading squad orders T-shirts that cost $18 each. The price per T-shirt decreases $0.15 for each T-shirt that is ordered. How many T-shirts should the squad order for the price per T-shirt to be no greater than $16.35? $18 - 0.15n \leq 16.35$; at least 11 T-shirts

Self-Assessment for Problem Solving

13. $4x - 3000 \geq 750$; $x \geq 938$ tokens
14. $p \leq \$70$

Learning Target
Write and solve two-step inequalities.

Success Criteria
- Apply properties of inequality to generate equivalent inequalities.
- Solve two-step inequalities using the basic operations.
- Apply two-step inequalities to solve real-life problems.

Review & Refresh

1. $x \leq -6$
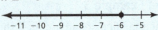

2. $d > 12$
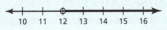

3. $g \geq -8$

4.
Flutes	7	21	28
Clarinets	4	12	16

$7:4, 21:12, 28:16$

5.
Boys	6	3	30
Girls	10	5	50

$6:10, 3:5, 30:50$

6. A

Concepts, Skills, & Problem Solving

7. $-2x + 4 \geq -6; x \geq -5$

8. $-2x + 2 > 6; x < -2$

9. $y < 1$

10. $p \geq -4$

11. $h > \dfrac{9}{2}$
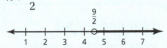

12. $m < 30$

13. $b \leq -6$

14. $r \geq 7$

15–20. See Additional Answers.

21. no; *Sample answer:* 4 should be multiplied by 3.

22. no; *Sample answer:* Divide by 3 first.

Assignment Guide and Concept Check

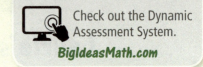

Scaffold assignments to support all students in their learning progression. The suggested assignments are a starting point. Continue to assign additional exercises and revisit with spaced practice to move every student toward proficiency.

Level	Assignment 1	Assignment 2
Emerging	3, 5, 6, 7, 9, 10, 11, 14, 15, 21, 22	16, 17, 18, 19, 23, 24, 26, 27
Proficient	3, 5, 6, 8, 10, 12, 14, 16, 21, 22, 24	18, 20, 23, 25, 26, 27
Advanced	3, 5, 6, 8, 10, 12, 18, 20, 21, 22, 24	25, 26, 27, 28, 29, 30

- Assignment 1 is for use after students complete the Self-Assessment for Concepts & Skills.
- Assignment 2 is for use after students complete the Self-Assessment for Problem Solving.
- The red exercises can be used as a concept check.

Review & Refresh Prior Skills

Exercises 1–3 Solving an Inequality
Exercises 4 and 5 Completing Ratio Tables
Exercise 6 Finding the Volume of a Rectangular Prism

Common Errors

- **Exercises 9–14** Students may incorrectly multiply or divide before adding or subtracting from both sides of the inequality. Remind students that they should work backward through the order of operations, or that they should start away from the variable and move toward it.
- **Exercises 11, 13, 14, 18, and 20** Students may forget to reverse the inequality symbol when multiplying or dividing by a negative number. Encourage students to write the inequality symbol that they should have in the solution before solving.
- **Exercises 15–20** If students distribute before solving, they may forget to distribute the number to the second term. Remind students that they need to distribute to everything within the parentheses. Encourage students to draw arrows to represent the multiplication.

A.7 Practice

▶ Review & Refresh

Solve the inequality. Graph the solution.

1. $-3x \geq 18$
2. $\frac{2}{3}d > 8$
3. $2 \geq \frac{g}{-4}$

Find the missing values in the ratio table. Then write the equivalent ratios.

4.
Flutes	7		28
Clarinets	4	12	

5.
Boys	6	3	
Girls	10		50

6. What is the volume of the cube?

   A. 8 ft^3
   B. 16 ft^3
   C. 24 ft^3
   D. 32 ft^3

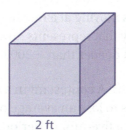

2 ft

▶ Concepts, Skills, & Problem Solving

USING ALGEBRA TILES Write the inequality modeled by the algebra tiles. Then solve the inequality using algebra tiles. Check your answer using properties of inequality. *(See Exploration 1, p. 503.)*

7. [algebra tiles] ≥ [algebra tiles]
8. [algebra tiles] > [algebra tiles]

SOLVING A TWO-STEP INEQUALITY Solve the inequality. Graph the solution.

9. $8y - 5 < 3$
10. $3p + 2 \geq -10$
11. $2 > 8 - \frac{4}{3}h$
12. $-2 > \frac{m}{6} - 7$
13. $-1.2b - 5.3 \geq 1.9$
14. $-1.3 \geq 2.9 - 0.6r$
15. $5(g + 4) > 15$
16. $4(w - 6) \leq -12$
17. $-8 \leq \frac{2}{5}(k - 2)$
18. $-\frac{1}{4}(d + 1) < 2$
19. $7.2 > 0.9(n + 8.6)$
20. $20 \geq -3.2(c - 4.3)$

 **YOU BE THE TEACHER** Your friend solves the inequality. Is your friend correct? Explain your reasoning.

21.
$\frac{x}{3} + 4 < 6$
$x + 4 < 18$
$x < 14$

22.
$3(w - 2) \geq 10$
$3w \geq 12$
$w \geq 4$

Section A.7 Solving Two-Step Inequalities 507

23. **MODELING REAL LIFE** The first jump in a unicycle high-jump contest is shown. The bar is raised 2 centimeters after each jump. Solve the inequality $2n + 10 \geq 26$ to find the numbers of additional jumps needed to meet or exceed the goal of clearing a height of 26 centimeters.

SOLVING AN INEQUALITY Solve the inequality. Graph the solution.

24. $9x - 4x + 4 \geq 36 - 12$

25. $3d - 7d + 2.8 < 5.8 - 27$

26. **MODELING REAL LIFE** A cave explorer is at an elevation of -38 feet. The explorer starts moving at a rate of -12 feet per minute. Write and solve an inequality that represents how long it will take the explorer to reach an elevation deeper than -200 feet.

27. **CRITICAL THINKING** A contestant in a weight-loss competition wants to lose an average of at least 8 pounds per month during a five-month period. Based on the progress report, how many pounds must the contestant lose in the fifth month to meet the goal?

Progress Report	
Month	Pounds Lost
1	12
2	9
3	5
4	8

28. **REASONING** A student theater charges $8.50 per ticket.

    a. The theater has already sold 70 tickets. How many more tickets does the theater need to sell to earn at least $750?

    b. The theater increases the ticket price by $1. Without solving an inequality, describe how this affects the total number of tickets needed to earn at least $750. Explain your reasoning.

29. **DIG DEEPER!** A zoo does not have room to add any more tigers to an enclosure. According to regulations, the area of the enclosure must increase by 150 square feet for each tiger that is added. The zoo is able to enlarge the 450 square foot enclosure for a total area no greater than 1000 square feet.

    a. Write and solve an inequality that represents this situation.

    b. Describe the possible numbers of tigers that can be added to the enclosure. Explain your reasoning.

30. **GEOMETRY** For what values of r will the area of the shaded region be greater than or equal to 12 square units?

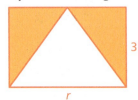

Mini-Assessment
Solve the inequality. Graph the solution.

1. $2x + 4 < 10$

   $x < 3$;

2. $3 \leq \dfrac{y}{-5} + 7$

   $y \leq 20$;

3. $-4.2 - 1.1b \leq 2.4$

   $b \geq -6$;

4. $\dfrac{2}{3}m + \dfrac{2}{3} \geq -\dfrac{1}{3}$

   $m \geq -\dfrac{3}{2}$;

5. You are selling subs to raise funds for a school field trip. You make a profit of $1.50 for each sub you sell. You have already sold 44 subs. How many more subs do you need to sell to raise at least $144?

   $1.5s + 44(1.5) \geq 144$; at least 52 subs

Concepts, Skills, & Problem Solving

23. $n \geq 8$ additional jumps

24. $x \geq 4$

25. $d > 6$

26. $-12x - 38 < -200$;
    $x > 13.5$ min

27. at least 6 lb

28. a. at least 19 tickets

    b. the number decreases; *Sample answer:* Each ticket costs $1 more, so fewer tickets earn the same amount.

29. a. $150x + 450 \leq 1000$; $x \leq 3\dfrac{2}{3}$

    b. 0, 1, 2, 3; *Sample answer:* Only nonnegative integers make sense for the problem.

30. $r \geq 8$ units

Section Resources

Surface Level	Deep Level
Resources by Chapter • Extra Practice • Reteach • Puzzle Time Student Journal • Self-Assessment • Practice Differentiating the Lesson Tutorial Videos Skills Review Handbook Skills Trainer	Resources by Chapter • Enrichment and Extension Graphic Organizers Dynamic Assessment System • Section Practice
Transfer Level	
Dynamic Assessment System • End-of-Chapter Quiz	Assessment Book • End-of-Chapter Quiz

Skills Needed

Exercise 1
- Finding a Missing Dimension
- Solving an Equation

Exercise 2
- Finding the Volume of a Rectangular Prism
- Writing and Solving an Inequality

Exercise 3
- Finding the Mean
- Solving a Two-Step Inequality

ELL Support

Discuss the word *property* in Exercise 1. Point out that it refers to land that belongs to someone. Discuss how that is different from its meaning in math. In math, a property is a rule.

Using the Problem-Solving Plan

1. $840
2. $t \geq 200$ min
3. $x \geq 18$

Performance Task

The *STEAM Video Performance Task* provides the opportunity for additional enrichment and greater depth of knowledge as students explore the mathematics of the chapter within a context tied to the chapter STEAM Video. The performance task and a detailed scoring rubric are provided at *BigIdeasMath.com*.

Laurie's Notes

Scaffolding Instruction

- The goal of this lesson is to help students become more comfortable with problem solving. These exercises combine writing and solving equations and inequalities with prior skills from other courses. The solution for Exercise 1 is worked out below, to help you guide students through the problem-solving plan. Use the remaining class time to have students work on the other exercises.
- **Emerging:** The goal for these students is to feel comfortable with the problem-solving plan. Allow students to work in pairs to write the beginning steps of the problem-solving plan for Exercise 2. Keep in mind that some students may only be ready to do the first step.
- **Proficient:** Students may be able to work independently or in pairs to complete Exercises 2 and 3.
- Visit each pair to review their plan for each problem. Ask students to describe their plans.

▶ Using the Problem-Solving Plan

Exercise 1

▷ **Understand the problem.** You know the area, height, and one base length of the trapezoid-shaped property. You are asked to find the cost of x feet of fencing, given that the fencing costs $7 per foot.

▷ **Make a plan.** Use the formula for the area of a trapezoid to find the length of fencing that you buy. Then multiply the length of fencing by $7 to find the total cost.

▷ **Solve and check.** Use the plan to solve the problem. Then check your solution.

- Find the length of fencing that you buy.

$A = \frac{1}{2}h(b_1 + b_2)$	Write formula for area of a trapezoid.
$15{,}750 = \frac{1}{2}(150)(90 + x)$	Substitute 150 for h, 90 for b_1, and x for b_2.
$15{,}750 = 75(90 + x)$	Simplify.
$15{,}750 = 6750 + 75x$	Distributive Property
$15{,}750 = 6750 + 75x$	
$\underline{-6750 \quad -6750}$	Subtraction Property of Equality
$9000 = 75x$	Simplify.
$\frac{9000}{75} = \frac{75x}{75}$	Division Property of Equality
$120 = x$	Simplify.

So, you buy 120 feet of fencing.

- Find the total cost.

$$120 \cdot 7 = 840$$

So, the total cost of the fence is $840.

- **Check:** Substitute 120 feet for x to verify the area.

$$15{,}750 = \frac{1}{2}(150)(90 + 120)$$
$$= \frac{1}{2}(150)(210)$$
$$= 15{,}750 \checkmark$$

A Connecting Concepts

▶ Using the Problem-Solving Plan

1. Fencing costs $7 per foot. You install x feet of the fencing along one side of a property, as shown. The property has an area of 15,750 square feet. What is the total cost of the fence?

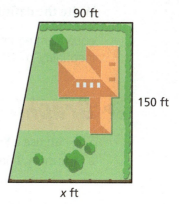

 You know the area, height, and one base length of the trapezoid-shaped property. You are asked to find the cost of x feet of fencing, given that the fencing costs $7 per foot.

 Use the formula for the area of a trapezoid to find the length of fencing that you buy. Then multiply the length of fencing by $7 to find the total cost.

 Use the plan to solve the problem. Then check your solution.

2. A pool is in the shape of a rectangular prism with a length of 15 feet, a width of 10 feet, and a depth of 4 feet. The pool is filled with water at a rate no faster than 3 cubic feet per minute. How long does it take to fill the pool?

3. The table shows your scores on 9 out of 10 quizzes that are each worth 20 points. What score do you need on the final quiz to have a mean score of at least 17 points?

Quiz Scores				
15	14	16	19	18
19	20	15	16	?

Performance Task

Distance and Brightness of the Stars

At the beginning of this chapter, you watched a STEAM Video called "Space Cadets." You are now ready to complete the performance task related to this video, available at BigIdeasMath.com. Be sure to use the problem-solving plan as you work through the performance task.

A Chapter Review

Go to *BigIdeasMath.com* to download blank graphic organizers.

▶ Review Vocabulary

Write the definition and give an example of each vocabulary term.

equivalent equations, *p. 466*
inequality, *p. 484*

solution of an inequality, *p. 484*

solution set, *p. 484*
graph of an inequality, *p. 486*

▶ Graphic Organizers

You can use a **Summary Triangle** to explain a concept. Here is an example of a Summary Triangle for **Addition Property of Equality**.

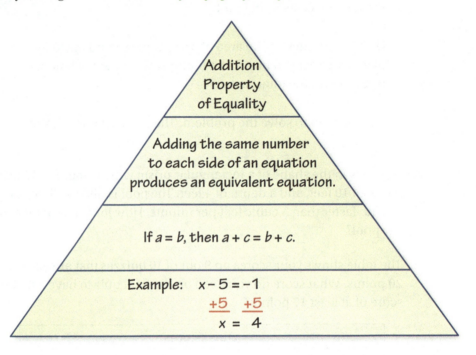

Choose and complete a graphic organizer to help you study the concept.

1. equivalent equations
2. Subtraction Property of Equality
3. Multiplication Property of Equality
4. Division Property of Equality
5. graphing inequalities
6. Addition and Subtraction Properties of Inequality
7. Multiplication and Division Properties of Inequality

"I finished my Summary Triangle about characteristics of hyenas."

Review Vocabulary

- As a review of the chapter vocabulary, have students revisit the vocabulary section in their *Student Journals* to fill in any missing definitions and record examples of each term.

Graphic Organizers

Sample answers:

1.

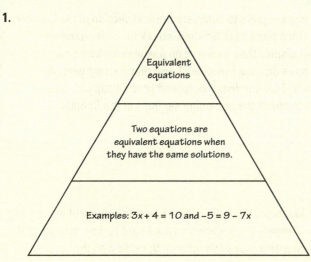

2.

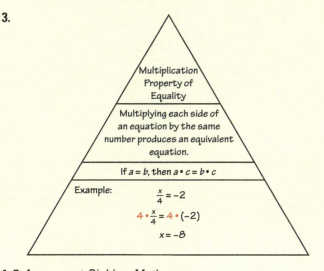

3.

[Multiplication Property of Equality summary triangle]

Multiplication Property of Equality

Multiplying each side of an equation by the same number produces an equivalent equation.

If $a = b$, then $a \cdot c = b \cdot c$

Example:
$$\frac{x}{4} = -2$$
$$4 \cdot \frac{x}{4} = 4 \cdot (-2)$$
$$x = -8$$

4–7. Answers at *BigIdeasMath.com*.

List of Organizers
Available at *BigIdeasMath.com*
Definition and Example Chart
Example and Non-Example Chart
Four Square
Information Frame
Summary Triangle

About this Organizer
A **Summary Triangle** can be used to explain a concept. Typically, the Summary Triangle is divided into 3 or 4 parts. Students write related categories in the middle part(s). Related categories may include: procedure, explanation, description, definition, theorem, or formula. In the bottom part, students write an example to illustrate the concept. A Summary Triangle can be used as an assessment tool, in which students complete the missing parts. Students may also place their Summary Triangles on note cards to use as a quick study reference.

T-510

Chapter Self-Assessment

1. $p = -1$
2. $q = -5$
3. $j = -20$
4. $b = 8$
5. $n = -\dfrac{1}{2}$
6. $v = -\dfrac{1}{24}$
7. $t = 4.9$
8. $\ell = -19.7$
9. $x + 5 = -4;\ x = -9$
10. $x + 5.62 + 3.65 + 5.62 = 23.59$; $x = 8.7$ ft
11. 7; The solution of $c + 5 = 12$ is $c = 7$.
12. $x = -24$
13. $y = -49$
14. $z = 3$
15. $w = 50$
16. $x = -2$
17. $y = -5$
18. $z = 6$
19. $w = -0.5$
20. $3y = -42;\ y = -14$
21. $\dfrac{t}{5} = -3.2;\ -16°F$
22. *Sample answer:* 7 of the same coins have a total value of $1.75. How much is each coin worth?

Chapter Self-Assessment

The Success Criteria Self-Assessment chart can be found in the *Student Journal* or online at *BigIdeasMath.com*.

ELL Support

Allow students to work in pairs to complete the first section of the Chapter Self-Assessment. Once pairs have finished, check for understanding by having each pair display their answers on a whiteboard for your review. Have two pairs discuss Exercise 11 and reach an agreement on their justifications. Monitor discussions and provide support. Use similar techniques to check the remaining sections of the Chapter Self-Assessment.

Common Errors

- **Exercises 1–8** Students may use the same operation instead of the inverse operation to solve. Simplify the equation on the board to demonstrate that this will not work. Students may have ignored the side with the variable when they made this mistake. Remind them to check their answers in the original equation.
- **Exercises 1–8** Students may add or subtract the number on the side of the equation without the variable. For example, $-14 + 14 = k + 6 + 14$ instead of $-14 - 6 = k + 6 - 6$. Remind students that they are trying to get the variable by itself, so they should start on the side with the variable and use the inverse of that operation.
- **Exercises 14, 15, 18, and 19** When the variable is multiplied by a negative number, students may not remember to keep the negative with the number and will really solve for $-x$ instead of x. Demonstrate an example of one of these problems on the board. Solve for $-x$ and ask students if x is by itself. If they do not realize it, remind them that there is a -1 in front of the variable and that they must divide by -1 to isolate the variable.

Chapter Self-Assessment

As you complete the exercises, use the scale below to rate your understanding of the success criteria in your journal.

1	2	3	4
I do not understand.	I can do it with help.	I can do it on my own.	I can teach someone else.

A.1 Solving Equations Using Addition or Subtraction (pp. 465–470)

Learning Target: Write and solve equations using addition or subtraction.

Solve the equation. Check your solution.

1. $p - 3 = -4$
2. $6 + q = 1$
3. $-2 + j = -22$
4. $b - 19 = -11$
5. $n + \dfrac{3}{4} = \dfrac{1}{4}$
6. $v - \dfrac{5}{6} = -\dfrac{7}{8}$
7. $t - 3.7 = 1.2$
8. $\ell + 15.2 = -4.5$

9. Write the word sentence as an equation. Then solve the equation.

    5 more than a number x is -4.

10. The perimeter of the trapezoid-shaped window frame is 23.59 feet. Write and solve an equation to find the unknown side length (in feet).

11. You are 5 years older than your cousin. How old is your cousin when you are 12 years old? Justify your answer.

A.2 Solving Equations Using Multiplication or Division (pp. 471–476)

Learning Target: Write and solve equations using multiplication or division.

Solve the equation. Check your solution.

12. $\dfrac{x}{3} = -8$
13. $-7 = \dfrac{y}{7}$
14. $-\dfrac{z}{4} = -\dfrac{3}{4}$
15. $-\dfrac{w}{20} = -2.5$
16. $4x = -8$
17. $-10 = 2y$
18. $-5.4z = -32.4$
19. $-6.8w = 3.4$

20. Write "3 times a number y is -42" as an equation. Then solve the equation.

21. The mean temperature change is $-3.2°F$ per day for 5 days. Write and solve an equation to find the total change over the 5-day period.

22. Describe a real-life situation that can be modeled by $7x = 1.75$.

A.3 Solving Two-Step Equations (pp. 477–482)

Learning Target: Write and solve two-step equations.

Solve the equation. Check your solution.

23. $-2c + 6 = -8$

24. $5 - 4t = 6$

25. $-3x - 4.6 = 5.9$

26. $\dfrac{w}{6} + \dfrac{5}{8} = -1\dfrac{3}{8}$

27. $3(3w - 4) = -20$

28. $-6y + 8y = -24$

29. The floor of a canyon has an elevation of -14.5 feet. Erosion causes the elevation to change by -1.5 feet per year. How many years will it take for the canyon floor to reach an elevation of -31 feet? Justify your solution.

A.4 Writing and Graphing Inequalities (pp. 483–488)

Learning Target: Write inequalities and represent solutions of inequalities on number lines.

Write the word sentence as an inequality.

30. A number w is greater than -3.

31. A number y minus $\dfrac{1}{2}$ is no more than $-\dfrac{3}{2}$.

Tell whether the given value is a solution of the inequality.

32. $5 + j > 8; j = 7$

33. $6 \div n \le -5; n = -3$

34. $7p \ge p - 12; p = -2$

Graph the inequality on a number line.

35. $q > -1.3$

36. $s < 1\dfrac{3}{4}$

37. The Enhanced Fujita scale rates the intensity of tornadoes based on wind speed and damage caused. An EF5 tornado is estimated to have wind speeds greater than 200 miles per hour. Write and graph an inequality that represents this situation.

A.5 Solving Inequalities Using Addition or Subtraction (pp. 489–494)

Learning Target: Write and solve inequalities using addition or subtraction.

Solve the inequality. Graph the solution.

38. $d + 12 < 19$

39. $t - 4 \le -14$

40. $-8 \le z + 6.4$

Common Errors

- **Exercises 23–28** Students may divide the coefficient first instead of adding or subtracting first. Tell students that while this is a valid method, they must remember to divide each part of the equation by the coefficient.
- **Exercise 27** Students may try to add or subtract without distributing. Remind students that when parentheses are present, they either need to use the Distributive Property or undo the multiplication first.
- **Exercises 35, 36, and 38–40** Students may shade the number line in the wrong direction. This often happens when the variable is on the right side of the inequality. Remind students to use test points to the left and right of the boundary point to determine which direction to shade the number line.
- **Exercises 35, 36, and 38–40** Students may draw a closed circle instead of an open circle and vice versa. Remind students that an open circle means the number is not included and a closed circle means that the number is included.
- **Exercises 38–40** Students may use the same operation instead of the inverse operation to isolate the variable. Remind students that when a number is added to the variable, they must subtract that number from each side. When a number is subtracted from the variable, they must add that number to each side. Remind students to check their answers in the original inequality.

Chapter Self-Assessment

23. $c = 7$
24. $t = -\dfrac{1}{4}$
25. $x = -3.5$
26. $w = -12$
27. $w = -\dfrac{8}{9}$
28. $y = -12$
29. 11 years; The solution of $-1.5x - 14.5 = -31$ is $x = 11$.
30. $w > -3$
31. $y - \dfrac{1}{2} \leq -\dfrac{3}{2}$
32. yes
33. no
34. yes
35. [number line showing open circle at −1.3]
36. [number line showing open circle at $1\frac{3}{4}$]
37. $s > 200$ [number line with open circle at 200]
38. $d < 7$ [number line with open circle at 7]
39. $t \leq -10$ [number line with closed circle at −10]
40. $z \geq -14.4$ [number line with closed circle at −14.4]

T-512

Chapter Self-Assessment

41. **a.** $p + 115 \leq 500$; $p \leq 385$ people

    b. yes; *Sample answer:* The cruise ship can hold less than or equal to 385 more people.

42. *Sample answer:* $x + 5 < 2$

43. $q < -3$

44. $r \geq -18$

45. $3 < s$

46. $-3p > 21$; $p < -7$

47. $\frac{3}{4}b \leq 24$; $b \leq 32$

48. $x > 4$

49. $z \geq -8$

50. $t > -7$

51. $q < -13$

52. $p \geq 21$

53. $j \geq 0.5$

54. $3.50x + 15 \geq 50$; $x \geq 10$ candles

Common Errors

- **Exercise 43** When there is a negative in the inequality, students may reverse the direction of the inequality symbol. Remind students that they only reverse the direction when they are multiplying or dividing by a negative number.
- **Exercises 43–45** Students may use the same operation instead of the inverse operation to isolate the variable. Remind students that when a number is multiplied to the variable, they must divide each side by that number. When the variable is divided by a number, they must multiply each side by that number. Remind students to check their answers in the original inequality.
- **Exercises 43–45** Students may shade the number line in the wrong direction. This often happens when the variable is on the right side of the inequality. Remind students to use test points to the left and right of the boundary point to determine which direction to shade the number line.
- **Exercises 44 and 45** Students may forget to reverse the inequality symbol when multiplying or dividing by a negative number. Remind students of this rule. Encourage students to substitute values into the original inequality to check that the solution is correct.
- **Exercises 48–50** Students may incorrectly multiply or divide before adding or subtracting from both sides of the inequality. Remind students that they should work backward through the order of operations, or that they should start away from the variable and move toward it.
- **Exercises 49, 50, and 52** Students may forget to reverse the inequality symbol when multiplying or dividing by a negative number. Encourage students to write the inequality symbol that they should have in the solution before solving.
- **Exercises 51–53** If students distribute before solving, they may forget to distribute the number to the second term. Remind students that they need to distribute to everything within the parentheses. Encourage students to draw arrows to represent the multiplication.

Chapter Resources

Surface Level	Deep Level
Resources by Chapter • Extra Practice • Reteach • Puzzle Time Student Journal • Practice • Chapter Self-Assessment Differentiating the Lesson Tutorial Videos Skills Review Handbook Skills Trainer Game Library	Resources by Chapter • Enrichment and Extension Graphic Organizers Game Library
Transfer Level	
STEAM Video Dynamic Assessment System • Chapter Test	Assessment Book • Chapter Tests A and B • Alternative Assessment • STEAM Performance Task

41. A small cruise ship can hold up to 500 people. There are 115 crew members on board the ship.

    a. Write and solve an inequality that represents the additional numbers of people that can board the ship.

    b. Can 385 more people board the ship? Explain.

42. Write an inequality that can be solved using the Subtraction Property of Inequality and has a solution of all numbers less than −3.

A.6 Solving Inequalities Using Multiplication or Division (pp. 495–502)

Learning Target: Write and solve inequalities using multiplication or division.

Solve the inequality. Graph the solution.

43. $6q < -18$ **44.** $-\dfrac{r}{3} \le 6$ **45.** $-4 > -\dfrac{4}{3}s$

46. Write the word sentence as an inequality. Then solve the inequality.

    The product of −3 and a number p is greater than 21.

47. You are organizing books on a shelf. Each book has a width of $\dfrac{3}{4}$ inch. Write and solve an inequality for the numbers of books b that can fit on the shelf.

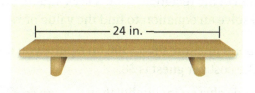

A.7 Solving Two-Step Inequalities (pp. 503–508)

Learning Target: Write and solve two-step inequalities.

Solve the inequality. Graph the solution.

48. $3x + 4 > 16$ **49.** $\dfrac{z}{-2} - 6 \le -2$ **50.** $-2t - 5 < 9$

51. $7(q + 2) < -77$ **52.** $-\dfrac{1}{3}(p + 9) \le 4$ **53.** $1.2(j + 3.5) \ge 4.8$

54. Your goal is to raise at least $50 in a charity fundraiser. You earn $3.50 for each candle sold. You also receive a $15 donation. Write and solve an inequality that represents the numbers of candles you must sell to reach your goal.

A Practice Test

Solve the equation. Check your solution.

1. $7x = -3$
2. $2(x + 1) = -2$
3. $\frac{2}{9}g = -8$
4. $z + 14.5 = 5.4$
5. $-14 = c - 10$
6. $\frac{2}{7}k - \frac{3}{8} = -\frac{19}{8}$

Write the word sentence as an inequality.

7. A number k plus 19.5 is less than or equal to 40.
8. A number q multiplied by $\frac{1}{4}$ is greater than -16.

Tell whether the given value is a solution of the inequality.

9. $n - 3 \leq 4$; $n = 7$
10. $-\frac{3}{7}m < 1 + m$; $m = -7$

Solve the inequality. Graph the solution.

11. $x - 4 > -6$
12. $-\frac{2}{9} + y \leq \frac{5}{9}$
13. $-6z \geq 36$
14. $-5.2 \geq \frac{p}{4}$
15. $4k - 8 \geq 20$
16. $-0.6 > -0.3(d + 6)$

17. You lose 0.3 point for stepping out of bounds during a gymnastics floor routine. Your final score is 9.124. Write and solve an equation to find your score without the penalty.

18. Half the area of the rectangle shown is 24 square inches. Write and solve an equation to find the value of x.

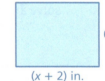

6 in.

$(x + 2)$ in.

19. You can spend no more than $100 on a party you are hosting. The cost per guest is $8.
    a. Write and solve an inequality that represents the numbers of guests you can invite to the party.
    b. What is the greatest number of guests that you can invite to the party? Explain your reasoning.

20. You have $30 to buy baseball cards. Each pack of cards costs $5. Write and solve an inequality that represents the numbers of packs of baseball cards you can buy and still have at least $10 left.

21. The sum of the lengths of any two sides of a triangle is greater than the length of the third side.
    a. Write and solve three inequalities for the previous statement using the triangle shown.
    b. What values for x make sense?

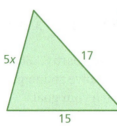

Practice Test Item References

Practice Test Questions	Section to Review
4, 5, 17	A.1
1, 3	A.2
2, 6, 18	A.3
7, 8, 9, 10	A.4
11, 12	A.5
13, 14, 19	A.6
15, 16, 20, 21	A.7

Test-Taking Strategies
Remind students to quickly look over the entire test before they start so that they can budget their time. On tests, it is really important for students to **Stop** and **Think**. When students hurry on a test dealing with positive and negative numbers, they often make "sign" errors. There are equations and inequalities on the test, so remind students to always check their solutions. When writing word phrases as inequalities, students can get confused by the subtle differences in wording. Encourage students to think carefully about which inequality symbol is implied by the wording.

Common Errors
- **Exercises 1–6** Students may use the same operation instead of the inverse operation to solve. Simplify the equation on the board to demonstrate that this will not work. Remind them to check their answers in the original equation.
- **Exercises 2 and 16** If students distribute before solving, they may forget to distribute the number to the second term. Remind students that they need to distribute to everything within the parentheses. Encourage students to draw arrows to represent the multiplication.
- **Exercises 11–16** Students may shade the number line in the wrong direction. This often happens when the variable is on the right side of the inequality. Remind students to use test points to the left and right of the boundary point to determine which direction to shade the number line.
- **Exercises 11–16** Students may draw a closed circle instead of an open circle and vice versa. Remind students that an open circle means the number is not included and a closed circle means that the number is included.
- **Exercises 13 and 16** Students may forget to reverse the inequality symbol when multiplying or dividing by a negative number. Encourage students to write the inequality symbol that they should have in the solution before solving.

Practice Test

1. $x = -\dfrac{3}{7}$ 2. $x = -2$
3. $g = -36$ 4. $z = -9.1$
5. $c = -4$ 6. $k = -7$
7. $k + 19.5 \leq 40$
8. $\dfrac{1}{4}q > -16$
9. yes
10. no
11. $x > -2$

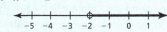

12. $y \leq \dfrac{7}{9}$

13. $z \leq -6$

14. $p \leq -20.8$

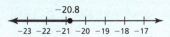

15. $k \geq 7$

16. $d > -4$

17. $x - 0.3 = 9.124;\ 9.424$
18. $6(x + 2) = 48;\ x = 6$ in.
19. **a.** $8g \leq 100;\ g \leq 12.5$
    b. 12; 12 is the largest whole number that satisfies the inequality.
20. $30 - 5c \geq 10;\ c \leq 4$ packs of cards
21. **a.** $5x + 17 > 15;\ x > -\dfrac{2}{5}$

   $5x + 15 > 17;\ x > \dfrac{2}{5}$

   $15 + 17 > 5x;\ x < 6\dfrac{2}{5}$

   b. values greater than $\dfrac{2}{5}$ and less than $6\dfrac{2}{5}$

Test-Taking Strategies

Available at *BigIdeasMath.com*

After Answering Easy Questions, Relax
Answer Easy Questions First
Estimate the Answer
Read All Choices before Answering
Read Question before Answering
Solve Directly or Eliminate Choices
Solve Problem before Looking at Choices
Use Intelligent Guessing
Work Backwards

About this Strategy

When taking a multiple-choice test, be sure to read each question carefully and thoroughly. After skimming the test and answering the easy questions, stop for a few seconds, take a deep breath, and relax. Work through the remaining questions carefully, using your knowledge and test-taking strategies. Remember, you already completed many of the questions on the test!

Cumulative Practice

1. B
2. I
3. A
4. F
5. 2.625

Item Analysis

1. **A.** The student multiplies instead of dividing.
   B. Correct answer
   C. The student switches the dividend and the divisor.
   D. The student sets the equation equal to 10 instead of −10.

2. **F.** The student finds the reciprocal of the product.
   G. The student finds the reciprocal of the first fraction before multiplying.
   H. The student finds the reciprocal of the second fraction before multiplying.
   I. Correct answer

3. **A.** Correct answer
   B. The student multiplies both sides of $\frac{x}{-4} \geq -1$ by 4 instead of −4
   C. The student thinks $-9 + 8 = 1$ instead of −1.
   D. The student does not reverse the inequality symbol when multiplying both sides of the inequality by a negative number.

4. **F.** Correct answer
   G. The student adds $\frac{1}{8}$ to both sides of the equation instead of subtracting.
   H. The student multiplies by the reciprocal of $-\frac{3}{4}$ before subtracting $\frac{1}{8}$ from both sides of the equation.
   I. The student multiplies by $-\frac{3}{4}$ instead of the reciprocal before subtracting $\frac{1}{8}$ from both sides of the equation.

5. **Gridded Response:** Correct answer: 2.625

   Common error: The student multiplies the whole number and the numerator to get $\frac{10}{8} = 1.25$.

A Cumulative Practice

1. Which equation represents the word sentence?

   The quotient of a number b and 0.3 equals negative 10.

   A. $0.3b = 10$ **B.** $\dfrac{b}{0.3} = -10$

   C. $\dfrac{0.3}{b} = -10$ **D.** $\dfrac{b}{0.3} = 10$

   Test-Taking Strategy
   After Answering Easy Questions, Relax

   "After answering the easy questions, relax and try the harder ones. For this, $2x = 12$, so $x = 6$ hyenas."

2. What is the value of the expression?

   $$-\dfrac{3}{8} \cdot \dfrac{2}{5}$$

   F. $-\dfrac{20}{3}$ **G.** $-\dfrac{16}{15}$

   H. $-\dfrac{15}{16}$ **I.** $-\dfrac{3}{20}$

3. Which graph represents the inequality?

   $$\dfrac{x}{-4} - 8 \geq -9$$

   A. [number line from −3 to 6, shaded left from 4]

   B. [number line from −6 to 3, shaded right from −4]

   C. [number line from −6 to 3, shaded left from −4]

   D. [number line from −3 to 6, shaded right from 4]

4. Which equation is equivalent to $-\dfrac{3}{4}x + \dfrac{1}{8} = -\dfrac{3}{8}$?

   F. $-\dfrac{3}{4}x = -\dfrac{3}{8} - \dfrac{1}{8}$

   G. $-\dfrac{3}{4}x = -\dfrac{3}{8} + \dfrac{1}{8}$

   H. $x + \dfrac{1}{8} = -\dfrac{3}{8} \cdot \left(-\dfrac{4}{3}\right)$

   I. $x + \dfrac{1}{8} = -\dfrac{3}{8} \cdot \left(-\dfrac{3}{4}\right)$

5. What is the decimal form of $2\dfrac{5}{8}$?

6. What is the value of the expression when $x = -5$, $y = 3$, and $z = -1$?

$$\frac{x^2 - 3y}{z}$$

   A. -34

   B. -16

   C. 16

   D. 34

7. Which expression is equivalent to $9h - 6 + 7h - 5$?

   F. $3h + 2$

   G. $16h + 1$

   H. $2h - 1$

   I. $16h - 11$

8. Your friend solved the equation $-96 = -6(x - 15)$.

$$-96 = -6(x - 15)$$
$$-96 = -6x - 90$$
$$-96 + 90 = -6x - 90 + 90$$
$$-6 = -6x$$
$$\frac{-6}{-6} = \frac{-6x}{-6}$$
$$1 = x$$

   What should your friend do to correct her error?

   A. First add 6 to both sides of the equation.

   B. First subtract x from both sides of the equation.

   C. Distribute the -6 to get $6x - 90$.

   D. Distribute the -6 to get $-6x + 90$.

9. Which expression does *not* represent the perimeter of the rectangle?

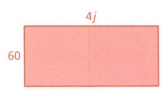

   F. $4j(60)$

   G. $8j + 120$

   H. $2(4j + 60)$

   I. $8(j + 15)$

Item Analysis (continued)

6. **A.** The student finds $x^2 + 3y$ instead of $x^2 - 3y$.
   B. Correct answer
   C. The student substitutes 1 instead of −1 for z.
   D. The student finds $x^2 + 3y$ instead of $x^2 - 3y$ and substitutes 1 instead of −1 for z.

7. **F.** The student does not combine like terms. The student incorrectly combines $9h - 6$ to get $3h$ and $7h - 5$ to get 2.
   G. The student subtracts 5 from 6 instead −6.
   H. The student subtracts 9h and 7h instead of adding and adds −6 and 5 instead of subtracting.
   I. Correct answer

8. **A.** The student thinks that the inverse operation of multiplying by −6 is adding 6.
   B. The student does not distribute the −6 before subtracting.
   C. The student ignores the negative sign and distributes 6 to the terms inside of the parentheses.
   D. Correct answer

9. **F.** Correct answer
   G The student does not realize that the expression $8j + 120$ is equivalent to $4j + 60 + 4j + 60$.
   H. The student does not realize that the expression is a factored form of the perimeter, $8j + 120$.
   I. The student does not realize that the expression is a factored form of the perimeter, $8j + 120$.

Cumulative Practice

6. B
7. I
8. D
9. F

Cumulative Practice

10. $-\dfrac{11}{24}$

11. *Part A* at least 48 more T-shirts; The inequality is $20 + 10t \geq 500$.

    Part B at least 63 T-shirts; The inequality is $8t \geq 500$.

    Part C your friend; at least 13 more T-shirts; You must sell at least 50 total T-shirts and your friend must sell at least 63 total T-shirts.

12. A
13. H
14. A

Item Analysis (continued)

10. **Gridded Response:** Correct answer: $-\dfrac{11}{24}$

    Common error: The student subtracts the numerators and subtracts the denominators to get $\dfrac{-2}{4} = -\dfrac{1}{2}$.

11. **4 points** The student's work and explanations demonstrate a thorough understanding of writing and solving inequalities. The student identifies the correct quantities, operations, and inequality symbols, and the solutions are clear, neat, and correct. In Part A, the student finds that you must sell at least 48 more T-shirts. In Part B, the student finds that your friend must sell at least 63 T-shirts. In Part C, the student finds that your friend must sell at least 13 more T-shirts than you, because he must sell at least 63 and you must sell at least 50.

    3 points The student's work and explanations demonstrate an essential but less than thorough understanding of writing and solving inequalities. There may be one error made, but subsequent work is consistent with the error.

    2 points The student's work and explanations demonstrate a partial but limited understanding of writing and solving inequalities. The student sets up one or more of the three problem situations incorrectly.

    1 point The student's work and explanations demonstrate a very limited understanding of writing and solving inequalities.

    0 points The student provides no response, a completely incorrect or incomprehensible response, or a response that demonstrates insufficient understanding of writing and solving inequalities.

12. **A.** Correct answer
    B. The student thinks the product of two negative numbers is negative.
    C. The student finds $-\dfrac{2}{3} - \dfrac{4}{9}$ instead of $-\dfrac{2}{3} - \left(-\dfrac{4}{9}\right)$.
    D. The student multiplies by the reciprocal of the dividend instead of the reciprocal of the divisor.

13. **F.** The student reverses the multiplicative relationship.
    G. The student does not distribute the 2 to the 10.
    H. Correct answer
    I. The student adds 2 to $6c + 10$ instead of multiplying by 2.

14. **A.** Correct answer
    B. The student finds the difference instead of the sum.
    C. The student adds $\dfrac{4}{5}$ to $-\dfrac{2}{3}$ instead of adding $-\dfrac{4}{5}$ to $-\dfrac{2}{3}$.
    D. The student finds the product instead of the sum.

10. What is the value of the expression?

$$\frac{5}{12} - \frac{7}{8}$$

11. You are selling T-shirts to raise money for a charity. You sell the T-shirts for $10 each.

   Part A You have already sold 2 T-shirts. How many more T-shirts must you sell to raise at least $500? Explain.

   Part B Your friend is raising money for the same charity and has not sold any T-shirts previously. He sells the T-shirts for $8 each. What are the total numbers of T-shirts he can sell to raise at least $500? Explain.

   Part C Who has to sell more T-shirts in total? How many more? Explain.

12. Which expression has the same value as $-\frac{2}{3} - \left(-\frac{4}{9}\right)$?

    A. $-\frac{1}{3} + \frac{1}{9}$

    B. $-\frac{2}{3} \times \left(-\frac{1}{3}\right)$

    C. $-\frac{1}{3} - \frac{7}{9}$

    D. $\frac{3}{2} \div \left(-\frac{1}{3}\right)$

13. You recycle $(6c + 10)$ water bottles. Your friend recycles twice as many water bottles as you recycle. Which expression represents the amount of water bottles your friend recycles?

    F. $3c + 5$

    G. $12c + 10$

    H. $12c + 20$

    I. $6c + 12$

14. What is the value of the expression?

    $$-\frac{4}{5} + \left(-\frac{2}{3}\right)$$

    A. $-\frac{22}{15}$

    B. $-\frac{2}{15}$

    C. $\frac{2}{15}$

    D. $\frac{8}{15}$

B Probability

- **B.1** Probability
- **B.2** Experimental and Theoretical Probability
- **B.3** Compound Events
- **B.4** Simulations

Chapter Learning Target:
Understand probability.

Chapter Success Criteria:
- I can identify the possible outcomes of a situation.
- I can explain the meaning of experimental and theoretical probability.
- I can make predictions using probabilities.
- I can solve real-life problems using probability.

STEAM Video: "Massively Multiplayer Rock Paper Scissors"

Laurie's Notes

Chapter B Overview

This is students' first formal introduction to probability, but it is not their first experience with random events. They have heard a weather forecaster say that there is an 80% chance of rain or thought about the possible outcomes in a game. In other words, students have an idea about chance and fairness. They have flipped coins, rolled number cubes, and worked with spinners. Understanding that probability is about how likely an event is on a continuum from 0 (impossible) to 1 (certain) is generally not the challenge. Many students have difficulty understanding the language of probability and correctly interpreting a problem.

This is a chapter that can be enriched by the use of online simulators (number cubes, spinners), probability games, and experimentation. Graphing calculators have apps for modeling probability experiments. Students need these experiences to fully understand that the outcomes of previous trials do not predict the outcome of another trial. For example, rolling an even number five times in a row on a number cube does not predict the outcome of the next roll.

The vocabulary of probability is presented in the first lesson. It is most effective to use the vocabulary in the context of an experiment. The exploration in Section B.1 provides this opportunity using spinners. Experimental probability and theoretical probability are then introduced.

The sample space of an experiment is the set of all possible outcomes for the experiment. Students often invent their own methods for finding and recording a sample space for an experiment. While their methods may not be efficient or well-organized, they may well be correct. Knowing how to determine the number of possible outcomes for an event or experiment is essential to solving probability problems.

The chapter concludes with a lesson on simulations. Simulations provide experiences that are necessary for helping students to develop an understanding of theoretical probability. Students need to connect the results of the experiment with the expected outcome. Look for online support to add interest and challenge when teaching this lesson.

Suggested Pacing

Chapter Opener	1 Day
Section 1	1 Day
Section 2	1 Day
Section 3	1 Day
Section 4	2 Days
Connecting Concepts	1 Day
Chapter Review	1 Day
Chapter Test	1 Day
Total Chapter B	9 Days
Year-to-Date	23 Days

Chapter Learning Target
Understand probability.

Chapter Success Criteria
- Identify the possible outcomes of a situation.
- Explain the meaning of experimental and theoretical probability.
- Make predictions using probabilities.
- Solve real-life problems using probability.

Chapter B Learning Targets and Success Criteria

Section	Learning Target	Success Criteria
B.1 Probability	Understand how the probability of an event indicates its likelihood.	• Identify possible outcomes of an experiment. • Use probability and relative frequency to describe the likelihood of an event. • Use relative frequency to make predictions.
B.2 Experimental and Theoretical Probability	Develop probability models using experimental and theoretical probability.	• Explain the meanings of experimental probability and theoretical probability. • Find experimental and theoretical probabilities. • Use probability to make predictions.
B.3 Compound Events	Find sample spaces and probabilities of compound events.	• Find the sample space of two or more events. • Find the total number of possible outcomes of two or more events. • Find probabilities of compound events.
B.4 Simulations	Design and use simulations to find probabilities of compound events.	• Design a simulation to model a real-life situation. • Recognize favorable outcomes in a simulation. • Use simulations to find experimental probabilities.

Progressions

Through the Grades

Grade 6	Grade 7	Grade 8
• Find percent as a rate per 100; solve problems involving finding the whole, given a part and the percent. • Summarize numerical data sets in relation to their context.	• Understand that probability is the likelihood of an event occurring, expressed as a number from 0 to 1. • Approximate the probability of a chance event and predict the approximate relative frequency given the probability. • Develop probability models and use them to find probabilities. • Find the probabilities of compound events.	• Construct and interpret a two-way table summarizing data. Use relative frequencies to describe possible association between the two variables.

Through the Chapter

Standard	B.1	B.2	B.3	B.4
Understand that the probability of a chance event is a number between 0 and 1 that expresses the likelihood of the event occurring. Larger numbers indicate greater likelihood. A probability near 0 indicates an unlikely event, a probability around $\frac{1}{2}$ indicates an event that is neither unlikely nor likely, and a probability near 1 indicates a likely event.	★			
Approximate the probability of a chance event by collecting data on the chance process that produces it and observing its long-run relative frequency, and predict the approximate relative frequency given the probability.	●	★		
Develop a uniform probability model by assigning equal probability to all outcomes, and use the model to determine probabilities of events.		★		
Develop a probability model (which may not be uniform) by observing frequencies in data generated from a chance process.	●	★		
Understand that, just as with simple events, the probability of a compound event is the fraction of outcomes in the sample space for which the compound event occurs.			★	★
Represent sample spaces for compound events using methods such as organized lists, tables and tree diagrams. For an event described in everyday language (e.g., "rolling double sixes"), identify the outcomes in the sample space which compose the event.			★	
Design and use a simulation to generate frequencies for compound events.				★

Key
▲ = preparing ★ = complete
● = learning ■ = extending

STEAM Video

1. $33.\overline{3}\%$; $33.\overline{3}\%$; $33.\overline{3}\%$

2. 5 times; *Sample answer:* Every time you play Rock Paper Scissors, you have a $33.\overline{3}\%$ chance of winning.

   $15 \times \dfrac{1}{3} = 5$ times

Performance Task

Sample answer: A game is fair if the player has an equal chance of winning or losing. For example, suppose a spinner is 50% colored red and 50% colored blue. A player spins the spinner and has an equal chance to land on both colors; A game is unfair if the player does not have an equal chance of winning or losing. For example, suppose a spinner is 75% colored red and 25% colored blue. A player has a better chance to land on the red portion than the blue portion.

Mathematical Practices

Students have opportunities to develop aspects of the mathematical practices throughout the chapter. Here are some examples.

1. **Make Sense of Problems and Persevere in Solving Them**
   B.2 Exercise 29, *p. 535*
2. **Reason Abstractly and Quantitatively**
   B.3 Exercise 32, *p. 544*
3. **Construct Viable Arguments and Critique the Reasoning of Others**
   B.2 Math Practice note, *p. 529*
4. **Model with Mathematics**
   B.4 Exercise 17, *p. 550*
5. **Use Appropriate Tools Strategically**
   B.4 Math Practice note, *p. 545*
6. **Attend to Precision**
   B.4 Math Practice note, *p. 546*
7. **Look for and Make Use of Structure**
   B.3 Math Practice note, *p. 537*
8. **Look for and Express Regularity in Repeated Reasoning**
   B.3 Exercise 35, *p. 544*

Laurie's Notes

STEAM Video

Before the Video
- To introduce the STEAM Video, read aloud the first paragraph of Massively Multiplayer Rock Paper Scissors and discuss the prompt with your students.
- "Describe a real-life situation where it is helpful to describe the percent of times that a particular outcome occurs."

During the Video
- The video shows Enid and Tory playing an extended version of Rock Paper Scissors that allows multiple people to play.
- Pause the video at 3:01 and ask, "What two types of probabilities are Enid and Tory calculating?" experimental probability and theoretical probability
- Watch the remainder of the video.

After the Video
- "What could cause the experimental probabilities to get closer to the theoretical probabilities?" Playing many more rounds of the game.
- Have students work with a partner to answer Questions 1 and 2.
- As students discuss and answer the questions, listen for understanding of finding probabilities and using them to make predictions.

Performance Task

- Use this information to spark students' interest and promote thinking about real-life problems.
- Ask, "In what ways can a game of chance be considered fair? unfair? Explain your reasoning."
- After completing the chapter, students will have gained the knowledge needed to complete "Fair and Unfair Carnival Games."

STEAM Video

Massively Multiplayer Rock Paper Scissors

Rock

Paper

Scissors

You can use *experimental probability* to describe the percent of times that you win, lose, or tie in Rock Paper Scissors. Describe a real-life situation where it is helpful to describe the percent of times that a particular outcome occurs.

Watch the STEAM Video "Massively Multiplayer Rock Paper Scissors." Then answer the following questions.

1. The table shows the ways that you can win, lose, or tie in Rock Paper Scissors. You and your opponent throw the signs for rock, paper, or scissors at random. What percent of the time do you expect to win? lose? tie?

		Your Throw		
		Rock	Paper	Scissors
Opponent's Throw	Rock	tie	win	lose
	Paper	lose	tie	win
	Scissors	win	lose	tie

2. You play Rock Paper Scissors 15 times. About how many times do you expect to win? Explain your reasoning.

Performance Task

Fair and Unfair Carnival Games

After completing this chapter, you will be able to use the concepts you learned to answer the questions in the *STEAM Video Performance Task*.

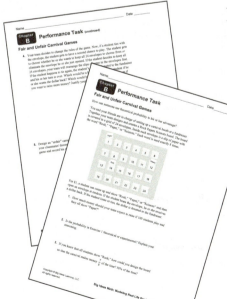

You will be given information about a version of Rock Paper Scissors used at a carnival. Then you will be asked to design your own "unfair" carnival game using a spinner or a number cube, and test your game with a classmate.

In what ways can a game of chance be considered fair? unfair? Explain your reasoning.

519

Getting Ready for Chapter B

Chapter Exploration

Work with a partner.

1. Play Rock Paper Scissors 30 times. Tally your results in the table.
2. How many possible results are there?
3. Of the possible results, in how many ways can Player A win? In how many ways can Player B win? In how many ways can there be a tie?
4. Is one of the players more likely to win than the other player? Explain your reasoning.

GAME RULES
Rock **breaks** scissors.
Paper **covers** rock.
Scissors **cut** paper.

Vocabulary

The following vocabulary terms are defined in this chapter. Think about what each term might mean and record your thoughts.

probability   theoretical probability   simulation

relative frequency   sample space

experimental probability   compound event

Laurie's Notes

Chapter Exploration

- Although most students will be familiar with this game, you may want to review the rules as a class.
- ❓ "Do you think that all pairs will get the exact same results?" Students should realize that it is unlikely.
- Allow time for students to complete the exploration.
- ❓ "Do your results in Exercise 1 support your answer in Exercise 4? Why or why not?" Answers will vary. Listen for understanding that although the players are equally likely to win, the actual results may vary.
- If time permits, combine the data of all pairs in a large table on the board. Then ask students if the collective data supports the answer in Exercise 4.

Vocabulary

- These terms represent some of the vocabulary that students will encounter in Chapter B. Discuss the terms as a class.
- Where have students heard the word *simulation* outside of a math classroom? In what contexts? Students may not be able to write the actual definition, but they may write phrases associated with a simulation.
- Allowing students to discuss these terms now will prepare them for understanding the terms as they are presented in the chapter.
- When students encounter a new definition, encourage them to write in their *Student Journals*. They will revisit these definitions during the Chapter Review.

ELL Support

Students may be familiar with the word *probable*. Say that if something is probable, it might happen but it might not. Provide examples of its use or ask students to offer their ideas. Explain that the mathematical term *probability* is related to the word *probable*. A number is used to represent the probability that an event will happen. That number will vary depending on the event. Point out that *vary* and *very* are two different words. *Vary* means "change" and *very* is used to intensify the meaning of a word.

Topics for Review

- Converting Between Fractions, Decimals, and Percents
- Multiplying Fractions
- Writing Ratios

Chapter Exploration

1. Answers will vary. Students should play Rock Paper Scissors 30 times and record their results in the table.
2. 9 results
3. 3 ways; 3 ways; 3 ways
4. no; Both players have 3 out of 9 possible ways of winning.

Learning Target
Understand how the probability of an event indicates its likelihood.

Success Criteria
- Identify possible outcomes of an experiment.
- Use probability and relative frequency to describe the likelihood of an event.
- Use relative frequency to make predictions.

Warm Up
Cumulative, vocabulary, and prerequisite skills practice opportunities are available in the *Resources by Chapter* or at *BigIdeasMath.com*.

ELL Support
Explain the meaning of the word *likelihood*. Point out that it means something different from the word *like*. If you like something, you enjoy it. If something is likely, it is expected to happen. The word *likelihood* is related to *likely*. The likelihood that something will happen is the expectation that it will happen.

Teaching Strategy
Students can make spinners by unfolding the end of a paper clip and placing the point of a pencil inside the opposite end, located in the center of the spinner.

Exploration 1
a. See Additional Answers.
b. Answers will vary.
c. See Additional Answers.

T-521

Laurie's Notes

Preparing to Teach
- Students should be familiar with organizing the results of an **experiment** in a table.
- In this exploration, students will gain a conceptual sense of **probability** by performing activities to determine the likelihood of an **event**. They will pursue the concept of possible **outcomes**, which leads to describing the likelihood of an event.

Motivate
- A county in a U.S. state is often named after a person, such as a president. In fact, there are 31 states in the U.S. with a county named Washington. Sometimes the county is named after a historical figure. Madison is a county name in 20 states and Calhoun is a county name in 11 states.
- Draw a spinner representing this information.

Key:
C – Calhoun   M – Madison   W – Washington

- ❓ "If you spin the spinner 100 times, how many times would you expect it to land on Washington? Explain." 50; There are 62 different counties represented and half of them are named Washington.

Exploration 1
- In this exploration, students will consider spinners with different-sized sections. Electronic spinners are available at *BigIdeasMath.com*. If students do not have access to these spinners, they can make spinners as described in the Teaching Strategy.
- ❓ "How does the size of a section affect the likelihood?" The smaller the section, the less likely the spinner will land on it.
- To save time in part (b), you could have each partner complete a different frequency table.
- ❓ After pairs complete part (b), ask, "Do your results support your answer in part (a)?" Answers will vary.
- ❓ "If not, are your answers in part (a) incorrect?" Listen for understanding that you may be more likely to spin certain numbers, but actual spins may vary.
- ❓ "What might affect your results?" *Sample answers:* a faulty spinner or the angle of the spinner
- If time permits, combine the data of all pairs in two large tables on the board. Then ask students if the collective data supports the answers in part (a).
- After pairs complete part (c), ask several pairs to share their answers with the class. Students may describe the percent of times they spun each number (experimental probability) or the percent of the spinner taken up by each section (theoretical probability).

B.1 Probability

Learning Target: Understand how the probability of an event indicates its likelihood.

Success Criteria:
- I can identify possible outcomes of an experiment.
- I can use probability and relative frequency to describe the likelihood of an event.
- I can use relative frequency to make predictions.

EXPLORATION 1

Determining Likelihood

Work with a partner. Use the spinners shown.

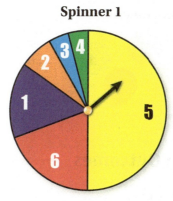

Spinner 1

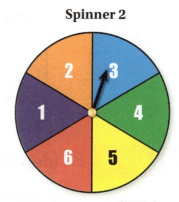

Spinner 2

a. For each spinner, determine which numbers you are more likely to spin and which numbers you are less likely to spin. Explain your reasoning.

b. Spin each spinner 20 times and record your results in two tables. Do the data support your answers in part (a)? Explain why or why not.

Spinner 1	
Number	Frequency
1	
2	
3	
4	
5	
6	

Spinner 2	
Number	Frequency
1	
2	
3	
4	
5	
6	

Math Practice

Recognize Usefulness of Tools

How does organizing the data in tables help you to interpret the results?

c. How can you use percents to describe the likelihood of spinning each number? Explain.

Section B.1 Probability 521

B.1 Lesson

Key Vocabulary
experiment, *p. 522*
outcomes, *p. 522*
event, *p. 522*
favorable outcomes, *p. 522*
probability, *p. 523*
relative frequency, *p. 524*

Key Idea

Outcomes and Events

An **experiment** is an investigation or a procedure that has varying results. The possible results of an experiment are called **outcomes**. A collection of one or more outcomes is an **event**. The outcomes of a specific event are called **favorable outcomes**.

For example, randomly choosing a marble from a group of marbles is an experiment. Each marble in the group is an outcome. Selecting a green marble from the group is an event.

Possible outcomes

Event: Choosing a green marble
Number of favorable outcomes: 2

EXAMPLE 1   Identifying Outcomes

You spin the spinner.

a. **How many possible outcomes are there?**

The possible outcomes are spinning a 1, 2, 1, 3, 1, or 4. So, there are six possible outcomes.

b. **What are the favorable outcomes of spinning an even number?**

The favorable outcomes of spinning an even number are 2 and 4.

even	*not* even
2, 4	1, 1, 3, 1

c. **In how many ways can spinning a number less than 2 occur?**

The possible outcomes of spinning a number less than 2 are 1, 1, and 1. So, spinning a number less than 2 can occur in 3 ways.

less than 2	*not* less than 2
1, 1, 1	2, 3, 4

Try It

1. You randomly choose one of the tiles shown from a hat.

    a. How many possible outcomes are there?

    b. What are the favorable outcomes of choosing a vowel?

    c. In how many ways can choosing a consonant occur?

522   Chapter B   Probability

Laurie's Notes

Scaffolding Instruction
- As students continue to conduct experiments, they will begin to understand how outcomes are affected by events that are *not* equally likely.
- **Emerging:** After the exploration, students may not be able to make predictions nor draw conclusions. The examples will help them master the success criteria.
- **Proficient:** Students have an understanding of probability and possible outcomes. After students review the Key Ideas, they should work through Examples 2 and 3 before completing the Try It and Self-Assessment exercises.

Scaffold instruction to support all students in their learning. Learning is individualized and you may want to group students differently as they move in and out of these levels with each skill and concept. Student self-assessment and feedback help guide your instructional decisions about how and when to layer support for all students to become proficient learners.

Key Idea
- Discuss the vocabulary words: **experiment**, **outcomes**, **event**, and **favorable outcomes**. You can relate the vocabulary to the exploration and to rolling two number cubes.
- ❓ "What does it mean to perform an experiment at *random*?" All of the possible outcomes are equally likely.
- Ask students to identify the favorable outcomes for the events of choosing each color of marble. green (2), blue (1), red (1), yellow (1), purple (1)
- Be sure students understand that there can be more than one favorable outcome.
- ❓ "What are some other examples of experiments and events? What are the favorable outcomes for these events?" *Sample answer:* An experiment is rolling a number cube with the numbers 1–6. An event is rolling a number greater than 4, with favorable outcomes of 5 and 6.

EXAMPLE 1
- In part (a), students may say there are four possible outcomes (1, 2, 3, or 4). Remind them to count each section of the spinner as a possible outcome.
- Work through parts (b) and (c) as shown.
- ❓ "Would it make a difference if the sections with the 1s were in consecutive locations on the spinner? Explain." No, the answers would be the same. Only the size of the sections matter, not the locations.
- ❓ "What are the favorable outcomes of spinning a prime number?" 2 and 3
- ❓ "In how many ways can spinning a number greater than 4 occur?" 0 ways

Try It
- Have students work in pairs to complete the exercise.

Extra Example 1
You roll a number cube.
a. How many possible outcomes are there? 6
b. What are the favorable outcomes of rolling an odd number? 1, 3, and 5
c. In how many ways can rolling a number greater than 4 occur? 2 ways

Try It
1. a. 8
   b. A, E, A
   c. 5

Extra Example 2

There is a 20% chance of snow flurries, a 65% chance of rain, and a 50% chance or sunshine tomorrow. Describe the likelihood of each event.

a. There is snow tomorrow. unlikely

b. There is rain tomorrow. likely

c. There is sunshine tomorrow. equally likely to happen or not happen

Try It

2. unlikely
3. certain

Laurie's Notes

Key Idea

- Discuss possible events which have probabilities near each benchmark.
- Make them personal for your situation, if possible.
  Examples:
    the sun rising tomorrow = 1
    math homework = 0.75
    winning the softball game = 0.50
    skipping breakfast = 0.25
    a winter in Vermont with no snow = 0
- Spend time discussing what *equally likely* means. Give examples of events that are equally likely and not equally likely.
    Equally likely: number cube
    Not equally likely: spinner with sections that are not all the same size

EXAMPLE 2

- "Has anyone heard a weather report for tomorrow?" Try to turn student responses into a percent or fraction. For example, you can translate "it is supposed to be nice tomorrow" into "there is a 90% chance of sunshine."
- Work through each part as shown.
- Be sure students understand that probabilities can be represented as fractions, decimals, or percents.

Try It

- Discuss the answers as a class.

ELL Support

After demonstrating Example 2, have students work in pairs to complete Try It Exercises 2 and 3. Have one student ask another, "What is the likelihood that you land a jump on a snowboard?" Expect students to perform according to their language levels.

Beginner: State one-word answers such as, "unlikely."

Intermediate: Use phrases or simple sentences such as, "It is unlikely."

Advanced: Use detailed sentences such as, "It is unlikely that you will land a jump on a snowboard."

Key Idea

Probability

The **probability** of an event is a number that represents the likelihood that the event will occur. Probabilities are between 0 and 1, including 0 and 1. The diagram relates likelihoods (above the diagram) and probabilities (below the diagram).

Probabilities can be written as fractions, decimals, or percents.

EXAMPLE 2 **Describing Likelihood**

There is an 80% chance of rain, a 50% chance of thunderstorms, and a 15% chance of hail tomorrow. Describe the likelihood of each event.

a. **There is rain tomorrow.**

The probability of rain tomorrow is 80%.

▸ Because 80% is close to 75%, it is *likely* that there will be rain tomorrow.

b. **There are thunderstorms tomorrow.**

The probability of thunderstorms tomorrow is 50%.

▸ Because the probability is 50%, thunderstorms are *equally likely to happen or not happen*.

c. **There is hail tomorrow.**

The probability of hail tomorrow is 15%.

▸ Because 15% is between 0% and 25%, it is *unlikely* that there will be hail tomorrow.

Try It Describe the likelihood of the event given its probability.

2. The probability that you land a jump on a snowboard is $\frac{1}{10}$.

3. There is a 100% chance that the temperature will be less than 120°F tomorrow.

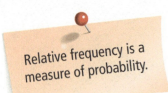

Relative frequency is a measure of probability.

When you conduct an experiment, the **relative frequency** of an event is the fraction or percent of the time that the event occurs.

$$\text{relative frequency} = \frac{\text{number of times the event occurs}}{\text{total number of times you conduct the experiment}}$$

EXAMPLE 3   Using Relative Frequencies

You flip a bottle and record the number of times it lands upright and the number of times it lands on its side. Describe the likelihood that the bottle lands upright on your next flip.

Upright	II
Side	||||| ||||| ||||| ||||| III

The bottle landed upright 2 times in a total of 25 flips.

$$\text{relative frequency} = \frac{\text{number of times the event occurs}}{\text{total number of times you conduct the experiment}}$$

$$= \frac{2}{25} \quad \begin{array}{l}\leftarrow \text{The bottle landed upright 2 times.} \\ \leftarrow \text{There was a total of 25 flips.}\end{array}$$

▸ The relative frequency is $\frac{2}{25}$, or 8%. So, it is unlikely that the bottle lands upright.

Try It

Shots Made	||||| ||||
Shots Missed	|||||	

4. You attempt three-point shots on a basketball court and record the number of made and missed shots. Describe the likelihood of each event.

   a. You make your next shot.   b. You miss your next shot.

Self-Assessment for Concepts & Skills

Solve each exercise. Then rate your understanding of the success criteria in your journal.

5. **IDENTIFYING OUTCOMES** You roll a number cube. What are the possible outcomes?

6. **USING RELATIVE FREQUENCIES** A bag contains only red marbles and blue marbles. You randomly draw a marble from the bag and replace it. The table shows the results of repeating this experiment. Find the likelihood of each event.

Red	||||| ||||| ||||| ||||| I
Blue	||||| ||||| ||||| ||||| I

   a. The next marble you choose is red.

   b. The next marble you choose is neither red nor blue.

Laurie's Notes

Discuss

- Ask ten students to stand at the front of the room. Hand each one a penny.
- ❓ "If [Student 1] flips his or her penny, what is the probability it will land on heads?" $\frac{1}{2}$ "If [Student 4] flips his or her penny, what is the probability it will land on heads?" $\frac{1}{2}$
- ❓ "If all of the students flip their pennies, what is the probability they will all land on heads?" Students will likely say $\frac{1}{2}$.
- ❓ Have all 10 students flip their pennies and then ask, "Did everyone's penny land on heads?" It is unlikely that all 10 pennies will land on heads.
- Discuss the definition of **relative frequency** and relate it to flipping pennies.
- Make sure students understand that flipping a coin 10 times and having it land on heads about half the time is a different experiment than flipping 10 coins and asking how likely it is that all 10 coins land on heads.
- **Note:** The number of times an event occurs is the same as counting the number of favorable outcomes.
- Explain that when you are finding a relative frequency, you are finding a probability. Essentially, students are finding an experimental probability, but they will not learn about experimental and theoretical probabilities until the next section. Experimental and theoretical probabilities are based on an understanding of relative frequency.

EXAMPLE 3

- This is not a chance event because the amount of water may change the results and there is skill involved in the way the bottle is flipped. Explain that you can still use relative frequencies to assess the likelihood of future results.
- Work through the problem as shown.
- ❓ **Extension:** "Imagine that you flip a bottle 25 times and it lands on its side each time. Can you conclude that it will land on its side on your next flip?" no

Try It

- **Think-Pair-Share:** Students should read the exercise independently and then work in pairs to complete both parts. Then have each pair compare their answers and reasoning with another pair.

✓ Self-Assessment for Concepts & Skills

- ⊙ These exercises give students an opportunity to check their understanding of the vocabulary and the success criteria.
- **Neighbor Check:** Have students work independently and the have their neighbors check their work. Have students discuss any discrepancies.

The Success Criteria Self-Assessment chart can be found in the *Student Journal* or online at *BigIdeasMath.com*.

Extra Example 3

The bar graph shows the results of rolling a number cube 50 times. Describe the likelihood of rolling a prime number.

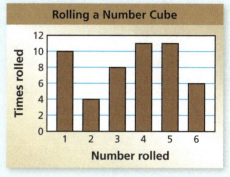

unlikely

Try It

4. a. equally likely
   b. equally likely

ELL Support

Allow students to work in pairs for extra support and to practice language. Have neighboring pairs check each other's work as described in Laurie's Notes. When they have completed the Self-Assessment for Concepts & Skills exercises, have each pair display their answers on a whiteboard for your review.

Self-Assessment
for Concepts & Skills

5. 1, 2, 3, 4, 5, 6
6. a. equally likely
   b. impossible

Extra Example 4

During a trivia game, you are asked 32 questions. You answer 6 questions correctly. Out of 48 questions, how many questions can you expect to answer correctly? **about 9 questions**

Self-Assessment
for Problem Solving

7. 24 days; $180 \times \dfrac{2}{15} = 24$ days

8. unlikely; *Sample answer:* 75% of 40% is $\dfrac{3}{4} \cdot \dfrac{4}{10} = \dfrac{3}{10}$, or 30%.

Learning Target
Understand how the probability of an event indicates its likelihood.

Success Criteria
- Identify possible outcomes of an experiment.
- Use probability and relative frequency to describe the likelihood of an event.
- Use relative frequency to make predictions.

Laurie's Notes

EXAMPLE 4

- **Make Sense of Problems and Persevere in Solving Them:** Ask a volunteer to read the problem. Then ask another volunteer to explain the problem. If no one can, have another student read the problem and then ask for an explanation. Students need to be able to understand the problem on their own, practice is the only way it will happen.
- Continue working through the problem-solving plan.
- ❓ "Why do you add 10 and 7?" Both +3 points and +1 point are favorable outcomes. The frequency of +3 points is 10 and the frequency of +1 point is 7, so you add 10 and 7.
- Some students may choose to use a proportion to solve for the percent.
- Remind students to always check that they have answered the question.
- ❓ **Construct Viable Arguments and Critique the Reasoning of Others:** "Do you expect to draw a positive point value exactly 30 times every 35 turns? Explain your reasoning to a classmate." no Listen for understanding that the results may vary in the same way that flipping a coin two times will not always result in one landing on heads and the other landing on tails.

✓ Self-Assessment for Problem Solving

- The goal for all students is to feel comfortable with the problem-solving plan. It is important for students to problem-solve in class, where they may receive support from you and their peers. Keep in mind that some students may only be ready for the first step.
- Have students use *Paired Verbal Fluency* as they work through the problem-solving plan for these problems. Partners should take turns speaking first.

The Success Criteria Self-Assessment chart can be found in the *Student Journal* or online at *BigIdeasMath.com*.

Closure

- **Exit Ticket:**
  - You flip a coin 100 times. How many times can you expect to flip heads? about 50 times
  - A bag contains 3 red chips and 9 blue chips. You draw a chip and replace it 100 times. How many times can you expect to draw a blue chip? about 75 times

EXAMPLE 4 Modeling Real Life

Each turn in a game, you randomly draw a token from a bag and replace it. The table shows the number of times you draw each type of token. How many times can you expect to draw a positive point value in 35 turns?

Token	Frequency
+3 points	⦀⦀⦀⦀⦀ ⦀⦀⦀⦀⦀
+1 point	⦀⦀⦀⦀⦀ ⦀⦀
−2 points	⦀⦀⦀

Understand the problem. You are given the number of times that you draw each type of token from a bag. You are asked to determine the number of times you can expect to draw a positive point value in 35 turns.

Make a plan. Find the relative frequency of drawing a positive point value. Then use the relative frequency and the percent equation to answer the question.

Solve and check. The favorable outcomes of drawing a positive point value are drawing a +3 token or a +1 token. So, the relative frequency of drawing a positive point value is $\frac{10 + 7}{20} = \frac{17}{20}$, or 85%.

To determine the number of times you can expect to draw a positive point value, answer the question "What is 85% of 35?"

$a = p\% \cdot w$ Write percent equation.

$= 0.85 \cdot 35$ Substitute 0.85 for $p\%$ and 35 for w.

$= 29.75$ Multiply.

▸ You can expect to draw a positive point value about 30 times.

Check Reasonableness
The table shows that positive point values are drawn 17 of 20 times. So, in 35 turns, you can expect to draw positive point values less than $17 \times 2 = 34$ times. ✓

Self-Assessment for Problem Solving

Solve each exercise. Then rate your understanding of the success criteria in your journal.

7. The table shows the number of days you have a pop quiz and the number of days you do not have a pop quiz in three weeks of school. How many days can you expect to have a pop quiz during a 180-day school year? Explain.

Pop Quiz	No Pop Quiz
⦀⦀	⦀⦀⦀⦀⦀ ⦀⦀⦀⦀⦀ ⦀⦀⦀

8. In a football game, the teams pass the ball on 40% of the plays. Of the passes thrown, greater than 75% are completed. You watch the film of a randomly chosen play. Describe the likelihood that the play results in a complete pass. Explain your reasoning.

B.1 Practice

Review & Refresh

An account earns simple interest. Find the interest earned.

1. $700 at 3% for 4 years
2. $650 at 2% for 6 years
3. $480 at 1.5% for 5 years
4. $1200 at 2.8% for 30 months

Write the indicated ratio. Then find and interpret the value of the ratio.

5. rolled oats : chopped peanuts
6. sunflower seeds to pumpkin seeds
7. pumpkin seeds : rolled oats

Granola	
(dry ingredients)	
rolled oats	2 cups
chopped peanuts	1/2 cup
sunflower seeds	1/3 cup
pumpkin seeds	1/4 cup

Solve the inequality. Graph the solution.

8. $x + 5 < 9$
9. $b - 2 \geq -7$
10. $1 > -\dfrac{w}{3}$
11. $6 \leq -2g$

Concepts, Skills, & Problem Solving

DETERMINING LIKELIHOOD Determine which numbers you are more likely to spin and which numbers you are less likely to spin. Explain your reasoning. (See Exploration 1, p. 521.)

12.
13.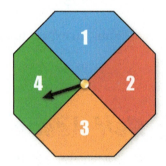

IDENTIFYING OUTCOMES You spin the spinner shown.

14. How many possible outcomes are there?
15. What are the favorable outcomes of spinning a number no greater than 3?
16. In how many ways can spinning an even number occur?
17. In how many ways can spinning a prime number occur?

526 Chapter B Probability

Assignment Guide and Concept Check

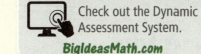

Check out the Dynamic Assessment System.
BigIdeasMath.com

Scaffold assignments to support all students in their learning progression. The suggested assignments are a starting point. Continue to assign additional exercises and revisit with spaced practice to move every student toward proficiency.

Level	Assignment 1	Assignment 2
Emerging	4, 7, 9, 10, 12, 14, 15, 16, 17, 19, 21, 29	23, 24, 25, 27, 30, 31, 32, 33, 34, 36, 39
Proficient	4, 7, 9, 10, 12, 14, 15, 16, 17, 18, 20, 29	22, 24, 26, 28, 30, 31, 32, 34, 35, 36, 37, 38, 39
Advanced	4, 7, 9, 10, 12, 14, 16, 17, 20, 22, 24, 30	26, 28, 31, 32, 35, 37, 38, 39, 40, 41

- Assignment 1 is for use after students complete the Self-Assessment for Concepts & Skills.
- Assignment 2 is for use after students complete the Self-Assessment for Problem Solving.
- The red exercises can be used as a concept check.

Review & Refresh Prior Skills

Exercises 1–4 Finding Interest Earned
Exercises 5–7 Writing and Interpreting Ratios
Exercises 8–11 Solving an Inequality

Review & Refresh

1. $84
2. $78
3. $36
4. $84
5. $2 : \frac{1}{2}$; The amount of rolled oats in the recipe is 4 times the amount of chopped peanuts.
6. $\frac{1}{3} : \frac{1}{4}$; The amount of sunflower seeds in the recipe is $\frac{4}{3}$ the amount of pumpkin seeds.
7. $\frac{1}{4} : 2$; The amount of pumpkin seeds in the recipe is $\frac{1}{8}$ the amount of rolled oats.
8. $x < 4$

9. $b \geq -5$
   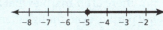
10. $w > -3$

11. $g \leq -3$

Concepts, Skills, & Problem Solving

12. more likely: 2, 4, 5; less likely: 1, 3, 6
    Sample answer: The numbers 2, 4, and 5 have a greater area than the numbers 1, 3, and 6, so you are more likely to spin them.

13. equal chance; *Sample answer:* All numbers have the same area, so you are equally likely to spin each number.

14. 8
15. 1, 2, 3
16. 4 ways
17. 4 ways

T-526

Concepts, Skills, & Problem Solving

18. **a.** 2 ways
    b. blue, blue
19. **a.** 1 way
    b. green
20. **a.** 2 ways
    b. purple, purple
21. **a.** 1 way
    b. yellow
22. **a.** 6 ways
    b. yellow, green, blue, blue, purple, purple
23. **a.** 7 ways
    b. red, red, red, purple, purple, green, yellow
24. no; There are 7 marbles that are *not* purple, even though there are only 4 colors.
25. false; red
26. false; five
27. true
28. false; eight
29. likely
30. impossible
31. certain
32. unlikely
33. You are equally likely to be chosen or not chosen.
34. **a.** equally likely
    b. equally likely

Common Errors

- **Exercises 18–23** Students may forget to include the repeats of a color when describing the favorable outcomes and how many ways the event can occur. Ask students to describe how many times you could choose a specific color from the bag if you happened to choose the same color each time (without replacing). For example, if the event is choosing a red marble, you can choose a red marble three times before there are no more red marbles in the bag. So, the event can occur three times.

IDENTIFYING OUTCOMES You randomly choose one marble from the bag. (a) Find the number of ways the event can occur. (b) Find the favorable outcomes of the event.

18. Choosing blue

19. Choosing green

20. Choosing purple

21. Choosing yellow

22. Choosing *not* red

23. Choosing *not* blue

24. **YOU BE THE TEACHER** Your friend finds the number of ways that choosing *not* purple can occur. Is your friend correct? Explain your reasoning.

purple	*not* purple
purple	red, blue, green, yellow

Choosing *not* purple can occur in 4 ways.

CRITICAL THINKING Tell whether the statement is *true* or *false*. If it is false, change the italicized word to make the statement true.

25. Spinning blue and spinning *green* have the same number of favorable outcomes on Spinner A.

26. There are *three* possible outcomes of spinning Spinner A.

27. Spinning *red* can occur in four ways on Spinner B.

28. Spinning not green can occur in *three* ways on Spinner B.

DESCRIBING LIKELIHOOD Describe the likelihood of the event given its probability.

29. Your soccer team wins $\frac{3}{4}$ of the time.

30. There is a 0% chance that you will grow 12 feet.

31. The probability that the sun rises tomorrow is 1.

32. It rains on $\frac{1}{5}$ of the days in June.

33. **MODELING REAL LIFE** You have a 50% chance of being chosen to explain a math problem in front of the class. Describe the likelihood that you are chosen.

34. **MODELING REAL LIFE** You roll a number cube and record the number of times you roll an even number and the number of times you roll an odd number. Describe the likelihood of each event.

Even	||||| ||||| ||||| ||||| |||||	
Odd	||||| ||||| ||||| ||||| ||||

a. You roll an even number on your next roll.

b. You roll an odd number on your next roll.

35. **MP REASONING** You want to determine whether a coin is *fair*. You flip the coin and record the number of times you flip heads and the number of times you flip tails.

Heads	|||| |||| |||| |||| ||
Tails	|||

   a. Describe the likelihood that you flip heads on your next flip.
   b. Describe the likelihood that you flip tails on your next flip.
   c. Do you think the coin is a *fair* coin? Explain.

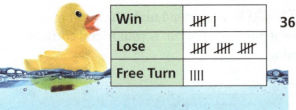

36. **MP LOGIC** At a carnival, each guest randomly chooses 1 of 50 rubber ducks and then replaces it. The table shows the numbers of each type of duck that have been drawn so far. Out of 150 draws, how many can you expect to *not* be a losing duck? Justify your answer.

37. **CRITICAL THINKING** A dodecahedron has twelve sides numbered 1 through 12. Describe the likelihood that each event will occur when you roll the dodecahedron. Explain your reasoning.

   a. rolling a 1
   b. rolling a multiple of 3
   c. rolling a number greater than 6

38. **DIG DEEPER!** A bargain bin contains classical CDs and rock CDs. There are 60 CDs in the bin. Choosing a rock CD and *not* choosing a rock CD have the same number of favorable outcomes. How many rock CDs are in the bin?

39. **MP REASONING** You randomly choose one of the cards and set it aside. Then you randomly choose a second card. Describe how the number of possible outcomes changes after the first card is chosen.

MP STRUCTURE A Punnett square is a grid used to show possible gene combinations for the offspring of two parents. In the Punnett square shown, a boy is represented by *XY*. A girl is represented by *XX*.

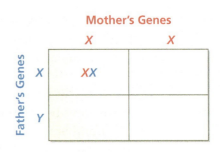

40. Complete the Punnett square. Explain why the events "having a boy" and "having a girl" are equally likely.

41. Two parents each have the gene combination *Cs*. The gene *C* is for curly hair. The gene *s* is for straight hair. Any gene combination that includes a *C* results in curly hair. When all outcomes are equally likely, what is the probability of a child having curly hair?

Mini-Assessment

You randomly choose one number below.

   10, 11, 12, 13, 14, 15, 16, 17, 18, 19

1. What are the favorable outcomes of choosing an even number?
   10, 12, 14, 16, 18
2. In how many ways can choosing an odd number less than 15 occur?   2 ways
3. In how many ways can choosing a number *not* divisible by 3 occur?   7 ways

Describe the likelihood of the event given its probability.

4. Your basketball team wins 50% of the time.   equally likely to happen or not happen
5. It snows on $\frac{2}{3}$ of the days in November.   likely

Section Resources

Surface Level	Deep Level
Resources by Chapter • Extra Practice • Reteach • Puzzle Time Student Journal • Self-Assessment • Practice Differentiating the Lesson Tutorial Videos Skills Review Handbook Skills Trainer	Resources by Chapter • Enrichment and Extension Graphic Organizers Dynamic Assessment System • Section Practice

Concepts, Skills, & Problem Solving

35. **a.** likely
    b. unlikely
    c. no; *Sample answer:* A fair coin would result in an equal number of heads and tails for the relative frequency.

36. 60 ducks; $\frac{6+4}{25} = \frac{10}{25}$, or 40% and $150 \times 0.4 = 60$ ducks

37. **a.** unlikely; Rolling a 1 has a probability of $\frac{1}{12}$, or $8.\overline{3}$%, which is unlikely.
    b. unlikely; Rolling a multiple of 3 has a probability of $\frac{1}{3}$, or $33.\overline{3}$%, which is unlikely.
    c. equally likely to happen or not happen; Rolling a number greater than 6 has a probability of $\frac{1}{2}$, or 50%, which is equally likely to happen or not happen.

38. 30 rock CDs

39. With all five cards available, the number of possible outcomes is 5. With only four cards left, the number of possible outcomes is reduced to 4.

40.
	Mother's Genes	
	X	X
Father's Genes X	XX	XX
Y	XY	XY

There are 2 combinations for each.

41. $\frac{3}{4}$, or 75%

Learning Target
Develop probability models using experimental and theoretical probability.

Success Criteria
- Explain the meanings of experimental probability and theoretical probability.
- Find experimental and theoretical probabilities.
- Use probability to make predictions.

Warm Up
Cumulative, vocabulary, and prerequisite skills practice opportunities are available in the *Resources by Chapter* or at *BigIdeasMath.com*.

ELL Support
Students may be familiar with the word *experiment* from science class. Point out that when you conduct an experiment you perform trials to see what happens. Each time you try an experiment is a trial. Probability that is based on repeated trials of an experiment is called *experimental probability*. For example, if you flip a coin, it will land on heads or tails. You experiment by flipping a coin multiple times to see what happens. Then you use a formula to calculate the experimental probability of flipping heads.

Exploration 1
a. Answers will vary. Students should notice that even though their results may differ, they tend to be close to each other.

b–d. See Additional Answers.

Laurie's Notes

Preparing to Teach
- Students have used probability and relative frequency to describe the likelihood of an event and to make predictions.
- **Attend to Precision:** Mathematically proficient students communicate precisely to others. In this exploration, students should pay close attention to the equally likely aspect of the outcomes based upon the relative frequencies of the experiments.

Motivate
- Play *Mystery Bag*. Before students arrive, place 10 cubes of the same shape and size in a paper bag; five of one color and five of a second color.
- Ask a volunteer to be the detective.
- ? "There are 10 cubes in my bag. Can you guess what color they are?" not likely
- Let the student remove a cube and look at its color.
- ? "Can you guess what color my cubes are?" not likely
- Replace the cube. Let the student pick again and see the color. Repeat your question. Try this 5–8 times until the student is ready to guess. The number of trials will depend upon the results and the student. You want students to see that they are collecting data and making a prediction.

Exploration 1
- ? "In Experiment 1, is each outcome equally likely?" yes
- Be aware of student safety for Experiment 2. Instruct students to toss the thumbtacks carefully, so that they stay on the table and no one is hurt.
- A thumbtack is used to demonstrate a probability model that is *not* uniform. A paper cup could also work. The thumbtacks or paper cups must be identical.
- ? "What are the possible outcomes of tossing a thumbtack?" landing point up or landing on its side Landing point down on a hard surface is not possible.
- ? "Do you think the two outcomes are equally likely?" Answers will vary.
- ? "Do you think that all pairs will get the exact same results for each experiment?" Students should realize that it is unlikely.
- ? "What do you think the relative frequency will be for each experiment?" Have students write their predictions on a piece of paper before performing the experiments.
- **Use Appropriate Tools Strategically:** Combine the results for each experiment. As the data are gathered and recorded, several students with calculators can summarize the results.
- ? "Did the relative frequency change when the results were combined for Experiment 1? for Experiment 2?" Answers will vary. Be sure students understand that as the number of trials increases, the relative frequency should get closer to the expected probability.
- "Compare your relative frequencies to your predictions." Answers will vary.
- ? "If there are only two possible outcomes, are they always equally likely to occur?" no
- Have pairs complete parts (b)–(d) and then discuss as a class.

B.2 Experimental and Theoretical Probability

Learning Target: Develop probability models using experimental and theoretical probability.

Success Criteria:
- I can explain the meanings of experimental probability and theoretical probability.
- I can find experimental and theoretical probabilities.
- I can use probability to make predictions.

EXPLORATION 1

Conducting Experiments

Work with a partner. Conduct the following experiments and find the relative frequencies.

Experiment 1

- Flip a quarter 25 times and record whether each flip lands heads up or tails up.

Experiment 2

- Toss a thumbtack onto a table 25 times and record whether each toss lands point up or on its side.

a. Combine your results with those of your classmates. Do the relative frequencies change? What do you notice?

b. Everyone in your school conducts each experiment and you combine the results. How do you expect the relative frequencies to change? Explain.

c. How many times in 1000 flips do you expect a quarter to land heads up? How many times in 1000 tosses do you expect a thumbtack to land point up? Explain your reasoning.

d. In a *uniform probability model*, each outcome is equally likely to occur. Can you use a uniform probability model to describe either experiment? Explain.

Math Practice

Use Definitions
You know the number of possible outcomes in a uniform probability model. Can you find the probability of each outcome? Explain your reasoning.

B.2 Lesson

Key Vocabulary
experimental probability, *p. 530*
theoretical probability, *p. 530*

Key Idea

Experimental Probability

Probability that is based on repeated trials of an experiment is called **experimental probability**.

$$P(\text{event}) = \frac{\text{number of times the event occurs}}{\text{total number of trials}}$$

EXAMPLE 1 Finding an Experimental Probability

The table shows the results of spinning a penny 25 times. What is the experimental probability of spinning heads?

Heads	Tails
6	19

Heads was spun 6 times in a total of $6 + 19 = 25$ spins.

$$P(\text{event}) = \frac{\text{number of times the event occurs}}{\text{total number of trials}}$$

$P(\text{heads}) = \dfrac{6}{25}$ ← Heads was spun 6 times.
  ← There was a total of 25 spins.

Experimental probabilities are found the same way as relative frequencies.

▶ The experimental probability is $\dfrac{6}{25}$, 0.24, or 24%.

Try It The table shows the results of rolling a number cube 50 times. Find the experimental probability of the event.

Number Rolled	1	2	3	4	5	6
Frequency	10	4	8	11	11	6

1. rolling a 3
2. rolling an odd number

Key Idea

Theoretical Probability

When all possible outcomes are equally likely, the **theoretical probability** of an event is the quotient of the number of favorable outcomes and the number of possible outcomes.

$$P(\text{event}) = \frac{\text{number of favorable outcomes}}{\text{number of possible outcomes}}$$

Laurie's Notes

Scaffolding Instruction
- In the exploration, students should have gained an intuitive understanding of experimental and theoretical probabilities.
- **Emerging:** Students may have difficulty distinguishing between the two types of probabilities. They will benefit from guided instruction for the Key Ideas and examples.
- **Proficient:** Students easily differentiate between the two types of probabilities, but they have not learned their formal names. They need to review the Key Ideas. Then have students work through Examples 3 and 4 before proceeding to the Self-Assessment exercises.

Key Idea
- ❓ Before displaying the Key Idea, ask, "What do you think experimental probability and theoretical probability mean?" Let students speculate about the meanings.
- Discuss **experimental probability** and make connections to the experiments in the exploration and to relative frequencies that students found.

EXAMPLE 1
- Point out the push pin note. Explain that relative frequency is the same as experimental probability.
- ❓ "What information is given in the table that will help answer the question?" The total number of times heads and tails were rolled.
- ❓ "How do you write a fraction as a percent?" *Sample answer:* Write an equivalent fraction with a denominator of 100. Then write the numerator with the percent symbol.
- **FYI:** This data was collected using pennies with the Lincoln Memorial on the back. These pennies land tails up about 80% of the time. If students have other pennies, you could have them conduct the experiment with those pennies and compare the experimental probabilities.
- ❓ "Why would the results be different for different coins?" *Sample answer:* Different engravings may leave more metal on one side than the other. This may make students wonder about the coins flipped at football games.

Try It
- **Neighbor Check:** Have students work independently and then have their neighbors check their work. Have students discuss any discrepancies.
- ❓ "What do you notice about $P(\text{odd})$ and $P(\text{even})$?" The sum is 1.

Key Idea
- Write the Key Idea.
- Discuss **theoretical probability** and give several examples with which students would be familiar, such as cards, number cubes, and marbles in a bag. Stress that the outcomes must be equally likely.

Scaffold instruction to support all students in their learning. Learning is individualized and you may want to group students differently as they move in and out of these levels with each skill and concept. Student self-assessment and feedback help guide your instructional decisions about how and when to layer support for all students to become proficient learners.

Extra Example 1
The table shows the results of rolling a number cube 30 times. What is the experimental probability of rolling a multiple of 3?

Number Rolled	Frequency
1	2
2	5
3	7
4	6
5	5
6	5

$\frac{2}{5}$, 0.4, or 40%

ELL Support
After demonstrating Example 1, have students work in pairs to complete Try It Exercises 1 and 2. Have one student ask another, "How many times is a three rolled? How many times is the number cube rolled? What is the experimental probability?" Have students switch roles.

Beginner: State the numbers.

Intermediate: Use phrases such as, "eight times."

Advanced: Use detailed sentences such as, "A three is rolled eight times."

Try It
1. $\frac{4}{25}$, 0.16, or 16%

2. $\frac{29}{50}$, 0.58, or 58%

Extra Example 2

The letters in the word JACKSON are placed in a hat. You randomly choose a letter from the hat. What is the theoretical probability of choosing a vowel? $\frac{2}{7}$, or about 29%

Try It

3. $\frac{1}{7}$, or about 14.3%

Extra Example 3

Use the bar graph from Example 3. How does the experimental probability of rolling an even number compare with the theoretical probability? The experimental probability of rolling an even number is 51%, which is close to the theoretical probability of 50%.

Try It

4. The experimental probability of rolling a number greater than 1 is 84%, which is close to the theoretical probability of 83.$\overline{3}$%.

Laurie's Notes

EXAMPLE 2

- Work through the example.
- ❓ "What is the probability of *not* choosing a vowel?" $\frac{4}{7}$, or about 57%
- ❓ "How do you write $\frac{3}{7}$ as a percent?" *Sample answer:* Divide 3 by 7 and write as a decimal. Then write the decimal as a percent.

Try It

- **Think-Pair-Share:** Students should read the question independently and then work in pairs to answer the question. Then have each pair compare their answer with another pair and discuss any discrepancies.

EXAMPLE 3

- Compare the bar graph in Example 3 with the table in Example 1.
- ❓ "Which method of displaying data do you prefer? Why?" Answers will vary.
- Work through the example as shown.
- **Reason Abstractly and Quantitatively:** Revisit the exploration and discuss the fact that as the number of trials increase, the experimental probability gets closer and closer to the theoretical probability.

Try It

- **Neighbor Check:** Have students work independently and then have their neighbors check their work. Have students discuss any discrepancies.

EXAMPLE 2 Finding a Theoretical Probability

You randomly choose one of the letters shown. What is the theoretical probability of choosing a vowel?

$$P(\text{vowel}) = \frac{\text{number of favorable outcomes}}{\text{number of possible outcomes}} = \frac{3}{7}$$

← There are 3 vowels.
← There is a total of 7 letters.

▸ The probability of choosing a vowel is $\frac{3}{7}$, or about 43%.

Try It

3. What is the theoretical probability of randomly choosing an X?

EXAMPLE 3 Comparing Probabilities

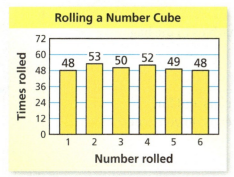

Rolling a Number Cube

The bar graph shows the results of rolling a number cube 300 times. How does the experimental probability of rolling an odd number compare with the theoretical probability?

Step 1: Find the experimental probability of rolling an odd number.

The bar graph shows 48 ones, 50 threes, and 49 fives. So, an odd number was rolled $48 + 50 + 49 = 147$ times in a total of 300 rolls.

$$P(\text{odd}) = \frac{\text{number of times an odd number was rolled}}{\text{total number of rolls}}$$

$$= \frac{147}{300}$$

$$= \frac{49}{100}, \text{ or } 49\%$$

In general, as the number of trials increases, the experimental probability gets closer to the theoretical probability.

Step 2: Find the theoretical probability of rolling an odd number.

$$P(\text{odd}) = \frac{\text{number of favorable outcomes}}{\text{number of possible outcomes}} = \frac{3}{6} = \frac{1}{2}, \text{ or } 50\%$$

▸ The experimental probability of rolling an odd number is 49%, which is close to the theoretical probability of 50%.

Try It

4. How does the experimental probability of rolling a number greater than 1 compare with the theoretical probability?

EXAMPLE 4 Using an Experimental Probability

A bag contains 50 marbles. You randomly draw a marble from the bag, record its color, and then replace it. The table shows the results after 30 draws. Predict the number of red marbles in the bag.

Color	Frequency
Blue	3
Green	12
Red	9
Yellow	6

Find the experimental probability of drawing a red marble.

$$P(\text{event}) = \frac{\text{number of times the event occurs}}{\text{total number of trials}}$$

$$P(\text{red}) = \frac{9}{30} = \frac{3}{10}$$

You draw red 9 times.

You draw a total of 30 marbles.

To make a prediction, multiply the probability of drawing red by the total number of marbles in the bag.

$$\frac{3}{10} \cdot 50 = 15$$

▶ So, you can predict that there are 15 red marbles in the bag.

Try It

5. An inspector randomly selects 200 pairs of jeans and finds 5 defective pairs. About how many pairs of jeans do you expect to be defective in a shipment of 5000?

Self-Assessment for Concepts & Skills

Solve each exercise. Then rate your understanding of the success criteria in your journal.

6. **VOCABULARY** Explain what it means for an event to have a theoretical probability of 0.25 and an experimental probability of 0.3.

7. **DIFFERENT WORDS, SAME QUESTION** You flip a coin and record the results in the table. Which is different? Find "both" answers.

Heads	Tails
32	28

What is the experimental probability of flipping heads?

What fraction of the flips can you expect a result of heads?

What percent of the flips result in heads?

What is the relative frequency of flipping heads?

Laurie's Notes

EXAMPLE 4

- ❓ "Does it seem reasonable to use information from 30 draws to predict the total number of red marbles in a bag of 50 marbles?" yes
- **Big Idea:** The experimental probability is used to make a prediction when you expect a trend to continue, or you believe the experiment reflects what might be true about a larger population.
- Work through the problem as shown.
- ❓ "Does this mean there are exactly 15 red marbles in the bag? Explain." No, it is a prediction based on the given information, so the actual number may differ.

Try It

- Students should solve the problem on whiteboards. Use *Popsicle Sticks* to solicit responses.
- Using *Paired Verbal Fluency* have students take turns answering the following questions.
    - What is the meaning of experimental probability? theoretical probability?
    - How do you find experimental probability? theoretical probability?
    - How can you use probability to make predictions?

Formative Assessment Tip

Talk Moves

This technique helps facilitate classroom discussion. Prompt students to answer a question and provide adequate *Wait Time* for students to respond. After a student shares an answer, repeat the answer to emphasize and clarify what the student said. Leave room for the student to agree, disagree, or elaborate by saying, "So you are saying ____. Do I have that right?" Then ask a student to restate what another student has said to ensure that students are listening carefully. Continue asking students to evaluate, critique, and use the responses and strategies discussed.

✓ Self-Assessment for Concepts & Skills

- Use *Talk Moves* to discuss students' answers in Exercise 6.
- **Neighbor Check:** Have students work independently on Exercise 7 and then have their neighbors check their work. Have students discuss any discrepancies.

ELL Support

Allow students to work in pairs to discuss and solve the exercises. Have two pairs present their answers to one another. Encourage questions and discussion. Monitor discussions and provide support as needed. When students have finished, discuss answers with the class.

The Success Criteria Self-Assessment chart can be found in the *Student Journal* or online at *BigIdeasMath.com*.

Extra Example 4

You randomly check 100 bags of pretzels and find 3 unsealed bags. About how many bags of pretzels do you expect to be unsealed in a shipment of 3000? 90 bags

Try It

5. 125

Self-Assessment for Concepts & Skills

6. The theoretical probability means that 25% of the time this event is expected to occur. The experimental probability means that the event actually occurred 30% of the time.

7. "What fraction of the flips can you expect a result of heads?"; $\frac{1}{2}$; The others are equal to $\frac{8}{15}$, or about 53.3%.

Extra Example 5

The theoretical probability of randomly choosing a red marble from a bag is $\frac{5}{8}$. There are 40 marbles in the bag.

a. How many marbles are red? 25

b. You randomly draw a marble and replace it. About how many times can you expect to draw a red marble in 56 trials? 35

Self-Assessment
for Problem Solving

8. 140; $\frac{2}{40} = \frac{7}{t}$; $t = 140$

9. $\frac{35}{79}$, or about 44%;

   There are 36 hip-hop songs on the playlist. After choosing 1 hip-hop song, 35 hip-hop songs remain out of 79 songs.

Learning Target
Develop probability models using experimental and theoretical probability.

Success Criteria
- Explain the meanings of experimental probability and theoretical probability.
- Find experimental and theoretical probabilities.
- Use probability to make predictions.

Laurie's Notes

EXAMPLE 5

- ❓ "What is the probability of winning a bobblehead?" $\frac{1}{6}$
- ❓ "If the spinner has 6 sections, how many bobblehead sections are there?" 1
- ❓ "Because there are 18 sections on the prize wheel, what do you know about the number of bobblehead sections?" There are 3.
- Write the proportion and solve.
- Complete part (b) as shown.
- Make sure students understand how this prediction is different from the prediction in Example 4. In Example 4, students are predicting the structure of the generating mechanism by drawing several random selections. In this example, students know the structure and are anticipating the relative frequency.

✓ Self-Assessment for Problem Solving

- Students may benefit from trying the exercises independently and then working with peers to refine their work. It is important to provide time in class for problem solving, so that students become comfortable with the problem-solving plan.
- Students should solve the problems independently before comparing and discussing their answers with a partner.

The Success Criteria Self-Assessment chart can be found in the *Student Journal* or online at *BigIdeasMath.com*.

Closure

❓ Use the colored cubes in the Mystery Bag from the Motivate. Reveal the contents, or use a different color ratio if you wish. Ask, "If the contents of the Mystery Bag came from a bag of 1000 colored cubes, how many of each color would you predict in the bag of 1000?" Answers will vary depending upon materials.

EXAMPLE 5 Modeling Real Life

The theoretical probability of winning a bobblehead when spinning a prize wheel is $\frac{1}{6}$. The wheel has 18 sections.

a. How many sections have a bobblehead as a prize?

Use the equation for theoretical probability.

$$P(\text{bobblehead}) = \frac{\text{number of bobblehead sections}}{\text{total number of sections}}$$

$\frac{1}{6} = \frac{s}{18}$ Substitute. Let s be the number of bobblehead sections.

$3 = s$ Multiply each side by 18.

▸ So, 3 sections have a bobblehead as a prize.

b. The prize wheel is spun 540 times. About how many bobbleheads do you expect to be won?

To make a prediction, multiply the probability of winning a bobblehead by the total number of times the wheel is spun.

$\frac{1}{6} \cdot 540 = 90$

▸ So, you can predict about 90 bobbleheads will be won.

Self-Assessment for Problem Solving

Solve each exercise. Then rate your understanding of the success criteria in your journal.

Ticket	Frequency
Win	2
Lose	29
Draw again	9

8. Contestants randomly draw a ticket from a hat and replace it. The table shows the results after 40 draws. There are 7 winning tickets in the hat. Predict the total number of tickets in the hat. Explain.

9. **DIG DEEPER!** You randomly choose two different songs on a music playlist that has 80 songs. The probability that the first song is a hip-hop song is 45%. The first song you choose is a hip-hop song. What is the probability that the second song is also a hip-hop song? Explain your reasoning.

B.2 Practice

Go to *BigIdeasMath.com* to get HELP with solving the exercises.

▶ Review & Refresh

Describe the likelihood of the event given its probability.

1. You randomly guess the correct answer of a multiple choice question $\frac{1}{4}$ of the time.

2. There is a 95% chance that school will *not* be cancelled tomorrow.

Find the annual interest rate.

3. $I = \$16$, $P = \$200$, $t = 2$ years

4. $I = \$26.25$, $P = \$500$, $t = 18$ months

Tell whether *x* and *y* are proportional.

5.
x	1	3	9
y	8	24	75

6.
x	0.75	1.5	2.25
y	0.3	0.6	0.9

▶ Concepts, Skills, & Problem Solving

CONDUCTING AN EXPERIMENT Use the bar graph below to find the relative frequency of the event. (See Exploration 1, p. 529.)

7. spinning a 6

8. spinning an even number

FINDING AN EXPERIMENTAL PROBABILITY
Use the bar graph to find the experimental probability of the event.

9. spinning a number less than 3

10. *not* spinning a 1

11. spinning a 1 or a 3

12. spinning a 7

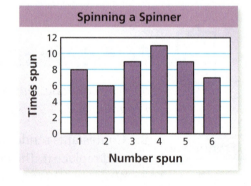

 There are 6 possible outcomes. So, the experimental probability of spinning a 4 is $\frac{1}{6}$.

13. **YOU BE THE TEACHER** Your friend uses the bar graph above to find the experimental probability of spinning a 4. Is your friend correct? Explain your reasoning.

14. **MODELING REAL LIFE** You check 20 laser pointers at random. Three of the laser pointers are defective. What is the experimental probability that a laser pointer is defective?

534 Chapter B Probability

Assignment Guide and Concept Check

Scaffold assignments to support all students in their learning progression. The suggested assignments are a starting point. Continue to assign additional exercises and revisit with spaced practice to move every student toward proficiency.

Level	Assignment 1	Assignment 2
Emerging	2, 4, 6, 7, 9, 10, 13, 15, 16, 17, 23	11, 12, 14, 18, 19, 20, 21, 24, 27, 28, 29, 30
Proficient	2, 4, 6, 8, 10, 11, 13, 15, 18, 19, 22	12, 14, 20, 21, 24, 26, 27, 28, 29, 30
Advanced	2, 4, 6, 8, 10, 11, 13, 15, 19, 20, 24	21, 26, 27, 28, 29, 30, 31, 32

- Assignment 1 is for use after students complete the Self-Assessment for Concepts & Skills.
- Assignment 2 is for use after students complete the Self-Assessment for Problem Solving.
- The red exercises can be used as a concept check.

Review & Refresh Prior Skills

Exercises 1 and 2 Describing Likelihood
Exercises 3 and 4 Finding an Annual Interest Rate
Exercises 5 and 6 Identifying Proportional Relationships

Common Errors

- **Exercises 9–12** Students may forget to total all of the trials before writing the experimental probability. They may have an incorrect number of trials in the denominator. Remind students that they need to know the total number of trials when finding the probability.

Review & Refresh

1. unlikely
2. likely
3. 4%
4. 3.5%
5. no
6. yes

Concepts, Skills, & Problem Solving

7. $\frac{7}{50}$, or 14%
8. $\frac{12}{25}$, or 48%
9. $\frac{7}{25}$, or 28%
10. $\frac{21}{25}$, or 84%
11. $\frac{17}{50}$, or 34%
12. 0, or 0%
13. no; Your friend found the theoretical probability.
14. $\frac{3}{20}$, or 15%

Concepts, Skills, & Problem Solving

15. $\frac{1}{3}$, or about 33.3%

16. $\frac{1}{6}$, or about 16.7%

17. $\frac{1}{2}$, or 50%

18. $\frac{1}{2}$, or 50%

19. 1, or 100%

20. 0, or 0%

21. $\frac{25}{26}$, or about 96.2%

22. theoretical: $\frac{1}{5}$, or 20%; experimental: $\frac{37}{200}$, or 18.5%; The experimental probability is close to the theoretical probability.

23. theoretical: $\frac{1}{5}$, or 20%; experimental: $\frac{39}{200}$, or 19.5%; The experimental probability is close to the theoretical probability.

24. theoretical: $\frac{1}{5}$, or 20%; experimental: $\frac{1}{5}$, or 20%; The probabilities are equal.

25. theoretical: $\frac{3}{5}$, or 60%; experimental: $\frac{120}{200}$, or 60%; The probabilities are equal.

26. theoretical; *Sample answer:* Using experimental probability would be very time consuming to spin the spinner 10,000 times.

27. 38 vowels

28. **a.** 30 chips

    b. 6 contestants

29. **a.** $\frac{4}{9}$, or about 44.4%

    b. 5 males

Common Errors

- **Exercises 15–20** Students may write a different probability than what is asked, or forget to include a favorable outcome. For example, a student may not realize that there are two red sections and will write the probability of spinning red as $\frac{1}{6}$ instead of $\frac{1}{3}$. Remind students to read the event carefully and to write the favorable outcomes before finding the probability.

- **Exercise 28** Students may write an incorrect proportion when finding how many chips are in the bag. Encourage students to write the proportion in words before substituting and solving.

FINDING A THEORETICAL PROBABILITY Use the spinner to find the theoretical probability of the event.

15. spinning red

16. spinning a 1

17. spinning an odd number

18. spinning a multiple of 2

19. spinning a number less than 7

20. spinning a 9

21. REASONING Each letter of the alphabet is printed on an index card. What is the theoretical probability of randomly choosing any letter except Z?

COMPARING PROBABILITIES The bar graph shows the results of spinning the spinner below 200 times. Compare the theoretical and experimental probabilities of the event.

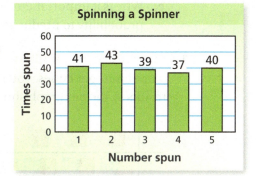

22. spinning a 4

23. spinning a 3

24. spinning a number greater than 4

25. spinning an odd number

26. REASONING Should you use *theoretical* or *experimental* probability to predict the number of times you will spin a 3 in 10,000 spins? Explain.

27. MODELING REAL LIFE A board game uses a bag of 105 lettered tiles. You randomly choose a tile and then return it to the bag. The table shows the number of vowels and the number of consonants after 50 draws. Predict the number of vowels in the bag.

Vowel	Consonant

28. MODELING REAL LIFE On a game show, a contestant randomly draws a chip from a bag and replaces it. Each chip says either *win* or *lose*. The theoretical probability of drawing a winning chip is $\frac{3}{10}$. The bag contains 9 winning chips.

 a. How many chips are in the bag?

 b. Out of 20 contestants, how many do you expect to draw a winning chip?

29. PROBLEM SOLVING There are 8 females and 10 males in a class.

 a. What is the theoretical probability that a randomly chosen student is female?

 b. One week later, there are 27 students in the class. The theoretical probability that a randomly chosen student is a female is the same as last week. How many males joined the class?

30. **NUMBER SENSE** The table at the right shows the results of flipping two coins 12 times each.

HH	HT	TH	TT
2	6	3	1

   a. What is the experimental probability of flipping two tails? Using this probability, how many times can you expect to flip two tails in 600 trials?

HH	HT	TH	TT
23	29	26	22

   b. The table at the left shows the results of flipping the same two coins 100 times each. What is the experimental probability of flipping two tails? Using this probability, how many times can you expect to flip two tails in 600 trials?

   c. Why is it important to use a large number of trials when using experimental probability to predict results?

31. **COMPARING PROBABILITIES** The table shows the possible outcomes of rolling a pair of number cubes. You roll a pair of number cubes 60 times and record your results in the bar graph shown.

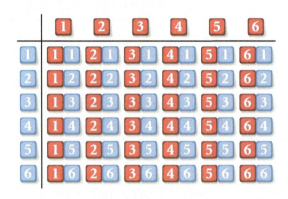
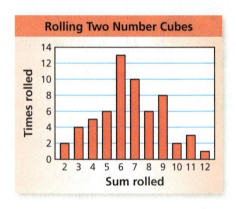

   a. Compare the theoretical and experimental probabilities of rolling each sum.

   b. Which sum do you expect to be most likely after 500 trials? 1000 trials? Explain your reasoning.

   c. Predict the experimental probability of rolling each sum after 10,000 trials. Explain your reasoning.

32. **PROJECT** When you toss a paper cup into the air, there are three ways for the cup to land: *open-end up*, *open-end down*, or *on its side*.

   a. Toss a paper cup 100 times and record your results. Do the outcomes for tossing the cup appear to be equally likely? Explain.

   b. Predict the number of times each outcome will occur in 1000 tosses. Explain your reasoning.

   c. Suppose you tape a quarter to the bottom of the cup. Do you think the cup will be *more likely* or *less likely* to land open-end up? Justify your answer.

Mini-Assessment

You have three sticks. Each stick has one red side and one blue side. You throw the sticks 10 times and record the results. Use the table to find the experimental probability of the event.

Outcome	Frequency
3 red	3
3 blue	2
2 blue, 1 red	4
2 red, 1 blue	1

1. 3 blue $\frac{1}{5}$, or 20%

2. 2 blue, 1 red $\frac{2}{5}$, or 40%

3. *not* all blue $\frac{4}{5}$, or 80%

Use the spinner to determine the theoretical probability of the event.

4. spinning purple $\frac{1}{6}$, or about 17%

5. spinning a 3 $\frac{1}{6}$, or about 17%

6. spinning an even number $\frac{1}{2}$, or 50%

7. spinning a multiple of 3 $\frac{1}{3}$, or about 33%

Section Resources

Surface Level	Deep Level
Resources by Chapter • Extra Practice • Reteach • Puzzle Time Student Journal • Self-Assessment • Practice Differentiating the Lesson Tutorial Videos Skills Review Handbook Skills Trainer	Resources by Chapter • Enrichment and Extension Graphic Organizers Dynamic Assessment System • Section Practice
Transfer Level	
Dynamic Assessment System • Mid-Chapter Quiz	Assessment Book • Mid-Chapter Quiz

Concepts, Skills, & Problem Solving

30. a. $\frac{1}{12}$; 50 times

    b. $\frac{11}{50}$; 132 times

    c. A larger number of trials should result in a more accurate probability, which gives a more accurate prediction.

31. a.

    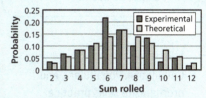

    b. As the number of trials increases, the most likely sum will change from 6 to 7.

    c. *Sample answer:* The experimental probability should approach the theoretical probability.

32. a. Check students' work. The cup should land on its side most of the time.

    b. Check students' work.

    c. more likely; Due to the added weight, the cup will be more likely to hit open-end up and thus more likely to land open-end up. Some students may justify by performing multiple trials with a quarter taped to the bottom of the cup.

Learning Target
Find sample spaces and probabilities of compound events.

Success Criteria
- Find the sample space of two or more events.
- Find the total number of possible outcomes of two or more events.
- Find probabilities of compound events.

Warm Up
Cumulative, vocabulary, and prerequisite skills practice opportunities are available in the *Resources by Chapter* or at BigIdeasMath.com.

ELL Support
Explain that the meaning of *compound* is similar to the opposite of *simple*. The word *simple* often refers to a single event or idea. The word *compound* refers to multiple events or ideas. Typically, there are more than two possible outcomes for a compound event. The set of possible outcomes is known as the sample space. Students may be familiar with the word *sample*. Explain that a sample space is not related to the act of trying a sample of an item.

Exploration 1
a. 10 outcomes; 1000 combinations

b. *Sample answer:* Multiply to find the total number of possible combinations: $10 \times 10 \times 10 = 1000$ combinations.

c. 64,000 combinations

d. 10,000 combinations

e. See Additional Answers.

T-537

Laurie's Notes

Check out the Dynamic Classroom.
BigIdeasMath.com

Preparing to Teach
- Students have counted the number of outcomes of an event. Now they will extend their understanding to find the total number of possible outcomes of two or more events.
- **Make Sense of Problems and Persevere in Solving Them:** Mathematically proficient students use visual models to represent problems. In this lesson, tree diagrams will be used to visualize the possible outcomes of events.

Motivate
- Display 3 different cups on your desk. I like to use a ceramic cup, a travel mug, and a foam cup. In addition, have a tea bag and hot cocoa mix.
- Tell students: You are thirsty. You have three different cups to select from and two different beverages.
- ❓ "How many different ways can I select a cup and a beverage?" The answer of 6 may or may not be obvious. Hold up the travel mug and tea bag, and then the travel mug and cocoa. Repeat for the other two cups.
- ❓ "How many different ways if I add another cup, say a plastic cup?" 8 ways
- ❓ "How many different ways if I add another beverage, say coffee?" 9 ways

Exploration 1
- If your school has lockers with combination locks, discuss how they operate.
- ❓ Ask, "Do any of you have combination locks for your bike, skis, or other possessions?" Answers will vary.
- In parts (a) and (b), students are guided with questions to help them reason about the number of possible outcomes. If available, a 10-sided die can be used to model the situation.
- ❓ "If the digits 0–9 are used, how many outcomes are there for each wheel?" 10
- Students may not think to multiply 10 three times to find the number of possible combinations, but they should be able to reason that the combination will be a number from 000 to 999. So, there are 1000 possible outcomes.
- When students finish part (b), make sure they understand the possible number of combinations is a result of multiplication: 10 • 10 • 10. This prepares them for parts (c) and (d), laying the foundation for the **Fundamental Counting Principle.**
- If students are not familiar with the lock in part (c), tell them that the first number is selected by turning the dial to the right, the second by turning left, and the last by turning right. So, a combination can repeat a number.
- "In part (c), how many possible outcomes are there when the dial is turned to the right? to the left?" 40; 40
- If students have made sense of parts (a) and (b), they will understand that the number of combinations in part (c) is 40 • 40 • 40.
- It may be helpful for some students if sample combinations are listed. For instance, in part (d), possible combinations are 4AK0, 4AK1, 4AK2, etc.
- **Attend to Precision:** Ask a volunteer to explain his or her reasoning for parts (d) and (e).

B.3 Compound Events

Learning Target: Find sample spaces and probabilities of compound events.

Success Criteria:
- I can find the sample space of two or more events.
- I can find the total number of possible outcomes of two or more events.
- I can find probabilities of compound events.

EXPLORATION 1

Comparing Combination Locks

Work with a partner. You are buying a combination lock. You have three choices.

a. One lock has 3 wheels. Each wheel is numbered from 0 to 9. How many possible outcomes are there for each wheel? How many possible combinations are there?

b. How can you use the number of possible outcomes on each wheel to determine the number of possible combinations?

c. Another lock has one wheel numbered from 0 to 39. Each combination uses a sequence of three numbers. How many possible combinations are there?

Math Practice

View as Components
What is the number of possible outcomes for each wheel of the lock? Explain.

d. Another lock has 4 wheels as described. How many possible combinations are there?

Wheel 1: 0–9
Wheel 2: A–J
Wheel 3: K–T
Wheel 4: 0–9

e. For which lock are you least likely to guess the combination? Why?

B.3 Lesson

The set of all possible outcomes of one or more events is called the **sample space**. You can use tables and tree diagrams to find the sample space of two or more events.

EXAMPLE 1 Finding a Sample Space

Key Vocabulary
sample space, *p. 538*
Fundamental Counting Principle, *p. 538*
compound event, *p. 540*

You randomly choose a bread and type of sandwich. Find the sample space. How many different sandwiches are possible?

Bread
- Wheat
- Sourdough

Type
- Ham
- Turkey
- Steak
- Chicken

Use a tree diagram to find the sample space.

Bread	Type	Outcome
Wheat	Ham	Wheat Ham
	Turkey	Wheat Turkey
	Steak	Wheat Steak
	Chicken	Wheat Chicken
Sourdough	Ham	Sourdough Ham
	Turkey	Sourdough Turkey
	Steak	Sourdough Steak
	Chicken	Sourdough Chicken

There are 8 different outcomes in the sample space. So, there are 8 different sandwiches possible.

Try It

1. **WHAT IF?** The sandwich shop adds a multi-grain bread. Find the sample space. How many sandwiches are possible?

You can use the sample space or the **Fundamental Counting Principle** to find the total number of possible outcomes of two or more events.

The Fundamental Counting Principle can be extended to more than two events.

 Key Idea

Fundamental Counting Principle

An event M has m possible outcomes. An event N has n possible outcomes. The total number of outcomes of event M followed by event N is $m \times n$.

Laurie's Notes

Scaffolding Instruction
- Students explored how the number of choices on locks affected the total number of combinations possible. Now they will build upon their understanding to find sample spaces and probabilities of compound events.
- **Emerging:** Students may be able to find the sample space for a small number of outcomes, like flipping a coin, but struggle with larger sample spaces. They will benefit from guided instruction for the examples and the Key Idea.
- **Proficient:** Students intuitively understand how to use tree diagrams and tables to find sample spaces and probabilities. They should review the definitions, Examples 1–4, and the Key Idea before completing the Try It and Self-Assessment exercises.

Discuss
- Today's lesson is about outcomes of one event followed by one or more other events.
- Define **sample space**. Give examples.

EXAMPLE 1
- ❓ Refer to the sandwich shop menu and ask, "How many types of bread are available?" 2 Write the possible breads with space between them as shown.
- ❓ "For either bread, how many different types of sandwich can you order?" 4 List the 4 types with each bread using the tree diagram as shown.
- **Make Sense of Problems and Persevere in Solving Them:** The tree diagram helps students visualize the 8 outcomes in the sample space.
- **Extension:** Add a size to each (half and whole). Have students determine the number of possible outcomes. 16

Try It
- Use *Popsicle Sticks* to solicit responses.

Key Idea
- Write the **Fundamental Counting Principle.**
- Revisit previous problems to see if the Fundamental Counting Principle gives the same answer.
- **Look for and Express Regularity in Repeated Reasoning:** Point out the push-pin note. Tell students that events A, B, and C have a, b, and c outcomes respectively, and then ask them to find the total number of possible outcomes of event A followed by event B followed by event C.

Scaffold instruction to support all students in their learning. Learning is individualized and you may want to group students differently as they move in and out of these levels with each skill and concept. Student self-assessment and feedback help guide your instructional decisions about how and when to layer support for all students to become proficient learners.

Extra Example 1
At a taco truck, you can choose sour cream, salsa, or guacamole on either a beef or chicken taco. You randomly choose a topping and meat. Find the sample space. How many different tacos are possible?
sour cream beef
sour cream chicken
salsa beef
salsa chicken
guacamole beef
guacamole chicken; 6

Try It
1. Sample space: Wheat Ham, Wheat Turkey, Wheat Steak, Wheat Chicken, Sourdough Ham, Sourdough Turkey, Sourdough Steak, Sourdough Chicken, Multi-grain Ham, Multi-grain Turkey, Multi-grain Steak, Multi-grain Chicken; 12 sandwiches

Extra Example 2

Find the total number of possible outcomes of rolling two number cubes. **36**

> **Formative Assessment Tip**
>
> **Chalkboard Splash**
> This technique allows students to solve a problem, while others critique their reasoning. Several students respond to a prompt at the same time on the board. *Chalkboard Splash* is a good way to show multiple representations of the same problem. To be informative, students must show all steps. Once complete, allow the rest of the class to ask questions. The students at the board will need to be able to defend and explain their reasoning. *Chalkboard Splash* allows you to check students' conceptual knowledge and ability to construct a viable argument.

Try It

2. 20 possible outcomes

Extra Example 3

How many different outfits can you make from 5 T-shirts, 3 pairs of jeans, and 2 pairs of shoes? **30**

Try It

3. 100 possible outfits

Laurie's Notes

EXAMPLE 2

- Use a number cube and coin to model this example.
- Work through the example using each method.
- Discuss the efficiency of using the Fundamental Counting Principle instead of a table. If you only need to know the number of outcomes, the Fundamental Counting Principle should be used. The table, however, shows the sample space instead of just the number of outcomes.
- ? "Is the answer the same if the coin is flipped first followed by rolling the number cube? Explain." *Yes, the order changes but the number of outcomes is the same.*

Try It

- This exercise could be modeled using a spinner and five pieces of paper.
- **Chalkboard Splash:** Choose two students to put their work on the board. Look for different approaches. Encourage other students to ask questions.

EXAMPLE 3

- Ask a volunteer to tell how many of each type of clothing is shown in the picture.
- In working through this problem there will be students who suggest that certain shoes would not be worn with certain jeans, and so on. Remind students that the question is, "How many different outfits *can* you make, not would you wear the outfit."
- ? "Would you want to make a tree diagram or table to answer this question? Explain." *No, it would take a long time to list the possible outcomes. The Fundamental Counting Principle is more efficient in finding the number of different outfits possible.*

Try It

- Have students solve this problem on whiteboards prior to discussing as a class.

> **ELL Support**
>
> After demonstrating Example 3, have students practice language by working in groups to complete Try It Exercise 3. Have groups consider these guiding questions: How many possible outcomes are there for T-shirts? pairs of jeans? pairs of shoes? What do you do with these numbers? How many different outfits are possible?
>
> **Beginner:** State numbers and one-word answers to the guiding questions.
>
> **Intermediate:** Use phrases or simple sentences such as, "There are four pairs of jeans."
>
> **Advanced:** Use detailed sentences such as, "Choosing a pair of jeans has four possible outcomes."

EXAMPLE 2 Finding the Total Number of Possible Outcomes

Find the total number of possible outcomes of rolling a number cube and flipping a coin.

Method 1: Use a table to find the sample space. Let H = heads and T = tails.

	1	2	3	4	5	6
🪙 (H)	1H	2H	3H	4H	5H	6H
🪙 (T)	1T	2T	3T	4T	5T	6T

▶ There are 12 possible outcomes.

Method 2: Use the Fundamental Counting Principle. Identify the number of possible outcomes of each event.

  Event 1: Rolling a number cube has 6 possible outcomes.
  Event 2: Flipping a coin has 2 possible outcomes.

  $6 \times 2 = 12$ Fundamental Counting Principle

▶ There are 12 possible outcomes.

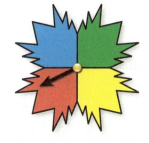

Try It

2. Find the total number of possible outcomes of spinning the spinner and randomly choosing a number from 1 to 5.

EXAMPLE 3 Finding the Total Number of Possible Outcomes

How many different outfits can you make from the T-shirts, jeans, and shoes in the closet?

Use the Fundamental Counting Principle. Identify the number of possible outcomes for each event.

  Event 1: Choosing a T-shirt has 7 possible outcomes.
  Event 2: Choosing jeans has 4 possible outcomes.
  Event 3: Choosing shoes has 3 possible outcomes.

  $7 \times 4 \times 3 = 84$ Fundamental Counting Principle

▶ So, you can make 84 different outfits.

Try It

3. How many different outfits can you make from 4 T-shirts, 5 pairs of jeans, and 5 pairs of shoes?

A **compound event** consists of two or more events. As with a single event, the probability of a compound event is the quotient of the number of favorable outcomes and the number of possible outcomes.

EXAMPLE 4 Finding the Probability of a Compound Event

In Example 2, what is the probability of rolling a number greater than 4 and flipping tails?

There are two favorable outcomes in the sample space for rolling a number greater than 4 and flipping tails: 5T and 6T.

$$P(\text{event}) = \frac{\text{number of favorable outcomes}}{\text{number of possible outcomes}}$$

$$P(\text{greater than 4 and tails}) = \frac{2}{12} \qquad \text{Substitute.}$$

$$= \frac{1}{6} \qquad \text{Simplify.}$$

 The probability is $\frac{1}{6}$, or $16\frac{2}{3}\%$.

Try It

4. In Example 2, what is the probability of rolling at most 4 and flipping heads?

Self-Assessment for Concepts & Skills

Solve each exercise. Then rate your understanding of the success criteria in your journal.

5. **FINDING THE SAMPLE SPACE** You randomly choose a flower and ornament for a display case. Find the sample space. How many different displays are possible?

6. **FINDING THE TOTAL NUMBER OF POSSIBLE OUTCOMES** You randomly choose a number from 1 to 5 and a letter from A to D. Find the total number of possible outcomes.

7. **WHICH ONE DOESN'T BELONG?** You roll a number cube and flip a coin. Which probability does *not* belong with the other three? Explain your reasoning.

Flower
- Daffodil
- Hyacinth
- Tulip

Ornament
- Figurine
- Trophy

$P(\text{less than 2 and heads})$ $P(\text{greater than 2 and tails})$

$P(\text{less than 2 and tails})$ $P(\text{greater than 5 and heads})$

Laurie's Notes

Discuss
- Define a **compound event**. Refer to the first three examples and explain that they all involved compound events. Tell students that the next step is to determine probabilities of compound events.
- Define the probability of a compound event: the ratio of the number of favorable outcomes to the number of possible outcomes.

EXAMPLE 4
- ❓ "How many possible outcomes are there when you roll a number cube and flip a coin as in Example 2?" 12
- ❓ "How many favorable outcomes are there for rolling a number greater than 4 and flipping tails? Explain." 2; The favorable outcomes are rolling a 5 and flipping tails (5T) and rolling a 6 and flipping tails (6T).
- So, $P(\text{rolling a number greater than 4 and flipping tails}) = \frac{2}{12} = \frac{1}{6}$.
- Students should now see the value in creating tree diagrams and tables to find sample spaces. When finding probabilities, they can help easily identify the number of favorable outcomes and number of possible outcomes.

Try It
- Have students solve this problem on whiteboards.

✓ Self-Assessment for Concepts & Skills
- **Think-Alouds:** Say, "The steps I will use in solving Exercise 5 are…" Ask Partner A to think aloud for Partner B to hear how he or she will solve the problem. Allow students 3–5 minutes to discuss the problems, alternating roles for each one. Then have students solve independently before comparing and discussing answers with their partners.
- ⦿ Have students use *Fist of Five* to indicate their understanding of each success criterion.

ELL Support
Allow students to work in pairs for extra support and to practice language. When they have completed Exercises 5 and 6, have pairs display their answers on whiteboards for your review. Have two pairs discuss their answers for Exercise 7 and then present their ideas to the class.

The Success Criteria Self-Assessment chart can be found in the *Student Journal* or online at *BigIdeasMath.com*.

Extra Example 4
In Example 2, what is the probability of rolling an even number and flipping heads? $\frac{1}{4}$, or 25%

Try It
4. $\frac{1}{3}$, or $33\frac{1}{3}\%$

Self-Assessment for Concepts & Skills
5. Sample space: Daffodil Figurine, Daffodil Trophy, Hyacinth Figurine, Hyacinth Trophy, Tulip Figurine, Tulip Trophy; 6 possible displays
6. 20 possible outcomes
7. $P(\text{greater than 2 and tails})$; The other 3 probabilities are $\frac{1}{6} \cdot \frac{1}{2} = \frac{1}{12}$.

Extra Example 5

You flip three dimes. What is the probability of flipping three heads?

$\frac{1}{8}$, or 12.5%

Self-Assessment for Problem Solving

8. 288 possible vacation packages

9. $\frac{3}{25}$, or 12%

Learning Target

Find sample spaces and probabilities of compound events.

Success Criteria

- Find the sample space of two or more events.
- Find the total number of possible outcomes of two or more events.
- Find probabilities of compound events.

T-541

Laurie's Notes

EXAMPLE 5

- **Model with Mathematics:** Read the problem and ask students to draw a tree diagram to find the sample space. Ask students how to use the sample space to find the indicated probability.
- ❓ "If you use the Fundamental Counting Principle, how many possible outcomes are there?" $2 \cdot 2 \cdot 2 = 8$
- Continue to work through the problem as shown.
- Remind students to always check that they answered the question and that their solution makes sense.
- **Another Method:** Students may recognize that the only way *not* to win at least one prize is to win zero prizes (NNN). Because $P(\text{zero prizes}) = \frac{1}{8}$, $P(\text{at least one prize}) = 1 - \frac{1}{8} = \frac{7}{8}$.
- ❓ **Extension:** "What is the probability of winning exactly one prize? two prizes?" $\frac{2}{8} = \frac{1}{4}$, or 25%; $\frac{3}{8}$, or 37.5%

✓ Self-Assessment for Problem Solving

- Allow time in class for students to practice using the problem-solving plan. Remember, some students may only be able to complete the first step.
- For Exercise 8, discuss as a class the different available vacation packages (the sample space).
- For Exercise 9, ask a student to read the problem and another to explain it. Then have each student discuss different strategies with a partner before sharing with the class. After discussing, students should solve the problem independently.

The Success Criteria Self-Assessment chart can be found in the *Student Journal* or online at *BigIdeasMath.com*.

Closure

- **Writing Prompt:**
  The Fundamental Counting Principle is used to . . .
  Tree diagrams and tables can be used to . . .

EXAMPLE 5 Modeling Real Life

On a game show, you choose one box from each pair of boxes shown. In each pair, one box contains a prize and the other does not. What is the probability of winning at least one prize?

Choice 1

Choice 2

Choice 3

Use a tree diagram to find the sample space. Let P = prize and N = no prize. Circle the outcomes in which you win 1, 2, or 3 prizes.

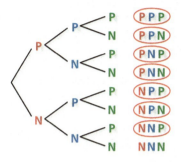

There are seven favorable outcomes in the sample space for winning at least one prize.

$$P(\text{event}) = \frac{\text{number of favorable outcomes}}{\text{number of possible outcomes}}$$

$P(\text{at least one prize}) = \dfrac{7}{8}$ Substitute.

▸ The probability of winning at least one prize is $\dfrac{7}{8}$, or 87.5%.

Self-Assessment for Problem Solving

Solve each exercise. Then rate your understanding of the success criteria in your journal.

8. A tour guide organizes vacation packages at a beachside town. There are 7 hotels, 5 cabins, 4 meal plans, 3 escape rooms, and 2 amusement parks. The tour guide chooses either a hotel or a cabin and then selects one of each of the remaining options. Find the total number of possible vacation packages.

9. **DIG DEEPER!** A fitness club with 100 members offers one free training session per member in either running, swimming, or weightlifting. Thirty of the fitness center members sign up for the free session. The running and swimming sessions are each twice as popular as the weightlifting session. What is the probability that a randomly chosen fitness club member signs up for a free running session?

B.3 Practice

Go to *BigIdeasMath.com* to get HELP with solving the exercises.

▶ Review & Refresh

Use the bar graph to find the experimental probability of the event.

1. rolling a 5
2. rolling a 2 or 6
3. rolling at least a 3
4. rolling a number less than or equal to 4

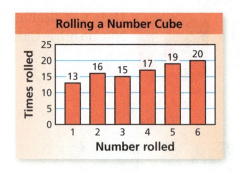

Find the product.

5. $3 \cdot 2$
6. $5(-3)$
7. $-6(-2)$

▶ Concepts, Skills, & Problem Solving

COMPARING PASSWORDS Determine which password is less likely to be guessed. (See Exploration 1, p. 537.)

8. a password with 3 numbers or a password with 3 capital letters
9. a password with 6 numbers or a password with 4 capital letters

USING A TREE DIAGRAM Use a tree diagram to find the sample space and the total number of possible outcomes.

10.
Birthday Party	
Activity	Miniature golf, Laser tag, Roller skating
Time	1:00 P.M.–3:00 P.M., 6:00 P.M.–8:00 P.M.

11.
New School Mascot	
Type	Lion, Bear, Hawk, Dragon
Style	Realistic, Cartoon

12.
Party Favor	
Item	Keychain, Magnet
Color	Blue, Green, Red

13.
Fidget Toy	
Type	Cube, Necklace, Spinner
Frame	Metal, Plastic, Rubber

14. **YOU BE THE TEACHER** Your friend finds the total number of ways that you can answer a quiz with five true-false questions. Is your friend correct? Explain your reasoning.

> $2 + 2 + 2 + 2 + 2 = 10$
> You can answer the quiz in 10 different ways.

542   Chapter B   Probability

Assignment Guide and Concept Check

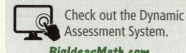

Scaffold assignments to support all students in their learning progression. The suggested assignments are a starting point. Continue to assign additional exercises and revisit with spaced practice to move every student toward proficiency.

Level	Assignment 1	Assignment 2
Emerging	4, 7, 8, 10, 11, 14, 15, 16, 19, 21, 23, 27	12, 13, 17, 18, 20, 22, 26, 28, 30, 31, 35
Proficient	4, 7, 8, 10, 12, 14, 16, 17, 19, 22, 24, 28	13, 18, 20, 26, 30, 31, 32, 33, 34, 35
Advanced	4, 7, 8, 10, 12, 14, 16, 18, 19, 24, 26, 30	32, 33, 34, 35, 36, 37

- Assignment 1 is for use after students complete the Self-Assessment for Concepts & Skills.
- Assignment 2 is for use after students complete the Self-Assessment for Problem Solving.
- The red exercises can be used as a concept check.

Review & Refresh Prior Skills

Exercises 1–4   Finding an Experimental Probability
Exercises 5–7   Multiplying Integers

Review & Refresh

1. $\frac{19}{100}$, or 19%
2. $\frac{9}{25}$, or 36%
3. $\frac{71}{100}$, or 71%
4. $\frac{61}{100}$, or 61%
5. 6
6. −15
7. 12

Concepts, Skills, & Problem Solving

8. a password with 3 capital letters
9. a password with 6 numbers
10. Sample space: Miniature golf 1 P.M.–3 P.M., Miniature golf 6 P.M.–8 P.M., Laser tag 1 P.M.–3 P.M., Laser tag 6 P.M.–8 P.M., Roller skating 1 P.M.–3 P.M., Roller skating 6 P.M.–8 P.M.; 6 possible outcomes
11. Sample space: Realistic Lion, Realistic Bear, Realistic Hawk, Realistic Dragon, Cartoon Lion, Cartoon Bear, Cartoon Hawk, Cartoon Dragon; 8 possible outcomes
12. Sample space: Keychain Blue, Keychain Green, Keychain Red, Magnet Blue, Magnet Green, Magnet Red; 6 possible outcomes
13. Sample space: Cube Metal, Cube Plastic, Cube Rubber, Necklace Metal, Necklace Plastic, Necklace Rubber, Spinner Metal, Spinner Plastic, Spinner Rubber; 9 possible outcomes
14. no; The possible outcomes of each question should be multiplied, not added.

T-542

Concepts, Skills, & Problem Solving

15. 12 possible outcomes
16. 20 possible outcomes
17. 24 possible outcomes
18. 36 possible outcomes
19. a. tree diagram or the Fundamental Counting Principle
    b. 12 possible outcomes
20. $\frac{1}{36}$, or $2\frac{7}{9}\%$
21. $\frac{1}{10}$, or 10%
22. $\frac{1}{5}$, or 20%
23. $\frac{1}{5}$, or 20%
24. 0, or 0%
25. $\frac{2}{5}$, or 40%
26. $\frac{3}{10}$, or 30%
27. $\frac{1}{18}$, or $5\frac{5}{9}\%$
28. $\frac{1}{9}$, or $11\frac{1}{9}\%$
29. $\frac{1}{9}$, or $11\frac{1}{9}\%$
30. $\frac{2}{9}$, or $22\frac{2}{9}\%$

Common Errors

- **Exercises 15–18** Students may add the number of possible outcomes for each event rather than multiply them. Remind students that the total number of outcomes of two or more events is found by multiplying the number of possible outcomes of each event.
- **Exercises 21–30** Students may find the probability of each individual event. Remind students that they are finding the probability of a *compound event*, so they need to find the ratio of the number of favorable outcomes to the number of possible outcomes using tables, tree diagrams, or the Fundamental Counting Principle.

USING THE FUNDAMENTAL COUNTING PRINCIPLE Use the Fundamental Counting Principle to find the total number of possible outcomes.

15.
Beverage	
Size	Small, Medium, Large
Flavor	Orange juice, Apple juice, Lemonade, Milk

16.
Fitness Tracker	
Battery	1 day, 3 days, 5 days, 7 days
Color	Silver, Green, Blue, Pink, Black

17.
Clown	
Suit	Dotted, Striped, Checkered
Wig	Single color, Multicolor
Talent	Balloon animals, Juggling, Unicycle, Magic

18.
Meal	
Appetizer	Soup, Spinach dip, Salad
Entrée	Chicken, Beef, Spaghetti, Fish
Dessert	Yogurt, Fruit, Rice pudding

19. **MP CHOOSE TOOLS** You randomly choose one of the marbles. Without replacing the first marble, you choose a second marble.

    a. Name two ways you can find the total number of possible outcomes.

    b. Find the total number of possible outcomes.

20. **FINDING A PROBABILITY** You roll two number cubes. What is the probability of rolling double threes?

FINDING THE PROBABILITY OF A COMPOUND EVENT You spin the spinner and flip a coin. Find the probability of the compound event.

21. spinning a 1 and flipping heads

22. spinning an even number and flipping heads

23. spinning a number less than 3 and flipping tails

24. spinning a 6 and flipping tails

25. *not* spinning a 5 and flipping heads

26. spinning a prime number and *not* flipping heads

FINDING THE PROBABILITY OF A COMPOUND EVENT You spin the spinner, flip a coin, and then spin the spinner again. Find the probability of the compound event.

27. spinning blue, flipping heads, then spinning a 1

28. spinning an odd number, flipping heads, then spinning yellow

29. spinning an even number, flipping tails, then spinning an odd number

30. *not* spinning red, flipping tails, then *not* spinning an even number

31. **MP REASONING** You randomly guess the answers to two questions on a multiple-choice test. Each question has three choices: A, B, and C.

    a. What is the probability that you guess the correct answers to both questions?

    b. Suppose you can eliminate one of the choices for each question. How does this change the probability that both of your guesses are correct?

32. **MP REASONING** You forget the last two digits of your cell phone password.

    a. What is the probability that you randomly choose the correct digits?

    b. Suppose you remember that both digits are even. How does this change the probability that you choose the correct digits?

33. **MP MODELING REAL LIFE** A combination lock has 3 wheels, each numbered from 0 to 9. You try to guess the combination by writing five different numbers from 0 to 999 on a piece of paper. Find the probability that the correct combination is written on the paper.

34. **MP MODELING REAL LIFE** A train has one engine and six train cars. Find the total number of ways an engineer can arrange the train. (The engine must be first.)

35. **MP REPEATED REASONING** You have been assigned a nine-digit identification number.

    a. Should you use the Fundamental Counting Principle or a tree diagram to find the total number of possible identification numbers? Explain.

    b. How many identification numbers are possible?

    c. **RESEARCH** Use the Internet to find out why the possible number of Social Security numbers is not the same as your answer to part (b).

36. **DIG DEEPER!** A social media account password includes a number from 0 to 9, an uppercase letter, a lowercase letter, and a special character, in that order.

    a. There are 223,080 password combinations. How many special characters are there?

    b. What is the probability of guessing the account password if you know the number and uppercase letter, but forget the rest?

37. **MP PROBLEM SOLVING** From a group of 5 scientists, an environmental committee of 3 people is selected. How many different committees are possible?

Mini-Assessment

1. Use a tree diagram to find the sample space and the total number of possible outcomes.

Snack	
Fruit	Apple, Banana, Pear
Drink	Water, Iced tea, Milk

Sample space: Apple and Water, Apple and Iced tea, Apple and Milk, Banana and Water, Banana and Iced tea, Banana and Milk, Pear and Water, Pear and Iced tea, Pear and Milk; 9 possible outcomes

2. Use the Fundamental Counting Principle to find the total number of possible outcomes.

Shirt	
Size	S, M, L, XL
Color	White, Blue, Red, Black, Gray
Style	T-shirt, Dress shirt

40

3. What is the probability of randomly choosing a banana and milk in Exercise 1? $\frac{1}{9}$, or $11\frac{1}{9}\%$

Section Resources

Surface Level	Deep Level
Resources by Chapter • Extra Practice • Reteach • Puzzle Time Student Journal • Self-Assessment • Practice Differentiating the Lesson Tutorial Videos Skills Review Handbook Skills Trainer	Resources by Chapter • Enrichment and Extension Graphic Organizers Dynamic Assessment System • Section Practice

Concepts, Skills, & Problem Solving

31. a. $\frac{1}{9}$, or about 11.1%

    b. It increases the probability that your guesses are correct to $\frac{1}{4}$, or 25%, because you are only choosing between 2 choices for each question.

32. a. $\frac{1}{100}$, or 1%

    b. It increases the probability that your choice is correct to $\frac{1}{25}$, or 4%, because each digit could be 0, 2, 4, 6, or 8.

33. There are 1000 possible combinations. With 5 tries, you would guess 5 out of the 1000 possibilities. So, the probability of getting the correct combination is $\frac{5}{1000}$, or 0.5%.

34. 720 ways

35. a. Fundamental Counting Principle; The Fundamental Counting Principle is more efficient. A tree diagram would be too large.

    b. 1,000,000,000 or one billion

    c. *Sample answer:* Not all possible number combinations are used for Social Security Numbers (SSN). SSNs are coded into geographical, group, and serial numbers. Some SSNs are reserved for commercial use and some are forbidden for various reasons.

36. a. 33 special characters

    b. $\frac{1}{858}$, or about 0.1166%

37. 10 ways

Learning Target
Design and use simulations to find probabilities of compound events.

Success Criteria
- Design a simulation to model a real-life situation.
- Recognize favorable outcomes in a simulation.
- Use simulations to find experimental probabilities.

Warm Up
Cumulative, vocabulary, and prerequisite skills practice opportunities are available in the *Resources by Chapter* or at BigIdeasMath.com.

ELL Support
Provide students with examples of simulations from everyday life. For example, at a game arcade there may be a simulation of driving a racecar. Video games are simulations of many different experiences. Pilots use simulations to learn how to fly a plane. These examples of simulations reproduce the conditions of a situation or process. In math, a simulation is an experiment designed to reproduce the conditions of a situation or process.

Exploration 1
a. *Sample answer:* yes; If the player makes 80% of her free throws, she can be expected to make 0.8 • 3 = 2.4 of her next three shots.

b. *Sample answer:* The digits 0 to 7 represent made shots and the digits of 8 and 9 represent missed shots.

c. See Additional Answers.

d. See Additional Answers.

T-545

Laurie's Notes

Preparing to Teach
- In the previous lesson, students found probabilities of compound events using tree diagrams, tables, and the Fundamental Counting Principle. Now they will design and use simulations to find probabilities of compound events.
- **Attend to Precision:** Mathematically proficient students communicate precisely to others. Students need to precisely describe the simulation they design to study situations that are impractical to create in real life.

Motivate
- Tell students that you heard the next social studies exam will include 10 true-false questions.
- ❓ "Assume you don't read the questions. How do you think you could find the probability of randomly guessing the correct answer to *at least* 7 questions?" Students will have a range of ideas about this.
- Explain that this is an event that you probably don't want to perform. Studying is a much better option; however, you can *simulate* the results.

Exploration 1
- Allow time for partners to discuss part (a). Then have students vote *yes* or *no*. Ask several students to explain their reasoning. Some students may say that she makes 80% of her free throw attempts and 80% of 3 is 2.4. So, she is likely to make two of her next three free throws.
- ❓ "In part (b), why do the numbers have three digits?" To represent her next three free throws. "How do the numbers model the situation?" You can select 8 digits to represent made shots and 2 digits to represent missed shots.
- ❓ "Why should you select 8 digits to represent made shots?" Because she makes 80% of her free throw. "Does it matter which 8 digits you choose?" no
- Using 1–8 as favorable outcomes, 838 represents making all three free throws and 937 represents missing the first free throw and making the last two.
- **Look for and Make Use of Structure:** Ask several pairs to choose different digits to represent made shots (e.g., 2–9 or 0, 1, 2, 3, 4, 6, 8, 9). Discuss how the meanings of the numbers can change depending on the digits used to represent made shots. For example, if 2–9 represent made shots, then 937 represents making all three free throws.
- Have pairs complete part (c) and then discuss as a class.
- ❓ "Do all pairs have the same results?" Answers will vary.
- ❓ "How can you make your estimated probability more accurate?" Sample answer: Conduct more trials. Help students realize that with more trials, the estimated probability will get closer to the theoretical probability regardless of which digits they choose to represent made shots.
- Explain that a **simulation** imitates a real-life situation using a process that can be easily reproduced, such as flipping a coin or using a random number generator. Simulations allow you to study the situation and make predictions.
- In part (d), students will likely describe a simulation similar to the one in part (b), but use four-digit numbers to represent her next four free throws and 6 digits to represent made shots. Ask several pairs to share their simulations.

B.4 Simulations

Learning Target: Design and use simulations to find probabilities of compound events.

Success Criteria:
- I can design a simulation to model a real-life situation.
- I can recognize favorable outcomes in a simulation.
- I can use simulations to find experimental probabilities.

EXPLORATION 1

Using a Simulation

Work with a partner. A basketball player makes 80% of her free throw attempts.

a. Is she likely to make at least two of her next three free throws? Explain your reasoning.

b. The table shows 30 randomly generated numbers from 0 to 999. Let each number represent three shots. How can you use the digits of these numbers to represent made shots and missed shots?

838	617	282	341	785
747	332	279	082	716
937	308	800	994	689
198	025	853	591	813
672	289	518	649	540
865	631	227	004	840

c. Use the table to estimate the probability that of her next three free throws, she makes

- exactly two free throws.
- at most one free throw.
- at least two free throws.
- at least two free throws in a row.

Choose Tools
What tools can you use to randomly generate data?

d. The experiment used in parts (b) and (c) is called a *simulation*. Another player makes $\frac{3}{5}$ of her free throws. Describe a simulation that can be used to estimate the probability that she makes three of her next four free throws.

Section B.4 Simulations 545

B.4 Lesson

Key Vocabulary
simulation, *p. 546*

A **simulation** is an experiment that is designed to reproduce the conditions of a situation or process. Simulations allow you to study situations that are impractical to create in real life.

EXAMPLE 1 Simulating Outcomes That Are Equally Likely

A dog has three puppies. The gender of each puppy is equally likely.

a. **Design a simulation involving 20 trials that you can use to model the genders of the puppies.**

Choose an experiment that has two equally likely outcomes for each event (gender), such as flipping three coins. Let heads (H) represent a male and tails (T) represent a female.

b. **Use your simulation to find the experimental probability that all three puppies are males.**

To find the experimental probability, perform 20 trials of the simulation. The table shows the results. Find the number of outcomes that represent 3 males, HHH.

HTH	HTT	HTT	HTH	HTT
TTT	HTT	HHH	TTT	HTT
HTH	HTT	HHH	HTH	HTT
HTT	HTH	TTT	HTT	HTH

Math Practice

Communicate Precisely
Describe a simulation involving a number cube that you can use to find the probability in part (b).

$$P(\text{three males}) = \frac{2}{20} = \frac{1}{10}$$

HHH occurred 2 times.
There is a total of 20 trials.

▸ The experimental probability is $\frac{1}{10}$, 0.1, or 10%.

Try It

1. You randomly guess the answers to four true-false questions.

   a. Design a simulation that you can use to model the answers.

   b. Use your simulation to find the experimental probability that you answer all four questions correctly.

Laurie's Notes

Scaffolding Instruction
- Students explored using a simulation to make predictions. Now they will design and use simulations to find experimental probabilities.
- **Emerging:** Students may understand that simulations can be used to estimate probabilities but struggle with designing a simulation to model the situation. They will benefit from guided instruction for the examples.
- **Proficient:** Students understand the design and use of simulations. They should work through Examples 1 and 2 independently before completing the Try It and Self-Assessment exercises.

Discuss
- Define **simulation** and give an example. Explain that simulations should be kept simple, allowing you to repeatedly duplicate the results of an event.
- To perform a simulation: (a) state the situation, (b) describe a model that randomly generates appropriate outcomes, (c) use the model repeatedly and record the results, and (d) use the results to make a conclusion.
- Students know that experimental probability approximates theoretical probability as the number of trials increases. So, simulations can be designed to accurately approximate theoretical probabilities.

EXAMPLE 1
- ❓ "How can you simulate an event that has two equally likely outcomes?" Answers will vary. Students will likely mention flipping coins.
- ❓ "If heads (H) represents a male dog and tails (T) represents a female dog, what outcome represents 3 male dogs?" HHH
- Students should view the data and interpret the first few results.
- The table shows that 2 out of 20, or 10% of the results represent 3 male dogs. Encourage students to run a simulation and create their own tables.
- ❓ "What is the theoretical probability that all three dogs are male?" $\frac{1}{8}$, 0.125, or 12.5% You could make a tree diagram similar to the one in Section B.3 Example 5, which represents the sample space of two equally likely outcomes chosen three times.
- ❓ "How does the theoretical probability compare to the experimental probability found in the simulation?" The theoretical probability (12.5%) is greater than the experimental probability (10%).
- ❓ "How can the two probabilities become closer?" Conduct more trials.
- **Extension:** Ask students to use the table to find the experimental probability that all three dogs are (a) female and (b) of the same gender. $\frac{3}{20}$, 0.15, or 15%; $\frac{1}{4}$, 0.25, or 25%

Try It
- Have students work with a partner and present their results. Discuss the different simulations that students create and their results.

Extra Example 1
A cat has four kittens. The gender of each kitten is equally likely.

a. Design a simulation involving 25 trials that you can use to model the genders of the kittens.
Flip four coins, let H = male and T = female.

b. Use your simulation to find the experimental probability that all four kittens are of the same gender.
Answers will vary, but the theoretical probability is $\frac{1}{16}$, 0.0625, or 6.25%.

ELL Support
After demonstrating Example 1, have students practice language by working in groups to complete Try It Exercise 1. Have groups consider these guiding questions: How many equally likely outcomes are there for each question? How will you label each of the outcomes? How many times will you perform the experiment? What is the experimental probability of answering all four questions correctly? Expect students to perform according to their language levels.

Beginner: State numbers and one-word answers to the guiding questions.

Intermediate: Use phrases or simple sentences such as, "two outcomes."

Advanced: Use detailed sentences such as, "There are two equally likely outcomes for each question."

Try It
1. a. Answers will vary.
   b. Answers will vary, but the theoretical probability is $\frac{1}{16}$, 0.0625, or 6.25%.

Formative Assessment Tip

Wait Time

Wait Time is the interval between a question being posed and a student (or teacher) response. Silence can be uncomfortable in a classroom, but research has shown that increasing *Wait Time* increases class participation and answers become more detailed. For complex, higher-order thinking questions, increased *Wait Time* is necessary. With increased participation, you will learn more about your students' progress and learning.

Extra Example 2

You randomly select a pair of pants and a shirt from your closet. You have a 70% chance of selecting blue pants and a 40% chance of selecting a red shirt. Design and use a simulation involving 50 randomly generated numbers to estimate the probability of selecting blue pants and a red shirt. *Randomly generate 50 numbers from 0 to 99 on a graphing calculator, let the digits 1–7 in the tens place represent selecting blue pants and let the digits 1–4 in the ones place represent selecting a red shirt; Answers will vary, but the theoretical probability is $\frac{7}{25}$, 0.28, or 28%.*

Try It

2. See Additional Answers.

ELL Support

Allow students to work in groups to design and use a simulation in Exercise 3. Then have students work on Exercise 4 in pairs. Ask each pair to display their answer on a whiteboard for your review.

Self-Assessment
for Concepts & Skills

3. See Additional Answers.

4. See Additional Answers.

Laurie's Notes

EXAMPLE 2

❓ "Is it possible to simulate a situation with outcomes that are not equally likely?" Students may say no at first. If you tell them to consider a number cube or different colors of marbles in a bag, they may change their minds.

- **Use Appropriate Tools Strategically:** In this simulation, a graphing calculator generates random whole numbers between 0 and 99 using the *randInt* feature. The syntax is *randInt(a,b,c)* where *a* and *b* represent the range of numbers and *c* represents how many are generated. You can use the right arrow key to scroll through the results. Commands and syntax may vary for different graphing calculators. The calculator will not display leading zeros, so write one-digit numbers with a zero in the tens place (i.e., 1 = 01).

- **Look for and Make Use of Structure:** It is unlikely that students will know the probability of winning both games can be found by multiplying their individual probabilities. You could explain a theoretical approach.

  - You have a 60% chance of winning a board game, so out of 5 board games you expect to win 3 times. You have a 20% chance of winning a card game, so out of 5 card games you expect to win 1 time.

Board Win	Board Win	Board Win	Board Lose	Board Lose
Card Lose / Card Lose	Card Lose / Card Lose	Card Lose / Card Lose	Card Lose / Card Lose	Card Lose / Card Lose
Card Lose / Card Lose	Card Lose / Card Lose	Card Lose / Card Lose	Card Lose / Card Lose	Card Lose / Card Lose
Card Win	Card Win	Card Win	Card Win	Card Win

There are 3 favorable outcomes out of 25 possible outcomes, so the theoretical probability of winning both games is $\frac{3}{25}$, 0.12, or 12%.

- Discuss the push-pin note. You could have students find the experimental probability using different groups of digits.

❓ "If different digits are used to represent winning the board or card game, will the experimental probability change?" Students should realize that although the probabilities may not be identical, they should be close. Give sufficient *Wait Time* before asking volunteers to share their ideas.

⊙ "Can you think of any other simulations that could be used to model this situation?" Discuss the possibilities students suggest.

Try It

- Have students work with a partner and then share with the class.

✓ Self-Assessment for Concepts & Skills

❓ "Why are simulations useful?" They allow you to study situations that are impractical to create in real life. "Will more trials make the results *more* or *less* accurate? Explain." more accurate; The more trials you conduct, the closer the experimental probability will be to the theoretical probability.

- Have students work with a partner and then share their results.

The Success Criteria Self-Assessment chart can be found in the *Student Journal* or online at *BigIdeasMath.com*.

EXAMPLE 2 **Simulating Outcomes That Are Not Equally Likely**

You have a 60% chance of winning a board game and a 20% chance of winning a card game. Design and use a simulation involving 50 randomly generated numbers to estimate the probability of winning both games.

> The digits 1–6 and 1–2 are chosen because they have a 60% and 20% chance of being randomly generated for each digit.

Use a simulation with randomly generated numbers from 0 to 99. Let the digits 1 through 6 in the tens place represent winning the board game. Let the digits 1 and 2 in the ones place represent winning the card game.

Use the random number generator on a graphing calculator to generate the numbers. The table shows the results. Find the number of outcomes that represent winning both games.

```
randInt(0,99,50)
{52 66 73 68 75…
```

52	66	73	68	75	28	35	47	48	02
16	68	49	03	77	35	92	78	06	06
58	18	89	39	24	80	32	41	77	21
32	40	96	59	86	01	12	00	94	73
40	71	28	61	01	24	37	25	03	25

$P(\text{win both games}) = \dfrac{7}{50}$ ← 7 numbers meet the criteria.
← There is a total of 50 trials.

▶ The experimental probability is $\dfrac{7}{50}$, 0.14, or 14%.

Try It

2. A baseball team wins 70% of the time. Design and use a simulation to estimate the probability that the team wins the next three games.

Self-Assessment for Concepts & Skills

Solve each exercise. Then rate your understanding of the success criteria in your journal.

3. **SIMULATING OUTCOMES** Four multiple-choice questions on a quiz each have five answer choices. You randomly guess the answer to each question. Design and use a simulation to find the experimental probability that you answer all of the questions correctly.

4. **SIMULATING OUTCOMES** You select a marble from a bag and a chip from a box. You have a 20% chance of choosing a green marble and a 90% chance of choosing a red chip. Estimate the probability that you choose a green marble and a red chip.

EXAMPLE 3 **Modeling Real Life**

Each school year, there is a 40% chance that weather causes one or more days of school to be canceled. Estimate the probability that weather causes a cancellation at least 3 years in a row in the next 4 years.

Use a simulation involving 50 randomly generated four-digit numbers to estimate the probability. Let the digits 1 through 4 represent years with a cancellation.

Use a random number table in a spreadsheet to generate the numbers. The spreadsheet shows the results. Find the number of outcomes in which the digits 1 through 4 occur at least three times in a row.

To create a four-digit random number table in a spreadsheet, enter =INT(RAND()*10000) into each cell.

	A	B	C	D	E	F
1	6527	4621	7810	3510	1408	
2	8141	0676	2535	8172	4095	
3	3450	7780	6435	8672	7537	
4	5063	1925	5137	9485	9437	
5	3299	2364	8034	8063	1323	
6	2556	1519	2735	2796	3987	
7	3771	7417	9177	4308	2723	
8	7593	7289	5091	0351	2179	
9	1479	0511	4550	8242	9407	
10	6910	8079	6142	6823	6138	
11						

$$P\binom{\text{cancellation at least 3 years}}{\text{in a row in the next 4 years}} = \frac{4}{50} = \frac{2}{25}$$

4 numbers meet the criteria.

There is a total of 50 trials.

▶ The experimental probability is $\frac{2}{25}$, 0.08, or 8%.

Self-Assessment for Problem Solving

Solve each exercise. Then rate your understanding of the success criteria in your journal.

5. Each day there is a 50% chance that your tablet overheats. Estimate the probability that your tablet overheats on exactly 2 of the next 3 days.

6. **DIG DEEPER!** The probability that a homeowner needs a plumber this year is 22%. The probability that the homeowner needs a septic tank specialist is 14%. Estimate the probability that the homeowner needs a plumber, but not a septic tank specialist.

Laurie's Notes

EXAMPLE 3

- ❓ "What is the chance that weather causes a school cancellation?" 40%
- The push-pin note shows how to randomly generate four-digit numbers in a spreadsheet. This could also be done using a graphing calculator.
- ❓ "If you randomly generate 50 numbers from 0 to 9999, what numbers represent school being canceled at least 3 years in a row in the next 4 years?" numbers with 1, 2, 3, or 4 in the first or last three digits
- ❓ "Why do the digits 1, 2, 3, and 4 represent years with a cancellation?" Because there is a 40% chance, so you use four of the ten digits.
- From the table, 4 out of 50, or 8% of the results represent a cancellation in at least 3 years in a row out of the next 4 years.
- Make sure students understand that assigning digits 1–4 to represent a school cancellation was arbitrary. They can use other digits, such as 0–3. Have students calculate the probability using different digits and then compare the results.

✓ Self-Assessment for Problem Solving

- Encourage students to use a Four Square to complete these exercises. For these problems, students may want to change "Make a plan" to "Design a simulation." Until students become comfortable with the problem-solving plan, they may only be ready to complete the first square.
- Have students work in pairs. Each partner should solve a different problem and then explain the simulation and solution to the other.

The Success Criteria Self-Assessment chart can be found in the *Student Journal* or online at *BigIdeasMath.com*.

Closure

- **Exit Ticket:** Design and use a simulation to find the experimental probability that you correctly guess at least 7 of the 10 true-false questions in the Motivate. *Sample answer:* Flip ten coins . Let heads represent a correct answer and T represent an incorrect answer. Run 50 trials; Answers will vary, but the theoretical probability is $\frac{11}{64}$, 0.171875, or 17.1875%.

Extra Example 3

Each school year, there is a 20% chance that the weather causes one or more days of school to be canceled. Estimate the probability that weather causes a cancellation in exactly 2 years of the next 5 years. Answers will vary, but the theoretical probability is $\frac{128}{625}$, 0.2048, or 20.48%.

Self-Assessment for Problem Solving

5. Answers will vary, but the theoretical probability is $\frac{3}{8}$, 0.375, or 37.5%.

6. Answers will vary, but the theoretical probability is $\frac{473}{2500}$, 0.1892, or 18.92%.

Learning Target
Design and use simulations to find probabilities of compound events.

Success Criteria
- Design a simulation to model a real-life situation.
- Recognize favorable outcomes in a simulation.
- Use simulations to find experimental probabilities.

Review & Refresh

1. $\frac{7}{40}$, or 17.5%
2. $\frac{1}{20}$, or 5%
3. $5a - 10$
4. $-21x - 7$
5. $-3p + 8$

Concepts, Skills, & Problem Solving

6. $\frac{1}{2}$, or 50%
7. $\frac{2}{15}$, or $13.\overline{3}$%
8. Answers will vary, but the theoretical probability is $\frac{7}{8}$, 0.875, or 87.5%.
9. Answers will vary, but the theoretical probability is $\frac{5}{32}$, 0.15625, or 15.625%.
10. Answers will vary, but the theoretical probability is $\frac{1}{16}$, 0.0625, or 6.25%; Answers will vary, but the theoretical probability is $\frac{9}{16}$, 0.5625, or 56.25%.
11. Answers will vary, but the theoretical probability is $\frac{25}{27}$, about 0.9259, or about 92.59%.

Assignment Guide and Concept Check

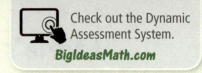

Scaffold assignments to support all students in their learning progression. The suggested assignments are a starting point. Continue to assign additional exercises and revisit with spaced practice to move every student toward proficiency.

Level	Assignment 1	Assignment 2
Emerging	2, 5, 6, 8, 9, 12, 14	7, 10, 11, 13, 15, 16, 18
Proficient	2, 5, 7, 9, 10, 12, 14	11, 13, 15, 16, 17, 18
Advanced	2, 5, 7, 9, 10, 12, 14	11, 13, 15, 17, 18, 19

- Assignment 1 is for use after students complete the Self-Assessment for Concepts & Skills.
- Assignment 2 is for use after students complete the Self-Assessment for Problem Solving.
- The red exercises can be used as a concept check.

Review & Refresh Prior Skills

Exercises 1 and 2 Finding the Probability of a Compound Event
Exercises 3–5 Using the Distributive Property

Common Errors

- **Exercise 8** Students may find the experimental probability that *exactly* one of your next three seeds sprouts instead of *at least* one. Remind students to read the problem carefully to determine what is being asked.
- **Exercise 11** Students may misinterpret *fewer than* and include two spins landing on reward A in their favorable outcomes. Remind students to read the problem carefully to determine what is being asked.

B.4 Practice

Go to *BigIdeasMath.com* to get HELP with solving the exercises.

▶ Review & Refresh

You flip a coin and roll the 20-sided figure. Find the probability of the compound event.

1. Flipping tails and rolling at least a 14

2. Flipping heads and rolling less than 3

Simplify the expression.

3. $5(a - 2)$
4. $-7(1 + 3x)$
5. $-1(3p - 8)$

▶ Concepts, Skills, & Problem Solving

USING A SIMULATION A medicine is effective for 80% of patients. The table shows 30 randomly generated numbers from 0 to 999. Use the table to estimate the probability of the event. (See Exploration 1, p. 545.)

463	013	231	898	139
365	492	565	188	465
438	751	961	646	598
045	241	940	901	467
151	774	538	380	509
251	924	401	549	859

6. The medicine is effective on each of three patients.

7. The medicine is effective on fewer than two of the next three patients.

SIMULATING OUTCOMES Design and use a simulation to find the experimental probability.

8. In your indoor garden, 50% of seeds sprout. What is the experimental probability that at least one of your next three seeds sprouts?

9. An archer hits a target 50% of the time. What is the experimental probability that the archer hits the target exactly four of the next five times?

10. A bank randomly selects one of four free gifts to send to each new customer. Gifts include a calculator, a keychain, a notepad, and a pen. What is the experimental probability that the next two new customers both receive calculators? that neither receives a calculator?

11. Employees spin a reward wheel. The wheel is equally likely to stop on each of six rewards labeled A–F. What is the experimental probability that fewer than two of the next three spins land on reward A?

Section B.4 Simulations 549

USING NUMBER CUBES Design and use a simulation with number cubes to estimate the probability.

12. Your lawn mower does not start on the first try $\frac{1}{6}$ of the time. Estimate the probability that your lawn mower will not start on the first try exactly one of the next two times you mow the lawn.

13. An application on your phone correctly identifies four out of every six songs. Estimate the probability that at least three of the next four songs are correctly identified.

SIMULATING OUTCOMES Design and use a simulation to find the experimental probability.

14. Two beakers are used in a lab test. What is the experimental probability that there are reactions in both beakers during the lab test?

Probability of Reaction	
Beaker 1	80%
Beaker 2	50%

15. You use a stain remover on two separate stains on a shirt. What is the experimental probability that the stain remover removes both the mud stain and the food stain?

Probability of Stain Removal	
Mud	90%
Food	80%

16. **DIG DEEPER!** The probability that a computer crashes one or more times in a month is 10%. Estimate the probability that the computer crashes at least one or more times per month for two months in a row during the first half of the year.

17. **MODELING REAL LIFE** You visit an orchard. The probability that you randomly select a ripe apple is 92%. The probability that you randomly select a ripe cherry is 86%. Estimate the probability that you pick an apple that is ripe and a cherry that is not ripe.

18. **CRITICAL THINKING** You use a simulation to find an experimental probability. How does the experimental probability compare to the theoretical probability as the number of trials increases?

19. **LOGIC** At a restaurant, 30% of customers donate to charity in exchange for a coupon. Estimate the probability that it will take at least four customers to find one who donates.

Common Errors

- **Exercise 16** Students may find the experimental probability that the computer crashes in any two months during the first half of the year instead of two months *in a row*. Remind students to read the problem carefully to determine what is being asked.

Mini-Assessment

1. You randomly guess on five true-false questions. Design and use a simulation to find the experimental probability that you correctly answer exactly 3 questions. *Sample answer:* Flip five coins. Let heads represent a correct answer and tails represent an incorrect answer. Run 50 trials; Answers will vary, but the theoretical probability is $\frac{5}{16}$, 0.3125, or 31.25%.

2. At a shopping mall, 40% of shoppers are willing to take a survey. Estimate the probability that out of the next 5 random shoppers, there will be 3 or more in a row that are willing to take the survey. Answers will vary, but the theoretical probability is $\frac{344}{3125}$, 0.11008, or 11.008%.

Section Resources

Surface Level	Deep Level
Resources by Chapter • Extra Practice • Reteach • Puzzle Time Student Journal • Self-Assessment • Practice Differentiating the Lesson Tutorial Videos Skills Review Handbook Skills Trainer	Resources by Chapter • Enrichment and Extension Graphic Organizers Dynamic Assessment System • Section Practice
Transfer Level	
Dynamic Assessment System • End-of-Chapter Quiz	Assessment Book • End-of-Chapter Quiz

Concepts, Skills, & Problem Solving

12. Answers will vary, but the theoretical probability is $\frac{5}{18}$, about 0.277, or about 27.7%.

13. Answers will vary, but the theoretical probability is $\frac{16}{27}$, about 0.5926, or about 59.26%.

14. Answers will vary, but the theoretical probability is $\frac{2}{5}$, 0.4, or 40%.

15. Answers will vary, but the theoretical probability is $\frac{18}{25}$, 0.72, or 72%.

16. Answers will vary.

17. Answers will vary, but the theoretical probability is $\frac{161}{1250}$, 0.1288, or 12.88%.

18. *Sample answer:* The experimental probability should get closer and closer to the theoretical probability as the number of trials increase.

19. Answers will vary, but the theoretical probability is $\frac{343}{1000}$, 0.343, or 34.3%.

Skills Needed

Exercise 1
- Finding an Experimental Probability
- Finding a Theoretical Probability
- Simulating Outcomes
- Writing and Interpreting Ratios

Exercise 2
- Finding an Experimental Probability
- Finding a Theoretical Probability
- Finding the Percent Error
- Using an Experimental Probability
- Using a Theoretical Probability

Exercise 3
- Finding a Theoretical Probability
- Identifying Outcomes
- Multiplying Integers

ELL Support

Before having students solve Exercise 2, discuss the experience of playing board games. Have students share what they know. Explain what a board game is if they are unfamiliar with one.

Using the Problem-Solving Plan

1. Answers will vary, but the theoretical probability is $\frac{7}{250}$, 0.028, or 2.8%.

2. a. 9 times
   b. 25%

3. See Additional Answers.

Performance Task

The *STEAM Video Performance Task* provides the opportunity for additional enrichment and greater depth of knowledge as students explore the mathematics of the chapter within a context tied to the chapter STEAM Video. The performance task and a detailed scoring rubric are provided at *BigIdeasMath.com*.

T-551

Laurie's Notes

Scaffolding Instruction

- The goal of this lesson is to help students become more comfortable with problem solving. These exercises combine finding and using probabilities with prior skills from other chapters and courses. The solution for Exercise 1 is worked out below, to help you guide students through the problem-solving plan. Use the remaining class time to have students work on the other exercises.
- **Emerging:** The goal for these students is to feel comfortable with the problem-solving plan. Allow students to work in pairs to write the beginning steps of the problem-solving plan for Exercise 2. Keep in mind that some students may only be ready to do the first step.
- **Proficient:** Students may be able to work independently or in pairs to complete Exercises 2 and 3.
- Visit each pair to review their plan for each problem. Ask students to describe their plans.

▶ Using the Problem-Solving Plan

Exercise 1

▷ **Understand the problem.** You know the ratio of gift cards to bicycles awarded in the contest. You want to find the probability that at least two of three randomly selected winners receive bicycles.

▷ **Make a plan.** Use the ratio to find the theoretical probability that a randomly selected winner receives a bicycle. Then use a simulation involving 50 randomly generated three-digit numbers to estimate the probability that at least two of three randomly selected winners receive bicycles.

▷ **Solve and check.** Use the plan to solve the problem. Then check your solution.

- Find the theoretical probability that a randomly selected winner receives a bicycle.

  $P(\text{bicycle}) = \dfrac{\text{number of bicycle winners}}{\text{total number of winners}} = \dfrac{1}{10}$, or 10%

- Use a simulation to estimate the probability. Let the digit 1 represent a bicycle winner and use the random number generator on a graphing calculator to generate numbers from 0 to 999.

908	146	514	405	733	043	339	995	200	798
951	220	007	935	108	006	548	855	977	278
275	(121)	052	722	012	421	307	972	028	837
618	205	984	724	301	249	946	925	042	(113)
696	985	632	312	085	997	198	398	(117)	369

$P\begin{pmatrix}\text{at least two of three} \\ \text{winners receive bicycles}\end{pmatrix} = \dfrac{3}{50}$

The experimental probability is $\dfrac{3}{50}$, 0.06, or 6%.

- **Check:** You could run another trial and compare the probabilities or verify that

$P\begin{pmatrix}\text{at least two of three} \\ \text{winners receive bicycles}\end{pmatrix} + P\begin{pmatrix}\text{less than two of three} \\ \text{winners receive bicycles}\end{pmatrix} = 1.$

$\dfrac{3}{50} \quad + \quad \dfrac{47}{50} \quad = 1 \checkmark$

Connecting Concepts

Using the Problem-Solving Plan

1. In an Internet contest, gift cards and bicycles are given as prizes in the ratio 9 : 1. Estimate the probability that at least two of three randomly selected winners receive bicycles.

Understand the problem. You know the ratio of gift cards to bicycles awarded in the contest. You want to find the probability that at least two of three randomly selected winners receive bicycles.

Make a plan. Use the ratio to find the theoretical probability that a randomly selected winner receives a bicycle. Then use a simulation involving 50 randomly generated three-digit numbers to estimate the probability that at least two of three randomly selected winners receive bicycles.

Solve and check. Use the plan to solve the problem. Then check your solution.

2. A board game uses the spinner shown.

    a. Use theoretical probability to predict the number of times you will spin a number greater than or equal to 8 in 30 spins.

    b. You play the game and record the results of 30 spins. Find the percent error of your prediction in part (a).

Number Spun	1	2	3	4	5	6	7	8	9	10
Frequency	2	2	3	1	3	3	4	3	4	5

3. The tiles shown are placed in a bag. You randomly select one of the tiles, return it to the bag, and then randomly select another tile. What is the probability that the product of the numbers on the tiles selected is greater than zero? Justify your answer.

Performance Task

Fair and Unfair Carnival Games

At the beginning of this chapter, you watched a STEAM Video called "Massively Multiplayer Rock Paper Scissors." You are now ready to complete the performance task related to this video, available at *BigIdeasMath.com*. Be sure to use the problem-solving plan as you work through the performance task.

Review Vocabulary

Write the definition and give an example of each vocabulary term.

experiment, *p. 522*
outcomes, *p. 522*
event, *p. 522*
favorable outcomes, *p. 522*
probability, *p. 523*
relative frequency, *p. 524*
experimental probability, *p. 530*
theoretical probability, *p. 530*
sample space, *p. 538*
Fundamental Counting Principle, *p. 538*
compound event, *p. 540*
simulation, *p. 546*

Graphic Organizers

You can use a **Four Square** to organize information about a concept. Each of the four squares can be a category, such as definition, vocabulary, example, non-example, words, algebra, table, numbers, visual, graph, or equation. Here is an example of a Four Square for *probability*.

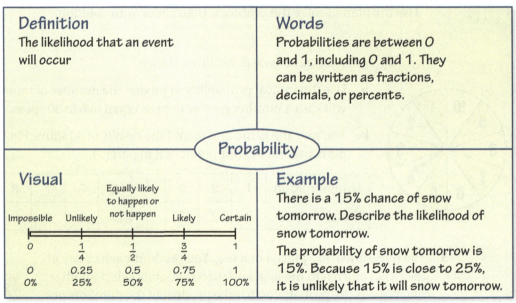

Choose and complete a graphic organizer to help you study the concept.

1. favorable outcomes
2. relative frequency
3. experimental probability
4. theoretical probability
5. Fundamental Counting Principle
6. compound event
7. simulation

"My **Four Square** shows that my new red skateboard is faster than my old blue skateboard."

Review Vocabulary

- As a review of the chapter vocabulary, have students revisit the vocabulary section in their *Student Journals* to fill in any missing definitions and record examples of each term.

Graphic Organizers

Sample answers:

1.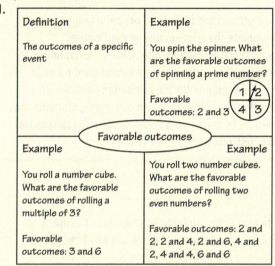

2.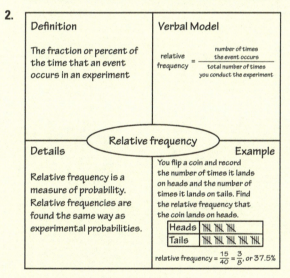

3–7. Answers at *BigIdeasMath.com*.

List of Organizers

Available at *BigIdeasMath.com*
Definition and Example Chart
Example and Non-Example Chart
Four Square
Information Frame
Summary Triangle

About this Organizer

A **Four Square** can be used to organize information about a concept. Students write the concept in the oval. Then students use each of the four squares surrounding the oval to represent a related category. Related categories may include: definition, vocabulary, example, non-example, words, algebra, table, numbers, visual, graph, or equation. Encourage students to use categories that will help them study the concept. Students can place their Four Squares on note cards to use as a quick study reference.

Chapter Self-Assessment

1. 7 possible outcomes
2. blue, red
3. 5 ways
4. a. 2
   b. green 1, purple 1
5. a. 3
   b. orange 3, blue 3, purple 3
6. a. 5
   b. green 1, purple 1, orange 3, blue 3, purple 3
7. a. 3
   b. blue 2, orange 2, green 2
8. a. 8
   b. green 1, purple 1, blue 2, orange 2, green 2, orange 3, blue 3, purple 3
9. a. 5
   b. green 1, purple 1, blue 2, orange 2, green 2
10. impossible
11. unlikely
12. likely
13. equally likely to happen or not happen
14. a. likely
    b. 10 or 11 rebounds

Chapter Self-Assessment

The Success Criteria Self-Assessment chart can be found in the *Student Journal* or online at *BigIdeasMath.com*.

ELL Support

Allow students extra support and the chance to practice language by working in pairs to complete the first section of the Chapter Self-Assessment. Once pairs have finished, check for understanding by asking each pair to display their answers on a whiteboard for your review. Use this and other techniques for the remaining sections as appropriate. For sections that include discussion questions, students may benefit from grouping two pairs and having them reach a consensus for the answers. Monitor discussions and provide support.

Common Errors

- **Exercises 1–3** Students may forget to include, or include too many, favorable outcomes. Encourage students to write out all of the possible outcomes and then circle the favorable outcomes for the given event.

Chapter Self-Assessment

As you complete the exercises, use the scale below to rate your understanding of the success criteria in your journal.

1	2	3	4
I do not understand.	I can do it with help.	I can do it on my own.	I can teach someone else.

B.1 Probability (pp. 521–528)

Learning Target: Understand how the probability of an event indicates its likelihood.

You randomly choose one toy race car.

1. How many possible outcomes are there?

2. What are the favorable outcomes of choosing a car that is *not* green?

3. In how many ways can choosing a green car occur?

You spin the spinner. (a) Find the number of ways the event can occur. (b) Find the favorable outcomes of the event.

4. spinning a 1

5. spinning a 3

6. spinning an odd number

7. spinning an even number

8. spinning a number greater than 0

9. spinning a number less than 3

Describe the likelihood of the event given its probability.

10. There is a 0% chance of snow in July for Florida.

11. The probability that you are called on to answer a question in class is $\frac{1}{25}$.

12. There is an 85% chance the bus is on time.

13. The probability of flipping heads on a coin is 0.5.

14. During a basketball game, you record the number of rebounds from missed shots for each team. (a) Describe the likelihood that your team rebounds the next missed shot. (b) How many rebounds should your team expect to have in 15 missed shots?

Your Team	|||| ||
Opposing Team	|||

Chapter Review 553

B.2 Experimental and Theoretical Probability (pp. 529–536)

Learning Target: Develop probability models using experimental and theoretical probability.

The bar graph shows the results of spinning a spinner 100 times. Use the bar graph to find the experimental probability of the event.

15. spinning a 2
16. spinning an even number
17. *not* spinning a 5
18. spinning a number less than 3
19. In Exercise 16, how does the experimental probability of spinning an even number compare with the theoretical probability?

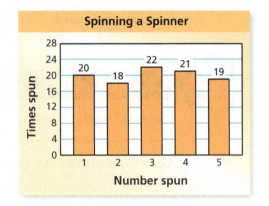

Use the spinner to find the theoretical probability of the event.

20. spinning blue
21. spinning a 1
22. spinning an even number
23. spinning a 4

24. The theoretical probability of choosing a red grape from a bag of grapes is $\frac{2}{9}$. There are 8 red grapes in the bag. How many grapes are in the bag?

25. The theoretical probability of choosing Event A is $\frac{2}{7}$. What is the theoretical probability of *not* choosing Event A? Explain your reasoning.

B.3 Compound Events (pp. 537–544)

Learning Target: Find sample spaces and probabilities of compound events.

26. You have 6 bracelets and 15 necklaces. Find the number of ways you can wear one bracelet and one necklace.

27. Use a tree diagram to find how many different home theater systems you can make from 6 DVD players, 8 TVs, and 3 brands of speakers.

28. A red, green, and blue book are on a shelf. You randomly pick one of the books. Without replacing the first book, you choose another book. What is the probability that you picked the red and blue book?

Common Errors

- **Exercises 15–18** Students may forget to total all of the trials before writing the experimental probability. They may have an incorrect number of trials in the denominator. Remind students that they need to know the total number of trials when finding the probability.
- **Exercises 20–23** Students may write a different probability than what is asked, or forget to include a favorable outcome. For example, a student may not realize that there are two blue sections and will write the probability of spinning blue as $\frac{1}{8}$ instead of $\frac{1}{4}$. Remind students to read the event carefully and to write the favorable outcomes before finding the probability.
- **Exercise 26** Students may add the number of possible outcomes for each event rather than multiply them. Remind students that the total number of outcomes of two or more events is found by multiplying the number of possible outcomes of each event.
- **Exercise 28** Students may find the probability of each individual event. Remind students that they are finding the probability of a *compound event*, so they need to find the ratio of the number of favorable outcomes to the number of possible outcomes using tables, tree diagrams, or the Fundamental Counting Principle.

Chapter Self-Assessment

15. $\frac{9}{50}$, 0.18, or 18%
16. $\frac{39}{100}$, 0.39, or 39%
17. $\frac{81}{100}$, 0.81, or 81%
18. $\frac{19}{50}$, 0.38, or 38%
19. The theoretical probability of spinning an even number is 40%. The experimental probability is 39%, which is close to the theoretical probability.
20. $\frac{1}{4}$, or 25%
21. $\frac{3}{8}$, or 37.5%
22. $\frac{5}{8}$, or 62.5%
23. $\frac{1}{8}$, or 12.5%
24. 36 grapes
25. $\frac{5}{7}$; *Sample answer:* The probability of not choosing Event A is $1 - \frac{2}{7} = \frac{5}{7}$.
26. 90 ways
27. 144 home theater systems
28. $\frac{1}{3}$, or $33.\overline{3}\%$

Chapter Self-Assessment

29. $\frac{1}{8}$, or 12.5%

30. *Sample answer:* You spin a spinner with five equal sections numbered 1 through 5. The probability of spinning a number less than 5 on each of two spins is $\frac{16}{25} = 64\%$.

31. $\frac{14}{15}$, or $93.\overline{3}\%$

32. Answers will vary, but the theoretical probability is $\frac{21}{100}$, 0.21, or 21%.

33. a. Answers will vary.

    b. Answers will vary, but the theoretical probability is $\frac{12}{25}$, 0.48, or 48%.

34. Answers will vary, but the theoretical probability is $\frac{76}{625}$, 0.1216, or 12.16%.

35. Answers will vary, but the theoretical probability is $\frac{2}{25}$, 0.08, or 8%.

Common Errors

- **Exercises 29 and 31** Students may find the probability of each individual event. Remind students that they are finding the probability of a *compound event*, so they need to find the ratio of the number of favorable outcomes to the number of possible outcomes using tables, tree diagrams, or the Fundamental Counting Principle.

Chapter Resources

Surface Level	Deep Level
Resources by Chapter • Extra Practice • Reteach • Puzzle Time Student Journal • Practice • Chapter Self-Assessment Differentiating the Lesson Tutorial Videos Skills Review Handbook Skills Trainer Game Library	Resources by Chapter • Enrichment and Extension Graphic Organizers Game Library
Transfer Level	
STEAM Video Dynamic Assessment System • Chapter Test	Assessment Book • Chapter Tests A and B • Alternative Assessment • STEAM Performance Task

29. You flip two coins and roll a number cube. What is the probability of flipping two tails and rolling an even number?

30. Describe a compound event that has a probability between 50% and 80%.

31. Your science teacher sets up six flasks. Two of the flasks contain water and four of the flasks contain hydrogen peroxide. A reaction occurs when you add yeast to hydrogen peroxide. You add yeast to two of the flasks. What is the probability that at least one reaction will occur?

B.4 Simulations (pp. 545–550)

Learning Target: Design and use simulations to find probabilities of compound events.

32. You select a marble from two different bags. You have a 30% chance of choosing a blue marble from the first bag and a 70% chance of choosing a blue marble from the second bag. Design and use a simulation to estimate the probability that you choose a blue marble from both bags.

33. A cereal company is including a prize in each box. There are 5 different prizes, all of which are equally likely.

    a. Describe a simulation involving 50 trials that you can use to model the prizes in the next 3 boxes of cereal you buy.

    b. Use your simulation to find the experimental probability that all three boxes contain a different prize.

34. In the past month, your cell phone has lost its entire charge on 40% of days. Design and use a simulation to estimate the experimental probability that your cell phone loses its entire charge on exactly 2 of the next 5 days.

35. You and your friends form a team in gym class. You have an 80% chance of winning a game of basketball and a 10% chance of winning a game of soccer. Design and use a simulation involving 50 randomly generated numbers to estimate the probability of winning both games.

B Practice Test

You randomly choose one game piece. (a) Find the number of ways the event can occur. (b) Find the favorable outcomes of the event.

1. choosing green
2. choosing *not* yellow

Find the sample space and the total number of possible outcomes.

3.
Sunscreen	
SPF	10, 15, 30, 45, 50
Type	Lotion, Spray, Gel

4.
Calculator	
Type	Basic display, Scientific, Graphing, Financial
Color	Black, White, Silver

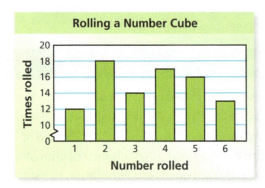

Use the bar graph to find the experimental probability of the event.

5. rolling a 1 or a 2
6. rolling an odd number
7. *not* rolling a 5
8. rolling a number less than 7

Use the spinner to find the theoretical probability of the event(s).

9. spinning an even number
10. spinning a 1 and then a 2

11. You randomly choose one of the pens shown. What is the theoretical probability of choosing a black pen?

12. You randomly choose one of the pens shown. Your friend randomly chooses one of the remaining pens. What is the probability that you and your friend both choose a blue pen?

13. There is an 80% chance of a thunderstorm on Saturday. Describe the likelihood that there is *not* a thunderstorm on Saturday.

14. You are helping to remodel a bathroom. The probability that a randomly selected tile is cracked is 40%. For every 10 boards, there is 1 that is warped. Design and use a simulation to estimate the experimental probability that the next tile you select is cracked and the next board you select is *not* warped.

Practice Test Item References

Practice Test Questions	Section to Review
1, 2, 13	B.1
5, 6, 7, 8, 9, 11	B.2
3, 4, 10, 12	B.3
14	B.4

Test-Taking Strategies

Remind students to quickly look over the entire test before they start so that they can budget their time. There is a lot of vocabulary in this chapter, so students should have been making flashcards as they worked through the chapter. Encourage students to jot down words that they mix up on the back of the test before they start. Have them use the **Stop** and **Think** strategy before they write their answers.

 Common Errors

- **Exercises 1 and 2** Students may forget to include, or include too many, favorable outcomes. Encourage students to write out all of the possible outcomes and then circle the favorable outcomes for the given event.
- **Exercises 5–8** Students may forget to total all of the trials before writing the experimental probability. They may have an incorrect number of trials in the denominator. Remind students that they need to know the total number of trials when finding the probability.
- **Exercise 12** Students may find the probability of each individual event. Remind students that they are finding the probability of a *compound event*, so they need to find the ratio of the number of favorable outcomes to the number of possible outcomes using tables, tree diagrams, or the Fundamental Counting Principle.

Practice Test

1. **a.** 1
   b. green
2. **a.** 5
   b. red, blue, red, green, blue
3. 15
4. 12
5. $\frac{1}{3}$, or $33.\overline{3}\%$
6. $\frac{7}{15}$, or $46.\overline{6}\%$
7. $\frac{37}{45}$, or $82.\overline{2}\%$
8. 1, or 100%
9. $\frac{4}{9}$, or $44.\overline{4}\%$
10. $\frac{1}{81}$, or about 1.2%
11. $\frac{2}{5}$, or 40%
12. $\frac{1}{10}$, or 10%
13. unlikely
14. Answers will vary, but the theoretical probability is $\frac{9}{25}$, 0.36, or 36%.

Test-Taking Strategies

Available at *BigIdeasMath.com*
After Answering Easy Questions, Relax
Answer Easy Questions First
Estimate the Answer
Read All Choices before Answering
Read Question before Answering
Solve Directly or Eliminate Choices
Solve Problem before Looking at Choices
Use Intelligent Guessing
Work Backwards

About this Strategy

When taking a multiple-choice test, be sure to read each question carefully and thoroughly. Sometimes you may not know the answer. So… guess intelligently! Look at the choices and choose the ones that are reasonable answers.

Cumulative Practice

1. C
2. $\frac{1}{5}$, or 20%

Item Analysis

1. **A.** The student does not understand the concepts of certainty and likelihood.

   B. The student does not understand the difference between likely and unlikely.

   C. Correct answer

   D. The student does not understand that even a highly unlikely event is not impossible.

2. **Gridded Response:** Correct answer: $\frac{1}{5}$, or 20%

   Common error: The student only considers that Sunday is one day of the week and gets an answer of $\frac{1}{7}$.

Cumulative Practice

1. A school athletic director asked each athletic team member to name his or her favorite professional sports team. The results are below:

   - D.C. United: 3
   - Florida Panthers: 8
   - Jacksonville Jaguars: 26
   - Jacksonville Sharks: 7
   - Miami Dolphins: 22
   - Miami Heat: 15
   - Miami Marlins: 20
   - Minnesota Lynx: 4
   - New York Knicks: 5
   - Orlando Magic: 18
   - Tampa Bay Buccaneers: 17
   - Tampa Bay Lightning: 12
   - Tampa Bay Rays: 28
   - Other: 6

   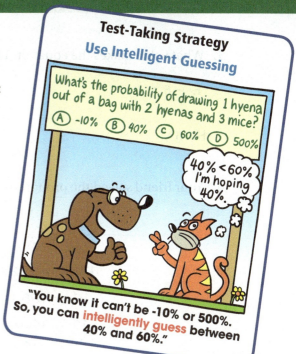

   One athletic team member is picked at random. What is the likelihood that this team member's favorite professional sports team is *not* located in Florida?

   A. certain
   B. likely, but not certain
   C. unlikely, but not impossible
   D. impossible

2. Each student in your class voted for his or her favorite day of the week. Their votes are shown in the circle graph:

   Favorite Day of the Week

   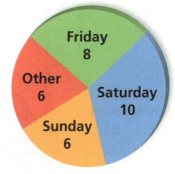

   Friday 8
   Other 6
   Saturday 10
   Sunday 6

   A student from your class is picked at random. What is the probability that this student's favorite day of the week is Sunday?

3. What value makes the equation $11 - 3x = -7$ true?

    F. -6 **G.** $-\dfrac{4}{3}$

    H. 6 **I.** 54

4. Your friend solved the proportion in the box below.

$$\frac{16}{40} = \frac{p}{27}$$
$$16 \cdot p = 40 \cdot 27$$
$$16p = 1080$$
$$\frac{16p}{16} = \frac{1080}{16}$$
$$p = 67.5$$

What should your friend do to correct the error that he made?

A. Add 40 to 16 and 27 to p.

B. Subtract 16 from 40 and 27 from p.

C. Multiply 16 by 27 and p by 40.

D. Divide 16 by 27 and p by 40.

5. Which value is a solution of the inequality?

$$3 - 2y < 7$$

    F. -6 **G.** -3

    H. -2 **I.** -1

6. A spinner is divided into eight equal sections, as shown. You spin the spinner twice. What is the probability that the arrow will stop in a yellow section both times?

Item Analysis (continued)

3. **F.** The student thinks the quotient of −18 and −3 is negative instead of positive.

   G. The student adds 11 to −7 instead of subtracting.

   H. Correct answer

   I. The student multiplies −18 by −3 instead of dividing.

4. **A.** The student incorrectly thinks that proportions involve addition.

   B. The student incorrectly thinks that proportions involve subtraction.

   C. Correct answer

   D. The student switches 40 and 27 in the proportion, resulting in a proportion that is not equivalent to the original proportion.

5. **F.** The student chooses the least possible answer, because the inequality symbol is *less than*.

   G. The student does not switch the inequality sign when dividing the inequality by a negative number and gets $y < -2$.

   H. The student solves the problem as an equation instead of an inequality.

   I. Correct answer

6. **Gridded Response:** Correct answer: $\frac{1}{16}$, or 6.25%

   Common error: The student finds the probability that the arrow will stop in a yellow section one time instead of two times and gets an answer of $\frac{1}{4}$, or 25%.

Cumulative Practice

3. H
4. C
5. I
6. $\frac{1}{16}$, or 6.25%

Cumulative Practice

7. A

8. H

9. *Part A* favorable outcomes: 3
possible outcomes: 6

Part B $\frac{1}{4}$, or 25%

10. B

11. G

Item Analysis (continued)

7. **A.** Correct answer

   B. The student thinks that 25% = $25 and subtracts $25 from $123.75.

   C. The student thinks that 25% = $0.25 and either adds $0.25 to or subtracts $0.25 from $123.75.

   D. The student thinks that 25% = $25 and adds $25 to $123.75.

8. **F.** The student finds what percent $6 is of $15.

   G. The student subtracts $6 from $15 to get $9 and thinks this means 90%.

   H. Correct answer

   I. The student finds what percent $15 is of $6.

9. **2 points** The student's work and explanations demonstrate a thorough understanding of finding probability. In Part A, the student finds the number of favorable outcomes is 3 and the number of possible outcomes is 6. In Part B, the student finds the probability is $\frac{1}{4}$, or 25%. The student provides clear and complete work and explanations.

   1 point The student's work and explanations demonstrate a partial but limited understanding of finding probability. The student finds the correct answers for Part A, but the answer for Part B is incorrect. The student shows some correct work and explanation.

   0 points The student provides no response, a completely incorrect or incomprehensible response, or a response that demonstrates insufficient understanding of finding probability.

10. **A.** The student finds the interest earned instead of the balance.

    B. Correct answer

    C. The student incorrectly writes 5% as 0.5 in the simple interest formula.

    D. The student does not write the interest rate as a decimal in the simple interest formula and finds the interest earned for a 500% interest rate instead of the balance.

11. **F.** The student divides incorrectly or converts measures incorrectly to choose an incorrect box.

    G. Correct answer

    H. The student divides incorrectly or converts measures incorrectly to choose an incorrect box.

    I. The student divides incorrectly or converts measures incorrectly to choose an incorrect box.

7. A pair of running shoes is on sale for 25% off the original price. Which price is closest to the sale price of the running shoes?

   A. $93 **B.** $99

   C. $124 **D.** $149

8. The value of a baseball card was $6 when it was sold. The value of this card is now $15. What is the percent increase in the value of the card?

   F. 40% **G.** 90%

   H. 150% **I.** 250%

9. You roll a number cube twice. You want to roll two even numbers.

   Part A Find the number of favorable outcomes and the number of possible outcomes of each roll.

   Part B Find the probability of rolling two even numbers. Explain your reasoning.

10. You put $600 into an account. The account earns 5% simple interest per year. What is the balance after 4 years?

   A. $120 **B.** $720

   C. $1800 **D.** $12,600

11. You are comparing the prices of four boxes of cereal. Two of the boxes contain free extra cereal.

   • Box F costs $3.59 and contains 16 ounces.
   • Box G costs $3.79 and contains 16 ounces, plus an additional 10% for free.
   • Box H costs $4.00 and contains 500 grams.
   • Box I costs $4.69 and contains 500 grams, plus an additional 20% for free.

   Which box has the least unit cost?

   F. Box F **G.** Box G

   H. Box H **I.** Box I

C Statistics

- **C.1** Samples and Populations
- **C.2** Using Random Samples to Describe Populations
- **C.3** Comparing Populations
- **C.4** Using Random Samples to Compare Populations

Chapter Learning Target:
Understand statistics.

Chapter Success Criteria:
- I can determine the validity of a conclusion.
- I can explain variability in samples of a population.
- I can solve a problem using statistics.
- I can compare populations.

STEAM Video: "Comparing Dogs"

Laurie's Notes

Chapter C Overview

In earlier grades, students' study of *measurement and data* was focused on collecting and displaying data in bar graphs, line plots, and picture graphs. In the previous course, students learned about statistical questions, collecting and summarizing data, and discussing distributions of data in dot plots, histograms, and box-and-whisker plots.

This chapter builds on prior work with single data distributions. Two data distributions are compared to answer questions about the differences between the populations. Collecting data through the process of random sampling is a big idea in this chapter. To describe populations and draw valid conclusions, students need to read critically and consider how the data was collected.

Example:
A power company has proposed the construction of a new power line in the northern region of a state to meet the demands of customers in a neighboring state. They surveyed 1000 randomly chosen customers to gauge their support of the project. The table shows the results of the survey.

Support	Do Not Support	Undecided
680	194	126

Is the sample *biased* or *unbiased*? What conclusions can be drawn from the data? Students should recognize that the sample may be biased if none of the customers surveyed are from the northern region of the state, where the power line would be constructed.

The last two lessons examine the visual overlap of two numerical data distributions (double box-and-whisker plots, double dot plots, back-to-back stem-and-leaf plots) to draw informal inferences about the populations. In the power line example, the data is categorical. If customers from each state were asked about the cost of electricity (maximum price per kilowatt-hour), then the data would be numerical and there would be two populations. You can compare the measures of center and variability for each population and consider conclusions that can be drawn.

The mathematics of this chapter is not difficult, however, the language can be challenging. Continue to focus students' understanding on the bigger ideas: measures of center, variability, and random sampling.

Suggested Pacing

Chapter Opener	1 Day
Section 1	1 Day
Section 2	1 Day
Section 3	2 Days
Section 4	2 Days
Connecting Concepts	1 Day
Chapter Review	1 Day
Chapter Test	1 Day
Total Chapter C	**10 Days**
Year-to-Date	33 Days

Chapter Learning Target
Understand statistics.

Chapter Success Criteria
- Determine the validity of a conclusion.
- Explain variability in samples of a population.
- Solve a problem using statistics.
- Compare populations.

Chapter C Learning Targets and Success Criteria

Section	Learning Target	Success Criteria
C.1 Samples and Populations	Understand how to use random samples to make conclusions about a population.	• Explain why a sample is biased or unbiased. • Explain why conclusions made from a biased sample may not be valid. • Use an unbiased sample to make a conclusion about a population.
C.2 Using Random Samples to Describe Populations	Understand variability in samples of a population.	• Use multiple random samples to make conclusions about a population. • Use multiple random samples to examine variation in estimates.
C.3 Comparing Populations	Compare populations using measures of center and variation.	• Find the measures of center and variation of a data set. • Describe the visual overlap of two data distributions numerically. • Determine whether there is a significant difference in the measures of center of two data sets.
C.4 Using Random Samples to Compare Populations	Use random samples to compare populations.	• Compare random samples using measures of center and variation. • Recognize whether random samples are likely to be representative of a population. • Compare populations using multiple random samples.

Progressions

Through the Grades

Grade 6	Grade 7	Grade 8
• Recognize statistical questions as ones anticipating variability. • Recognize that a measure of center for a numerical data set summarizes all of its values with a single number, and a measure of variation describes how its values vary with a single number. • Display data on number lines, including dot plots, stem-and-leaf plots, histograms, and box-and-whisker plots. • Use measures of center to summarize all of the values in a data set with a single number, and use measures of variation to summarize how all of the values in a data set vary with a single number. • Choose appropriate measures of center and variation based on shape.	• Understand representative samples (random samples) and populations. • Use samples to draw inferences about populations. • Compare two populations from random samples using measures of center and variability.	• Construct and interpret scatter plots. • Find and assess lines of fit for scatter plots. • Construct and interpret a two-way table summarizing data. Use relative frequencies to describe possible association between the two variables.

Through the Chapter

Standard	C.1	C.2	C.3	C.4
Understand that statistics can be used to gain information about a population by examining a sample of the population; generalizations about a population from a sample are valid only if the sample is representative of that population. Understand that random sampling tends to produce representative samples and support valid inferences.	★			
Use data from a random sample to draw inferences about a population with an unknown characteristic of interest. Generate multiple samples (or simulated samples) of the same size to gauge the variation in estimates or predictions.	●	●		★
Informally assess the degree of visual overlap of two numerical data distributions with similar variabilities, measuring the difference between the centers by expressing it as a multiple of a measure of variability.			★	
Use measures of center and measures of variability for numerical data from random samples to draw informal comparative inferences about two populations.				★

Key
▲ = preparing ★ = complete
● = learning ■ = extending

Laurie's Notes

STEAM Video

STEAM Video

1. The population is Devo and Etta because they are the only dogs shown in the video. A sample is just Devo, because Devo is one of the dogs in the population.

2. **a.** *Sample answer:* One sample is Golden Retriever. Golden Retrievers are one group of dogs in the *Canis lupus* species.

   b. You would use a sample because it is not possible to measure every single animal.

   c. The *Canis lupus* species is one group of animals. So, the species is a sample of all animals.

Before the Video
- To introduce the STEAM Video, read aloud the first paragraph of Comparing Dogs and discuss the question with your students.
- ❓ "How are dogs and wolves similar?"

During the Video
- The video shows two people discussing different characteristics that dogs can have.
- ❓ Pause the video at 1:46 and ask, "How can you classify species?" By studying breeding patterns, bone patterns, or DNA.
- Watch the remainder of the video.

After the Video
- Have students work with a partner to answer Questions 1 and 2.
- As students discuss and answer the questions, listen for understanding of populations and samples.

Performance Task

Sample answer: to see how the groups are similar or different

Performance Task
- Use this information to spark students' interest and promote thinking about real-life problems.
- ❓ Ask, "Why might a researcher want to compare data from two different groups of wildlife?"
- After completing the chapter, students will have gained the knowledge needed to complete "Estimating Animal Populations."

Mathematical Practices

Students have opportunities to develop aspects of the mathematical practices throughout the chapter. Here are some examples.

1. **Make Sense of Problems and Persevere in Solving Them**
   C.3 Exercise 14, *p. 580*

2. **Reason Abstractly and Quantitatively**
   C.2 Math Practice note, *p. 572*

3. **Construct Viable Arguments and Critique the Reasoning of Others**
   C.3 Exercise 11, *p. 580*

4. **Model with Mathematics**
   C.2 Exercise 13, *p. 574*

5. **Use Appropriate Tools Strategically**
   C.3 Math Practice note *p. 575*

6. **Attend to Precision**
   C.1 Math Practice note, *p. 564*

7. **Look for and Make Use of Structure**
   C.3 Math Practice note, *p. 576*

8. **Look for and Express Regularity in Repeated Reasoning**
   C.1 Math Practice note, *p. 563*

STEAM Video

Comparing Dogs

Although dogs and wolves are the same species, they can have very different characteristics. How are dogs and wolves similar?

Watch the STEAM Video "Comparing Dogs." Then answer the following questions.

1. In the video, the dogs Devo and Etta are walking in a park. Describe the *population* of the dogs shown in the video. Then describe a *sample* of the dogs shown in the video. Explain your reasoning.

2. Dogs, wolves, and dingos are all the same species. This species is called *Canis lupus*.

   a. Describe one possible sample of the *Canis lupus* species. Explain your reasoning.

   b. You want to know the average height of an animal in the Canis lupus species. Would you use the entire population of the species or would you use a sample to gather data? Explain.

   c. The entire *Canis lupus* species is a sample of what population? Explain.

Performance Task

Estimating Animal Populations

After completing this chapter, you will be able to use the concepts you learned to answer the questions in the *STEAM Video Performance Task*. You will be given a double box-and-whisker plot that represents the weights of male and female gray wolves.

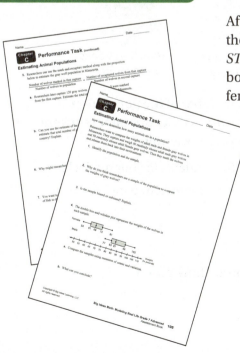

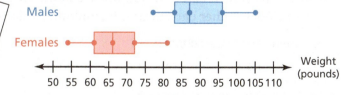

You will be asked to compare the weights of male and female gray wolves. Why might a researcher want to compare data from two different groups of wildlife?

561

Getting Ready for Chapter

Chapter Exploration

A **population** is an entire group of people or objects. A **sample** is a part of the population. You can use a sample to make an *inference*, or conclusion about a population.

Identify a population. → Select a sample. → Interpret the data in the sample. → Make an inference about the population.

Population → Sample → Interpretation → Inference

1. Work with a partner. Identify the population and the sample in each pair.

   a.

   The students in a school   The students in a math class

   b.

   The grizzly bears with GPS collars in a park   The grizzly bears in a park

   c.

   150 quarters   All quarters in circulation

   d.

   All fiction books in the library   10 fiction books in the library

2. Work with a partner. When a sample is random, each member of the population is equally likely to be selected. You want to know the favorite activity of students at your school. Tell whether each sample is random. Explain your reasoning.

   a. members of the school band
   b. students in your math class
   c. students who enter your school in a morning
   d. school newspaper readers

Vocabulary

The following vocabulary terms are defined in this chapter. Think about what each term might mean and record your thoughts.

population   unbiased sample
sample   biased sample

Laurie's Notes

Check out the digital flash cards.
BigIdeasMath.com

Chapter Exploration

- Ask a volunteer to read the paragraph at the top of the page.
- Discuss the meanings of *population* and *sample*. Give a few examples of each. Then ask volunteers to share their own examples.
- Have pairs complete Exercise 1 and then compare their answers with another pair. Discuss any discrepancies as a class.
- Ask a volunteer to read Exercise 2 and then discuss the meaning of the word *random*.
- Have pairs complete Exercise 2 and then compare their answers with another pair. Discuss any discrepancies as a class.

ELL Support

Students may be familiar with the word *sample* from everyday life. If they are familiar with samples, have students share their experiences. Explain that a sample may be a small taste of food, a small card with a paint color, or a small swatch of cloth. All are examples that give you an idea of what a larger amount of the substance or material is like. When working with samples in statistics, you look at a small part of a larger group. That small part gives you an idea of what the larger group is like.

Vocabulary

- These terms represent some of the vocabulary that students will encounter in Chapter C. Discuss the terms as a class.
- Where have students heard the term *population* outside of a math classroom? In what contexts?
- Allowing students to discuss these terms now will prepare them for understanding the terms as they are presented in the chapter.
- When students encounter a new definition, encourage them to write in their *Student Journals*. They will revisit these definitions during the Chapter Review.

Topics for Review

- Box-and-Whisker Plots
- Dot Plots
- Measures of Center
- Measures of Variation
- Stem-and-Leaf Plots

Chapter Exploration

1. a. Population: the students in a school
      Sample: the students in a math class

   b. Population: the grizzly bears in a park
      Sample: the grizzly bears with GPS collars in a park

   c. Population: all quarters in circulation
      Sample: 150 quarters

   d. Population: all books in a library
      Sample: 10 fiction books

2. a. no; Not every student in your school is equally likely to be selected. Not all students are in the band.

   b. no; Not every student in your school is equally likely to be selected. You are only surveying students from one class.

   c. yes; Every student in school is equally likely to be selected.

   d. no; Not every student in your school is equally likely to be selected. Not all students may read the school newspaper.

T-562

Learning Target
Understand how to use random samples to make conclusions about a population.

Success Criteria
- Explain why a sample is biased or unbiased.
- Explain why conclusions made from a biased sample may not be valid.
- Use an unbiased sample to make a conclusion about a population.

Warm Up
Cumulative, vocabulary, and prerequisite skills practice opportunities are available in the *Resources by Chapter* or at BigIdeasMath.com.

ELL Support
Students may know the word *population* from geography or science class. In everyday life, it is most commonly used to describe the number of people living in an area. In science, it refers to the number of individuals of the same species (plants or animals) living in an area. When used in mathematics, *population* refers to the entire group of people or objects from which statistical information is being collected.

Exploration 1
1. a. Population: all students at your school; *Sample answer:* boys, girls, your art class, band members, basketball players

    b. *Sample answer:* In all of the samples, each member of the population is not equally likely to be selected.

    c–d. See Additional Answers.

T-563

Laurie's Notes

Check out the Dynamic Classroom.
BigIdeasMath.com

Preparing to Teach
- In the previous course, students answered simple statistical questions about a data set. In the previous chapter, they learned the basics of probability that provide the foundation for studying statistics. Students need to understand that a sample must be randomly selected from equally likely choices to make a valid conclusion.
- **Construct Viable Arguments and Critique the Reasoning of Others:** Mathematically proficient students understand and use stated assumptions and previously established results in constructing arguments. They reason about data and make plausible arguments that take into account the context from which the data arose.

Motivate
- Conduct a quick survey of your class. Ask a couple of fun questions and then ask a question related to math.
  - How many of you can roll your tongue?
  - Who likes spicy brown mustard better than yellow mustard?
  - Can you simplify a fraction?
- Discuss each of the questions: Who would ask the question? Why might the question be asked? Point out the following:
  - Tongue rolling is a frequently used example of a simple genetic trait.
  - The second question doesn't allow an option for a person who dislikes both mustards to answer.
  - Teachers frequently survey students to help guide instruction.
- Define **population** and **sample**. For this survey, the students in the school could be the *population* and the students in your class are the *sample*.
- Remind students that a survey is not the only way you can collect data from a sample, but it is likely the most common method.

Exploration 1
- "What are the characteristics of a random sample?" Answers will vary.
- List all of the suggested samples on the board. Discuss whether each sample provides a random, equally likely selection. A sample selected *at random* is also called a *random sample*. Students should explain their reasoning.
- "Why do you think a sample is taken instead of trying to survey an entire population?" It may take too long or be impossible.
- When discussing part (c), point out that the second sample uses ratio language. This is intentional, as students will use ratio reasoning to make conclusions about populations later in the lesson.
- When students are finished, ask volunteers to share their survey questions. Discuss each question and suggested sample. Students should be deciding if the sampling method will result in a random sample. Utilize *Talk Moves*.
- **Extension:** Ask students to conduct their surveys and display their results. Then ask, "Would you change any part of your survey to make it more accurate? Explain." Answers will vary.

C.1 Samples and Populations

Learning Target: Understand how to use random samples to make conclusions about a population.

Success Criteria:
- I can explain why a sample is biased or unbiased.
- I can explain why conclusions made from a biased sample may not be valid.
- I can use an unbiased sample to make a conclusion about a population.

A **population** is an entire group of people or objects. A **sample** is a part of a population. You can gain information about a population by examining samples of the population.

EXPLORATION 1
Using Samples of Populations

Work with a partner. You want to make conclusions about the favorite extracurricular activities of students at your school.

a. Identify the population. Then identify five samples of the population.

b. When a sample is selected *at random*, each member of the population is equally likely to be selected. Are any of the samples in part (a) selected at random? Explain your reasoning.

c. How are the samples below different? Is each conclusion valid? Explain your reasoning.

You ask 20 members of the school band about their favorite activity. The diagram shows the results. You conclude that band is the favorite activity of 70% of the students in your school.

Favorite Activity

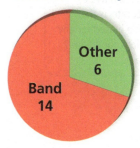

Band 14
Other 6

You ask every eighth student who enters the school about their favorite activity. One student says glee club for every nine that name a different activity. You conclude that glee club is the favorite activity of 10% of the students in your school.

Math Practice

Maintain Oversight

Can the size of a sample affect the validity of a conclusion about a population? Explain.

d. **CHOOSE TOOLS** Write a survey question about a topic that interests you. How can you choose people to survey so that you can use the results to make a valid conclusion?

Section C.1 Samples and Populations 563

C.1 Lesson

Key Vocabulary
population, *p. 563*
sample, *p. 563*
unbiased sample, *p. 564*
biased sample, *p. 564*

An **unbiased sample** is representative of a population. It is selected at random and is large enough to provide accurate data.

A **biased sample** is not representative of a population. One or more parts of the population are favored over others.

EXAMPLE 1   Identifying an Unbiased Sample

You want to estimate the number of students in a high school who ride a bus to school. Which sample is unbiased?

- **A.** 4 students in the hallway
- **B.** all students on the soccer team
- **C.** 50 twelfth-grade students at random
- **D.** 100 students at random during lunch

Choice A is not large enough to provide accurate data.

Choice B is not selected at random.

Choice C is not representative of the population because twelfth-grade students are favored over other students.

Choice D is representative of the population because it is selected at random and is large enough to provide accurate data.

▸ So, the correct answer is **D**.

Math Practice

Communicate Precisely
Explain why conclusions made from the sample in Choice C may be inaccurate. Is the sample biased for any possible population? Explain.

Try It

1. **WHAT IF?** You want to estimate the number of twelfth-grade students in a high school who ride a bus to school. Which sample is unbiased? Explain.

2. You want to estimate the number of eighth-grade students in your school who find it relaxing to listen to music. You consider two samples.

   - fifteen randomly selected members of the band
   - every fifth student whose name appears on an alphabetical list of eighth-grade students

   Which sample is unbiased? Explain.

Laurie's Notes

Scaffolding Instruction
- Students identified samples and populations in the exploration. Now they will identify biased and unbiased samples and determine if a sample can be used to draw conclusions and make predictions about a population.
- **Emerging:** Students need practice distinguishing between biased and unbiased samples and using samples to make conclusions. They will benefit from guided instruction for the examples.
- **Proficient:** Students understand how to identify samples and populations. They need to review the definitions and examples to understand the difference between biased and unbiased samples. Then have students complete the Try It and Self-Assessment exercises.

Discuss
- Define **unbiased sample** and **biased sample**. Give a few examples of each. Then ask students to write the definitions in their own words and share an example of each type of sample.
- The size of a sample can have a great influence on the results. A sample that is not large enough may not be unbiased and a sample that is too large may be too cumbersome to use. As a rule of thumb, a sample of 30 is usually large enough to provide accurate data for modest population sizes.

EXAMPLE 1
- Work through the problem and discuss why the first three samples are not reasonable.
- ? "What other samples might not be reasonable?" Answers will vary.

Try It
- ? "How has the population changed in Exercise 1?" The population was students in a high school but now it is just twelfth-grade students.
- **Neighbor Check:** Have students work independently and then have their neighbors check their work. Have students discuss any discrepancies using *Accountable Language Stems*.
- ? "Why is selecting every fifth student from an alphabetized list considered random?" *Sample answer:* Because the list includes all of the population and an alphabetized list has no bias related to listening to music.
- ? "If the list was the names of all band members would it be unbiased? Explain." No, it is not representative of the population because band students are favored.

ELL Support
Have students work in groups to complete Try It Exercises 1 and 2. Have them discuss the questions: Does the sample represent the whole population? Is it random? Expect students to perform according to their language levels.

Beginner: State "yes," "no," or one-word answers to the guiding questions.

Intermediate: Use simple sentences such as, "It is not representative."

Advanced: Use detailed sentences such as, "Four students in the hallway is not representative because it is not large enough to provide accurate data."

Formative Assessment Tip

Accountable Language Stems
Students are often asked to discuss their ideas and any discrepancies, but they may not understand what you are asking them to do. *Accountable Language Stems* help students resist the urge to say anything that comes to mind, while challenging them to check the quality of claims and arguments in a respectful manner. You can provide specific sentence stems for a particular problem or post various stems around the room for students to refer to.

Examples:
- "I agree with ___ because ___."
- "I disagree with ___ because ___."
- "I'm not sure I agree with what ___ said, because ___."
- "I can see that ___; however, I disagree with ___."
- "I'm not sure I understood you when you said ___. Could you say more about that?"
- "I want to know more about ___."

Accountable Language Stems help student learn to "talk" with their partners or neighbors. They also support class discussions.

Extra Example 1
You want to estimate the number of students in your school who start their math homework right after school. Which sample is unbiased?

A. every tenth student who arrives in the school

B. 3 students in the cafeteria

C. all students in the math club

D. 40 sixth-grade students at random

A

Try It
1. C
2. second sample; It is selected at random and is large enough to provide accurate data.

Extra Example 2

You want to know how the residents of your town feel about a ban on texting while driving. Determine whether each conclusion is valid.

a. You survey 200 residents at random. The table shows the results. You conclude that 82% of the residents of your town support the ban.

Ban on Texting	
Support	164
Do Not Support	36

The sample is unbiased, and the conclusion is valid.

b. You survey the first 15 residents who drive into your neighborhood. The diagram shows the results. You conclude that $33\frac{1}{3}$% of the residents of your town support the ban.

Ban on Texting

The sample is biased, and the conclusion is not valid.

Try It

3. no; The sample is biased because it is not large enough and it is not representative of the residents of the town.

Self-Assessment for Concepts & Skills

4. biased; *Sample answer:* The sample is not representative of all students in your school.

5. yes; *Sample answer:* The sample is representative of the population, selected at random, and large enough to produce accurate data.

Laurie's Notes

EXAMPLE 2

- **Construct Viable Arguments and Critique the Reasoning of Others:** Ask a volunteer to read part (a). Then ask whether the conclusion is valid. Students should recognize that the sample is biased because the survey was not random—you only surveyed nearby residents.
- Ask a volunteer to read part (b). Then ask whether the conclusion is valid. Students should recognize that the sample is random and large enough to provide accurate data, so it is an unbiased sample.
- **Extension:** "If there are 2000 residents in the town, then how many would you expect to be in favor of the new landfill?" 40% of 2000, or 800 residents

Try It

- **Think-Pair-Share:** Students should read the exercise independently and then work in pairs to complete the exercise. Then have each pair compare their answer with another pair and discuss any discrepancies. Encourage students to use *Accountable Language Stems*.
- Use *Popsicle Sticks* to solicit responses.

✓ Self-Assessment for Concepts & Skills

- Divide students into 3 or 6 groups. Assign each group a success criterion. Allow time for groups to prepare an explanation or example of the success criterion they were assigned. Then have each group present their explanation or example to the class.
- **Think-Pair-Share:** Students should read each exercise independently and then work in pairs to complete the exercises. Then have each pair compare their answers with another pair and discuss any discrepancies.

The Success Criteria Self-Assessment chart can be found in the *Student Journal* or online at *BigIdeasMath.com*.

ELL Support

Have students work as described in Laurie's Notes, working in groups and pairs to practice language. Ask groups to present their explanations for Exercise 4 to the class. For Exercise 5, ask students if *80% of the audience members support production of a new musical* is valid and have students use a thumbs up to answer *yes* or a thumbs down to answer *no*. Discuss students' explanations as a class.

The results of an unbiased sample are proportional to the results of the population. So, you can use unbiased samples to make conclusions about a population. Biased samples are not representative of a population. So, you should not use them to make conclusions about a population.

EXAMPLE 2 Determining Whether Conclusions Are Valid

You want to know how the residents of your town feel about adding a new landfill. Determine whether each conclusion is valid.

a. **You survey the 100 residents who live closest to the new landfill. The diagram shows the results. You conclude that 10% of the residents of your town support the new landfill.**

The sample is not representative of the population because residents who live close to the landfill may be less likely to support it.

▸ So, the sample is biased, and the conclusion is not valid.

New Landfill	
Support	40
Do Not Support	60

b. **You survey 100 residents at random. The table shows the results. You conclude that 60% of the residents of your town do not support the new landfill.**

The sample is representative of the population because it is selected at random and is large enough to provide accurate data.

▸ So, the sample is unbiased, and the conclusion is valid.

Try It

3. Four out of five randomly chosen teenagers support the new landfill. So, you conclude that 80% of the residents of your town support the new landfill. Is the conclusion valid? Explain.

Self-Assessment for Concepts & Skills

Solve each exercise. Then rate your understanding of the success criteria in your journal.

4. **WRITING** You want to estimate the number of students in your school who play a school sport. You ask 40 honors students at random whether they play a school sport. Is this sample biased or unbiased? Explain.

5. **ANALYZING A CONCLUSION** You survey 50 randomly chosen audience members at a theater about whether the theater should produce a new musical. The diagram shows the results. You conclude that 80% of the audience members support production of a new musical. Is your conclusion valid? Explain.

EXAMPLE 3   Modeling Real Life

You ask 75 randomly chosen students at a school how many movies they watch each week. There are 1200 students in the school. Estimate the number of students in the school who watch one movie each week.

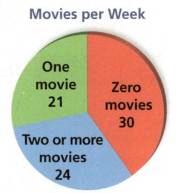

Movies per Week
- One movie: 21
- Zero movies: 30
- Two or more movies: 24

Understand the problem.

You are given the numbers of movies watched each week by a sample of 75 students. You are asked to make an estimate about the population, all students in the school.

Make a plan.

The sample is representative of the population because it is selected at random and is large enough to provide accurate data. So, the sample is unbiased and its results are proportional to the results of the population. Use a ratio table to estimate the number of students in the school who watch one movie each week.

Solve and check.

×4   ×4

Students (one movie)	21	84	336
Total Students	75	300	1200

×4   ×4

Another Method
Use a proportion.
$$\frac{21}{75} = \frac{n}{1200}$$
$$336 = n \checkmark$$

So, about 336 students in the school watch one movie each week.

Self-Assessment for Problem Solving

Solve each exercise. Then rate your understanding of the success criteria in your journal.

6. You want to estimate the mean photo size on your cell phone. You choose 30 photos at random from your phone. The total size of the sample is 186 megabytes. Explain whether you can use the sample to estimate the mean size of photos on your cell phone. If so, what is your estimate?

7. **DIG DEEPER!** You ask 50 randomly chosen employees of a company how many books they read each month. The diagram shows the results. There are 600 people employed by the company. Estimate the number of employees who read at least one book each month.

Books per Month
- Zero books: 14
- One book: 19
- Two books: 7
- Three or more books: 10

Laurie's Notes

EXAMPLE 3

- Read and discuss the information given.
- ❓ "Why is this sample unbiased?" The sample is representative of the population, the students were selected at random, and the sample is large enough to provide accurate data.
- ❓ "How many students were surveyed?" 75 students "How many of them watch one movie each week?" 21 students
- Create a ratio table to solve the problem as shown.
- Discuss the Another Method note and step through the ratio reasoning used to write the proportion.
  - Because the sample is unbiased,
    the ratio of (students in the sample that watched one movie) : (total students in the sample)
    is proportional to
    the ratio of (students in the school that watched one movie) : (total students in the school).
    So, the values of these ratios must be equal.

    $$\frac{\text{students in sample (one movie)}}{\text{total students in sample}} = \frac{\text{students in school (one movie)}}{\text{total students in school}}$$

- ❓ "What steps are needed to arrive at the answer, $336 = n$?" Use the Cross Products Property and then the Division Property of Equality or multiply each side by 1200 (Multiplication Property of Equality).
- ❓ "Can you think of any other methods for solving this problem?" Students may suggest calculating the percent of the sample that watch one movie (28%) and then finding 28% of the total students in the school.
- ❓ **Extension:** "How can you find the number of students that watched zero movies each week?" *Sample answer:* Make a ratio table similar to the table for students that watched one movie and then multiply both quantities by 16.

✓ Self-Assessment for Problem Solving

- The goal for all students is to feel comfortable with the problem-solving plan. It is important for students to problem-solve in class, where they may receive support from you and their peers. Keep in mind that some students may only be ready for the first step.
- Students should complete the problems independently before sharing with a group.

The Success Criteria Self-Assessment chart can be found in the *Student Journal* or online at *BigIdeasMath.com*.

Closure

- **Exit Ticket:** What survey question would you ask to find out what vegetable should be served more often for the lunch program at your school? What would be your sample? *Answers will vary.* If a sample only includes students, discuss whether that is really an unbiased sample.

Extra Example 3

You ask 50 randomly chosen students at a school to name their favorite sport. There are 600 students in the school. Estimate the number of students in the school who would name soccer as their favorite sport.

Favorite Sport	Number of Students
Football	8
Soccer	12
Basketball	20
Baseball	10

144 students

Self-Assessment for Problem Solving

6. yes; The photos are chosen at random and the sample size is large enough to produce accurate data; 6.2 megabytes

7. 432 employees

Learning Target

Understand how to use random samples to make conclusions about a population.

Success Criteria

- Explain why a sample is biased or unbiased.
- Explain why conclusions made from a biased sample may not be valid.
- Use an unbiased sample to make a conclusion about a population.

Review & Refresh

1. Answers will vary, but the theoretical probability is $\frac{9}{50}$, 0.18, or 18%.

2. Answers will vary, but the theoretical probability is $\frac{8}{25}$, 0.32, or 32%.

3. $x < 7$
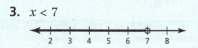

4. $q \geq -3$

5. $r > \frac{4}{3}$

Concepts, Skills, & Problem Solving

6. no; $\frac{20}{50} = 0.4 = 40\%$

7. yes; $\frac{5}{50} = 0.1 = 10\%$

8. Population: Residents of New Jersey
   Sample: Residents of Ocean County

9. Population: All cards in a deck
   Sample: 4 cards

10. unbiased; The sample is representative of the population, selected at random, and large enough to provide accurate data.

11. biased; The sample is not representative of the population because people who go to a park are more likely to think that the park needs to be remodeled.

Assignment Guide and Concept Check

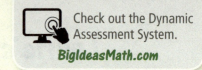

Check out the Dynamic Assessment System.
BigIdeasMath.com

Scaffold assignments to support all students in their learning progression. The suggested assignments are a starting point. Continue to assign additional exercises and revisit with spaced practice to move every student toward proficiency.

Level	Assignment 1	Assignment 2
Emerging	2, 5, 6, 8, 10, 14	7, 9, 11, 12, 13, 15, 17, 18
Proficient	2, 5, 6, 7, 8, 9, 10, 11, 14, 15	12, 13, 16, 17, 18, 19
Advanced	2, 5, 6, 7, 8, 9, 10, 11, 14, 15	12, 13, 16, 17, 19, 20

- Assignment 1 is for use after students complete the Self-Assessment for Concepts & Skills.
- Assignment 2 is for use after students complete the Self-Assessment for Problem Solving.
- The red exercises can be used as a concept check.

Review & Refresh Prior Skills

Exercises 1 and 2 Simulating Outcomes
Exercises 3–5 Solving a Two-Step Inequality

Common Errors

- **Exercises 8 and 9** Students may get confused with the words *population* and *sample*. Encourage students to think about what it means to eat a sample of something and then compare the whole to the population.

T-567

C.1 Practice

Go to BigIdeasMath.com to get HELP with solving the exercises.

Review & Refresh

Design a simulation that you can use to model the situation. Then use your simulation to find the experimental probability.

1. The probability that a meal at a restaurant is overcooked is 10%. Estimate the probability that exactly 1 of the next 2 meals is overcooked.

2. The probability that you see a butterfly during a nature center tour is 80%. The probability that you see a turtle is 40%. What is the probability of seeing both?

Solve the inequality. Graph the solution.

3. $2x - 5 < 9$
4. $5q + 2 \geq -13$
5. $2 > 6 - 3r$

Concepts, Skills, & Problem Solving

USING SAMPLES OF POPULATIONS You ask 50 randomly chosen artists in your town about their favorite art form. Determine whether your conclusion is valid. Justify your answer. *(See Exploration 1, p. 563.)*

6. You conclude that drawing is the favorite art form of 60% of artists in your town.

7. You conclude that ceramics is the favorite art form of 10% of people in your town.

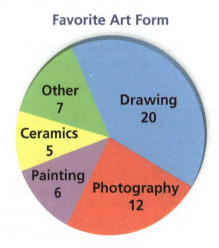

Favorite Art Form
- Other 7
- Drawing 20
- Ceramics 5
- Painting 6
- Photography 12

IDENTIFYING POPULATIONS AND SAMPLES Identify the population and the sample.

8.
Residents of New Jersey | Residents of Ocean County

9.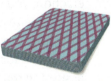
4 cards | All cards in a deck

IDENTIFYING BIASED AND UNBIASED SAMPLES Determine whether the sample is *biased* or *unbiased*. Explain.

10. You want to estimate the number of books students in your school read over the summer. You survey every fourth student who enters the school.

11. You want to estimate the number of people in a town who think that a park needs to be remodeled. You survey every 10th person who enters the park.

Section C.1   Samples and Populations   567

12. **MODELING REAL LIFE** You want to determine the number of students in your school who have visited a science museum. You survey 50 students at random. Twenty have visited a science museum, and thirty have not. So, you conclude that 40% of the students in your school have visited a science museum. Is your conclusion valid? Explain.

13. **USING A SAMPLE** Which sample is better for making an estimate? Explain.

Estimate the number of defective pencils produced per day.	
Sample A	A random sample of 500 pencils from 20 machines
Sample B	A random sample of 500 pencils from 1 machine

CONDUCTING SURVEYS Determine whether you should survey the population or a sample. Explain.

14. You want to know the average height of seventh graders in the United States.

15. You want to know the favorite types of music of students in your homeroom.

16. **CRITICAL THINKING** Does increasing the size of a sample necessarily make the sample more representative of a population? Give an example to support your explanation.

17. **LOGIC** A person surveys residents of a town to determine whether a skateboarding ban should be overturned. Describe how the person can conduct the survey so that the sample is biased toward overturning the ban.

Favorite Way to Eliminate Waste	
Reducing	14
Reusing	4
Recycling	2

18. **MODELING REAL LIFE** You ask 20 randomly chosen environmental scientists from your state to name their favorite way to eliminate waste. There are 200 environmental scientists in your state. Estimate the number of environmental scientists in your state whose favorite way to eliminate waste is recycling.

19. **MODELING REAL LIFE** To predict the result of a mayoral election, you survey 50 likely voters at random. The diagram shows the results. Describe whether the sample can be used to predict the outcome of the election. If so, what is your prediction for the number of votes received by the winner assuming that 500 people vote?

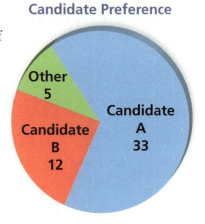

Number of Dogs	Frequency
1	54
2	38
3	3
4	1
5	4

20. **DIG DEEPER!** You ask 100 randomly chosen dog owners in your town how many dogs they own. The results are shown in the table. There are 500 dog owners in your town.

   a. Estimate the median number of dogs per dog owner in your town. Justify your answer.

   b. Estimate the mean number of dogs per dog owner in your town. Justify your answer.

Common Errors

- **Exercises 14 and 15** Students may not understand why you may or may not want to question the entire population for a survey. Ask them to estimate the population size for each survey and then ask if it would be reasonable to ask everyone in that population for a response.

Mini-Assessment

1. You want to estimate the number of students in your school who play a sport. You survey the first 10 students who arrive for lunch.
   a. Identify the population and the sample of your survey. all students in your school; first 10 students who arrive for lunch
   b. Determine whether the sample is *biased* or *unbiased*. Explain. biased; The sample is not selected at random and is not large enough to provide accurate data.

2. You ask 120 randomly chosen people at a stadium to name their favorite stadium food. There are about 50,000 people in the stadium. Estimate the number of people in the stadium whose favorite stadium food is nachos.

Favorite Stadium Food	
Nachos	24
Hot Dog	55
Peanuts	16
Popcorn	25

about 10,000 people

Section Resources

Surface Level	Deep Level
Resources by Chapter • Extra Practice • Reteach • Puzzle Time Student Journal • Self-Assessment • Practice Differentiating the Lesson Tutorial Videos Skills Review Handbook Skills Trainer	Resources by Chapter • Enrichment and Extension Graphic Organizers Dynamic Assessment System • Section Practice

Concepts, Skills, & Problem Solving

12. yes; The sample is representative of the population, selected at random, and large enough to provide accurate data. So, the sample is unbiased and the conclusion is valid.

13. Sample A; It is representative of the population.

14. a sample; It is much easier to collect sample data in this situation.

15. a population; There are few enough students in your homeroom to not make the surveying difficult.

16. no; You can have a large sample that is not representative of a population. *Sample answer:* You survey residents of a town about a new power plant being built, but you only survey residents who will live close to the power plant. This could result in a large sample that is not representative of the residents in the town.

17. *Sample answer:* The person could ask, "Do you agree with the town's unfair ban on skateboarding on public property?"

18. 20 environmental scientists

19. yes; The sample is representative of the population, selected at random, and large enough to provide accurate data; 330 votes

20. a. 1; Because 54 of the 100 dog owners sampled (over half) have 1 dog, you can conclude that the median is 1.

    b. 1.63 dogs per dog owner; $\dfrac{163 \text{ dogs}}{100 \text{ dog owners}} = 1.63$ dogs per dog owner

T-568

Learning Target
Understand variability in samples of a population.

Success Criteria
- Use multiple random samples to make conclusions about a population.
- Use multiple random samples to examine variation in estimates.

Warm Up
Cumulative, vocabulary, and prerequisite skills practice opportunities are available in the *Resources by Chapter* or at BigIdeasMath.com.

ELL Support
Explain that information among samples may vary. This means that the information can differ or change from sample to sample. Explain the difference between *vary* and *very*. The differences among samples are known as the variability. You may want to review the parts of speech – *vary* (verb), *variable* (adjective), *variability* (noun).

Exploration 1
a. a seventh grader that has visited a planetarium
b. Answers will vary.
c. Answers will vary.
d. Answers will vary, but will be close to the stated probability of 60%.

T-569

Laurie's Notes

Check out the Dynamic Classroom.
BigIdeasMath.com

Preparing to Teach
- Students have identified biased and unbiased samples and determined whether a sample can be used to draw conclusions and make predictions about a population. In this lesson, students will generate multiple samples of data and draw inferences about a population.

Motivate
- ❓ "Are you familiar with different groups that poll large groups of people?" Students may have heard of the Gallup Poll or Rasmussen Reports.
- ❓ "Have any of you or has someone you know ever been asked to participate in a survey, perhaps at the mall or on the telephone?" Answers will vary.
- Explain that in the exploration, students will compare multiple samples to make an inference about a population.

Teaching Strategy
You can mark uncooked beans with a permanent marker or soak them in a mixture of food coloring (red or blue works best). After soaking, allow the beans to air dry on newspaper. They will return to their original size. Fill bags with beans using a ratio of 6 to 4, marked to unmarked. Preparing the bags beforehand saves valuable class time and the bags of beans can be reused.

Exploration 1
- **Note:** You can substitute other materials for the packing peanuts, such as colored tiles, marbles, or uncooked beans (see the Teaching Strategy).
- The goal is for students to see that there will be variability in samples. They should have a sense of this from using simulations.
- There are no wrong answers in part (b), just data collection. It might be interesting to see what happens if each pair simulates a different number of students.
- For part (d), draw a large table on the board and have each pair record their percent. Students should begin to notice the variability in the percents.
- Students used dot plots in the previous course. You may need to remind them that a dot plot uses a number line to show the number of times each value in a data set occurs. Dot plots show the spread and distribution of a data set.

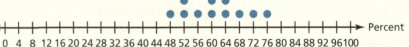

- After pairs create a dot plot, discuss the variation in the data as a class.
- ❓ "What percent of marked peanuts did you expect to have?" 60% "Why might the average of all the percents be closer to the expected percent than an individual pair's percent?" There are more random samples involved.
- Students will use technology to produce simulations with a large number of samples in Example 3. This will help them have an idea of how much variability to expect in certain situations.

C.2 Using Random Samples to Describe Populations

Learning Target: Understand variability in samples of a population.

Success Criteria:
- I can use multiple random samples to make conclusions about a population.
- I can use multiple random samples to examine variation in estimates.

EXPLORATION 1

Exploring Variability in Samples

Work with a partner. Sixty percent of all seventh graders have visited a planetarium.

a. Design a simulation using packing peanuts. Mark 60% of the packing peanuts and put them in a paper bag. What does choosing a marked peanut represent?

Math Practice

Make Conjectures
How many marked peanuts do you expect to draw in 30 trials? Explain your reasoning.

b. Simulate a sample of 25 students by choosing peanuts from the bag, replacing the peanut each time. Record the results.

c. Find the percent of students in the sample who have visited a planetarium. Compare this value to the actual percent of all seventh graders who have visited a planetarium.

d. Record the percent in part (c) from each pair in the class. Use a dot plot to display the data. Describe the variation in the data.

Section C.2 Using Random Samples to Describe Populations 569

C.2 Lesson

You have used unbiased samples to make conclusions about populations. Different samples often give slightly different conclusions due to variability in the sample data.

EXAMPLE 1   Using Multiple Random Samples

You and a group of friends want to know how many students in your school prefer pop music. There are 840 students in your school. Each person in the group randomly surveys 20 students. The table shows the results.

	Favorite Type of Music			
	Country	Pop	Rock	Rap
You	2	13	4	1
Friend A	3	8	7	2
Friend B	4	10	5	1
Friend C	5	10	4	1
Friend D	5	9	3	3

a. Use each sample to make an estimate for the number of students in your school who prefer pop music.

In your sample, 13 out of 20, or 65% of the students chose pop music. So, you can estimate that $0.65(840) = 546$ students in your school prefer pop music. Make estimates for the other samples.

	You	Friend A	Friend B	Friend C	Friend D
Estimate	546	336	420	420	378

 So, the estimates are that 336, 378, 420, 420, and 546 students prefer pop music.

b. Describe the center and the variation of the estimates.

 The estimates have a median of 420 students and a range of $546 - 336 = 210$ students.

Try It

1. Use each sample to make an estimate for the number of students in your school who prefer rap music. Describe the center and the variation of the estimates.

Laurie's Notes

Scaffolding Instruction

- In the exploration, students explored the variability in different samples of a population. Now they will discover that different samples may lead to different conclusions due to variability in the sample data.
- **Emerging:** Students may be able to find results of sampling but struggle in applying the information to make conclusions. They will benefit from guided instruction for the examples.
- **Proficient:** Students are able to conduct simulations and draw conclusions from the results. They understand the variability in the sample data. Students should review the examples before completing the Try It and Self-Assessment exercises.

Scaffold instruction to support all students in their learning. Learning is individualized and you may want to group students differently as they move in and out of these levels with each skill and concept. Student self-assessment and feedback help guide your instructional decisions about how and when to layer support for all students to become proficient learners.

EXAMPLE 1

- **Make Sense of Problems and Persevere in Solving Them:** Read the introduction and context for the problem. Make sure students understand that more than one random sample is being taken of the 840 students.
- ❓ "How can an unbiased sample be used to make an inference about a population?" Students may describe using a ratio table to make a population estimate, as they did in the previous section. The ratio table showed the proportionality involved. Now they will use a different strategy.
- Give sufficient time for students to use each sample to make an estimate.
- Use *Popsicle Sticks* to solicit an estimate for each sample.
- In part (b), the median and the range are used to describe the center and the variation of the estimates. Students studied these terms in the previous course, but they may need a quick review.
- ❓ "How do you find the median of a set of data?" Order the data and find the middle value or the mean of the two middle values.
- ❓ "What is the median of the estimates?" 420 students
- ❓ "What is the range of a set of data?" the difference between the greatest value and the least value
- ❓ "What is the range of the estimates?" 210 students

Try It

- Students should work with a partner.

ELL Support

After demonstrating Example 1, have students work in pairs to complete Try It Exercise 1. Have one student calculate the estimates for You and Friend A, while the other student calculates the estimates for Friends B, C, and D. Then have both students find the center and the variation of the estimates.

Beginner: Calculate and state numbers.

Intermediate: Use simple sentences such as, "In Friend B's sample, five percent prefer rap music."

Advanced: Use detailed sentences such as, "If five percent of the sample prefer rap music, then about forty-two students in your school prefer rap music."

Extra Example 1

You and a group of friends want to know how many students in your school prefer popcorn. There are 500 students in your school. Each person in the group randomly surveys 25 students. The table shows the results.

	Favorite Type of Snack		
	Nachos	Popcorn	Pretzels
You	15	9	1
Friend A	11	11	3
Friend B	13	7	5
Friend C	8	10	7

a. Use each sample to make an estimate for the number of students in your school who prefer popcorn. 140, 180, 200, and 220

b. Describe the center and the variation of the estimates. The estimates have a median of 190 students and a range of 80 students.

Try It

1. 42, 84, 42, 42, 126; median: 42 students; range: 84 students

Extra Example 2

You want to know the mean number of hours students spend studying each week. At each of five schools you randomly survey 12 students. Your results are shown.

Hours Spent Studying Each Week
A: 2, 4, 3, 5, 6, 7, 8, 4, 7, 4, 10, 6
B: 3, 8, 8, 9, 11, 3, 5, 7, 6, 10, 6, 8
C: 8, 5, 4, 9, 8, 7, 5, 10, 11, 8, 5, 4
D: 6, 7, 8, 9, 4, 3, 10, 8, 5, 6, 4, 8
E: 3, 7, 4, 5, 6, 5, 7, 12, 8, 5, 6, 4

a. Use each sample to make an estimate for the mean number of hours students spend studying each week. Describe the variation of the estimates. The estimates have a range of 1.5 hours.

b. Use all five samples to make one estimate for the mean number of hours students spend studying each week. 6.4 hours

Try It

2. a. 4.5, 7, 7.5, 8, 8, 8.5; range: 4 hours
   b. 7 hours

Self-Assessment
for Concepts & Skills

3. 168, 294, 210, 168, 126; median: 168 students; range: 168 students

4. $4.7\overline{6}$ hours

Laurie's Notes

EXAMPLE 2

- Discuss with students the description of the samples. The students surveyed all have part-time jobs and are from six different schools.
- In part (a), students are asked to describe the variation of the estimates, but first they must find the estimates by calculating the mean of each sample.
- Students calculated means in the previous course, but they may need a quick review. Remind students that mean, median, and mode are types of averages used in statistics.
- ? "How do you find the mean of a set of data?" Divide the sum of the data by the number of data values.
- **Use Appropriate Tools Strategically:** Students can use calculators to quickly find the mean of each sample.
- ? "What is the greatest estimate?" 9 hours "What is the least estimate?" 5 hours
- ? "What is the range of the estimates?" 4 hours
- Work through part (b) as shown.
- Students may realize that they can use the sums from part (a) to find the sum of data from all six samples.

Try It

- Students should solve this problem on whiteboards.

✓ Self-Assessment for Concepts & Skills

- ⊙ Remind students of how the Motivate mentioned polling large groups of people. The examples showed variations in estimates caused by variations in multiple random samples. Have students use *Think-Pair-Share* to discuss the following questions.
  - Who might want to poll large groups of people?
  - What information could they be trying to find?
  - How might they use that information?
  - How could their conclusions about a population be misleading?
- **Neighbor Check:** Have students complete Exercise 4 independently and then have their neighbors check their work. Have students discuss any discrepancies.

ELL Support

Allow students to work in pairs for extra support and to practice language. Have two pairs discuss their answers. Encourage questions and discussion. Monitor and provide support as needed. Have pairs display their estimates on whiteboards for your review. Discuss the answers as a class.

The Success Criteria Self-Assessment chart can be found in the *Student Journal* or online at *BigIdeasMath.com*.

EXAMPLE 2 Estimating an Average of a Population

Hours Worked Each Week
- A: 6, 8, 6, 6, 7, 4, 10, 8, 7, 8
- B: 10, 4, 4, 6, 8, 6, 7, 12, 8, 8
- C: 10, 9, 8, 6, 5, 8, 6, 6, 9, 10
- D: 4, 8, 4, 4, 5, 4, 4, 6, 5, 6
- E: 6, 8, 8, 6, 12, 4, 10, 8, 6, 12
- F: 10, 4, 8, 9, 6, 8, 7, 12, 16, 10

You want to know the mean number of hours students with part-time jobs work each week. At each of six schools you randomly survey 10 students with part-time jobs. Your results are shown.

a. **Use each sample to make an estimate for the mean number of hours students with part-time jobs work each week. Describe the variation of the estimates.**

Find the mean of each sample.

Sample	A	B	C	D	E	F
Mean	$\frac{70}{10}=7$	$\frac{73}{10}=7.3$	$\frac{77}{10}=7.7$	$\frac{50}{10}=5$	$\frac{80}{10}=8$	$\frac{90}{10}=9$

▶ So, the six estimates are that students with part-time jobs work 5, 7, 7.3, 7.7, 8, and 9 hours each week. The estimates have a range of $9 - 5 = 4$ hours.

b. **Use all six samples to make one estimate for the mean number of hours students with part-time jobs work each week.**

The mean of all sample data is $\frac{440}{60} = 7.\overline{3}$ hours.

▶ So, you can estimate that students with part-time jobs work $7.\overline{3}$ hours each week.

Try It

2. Repeat Example 2, but estimate the medians instead of the means.

Self-Assessment for Concepts & Skills

Solve each exercise. Then rate your understanding of the success criteria in your journal.

3. **USING MULTIPLE RANDOM SAMPLES** Use each sample in Example 1 to make an estimate for the number of students in your school who prefer rock music. Describe the variation of the estimates.

Hours Practiced Each Week
- A: 6, 5, 5, 6, 4, 6, 8, 5, 2, 6
- B: 0, 6, 6, 5, 4, 5, 6, 3, 4, 9
- C: 4, 5, 6, 4, 3, 2, 2, 3, 12, 1

4. **ESTIMATING AN AVERAGE OF A POPULATION** You want to know the mean number of hours music students at your school practice each week. At each of three music classes you randomly survey 10 students. Your results are shown. Use all three samples to make one estimate for the mean number of hours music students practice each week.

You can use technology to perform simulations with large numbers of trials.

EXAMPLE 3 Modeling Real Life

As stated in Exploration 1, 60% of all seventh graders have visited a planetarium. Use technology to simulate choosing 200 random samples of 50 students each. How closely do the samples estimate the percent of all seventh graders who have visited a planetarium?

The actual percentage is 60%, the number of samples is 200, and the sample size is 50. Use technology to run the simulation.

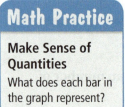

Math Practice

Make Sense of Quantities
What does each bar in the graph represent?

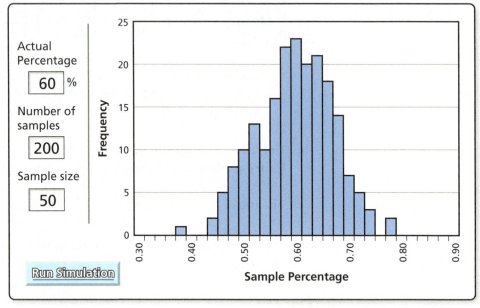

Available at *BigIdeasMath.com*

The estimates are clustered around 60%. Most are between 45% and 70%.

▸ So, most of the samples are within 15% of the actual percentage.

Self-Assessment for Problem Solving

Solve each exercise. Then rate your understanding of the success criteria in your journal.

5. Repeat Example 3 with the assumption that 50% of all seventh graders have visited a planetarium.

6. Forty percent of all seventh graders have visited a state park. How closely do 200 random samples of 50 students estimate the percent of seventh graders who have visited a state park? Use a simulation to support your answer.

Laurie's Notes

EXAMPLE 3

- **Model with Mathematics:** In the exploration, students found random samples of size 25 using packing peanuts. In this example, students are asked to choose 200 random samples of size 50. Using packing peanuts to simulate 200 samples would be unreasonable. Make sure students understand the change in approach and what the technology is simulating in this context.
- To complete this efficiently, students should use technology to simulate the samples and then analyze the results.
- **Look for and Express Regularity in Repeated Reasoning:** A simulator can be found at *BigIdeasMath.com*. Tell students to enter the actual percentage, the number of samples, and the sample size. Ask students what happens when you repeatedly run the simulation. They should see that while the graph changes, the variability stays relatively consistent.
- **Attend to Precision:** Be sure students understand that *within 15%* means 15% in either direction. Also, *within 15%* is sometimes described as *plus or minus 15%*.

✓ Self-Assessment for Problem Solving

- Encourage students to use a Four Square to complete these exercises. Until students become comfortable with the problem-solving plan, they may only be ready to complete the first square.
- Students should work in groups, taking turns reading and explaining the problems. They should complete their Four Squares independently and then compare with the group and discuss any discrepancies.

The Success Criteria Self-Assessment chart can be found in the *Student Journal* or online at *BigIdeasMath.com*.

Closure

- **Writing Prompt:** Why is it better to make inferences about a population based on multiple samples instead of only one sample? What additional information do you gain by taking multiple random samples? Explain.

Extra Example 3

Eighty-four percent of all middle school students own a cell phone. Use technology to simulate choosing 150 random samples of 50 students each. How closely do the samples estimate the percent of all middle school students who own a cell phone? *Answers will vary.*

Self-Assessment for Problem Solving

5. Answers will vary.
6. Answers will vary.

Learning Target
Understand variability in samples of a population.

Success Criteria
- Use multiple random samples to make conclusions about a population.
- Use multiple random samples to examine variation in estimates.

Review & Refresh

1. valid
2. invalid
3. $\frac{x}{100} = \frac{12}{30}$; 40%
4. $\frac{x}{100} = \frac{17}{68}$; 25%

Concepts, Skills, & Problem Solving

5. yes; $\frac{14}{50} = 28\%$, which is close to 30%
6. no; $\frac{3}{30} = 10\%$, which is not close to 30%
7. a. 330, 360, 420
   b. median: 360 customers; range: 90 customers
8. a. 330, 300, 270, 300, 360
   b. median: 300 customers; range: 90 customers

Assignment Guide and Concept Check

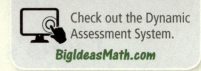

Scaffold assignments to support all students in their learning progression. The suggested assignments are a starting point. Continue to assign additional exercises and revisit with spaced practice to move every student toward proficiency.

Level	Assignment 1	Assignment 2
Emerging	2, 4, 5, 7	6, 8, 9, 10, 11, 12, 15
Proficient	2, 4, 5, 7, 9, 10	6, 8, 11, 12, 13, 15
Advanced	2, 4, 6, 8, 9, 10	11, 12, 13, 14, 15

- Assignment 1 is for use after students complete the Self-Assessment for Concepts & Skills.
- Assignment 2 is for use after students complete the Self-Assessment for Problem Solving.
- The red exercises can be used as a concept check.

Review & Refresh Prior Skills

Exercises 1 and 2 Using Samples of Populations
Exercises 3 and 4 Using the Percent Proportion

Common Errors

- **Exercises 5 and 6** Students may not calculate the percent of seventh graders in the sample that own a bracelet and incorrectly compare the number of students in the sample that own a bracelet to 30%. Remind students that they need to calculate the percent first.

C.2 Practice

Review & Refresh

You ask 100 randomly chosen high school students whether they support a new college in your town. Determine whether your conclusion is valid.

1. You conclude that 85% of high school students in your town support the new college.

2. You conclude that 15% of residents in your town do not support the new college.

New College	
Support	85
Do not support	15

Write and solve a proportion to answer the question.

3. What percent of 30 is 12?

4. 17 is what percent of 68?

Concepts, Skills, & Problem Solving

EXPLORING VARIABILITY IN SAMPLES Thirty percent of all seventh graders own a bracelet. Explain whether the sample closely estimates the percentage of seventh graders who own a bracelet. (See Exploration 1, p. 569.)

5. 50 seventh graders, 14 own a bracelet

6. 30 seventh graders, 3 own a bracelet

	Vegetable Preference	
	Fresh	Canned
A	11	9
B	14	6
C	12	8

7. **USING MULTIPLE RANDOM SAMPLES** A store owner wants to know how many of her 600 regular customers prefer canned vegetables. Each of her three cashiers randomly surveys 20 regular customers. The table shows the results.

   a. Use each sample to make an estimate for the number of regular customers of the store who prefer fresh vegetables.

   b. Describe the variation of the estimates.

8. **USING MULTIPLE RANDOM SAMPLES**
   An arcade manager wants to know how many of his 750 regular customers prefer to visit in the winter. Each of five staff members randomly surveys 25 regular customers. The table shows the results.

   a. Use each sample to make an estimate for the number of regular customers who prefer to visit in the winter.

   b. Describe the variation of the estimates.

Preferred Season to Visit the Arcade				
	Spring	Summer	Fall	Winter
A	4	4	6	11
B	5	3	7	10
C	6	5	5	9
D	4	5	6	10
E	4	4	5	12

9. ESTIMATING A MEAN OF A POPULATION A park ranger wants to know the mean number of nights students in your school plan to camp next summer. The park ranger randomly surveys 10 students from each class. The results are shown.

Nights Camping
A: 0, 5, 2, 3, 0, 6, 0, 10, 3, 0
B: 14, 0, 0, 6, 5, 0, 1, 2, 2, 5
C: 8, 8, 2, 3, 4, 1, 0, 0, 0, 6
D: 10, 10, 5, 6, 1, 0, 0, 0, 4, 0

a. Use each sample to make an estimate for the mean number of nights students in your school plan to camp next summer. Describe the variation of the estimates.

b. Use all four samples to make one estimate for the mean number of nights students plan to camp next summer.

10. ESTIMATING A MEDIAN OF A POPULATION Repeat Exercise 9, but estimate the medians instead of the means.

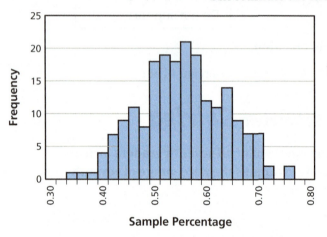

11. DESCRIBING SAMPLE VARIATION Fifty-five percent of doctors at a hospital prescribe a particular medication. A simulation with 200 random samples of 50 doctors each is shown. Describe how the sample percentages vary.

12. MODELING REAL LIFE Sixty percent of vacationers enjoy water parks. Use technology to generate 20 samples of size 100. How closely do the samples estimate the percent of all vacationers who enjoy water parks?

13. MODELING REAL LIFE Thirty percent of all new wooden benches have a patch of chipped paint. Use technology to simulate 100 random samples of 10 wooden benches. How closely do the samples estimate the percent of all wooden benches with a patch of chipped paint?

14. DIG DEEPER! You want to predict whether a proposal will be accepted by likely voters. You randomly sample 3 different groups of 100 likely voters. The results are shown. Do you expect the proposal to be accepted? Justify your answer.

	Proposal	
	Support	Oppose
Sample A	48	52
Sample B	52	48
Sample C	47	53

15. CRITICAL THINKING Explain why public opinion polls use sample sizes of more than 1000 people instead of using a smaller sample size.

Mini-Assessment

1. You and a group of friends want to know how many students in your school prefer watching football. There are 820 students in your school. Each person in the group randomly surveys 20 students. The table shows the results.

	Favorite Sport to Watch			
	Baseball	Basketball	Football	Soccer
You	5	4	9	2
Friend A	7	3	7	3
Friend B	7	2	5	6
Friend C	4	7	9	0
Friend D	3	5	4	8

   a. Use each sample to make an estimate for the number of students in your school who prefer watching football. *164, 205, 287, 369, and 369*
   b. Describe the center and the variation of the estimates. *The estimates have a median of 287 students and a range of 205 students.*

2. You want to know the mean number of hours students spend using technology each week. At each of six schools you randomly survey 8 students. Your results are shown.

   Hours Spent Using Technology Each Week
   A: 14, 18, 20, 16, 15, 7, 22, 24
   B: 18, 14, 12, 20, 12, 14, 18, 22
   C: 15, 21, 25, 24, 16, 18, 20, 21
   D: 25, 21, 30, 28, 20, 22, 24, 26
   E: 12, 18, 20, 18, 26, 15, 20, 21
   F: 18, 20, 24, 20, 14, 18, 16, 10

   a. Use each sample to make an estimate for the mean number of hours students spend using technology each week. Describe the variation of the estimates. *The estimates have a range of 8.25 hours.*
   b. Use all six samples to make one estimate for the mean number of hours students spend using technology each week. *19 hours*

Section Resources

Surface Level	Deep Level
Resources by Chapter • Extra Practice • Reteach • Puzzle Time Student Journal • Self-Assessment • Practice Differentiating the Lesson Tutorial Videos Skills Review Handbook Skills Trainer	Resources by Chapter • Enrichment and Extension Graphic Organizers Dynamic Assessment System • Section Practice
Transfer Level	
Dynamic Assessment System • Mid-Chapter Quiz	Assessment Book • Mid-Chapter Quiz

Concepts, Skills, & Problem Solving

9. a. 2.9, 3.5, 3.2, 3.6; median: 3.35 nights; range: 0.7 night
   b. 3.3 nights

10. a. 2.5, 2, 2.5, 2.5; median: 2.5 nights; range: 0.5 night
    b. 2.375 nights

11. *Sample answer:* Most of the samples are within 15% of the actual percentage.

12. Answers will vary.

13. Answers will vary.

14. *Sample answer:* no; Sample results suggest only 49% support, but it is possible that the true percent is greater than 50% due to sampling variability.

15. *Sample answer:* The larger the sample size, the closer the sample estimate will be to the theoretical percentage.

Learning Target
Compare populations using measures of center and variation.

Success Criteria
- Find the measures of center and variation of a data set.
- Describe the visual overlap of two data distributions numerically.
- Determine whether there is a significant difference in the measures of center of two data sets.

Warm Up
Cumulative, vocabulary, and prerequisite skills practice opportunities are available in the *Resources by Chapter* or at *BigIdeasMath.com*.

ELL Support
Explain that when you compare populations, you compare their measures of center and measures of variation. *Variation* is a noun related to the verb *vary*. Measures of variation describe the distribution of a data set, how the data vary.

Exploration 1
a. See Additional Answers.
b. *Sample answer:* talk about how many values are in both data distributions and how much overlap there is; using measures of center and measures of variation
c. *Sample answer:* the stem-and-leaf plot; The more the two graphs overlap, the less significant the differences are.

T-575

Laurie's Notes

Check out the Dynamic Classroom.
BigIdeasMath.com

Preparing to Teach
- In the previous course, students found measures of center and measures of variation. Now they will use these measures to compare populations in a variety of data displays.
- **Reason Abstractly and Quantitatively:** Mathematically proficient students make sense of quantities and their relationships in problem situations. They use the overlap of two data distributions to visually compare the data sets.

Motivate
- Display the double box-and-whisker plot showing the electricity produced (in kilowatt-hours, kWh) each day in July from solar panels on two houses.

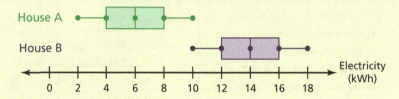

- Ask questions comparing the box-and-whisker plots.
- ❓ "Were there days in which House A generated more electricity than House B?" no
- ❓ "Could there have been days in which both houses generated the same amount of electricity?" yes

Exploration 1
- **Reason Abstractly and Quantitatively:** The analysis of each plot will provide insight into students' understanding of each type of data display.
- ❓ "What is the first data display called?" double box-and-whisker plot "What is the second data display called?" double dot plot "What is the third data display called?" back-to-back stem-and-leaf plot
- Ask students to summarize what is known about each data set in each of the three displays.
  - ❓ "Do you know how many students are represented in the box-and-whisker plot? the dot plot? the stem-and-leaf plot?" no; yes; yes
- Students may need a quick review of mean, MAD, and the five-number summary. Remind students that a box-and-whisker plot can be used to find the five-number summary but not the mean nor the MAD. A dot plot or a stem-and-leaf plot can be used to find all three.
- In part (b), students should describe the overlap using measures of center and the least and greatest values in the overlap.
- In part (c), students need to see that the when the overlap of two data sets is great, their differences are less significant. Help them understand that there are two things that impact the significance: the amount of difference in the means (or medians) and the amount of variation.

Comparing Populations

Learning Target: Compare populations using measures of center and variation.

Success Criteria:
- I can find the measures of center and variation of a data set.
- I can describe the visual overlap of two data distributions numerically.
- I can determine whether there is a significant difference in the measures of center of two data sets.

EXPLORATION 1 Comparing Two Data Distributions

Work with a partner.

a. Does each data display show *overlap*? Explain.

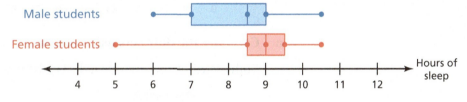

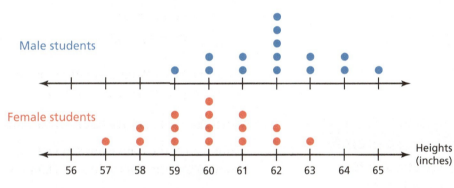

Ages of People in Two Exercise Classes

10:00 A.M. Class		8:00 P.M. Class
	1	8 9
	2	1 2 2 7 9 9
	3	0 3 4 5 7
9 7 3 2 2 2	4	0
7 5 4 3 1	5	
7 0 0	6	
0	7	

Key: 2 | 4 | 0 = 42 and 40 years

Math Practice

Recognize Usefulness of Tools

What are the advantages of each type of data display? Which do you prefer? Explain.

b. How can you describe the overlap of two data distributions using words? How can you describe the overlap numerically?

c. In which pair of data sets is the difference in the measures of center the most significant? Explain your reasoning.

C.3 Lesson

Use the mean and the mean absolute deviation (MAD) to compare two populations when both distributions are symmetric. Use the median and the interquartile range (IQR) when either one or both distributions are skewed.

EXAMPLE 1 **Comparing Populations**

Two data sets contain an equal number of values. The double box-and-whisker plot represents the values in the data sets.

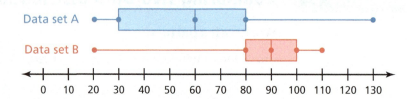

a. **Compare the data sets using measures of center and variation.**

Both distributions are skewed. Use the median and the IQR.

Data set A	Data set B
Median = 60	Median = 90
IQR = 80 − 30 = 50	IQR = 100 − 80 = 20

 So, Data set B has a greater measure of center, and Data set A has a greater measure of variation.

b. **Which data set is more likely to contain a value of 95?**

About 25% of the data values in Data set A are between 80 and 130. About 50% of the data values in Data set B are between 80 and 100.

 So, Data set B is more likely to contain a value of 95.

c. **Which data set is more likely to contain a value that differs from the center by at least 30?**

The IQR of Data set A is 50 and the IQR of Data set B is 20. This means it is more common for a value to differ from the center by 30 in Data set A than in Data set B.

So, Data set A is more likely to contain a value that differs from the center by at least 30.

Math Practice

Look for Structure
Explain how you know that about 50% of the data values in Data set B are between 80 and 100.

Try It

1. Which data set is more likely to contain a value of 70?

2. Which data set is more likely to contain a value that differs from the center by no more than 3?

Laurie's Notes

Scaffolding Instruction
- Students have explored the overlap between data sets. Now they will compare two populations using measures of center, measures of variation, and overlap.
- **Emerging:** Students may understand the different types of data displays, but struggle with the analysis. They will benefit from guided instruction for the examples.
- **Proficient:** Students can use measures of center, variation, and overlap to compare populations. They should review the examples and then use the Self-Assessment exercises to check their understanding.
- **Note:** This section only covers cases where the variabilities are similar. Students can informally reason about whether differences in the measures of center are significant for samples with a large difference in variation by making observations of data displays.

Discuss
- Remind students that in the previous course, they used the mean and the MAD to describe symmetric distributions of data. They used the median and the IQR to describe skewed distributions of data.
- Tell students that when comparing two populations, they should use the mean and the MAD when *both* distributions are symmetric. If either one or both of the distributions are skewed, they should use the median and the IQR.

EXAMPLE 1
- Ask a volunteer to read part (a).
- ❓ "What do you notice about the distributions?" They are both skewed, one to the right and the other to the left.
- ❓ "How do you describe the centers and variation of skewed distributions?" using the median and the IQR
- Give students time to find the median and the IQR. Use *Popsicle Sticks* to solicit answers.
- Work through parts (b) and (c) as shown.

Try It
- **Neighbor Check:** Have students work independently and then have their neighbors check their work. Have students discuss any discrepancies.

ELL Support

Have students work in pairs to complete Try It Exercises 1 and 2. As they discuss each exercise, have them ask, "What is the median? What is the IQR?" Expect students to perform according to their language levels.

Beginner: State numbers and one-word answers.

Intermediate: Use simple sentences such as, "Data set A is more likely."

Advanced: Use detailed sentences such as, "Data set A is more likely to contain a value of seventy because about fifty percent of the data values are between thirty and eighty."

Scaffold instruction to support all students in their learning. Learning is individualized and you may want to group students differently as they move in and out of these levels with each skill and concept. Student self-assessment and feedback help guide your instructional decisions about how and when to layer support for all students to become proficient learners.

Extra Example 1
Two data sets contain an equal number of values. The double box-and-whisker plot represents the values in the data sets.

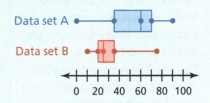

a. Compare the data sets using measures of center and variation. Data set A has a greater measure of center and a greater measure of variation.

b. Which data set is more likely to contain a value of 65? Data set A

c. Which data set is more likely to contain a value that differs from the center by at least 35? Data set A

Try It
1. Data set A
2. Data set B

T-576

Extra Example 2
The double dot plot shows two data sets. Express the difference in the measures of center as a multiple of the measure of variation.

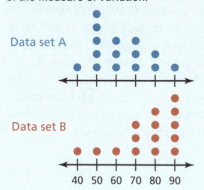

The difference in the medians is 1 times the IQR.

ELL Support

Have students work in pairs for extra support and to practice language as they complete the Self-Assessment for Concepts & Skills exercises. Have two pairs discuss their answers. Monitor and provide support as needed. For Exercise 4, have pairs display their measures of center and variation on whiteboards for your review.

Try It

3. The mean of Data set A increases by 30 to 84 and the MAD does not change, so Data set A still has a greater mean time. The difference in the means is now 3.5 times the MAD. The number is greater, indicating less overlap in the data.

Self-Assessment
for Concepts & Skills

4. Data set A has a greater mean and a greater MAD; The difference in the means is 1.25 to 1.5 times the MAD.

5. See Additional Answers.

T-577

Laurie's Notes

Discuss

- Discuss the push-pin note and the first paragraph. Students need to realize that when two data sets have similar variability, the difference in the measures of center is less significant when the sets have a lot of overlap.
  - For example, in each double box-and-whisker plot below the difference in the medians is the same, but the difference is more significant in the first plot because there is less variation.

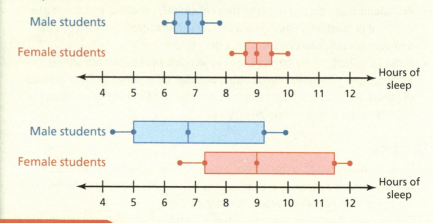

EXAMPLE 2

- "How can you describe the distributions shown in the display?" Both distributions are approximately symmetric. "How do you describe the centers and variation of symmetric distributions?" using the mean and the MAD
- **Use Appropriate Tools Strategically:** Students can use a calculator to quickly compute the mean and the MAD. Split the class with each half computing one of the two means and the associated MAD.
- "Do the dot plots overlap?" yes "Do you think you can *measure* the overlap?" Students may think it can be measured but are unsure of what it means.
- **Look for and Make Use of Structure:** Students need to express the difference in the means as a multiple of the MAD, so they must divide the difference in the means by the MAD. The difference must be positive. Students can either subtract the smaller number from the greater number or find the absolute value of the difference.
- In this case, the difference in the means is about 1.6 times the MAD. Make sure students understand this number describes the visual overlap between the data. In general, the greater the value, the less the overlap.

Try It

- Have students work with a partner.

✓ Self-Assessment for Concepts & Skills

- **Which One Doesn't Belong:** See page T-578 for a description of *Which One Doesn't Belong*.
- ⊙ Have students use *Thumbs Up* to indicate their understanding of the first two success criteria.

The Success Criteria Self-Assessment chart can be found in the *Student Journal* or online at *BigIdeasMath.com*.

Less visual overlap indicates a more significant difference in the measures of center.

When two populations have similar variabilities, the visual overlap of the data can be described by writing the difference in the measures of center as a multiple of the measure of variation. Greater values indicate less visual overlap.

EXAMPLE 2 Describing Visual Overlap

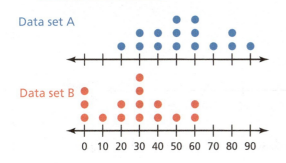

The double dot plot shows two data sets. Express the difference in the measures of center as a multiple of the measure of variation.

Both distributions are approximately symmetric. Use the mean and the MAD to describe the centers and variations.

Data set A

$$\text{Mean} = \frac{810}{15} = 54$$

$$\text{MAD} = \frac{244}{15} \approx 16$$

Data set B

$$\text{Mean} = \frac{420}{15} = 28$$

$$\text{MAD} = \frac{236}{15} \approx 16$$

$$\frac{\text{difference in means}}{\text{MAD}} = \frac{26}{16} \approx 1.6$$

 So, the difference in the means is about 1.6 times the MAD.

Try It

3. **WHAT IF?** Each value in the dot plot for Data set A increases by 30. How does this affect your answers? Explain.

Self-Assessment for Concepts & Skills

Solve each exercise. Then rate your understanding of the success criteria in your journal.

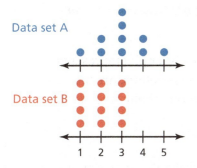

4. **COMPARING POPULATIONS** The double dot plot shows two data sets. Compare the data sets using measures of center and variation. Then express the difference in the measures of center as a multiple of the measure of variation.

5. **WHICH ONE DOESN'T BELONG?** You want to compare two populations represented by skewed distributions. Which measure does *not* belong with the other three? Explain your reasoning.

Median of first data set	Median of second data set
IQR of first data set	MAD of second data set

Section C.3 Comparing Populations

When the difference in the measures of center is at least 2 times the measure of variation, the difference is significant.

EXAMPLE 3 Modeling Real Life

The double box-and-whisker plot represents the heights of rollercoasters at two amusement parks. Are the rollercoasters significantly taller at one park than at the other park?

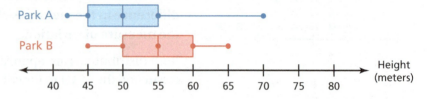

The distribution for Park A is skewed, so use the median and the IQR to describe the centers and variations.

Park A	Park B
Median = 50	Median = 55
IQR = 55 − 45 = 10	IQR = 60 − 50 = 10

Because the variabilities are similar, you can describe the visual overlap by expressing the difference in the medians as a multiple of the IQR.

$$\frac{\text{difference in medians}}{\text{IQR}} = \frac{5}{10} = 0.5$$

Because the quotient is less than 2, the difference in the medians is not significant.

 The rollercoasters are not significantly taller at one park than at the other park.

 ## Self-Assessment for Problem Solving

Solve each exercise. Then rate your understanding of the success criteria in your journal.

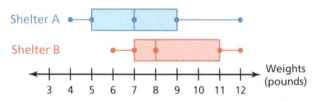

6. The double box-and-whisker plot represents the weights of cats at two shelters. Are the cats significantly heavier at one shelter than at the other? Explain.

7. **DIG DEEPER!** Tornadoes in Region A travel significantly farther than tornadoes in Region B. The tornadoes in Region A travel a median of 10 miles. Create a double box-and-whisker plot that can represent the distances traveled by the tornadoes in the two regions.

Laurie's Notes

Formative Assessment Tip

Which One Doesn't Belong

This technique is one that you should be quite familiar with because it is often used in the Self-Assessment for Concepts & Skills exercises! Students are presented with four expressions, quantities, images, or words and asked which one does not belong with the other three. They are also expected to give a reason for their choice, which can be quite informative.

Used at the end of instruction, *Which One Doesn't Belong* informs you as to how students have conceptualized and made connections in their learning. Used at the beginning of a lesson, this technique can inform you about what knowledge students already have about the topic.

Discuss

- Ask students to describe what they believe is meant by a "significant" difference in measures of center.
- Discuss the paragraph at the top of the page. Explain that *at least 2 times* is not a strict rule, just a general guideline.

EXAMPLE 3

- ❓ "Which measure of center and variation should you use to compare the data sets? Explain." median and IQR; The distribution of Park A is skewed. Some students may also recognize that because the individual data values are not given, you cannot find the mean or the MAD.
- Calculate the quotient of the difference in the medians and the IQR.
- ❓ Ask, "Is the difference in the medians at least 2 times the IQR?" no "What does this tell you?" The rollercoasters are not significantly taller at one park than the other park.

✓ Self-Assessment for Problem Solving

- Allow time in class for students to practice using the problem-solving plan. Remember, some students may only be able to complete the first step.
- Have students work with a partner to solve the problems and then present their work to the class.

The Success Criteria Self-Assessment chart can be found in the *Student Journal* or online at *BigIdeasMath.com*.

Closure

- **One-Minute Card:** To compare two populations…
- Collect the cards as the students leave. Begin the next class with a discussion of any misunderstandings.

Extra Example 3

The double box-and-whisker plot represents the numbers of electrical outlets per room for two houses. Is the number of electrical outlets per room significantly greater for one house than the other house?

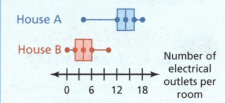

Yes, the number of electrical outlets per room for House A is significantly greater than for House B.

Self-Assessment
for Problem Solving

6. no; The difference in the medians as a multiple of IQR is 0.25, which is less than 2.

7. See Additional Answers.

Learning Target

Compare populations using measures of center and variation.

Success Criteria

- Find the measures of center and variation of a data set.
- Describe the visual overlap of two data distributions numerically.
- Determine whether there is a significant difference in the measures of center of two data sets.

▶ Review & Refresh

1. yes; $\frac{4}{15}$, or $26.\overline{6}\%$, is close to 20%.

2. no; $\frac{6}{10}$, or 60%, is not close to 20%.

3. 30 kilometers per hour

4. $2.28 per can

▶ Concepts, Skills, & Problem Solving

5. no; *Sample answer:* none of the sets have similar values

6. yes; *Sample answer:* Because there is less visual overlap in the graphs, there is a more significant difference in the measures of center.

7. Data set A has a greater median and Data set B has a greater range and greater IQR.

8. Data set A

9. Data set B

10. The difference in the means is about 3.86 times the MAD.

Assignment Guide and Concept Check

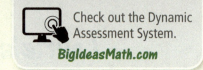

Scaffold assignments to support all students in their learning progression. The suggested assignments are a starting point. Continue to assign additional exercises and revisit with spaced practice to move every student toward proficiency.

Level	Assignment 1	Assignment 2
Emerging	2, 4, 5, 7, 8, 9, 10	6, 11, 12, 13
Proficient	2, 4, 5, 6, 7, 8, 9, 10	11, 12, 13
Advanced	2, 4, 5, 6, 7, 8, 9, 10	11, 13, 14

- Assignment 1 is for use after students complete the Self-Assessment for Concepts & Skills.
- Assignment 2 is for use after students complete the Self-Assessment for Problem Solving.
- The red exercises can be used as a concept check.

Review & Refresh Prior Skills

Exercises 1 and 2 Exploring Variability in Samples
Exercises 3 and 4 Finding Unit Rates

Common Errors

- **Exercises 6 and 7** Students may use the wrong measures of center and variation when comparing populations. Remind students to use the mean and the MAD when *both* distributions are symmetric. Otherwise, use the median and IQR.

T-579

C.3 Practice

Go to *BigIdeasMath.com* to get HELP with solving the exercises.

▶ Review & Refresh

Twenty percent of all seventh graders have watched a horse race. Explain whether the sample closely estimates the percentage of seventh graders who have watched a horse race.

1. In a sample of 15 seventh graders, 4 have watched a horse race.
2. In a sample of 10 seventh graders, 6 have watched a horse race.

Find the unit rate.

3. 60 kilometers in 2 hours
4. $11.40 for 5 cans

▶ Concepts, Skills, & Problem Solving

COMPARING TWO DATA DISTRIBUTIONS The double box-and-whisker plot represents the values in two data sets. *(See Exploration 1, p. 575.)*

5. Does the data display show *overlap*? Explain.

6. Is there a significant difference in the measures of center for the pair of data sets? Explain.

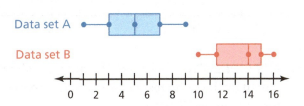

COMPARING POPULATIONS Two data sets contain an equal number of values. The double box-and-whisker plot represents the values in the data sets.

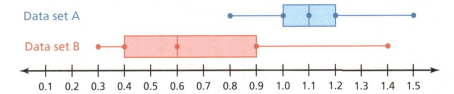

7. Compare the data sets using measures of center and variation.

8. Which data set is more likely to contain a value of 1.1?

9. Which data set is more likely to contain a value that differs from the center by 0.3?

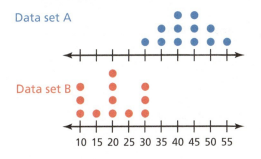

10. **DESCRIBING VISUAL OVERLAP** The double dot plot shows the values in two data sets. Express the difference in the measures of center as a multiple of the measure of variation.

Section C.3 Comparing Populations 579

11. **MP YOU BE THE TEACHER** The distributions of attendance at basketball games and volleyball games at your school are symmetric. Your friend makes a conclusion based on the calculations shown below. Is your friend correct? Explain your reasoning.

> Volleyball Game Attendance: Mean = 80, MAD = 20
> Basketball Game Attendance: Mean = 160, MAD = 20
>
> The difference in means is four times the MAD, so attendance at basketball games is significantly greater than attendance at volleyball games.

12. **MP MODELING REAL LIFE** The double box-and-whisker plot represents the goals scored per game by two hockey teams during a 20-game season. Is the number of goals scored per game significantly greater for one team than the other? Explain.

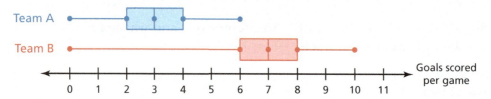

13. **MP MODELING REAL LIFE** The dot plots show the test scores for two classes taught by the same teacher. Are the test scores significantly greater for one class than the other? Explain.

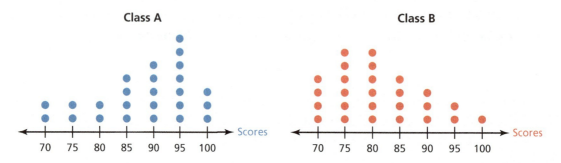

14. **MP PROBLEM SOLVING** A scientist experiments with mold colonies of equal area. She adds a treatment to half of the colonies. After a week, she measures the area of each colony. If the areas are significantly different, the scientist will repeat the experiment. The results are shown. Should the scientist repeat the experiment? Justify your answer.

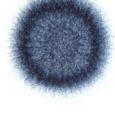

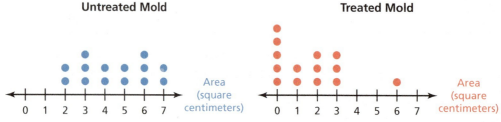

Common Errors

- **Exercises 11–14** Students may use the wrong measures of center and variation when comparing populations. Remind students to use the mean and the MAD when *both* distributions are symmetric. Otherwise, use the median and IQR.

Mini-Assessment

The double dot plot shows the final grades of females in a seventh grade math class and females in an eighth grade math class.

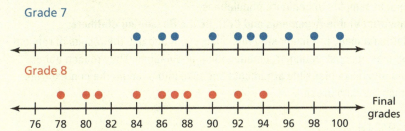

1. Compare the populations using measures of center and variation. Seventh grade females have a greater mean final grade, and the variations are the same.
2. Express the difference in the measures of center as a multiple of the measure of variation. The difference in the means is about 1.4 times the MAD.
3. Are the final grades significantly greater for one class than the other? Explain. No, the quotient of the difference in the means and the MAD is less than 2.

Concepts, Skills, & Problem Solving

11. yes; Because the difference in means is greater than two times the MAD, the attendance is significantly greater.

12. yes; The difference in the medians is 2 times the IQR.

13. no; The difference in the medians is 0.8 to 1 times the IQR.

14. no; Because the difference in the median areas as a multiple of the IQR is 1 (less than 2), the areas are not significantly different.

Section Resources

Surface Level	Deep Level
Resources by Chapter • Extra Practice • Reteach • Puzzle Time Student Journal • Self-Assessment • Practice Differentiating the Lesson Tutorial Videos Skills Review Handbook Skills Trainer	Resources by Chapter • Enrichment and Extension Graphic Organizers Dynamic Assessment System • Section Practice

Learning Target
Use random samples to compare populations.

Success Criteria
- Compare random samples using measures of center and variation.
- Recognize whether random samples are likely to be representative of a population.
- Compare populations using multiple random samples.

Warm Up
Cumulative, vocabulary, and prerequisite skills practice opportunities are available in the *Resources by Chapter* or at BigIdeasMath.com.

ELL Support
Discuss the meaning of the word *random*. Explain that random can be described using phrases such as "without pattern," "not having regularity," or "being equally likely." Point out that the word *likely* means something is expected to happen. It does not mean that you will *like* something. Give examples of sentences using the word *random*. Then have students share their own examples.

Exploration 1
a. See Additional Answers.

b. no; *Sample answer:* The sample taken was random, but the sample size is not large enough to provide accurate data.

c. The medians in the double box-and-whisker plot are greater and the IQRs in the double box-and-whisker plot are lesser.

d. See Additional Answers.

e. See Additional Answers.

T-581

Laurie's Notes

Check out the Dynamic Classroom.
BigIdeasMath.com

Preparing to Teach
- In the previous lesson, students compared populations using measures of center and variation. They also determined whether there was a significant difference in the measures of center of two data sets. Now students will use random samples to compare populations.
- **Construct Viable Arguments and Critique the Reasoning of Others:** Mathematically proficient students understand and use the results of random samples in constructing arguments about populations. They reason about data and make plausible arguments that take into account the context from which the data arose.

Motivate
- "Has your favorite TV show ever been cancelled?" Answers will vary.
- "Why do you think it was cancelled?" If a student does not mention low ratings, suggest that it could be a reason.
- "Where do the ratings come from?" Students should recognize that not every person who has watched the show is asked to give his or her rating. A *sample* of the people watching is asked and the results of the survey are used to predict the entire population's opinions.
- "Can you think of any other examples where you would want to use a random sample to make a conclusion rather than using the entire population?" *Sample answer:* predicting election results
- "Do you think conclusions from samples are always accurate?" no
- Tell students that today they will learn how to compare random samples of data and draw conclusions.

Exploration 1
- "How will you compare the data?" using measures of center and variation
- "Which measure of center and variation should you use and why?" median and IQR; Both sets of data are skewed.
- After pairs complete part (b), ask several pairs to share their answers and reasoning. Students should realize that the samples are much too small to represent all male and female students in your state.
- "What happens if the sample is too small?" Conclusions may not be accurate.
- Ask a volunteer to read part (c) aloud.
- "Do you think that this sampling will produce more accurate conclusions? Explain." Yes, more random samples will produce more reliable conclusions.
- In part (c), students should recognize that the variations of the distributions in the box-and-whisker plot are much smaller than the variations of the distributions of the data in the tables.
- In part (d), students should recognize that they are more likely to make accurate comparisons of the populations using the data in the box-and-whisker plot because the variations are smaller and the number of samples is greater.
- **Turn and Talk:** Have students discuss part (e) and the Math Practice note.

C.4 Using Random Samples to Compare Populations

Learning Target: Use random samples to compare populations.

Success Criteria:
- I can compare random samples using measures of center and variation.
- I can recognize whether random samples are likely to be representative of a population.
- I can compare populations using multiple random samples.

EXPLORATION 1

Using Random Samples

Work with a partner. You want to compare the numbers of hours spent on homework each week by male and female students in your state. You take a random sample of 15 male students and 15 female students throughout the state.

Male Students				
1.5	3	0	2.5	1
8	2.5	1	3	0
6.5	1	5	0	5

Female Students				
4	0	3	1	1
5	1	3	5.5	10
2	0	6	3.5	2

a. Compare the data in each sample.

b. Are the samples likely to be representative of all male and female students in your state? Explain.

c. You take 100 random samples of 15 male students in your state and 100 random samples of 15 female students in your state and record the median of each sample. The double box-and-whisker plot shows the distributions of the sample medians. Compare the distributions in the double box-and-whisker plot with the distributions of the data in the tables.

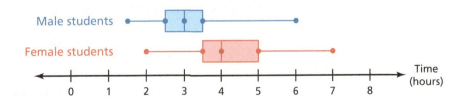

Math Practice

Build Arguments
How does taking multiple random samples allow you to make conclusions about two populations?

d. What can you conclude from the double box-and-whisker plot? Explain.

e. How can you use random samples to make accurate comparisons of two populations?

C.4 Lesson

You do not need to have all of the data from two populations to make comparisons. You can use random samples to make comparisons.

EXAMPLE 1 Comparing Random Samples

Two bags each contain 1000 numbered tiles. The double box-and-whisker plot represents a random sample of 12 numbers from each bag. Compare the samples using measures of center and variation. Can you determine which bag contains tiles with greater numbers?

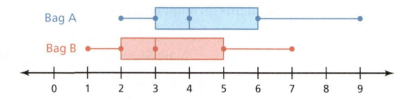

Both distributions are skewed right, so use the median and the IQR.

Bag A	Bag B
Median = 4	Median = 3
IQR = 6 − 3 = 3	IQR = 5 − 2 = 3

▶ The variation in the samples is about the same, but the sample from Bag A has a greater median. The sample size is too small, however, to conclude that tiles in Bag A generally have greater numbers than tiles in Bag B.

You are more likely to make valid comparisons when the sample size is large and there is little variability in the data.

Try It

1. The double dot plot shows the weekly reading habits of a random sample of 10 students in each of two schools. Compare the samples using measures of center and variation. Can you determine which school's students read less? Explain.

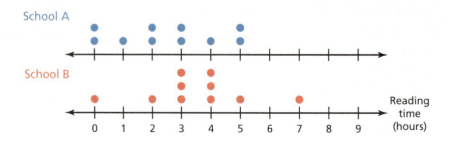

Laurie's Notes

Scaffolding Instruction
- In the exploration, students began to compare random samples. Now they will continue comparing random samples, but in a more precise manner.
- **Emerging:** Students may understand that comparisons can be made using multiple random samples, but they need help formalizing the process. They will benefit from guided instruction for the examples.
- **Proficient:** Students are able to transfer prior work with random samples and comparing populations to compare random samples and draw conclusions. They should work through the Try It exercises before completing the Self-Assessment exercises.

EXAMPLE 1
- Point out the push-pin note and remind students that to make valid comparisons they need a sample size of at least 30. Students may recognize that the sample size of 12 is too small, but they can still practice comparing samples.
- **?** If students question why the sample size matters, ask, "If you flip a coin one time and it lands on tails, can you assume that the coin will always land on tails?" no
- Work through the problem and reasoning as shown.

Try It
- **Think-Pair-Share:** Students should read the problem independently and then work in pairs to answer the question. Have each pair compare their answers with another pair and discuss any discrepancies.

ELL Support

After demonstrating Example 1, have students practice language by working in groups to complete Try It Exercise 1. Have groups consider the measures of center and variation for each sample and compare their ideas. Expect students to perform according to their language levels.

Beginner: State numbers and one-word answers.

Intermediate: Use simple sentences such as, "School A has a greater mean. The MADs are about the same. No, the sample size is too small."

Advanced: Use detailed sentences such as, "The MAD for School A is one and one-half hours and the MAD for School B is one and three-tenths hours. School B has a greater mean, but the sample size is too small to conclude that students in School B generally spend more time reading than students in School A."

Scaffold instruction to support all students in their learning. Learning is individualized and you may want to group students differently as they move in and out of these levels with each skill and concept. Student self-assessment and feedback help guide your instructional decisions about how and when to layer support for all students to become proficient learners.

Extra Example 1
Two boxes each contain 500 numbered tokens. The double box-and-whisker plot represents a random sample of 10 numbers from each box. Compare the samples using measures of center and variation. Can you determine which box contains tokens with greater numbers?

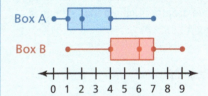

Box B has a greater median; The IQRs are about the same; No, the sample size is too small.

Try It

1. School A: mean = 2.5, MAD = 1.5
   School B: mean = 3.5, MAD = 1.3
   no; The sample size is too small to make a conclusion.

Extra Example 2

The double box-and-whisker plot represents the medians of 50 random samples of 10 numbers from each box in Extra Example 1. Compare the variability of the sample medians to the variability of the samples in Extra Example 1. Can you determine which box contains tokens with greater numbers?

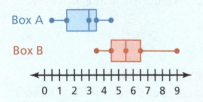

The IQR of the sample medians for each box is 2, which is less than the IQR of the samples in Extra Example 1. Most of the sample medians for Box B are greater than the sample medians for Box A; Yes, tokens in Box B generally have greater numbers than tokens in Box A.

Try It

2. yes

Self-Assessment
for Concepts & Skills

3. Box A: mean = 5.5, MAD = 1.25
   Box B: mean = 1.5, MAD = 1.25
   no; The sample size is too small to make a conclusion.

4. yes; *Sample answer:* The IQR of the sample medians is 2.5 for each crate. Most of the sample medians for Crate B are greater than the sample medians for Crate A. So, in general, Crate B contains objects that weigh more than objects in Crate A.

T-583

Laurie's Notes

EXAMPLE 2

- Ask a volunteer to read the problem aloud.
- Ask students to compare the data in this example to the data in Example 1.
- ? "What do the data in the box-and-whisker plot represent in Example 1?" the numbers drawn
- ? "What do the data in this box-and-whisker plot represent?" the medians of each sample of 12
- Be sure students understand that the data in Example 1 represent 12 numbers drawn from each bag. In this example, the data represent the *medians* of 50 random samples of 12 numbers from each bag.
- ? "Would you expect conclusions to be more accurate in this example than in Example 1? Explain." Yes, this example uses many more samples.
- Work through the problem and reasoning as shown.

Try It

- Students should work with a partner and then share their results with the class.

Formative Assessment Tip

Three-Minute Pause

This technique is used when a lesson involves a particularly large amount of information or a lengthy process. After a period of instruction, you take a three-minute break and students work with partners or small groups to process the information they have just learned. They might ask one another questions or clarify what their understanding is, relative to the exploration or instruction they have just experienced.

The break in instruction allows students to resolve questions and ask for feedback from peers. Once the three minutes are up, the instruction continues until the next *Three-Minute Pause*. After the final *Three-Minute Pause*, any lingering questions can be written down and used to clarify concepts taught in the lesson.

✓ Self-Assessment for Concepts & Skills

- ⊙ This is a good time for a *Three-Minute Pause*. Pause three minutes for students to confer with partners and reflect on their understanding. Have them discuss each of the success criteria and any questions they still have. Then have pairs write any remaining questions on index cards for class discussion later in the lesson.
- **Neighbor Check:** Have students work independently and then have their neighbors check their work. Have students discuss any discrepancies.

ELL Support

Allow students to work in pairs. For Exercise 3, ask which box they believe contains tiles with greater numbers and have students hold up 1 finger for Box A or 2 fingers for Box B. For Exercise 4, ask which crate weighs more and use a similar technique to indicate Crate A or Crate B.

The Success Criteria Self-Assessment chart can be found in the *Student Journal* or online at *BigIdeasMath.com*.

EXAMPLE 2 Using Multiple Random Samples

The double box-and-whisker plot represents the medians of 50 random samples of 12 numbers from each bag in Example 1. Compare the variability of the sample medians to the variability of the samples in Example 1. Can you determine which bag contains tiles with greater numbers?

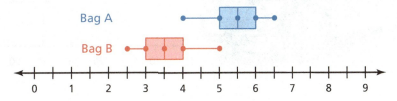

Bag A
Median = 5.5
IQR = 6 − 5 = 1

Bag B
Median = 3.5
IQR = 4 − 3 = 1

▸ The IQR of the sample medians for each bag is 1, which is less than the IQR of the samples in Example 1. Most of the sample medians for Bag A are greater than the sample medians for Bag B. So, tiles in Bag A generally have greater numbers than tiles in Bag B.

Try It

2. **WHAT IF?** Each value in the box-and-whisker plot of the sample medians for Bag A decreases by 2. Does this change your answer?

 Self-Assessment for Concepts & Skills

Solve each exercise. Then rate your understanding of the success criteria in your journal.

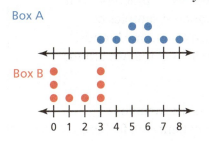

3. **COMPARING RANDOM SAMPLES** Two boxes each contain 600 numbered tiles. The double dot plot shows a random sample of 8 numbers from each box. Compare the samples using measures of center and variation. Can you determine which box contains tiles with greater numbers? Explain.

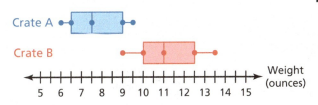

4. **USING MULTIPLE RANDOM SAMPLES** Two crates each contain 750 objects. The double box-and-whisker plot shows the median weights of 50 random samples of 10 objects from each crate. Can you determine which crate weighs more? Explain.

EXAMPLE 3 Modeling Real Life

The double box-and-whisker plot represents the medians of 50 random samples of 10 speeding tickets issued in two states. Compare the costs of speeding tickets in the two states.

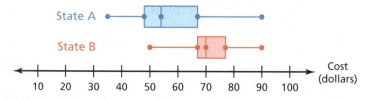

There is enough data to draw conclusions about the costs of speeding tickets in the two states. Find the measures of center and variation for the sample medians from each state. Then compare the data.

State A
Median ≈ 54
IQR ≈ 67 − 48 = 19

State B
Median = 70
IQR ≈ 77 − 67 = 10

The variation for State A is greater than the variation for State B, and the measure of center for State B is greater than the measure of center for State A.

▸ So, you can conclude that the cost of speeding tickets varies more in State A, but speeding tickets generally cost more in State B.

 ## Self-Assessment for Problem Solving

Solve each exercise. Then rate your understanding of the success criteria in your journal.

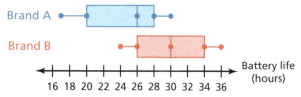

5. The double box-and-whisker plot represents the medians of 100 random samples of 20 battery lives for two cell phone brands. Compare the battery lives of the two brands.

6. The double box-and-whisker plot represents the medians of 50 random samples of 10 wait times at two patient care facilities. Which facility should you choose? Explain your reasoning.

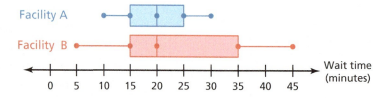

Laurie's Notes

EXAMPLE 3

- Ask a volunteer to read the problem.
- As you work through the solution, ask students to point out the different steps of the problem-solving plan.
- ? "Is there enough data to make a valid comparison?" yes
- ? "What do you notice about the distributions?" They are both skewed.
- ? "How do you describe the centers and variation of skewed distributions?" using the median and the IQR
- Give students time to find the medians and the IQRs.
- Use *Popsicle Sticks* to solicit explanations of how to find the medians and the IQRs.
- Remind students that they need to find the *answer*, not just find the measures of center and variation.
- **Construct Viable Arguments and Critique the Reasoning of Others:** Based on the measures of center and variation, students should conclude that it is reasonable to assume that speeding tickets generally cost more in State B than in State A.

✓ Self-Assessment for Problem Solving

- Students may benefit from trying the exercises independently and then working with peers to refine their work. It is important to provide time in class for problem solving, so that students become comfortable with the problem-solving plan.
- Students should work independently and then *Turn and Talk* with a neighbor to resolve any discrepancies.

The Success Criteria Self-Assessment chart can be found in the *Student Journal* or online at *BigIdeasMath.com*.

Closure

- Discuss the questions on the index cards from the *Three-Minute Pause*.

Extra Example 3

The double box-and-whisker plot represents the medians of 50 random samples of 10 concerts held at two theaters. Compare the costs of concert tickets at the two theaters.

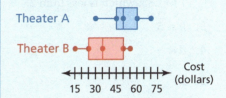

The cost of concert tickets varies more in Theater B, but concert tickets generally cost more in Theater A.

Self-Assessment for Problem Solving

5. *Sample answer:* The variation of battery lives for both brands are the same. The measures of center for Brand B is greater than the measure of center for Brand A. You can conclude that Brands B's batteries will last longer than Brand A's batteries.

6. Facility A; *Sample answer:* The measure of center for both facilities is the same, but the variation of wait times for Facility A is much smaller.

Learning Target

Use random samples to compare populations.

Success Criteria

- Compare random samples using measures of center and variation.
- Recognize whether random samples are likely to be representative of a population.
- Compare populations using multiple random samples.

Review & Refresh

1. Data set B has a greater median and a greater IQR.

2. no; The difference in the medians as a multiple of IQR is 1 to 1.33, which is less than 2.

3. $b = 5$

4. $d = -5$

5. $z = \frac{2}{3}$

Concepts, Skills, & Problem Solving

6. yes

7. non-teachers spend more time on recreation each week than teachers; *Sample answer:* 75% of non-teachers spend at least 6 hours on recreation. 50% of teachers spend less than 5 hours on recreation.

8. yes; *Sample answer:* The variation for College A and College B are the same, but the measure of center for College B is greater than the measure of center for College A. You can conclude that College B's athletes generally spend more time running than College A's athletes.

9. yes; *Sample answer:* The variation for Lake A and Lake B are the same, but the measure of center for Lake A is greater than the measure of center for Lake B. You can conclude that Lake A generally contains larger fish than Lake B.

Assignment Guide and Concept Check

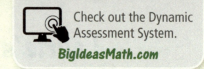

Scaffold assignments to support all students in their learning progression. The suggested assignments are a starting point. Continue to assign additional exercises and revisit with spaced practice to move every student toward proficiency.

Level	Assignment 1	Assignment 2
Emerging	1, 2, 5, 6, 7, 8, 9	10, 11, 12
Proficient	1, 2, 5, 6, 7, 8, 9	10, 11, 12
Advanced	1, 2, 5, 6, 7, 8, 9	10, 12, 13

- Assignment 1 is for use after students complete the Self-Assessment for Concepts & Skills.
- Assignment 2 is for use after students complete the Self-Assessment for Problem Solving.
- The red exercises can be used as a concept check.

Review & Refresh Prior Skills

Exercises 1 and 2 Comparing Populations
Exercises 3–5 Solving an Equation

Common Errors

- **Exercise 8** Students may use the wrong measures of center and variation when comparing samples. Remind students to use the mean and the MAD when *both* distributions are symmetric. Otherwise, use the median and the IQR.

C.4 Practice

Review & Refresh

The double dot plot shows the values in two data sets.

1. Compare the data sets using measures of center and variation.

2. Are the values of one data set significantly greater than the values of the other data set? Explain.

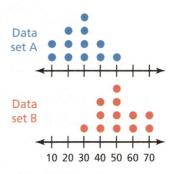

Solve the equation. Check your solution.

3. $5b - 3 = 22$
4. $1.5d + 3 = -4.5$
5. $4 = 9z - 2$

Concepts, Skills, & Problem Solving

USING RANDOM SAMPLES You want to compare the numbers of hours spent on recreation each week by teachers and non-teachers in your state. You take 100 random samples of 15 teachers and 100 random samples of 15 non-teachers throughout the state and record the median value of each sample. The double box-and-whisker plot shows the distributions of sample medians. *(See Exploration 1, p. 581.)*

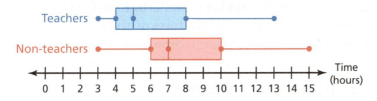

6. Are the samples likely to be representative of all teachers and non-teachers in your state?

7. What can you conclude from the double box-and-whisker plot? Explain.

8. **COMPARING RANDOM SAMPLES** The double dot plot shows the weekly running habits of athletes at two colleges. Compare the samples using measures of center and variation. Can you determine which college's athletes spend more time running? Explain.

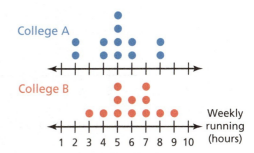

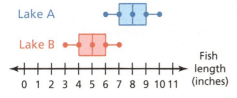

9. **USING MULTIPLE RANDOM SAMPLES** Two lakes each contain about 2000 fish. The double box-and-whisker plot shows the medians of 50 random samples of 14 fish lengths from each lake. Can you determine which lake contains longer fish? Explain.

10. **MODELING REAL LIFE** Two laboratories each produce 800 chemicals. A chemist takes 10 samples of 15 chemicals from each lab, and records the number that pass an inspection. Are the samples likely to be representative of all the chemicals for each lab? If so, which lab has more chemicals that will pass the inspection? Justify your answer.

Research Lab A				
14	13	15	15	14
14	15	15	13	12

Research Lab B				
12	10	12	14	11
9	14	11	11	15

11. **MODELING REAL LIFE** A farmer grows two types of corn seedlings. There are 1000 seedlings of each type. The double box-and-whisker plot represents the median growths of 50 random samples of 7 corn seedlings of each type. Compare the growths of each type of corn seedling. Justify your result.

    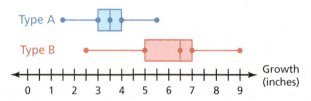

12. **DIG DEEPER!** You want to compare the number of words per sentence in a sports magazine to the number of words per sentence in a political magazine.

    a. The data represent random samples of the number of words in 10 sentences from each magazine. Compare the samples using measures of center and variation. Can you use the data to make a valid comparison about the magazines? Explain.

    Sports magazine: 9, 21, 15, 14, 25, 26, 9, 19, 22, 30
    Political magazine: 31, 22, 17, 5, 23, 15, 10, 20, 20, 17

    b. The double box-and-whisker plot represents the means of 200 random samples of 20 sentences from each magazine. Compare the variability of the sample means to the variability of the sample numbers of words in part (a).

    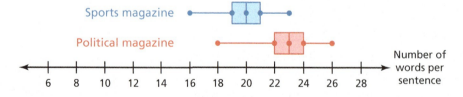

    c. Make a conclusion about the numbers of words per sentence in each magazine.

13. **PROJECT** You want to compare the average amounts of time students in sixth, seventh, and eighth grade spend on homework each week.

    a. Design an experiment involving random sampling that can help you make a comparison.

    b. Perform the experiment. Can you make a conclusion about which grade spends the most time on homework? Explain your reasoning.

Common Errors

- **Exercises 11 and 12** Students may use the wrong measures of center and variation when comparing samples. Remind students to use the mean and the MAD when *both* distributions are symmetric. Otherwise, use the median and the IQR.

Mini-Assessment

1. Two baskets each contain 600 numbered chips. The double box-and-whisker plot represents a random sample of 15 numbers from each basket. Compare the samples using measures of center and variation. Can you determine which basket contains chips with greater numbers?

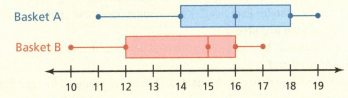

Basket A has a greater median; The IQRs are about the same; No, the sample size is too small.

2. The double box-and-whisker plot represents the medians of 50 random samples of 12 prices of sweatshirts at two stores. Compare the costs of sweatshirts at the two stores.

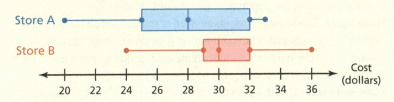

The cost of sweatshirts varies more in Store A, but sweatshirts generally cost more in Store B.

Section Resources

Surface Level	Deep Level
Resources by Chapter • Extra Practice • Reteach • Puzzle Time Student Journal • Self-Assessment • Practice Differentiating the Lesson Tutorial Videos Skills Review Handbook Skills Trainer	Resources by Chapter • Enrichment and Extension Graphic Organizers Dynamic Assessment System • Section Practice
Transfer Level	
Dynamic Assessment System • End-of-Chapter Quiz	Assessment Book • End-of-Chapter Quiz

Concepts, Skills, & Problem Solving

10. yes; Lab A; *Sample answer:* The mean and median are higher for Lab A than Lab B.

11. *Sample answer:* The measures of center and variation for Type B are greater than Type A. You can conclude that growths of the Type B corn seedlings are larger and vary by more than the Type A corn seedlings.

12. **a.** The mean and MAD for the sports magazine, 19 and 5.8, are close to the mean and MAD for the political magazine, 18 and 5.2. However, the sample size is small and the variability is too great to conclude that the number of words per sentence is about the same.

    b. The sample means vary much less than the sample numbers of words per sentence.

    c. The number of words per sentence is generally greater in the political magazine than in the sports magazine.

13. **a.** Check students' work. Experiments should include taking many samples of a manageable size from each grade level. This will be more doable if the work of sampling is divided among the whole class, and the results are pooled together.

    b. Check students' work. The data may or may not support a conclusion.

T-586

Skills Needed

Exercise 1
- Identifying Biased and Unbiased Samples
- Using the Percent Equation
- Using a Sample

Exercise 2
- Comparing Data Distributions
- Subtracting Integers

Exercise 3
- Simulating Outcomes
- Using a Sample

ELL Support

Explain that *a city's residents* means "the people living in a city." Point out that the total number of residents in a city is also considered the city's population. In Exercise 1, the city's population is the population being sampled.

Using the Problem-Solving Plan

1. 44,800 residents
2. yes
3. 34.83%

Performance Task

The *STEAM Video Performance Task* provides the opportunity for additional enrichment and greater depth of knowledge as students explore the mathematics of the chapter within a context tied to the chapter STEAM Video. The performance task and a detailed scoring rubric are provided at *BigIdeasMath.com*.

Laurie's Notes

Scaffolding Instruction

- The goal of this lesson is to help students become more comfortable with problem solving. These exercises combine describing and comparing populations with prior skills from other courses. The solution for Exercise 1 is worked out below, to help you guide students through the problem-solving plan. Use the remaining class time to have students work on the other exercises.
- **Emerging:** The goal for these students is to feel comfortable with the problem-solving plan. Allow students to work in pairs to write the beginning steps of the problem-solving plan for Exercise 2. Keep in mind that some students may only be ready to do the first step.
- **Proficient:** Students may be able to work independently or in pairs to complete Exercises 2 and 3.
- Visit each pair to review their plan for each problem. Ask students to describe their plans.

▶ Using the Problem-Solving Plan

Exercise 1

 Understand the problem. You are given the numbers of sporting events attended each month by a sample of 1500 residents. You are asked to make an estimate about the population, all residents of the city.

 Make a plan. The sample is representative of the population because it is selected at random and is large enough to provide accurate data. So, find the percent of people in the survey that attend at least one sporting event each month, and use the percent equation to make an estimate.

 Solve and check. Use the plan to solve the problem. Then check your solution.

- Find the percent of people in the survey that attend at least one sporting event each month.

$$\text{percent of people in the survey who attend at least one sporting event} = \frac{477 + 276 + 87}{1500} = \frac{840}{1500} = 0.56, \text{ or } 56\%$$

- Use the percent equation to make an estimate.

$a = p\% \cdot w$ Write the percent equation.
$= 0.56 \cdot 80{,}000$ Substitute 0.56 for $p\%$ and 80,000 for w.
$= 44{,}800$ Simplify.

So, there are about 44,800 residents in the city who attend at least one sporting event each month.

- **Check:** Find the percent of residents that attend at least one sporting event each month to verify that it is equivalent to the percent of people in the survey who attend at least one sporting event each month, 56%.

$$\text{percent of residents who attend at least one sporting event} = \frac{44{,}800}{80{,}000} = 0.56, \text{ or } 56\% ✓$$

Connecting Concepts

Using the Problem-Solving Plan

1. In a city, 1500 randomly chosen residents are asked how many sporting events they attend each month. The city has 80,000 residents. Estimate the number of residents in the city who attend at least one sporting event each month.

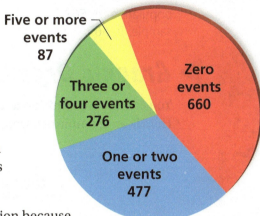

Sporting Events per Month

- Five or more events: 87
- Zero events: 660
- Three or four events: 276
- One or two events: 477

Understand the problem. You are given the numbers of sporting events attended each month by a sample of 1500 residents. You are asked to make an estimate about the population, all residents of the city.

Make a plan. The sample is representative of the population because it is selected at random and is large enough to provide accurate data. So, find the percent of people in the survey that attend at least one sporting event each month, and use the percent equation to make an estimate.

Solve and check. Use the plan to solve the problem. Then check your solution.

2. The dot plots show the values in two data sets. Is the difference in the measures of center for the data sets significant?

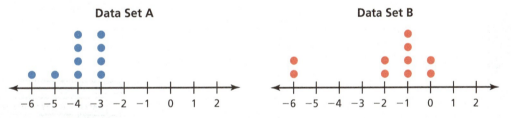

Data Set A

Data Set B

3. You ask 60 randomly chosen students whether they support a later starting time for school. The table shows the results. Estimate the probability that at least two out of four randomly chosen students do not support a later starting time.

Yes	No
42	18

Performance Task

Estimating Animal Populations

At the beginning of the this chapter, you watched a STEAM Video called "Comparing Dogs." You are now ready to complete the performance task related to this video, available at *BigIdeasMath.com*. Be sure to use the problem-solving plan as you work through the performance task.

Chapter Review

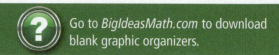

Go to *BigIdeasMath.com* to download blank graphic organizers.

Review Vocabulary

Write the definition and give an example of each vocabulary term.

population, *p. 563*
sample, *p. 563*
unbiased sample, *p. 564*
biased sample, *p. 564*

Graphic Organizers

You can use a **Definition and Example Chart** to organize information about a concept. Here is an example of a Definition and Example Chart for the vocabulary term *sample*.

Sample: part of a population

Example
unbiased sample: 100 seventh-grade students selected randomly during lunch

Example
biased sample: the seventh-grade students at your lunch table

Choose and complete a graphic organizer to help you study each topic.

1. population
2. shape of a distribution
3. mean absolute deviation (MAD)
4. interquartile range (IQR)
5. double box-and-whisker plot
6. double dot plot

"Here is my **Definition and Example Chart**. I read in the news that a cat once floated over this waterfall in a barrel."

Review Vocabulary

- As a review of the chapter vocabulary, have students revisit the vocabulary section in their *Student Journals* to fill in any missing definitions and record examples of each term.

Graphic Organizers

Sample answers:

1. **Population:** an entire group of people or objects
   - Example: all seventh-grade students in a school
   - Example: all residents in a city
   - Example: all books in a library

2. **Shape of a distribution:** a description of how data are distributed in a data display
   - Example: skewed left:
   - Example: symmetric:
   - Example: skewed right:

3. **Mean absolute deviation (MAD):** an average of how much data values differ from the mean
   - Example: Find the mean absolute deviation of the data:
     2, 3, 4, 5, 6
     mean $= \frac{20}{5} = 4$ MAD $= \frac{2+1+0+1+2}{5} = \frac{6}{5} = 1.2$
   - Example: Find the mean absolute deviation of the data:
     8, 9, 4, 5, 7, 3
     mean $= \frac{36}{6} = 6$ MAD $= \frac{2+3+2+1+1+3}{6} = \frac{12}{6} = 2$
   - Example: Find the mean absolute deviation of the data:
     10, 15, 14, 11, 10, 18, 13
     mean $= \frac{91}{7} = 13$ MAD $= \frac{3+2+1+2+3+5+0}{7} = \frac{16}{7} \approx 2.3$

4–6. Answers at *BigIdeasMath.com*.

List of Organizers
Available at *BigIdeasMath.com*
Definition and Example Chart
Example and Non-Example Chart
Four Square
Information Frame
Summary Triangle

About this Organizer

A **Definition and Example Chart** can be used to organize information about a concept. Students fill in the top rectangle with a term and its definition or description. Students fill in the rectangles that follow with examples to illustrate the term. Each sample answer shows three examples, but students can show more or fewer examples. Definition and Example Charts are useful for concepts that can be illustrated with more than one type of example.

Chapter Self-Assessment

1. biased; The sample is not selected at random and is not representative of the population because students in the biology club like biology.

2. *Sample answer:* biased: Randomly selecting 50 male athletes from your school. unbiased: Randomly selecting 50 athletes from your school.

3. no; The sample is not representative of the population because people going to the baseball stadium are more likely to support building a new baseball stadium. So, the sample is biased and the conclusion is not valid.

4. Sample B; It is a larger sample.

5. 696 students

6. sample; It is much easier to collect sample data in this situation.

Chapter Self-Assessment

The Success Criteria Self-Assessment chart can be found in the *Student Journal* or online at *BigIdeasMath.com*.

ELL Support

Allow students extra support and the chance to practice language by working in pairs to complete the first section of the Chapter Self-Assessment. Once pairs have finished, have them present their explanations to another pair. Have all four participants in each group reach an agreement for each explanation and revise as necessary. Monitor discussions and provide support. Use similar techniques for the remaining sections of the Chapter Self-Assessment. You may want to have pairs or groups present some of the answers to the entire class for further review and discussion.

Common Errors

- **Exercise 6** Students may not understand why you may or may not want to question the entire population for a survey. Ask them to estimate the population size and then ask if it would be reasonable to ask everyone in that population for a response.

Chapter Self-Assessment

As you complete the exercises, use the scale below to rate your understanding of the success criteria in your journal.

1	2	3	4
I do not understand.	I can do it with help.	I can do it on my own.	I can teach someone else.

C.1 Samples and Populations (pp. 563–568)

Learning Target: Understand how to use random samples to make conclusions about a population.

1. You want to estimate the number of students in your school whose favorite subject is biology. You survey the first 10 students who arrive at biology club. Determine whether the sample is *biased* or *unbiased*. Explain.

2. You want to estimate the number of athletes who play soccer. Give an example of a biased sample. Give an example of an unbiased sample.

3. You want to know how the residents of your town feel about building a new baseball stadium. You randomly survey 100 people who enter the current stadium. Eighty support building a new stadium, and twenty do not. So, you conclude that 80% of the residents of your town support building a new baseball stadium. Is your conclusion valid? Explain.

4. Which sample is better for making an estimate? Explain.

Predict the number of students in a school who like gym class.	
Sample A	A random sample of 8 students from the yearbook
Sample B	A random sample of 80 students from the yearbook

5. You ask 125 randomly chosen students to name their favorite beverage. There are 1500 students in the school. Predict the number of students in the school whose favorite beverage is a sports drink.

Favorite Beverage	
Sports drink	58
Soda	36
Water	14
Other	17

6. You want to know the number of students in your state who have summer jobs. Determine whether you should survey the population or a sample. Explain.

C.2 Using Random Samples to Describe Populations (pp. 569–574)

Learning Target: Understand variability in samples of a population.

7. To pass a quality control inspection, the products at a factory must contain no critical defects, no more than 2.5% of products can contain major defects, and no more than 4% of products can contain minor defects. There are 40,000 products being shipped from a factory. Each inspector randomly samples 125 products. The table shows the results.

   a. Use each sample to make an estimate for the number of products with minor defects at the factory. Describe the center and the variation of the estimates.

   b. Use the samples to make an estimate for the percent of products with minor defects, with major defects, and with critical defects at the factory. Does the factory pass inspection? Explain.

	Type of Defect		
	Critical	Major	Minor
Inspector A	0	2	5
Inspector B	0	1	6
Inspector C	0	3	3
Inspector D	0	5	6

8. A scientist determines that 35% of packages of a food product contain a specific bacteria. Use technology to simulate choosing 100 random samples of 20 packages. How closely do the samples estimate the percent of all packages with the specific bacteria?

C.3 Comparing Populations (pp. 575–580)

Learning Target: Compare populations using measures of center and variation.

9. The double box-and-whisker plot represents the points scored per game by two football teams during the regular season.

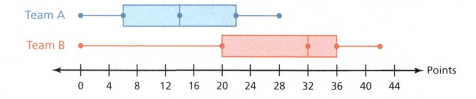

   a. Compare the data sets using measures of center and variation.

   b. Which team is more likely to score 18 points in a game?

Common Errors

- **Exercise 9** Students may use the wrong measures of center and variation when comparing populations. Remind students to use the mean and the MAD when *both* distributions are symmetric. Otherwise, use the median and IQR.

Chapter Self-Assessment

7. **a.** 1600 products; The estimates have a median of 1760 minor defects and a range of 960 defects.

   b. Critical defects: 0%, Major defects: 2.2%, Minor defects: 4%; yes; All percentages of defects fall under the allowable amount for the quality control inspection.

8. *Sample answer:* Most of the samples are within 20% of the actual percentage.

9. **a.** The IQRs are the same and Team B has a greater median.

   b. Team B

Chapter Self-Assessment

10. **a.** The difference in the means is 2 times the MAD.

    b. yes; The difference in the means is 2 times the MAD.

11. The median and IQR are greater for Model B; yes; *Sample answer:* The variation for Model A and Model B are close. Most of the sample medians for Model B are greater than the sample medians for Model A. So, in general, Model B has a better gas mileage than Model A.

12. yes; *Sample answer:* The variation for each age group is the same, but the measure of center for people in their thirties is greater than the measure of center for people in their twenties. So, in general, people in their thirties drive more than people in their twenties.

Common Errors

- **Exercises 10 and 11** Students may use the wrong measures of center and variation when comparing populations or samples. Remind students to use the mean and the MAD when *both* distributions are symmetric. Otherwise, use the median and IQR.

Chapter Resources

Surface Level	Deep Level
Resources by Chapter • Extra Practice • Reteach • Puzzle Time Student Journal • Practice • Chapter Self-Assessment Differentiating the Lesson Tutorial Videos Skills Review Handbook Skills Trainer Game Library	Resources by Chapter • Enrichment and Extension Graphic Organizers Game Library
Transfer Level	
STEAM Video Dynamic Assessment System • Chapter Test	Assessment Book • Chapter Tests A and B • Alternative Assessment • STEAM Performance Task

10. The dot plots show the ages of campers at two summer camps.

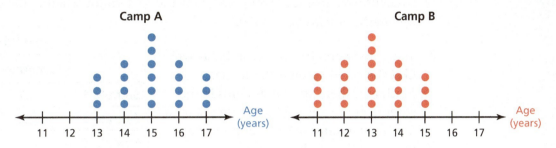

a. Express the difference in the measures of center as a multiple of the measure of variation.

b. Are the ages of campers at one camp significantly greater than at the other? Explain.

C.4 Using Random Samples to Compare Populations (pp. 581–586)

Learning Target: Use random samples to compare populations.

11. The double dot plot shows the median gas mileages of 10 random samples of 50 vehicles for two car models. Compare the samples using measures of center and variation. Can you determine which car model has a better gas mileage? Explain.

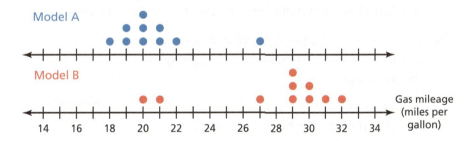

12. You compare the average amounts of time people in their twenties and thirties spend driving each week. The double box-and-whisker plot represents the medians of 100 random samples of 8 people from each age group. Can you determine whether one age group drives more than the other? Explain.

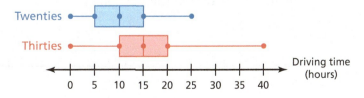

Chapter Review 591

C Practice Test

1. You want to estimate the number of students in your school who prefer to bring a lunch from home rather than buy one at school. You survey five students who are standing in the lunch line. Determine whether the sample is *biased* or *unbiased*. Explain.

2. You want to predict which candidate will likely be voted Seventh Grade Class President. There are 560 students in the seventh grade class. You randomly sample 3 different groups of 50 seventh-grade students. The results are shown.

	Candidate Preference	
	Candidate A	Candidate B
Sample 1	27	23
Sample 2	22	28
Sample 3	15	35

   a. Use each sample to make an estimate for the number of students in seventh grade that vote for Candidate A.

   b. Who do you expect to be voted Seventh Grade Class President? Explain.

3. Of 60 randomly chosen students from a school surveyed, 16 chose the aquarium as their favorite field trip. There are 720 students in the school. Predict the number of students in the school who choose the aquarium as their favorite field trip.

4. The double box-and-whisker plot shows the ages of the viewers of two television shows in a small town.

   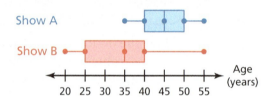

   a. Compare the data sets using measures of center and variation.

   b. Which show is more likely to have a 44-year-old viewer?

5. The double box-and-whisker plot shows the test scores for two French classes taught by the same teacher.

   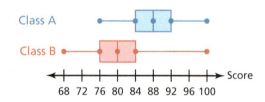

   a. Express the difference in the measures of center as a multiple of the measure of variation.

   b. Are the scores for one class significantly greater than for the other? Explain.

6. Two airplanes each hold about 400 pieces of luggage. The double dot plot shows a random sample of 8 pieces of luggage from each plane. Compare the samples using measures of center and variation. Can you determine which plane has heavier luggage? Explain.

   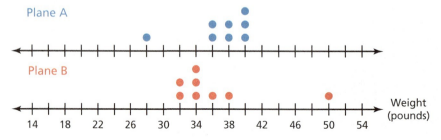

Practice Test Item References

Practice Test Questions	Section to Review
1, 3	C.1
2	C.2
4, 5	C.3
6	C.4

Test-Taking Strategies

Remind students to quickly look over the entire test before they start so that they can budget their time. There is a lot of vocabulary in this chapter, so students should have been making flashcards as they worked through the chapter. Encourage students to jot down words that they mix up on the back of the test before they start. Have them use the **Stop** and **Think** strategy before they write their answers.

Common Errors

- **Exercises 4–6** Students may use the wrong measures of center and variation when comparing populations or samples. Remind students to use the mean and the MAD when *both* distributions are symmetric. Otherwise, use the median and IQR.

Practice Test

1. biased; The sample size is too small and students standing in line are more likely to say they prefer to buy their lunches at school.

2. a. 302, 246, 168

   b. Candidate B; *Sample answer:* Using sample data provided, Candidate A is likely to receive about 43% of the votes and Candidate B is likely to receive about 57% of the votes.

3. 192 students

4. a. Show A has a greater median and Show B has a greater IQR.

   b. Show A

5. a. The difference in the medians is 1 times the IQR.

   b. no; Because the difference in the medians is less than 2 times the IQR, the scores are not significantly greater for one class than the other.

6. The IQRs are the same and Plane A has a greater median; no; The sample size is not large enough to provide accurate data.

Test-Taking Strategies

Available at *BigIdeasMath.com*
After Answering Easy Questions, Relax
Answer Easy Questions First
Estimate the Answer
Read All Choices before Answering
Read Question before Answering
Solve Directly or Eliminate Choices
Solve Problem before Looking at Choices
Use Intelligent Guessing
Work Backwards

About this Strategy

When taking a multiple-choice test, be sure to read each question carefully and thoroughly. Sometimes it is easier to solve the problem and then look for the answer among the choices.

Cumulative Practice

1. C
2. G
3. A
4. F

Item Analysis

1. **A.** The student writes the ratios in fraction form and incorrectly multiplies numerators with numerators and denominators with denominators, getting 20 = 20.
   B. The student thinks adding the same number (5) to each value in the ratio 2 : 3 forms an equivalent ratio.
   C. Correct answer
   D. The student thinks subtracting the same number (4) from each value in the ratio 12 : 8 forms an equivalent ratio.

2. **F.** The student finds what percent 60 is of 660.
   G. Correct answer
   H. The student finds 60% of 660 and misplaces the decimal point.
   I. The student thinks that the difference of the scores is equivalent to the percent.

3. **A.** Correct answer
   B. The student finds the number of students who say their favorite food is something other than pizza, tacos, or chicken.
   C. The student finds the number of students who say their favorite food is tacos.
   D. The student finds the number of students who say their favorite food is pizza.

4. **F.** Correct answer
   G. The student subtracts 5 from 6 instead of 6 from 5.
   H. The student adds 5 and 6 instead of subtracting.
   I. The student multiplies 5 and 6 instead of subtracting.

Cumulative Practice

1. Which of the ratios form a proportion?

   A. 5 to 2 and 4 to 10

   B. 2 : 3 and 7 : 8

   C. 3 to 2 and 15 to 10

   D. 12 : 8 and 8 : 4

2. A student scored 600 the first time she took the mathematics portion of a college entrance exam. The next time she took the exam, she scored 660. Her second score represents what percent increase over her first score?

   F. 9.1%   G. 10%

   H. 39.6%   I. 60%

3. You ask 100 randomly chosen students to name their favorite food. There are 1250 students in the school. Based on this sample, what is the number of students in the school whose favorite food is chicken?

Favorite Food	
Pizza	38
Tacos	36
Chicken	8
Other	18

   A. 100   B. 225

   C. 450   D. 475

4. Which value of p makes the equation $p + 6 = 5$ true?

   F. -1 G. 1

   H. 11   I. 30

Cumulative Practice   593

5. The table shows the costs for four cans of tomato soup. Which can has the lowest cost per ounce?

	Cost (dollars)	Number of Ounces
Can A	1.95	26
Can B	0.72	8
Can C	0.86	10.75
Can D	2.32	23.2

A. Can A
B. Can B
C. Can C
D. Can D

6. What value of y makes the equation $-3y = -18$ true?

7. The double dot plot shows the values in two data sets. Which sentence best represents the difference in the measures of center as a multiple of the measure of variation?

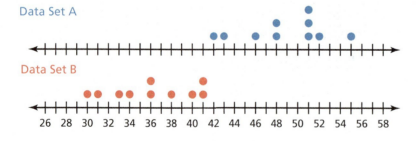

F. The difference of the means is about 3.3 times the MAD.

G. The difference of the means is about 3.8 times the MAD.

H. The difference of the means is 36 times the MAD.

I. The difference of the means is 48.7 times the MAD.

Item Analysis (continued)

5. **A.** Correct answer

   B. The student incorrectly thinks that Can B has the lowest cost per ounce because it has the lowest cost.

   C. The student thinks $0.08 per ounce is less than $0.075 per ounce.

   D. The student finds the least amount of ounces per dollar instead of the lowest cost per ounce.

6. **Gridded Response:** Correct answer: 6

   Common error: The student makes a sign error and gets −6.

7. **F.** The student finds the MAD instead of finding the difference in the means as a multiple of the MAD.

   G. Correct answer

   H. The student finds the mean for Data Set A instead of finding the difference in the means as a multiple of the MAD.

   I. The student finds the mean for Data Set B instead of finding the difference in the means as a multiple of the MAD.

Cumulative Practice

5. A
6. 6
7. G

T-594

Cumulative Practice

8. 20

9. A

10. *Part A* 270, 315, 360, 225, 90

    Part B 270 students

    Part C 252 students

Item Analysis (continued)

8. **Gridded Response:** Correct answer: 20

   Common error: The student thinks there is a pattern of adding 10 in the second column and gets 25.

9. **A.** Correct answer

   B. The student thinks the answer is *greater than* 11 instead of *greater than or equal to* 11.

   C. The student subtracts instead of dividing.

   D. The student multiplies instead of dividing.

10. **4 points** The student's work and explanations demonstrate a thorough understanding of using multiple random samples to make conclusions about a population and to examine variation in estimates. In Part A, the student correctly makes an estimate for each sample, getting 270, 315, 360, 225, and 90. In Part B, the student correctly determines that the estimates have a range of 270 students. In Part C, the student correctly makes one estimate for the number of students who prefer science in your school, getting 252 students. The student provides accurate work with clear and complete explanations.

    3 points The student's work and explanations demonstrate an essential but less than thorough understanding of using multiple random samples to make conclusions about a population and to examine variation in estimates.

    2 points The student's work and explanations demonstrate a partial but limited understanding of using multiple random samples to make conclusions about a population and to examine variation in estimates.

    1 point The student's work and explanations demonstrate a very limited understanding of using multiple random samples to make conclusions about a population and to examine variation in estimates.

    0 points The student provides no response, a completely incorrect or incomprehensible response, or a response that demonstrates insufficient understanding of using multiple random samples to make conclusions about a population and to examine variation in estimates.

8. What is the missing value in the ratio table?

x	y
$\frac{2}{3}$	5
2	15
$\frac{8}{3}$	
8	60

9. You are selling tomatoes. What is the minimum number of pounds of tomatoes you need to sell to earn at least $44?

A. 11 B. 12
C. 40 D. 176

10. You and a group of friends want to know how many students in your school prefer science. There are 900 students in your school. Each person randomly surveys 20 students. The table shows the results. Which subject do students at your school prefer?

	Favorite Subject			
	English	Math	Science	History
You	4	5	6	5
Friend A	2	4	7	7
Friend B	7	4	8	1
Friend C	3	6	5	6
Friend D	6	7	2	5

Part A Use each sample to make an estimate for the number of students in your school who prefer science.

Part B Describe the variation of the estimates.

Part C Use the samples to make one estimate for the number of students who prefer science in your school.

Cumulative Practice 595

D Geometric Shapes and Angles

- **D.1** Circles and Circumference
- **D.2** Areas of Circles
- **D.3** Perimeters and Areas of Composite Figures
- **D.4** Constructing Polygons
- **D.5** Finding Unknown Angle Measures

Chapter Learning Target:
Understand geometry.

Chapter Success Criteria:
- ■ I can explain how to find the circumference of a circle.
- ■ I can find the areas of circles and composite figures.
- ■ I can solve problems involving angle measures.
- ■ I can construct a polygon.

STEAM Video: "Track and Field"

Laurie's Notes

Chapter D Overview

If you ask students what geometry is about, you might hear "shapes, like squares, rectangles, triangles, and circles." They may mention solids, "boxes (prisms), cones, and pyramids." Students rarely mention the measurement aspect of these figures or any concepts related to spatial reasoning or spatial relationships. For many students, geometry is about what you see, meaning shapes and solids.

Of course, the geometry strand is much more. There is a measurement aspect that describes the dimension or size of an object. If the figure is two-dimensional, you want to know about the perimeter, circumference, and area. If the figure is three-dimensional, you want to know about the surface area and volume. There is also a reasoning component of geometry. What happens to the circumference (or area) of a circle when you double the radius? Is it possible to draw an isosceles triangle with side lengths of 4 centimeters and 10 centimeters?

This chapter is about measurement, reasoning, and angle relationships. Geometry software is recommended for several explorations and exercises. Supportive technology can be found at *BigIdeasMath.com*. Rulers, compasses, and protractors are also necessary tools.

Students can develop a conceptual understanding of the circumference and the area of a circle through exploration. Exploring these relationships is preferred over just memorizing the formulas. Students will then apply their understanding of circumference and area to composite figures. A common error students make when working with composite figures is forgetting to subtract the lengths that lie in the interior of a figure.

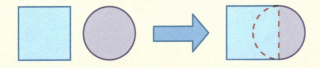

Remember, as you work through the chapter, be intentional in mentioning the units and asking questions like "What does a foot look like? What does a square meter look like?" What do students visualize when they hear these words?

The remaining lessons of the chapter focus on two specific goals for students: drawing (constructing) geometric shapes given conditions such as side lengths and angle measures and using facts about angle relationships to write and solve equations for an unknown angle measure. Both lessons are enhanced by using technology, specifically geometry software.

Suggested Pacing

Chapter Opener	1 Day
Section 1	1 Day
Section 2	1 Day
Section 3	1 Day
Section 4	1 Day
Section 5	1 Day
Connecting Concepts	1 Day
Chapter Review	1 Day
Chapter Test	1 Day
Total Chapter D	9 Days
Year-to-Date	42 Days

Chapter Learning Target
Understand geometry.

Chapter Success Criteria
- Explain how to find the circumference of a circle.
- Find the areas of circles and composite figures.
- Solve problems involving angle measures.
- Construct a polygon.

Chapter D Learning Targets and Success Criteria

Section	Learning Target	Success Criteria
D.1 Circles and Circumference	Find the circumference of a circle.	• Explain the relationship between the diameter and circumference of a circle. • Use a formula to find the circumference of a circle.
D.2 Areas of Circles	Find the area of a circle.	• Estimate the area of a circle. • Use a formula to find the area of a circle.
D.3 Perimeters and Areas of Composite Figures	Find perimeters and areas of composite figures.	• Use a grid to estimate perimeters and areas. • Identify the shapes that make up a composite figure. • Find the perimeters and areas of shapes that make up composite figures.
D.4 Constructing Polygons	Construct a polygon with given measures.	• Use technology to draw polygons. • Determine whether given measures result in one triangle, many triangles, or no triangle. • Draw polygons given angle measures or side lengths.
D.5 Finding Unknown Angle Measures	Use facts about angle relationships to find unknown angle measures.	• Identify adjacent, complementary, supplementary, and vertical angles. • Use equations to find unknown angle measures. • Find unknown angle measures in real-life situations.

Progressions

Through the Grades

Grade 6	Grade 7	Grade 8
• Find the areas of triangles, special quadrilaterals, and polygons. • Draw polygons in the coordinate plane given vertices and find lengths of sides.	• Draw geometric shapes with given conditions, focusing on triangles. • Solve problems involving the area and circumference of a circle. Understand pi and its estimates. • Use facts about supplementary, complementary, vertical, and adjacent angles. • Solve real-world and mathematical problems involving area of two-dimensional objects.	• Verify the properties of translations, reflections, and rotations. • Understand that figures are congruent (or similar) when they can be related by a sequence of translations, reflections, and rotations (and dilations). Describe a sequence that exhibits congruence (or similarity) between two figures. • Demonstrate that the sum of the interior angle measures of a triangle is 180° and apply this fact to find the unknown measures of angles and the sums of the angle measures of polygons. Classify and determine the measures of angles created when parallel lines are cut by a transversal. Use similar triangles to solve problems that include height and distance. • Know and apply the formulas for the volumes of cones, cylinders, and spheres.

Through the Chapter

Standard	D.1	D.2	D.3	D.4	D.5
Draw (freehand, with ruler and protractor, and with technology) geometric shapes with given conditions. Focus on constructing triangles from three measures of angles or sides, noticing when the conditions determine a unique triangle, more than one triangle, or no triangle.				★	
Know the formulas for the area and circumference of a circle and use them to solve problems; give an informal derivation of the relationship between the circumference and area of a circle.	●	●	★		
Use facts about supplementary, complementary, vertical, and adjacent angles in a multi-step problem to write and solve simple equations for an unknown angle in a figure.					★
Solve real-world and mathematical problems involving area, volume, and surface area of two- and three-dimensional objects composed of triangles, quadrilaterals, polygons, cubes, and right prisms.			●		

Key
▲ = preparing   ★ = complete
● = learning   ■ = extending

STEAM Video

1. about 100.06 m
2. *Sample answer:* The width of the rectangle is 2 times the distance around each semicircle divided by π.

Performance Task

The radius or diameter of the semicircle and the width of the track.

Mathematical Practices

Students have opportunities to develop aspects of the mathematical practices throughout the chapter. Here are some examples.

1. **Make Sense of Problems and Persevere in Solving Them**
   D.3 Exercise 20, *p. 618*
2. **Reason Abstractly and Quantitatively**
   D.4 Exercise 44, *p. 626*
3. **Construct Viable Arguments and Critique the Reasoning of Others**
   D.4 Exercise 24, *p. 625*
4. **Model with Mathematics**
   D.3 Math Practice note, *p. 613*
5. **Use Appropriate Tools Strategically**
   D.1 Exploration 1(b), *p. 599*
6. **Attend to Precision**
   D.1 Math Practice note, *p. 599*
7. **Look for and Make Use of Structure**
   D.4 Math Practice note, *p. 621*
8. **Look for and Express Regularity in Repeated Reasoning**
   D.2 Exercise 25, *p. 612*

Laurie's Notes

STEAM Video

Before the Video
- To introduce the STEAM Video, read aloud the first paragraph of Track and Field and discuss the question with your students.
- "How can competitors run in different lanes and have the same finish line?"

During the Video
- In the video, Alex and Robert are trying to figure out how the starting lines are determined for a race track.
- Pause the video at 1:40 and ask, "What shapes make up the track?" 2 semicircles and 1 rectangle
- "Why is each lane a different length?" *Sample answer:* Because of the curves of the semicircles.
- Watch the remainder of the video.

After the Video
- Have students work with a partner to answer Questions 1 and 2.
- As students discuss and answer the questions, they should begin to see a relationship between the circumference and the diameter of a circle.

Performance Task

- Use this information to spark students' interest and promote thinking about real-life problems.
- Ask, "Given a race track, what measures do you need to find the outer perimeter?"
- After completing the chapter, students will have gained the knowledge needed to complete "Finding the Area and Perimeter of a Track."

STEAM Video

Track and Field

Different lanes on a race track have different lengths. How can competitors run in different lanes and have the same finish line?

Watch the STEAM Video "Track and Field." Then answer the following questions.

1. A track consists of a rectangle and two semicircles. The dimensions of the rectangle formed by the innermost lane are shown. What is the distance around each semicircle on the 400-meter, innermost lane?

2. How does the width of the rectangle, 63.7 meters, compare to the distance around each semicircle? Explain.

Performance Task

Finding the Area and Perimeter of a Track

After completing this chapter, you will be able to use the concepts you learned to answer the questions in the *STEAM Video Performance Task*. You will be given the dimensions of a race track.

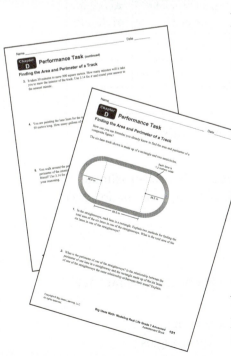

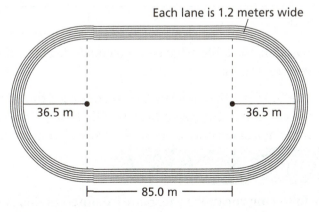

You will be asked to solve various perimeter and area problems about the track. Given a race track, what measures do you need to find the outer perimeter?

597

Getting Ready for Chapter D

Chapter Exploration

Work with a partner.

1. Perform the steps for each of the figures.
   - Measure the perimeter of the larger polygon to the nearest millimeter.
   - Measure the diameter of the circle to the nearest millimeter.
   - Measure the perimeter of the smaller polygon to the nearest millimeter.
   - Calculate the value of the ratio of the two perimeters to the diameter.
   - Take the average of the ratios. This average is the approximation of π (the Greek letter *pi*).

a.

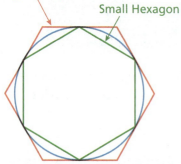

Large Hexagon
Small Hexagon

b.

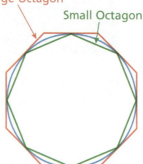

Large Octagon
Small Octagon

c.

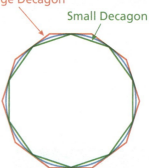

Large Decagon
Small Decagon

Sides	Large Perimeter	Diameter of Circle	Small Perimeter	Large Perimeter / Diameter	Small Perimeter / Diameter	Average of Ratios
6						
8						
10						

2. Based on the table, what can you conclude about the value of π? Explain your reasoning.

3. The Greek mathematician Archimedes used the above procedure to approximate the value of π. He used polygons with 96 sides. Do you think his approximation was more or less accurate than yours? Explain your reasoning.

Vocabulary

The following vocabulary terms are defined in this chapter. Think about what each term might mean and record your thoughts.

diameter of a circle
circumference
semicircle
composite figure
adjacent angles
vertical angles

Laurie's Notes

Check out the digital flash cards.
BigIdeasMath.com

Chapter Exploration

- Before students begin this exploration, review the names of several polygons.
- Ask, "What is the name of a polygon with 3 sides? 4 sides? 5 sides? 6 sides? 7 sides? 8 sides? 9 sides? 10 sides?" triangle; quadrilateral; pentagon; hexagon; heptagon; octagon; nonagon; decagon
- In this exploration, students will investigate the value of pi (π) by examining the relationship between the perimeters of several polygons and the diameter of a circle.
- Have pairs complete the table in Exercise 1 and then compare their answers with another pair. Discuss any discrepancies as a class.
- Allow time for pairs to complete Exercise 2 and then discuss their conclusions and reasoning as a class.
- **Think-Pair-Share:** Have students read Exercise 3 independently and then work with their partners to answer the question. Then ask pairs to share their ideas with the class.
- From their own investigations, students should recognize that as the number of sides of the polygon increases, the polygon gets closer to the circle. So, a polygon with 96 sides would produce a more accurate approximation of the value of π.

Vocabulary

- These terms represent some of the vocabulary that students will encounter in Chapter D. Discuss the terms as a class.
- Where have students heard the term *circumference* outside of a math classroom? In what contexts? Students may not be able to write the actual definition, but they may write phrases associated with *circumference*.
- Allowing students to discuss these terms now will prepare them for understanding the terms as they are presented in the chapter.
- When students encounter a new definition, encourage them to write in their *Student Journals*. They will revisit these definitions during the Chapter Review.

ELL Support

The mathematical discipline of geometry examines shapes and angles. The word *geometry* comes from the Latin word *geometria*, with the *geo-* prefix meaning "earth" and the Greek root word *metria*, meaning "measure." In other words, geometry "measures the shapes found on Earth." Ask students if they know other words with these roots. Explore their knowledge and offer examples if necessary.

- Examples for *geo-*: *geography* and *geology*
- Examples for *metria*: *metric* and *meter*

You may want to point out the differences in pronunciations and meanings of the words *angle* and *angel*.

Topics for Review

- Area
- Classifying Figures
- Drawing Angles
- Equations
- Exponents
- Intersection
- Lines
- Measuring Angles
- Perimeter
- Polygons
- Triangles

Chapter Exploration

1. See Additional Answers.

2. The value of π is about $\dfrac{22}{7} \approx 3.14$, because this is the approximation given in the last row of the table.

3. more accurate; *Sample answer:* The more sides for the polygons used by Archimedes, the closer the polygon resembles a circle. The more sides used, the closer the approximation is to the value of π.

Learning Target
Find the circumference of a circle.

Success Criteria
- Explain the relationship between the diameter and circumference of a circle.
- Use a formula to find the circumference of a circle.

Warm Up
Cumulative, vocabulary, and prerequisite skills practice opportunities are available in the *Resources by Chapter* or at BigIdeasMath.com.

ELL Support
Discuss the word *relationship*. Explain that a relationship is the description of a connection between things. The word is most commonly used to describe how people in a family are related. You may want to discuss students' understanding of family relationships. Then explain that the parts of a circle are also related. The *diameter* is the distance across the circle through the center and the *circumference* is the distance around the circle. In this section, students will learn more about how the diameter and the circumference of a circle are related.

Exploration 1
a. 4 in.
b. See Additional Answers.

Exploration 2
a. Check students' work.
b. circumference; *Sample answer:* roughly 3.14 times greater
c. See Additional Answers.
d. multiply the diameter by 3.14; 12.56 in.

T-599

Laurie's Notes

Preparing to Teach
- **Look for and Express Regularity in Repeated Reasoning:** Today's exploration gives students the opportunity to understand that *pi* is a calculable number. Students will discover that there is a constant relationship between the circumference and the diameter of a circle.

Motivate
- **Whole Class Activity:** How observant are your students? Tell them that you are going to give them 1 minute to write a list of objects in the room that have a special characteristic. Give them time to get scrap paper and a pencil.
- Announce that they need to list objects that are circular or have a **circle** on them. Go!
- Items will vary but expected items include: clock and/or watch face, bottom of coffee cup, pencil's eraser, pupils of your eyes, a student's glasses, metal feet on the chair, etc.

Exploration 1
- You may need to explain how to use a compass to draw a circle.
- **Use Appropriate Tools Strategically:** In part (b), let students spend a few minutes trying to figure out how they can approximate the **circumference** (string, ruler, cut small pieces of paper and form a line to measure, etc.). They may measure one-half or one-fourth of the circumference and then multiply by two or four.
- Have each pair share their methods and answers. The answers should be close to the same measurement. Discuss why they may differ.
- **Note:** If you choose not to use Exploration 2, you could expand this exploration by having students draw and measure several circles with different radii to explore the relationship between the **diameter** and circumference of a circle.

Exploration 2
- Students need a cylindrical object such as a can, paper towel or toilet paper roll, glass, etc. The objects should have different diameters. It is important that the objects do not change shape as students roll them.
- **Note:** Instead of rolling the objects on a flat surface, students could wrap string around the object and then measure the string with a ruler.
- If students are using cardboard objects, they could cut them and measure the circumferences with a ruler after rolling them.
- For part (c), draw a table on the board for pairs to record their diameters and circumferences. Students should recognize that each circumference is about 3 times as large as the corresponding diameter.
- **Big Idea:** The main goal of this exploration is to see there is a relationship between the diameter and circumference of a circle, not to calculate a close approximation of **pi**. Pi will be discussed later in the lesson.
- **Note:** You will use cans in Section E.2 so you may want to save them.

D.1 Circles and Circumference

Learning Target: Find the circumference of a circle.
Success Criteria:
- I can explain the relationship between the diameter and circumference of a circle.
- I can use a formula to find the circumference of a circle.

EXPLORATION 1

Using a Compass to Draw a Circle

Work with a partner. Set a compass to 2 inches and draw a circle.

a. Draw a line from one side of the circle to the other that passes through the center. What is the length of the line? This is called the *diameter* of the circle.

b. **MP CHOOSE TOOLS** Estimate the distance around the circle. This is called the *circumference* of the circle. Explain how you found your answer.

EXPLORATION 2

Exploring Diameter and Circumference

Work with a partner.

a. Roll a cylindrical object on a flat surface to find the circumference of the circular base.

b. Measure the diameter of the circular base. Which is greater, the diameter or the circumference? how many times greater?

c. Compare your answers in part (b) with the rest of the class. What do you notice?

d. Without measuring, how can you find the circumference of a circle with a given diameter? Use your method to estimate the circumference of the circle in Exploration 1.

Math Practice

Calculate Accurately
What other methods can you use to calculate the circumference of a circle? Which methods are more accurate?

D.1 Lesson

Key Vocabulary
circle, *p. 600*
center, *p. 600*
radius, *p. 600*
diameter, *p. 600*
circumference, *p. 601*
pi, *p. 601*
semicircle, *p. 602*

A **circle** is the set of all points in a plane that are the same distance from a point called the **center**.

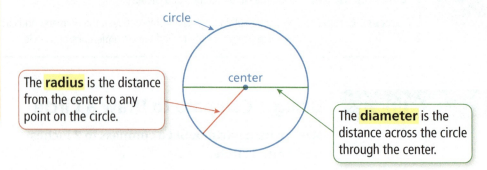

The **radius** is the distance from the center to any point on the circle.

The **diameter** is the distance across the circle through the center.

 Key Idea

Radius and Diameter

Words The diameter d of a circle is twice the radius r. The radius r of a circle is one-half the diameter d.

Algebra   **Diameter:** $d = 2r$ **Radius:** $r = \dfrac{d}{2}$

EXAMPLE 1   Finding a Radius and a Diameter

a. The diameter of a circle is 20 feet. Find the radius.

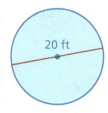

$r = \dfrac{d}{2}$ Radius of a circle

$= \dfrac{20}{2}$ Substitute 20 for *d*.

$= 10$ Divide.

▶ The radius is 10 feet.

b. The radius of a circle is 7 meters. Find the diameter.

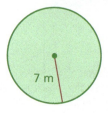

$d = 2r$ Diameter of a circle

$= 2(7)$ Substitute 7 for *r*.

$= 14$ Multiply.

▶ The diameter is 14 meters.

Try It

1. The diameter of a circle is 16 centimeters. Find the radius.
2. The radius of a circle is 9 yards. Find the diameter.

Laurie's Notes

Scaffolding Instruction
- Students have explored the relationship between the circumference and diameter of a circle. Now they will use a formula to find the circumference of a circle.
- **Emerging:** Students may recognize that there is a relationship between the diameter and circumference of a circle, but they need help formalizing the relationship. They will benefit from guided instruction for the Key Ideas and examples.
- **Proficient:** Students have begun to formalize the relationship between the diameter and circumference of a circle. They should review the vocabulary, Key Ideas, and examples before completing the Try It and Self-Assessment exercises.

Key Idea
- Draw a **circle** on the board and label the **center**, a **radius**, and a **diameter**. Discuss each term.
- Write the Key Idea.
- Discuss with students that if you know either the diameter or radius of a circle, you can find the other. There is a 2 : 1 relationship between the diameter and the radius.

EXAMPLE 1
- Work through each part as shown.
- **Attend to Precision:** Remind students to label their answers with the appropriate units.

Try It
- It helps some students to draw a sketch of a circle and label the given information. As visual learners, these students need to see the relationship instead of just reading the given information.

Scaffold instruction to support all students in their learning. Learning is individualized and you may want to group students differently as they move in and out of these levels with each skill and concept. Student self-assessment and feedback help guide your instructional decisions about how and when to layer support for all students to become proficient learners.

Extra Example 1
a. The diameter of a circle is 8 yards. Find the radius. 4 yd
b. The radius of a circle is 15 millimeters. Find the diameter. 30 mm

Try It
1. 8 cm
2. 18 yd

Extra Example 2

a. Find the circumference of a flying disc with a radius of 8 centimeters. Use 3.14 for π. about 50.24 cm

b. Find the circumference of a clock with a diameter of 21 inches. Use $\frac{22}{7}$ for π. about 66 in.

Try It

3. about 12.56 cm
4. about 44 ft
5. about 28.26 in.

ELL Support

After demonstrating Example 2, have students work in pairs to complete Try It Exercises 3–5. As they discuss each exercise, have them consider the following questions: Is the diameter or the radius given? What is the length of the diameter (or radius)? Which formula should you use? Which value of pi should you use? Expect students to perform according to their language levels.

Beginner: State numbers or one-word answers.

Intermediate: Use phrases or simple sentences such as, "The radius is two centimeters."

Advanced: Use detailed sentences such as, "The radius is two centimeters, so you multiply two times three and fourteen hundredths times two."

Laurie's Notes

Key Idea

- **Make Sense of Problems and Persevere in Solving Them:** Read the information at the top of the page. Note the two approximations of **pi** and how each is used in the problems that follow. Discuss the push-pin note.
- Write the Key Idea.
- **Common Misconception:** Students may know that pi is a number; however, when they see it in a formula, they can become confused. Students may ask if π is a variable. Pi is a constant whose value is approximately 3.14 or $\frac{22}{7}$. Remind students that πd means π times the diameter and $2\pi r$ means 2 times π times the radius.
- **Big Idea:** The ratio of the circumference to the diameter is pi. To get the formula for circumference, multiply both sides of the equation by the diameter.

$$\frac{\text{circumference}}{\text{diameter}} = \text{pi}$$

$$\frac{C}{d} = \pi$$

$$\cancel{d} \cdot \frac{C}{\cancel{d}} = \pi \cdot d$$

$$C = \pi d$$

EXAMPLE 2

- Work through each part as shown.
- Point out to students when to use the different forms of the circumference formula given a radius or a diameter.
- Remind students that the symbol $\approx$ means "approximately equal to."
- ? "Why is the equal sign replaced by the approximately equal ($\approx$) sign?" 3.14 is an approximation for π.
- ? "Why is $2 \times 3.14 \times 5$ equal to $2 \times 5 \times 3.14$?" Commutative Property of Multiplication
- Note that in part (b), the diameter is a multiple of 7, so $\frac{22}{7}$ is used as the approximation for π.
- **Note:** If students use the π key on their calculators, their answers may differ from those in the book. On standardized tests, students should always read the problem and/or formula sheet carefully to see which value of π they should use.

Try It

- **Think-Pair-Share:** Students should read each exercise independently and then work in pairs to complete the exercises. Then have each pair compare their answers with another pair and discuss any discrepancies.
- Check which estimate for π students used and why.

Math Practice

Use Definitions
Is pi a constant of proportionality? Explain your reasoning.

The distance around a circle is called the **circumference**. The ratio of the circumference to the diameter is the same for *every* circle and its value is represented by the Greek letter π, called **pi**. Two approximations for the value of π are 3.14 and $\frac{22}{7}$.

When the radius or diameter is a multiple of 7, it is easier to use $\frac{22}{7}$ as the estimate of π.

Key Idea

Circumference of a Circle

Words The circumference C of a circle is equal to π times the diameter d or π times twice the radius r.

Algebra $C = \pi d$ or $C = 2\pi r$

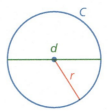

EXAMPLE 2 Finding Circumferences of Circles

5 in.

a. Find the circumference of the flying disc. Use 3.14 for π.

$C = 2\pi r$ Write formula for circumference.

$\approx 2 \cdot 3.14 \cdot 5$ Substitute 3.14 for π and 5 for r.

$= 31.4$ Multiply.

▶ The circumference is about 31.4 inches.

b. Find the circumference of the watch face. Use $\frac{22}{7}$ for π.

28 mm

$C = \pi d$ Write formula for circumference.

$\approx \frac{22}{7} \cdot 28$ Substitute $\frac{22}{7}$ for π and 28 for d.

$= 88$ Multiply.

▶ The circumference is about 88 millimeters.

Try It Find the circumference of the object. Use 3.14 or $\frac{22}{7}$ for π.

3.  2 cm

4.  14 ft

5.  9 in.

EXAMPLE 3 **Finding the Perimeter of a Semicircular Region**

A **semicircle** is one-half of a circle. Find the perimeter of the semicircular region.

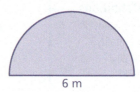
6 m

The straight side is 6 meters long. The distance around the curved part is one-half the circumference of a circle with a diameter of 6 meters.

$$\frac{C}{2} = \frac{\pi d}{2}$$ Divide the circumference by 2.

$$\approx \frac{3.14 \cdot 6}{2}$$ Substitute 3.14 for π and 6 for d.

$$= \frac{18.84}{2}$$ Multiply.

$$= 9.42$$ Divide.

 So, the perimeter is about $6 + 9.42 = 15.42$ meters.

Try It Find the perimeter of the semicircular region.

6.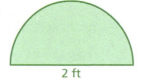
2 ft

7. 7 cm
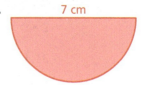

8.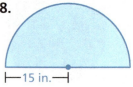
15 in.

 Self-Assessment for Concepts & Skills

Solve each exercise. Then rate your understanding of the success criteria in your journal.

9. **WRITING** Are there circles for which the value of the ratio of circumference to diameter is not equal to π? Explain.

10. **FINDING A PERIMETER** Find the perimeter of a semicircular region with a straight side that is 8 yards long.

11. **DIFFERENT WORDS, SAME QUESTION** Which is different? Find "both" answers.

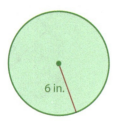
6 in.

What is the distance around the circle?

What is π times the radius?

What is the circumference of the circle?

What is π times the diameter?

Laurie's Notes

EXAMPLE 3

- Draw the diagram. It may be helpful to draw the other half of the semicircle as a dotted curve.
- Another way to visualize the distance around the curved part is to overlap a circle with a diameter of 6 meters with a semicircle with a straight side of 6 meters.
- Instead of first multiplying 3.14 and 6, you could divide 6 by 2 first and then multiply 3.14 by 3. This would require fewer decimal computations.
- **Common Error:** Students may find half the circumference and forget to add the distance across the diameter.
- **Extension:** Write and simplify a formula for the perimeter of a semicircle. $P = \pi r + d$, or $P = r(\pi + 2)$

Try It

- Students should solve the problems on whiteboards.

✓ Self-Assessment for Concepts & Skills

- Have students use *Visitor Explanation* with a neighbor to explain the relationship between the diameter and circumference of a circle and how to use a formula to find the circumference of a circle. As they take turns explaining, students should utilize *Accountable Language Stems*.
- **Neighbor Check:** Have students work independently and then have their neighbors check their work. Have students discuss any discrepancies.

> ### ELL Support
> Allow students to work in pairs instead of independently. Then have two pairs form a group to check their work. Have pairs display their answers to Exercise 10 on whiteboards for your review.

The Success Criteria Self-Assessment chart can be found in the *Student Journal* or online at *BigIdeasMath.com*.

Extra Example 3

A semicircle is one-half of a circle. Find the perimeter of the semicircular region.

about 25.7 yd

Try It

6. about 5.14 ft
7. about 18 cm
8. about 77.1 in.

Self-Assessment
for Concepts & Skills

9. no; *Sample answer:* The definition of π is the value of this ratio.
10. about 12.56 yd
11. What is π times the radius?; about 18.84 in.; about 37.68 in.

Extra Example 4
A roll of tape has a circumference of 32.6 inches. The circumference of the roll of tape decreases 7.5 inches after you use some of the tape. What is the radius of the roll after you use the tape? about 4.0 in.

Self-Assessment
for Problem Solving

12. about 207.24 in.

13. no; *Sample answer:* The radius of the dog's neck is 1.99 inches. The collar's radius needs to be 1.99 + 0.5, or 2.49 inches. The circumference of the collar is 15.64 inches, which is outside the range.

14. 4 times larger; *Sample answer:* The original circumference is $C = 2\pi r$. The new circumference will be $C = 2\pi(4r) = 8\pi r$, and $\frac{8\pi r}{2\pi r} = 4$.

Learning Target
Find the circumference of a circle.

Success Criteria
- Explain the relationship between the diameter and circumference of a circle.
- Use a formula to find the circumference of a circle.

Laurie's Notes

Formative Assessment Tip

KNWS Chart
This technique helps guide students through solving a word problem. Students complete a chart with the following columns as they work through the word problem.

K: What do you *know*?   **N:** What is *not* important?
W: *What* is the problem asking?   **S:** What *strategy* can you use?

Students can use their *KNWS Charts* to discuss and compare solving strategies with a partner. This technique helps students organize their thoughts and provides an effective process for problem solving.

EXAMPLE 4

- Ask a volunteer to read the problem aloud. Then ask another volunteer to explain the problem. If necessary, have another student re-read the problem.
- Model solving this problem using a *KNWS Chart*. A sample chart is shown.

K	N	W	S
• The circumference C of the roll of tape is 31.4 inches. • C decreases 10.5 inches.	• who uses the tape	• To find the radius of the roll of tape after the firefighter uses the tape.	• Use the formula for the circumference of a circle to find the radius of the roll after the firefighter uses the tape.

- Have students draw a diagram representing the top view of the tape using concentric circles.
- Work through the problem as shown, asking volunteers to explain each step.
- Remind students to always re-read the question and write a sentence to answer the question.

✓ Self-Assessment for Problem Solving

- The goal for all students is to feel comfortable with the problem-solving plan. It is important for students to problem-solve in class, where they may receive support from you and their peers. Keep in mind, some students may only be ready for the first step.
- Students should read each problem independently and make a plan for each problem. Then have students share and discuss their plans with a partner before solving the problems independently.

The Success Criteria Self-Assessment chart can be found in the *Student Journal* or online at BigIdeasMath.com.

Closure

- **Exit Ticket:** A coin has a diameter of 21 millimeters.
    a. What is the radius of the coin? 10.5 mm
    b. What is the circumference of the coin? about 66 mm

EXAMPLE 4 Modeling Real Life

The circumference of the roll of caution tape decreases 10.5 inches after a firefighter uses some of the tape. What is the radius of the roll after the firefighter uses the tape?

C = 31.4 in.

The radius and circumference of the roll are the radius and circumference of the circular bases of the roll. After the decrease, the circumference is $31.4 - 10.5 = 20.9$ inches.

Use the formula for the circumference of a circle to find the radius of a circle with a circumference of 20.9 inches.

$C = 2\pi r$	Write formula for circumference.
$20.9 \approx 2(3.14)r$	Substitute 20.9 for C and 3.14 for π.
$20.9 = 6.28r$	Multiply.
$3.3 \approx r$	Divide each side by 6.28.

▸ So, the radius of the roll is about 3.3 inches.

Self-Assessment for Problem Solving

Solve each exercise. Then rate your understanding of the success criteria in your journal.

12. The wheels of a monster truck are 66 inches tall. Find the distance the monster truck travels when the tires make one 360-degree rotation.

13. **DIG DEEPER!** The radius of a dog's collar should be at least 0.5 inch larger than the radius of the dog's neck. A dog collar adjusts to a circumference of 10 to 14 inches. Should the collar be worn by a dog with a neck circumference of 12.5 inches? Explain.

14. You resize a picture so that the radius of the midday Sun appears four times larger. How much larger does the circumference of the Sun appear? Explain.

D.1 Practice

> Go to **BigIdeasMath.com** to get HELP with solving the exercises.

▶ Review & Refresh

Two jars each contain 1000 numbered tiles. The double box-and-whisker plot represents a random sample of 10 numbers from each jar.

1. Compare the samples using measures of center and variation.

2. Can you determine which jar contains greater numbers? Explain.

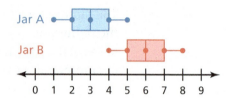

3. Find the percent of change from 24 to 18.

   A. 25% decrease   **B.** 25% increase   **C.** 75% increase   **D.** 75% decrease

▶ Concepts, Skills, & Problem Solving

EXPLORING DIAMETER AND CIRCUMFERENCE Estimate the circumference of the circular base of the object. (See Exploration 2, p. 599.)

4. tube of lip balm with radius 0.5 mm

5. D battery with radius 0.65 in.

FINDING A RADIUS Find the radius of the button.

6.  5 cm

7.  28 mm

8.  $3\frac{1}{2}$ in.

FINDING A DIAMETER Find the diameter of the object.

9. 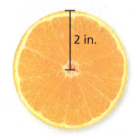 2 in.

10.  0.8 ft

11.  $\frac{3}{5}$ cm

FINDING A CIRCUMFERENCE Find the circumference of the object. Use 3.14 or $\frac{22}{7}$ for π.

12.  7 in.

13.  6 cm

14.  2 meters

604 Chapter D   Geometric Shapes and Angles

Assignment Guide and Concept Check

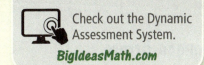

Scaffold assignments to support all students in their learning progression. The suggested assignments are a starting point. Continue to assign additional exercises and revisit with spaced practice to move every student toward proficiency.

Level	Assignment 1	Assignment 2
Emerging	1, 2, 3, 4, 6, 7, 9, 10, 12, 13, 15	8, 11, 14, 16, 17, 19, 21, 24, 29
Proficient	1, 2, 3, 5, 6, 8, 10, 11, 12, 14, 15	16, 17, 18, 19, 20, 22, 23, 24, 25, 26, 29
Advanced	1, 2, 3, 5, 6, 8, 10, 11, 12, 14, 16	18, 20, 22, 23, 24, 25, 26, 27, 28, 29, 30

- Assignment 1 is for use after students complete the Self-Assessment for Concepts & Skills.
- Assignment 2 is for use after students complete the Self-Assessment for Problem Solving.
- The red exercises can be used as a concept check.

Review & Refresh Prior Skills

Exercises 1 and 2 Comparing Random Samples
Exercise 3 Finding a Percent of Change

Common Errors

- **Exercises 6–11** Students may confuse what they are finding and halve the radius or double the diameter. Remind them that the radius is half the diameter. Encourage students to draw a line representing the radius or diameter for each problem so that they have a visual reference.
- **Exercises 12–14** Students may use the wrong formula for circumference when given a radius or diameter. Remind them of the different equations. If students are struggling with the two equations, tell them to use only one equation and to convert the dimension given to the one in the chosen formula.
- **Exercises 12–14** Students may use $\frac{22}{7}$ when it would be easier to use 3.14 and get frustrated. Remind students to use $\frac{22}{7}$ when the radius or diameter is a multiple of 7.

Review & Refresh

1. Jar A: Median: 3, IQR: 2; Jar B: Median: 6, IQR: 2
2. no; *Sample answer:* The sample size is too small to conclude that the tiles in Jar B have greater numbers than the tiles in Jar A.
3. A

Concepts, Skills, & Problem Solving

4. about 3.14 mm
5. about 4.08 in.
6. 2.5 cm
7. 14 mm
8. $1\frac{3}{4}$ in.
9. 4 in.
10. 1.6 ft
11. $1\frac{1}{5}$ cm
12. about 44 in.
13. about 18.84 cm
14. about 6.28 m

T-604

Concepts, Skills, & Problem Solving

15. about 7.71 ft
16. about 102.8 cm
17. about 1.42 mm
18. about 19.43 in.
19. a. about 25 m; about 50 m
    b. about 2 times greater
20. a. D; *Sample answer:* Figure D has the largest diameter, so its circumference is the greatest.
    b. B; *Sample answer:* Figure B has the smallest diameter, so its circumference is the least.
21. about 31.4 cm; about 62.8 cm
22. about 28.26 ft; about 44 ft
23. about 69.08 m; about 138.16 m
24. about 266,272 km

Common Errors

- **Exercises 15 and 16** Students may find the circumference of the circle and forget to divide by 2. Remind students that because it is a semicircle, they must divide the circumference of the circle by 2.
- **Exercises 15 and 16** Students may forget to add the diameter to the perimeter after they find the circumference part. Remind students that the perimeter includes all the sides, not just the curved part.
- **Exercise 20** Students may try to compare the radii or diameters without converting to the same units. Remind students that they need to have all the same units before comparing.
- **Exercises 21–23** Students may use the incorrect radius or diameter for the larger or smaller circle. Remind students that they will need to find the radius or diameter of the other circle.

FINDING THE PERIMETER OF A SEMICIRCULAR REGION Find the perimeter of the window.

15.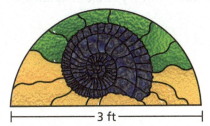
— 3 ft —

16.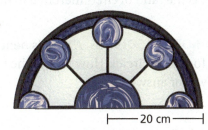
— 20 cm —

ESTIMATING A RADIUS Estimate the radius of the object.

17.
C = 8.9 mm

18.
C = 122 in.

19. **MP MODELING REAL LIFE** A circular sinkhole has a circumference of 75.36 meters. A week later, it has a circumference of 150.42 meters.

   a. Estimate the diameter of the sinkhole each week.
   b. How many times greater is the diameter of the sinkhole a week later?

20. **MP REASONING** Consider the circles A, B, C, and D.

   A.  8 ft
   B.  10 in.
   C. 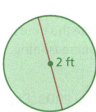 2 ft
   D. 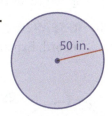 50 in.

   a. Without calculating, which circle has the greatest circumference? Explain.
   b. Without calculating, which circle has the least circumference? Explain.

FINDING CIRCUMFERENCES Find the circumferences of both circles.

21.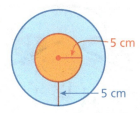
5 cm
5 cm

22.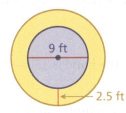
9 ft
2.5 ft

23.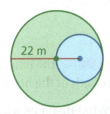
22 m

24. **MP MODELING REAL LIFE** A satellite is in an approximately circular orbit 36,000 kilometers from Earth's surface. The radius of Earth is about 6400 kilometers. What is the circumference of the satellite's orbit?

25. **MP STRUCTURE** The ratio of circumference to diameter is the same for every circle. Is the ratio of circumference to radius the same for every circle? Explain.

26. **MP PROBLEM SOLVING** A wire is bent to form four semicircles. How long is the wire? Justify your answer.

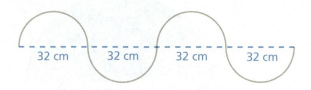

27. **CRITICAL THINKING** Explain how to draw a circle with a circumference of π^2 inches. Then draw the circle.

28. **DIG DEEPER!** "Lines" of latitude on Earth are actually circles. The Tropic of Cancer is the northernmost line of latitude at which the Sun appears directly overhead at noon. The Tropic of Cancer has a radius of 5854 kilometers.

    To qualify for an around-the-world speed record, a pilot must cover a distance no less than the circumference of the Tropic of Cancer, cross all meridians, and land on the same airfield where the flight began.

    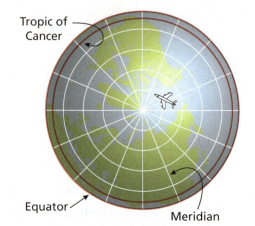

    a. What is the minimum distance that a pilot must fly to qualify for an around-the-world speed record?

    b. **RESEARCH** Estimate the time it will take for a pilot to qualify for the speed record. Explain your reasoning.

29. **MP PROBLEM SOLVING** Bicycles in the late 1800s looked very different than they do today.

    a. How many rotations does each tire make after traveling 600 feet? Round your answers to the nearest whole number.

    b. Would you rather ride a bicycle made with two large wheels or two small wheels? Explain.

30. **MP LOGIC** The length of the minute hand is 150% of the length of the hour hand.

    a. What distance will the tip of the minute hand move in 45 minutes? Justify your answer.

    b. In 1 hour, how much farther does the tip of the minute hand move than the tip of the hour hand? Explain how you found your answer.

Mini-Assessment

1. Find the radius of the circle.

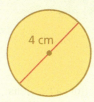

   2 cm

2. Find the diameter of the circle.

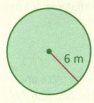

   12 m

Find the circumference of the circle. Use 3.14 or $\frac{22}{7}$ for π.

3.

   about 154 in.

4.

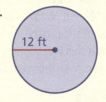

   about 75.36 ft

5. Find the perimeter of the window.

   about 20.56 ft

Section Resources

Surface Level	Deep Level
Resources by Chapter • Extra Practice • Reteach • Puzzle Time Student Journal • Self-Assessment • Practice Differentiating the Lesson Tutorial Videos Skills Review Handbook Skills Trainer	Resources by Chapter • Enrichment and Extension Graphic Organizers Dynamic Assessment System • Section Practice

Concepts, Skills, & Problem Solving

25. yes; Because $\frac{\text{circumference}}{\text{radius}} = \frac{2\pi r}{r} = 2\pi$, the ratio is the same for every circle.

26. about 200.96 cm; *Sample answer:* The circumference of each semicircle is about 50.24 cm. Because there are 4 semicircles, 4(50.24) = 200.96 cm.

27. The circle has a diameter of π inches, so use a diameter of about 3.1 inches.

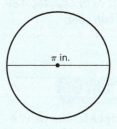

28. a. about 36,763 km
    b. Check students' work.

29. a. small tire: about 127 rotations; large tire: about 38 rotations
    b. *Sample answer:* A bicycle with large wheels would allow you to travel farther with each rotation of the pedal.

30. a. about 254.34 mm; First, find the length of the minute hand. Then, find $\frac{3}{4}$ of the circumference of a circle whose radius is the length of the minute hand.
    b. about 320.28 mm; Subtract $\frac{1}{12}$ the circumference of a circle whose radius is the length of the hour hand from the circumference of a circle whose radius is the length of the minute hand.

Learning Target
Find the area of a circle.

Success Criteria
- Estimate the area of a circle.
- Use a formula to find the area of a circle.

Warm Up
Cumulative, vocabulary, and prerequisite skills practice opportunities are available in the *Resources by Chapter* or at BigIdeasMath.com.

ELL Support
Students may be familiar with the word *area* as it is used in everyday language. Ask them to describe what area means. Then explain that in math the word *area* has a very specific meaning. It is the amount of surface covered by a figure. It is measured using square units, such as square feet. For example, a rectangle with a length of 2 feet and a width of 3 feet has an area of 6 square feet.

Exploration 1
Sample answer: 12 cm², 12.5 cm²; 12.5625 cm²; The grid with the smallest squares should be closest to the actual area of the circle because you can better estimate the number of squares in the circle.

Exploration 2
a. $A = \pi r^2$; height of parallelogram = r, base of parallelogram = $\dfrac{C}{2} = \dfrac{2\pi r}{2} = \pi r$, Area = $bh = \pi r^2$.

b. $r = 2$ cm; $A = \pi(2)^2 \approx 12.56$ cm²

T-607

Laurie's Notes

Preparing to Teach
- Students should know how to find areas of parallelograms from a previous course. Now they will relate their understanding of finding the area of a parallelogram to finding the area of a circle.
- **Reason Abstractly and Quantitatively:** In the explorations, students will use models to develop the formula for the area of a circle.

Motivate
- ❓ "At a pizza restaurant, you have a choice of ordering a 16-inch pizza or a 12-inch pizza for dinner. What measurement is being used to describe the pizza?" the diameter
- ❓ "Both pizzas are cut into the same number of pieces. Do both pizzas give you the same amount of pizza?" No, the size of the slices is different.
- ❓ "How would you figure out how many times more pizza you get with the 16-inch pizza than with the 12-inch pizza?" Listen for students to mention the idea of comparing the areas of the pizzas.
- Mention to students that after this lesson, they will be able to answer this question. You may want to return to this question at the end of the lesson.

Exploration 1
- Students need to determine the area of each grid square before finding the estimates.
- ❓ "What is the side length of each grid square in the first grid? the second grid? the third grid?" 1 centimeter; 0.5 centimeter; 0.25 centimeter
- ❓ "How can you use the first grid to estimate the area of the circle?" Count the shaded grid squares. "What about the partially shaded grid squares?" Combine them to approximate a full grid square.
- Students' estimates may or may not get closer to the actual area as the grid squares become smaller, depending on how they estimate.
- ❓ "What will you need to do differently in the second and third grid?" Divide the number of squares by 4 in the second grid and by 16 in the third grid (to convert to square centimeters).

Exploration 2
- **Note:** To make this exploration more hands on, you could have students draw circles, cut out equal sections, and rearrange them. This can be done before or after the exploration using 24 sections or another even number of sections.
- ❓ "What happens to the 'parallelogram' if you divide the circle into a large number of equal sections?" It will look more like a rectangle.
- ❓ "How do you find the area of a parallelogram?" $A = bh$
- ❓ "What is the length of the base?" $\frac{1}{2}C = \frac{1}{2}(2\pi r) = \pi r$ "What is the height?" r
- ❓ "What is the formula for the area of a circle?" $A = (\pi r)(r) = (\pi r^2)$
- ❓ "What is the relationship between the area and the circumference?" The area is half the circumference times the radius.

D.2 Areas of Circles

Learning Target: Find the area of a circle.

Success Criteria:
- I can estimate the area of a circle.
- I can use a formula to find the area of a circle.

EXPLORATION 1

Estimating the Area of a Circle

Work with a partner. Each grid contains a circle with a diameter of 4 centimeters. Use each grid to estimate the area of the circle. Which estimate should be closest to the actual area? Explain.

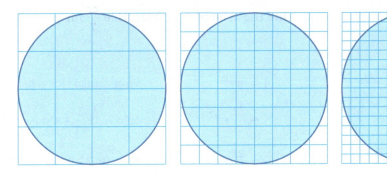

EXPLORATION 2

Writing a Formula for the Area of a Circle

Work with a partner. A student draws a circle with radius r and divides the circle into 24 equal sections. The student cuts out each section and arranges the sections to form a shape that resembles a parallelogram.

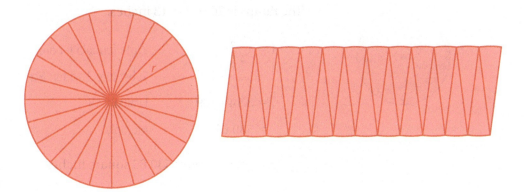

Math Practice

Interpret a Solution
Describe the relationship between the radius and the area of a circle.

a. Use the diagram to write a formula for the area A of a circle in terms of the radius r. Explain your reasoning.

b. Use the formula to check your estimates in Exploration 1.

Section D.2 Areas of Circles 607

D.2 Lesson

Area of a Circle

Words The area A of a circle is the product of π and the square of the radius r.

Algebra $A = \pi r^2$

EXAMPLE 1 Finding Areas of Circles

a. Find the area of the circle. Use $\dfrac{22}{7}$ for π.

Estimate
$3 \times 7^2 \approx 3 \times 50$
$= 150$

7 cm

$A = \pi r^2$ Write formula for area.

$\approx \dfrac{22}{7} \cdot 7^2$ Substitute $\dfrac{22}{7}$ for π and 7 for r.

$= \dfrac{22}{7} \cdot 49$ Evaluate 7^2. Divide out the common factor.

$= 154$ Multiply.

▶ The area is about 154 square centimeters.

Reasonable?
$154 \approx 150$ ✓

b. Find the area of the circle. Use 3.14 for π.

The radius is $26 \div 2 = 13$ inches.

Estimate
$3 \times 13^2 \approx 3 \times 170$
$= 510$

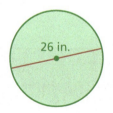

26 in.

$A = \pi r^2$ Write formula for area.

$\approx 3.14 \cdot 13^2$ Substitute 3.14 for π and 13 for r.

$= 3.14 \cdot 169$ Evaluate 13^2.

$= 530.66$ Multiply.

▶ The area is about 530.66 square inches.

Reasonable?
$530.66 \approx 510$ ✓

Try It

1. Find the area of a circle with a radius of 6 feet. Use 3.14 for π.

2. Find the area of a circle with a diameter of 28 meters. Use $\dfrac{22}{7}$ for π.

Laurie's Notes

Scaffolding Instruction
- In the exploration, students gained an intuitive understanding about how to find the area of a circle. Now they will use the formula to solve real-life problems.
- **Emerging:** Students may struggle with using the formula for the area of a circle. They will benefit from guided instruction for the examples.
- **Proficient:** Students understand the development and use of the formula for the area of a circle. They should review Example 2 before completing the Try It and Self-Assessment exercises.

Key Idea
- Discuss the formula, written in words and algebraically.
- **Common Error:** Students square the product of π and r, instead of just the radius.

EXAMPLE 1
- Work through each part as shown. Remind students that π can be rounded to 3 when estimating.
- **Common Error:** Make sure students are reading the figures correctly. A line segment from the center to the outside edge indicates a radius. A line segment across the circle through the center represents a diameter.
- ❓ "What would a reasonable answer be?" Answers will vary but should be similar to what is shown in the text.
- ❓ "In part (a), why is $\frac{22}{7}$ used as an estimate for π?" The radius is a multiple of 7.
- **Look for and Make Use of Structure:** In part (a), 7 is squared and then 7 is divided out in the next step. You could divide 7 out before squaring, but students have not done this with powers yet.

$$\frac{22}{7} \cdot 7^2 = \frac{22}{7} \cdot 7 \cdot 7 \quad \text{or} \quad \frac{22}{7} \cdot 7^2 = \frac{22}{1\,7} \cdot 7^2$$

- **Common Error:** For part (b), students may forget to divide the diameter by 2 to find the radius before substituting in the area formula.
- If students are not using calculators, ask them to give a reasonable estimate for 3.14×169 before they multiply.
- Remind students to label their answers with the appropriate units.

Try It
- **Teaching Strategy:** Have students draw a diagram to represent each written problem.
- **Neighbor Check:** Have students work independently and then have their neighbors check their work. Have students discuss any discrepancies.

Teaching Strategy
Many students view a diagram differently than a written problem, especially visual learners. When demonstrating examples without a diagram, be sure to draw one to represent the problem. Diagrams do not need to be drawn precisely to benefit student understanding. Visual learners will be aided by a simple diagram that includes the given information.

Scaffold instruction to support all students in their learning. Learning is individualized and you may want to group students differently as they move in and out of these levels with each skill and concept. Student self-assessment and feedback help guide your instructional decisions about how and when to layer support for all students to become proficient learners.

Extra Example 1
a. Find the area of a circle with a radius of 21 feet. Use $\frac{22}{7}$ for π. about 1386 ft^2

b. Find the area of a circle with a diameter of 12 meters. Use 3.14 for π. about 113.04 m^2

ELL Support
After demonstrating Example 1, have students work in pairs to complete Try It Exercises 1 and 2. Have one student ask another, "What is the radius? How do you find the area? What is the area?" Then have students switch roles.

Beginner: Write the formula and state numbers to answer the guiding questions.

Intermediate: Use simple sentences such as, "Multiply three and fourteen hundredths and six squared."

Advanced: Use detailed sentences such as, "To find the area, square six and then multiply by three and fourteen hundredths."

Try It
1. about 113.04 ft^2
2. about 616 m^2

Extra Example 2

Find the area of the semicircle.

about 127.17 in.²

Try It

3. about 189.97 cm²
4. about 25.12 m²
5. about 9.8125 yd²

Self-Assessment
for Concepts & Skills

6. 3 cm²; *Sample answer:* By increasing the number of squares inside the grid, a closer approximation to the area of the circle can be found.

7. $A = \dfrac{C^2}{4\pi}$

8. What is the area of a circle with a radius of 100 cm?; 31,400 cm²; about 7850 cm²

Laurie's Notes

EXAMPLE 2

- ❓ "How do you find the area of a semicircle?" Find $\frac{1}{2}$ the area of the circle.
- ❓ "What is the radius of the semicircle?" 15 feet
- Work through the problem as shown.
- **Extension:** If time permits and students are using the area formula correctly, try the following problems.
  - ❓ "If you make a mistake and use the diameter instead of the radius in the area formula, is the area doubled? Explain." No, the area is quadrupled.
  - "Find the area of the doughnut region." $8\pi \approx 25.12$ square inches

Try It

- Check to see that students recognize the difference in how a radius and a diameter are labeled.
- **Neighbor Check:** Have students work independently and then have their neighbors check their work. Have students discuss any discrepancies.

✓ Self-Assessment for Concepts & Skills

- Students should solve these problems independently and then work with a partner to discuss any discrepancies.
- Ask students to use *Thumbs Up* to indicate their understanding of each success criterion.

ELL Support

Allow students to work in pairs for extra support and to practice language. Have pairs display their estimates for Exercise 6 on whiteboards for your review. Have two pairs discuss all of their answers. Encourage questions. Monitor discussions and provide support as needed. Then discuss the answers as a class.

The Success Criteria Self-Assessment chart can be found in the *Student Journal* or online at *BigIdeasMath.com*.

EXAMPLE 2 **Finding the Area of a Semicircle**

Find the area of the semicircle.

The area of the semicircle is one-half the area of a circle with a diameter of 30 feet. The radius of the circle is $30 \div 2 = 15$ feet.

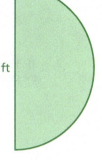

30 ft

$$\frac{A}{2} = \frac{\pi r^2}{2} \quad \text{Divide the area by 2.}$$

$$\approx \frac{3.14 \cdot 15^2}{2} \quad \text{Substitute 3.14 for } \pi \text{ and 15 for } r.$$

$$= \frac{3.14 \cdot 225}{2} \quad \text{Evaluate } 15^2.$$

$$= 353.25 \quad \text{Simplify.}$$

▶ So, the area of the semicircle is about 353.25 square feet.

Math Practice

Find General Methods

How can you find the area of one-fourth of a circle? three-fourths of a circle?

Try It Find the area of the semicircle.

3. 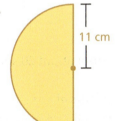 11 cm

4. 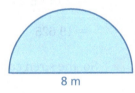 8 m

5. 5 yd

Self-Assessment for Concepts & Skills

Solve each exercise. Then rate your understanding of the success criteria in your journal.

6. **ESTIMATING AN AREA** The grid contains a circle with a diameter of 2 centimeters. Use the grid to estimate the area of the circle. How can you change the grid to improve your estimate? Explain.

7. **WRITING** Explain the relationship between the circumference and area of a circle.

8. **DIFFERENT WORDS, SAME QUESTION** Which is different? Find "both" answers.

What is the area of a circle with a diameter of 1 m?

What is the area of a circle with a diameter of 100 cm?

What is the area of a circle with a radius of 100 cm?

What is the area of a circle with a radius of 500 mm?

EXAMPLE 3 **Modeling Real Life**

A tsunami warning siren can be heard up to 2.5 miles away in all directions. From how many square miles can the siren be heard?

 Understand the problem.

You are given the description of a region in which a siren can be heard. You are asked to find the number of square miles within the range of the siren.

 Make a plan.

Two and a half miles from the siren in all directions is a circular region with a radius of 2.5 miles. So, find the area of a circle with a radius of 2.5 miles.

Solve and check.

$A = \pi r^2$ Write formula for area.

$\approx 3.14 \cdot 2.5^2$ Substitute 3.14 for π and 2.5 for r.

$= 3.14 \cdot 6.25$ Evaluate 2.5^2.

$= 19.625$ Multiply.

 So, the siren can be heard from about 20 square miles.

Check Reasonableness The number of square miles should be greater than $3 \cdot 2^2 = 12$, but less than $4 \cdot 3^2 = 36$. Because $12 < 20 < 36$, the answer is reasonable. ✓

 Self-Assessment for Problem Solving

Solve each exercise. Then rate your understanding of the success criteria in your journal.

9. A local event planner wants to cover a circular region with mud for an obstacle course. The region has a circumference of about 157 feet. The cost to cover 1 square foot with mud is $1.50. Approximate the cost to cover the region with mud.

10. **DIG DEEPER!** A manufacturer recommends that you use a frying pan with a radius that is within 1 inch of the radius of your stovetop burner. The area of the bottom of your frying pan is 25π square inches. The circumference of your cooktop burner is 9π inches. Does your frying pan meet the manufacturer's recommendation?

Laurie's Notes

EXAMPLE 3

- Ask a volunteer to read the problem aloud. Give time for students to process the information.
- **Teaching Strategy:** Have students draw a simple diagram on whiteboards to represent the problem and discuss any discrepancies.
- Work through the example as shown.
- Explain the Check Reasonableness note. Because π is between 3 and 4, the underestimate uses 3 for π and the overestimate uses 4 for π. Because 2.5 miles is between 2 miles and 3 miles, the underestimate uses 2 for the radius and the overestimate uses 3 for the radius.

✓ Self-Assessment for Problem Solving

- Allow time in class for students to practice using the problem-solving plan. Remember, some students may only be able to complete the first step.
- Students should independently make a plan for each problem and then check with a neighbor before solving.
- In Exercise 9, students may only find the area of the circular region because the lesson is on areas of circles. Remind students to always read the problem carefully to determine what is being asked.

The Success Criteria Self-Assessment chart can be found in the *Student Journal* or online at *BigIdeasMath.com*.

Closure

- Return to the question from the Motivate.
  - Find the areas of a 16-inch pizza and a 12-inch pizza. How many times larger is the 16-inch pizza than the 12-inch pizza? about 1.8 times
  - Students may find this easier to calculate if the area is kept in terms of π.

    Area of 16-inch pizza
    $A = \pi(8)^2$
    $= 64\pi$ square inches

    Area of 12-inch pizza
    $A = \pi(6)^2$
    $= 36\pi$ square inches

    Compare 64π and 36π. When you divide both quantities by π, you are comparing 64 and 36. $64 \div 36 \approx 1.8$, so the 16-inch pizza is about 1.8 times larger than the 12-inch pizza.
  - This situation can also be thought of as "how many times more toppings are needed for the larger pizza?"

Extra Example 3
The boundary of a wildlife refuge is located 6.2 miles away in all directions from the refuge headquarters. How many square miles are in the wildlife refuge? about 121 square miles

Self-Assessment for Problem Solving

9. about $2950
10. yes

Learning Target
Find the area of a circle.

Success Criteria
- Estimate the area of a circle.
- Use a formula to find the area of a circle.

Review & Refresh

1. about 28.26 cm
2. about 22 in.
3. 3 possible outcomes
4. 2 different ways

Concepts, Skills, & Problem Solving

5. about 6.75 cm^2
6. about 2.08 in.^{2}
7. about 254.34 mm^2
8. about 616 cm^2
9. about 314 in.^{2}
10. about 7.065 in.^{2}
11. about 3.14 cm^2
12. about 1.76625 ft^2

Assignment Guide and Concept Check

Scaffold assignments to support all students in their learning progression. The suggested assignments are a starting point. Continue to assign additional exercises and revisit with spaced practice to move every student toward proficiency.

Level	Assignment 1	Assignment 2
Emerging	2, 3, 4, 5, 7, 9, 11, 13, 17	6, 8, 10, 12, 14, 15, 16, 19, 20, 21, 25
Proficient	2, 3, 4, 6, 8, 10, 11, 13, 17, 18	12, 15, 16, 19, 20, 21, 23, 24, 25
Advanced	2, 3, 4, 6, 8, 10, 12, 13, 18, 19	15, 16, 20, 22, 23, 24, 25, 26

- Assignment 1 is for use after students complete the Self-Assessment for Concepts & Skills.
- Assignment 2 is for use after students complete the Self-Assessment for Problem Solving.
- The red exercises can be used as a concept check.

Review & Refresh Prior Skills

Exercises 1 and 2 Finding a Circumference
Exercises 3 and 4 Identifying Outcomes

Common Errors

- **Exercises 7–12** Students may write the incorrect units for the area. Remind students to carefully check the units and to square the units as well.
- **Exercises 7–12** Students may refer to the formula for circumference and forget to square the radius when finding the area. Remind students that the area formula uses the radius squared.
- **Exercises 10–12** Students may forget to divide the diameter by 2 to find the area. Remind students that they need the *radius* for the formula for the area of a circle.

D.2 Practice

 Go to **BigIdeasMath.com** to get HELP with solving the exercises.

▶ Review & Refresh

Find the circumference of the object. Use 3.14 or $\frac{22}{7}$ for π.

1.  9 cm

2.  7 in.

You spin the spinner shown.

3. How many possible outcomes are there?

4. In how many ways can spinning an odd number occur?

▶ Concepts, Skills, & Problem Solving

ESTIMATING AN AREA Use the grid to estimate the area of the circle. *(See Exploration 1, p. 607.)*

5. diameter of 3 centimeters

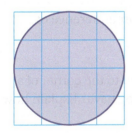

6. diameter of 1.6 inches

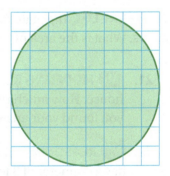

FINDING AN AREA Find the area of the circle. Use 3.14 or $\frac{22}{7}$ for π.

7.  9 mm

8.  14 cm

9. 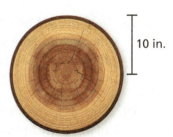 10 in.

10.  3 in.

11.  2 cm

12.  1.5 ft

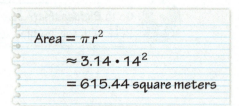

13. **YOU BE THE TEACHER** Your friend finds the area of a circle with a diameter of 7 meters. Is your friend correct? Explain.

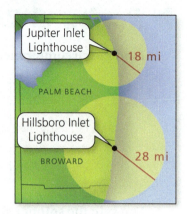

14. **MODELING REAL LIFE** The diameter of a flour tortilla is 12 inches. What is the total area of two tortillas?

15. **MODELING REAL LIFE** The diameter of a coaster is 7 centimeters. What is the total area of five coasters?

16. **PROBLEM SOLVING** The Hillsboro Inlet Lighthouse lights up how much more area than the Jupiter Inlet Lighthouse?

FINDING THE AREA OF A SEMICIRCLE Find the area of the semicircle.

17.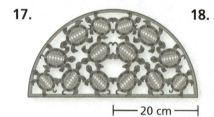
18.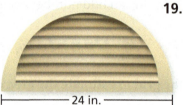
19.

20. **MODELING REAL LIFE** The plate for a microscope has a circumference of 100π millimeters. What is the area of the plate?

21. **MODELING REAL LIFE** A dog is leashed to the corner of a house. How much running area does the dog have? Explain how you found your answer.

22. **REASONING** Target A has a circumference of 20 feet. Target B has a diameter of 3 feet. Both targets are the same distance away. Which target is easier to hit? Explain your reasoning.

23. **MODELING REAL LIFE** A circular oil spill has a radius of 2 miles. After a day, the radius of the oil spill increases by 3 miles. By how many square miles does the area of the oil spill increase?

24. **FINDING AN AREA** Find the area of the circle in square yards.

25. **REPEATED REASONING** What happens to the circumference and the area of a circle when you double the radius? triple the radius? Justify your answer.

26. **CRITICAL THINKING** Is the area of a semicircle with a diameter of x *greater than*, *less than*, or *equal to* the area of a circle with a diameter of $\frac{1}{2}x$? Explain.

Common Errors
- **Exercises 17–19** Students may write the incorrect units for the area. Remind students to carefully check the units and to square the units as well.
- **Exercises 17–19** Students may forget to divide the area by 2. Remind students that they are finding the area of half of a circle, so the area is half the area of a whole circle.

Mini-Assessment

Find the area of the circle. Use 3.14 or $\frac{22}{7}$ for π.

1.

   about 3.14 ft²

2.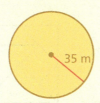

   about 3850 m²

3.

   about 200.96 in.²

4.

   about 379.94 cm²

5. Find the area of the rug.

   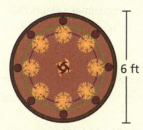

   about 28.26 ft²

Section Resources

Surface Level	Deep Level
Resources by Chapter • Extra Practice • Reteach • Puzzle Time Student Journal • Self-Assessment • Practice Differentiating the Lesson Tutorial Videos Skills Review Handbook Skills Trainer	Resources by Chapter • Enrichment and Extension Graphic Organizers Dynamic Assessment System • Section Practice

Concepts, Skills, & Problem Solving

13. no; The diameter was doubled instead of taking half of the diameter to find the radius.
14. about 226.08 in.²
15. about 192.33 cm²
16. about 1444.4 mi²
17. about 628 cm²
18. about 226.08 in.²
19. about 1.57 ft²
20. about 7850 mm²
21. about 942 ft²; *Sample answer:* The running area is $\frac{3}{4}$ the area of a circle with a radius of 20 feet.
22. Target A; *Sample answer:* Target A has a radius of about 3.18 feet and Target B has a radius of 1.5 feet. Target A is a larger target, so it is easier to hit.
23. about 65.94 mi²
24. about 7.07 yd²
25. See Additional Answers.
26. greater than; The circle's diameter is one-half as long, so it equals the radius of the semicircle. A diagram shows that the area of the semicircle is greater.

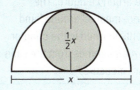

Learning Target
Find perimeters and areas of composite figures.

Success Criteria
- Use a grid to estimate perimeters and areas.
- Identify the shapes that make up a composite figure.
- Find the perimeters and areas of shapes that make up composite figures.

Warm Up
Cumulative, vocabulary, and prerequisite skills practice opportunities are available in the *Resources by Chapter* or at BigIdeasMath.com.

ELL Support
Explain that a composite figure is made up of more than one shape. It may contain rectangles, triangles, circles, or other geometric shapes. *Composite* is related to the word *compose*, which comes from the Latin language and means "put together." The perimeter is the distance around a figure. The prefix *peri-* means "around" and as students learned in the chapter opener, *meter* comes from the Latin word for "measure."

Exploration 1
Check students' work.

Laurie's Notes

Preparing to Teach
- **Make Sense of Problems and Persevere in Solving Them:** Students have worked with perimeter and area formulas. In making sense of **composite figures**, they need to view the figures as composed of smaller, familiar figures.

Motivate

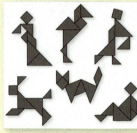
- Arrange a set of tangram pieces in a square. Tell students that the area of the square is 16 square units.
- ❓ "What are the dimensions of the square?" 4 units by 4 units
- Now rearrange all of the tangram pieces to make a new shape.
- ❓ "Can you find the area of each of these? Explain." Yes, the area is 16 square units because each new figure is composed of the same 7 pieces that made the square.

Exploration 1

- Share with students that builders and contractors submit bids for work that they want to do. If more than one bid is received, the consumer selects the builder or contractor based upon a number of factors, one of which is the cost that is quoted.
- In this exploration, assume that each pair of students is bidding on the job. They could even have a name for their two-person company. Their bid sheet (work done) should be neat and organized and easily understood by the pool's owner—you!
- Explain the phrase *$5 per linear foot* so that all students understand. In construction, when the width of material (in this case, the tile) is predetermined, the cost is given in terms of the length, not in terms of area (square feet). From the drawing, students should realize that side length of each tile is 1 linear foot.
- Students should count the number of tiles surrounding the pool to determine how much tile is needed and then multiply by $5 per linear foot.
- Students need to design the custom-made tarp for the pool. Encourage students to lower the cost by ordering an irregular-shaped tarp that covers only the surface of the pool with minimal overlap of the deck.
- Make sure each pair includes a labor charge based on the information given. They will set their own hourly wage. Is it realistic?
- Remind students to estimate their total profits.
- Discuss general results with the whole class. Compare the quotes, separating out the material and labor.
- **Extension:** List the hourly wage and the number of hours of labor that each company charges. Use this data to find the mean, median, and range of the hourly wages and the total labor charge.

T-613

D.3 Perimeters and Areas of Composite Figures

Learning Target: Find perimeters and areas of composite figures.

Success Criteria:
- I can use a grid to estimate perimeters and areas.
- I can identify the shapes that make up a composite figure.
- I can find the perimeters and areas of shapes that make up composite figures.

EXPLORATION 1

Submitting a Bid

Work with a partner. You want to bid on a project for the pool shown. The project involves ordering and installing the brown tile that borders the pool, and ordering a custom-made tarp to cover the surface of the pool. In the figure, each grid square represents 1 square foot.

- You pay $5 per linear foot for the tile.
- You pay $4 per square foot for the tarp.
- It takes you about 15 minutes to install each foot of tile.

a. Estimate the total cost for the tile and the tarp.

b. Write a bid for how much you will charge for the project. Include the hourly wage you will receive. Estimate your total profit.

Math Practice

Simplify a Situation

How does using a grid help you make approximations for the perimeter and area of the pool?

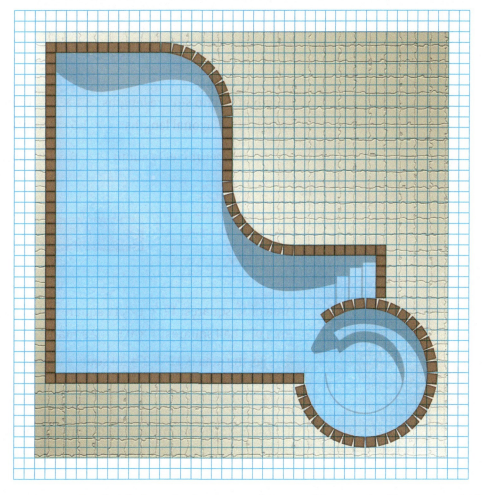

Section D.3 Perimeters and Areas of Composite Figures 613

D.3 Lesson

Key Vocabulary
composite figure, p. 614

A **composite figure** is made up of triangles, squares, rectangles, semicircles, and other two-dimensional figures.

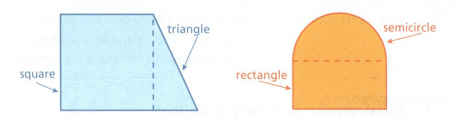

To find the perimeter of a composite figure, find the distance around the figure. To find the area of a composite figure, separate it into figures with areas you know how to find. Then find the sum of the areas of those figures.

EXAMPLE 1 Estimating Perimeter and Area

Estimate (a) the perimeter and (b) the area of the arrow.

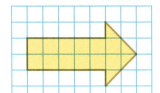

a.

Count the number of grid square lengths around the arrow. There are 14.

Count the number of diagonal lengths around the arrow. There are 4.

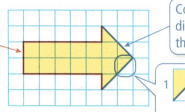

Estimate the diagonal length to be 1.5 units.

Length of 14 grid square lengths: $14 \times 1 = 14$ units

Length of 4 diagonal lengths: $4 \times 1.5 = 6$ units

 So, the perimeter is about $14 + 6 = 20$ units.

b.

Count the number of squares that lie entirely in the figure. There are 12.

Count the number of half squares in the figure. There are 4.

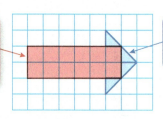

Area of 12 squares: $12 \times 1 = 12$ square units

Area of 4 half squares: $4 \times 0.5 = 2$ square units

 So, the area is $12 + 2 = 14$ square units.

Try It

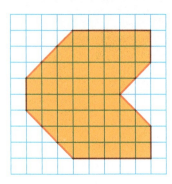

1. Estimate the perimeter and the area of the figure.

614 Chapter D Geometric Shapes and Angles

Laurie's Notes

Scaffolding Instruction

- In the exploration, students gained an intuitive understanding about how to find the perimeter and area of a composite figure. Now they will separate composite figures into familiar geometric shapes and use known formulas to find the perimeters and areas.
- **Emerging:** Students may be able to use grid squares to estimate perimeters and areas of composite figures, but they need guided instruction for using formulas.
- **Proficient:** Students can separate a composite figure into known shapes and then use formulas to find the perimeter and area of the composite figure. They should complete the Try It exercises before moving on to the Self-Assessment exercises.

Discuss

- Discuss the definition for a **composite figure** and how to find the perimeter and area of a composite figure.
- Display the composite figures below and ask students what shapes they would separate them into.

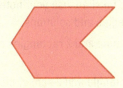 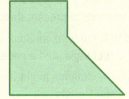

EXAMPLE 1

- **Common Error:** Students may think the diagonal of the square is 1 unit because the side lengths are 1 unit. Have them think about the *shortcut* of walking across the diagonal of a square versus walking the two side lengths. Have students cut out a square with 1-inch sides. Use this to compare the length of a side and the diagonal of the square.
- Students are asked to estimate the perimeter because the slanted sides are irrational numbers.
- Work through both parts as shown. Remind students that area is measured in square units.

Try It

- Ask a volunteer to share his or her thinking and solution to the problem.

Scaffold instruction to support all students in their learning. Learning is individualized and you may want to group students differently as they move in and out of these levels with each skill and concept. Student self-assessment and feedback help guide your instructional decisions about how and when to layer support for all students to become proficient learners.

Extra Example 1

Estimate (a) the perimeter and (b) the area of the arrow.

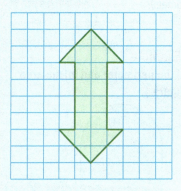

about 24 units; 16 square units

ELL Support

After demonstrating Example 1, have students work in groups to complete Try It Exercise 1. Have them consider the questions: How can you separate the figure? Is each partial square one-half square unit? Expect students to perform according to their language levels.

Beginner: Indicate answers to guiding questions by drawing and/or stating numbers and one-word answers.

Intermediate: Use phrases such as, "into rectangles and triangles."

Advanced: Use detailed sentences such as, "Separate the figure into four rectangles and four triangles."

Try It

1. about 31 units; 51 units^2

Teaching Strategy

When students are working alone or with partners on a problem, circulate to view different approaches. Make notes about the order in which you want to call on students, so you can control the sequence of responses. You do not want the first response to be the most polished or efficient. Look for work that clearly demonstrates the outcome(s).

Extra Example 2
Find (a) the perimeter and (b) the area of the figure.

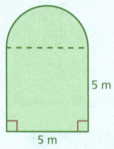

about 22.85 m; about 34.8125 m²

Try It

2. about 12.56 in.; about 10.28 in.²

Self-Assessment
for Concepts & Skills

3. about 30 units; 37 units²
4. 2 semicircles and 1 rectangle; about 36.84 ft; about 64.26 ft²

Laurie's Notes

EXAMPLE 2

- Draw the diagram for the problem.
- ❓ "What is the diameter of the semicircle?" 10 feet
- Explain to students that although the third side of the triangle is shown (which is also the diameter of the circle), it is not a part of the perimeter. It is needed to find both the circumference and the area of the semicircle.
- ❓ **Attend to Precision:** "Could $\frac{22}{7}$ be used for π?" yes "Why do you think 3.14 is used?" The diameter is 10, which is not a multiple of 7.

Try It

- Have students share their strategies for the exercise. Students might use a square and 4 semicircles or a square and 2 circles.

✓ Self-Assessment for Concepts & Skills

- **Teaching Strategy:** As students are working independently on these exercises, circulate and make notes about the order in which you want to call on students. When students are finished, use your notes to ask several students to present their strategies and solutions.
- In Exercise 3, students might use a triangle and 2 rectangles or a triangle, a rectangle, and a square.
- In Exercise 4, students might use a rectangle and 2 semicircles or a rectangle and 1 circle.
- **Fist of Five:** Ask students to indicate their understanding of each success criterion.

ELL Support

Have students work in pairs for extra support and to practice language. Then have pairs display their answers on whiteboards for your review.

The Success Criteria Self-Assessment chart can be found in the *Student Journal* or online at *BigIdeasMath.com*.

EXAMPLE 2 **Finding Perimeter and Area**

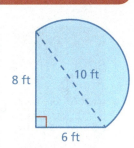

Find (a) the perimeter and (b) the area of the figure.

a. The figure is made up of a triangle and a semicircle.

The distance around the triangular part of the figure is $6 + 8 = 14$ feet. The distance around the semicircle is one-half the circumference of a circle with a diameter of 10 feet.

$$\frac{C}{2} = \frac{\pi d}{2}$$ Divide the circumference by 2.

$$\approx \frac{3.14 \cdot 10}{2}$$ Substitute 3.14 for π and 10 for d.

$$= 15.7$$ Simplify.

▶ So, the perimeter is about $14 + 15.7 = 29.7$ feet.

b. Find the area of the triangle and the area of the semicircle.

Area of Triangle

$$A = \frac{1}{2}bh$$

$$= \frac{1}{2}(6)(8)$$

$$= 24$$

Area of Semicircle

$$A = \frac{\pi r^2}{2}$$

$$\approx \frac{3.14 \cdot 5^2}{2}$$

$$= 39.25$$

The semicircle has a radius of $\frac{10}{2} = 5$ feet.

▶ So, the area is about $24 + 39.25 = 63.25$ square feet.

Try It

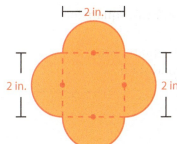

2. Find the perimeter and the area of the figure.

Self-Assessment for Concepts & Skills

Solve each exercise. Then rate your understanding of the success criteria in your journal.

3. **ESTIMATING PERIMETER AND AREA** Estimate the perimeter and area of the figure at the right.

4. **FINDING PERIMETER AND AREA** Identify the shapes that make up the figure at the left. Then find the perimeter and area of the figure.

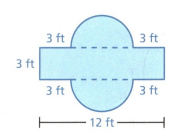

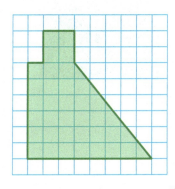

EXAMPLE 3 Modeling Real Life

The center circle of the basketball court has a radius of 3 feet and is painted blue. The rest of the court is stained brown. One gallon of wood stain covers 150 square feet. How many gallons of wood stain do you need to cover the brown portions of the court?

Understand the problem.

You are given dimensions of a basketball court. You are asked to determine the number of gallons of wood stain needed to stain the brown portions of the court when one gallon of wood stain covers 150 square feet.

Make a plan.

Find the entire area of the rectangular court. Then subtract the area of the center circle and divide by 150.

Solve and check.

Area of Rectangle

$A = \ell w$

$= 84(50)$

$= 4200$

Area of Circle

$A = \pi r^2$

$\approx 3.14 \cdot 3^2$

$= 28.26$

The area that is stained is about $4200 - 28.26 = 4171.74$ square feet.

▶ Because one gallon of wood stain covers 150 square feet, you need $4171.74 \div 150 \approx 27.8$ gallons of wood stain.

Check Reasonableness
The circle covers a small area of the court. So, it makes sense that you need just less than $\dfrac{84(50)}{150} = 28$ gallons of wood stain. ✓

Self-Assessment for Problem Solving

Solve each exercise. Then rate your understanding of the success criteria in your journal.

5. A farmer wants to seed and fence a section of land. Fencing costs $27 per yard. Grass seed costs $2 per square foot. How much does it cost to fence and seed the pasture?

6. **DIG DEEPER!** In each room shown, you plan to put down carpet and add a wallpaper border around the ceiling. Which room needs more carpeting? more wallpaper?

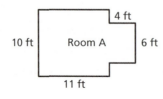
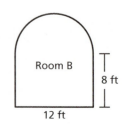

616 Chapter D Geometric Shapes and Angles

Laurie's Notes

EXAMPLE 3

- Ask a volunteer to read the problem aloud.
- ❓ "What are you asked to find?" the number of gallons of wood stain needed to cover the brown portions of the court
- ❓ "Do you need to find the perimeter or area of the brown portions of the court? How do you know?" area; You are staining an area of the court, not the distance around the court.
- **Look for and Make Use of Structure:** Ask students to explain how this composite figure is different from the ones in the previous examples. What will they do differently to calculate the area? They should realize that they must subtract the area of the circle from the area of the rectangle instead of adding the areas.
- Continue solving as shown.
- **Common Error:** Students may find the composite area and forget to find the number of gallons needed. Remind students to always re-read the question to make sure they have answered it.
- You may want to show students the unit analysis involved in the last step.

$$4171.74 \text{ ft}^2 \times \frac{1 \text{ gal}}{150 \text{ ft}^2} \approx 27.8 \text{ gallons}$$

✓ Self-Assessment for Problem Solving

- Encourage students to use a Four Square to complete these exercises. By now, students should be more comfortable with the problem-solving plan and be able to complete more than the first square.
- **Neighbor Check:** Have students work independently and then have their neighbors check their work. Have students discuss any discrepancies.

The Success Criteria Self-Assessment chart can be found in the *Student Journal* or online at *BigIdeasMath.com*.

Closure

- **Exit Ticket:** Find the perimeter and the area of the room.

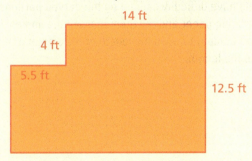

64 ft; 221.75 ft²

Extra Example 3
You are staining the pool deck shown. One gallon of wood stain covers 200 square feet. How many gallons of wood stain do you need to cover the deck?

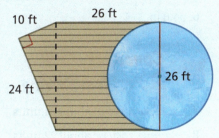

about 2.7 gallons

Self-Assessment
for Problem Solving

5. $475,740
6. Room B; Room A

Learning Target
Find perimeters and areas of composite figures.

Success Criteria
- Use a grid to estimate perimeters and areas.
- Identify the shapes that make up a composite figure.
- Find the perimeters and areas of shapes that make up composite figures.

Review & Refresh

1. about 50.24 mm^2
2. about 63.59 ft^2
3. 30 ft
4. 12 ft
5. 1 m
6. 4.8 in.

Concepts, Skills, & Problem Solving

7. *Sample answer:* about 24 units
8. *Sample answer:* about 22 units^2
9. about 19.5 units; 13.5 units^2
10. about 20 units; 24 units^2
11. about 24.6 units; about 41.1 units^2
12. 28 units; 32 units^2
13. about 19 units; 24 units^2
14. about 30.4 units; about 27.1 units^2

Assignment Guide and Concept Check

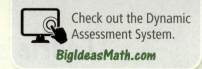

Scaffold assignments to support all students in their learning progression. The suggested assignments are a starting point. Continue to assign additional exercises and revisit with spaced practice to move every student toward proficiency.

Level	Assignment 1	Assignment 2
Emerging	2, 5, 6, 7, 9, 10, 11, 15, 16, 18	12, 13, 14, 17, 19, 20
Proficient	2, 5, 6, 8, 12, 13, 14, 15, 16, 18	17, 19, 20, 21, 22
Advanced	2, 5, 6, 8, 12, 13, 14, 16, 17, 18	19, 20, 21, 22, 23

- Assignment 1 is for use after students complete the Self-Assessment for Concepts & Skills.
- Assignment 2 is for use after students complete the Self-Assessment for Problem Solving.
- The red exercises can be used as a concept check.

Review & Refresh Prior Skills

Exercises 1 and 2 Finding an Area of a Circle
Exercises 3–6 Using a Scale

Common Errors

- **Exercises 9–14** When finding the perimeter, students may count the sides of the squares inside the figure. Remind students that they are finding the perimeter, so they only need to count the outside lengths.
- **Exercises 9–14** When finding the area, students may forget to count all the squares inside the figure and just count the ones along the border because this is what they do for perimeter. Remind students that the area includes everything inside the figure.
- **Exercises 11 and 14** Students have difficulty estimating the curved portions of the figure. Give students tracing paper and tell them to trace the line as straight instead of curved and compare it with the length of the side of a square to help them estimate the length.

D.3 Practice

? Go to *BigIdeasMath.com* to get HELP with solving the exercises.

▶ Review & Refresh

Find the area of the circle. Use 3.14 or $\frac{22}{7}$ for π.

1.

2.

Find the missing dimension. Use the scale 1 : 5.

	Item	Model	Actual
3.	House	Height: 6 ft	Height: ____ ft
4.	Garden hose	Length: ____ ft	Length: 20 yd
5.	Fountain	Depth: 20 cm	Depth: ____ m
6.	Bicycle wheel	Diameter: ____ in.	Diameter: 2 ft

▶ Concepts, Skills, & Problem Solving

ESTIMATING PERIMETER AND AREA You build a patio with a brick border. (See Exploration 1, p. 613.)

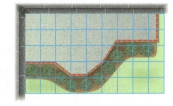

7. Estimate the perimeter of the patio.

8. Estimate the area of the patio.

ESTIMATING PERIMETER AND AREA Estimate the perimeter and the area of the shaded figure.

9.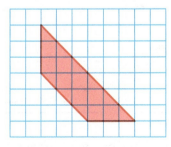

10.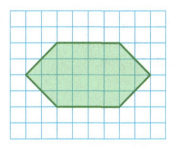

11.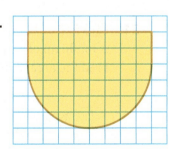

12.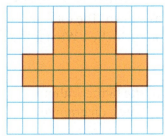

13.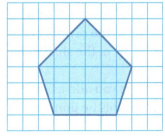

14.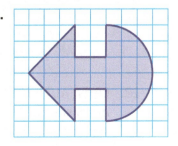

Section D.3   Perimeters and Areas of Composite Figures   617

FINDING PERIMETER AND AREA Find the perimeter and the area of the figure.

15.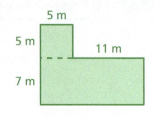

16.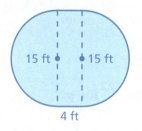

17.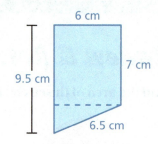

18. **MP YOU BE THE TEACHER** Your friend finds the perimeter of the figure. Is your friend correct? Explain your reasoning.

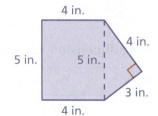

19. **MP LOGIC** A running track has six lanes. Explain why the starting points for the six runners are staggered. Draw a diagram as part of your explanation.

20. **MP PROBLEM SOLVING** You run around the perimeter of the baseball field at a rate of 9 feet per second. How long does it take you to run around the baseball field?

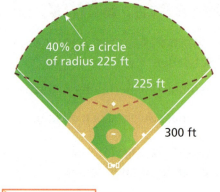

21. **MP STRUCTURE** The figure at the right is made up of a square and a rectangle. Find the area of the shaded region.

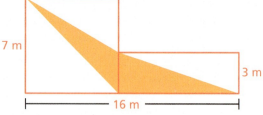

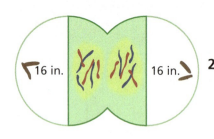

22. **DIG DEEPER!** Your friend makes a two-dimensional model of a dividing cell as shown. The total area of the dividing cell is 350 square inches. What is the area of the shaded region?

23. **CRITICAL THINKING** How can you add a figure to a composite figure without increasing its perimeter? Can this be done for all figures? Draw a diagram to support your answer.

Common Errors

- **Exercises 15–17** When finding the area, students may forget to include one of the areas of the composite figure or may count one area more than once. Tell students to separate the figure into several shapes. Draw and label each shape and then find the area of each. Finally, add the areas of each shape together for the area of the whole figure.

Mini-Assessment

Find the perimeter and the area of the figure.

1.
2.

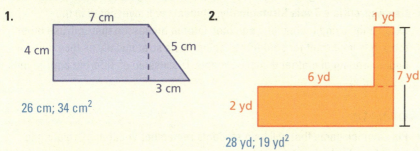

26 cm; 34 cm²

28 yd; 19 yd²

3.

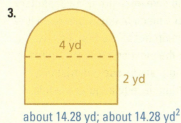

about 14.28 yd; about 14.28 yd²

4.

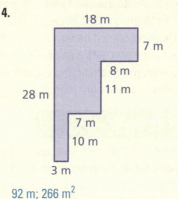

92 m; 266 m²

5. Find the perimeter and the area of the garden.

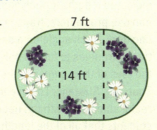

about 57.96 ft; about 251.86 ft²

Section Resources

Surface Level	Deep Level
Resources by Chapter • Extra Practice • Reteach • Puzzle Time Student Journal • Self-Assessment • Practice Differentiating the Lesson Tutorial Videos Skills Review Handbook Skills Trainer	Resources by Chapter • Enrichment and Extension Graphic Organizers Dynamic Assessment System • Section Practice
Transfer Level	
Dynamic Assessment System • Mid-Chapter Quiz	Assessment Book • Mid-Chapter Quiz

Concepts, Skills, & Problem Solving

15. 56 m; 137 m²
16. 55.1 ft; about 236.625 ft²
17. 29 cm; 49.5 cm²
18. no; The length of the rectangle was counted twice.
19. The starting points are staggered so that each runner can run the same distance and use the same finish line. This is necessary because the circumference is different for each lane. The diagram shows this because the diameter is greater in the outer lanes.

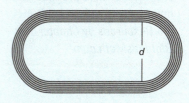

20. about 129.5 sec
21. 24 m²
22. about 149.04 in.²
23. *Sample answer:* By adding the triangle shown by the dashed line to the L-shaped figure, you *reduce* the perimeter.

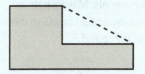

no; For the composite figure below, adding any figure increases its perimeter.

Learning Target
Construct a polygon with given measures.

Success Criteria
- Use technology to draw polygons.
- Determine whether given measures result in one triangle, many triangles, or no triangle.
- Draw polygons given angle measures or side lengths.

Warm Up
Cumulative, vocabulary, and prerequisite skills practice opportunities are available in the *Resources by Chapter* or at *BigIdeasMath.com*.

Teaching Strategy
If you prepare bags of materials for students, label them with the chapter and section number for reuse in following years. Store the prepared bags in a larger bag. Label and file the larger bag with other chapter materials. Make a note in your teaching edition of where the materials are stored.

ELL Support
Explain that a polygon is a figure with three or more angles. Triangles and rectangles are examples of polygons. The word *polygon* comes from the Greek and Latin languages and means "many angles." The prefix *poly-* means "many" and the root *-gon* refers to angles. In this lesson, students will learn how to draw polygons.

Exploration 1
a–c. See Additional Answers.

T-619

Laurie's Notes

Check out the Dynamic Classroom.
BigIdeasMath.com

Preparing to Teach
- Students should know how to classify two-dimensional figures based on properties, draw polygons, and draw angles. Now they will learn to construct polygons by hand given angle measures or side lengths.
- **Use Appropriate Tools Strategically:** Students will investigate in the exploration using technology and then later in the lesson they will use other tools. It is important for students to select tools strategically as they develop understanding of mathematical concepts. Discussion of different approaches is essential.

Motivate
- Play a quick game that will help students remember vocabulary relating to triangles. Divide the class into two groups and give each group a vocabulary word. Each group must write the definition on a piece of paper and hand it to you. Definitions must be written in complete sentences. The first team with a correct definition gets a point. The team with the most points at the end wins.
- Some examples: obtuse angle, acute angle, right angle, scalene triangle, isosceles triangle, right triangle, equilateral triangle, equiangular triangle

Exploration 1
- This exploration is best completed using technology. If geometry software is available, let students practice using it before starting the exploration.
- If technology is not available, students can use drinking straws cut to the indicated lengths for polygons (i)–(vii). For polygons (viii)–(xiv), students can use protractors, transparencies, and transparency markers. Students can draw each angle on a separate transparency and then layer the transparencies to form a polygon, if possible. Encourage students to extend the rays of their angles to the edges of the transparencies.
- **Teaching Strategy**: To save time, you could pre-cut straws and prepare reclosable bags with the necessary pieces for each pair of students. Tell students that all of the lengths of straws they need are in the bags.
- Tell students that the given measurements are the only side lengths or angle measures they should use. Students should not introduce other line segments or angles to complete a figure.
- As students complete part (a), they should draw and name the possible figures.
- ? Discuss students' answers in part (a). Go through each set of side lengths and angle measures, asking, "Were you able to form a polygon? If not, why wasn't it working? If so, did all pairs of students draw the same polygon?"
- **Construct Viable Arguments and Critique the Reasoning of Others:** Ask volunteers to explain the process they used to determine if a figure was possible. Encourage others to critique their reasoning.
- As you discuss parts (b) and (c), keep in mind that the goal of this exploration is for students to gain an informal understanding of angle sum rules and the Triangle Inequality Theorem.

D.4 Constructing Polygons

Learning Target: Construct a polygon with given measures.

Success Criteria:
- I can use technology to draw polygons.
- I can determine whether given measures result in one triangle, many triangles, or no triangle.
- I can draw polygons given angle measures or side lengths.

EXPLORATION 1   Using Technology to Draw Polygons

Work with a partner.

a. Use geometry software to draw each polygon with the given side lengths or angle measures, if possible. Complete the table.

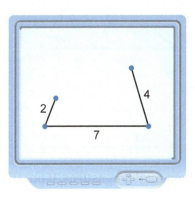

Side Lengths or Angle Measures	How many figures are possible?
i. 4 cm, 6 cm, 7 cm	
ii. 2 cm, 6 cm, 7 cm	
iii. 2 cm, 4 cm, 7 cm	
iv. 2 cm, 4 cm, 6 cm	
v. 2 in., 3 in., 3 in., 5 in.	
vi. 1 in., 1 in., 3 in., 6 in.	
vii. 1 in., 1 in., 3 in., 4 in.	
viii. 90°, 60°, 30°	
ix. 100°, 40°, 20°	
x. 50°, 60°, 70°	
xi. 20°, 80°, 100°	
xii. 20°, 50°, 50°, 60°	
xiii. 30°, 80°, 120°, 130°	
xiv. 60°, 60°, 120°, 120°	

Math Practice

Use Technology to Explore

How does geometry software help you learn about characteristics of triangles and quadrilaterals?

b. Without constructing, how can you tell whether it is possible to draw a triangle given three angle measures? three side lengths? Explain your reasoning.

c. Without constructing, how can you tell whether it is possible to draw a quadrilateral given four angle measures? four side lengths? Explain your reasoning.

Section D.4   Constructing Polygons   619

D.4 Lesson

You can draw a triangle with three given angle measures when the sum of the angle measures is 180°.

EXAMPLE 1 **Constructing Triangles Using Angle Measures**

Draw a triangle with angle measures of 30°, 60°, and 90°, if possible.

Because 30° + 60° + 90° = 180°, you can draw a triangle with the given angle measures.

Step 1: Draw the 30° angle.   **Step 2:** Draw the 60° angle.

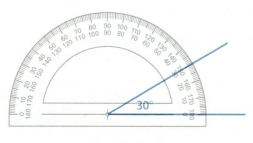

Step 3: Measure the remaining angle. The angle measure is 90°.

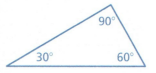

Try It Draw a triangle with the given angle measures, if possible.

1. 45°, 45°, 90°
2. 100°, 55°, 25°
3. 60°, 60°, 80°

EXAMPLE 2 **Constructing Triangles Using Angles and Sides**

Draw a triangle with side lengths of 3 centimeters and 4 centimeters that meet at a 20° angle.

Step 1: Draw a 20° angle.

Step 2: Use a ruler to mark 3 centimeters on one ray and 4 centimeters on the other ray.

Step 3: Draw the third side to form the triangle.

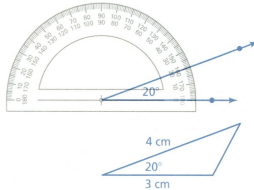

In Example 1, you can change the lengths of the sides to create many different triangles that meet the criteria. In Example 2, only one triangle is possible.

Try It

4. Draw a triangle with side lengths of 1 inch and 2 inches that meet at a 60° angle.

620 Chapter D Geometric Shapes and Angles

Laurie's Notes

Scaffolding Instruction

- In the exploration, students used technology to investigate constructing polygons given side lengths and angle measures. Now they will learn to construct polygons by hand, with the focus on triangles.
- **Emerging:** Students may struggle with using a protractor and may not understand the angle sum rules and the Triangle Inequality Theorem. They will benefit from guided instruction for the examples.
- **Proficient:** Students understand how to construct polygons using technology and have a good sense of the angle sum rules and the Triangle Inequality Theorem. They should review the examples to gain understanding of constructing polygons by hand. Then have students complete the Try It exercises before proceeding to the Self-Assessment exercises.

EXAMPLE 1

- No constraints are given for the side lengths. So, one way to draw the triangle is to draw the first given angle at one end of a segment, draw the second given angle at the other end, and extend the rays for the two angles until they intersect.
- **Teaching Tip:** Encourage students not to make tiny drawings. It can be difficult to measure angles when the side lengths are shorter than the radius of the protractor.
- **? Construct Viable Arguments and Critique the Reasoning of Others:** "Does the order in which you draw the angles matter? Explain." No, after you draw two angles, the third angle should have the measure of the remaining angle. Have half the students start with the 30° angle and the other half start with the 60° angle.
- Students should measure to verify that the third angle has the desired measure.
- **?** "How do you classify this triangle?" right scalene
- Students should compare their triangles to those of their neighbors. They should realize that many different-sized triangles can have angles of 30°, 60°, and 90°. They should understand that every neighbor's triangle should be a right scalene triangle. Point this out if they do not make this conclusion.

Try It

- Have students draw the triangles and then check with a neighbor.

EXAMPLE 2

- You may want to have students draw the sides in inches instead of centimeters to make the triangle a little larger and easier to draw.
- Students should compare their triangles to those of their neighbors. This time, each student should have the same sized triangle. Discuss the push-pin note.
- Repeat the construction but with the 4-centimeter leg horizontal (instead of the 3-centimeter leg). Have them "match up" this triangle with the original triangle. No matter the orientation, the triangles will be the same.
- **?** "How do you classify this triangle?" obtuse scalene

Try It

- Have students draw the triangle and then check with a neighbor.

Scaffold instruction to support all students in their learning. Learning is individualized and you may want to group students differently as they move in and out of these levels with each skill and concept. Student self-assessment and feedback help guide your instructional decisions about how and when to layer support for all students to become proficient learners.

Extra Example 1
Draw a triangle with angle measures of 35°, 45°, and 100°, if possible.

Try It

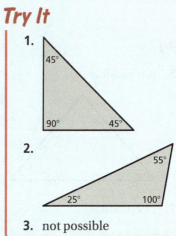

3. not possible

Extra Example 2
Draw a triangle with side lengths of 3 centimeters and 5 centimeters that meet at a 75° angle.

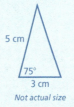

Not actual size

Try It

4.
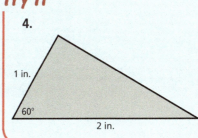

Extra Example 3

Draw a triangle with the given side lengths, if possible.

a. 8 cm, 4 cm, 4 cm not possible

b. 2.5 in., 5 in., 4 in.

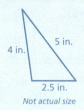
Not actual size

Try It

5. not possible

6.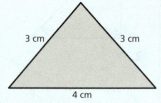

7. not possible

Laurie's Notes

Discuss

- Discuss the text at the top of the page. This is the Triangle Inequality Theorem, but it does not need to be formalized in this course.
- Students developed a sense of this in the exploration. Refer back to the exploration and review the sets of three side lengths that did not form a triangle.

  (iii) 2 cm, 4 cm, 7 cm   (iv) 2 cm, 4 cm, 6 cm
     2 cm + 4 cm < 7 cm   2 cm + 4 cm = 6 cm

EXAMPLE 3

- Make sure students know how to set their compasses to the appropriate length, place the point on a vertex, and draw the arc. Drawing the arcs helps students see how the intersection determines the side lengths.
- ❓ "Is it possible to draw a triangle with side lengths of 4 centimeters, 2 centimeters, and 3 centimeters? Explain." Yes, the sum of the lengths of any two sides is greater than the length of the third side.
- Work through the steps for drawing the triangle.
- Have students repeat the construction but start with a different side length. Have them "match up" this triangle with the original triangle. No matter the orientation, the triangles will be the same. Discuss the push-pin note.
- ❓ "How do you classify this triangle?" acute scalene
- ❓ "Is it possible to draw a triangle with side lengths of 2.5 inches, 1 inch, and 1 inch? Explain." No, the sum of 1 inch and 1 inch is 2 inches, which is less than 2.5 inches.
- Discuss the Check note and the Math Practice note with students.

Try It

- Have students draw the triangles and then check with a neighbor.

ELL Support

After demonstrating Example 3, have students practice language by working in pairs to complete Try It Exercises 5–7. Monitor discussions and provide support as needed. Expect students to perform according to their language levels.

Beginner: Draw a triangle, if possible.

Intermediate: Use simple sentences such as, "Two centimeters plus two centimeters is less than five centimeters."

Advanced: Use detailed sentences such as, "Because two centimeters plus two centimeters is less than five centimeters, it is not possible to draw a triangle."

You can draw a triangle with three given side lengths when the sum of the lengths of any two sides is greater than the length of the third side.

EXAMPLE 3 Constructing Triangles Using Side Lengths

Draw a triangle with the given side lengths, if possible.

a. **4 cm, 2 cm, 3 cm**

   The sum of the lengths of any two sides is greater than the length of the third side.

   4 cm + 2 cm > 3 cm   4 cm + 3 cm > 2 cm   2 cm + 3 cm > 4 cm

   So, you can draw a triangle with the given side lengths.

   Step 1: Draw a 4-centimeter side.

   Step 2: Use a compass to determine where the 2-centimeter side and the 3-centimeter side meet.

   Step 3: The third vertex can be at either intersection point. Draw the triangle.

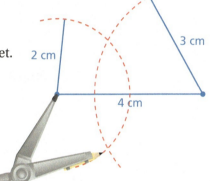

> In Example 3, only one triangle is possible. You can start with a different side length in Step 1, but the resulting triangle will have the same size and shape.

b. **2.5 in., 1 in., 1 in.**

   Because 1 in. + 1 in. < 2.5 in., it is not possible to draw the triangle.

   Check Try to draw the triangle. Draw a 2.5-inch side. Use a compass to show that the 1-inch sides cannot intersect.

   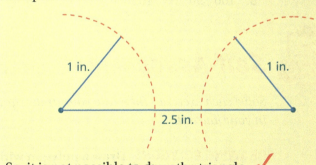

   So, it is not possible to draw the triangle. ✓

Math Practice

Look for Structure
How can you change one of the side lengths in part (b) so that they form a triangle? Compare answers with a classmate.

Try It Draw a triangle with the given side lengths, if possible.

5. 2 cm, 2 cm, 5 cm   6. 4 cm, 3 cm, 3 cm   7. 1 cm, 4 cm, 5 cm

You can draw a quadrilateral with four given angle measures when the sum of the angle measures is 360°.

EXAMPLE 4 Constructing a Quadrilateral

Draw a quadrilateral with angle measures of 60°, 120°, 70°, and 110°, if possible.

Because 60° + 120° + 70° + 110° = 360°, you can draw a quadrilateral with the given angle measures.

Step 1: Draw a 60° angle and a 120° angle that each have one side on a line.

Step 2: Draw the remaining side at a 70° angle.

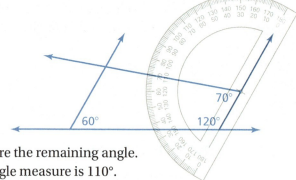

Step 3: Measure the remaining angle. The angle measure is 110°.

Try It Draw a quadrilateral with the given angle measures, if possible.

8. 100°, 90°, 65°, 105°

9. 100°, 40°, 20°, 20°

Self-Assessment for Concepts & Skills

Solve each exercise. Then rate your understanding of the success criteria in your journal.

DRAWING POLYGONS Draw a polygon with the given side lengths or angle measures, if possible.

10. 25 mm, 36 mm, 38 mm

11. 10°, 15°, 155°

12. 20°, 45°, 50°, 65°

13. 50°, 90°, 110°, 110°

14. USING SIDE LENGTHS Can you construct *one*, *many*, or *no* triangle(s) with side lengths of 3 inches, 4 inches, and 8 inches? Explain.

Laurie's Notes

Discuss
- Discuss the text at the top of the page.
- Students developed a sense of this in the exploration. Refer back to the exploration and review the set of four angle measures that did not form a quadrilateral.
  - (xii) 20°, 50°, 50°, 60°
    - 20° + 50° + 50° + 60° < 360°

EXAMPLE 4
- ❓ "Is it possible to draw a quadrilateral with angle measures of 60°, 120°, 70°, and 110°? Explain." Yes, the sum of the angle measures is 360°.
- Work through the steps for drawing the quadrilateral.
- Have students construct a quadrilateral with the angles in a different order. Because there are no constraints given for the side lengths, students can use any lengths they want.
- ❓ "Do the quadrilaterals look the same no matter what order the angles are drawn?" no

Try It
- Have students work independently.
- ❓ Ask, "What must be true about the angles of a quadrilateral?" The sum of the angle measures must be 360°.

✓ Self-Assessment for Concepts & Skills
- **Agree-Disagree Statement:** Ask students if they agree or disagree with each statement below. Students should explain why or why not.
  - Any three line segments can be used to make a triangle. disagree; If the sum of any two line segments is less than the length of the third line segment, then the line segments cannot make a triangle.
  - If you know two angle measures of a triangle, you can find the third angle measure. agree; If you know two angle measures, you can subtract their sum from 180° to find the third angle measure.
  - You can construct many triangles with angle measures of 40°, 60°, and 90°. disagree; The sum of the angle measures is 190°, not 180°. So, you cannot construct a triangle with those angle measures.
- Students should work independently on these problems and then check their answers with a neighbor.

ELL Support
Allow students to work in pairs. For Exercises 10–13, ask if it is possible to draw each figure and have students use a thumbs up to answer *yes* and a thumbs down to answer *no*. Have each pair compare their drawings with another pair. Solicit answers for Exercise 14 with hand signals—a 0 formed with a thumb and a finger for *no*, one finger raised for *one*, or a raised hand with all fingers extended for *many*. Discuss their answers as a class.

The Success Criteria Self-Assessment chart can be found in the *Student Journal* or online at *BigIdeasMath.com*.

Extra Example 4
Draw a quadrilateral with angle measures of 45°, 50°, 130°, and 135°, if possible.

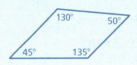

Try It
8. Sample answer:

9. not possible

Self-Assessment for Concepts & Skills

10.

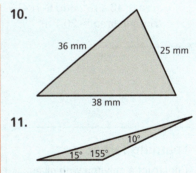

11.

12. not possible

13. Sample answer:

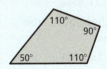

14. none; *Sample answer:* The sum of the lengths of any two sides of a triangle must be greater than the length of the third side of the triangle, and 3 + 4 ≯ 8.

Extra Example 5

You enclose a pasture using fences with lengths 5 meters, 12 meters, and 13 meters. Estimate the area of the pasture. about 30 square meters

Self-Assessment
for Problem Solving

15. See Additional Answers.

16. no; *Sample answer:* You need to know at least one of the side lengths of the triangle.

17. patio with sides 9 m, 10 m, 11 m; *Sample answer:* Using a scale drawing of each triangular patio, the base and height for each triangle can be measured. Then, convert the base and height to their actual size and apply the formula for area of a triangle for each: 9-10-11 triangle area ≈ 42.4 m^2, and 6-10-15 triangle area ≈ 20.1 m^2.

Learning Target
Construct a polygon with given measures.

Success Criteria
- Use technology to draw polygons.
- Determine whether given measures result in one triangle, many triangles, or no triangle.
- Draw polygons given angle measures or side lengths.

Laurie's Notes

EXAMPLE 5

- Ask a volunteer to read the problem aloud. Then ask another volunteer to explain what the problem is asking.
- ? "Can the given lengths form a triangle? Explain." Yes, the sum of the lengths of any two sides is greater than the length of the third side.
- ? "Is it reasonable to draw the given triangle? Explain." No, the lengths would not fit on a regular-sized piece of paper.
- ? "How can you draw a representation of the flower bed?" Make a scale drawing.
- Have students make a scale drawing of the flower bed.
- ? "How can you use your scale drawing to estimate the area of the flower bed?" Estimate the height and the length of the base of the triangle. Use the area formula for a triangle to estimate the area of the scale drawing and then convert the area to square yards.
- **Note:** The problem says to estimate but 6 square yards is actually an exact area because the flower bed is a right triangle. Although they could measure the angle, students cannot be certain that it is precisely 90°.
- Discuss the Another Method note with students.

✓ Self-Assessment for Problem Solving

- Students may benefit from making their plans independently before comparing with a partner and discussing any discrepancies. Then they should solve the problems independently. It is important to provide time in class for problem solving, so that students become comfortable with the problem-solving plan.
- Have students use *Thumbs Up* to indicate their understanding of the success criteria.

The Success Criteria Self-Assessment chart can be found in the *Student Journal* or online at *BigIdeasMath.com*.

Closure

- **Exit Ticket:** Draw a triangle with side lengths of 3 inches, 3 inches, and 4 inches, if possible.

Not actual size

T-623

EXAMPLE 5 Modeling Real Life

You enclose a flower bed using landscaping boards with lengths of 3 yards, 4 yards, and 5 yards. Estimate the area of the flower bed.

You know the lengths of boards used to enclose a triangular region. You are asked to estimate the area of the triangular region.

Draw a triangle with side lengths of 3 yards, 4 yards, and 5 yards using a scale of 1 cm : 1 yd. Use the drawing to estimate the base and height of the flower bed. Then use the formula for the area of a triangle to estimate the area.

Draw the triangle.

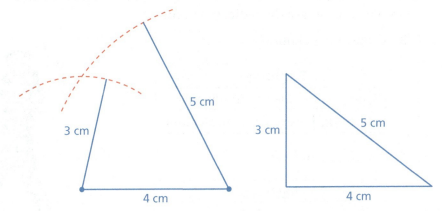

Another Method
Using a ruler, the height from the largest angle to the 5-centimeter side is about 2.4 centimeters. So, the area is about $\frac{1}{2}(2.4)(5) = 6$ yd². ✓

The shape of the flower bed appears to be a right triangle with a base length of 4 yards and a height of 3 yards.

▶ So, the area of the flower bed is about $A = \frac{1}{2}(4)(3) = 6$ square yards.

Self-Assessment for Problem Solving

Solve each exercise. Then rate your understanding of the success criteria in your journal.

15. A triangular pen has fence lengths of 6 feet, 8 feet, and 10 feet. Create a scale drawing of the pen.

16. The front of a cabin is the shape of a triangle. The angles of the triangle are 40°, 70°, and 70°. Can you determine the height of the cabin? If not, what information do you need?

17. **DIG DEEPER!** Two rooftops have triangular patios. One patio has side lengths of 9 meters, 10 meters, and 11 meters. The other has side lengths of 6 meters, 10 meters, and 15 meters. Which patio has a greater area? Explain.

D.4 Practice

Go to *BigIdeasMath.com* to get HELP with solving the exercises.

▶ Review & Refresh

Find the perimeter and area of the figure.

1.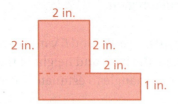

2.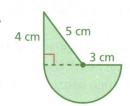

Use a tree diagram to find the sample space and the total number of possible outcomes of the indicated event.

3. choosing a toothbrush

Toothbrush	
Type	Electric, Traditional
Strength	Extra soft, Soft, Medium

4. choosing a toy hoop

Toy Hoop	
Size	Small, Medium, Large
Color	Blue, Green, Orange, Pink, Purple, Yellow

▶ Concepts, Skills, & Problem Solving

USING TECHNOLOGY TO DRAW POLYGONS Use geometry software to draw the polygon with the given side lengths or angle measures, if possible. (See Exploration 1, p. 619.)

5. 30°, 65°, 85°

6. 2 in., 3 in., 5 in.

7. 80°, 90°, 100°, 110°

8. 2 cm, 2 cm, 5 cm, 5 cm

CONSTRUCTING TRIANGLES USING ANGLE MEASURES Draw a triangle with the given angle measures, if possible.

9. 40°, 50°, 90°

10. 20°, 40°, 120°

11. 38°, 42°, 110°

12. 54°, 60°, 66°

13. **MP YOU BE THE TEACHER** Your friend determines whether he can draw a triangle with angle measures of 10°, 40°, and 130°. Is your friend correct? Explain your reasoning.

> 10° + 40° < 130°
>
> Because the sum of the measure of two angles is not greater than the measure of the third angle, you cannot draw a triangle.

624   Chapter D   Geometric Shapes and Angles

Assignment Guide and Concept Check

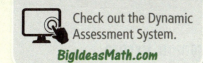

Scaffold assignments to support all students in their learning progression. The suggested assignments are a starting point. Continue to assign additional exercises and revisit with spaced practice to move every student toward proficiency.

Level	Assignment 1	Assignment 2
Emerging	2, 4, 5, 6, 9, 10, 13, 15, 19, 31	7, 8, 12, 17, 21, 22, 23, 25, 29, 33, 35, 41
Proficient	2, 4, 5, 8, 10, 12, 13, 14, 16, 18, 20, 32, 34	17, 21, 22, 23, 24, 26, 28, 30, 36, 37, 39, 41, 42
Advanced	2, 4, 5, 8, 10, 12, 13, 14, 16, 18, 20, 32, 34	23, 24, 26, 28, 30, 37, 38, 39, 40, 42, 43, 44

- Assignment 1 is for use after students complete the Self-Assessment for Concepts & Skills.
- Assignment 2 is for use after students complete the Self-Assessment for Problem Solving.
- The red exercises can be used as a concept check.

Review & Refresh Prior Skills
Exercises 1 and 2 Finding Perimeter and Area
Exercises 3 and 4 Using a Tree Diagram

Common Errors

- **Exercises 9–12** Students may use the wrong set of angles on a protractor. Encourage students to decide which set to use by comparing the angle measure to 90°.

Review & Refresh

1. 14 in.; 8 in.²

2. about 21.42 cm; about 20.13 cm²

3. Electric Extra Soft, Electric Soft, Electric Medium, Traditional Extra Soft, Traditional Soft, Traditional Medium; 6 possible outcomes

4. Small Blue, Small Green, Small Orange, Small Pink, Small Purple, Small Yellow, Medium Blue, Medium Green, Medium Orange, Medium Pink, Medium Purple, Medium Yellow, Large Blue, Large Green, Large Orange, Large Pink, Large Purple, Large Yellow; 18 possible outcomes

Concepts, Skills, & Problem Solving

5.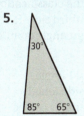

6. not possible

7. not possible

8. See Additional Answers.

9.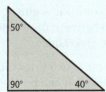

10.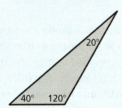

11. not possible

12. See Additional Answers.

13. no; *Sample answer:* Your friend was using the rule for side lengths. Because the sum of the angle measures is 180°, you can draw the triangle.

T-624

Concepts, Skills, & Problem Solving

14–17. See Additional Answers.

18. not possible

19. not possible

20. See Additional Answers.

21. [Triangle with sides 8 mm, 13 mm, and 12 mm]

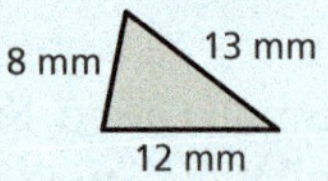

22. no; The sum of the lengths of the 2 shorter sides is 24 inches, which is less than the length of the third side, 25 inches.

23. yes; *Sample answer:* The sum of the lengths of any two sides is 12 inches, which is greater than the length of the third side, 6 inches.

24. no; Just because one angle is acute doesn't mean it will be an acute triangle. The classification depends on the third side. It could form a right angle or an obtuse angle.

25. many; With only 1 angle measure and 1 side length given, many triangles can be created.

26. many; You can change the angle formed by the two given sides to create many triangles.

27. one; Only one line segment can be drawn between the endpoints of the two given sides.

28. one; The other two sides will only intersect at one possible point.

29. one; The other angle measure will be 125°. You can draw the two angles that connect to the given side length. The other two sides will only intersect at one possible point.

30. a. See Additional Answers.

   b. by decreasing the side lengths opposite from angles *B* and *C*, or by increasing the side lengths opposite from angle *A*

Common Errors

- **Exercises 14–17** Students may use the wrong set of angles on a protractor. Encourage students to decide which set to use by comparing the angle measure to 90°.

CONSTRUCTING TRIANGLES USING ANGLES AND SIDES Draw a triangle with the given description.

14. side lengths of 1 inch and 2 inches meet at a 50° angle
15. side lengths of 7 centimeters and 9 centimeters meet at a 120° angle
16. a 95° angle connects to a 15° angle by a side of length 2 inches
17. a 70° angle connects to a 70° angle by a side of length 4 centimeters

CONSTRUCTING TRIANGLES USING SIDE LENGTHS Draw a triangle with the given side lengths, if possible.

18. 4 in., 5 in., 10 in.
19. 10 mm, 30 mm, 50 mm
20. 5 cm, 5 cm, 8 cm
21. 8 mm, 12 mm, 13 mm

22. **MP MODELING REAL LIFE** Can you construct a triangular case using two pieces of wood that are 12 inches long and one piece of wood that is 25 inches long? Explain.

23. **MP MODELING REAL LIFE** Can you construct a warning triangle using three pieces of plastic that are each 6 inches long? Explain.

24. **MP LOGIC** You are constructing a triangle. You draw the first angle, as shown. Your friend says that you must be constructing an acute triangle. Is your friend correct? Explain your reasoning.

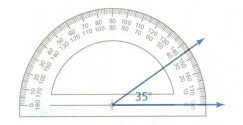

USING ANGLES AND SIDES Determine whether you can construct *one, many,* or *no* triangle(s) with the given description. Explain your reasoning.

25. a triangle with one angle measure of 60° and one side length of 4 centimeters
26. a scalene triangle with side lengths of 3 centimeters and 7 centimeters
27. an isosceles triangle with two side lengths of 4 inches that meet at an 80° angle
28. a triangle with one angle measure of 60°, one angle measure of 70°, and a side length of 10 centimeters between the two angles
29. a triangle with one angle measure of 20°, one angle measure of 35°, and a side of length 3 inches that is between the two angles

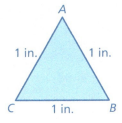

30. **MP REASONING** A triangle is shown.

    a. Construct a triangle with side lengths twice those of the triangle shown. Does the new triangle have the same angle measures?

    b. How can you change the side lengths of the triangle so that the measure of ∠A increases?

CONSTRUCTING QUADRILATERALS Draw a quadrilateral with the given angle measures, if possible.

31. 60°, 60°, 120°, 120°

32. 50°, 60°, 110°, 150°

33. 20°, 30°, 150°, 160°

34. 10°, 10°, 10°, 150°

CONSTRUCTING SPECIAL QUADRILATERALS Construct a quadrilateral with the given description.

35. a rectangle with side lengths of 1 inch and 2 inches

36. a kite with side lengths of 4 centimeters and 7 centimeters

37. a trapezoid with base angles of 40°

38. a rhombus with side lengths of 10 millimeters

39. **MP REASONING** A quadrilateral has side lengths of 6 units, 2 units, and 3 units as shown. How many quadrilaterals can be formed given a fourth side with a fixed length? Explain.

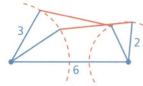

40. **MP REASONING** What types of quadrilaterals can you form using four side lengths of 7 units? Use drawings to support your conclusion.

41. **MP MODELING REAL LIFE** A triangular section of a farm is enclosed by fences that are 2 meters, 6 meters, and 7 meters long. Estimate the area of the section.

42. **MP MODELING REAL LIFE** A chemical spill expert sets up a triangular caution zone using cones. Cones A and B are 14 meters apart. Cones B and C are 22 meters apart. Cones A and C are 34 meters apart. Estimate the area of the caution zone.

43. **MP MODELING REAL LIFE** A search region is in the shape of an equilateral triangle. The measure of one side of the region is 20 miles. Make a scale drawing of the search region. Estimate the area of the search region.

44. **MP REASONING** A triangle has fixed side lengths of 2 and 14.

   a. How many triangles can you construct? Use the figure below to explain your reasoning.

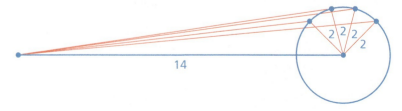

   b. Is the unknown side length of the triangle also fixed? Explain.

Common Errors

- **Exercises 31–34 and 37** Students may use the wrong set of angles on a protractor. Encourage students to decide which set to use by comparing the angle measure to 90°.

Mini-Assessment

1. Draw a triangle with angle measures of 20°, 70°, and 90°, if possible.

   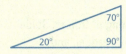

2. Draw a triangle with side lengths of 3 centimeters and 4 centimeters that meet at a 15° angle.

   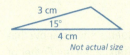
   Not actual size

3. Draw a triangle with side lengths of 2 inches, 3 inches, and 5 inches, if possible. not possible

4. Draw a quadrilateral with angle measures of 50°, 70°, 110°, and 150°, if possible. not possible

5. Draw a quadrilateral with angle measures of 40°, 60°, 120°, and 140°, if possible.

   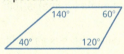

Section Resources

Surface Level	Deep Level
Resources by Chapter • Extra Practice • Reteach • Puzzle Time Student Journal • Self-Assessment • Practice Differentiating the Lesson Tutorial Videos Skills Review Handbook Skills Trainer	Resources by Chapter • Enrichment and Extension Graphic Organizers Dynamic Assessment System • Section Practice

Concepts, Skills, & Problem Solving

31. *Sample answer:*

    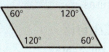

32. not possible

33. *Sample answer:*

    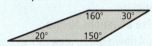

34. not possible

35–36. See Additional Answers.

37.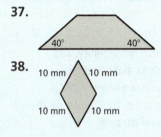

38.
    10 mm, 10 mm, 10 mm, 10 mm

39. infinitely many; *Sample answer:* The fourth side is a fixed length, but the angles are not fixed.

40. See Additional Answers.

41. about 5.56 m²

42. about 97.75 m²

43. *Sample answer:*

    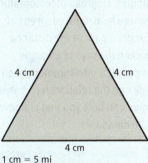
    1 cm = 5 mi

    about 173.2 mi²

44. a. infinitely many; *Sample answer:* At every point on the circle, another third side of the triangle could be made.

    b. no; *Sample answer:* The length changes depending on where the side with a length of 2 units is on the circle.

T-626

Learning Target
Use facts about angle relationships to find unknown angle measures.

Success Criteria
- Identify adjacent, complementary, supplementary, and vertical angles.
- Use equations to find unknown angle measures.
- Find unknown angle measures in real-life situations.

Warm Up
Cumulative, vocabulary, and prerequisite skills practice opportunities are available in the *Resources by Chapter* or at BigIdeasMath.com.

ELL Support
Explain that angles are measured in degrees. Students may be familiar with the word *degree* as it applies to measuring temperature. Point out that this type of measurement is not related to the measurement of angles. Degrees of temperature measure heat, while degrees of an angle measure the distance between the rays of an angle. Knowing the measurement of an angle and the relationships between angles can help you find unknown angle measures.

Exploration 1
a. See Additional Answers.
b. ∠BAC and ∠EAD, ∠BAE and ∠CAD; *Sample answer:* All vertical angles are opposite angles formed by the intersection of two lines.
c. See Additional Answers.
d. *Sample answer:* Vertical angles have the same measure.
e. Check students' work.

T-627

Laurie's Notes

Check out the Dynamic Classroom.
BigIdeasMath.com

Preparing to Teach
- Students should know basic vocabulary associated with angles from prior courses.
- **Construct Viable Arguments and Critique the Reasoning of Others**: Students will investigate and make conjectures about adjacent, vertical, and supplementary angles. Students need practice giving supporting evidence for their conjectures.

Motivate
- Because this chapter has focused on geometry, students should know that Euclid is credited for the study of geometry. He is often called the *Father of Geometry*. Euclid was a Greek mathematician best known for his 13 books on geometry known as *The Elements*. This work influenced the development of Western mathematics for more than 2000 years.

Exploration 1
- Remind students that the angle measure for a straight angle (or line) is 180°. Use a protractor to show the measure.
- Remind students of how angles are named. Discuss when there is a need for three letters instead of one. Remind them that when three letters are used, the middle letter is the vertex and the other two are points on the rays. Also discuss that ∠BAC and ∠CAB name the same angle because the vertex position is the same.
- Ask a volunteer to read the directions aloud. If students do not understand the meaning of *adjacent*, ask five students to stand in a line. Point out which pairs of students are adjacent and which are not.
- Make sure students understand that not all nonadjacent angles are vertical. **Vertical angles** cannot be adjacent, but this does not define them. A formal definition for vertical angles is given in the lesson.
- In part (c), students may need to be reminded of the definition for **supplementary angles** and how to use it to find angle measures.
- In part (d), students should notice that the angle measures are the same for each pair of vertical angles.
- Discuss students answers and reasoning for parts (c) and (d) as a class. Use *Accountable Language Stems* to encourage students to explain their answers in a way that all students understand.
- Students should be able to use their understanding from parts (c) and (d) to explain that the measures of the vertical angles are the same because they are supplementary to the same angle. After finding all the angle measures in the diagram, have pairs share and discuss their answers as a class.
- **Model:** Have students draw a pair of intersecting lines. Tell them to fold their papers over the vertex so that the rays overlap, visually demonstrating that the pair of vertical angles has the same measure. Repeat with the other two rays to show that a pair of intersecting lines produces two pairs of vertical angles with the same measures.

D.5 Finding Unknown Angle Measures

Learning Target: Use facts about angle relationships to find unknown angle measures.

Success Criteria:
- I can identify adjacent, complementary, supplementary, and vertical angles.
- I can use equations to find unknown angle measures.
- I can find unknown angle measures in real-life situations.

EXPLORATION 1 Using Rules About Angles

Work with a partner. The diagram shows pairs of *adjacent* angles and *vertical* angles. Vertical angles cannot be adjacent.

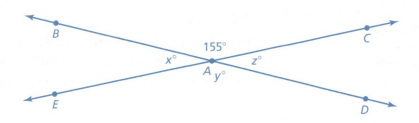

a. Which pair(s) of angles are adjacent angles? Explain.

b. Which pair(s) of angles are vertical angles? Explain.

c. Without using a protractor, find the values of x, y, and z. Explain your reasoning.

d. Make a conjecture about the measures of any two vertical angles.

e. Test your conjecture in part (d) using the diagram below. Explain why your conjecture is or is *not* true.

Math Practice

Use Definitions

How can you use the definition of supplementary angles to explain why your conjecture is or is *not* true?

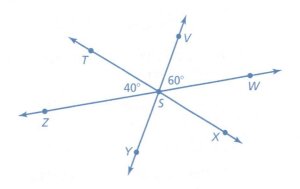

Section D.5 Finding Unknown Angle Measures 627

D.5 Lesson

Key Vocabulary
adjacent angles, *p. 628*
complementary angles, *p. 628*
supplementary angles, *p. 628*
vertical angles, *p. 628*

🔑 Key Ideas

Adjacent Angles
Words Two angles are **adjacent angles** when they share a common side and have the same vertex.

Complementary Angles
Words Two angles are **complementary angles** when the sum of their measures is 90°.

Supplementary Angles
Words Two angles are **supplementary angles** when the sum of their measures is 180°.

Vertical Angles
Words Two angles are **vertical angles** when they are opposite angles formed by the intersection of two lines. Vertical angles have the same measure because they are both supplementary to the same angle.

Reading
Angles that have the same measures are called *congruent angles*.

EXAMPLE 1   Naming Angles

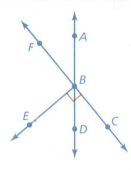

Name a pair of (a) adjacent angles, (b) complementary angles, (c) supplementary angles, and (d) vertical angles in the figure.

a. ∠ABC and ∠ABF share a common side and have the same vertex B.

▸ So, ∠ABC and ∠ABF are adjacent angles.

b. ∠EBC is a right angle. This means that the sum of the measure of ∠EBD and the measure of ∠CBD is 90°.

▸ So, ∠EBD and ∠CBD are complementary angles.

c. ∠ABC and ∠DBC make up a straight angle. This means that the sum of the measure of ∠ABC and the measure of ∠DBC is 180°.

▸ So, ∠ABC and ∠DBC are supplementary angles.

d. ∠ABF and ∠CBD are opposite angles formed by the intersection of two lines.

▸ So, ∠ABF and ∠CBD are vertical angles.

Try It

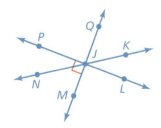

1. Name a pair of (a) adjacent angles, (b) complementary angles, (c) supplementary angles, and (d) vertical angles in the figure.

628   Chapter D   Geometric Shapes and Angles   🔊 Multi-Language Glossary at *BigIdeasMath.com*

Laurie's Notes

Scaffolding Instruction

- In the exploration, students investigated relationships between angles. They also named angles and found their measures. Now the pairs of angles will be formally defined. Students will identify different types of angles and use their relationships to find unknown angle measures.
- **Emerging:** Students may be comfortable identifying adjacent, vertical, and supplementary angles from the exploration, but they will need guided instruction for complementary angles and finding unknown angle measures.
- **Proficient:** Students are able to name and use all four types of angles. They should review the Key Ideas before completing the Try It and Self-Assessment exercises.

Key Ideas

- Students have worked with complementary, supplementary, and adjacent angles in previous courses, but they may need a quick review.
- Review the definitions for **adjacent angles**, **complementary angles**, and **supplementary angles**. Have students draw diagrams on whiteboards to represent each pair of angles and display them to the class.
- Discuss the definition for **vertical angles** and point out the Reading note.

EXAMPLE 1

- Draw the figure and ask students to identify the lines and rays. There are five rays, two pairs of rays are also collinear (on the same line). Only $\overrightarrow{BE}$ is not part of a line.
- **? Construct Viable Arguments and Critique the Reasoning of Others:** "When two lines intersect, will there always be one pair of obtuse angles and one pair of acute angles? Explain." No, the two lines could form four right angles.
- Remind students that the corner mark is used to designate a right angle.
- In part (a), some students may say ∠ABE and ∠CBE are also adjacent.
- **?** "Is ∠ABE adjacent to ∠FBE? Explain." Students may say "yes" because the definition is satisfied; however, adjacent angles do not overlap. In a geometry class, this will be included in the definition.
- In part (b), tell students that ∠EBD and ∠ABF are also complementary. Ask volunteers to explain why. ∠EBD and ∠CBD are complementary angles. ∠CBD and ∠ABF have the same measure because they are vertical angles. So, ∠EBD and ∠ABF must also be complementary angles.
- In part (c), students may have a variety of answers but make sure they only name *two* angles at a time.
- "Name a pair of vertical angles." Listen for the two pairs. One pair is acute (∠ABF and ∠CBD) and the other pair is obtuse (∠DBF and ∠ABC).
- **?** Students should notice that some angle pairs can be classified in more than one way. "What are two classifications for ∠ABC and ∠ABF?" adjacent and supplementary "Name another pair of angles with two classifications." *Sample answer:* ∠EBD and ∠CBD are adjacent and complementary.

Try It

- Students should write their answers on whiteboards for a quick check.

Scaffold instruction to support all students in their learning. Learning is individualized and you may want to group students differently as they move in and out of these levels with each skill and concept. Student self-assessment and feedback help guide your instructional decisions about how and when to layer support for all students to become proficient learners.

Extra Example 1
Name a pair of (a) adjacent angles, (b) complementary angles, (c) supplementary angles, and (d) vertical angles in the figure.

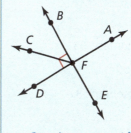

- **a.** Sample answer: ∠AFB and ∠BFC
- **b.** ∠BFC and ∠CFD
- **c.** Sample answer: ∠CFD and ∠AFC
- **d.** Sample answer: ∠AFB and ∠EFD

Try It
1. Sample answer:
   - **a.** ∠QJK and ∠KJL
   - **b.** ∠PJN and ∠NJM
   - **c.** ∠QJK and ∠KJM
   - **d.** ∠LJM and ∠QJP

Extra Example 2

Classify each pair of angles. Then find the value of *x*.

a.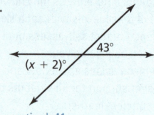
vertical; 41

b.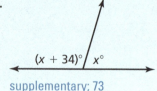
supplementary; 73

c.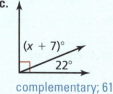
complementary; 61

Try It

2. supplementary; 95
3. vertical; 90
4. complementary; 31

Laurie's Notes

EXAMPLE 2

- "What do you know about the two angles in part (a)? Explain." They have the same measure (70°) because they are vertical angles.
- **Extension:** "In part (a), what are the measures of the two remaining angles? How do you know?" 110°; Any two adjacent angles in the figure form a straight angle, which measures 180°, and 180° − 70° = 110°.
- In parts (b) and (c), students practice writing and solving equations.
- "What do you know about the two angles in part (b)? Explain." The sum of their measures is 90° because they make up a right angle.
- Point out the Remember note. Explain that if the angles overlap, then their measures would not sum to the measure of the larger angle.
- Work through part (b) as shown.
- In part (c), students may think the two angles look like right angles. This is a good opportunity to discuss why students cannot find the measures based on the way a figure looks.
- "What do you know about the two angles in part (c)? Explain." The sum of their measures is 180° because they make up a straight angle.
- Work through part (c) as shown.
- Have students check their answers by substituting each value of *x* in the corresponding figure.

Try It

- **Neighbor Check:** Have students work independently and then have their neighbors check their work. Have students discuss any discrepancies.

ELL Support

After reviewing Example 2, have students work in groups to complete Try It Exercises 2–4. As they discuss each exercise, have them consider the questions: Are the angles vertical or adjacent? What do you know? What is the equation? What is the value of *x*? Expect students to perform according to their language levels.

Beginner: State numbers and one-word answers to the guiding questions.

Intermediate: Use simple sentences such as, "The angles are adjacent."

Advanced: Use detailed sentences such as, "Because one angle has a measure of eighty-five degrees and a straight angle has a measure of one hundred eighty degrees, you know that the other angle has a measure of ninety-five degrees."

EXAMPLE 2 Using Pairs of Angles

Classify each pair of angles. Then find the value of *x*.

a.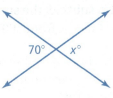

The angles are vertical angles. Vertical angles have the same measure.

▶ So, the value of *x* is 70.

> **Remember**
> When two or more adjacent angles form a larger angle, the sum of the measures of the smaller angles is equal to the measure of the larger angle.

b.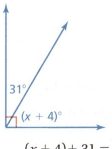

The angles are adjacent angles. Because the angles make up a right angle, the angles are also complementary angles, and the sum of their measures is 90°.

$(x + 4) + 31 = 90$ Write equation.

$x + 35 = 90$ Combine like terms.

$x = 55$ Subtract 35 from each side.

▶ So, the value of *x* is 55.

c.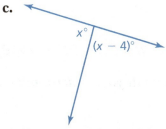

The angles are adjacent angles. Because the angles make up a straight angle, the angles are also supplementary angles, and the sum of their measures is 180°.

$x + (x - 4) = 180$ Write equation.

$2x - 4 = 180$ Combine like terms.

$2x = 184$ Add 4 to each side.

$x = 92$ Divide each side by 2.

▶ So, the value of *x* is 92.

Try It Classify the pair of angles. Then find the value of *x*.

2. 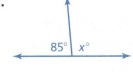   3. 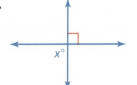   4.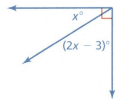

EXAMPLE 3 Finding an Angle Measure

Find the measure of ∠EAB.

To find the measure of ∠EAB, subtract the sum of the measures of ∠BAC and ∠EAC from 360°.

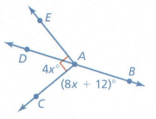

To find the measure of ∠BAC, find the value of x. ∠DAC and ∠BAC are supplementary angles. So, the sum of their measures is 180°.

$4x + (8x + 12) = 180$	Write equation.
$12x + 12 = 180$	Combine like terms.
$12x = 168$	Subtract 12 from each side.
$x = 14$	Divide each side by 12.

Remember
The sum of the measures of the angles around a point is equal to 360°.

So, the measure of ∠BAC is $8(14) + 12 = 124°$.

Because ∠EAC is a right angle, it has a measure of 90°.

▶ So, the measure of ∠EAB is $360 - (124 + 90) = 146°$.

Try It Find the measure of the indicated angle in the diagram.

5. ∠NJM   **6.** ∠KJP   **7.** ∠KJM

Self-Assessment for Concepts & Skills

Solve each exercise. Then rate your understanding of the success criteria in your journal.

8. NAMING ANGLES Name a pair of (a) adjacent angles, (b) complementary angles, (c) supplementary angles, and (d) vertical angles in the figure at the left.

FINDING ANGLE MEASURES Find the value of x.

9.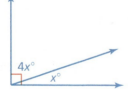

10.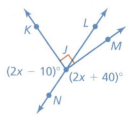

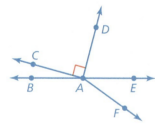

11. WHICH ONE DOESN'T BELONG? Which pair of angles does *not* belong with the other three? Explain your reasoning.

| ∠FBA, ∠FBE | ∠CBD, ∠DBF | ∠DBE, ∠DBC | ∠FBA, ∠EBD |

630 Chapter D Geometric Shapes and Angles

Laurie's Notes

EXAMPLE 3

- Draw the diagram on the board.
- Ask students to work with a partner to find the measure of ∠EAB. Tell students that there is more than one way to find it.
- Find pairs of students that used different methods. Have them share their methods and reasoning with the class. Use *Accountable Language Stems* to lead discussions and encourage students to use them as well.
- **Another Method:** If using the expression 360 − 90 − (8x + 12) for the measure of ∠EAB is not suggested, present it as another option.

Try It

- Have students use *Think-Pair-Share* to solve these problems.

✓ Self-Assessment for Concepts & Skills

- **Always-Sometimes-Never True:** Pose the following conjectures to students. Use *Popsicle Sticks* to solicit explanations.
  - Angles that touch are adjacent angles. sometimes; Adjacent angles share a common side and common vertex. Vertical angles share a common vertex, but they are not adjacent.
  - The sum of the measures of complementary angles is 90°. always
  - Vertical angles may also be adjacent angles. never; Adjacent angles share a common side, vertical angles cannot share a common side.
- Students should work independently on the problems and then share with a partner. Use *Popsicle Sticks* to solicit responses.

> ### ELL Support
> Have students work in pairs for extra support and to practice language. Have two pairs discuss their answers for Exercises 8 and 11 and reach an agreement. Monitor discussions and provide support as needed. Have pairs display their answers to Exercises 9 and 10 on whiteboards for your review.

The Success Criteria Self-Assessment chart can be found in the *Student Journal* or online at *BigIdeasMath.com*.

Extra Example 3

Find the measure of ∠XZW.

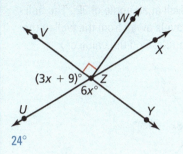

Try It

5. 60°
6. 150°
7. 120°

Self-Assessment
for Concepts & Skills

8. Sample answer:
   a. ∠DAE and ∠EAF
   b. ∠DAE and ∠CAB
   c. ∠CAB and ∠CAE
   d. none
9. 18
10. 60
11. ∠FBA, ∠EBD; The other pairs of angles are adjacent angles.

Extra Example 4

A racquetball bounces off a floor and hits a wall at an angle of 35°. The ball then travels away from the wall at the same angle. Find the value of x.

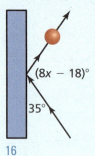

16

Self-Assessment
for Problem Solving

12. 120°; The three angles of the windmill make up an entire circle, so $x + x + x = 360$ and $x = 120$.

13. 120; *Sample answer:* The wall represents a straight angle, so $30 + y + 30 = 180$ and $y = 120$.

14. 40°

Learning Target
Use facts about angle relationships to find unknown angle measures.

Success Criteria
- Identify adjacent, complementary, supplementary, and vertical angles.
- Use equations to find unknown angle measures.
- Find unknown angle measures in real-life situations.

Laurie's Notes

EXAMPLE 4

- Draw the diagram on the board and ask a volunteer to read the problem. Then ask another volunteer to explain what the problem is asking.
- ❓ "What do you know about $\angle GAF$ and $\angle DAC$?" They are vertical angles, so they have the same measure.
- ❓ "What is the relationship between $\angle BAC$, $\angle DAC$, and $\angle EAD$?" They form a straight angle, so the sum of their measures is 180°.
- Write and solve the equation as shown.
- ❓ "How can you determine if the design meets the requirement?" Students should indicate that they will know the design meets the requirement if the measures of all the angles where two roads meet are at least 60°. If they find an angle less than 60°, they will know that the design does not meet the requirement.
- Allow students to finish the problem in small groups. Some groups may find all the angles, while others may stop when they find an angle that is less than 60°.
- **Model with Mathematics:** Discuss the different strategies that students use. Look for efficient methods and explain that if this were a test question, it might be best to stop when they find an angle with a measure less than 60°.

✓ Self-Assessment for Problem Solving

- Allow time in class for students to practice using the problem-solving plan. By now, students should be more comfortable with the problem-solving plan and be able to complete more than the first step.
- Have students work in pairs to make their plans before solving the problems independently.

The Success Criteria Self-Assessment chart can be found in the *Student Journal* or online at *BigIdeasMath.com*.

Formative Assessment Tip

Write Your Own

This technique allows students to practice writing and evaluating their own problems. You provide a description of the type of problem students are to create. Descriptions may be broad or specific. Students write and solve their own problems to check that the conditions are met and the problems are solved correctly.

Closure

- **Write Your Own:** Write a problem involving adjacent, complementary, supplementary, and/or vertical angles and their measures.
- Collect the problems as students leave. Redistribute the problems the next day for students to use as review. If time permits, put students in groups of 5 or 6 and have each group member solve one of the problems on a separate piece of paper and then pass the problem to the right. Repeat until all members of the group have solved all the problems. Then have students compare their answers and discuss any discrepancies.

EXAMPLE 4   Modeling Real Life

A city worker designs an intersection of three roads that will be constructed next year. The measure of the angle between any two roads must be at least 60° in order for vehicles to turn safely. Does the design shown meet the requirement?

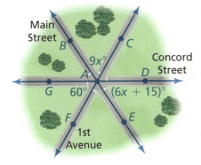

Because ∠GAF and ∠DAC are vertical angles, you know that the measure of ∠DAC is 60°. Because ∠BAC, ∠DAC, and ∠EAD make up a straight angle, you know that the sum of their measures is 180°. Use this information to write and solve an equation for x. Then determine whether any of the angle measures between two roads is less than 60°.

$9x + 60 + (6x + 15) = 180$	Write equation.
$15x + 75 = 180$	Combine like terms.
$15x = 105$	Subtract 75 from each side.
$x = 7$	Divide each side by 15.

∠EAD has a measure of $6(7) + 15 = 57°$.

▶ So, the measure of ∠EAD is less than 60°, and the design does not meet the requirement.

Self-Assessment for Problem Solving

Solve each exercise. Then rate your understanding of the success criteria in your journal.

12. What is the angle between any two windmill blades in the windmill at the left? Justify your answer.

13. A hockey puck strikes a wall at an angle of 30°. The puck then travels away from the wall at the same angle. Find the value of y. Explain your reasoning.

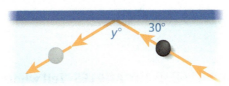

14. The laptop screen turns off when the angle between the keyboard and the screen is less than 20°. How many more degrees can the laptop screen close before the screen turns off?

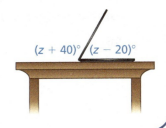

Section D.5   Finding Unknown Angle Measures

D.5 Practice

▶ Review & Refresh

Draw a triangle with the given side lengths, if possible.

1. 1 in., 3 in., 4 in.
2. 4 cm, 4 cm, 7 cm

Solve the inequality. Graph the solution.

3. $-8y \leq 40$
4. $1.1z > -3.3$
5. $\dfrac{1}{3}x \geq 2.5$

▶ Concepts, Skills, & Problem Solving

USING RULES ABOUT ANGLES The diagram shows pairs of *adjacent* angles and *vertical* angles. (See Exploration 1, p. 627.)

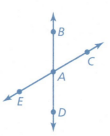

6. Which pair(s) of angles are adjacent angles? Explain.
7. Which pair(s) of angles are vertical angles? Explain.

NAMING ANGLES Use the figure shown.

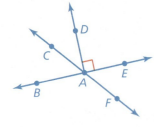

8. Name a pair of adjacent angles.
9. Name a pair of complementary angles.
10. Name a pair of supplementary angles.
11. Name a pair of vertical angles.

12. **YOU BE THE TEACHER** Your friend names a pair of angles with the same measure. Is your friend correct? Explain your reasoning.

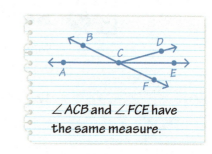

∠ACB and ∠FCE have the same measure.

ADJACENT AND VERTICAL ANGLES Tell whether the angles are *adjacent*, *vertical*, or *neither*. Explain.

13.
14.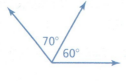
15.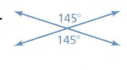

COMPLEMENTARY AND SUPPLEMENTARY ANGLES Tell whether the angles are *complementary*, *supplementary*, or *neither*. Explain.

16.
17.
18.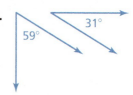

Assignment Guide and Concept Check

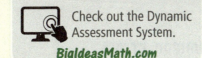

Check out the Dynamic Assessment System.
BigIdeasMath.com

Scaffold assignments to support all students in their learning progression. The suggested assignments are a starting point. Continue to assign additional exercises and revisit with spaced practice to move every student toward proficiency.

Level	Assignment 1	Assignment 2
Emerging	1, 2, 5, 6, 7, 8, 9, 10, 11, 12, 13, 17, 19, 20, 21, 22	15, 16, 23, 25, 26, 29, 30, 31, 32, 35, 43
Proficient	1, 2, 5, 6, 7, 8, 9, 10, 11, 12, 13, 15, 16, 18, 19, 23, 24, 25	26, 28, 29, 30, 31, 33, 36, 38, 40, 42, 43, 44, 46
Advanced	1, 2, 5, 6, 7, 8, 9, 10, 11, 12, 13, 15, 16, 18, 23, 26, 28	30, 31, 34, 37, 38, 40, 42, 43, 45, 46, 47, 48, 50

- Assignment 1 is for use after students complete the Self-Assessment for Concepts & Skills.
- Assignment 2 is for use after students complete the Self-Assessment for Problem Solving.
- The red exercises can be used as a concept check.

Review & Refresh Prior Skills
Exercises 1 and 2 Constructing Triangles Using Side Lengths
Exercises 3–5 Solving an Inequality

Common Errors
- **Exercises 16–18** Students may mix up the terms *complementary* and *supplementary*. Remind them of the definitions and use the alliteration that complementary angles are corners and supplementary angles are straight.

Review & Refresh

1. not possible
2. See Additional Answers.
3. $y \geq -5$

4. $z > -3$

5. $x \geq 7.5$

Concepts, Skills, & Problem Solving

6. See Additional Answers.
7. See Additional Answers.
8. *Sample answer:* ∠CAD and ∠DAE
9. *Sample answer:* ∠BAC and ∠CAD
10. *Sample answer:* ∠BAC and ∠CAE
11. *Sample answer:* ∠EAF and ∠CAB
12. yes; *Sample answer:* ∠ACB and ∠FCE are vertical angles and have the same measure.
13. neither; The angles do not share a common side (adjacent) nor are they opposite angles formed by two intersecting lines (vertical).
14. adjacent; The angles share a common side and have the same vertex.
15. vertical; The angles are opposite angles formed by the intersection of two lines.
16. neither; The sum of the measures of the angles is not 90° or 180°.
17. complementary; The sum of the measures of the angles is 90°.
18. complementary; The sum of the measures of the angles is 90°.

T-632

Concepts, Skills, & Problem Solving

19. no; $\angle LMN$ and $\angle PMQ$ are complementary, not supplementary.
20. complementary; 55
21. vertical; 128
22. supplementary; 63
23. vertical; 25
24. complementary; 15
25. supplementary; 20
26. complementary; 15
27. complementary; 55
28. supplementary; 31
29. $\angle 1 = 130°$, $\angle 2 = 50°$, $\angle 3 = 130°$; Sample answer: $\angle 2$ is a vertical angle to 50°, $\angle 1$ and $\angle 2$ are supplementary angles, $\angle 1$ and $\angle 3$ are vertical angles.
30. 53; Sample answer: $x°$ and $(2x + 21)°$ are supplementary angles, so $x + (2x + 21) = 180$ and $x = 53$.
31. 43
32. $\angle FGL = 10°$, $\angle LGK = 90°$, $\angle KGJ = 80°$, $\angle JGH = 10°$, $\angle FGH = 170°$
33. $\angle KJL = 80°$, $\angle NJM = 25°$, $\angle MJL = 75°$
34. $\angle BAD = 109°$, $\angle DAC = 111°$

Common Errors

- **Exercises 20–28** Students may think that there is not enough information to determine the value of x. Ask them to think about the information given in each figure. For instance, Exercise 20 shows two angles making up a right angle. So, the sum of the two angle measures must be 90°. Students can use this information to set up and solve a simple equation to find the value of x.

19. **YOU BE THE TEACHER** Your friend names a pair of supplementary angles. Is your friend correct? Explain.

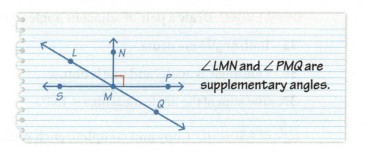
∠LMN and ∠PMQ are supplementary angles.

USING PAIRS OF ANGLES Classify the pair of angles. Then find the value of x.

20.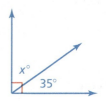

21.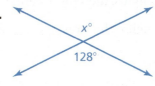

22.

23.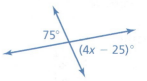

24.

25.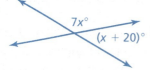

26.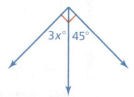

27.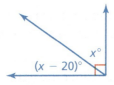

28.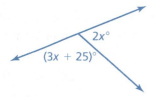

29. **MODELING REAL LIFE** What is the measure of each angle formed by the intersection? Explain.

30. **MODELING REAL LIFE** A tributary joins a river at an angle. Find the value of x. Explain.

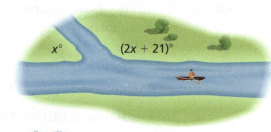

31. **MODELING REAL LIFE** The iron cross is a skiing trick in which the tips of the skis are crossed while the skier is airborne. Find the value of x in the iron cross shown.

FINDING ANGLE MEASURES Find all angle measures in the diagram.

32.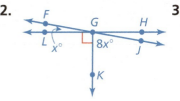

33.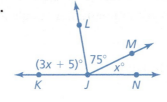

34.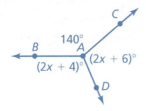

Section D.5   Finding Unknown Angle Measures   633

OPEN-ENDED Draw a pair of adjacent angles with the given description.

35. Both angles are acute.

36. One angle is acute, and one is obtuse.

37. The sum of the angle measures is 135°.

MP REASONING Copy and complete each sentence with *always, sometimes,* or *never*.

38. If x and y are complementary angles, then both x and y are _____ acute.

39. If x and y are supplementary angles, then x is _____ acute.

40. If x is a right angle, then x is _____ acute.

41. If x and y are complementary angles, then x and y are _____ adjacent.

42. If x and y are supplementary angles, then x and y are _____ vertical.

43. **MP REASONING** Draw a figure in which $\angle 1$ and $\angle 2$ are acute vertical angles, $\angle 3$ is a right angle adjacent to $\angle 2$, and the sum of the measure of $\angle 1$ and the measure of $\angle 4$ is 180°.

44. **MP STRUCTURE** Describe the relationship between the two angles represented by the graph shown at the right.

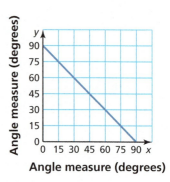

45. **MP STRUCTURE** Consider the figure shown at the left. Use a ruler to extend both rays into lines. What do you notice about the three new angles that are formed?

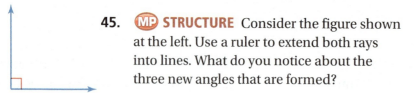

46. **OPEN-ENDED** Give an example of an angle that can be a supplementary angle but cannot be a complementary angle to another angle. Explain.

47. **MP MODELING REAL LIFE** The *vanishing point* of the picture is represented by point B.

   a. The measure of $\angle ABD$ is 6.2 times greater than the measure of $\angle CBD$. Find the measure of $\angle CBD$.

   b. $\angle FBE$ and $\angle EBD$ are congruent. Find the measure of $\angle FBE$.

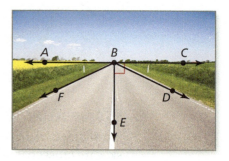

48. **CRITICAL THINKING** The measures of two complementary angles have a ratio of 3 : 2. What is the measure of the larger angle?

49. **MP REASONING** Two angles are vertical angles. What are their measures if they are also complementary angles? supplementary angles?

50. **MP PROBLEM SOLVING** Find the values of x and y.

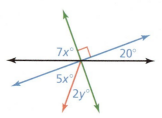

For Your Information
- **Exercise 47** Students may not understand what a *vanishing point* is. A vanishing point is a point in a perspective drawing to which parallel lines appear to converge.

Mini-Assessment
Classify the pair of angles. Then find the value of x.

1.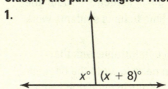
   adjacent and supplementary; 86

2.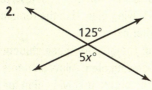
   vertical; 25

3.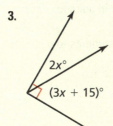
   adjacent and complementary; 15

4.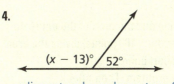
   adjacent and supplementary; 141

Section Resources

Surface Level	Deep Level
Resources by Chapter • Extra Practice • Reteach • Puzzle Time Student Journal • Self-Assessment • Practice Differentiating the Lesson Tutorial Videos Skills Review Handbook Skills Trainer	Resources by Chapter • Enrichment and Extension Graphic Organizers Dynamic Assessment System • Section Practice
Transfer Level	
Dynamic Assessment System • End-of-Chapter Quiz	Assessment Book • End-of-Chapter Quiz

Concepts, Skills, & Problem Solving

35. *Sample answer:*

36. *Sample answer:*

37. *Sample answer:*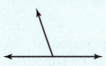

38. always
39. sometimes
40. never
41. sometimes
42. sometimes
43.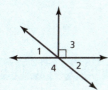

44. The two angles are complementary.

45. They are right angles.

46. *Sample answer:* 120°; It is supplementary with a 60° angle, but it is greater than 90°, so it cannot be complementary with another angle.

47. **a.** 25°
    b. 65°

48. 54°

49. 45°; 90°

50. $x = 10$; $y = 20$

T-634

Skills Needed

Exercise 1
- Finding an Area of a Circle
- Finding a Theoretical Probability

Exercise 2
- Finding the Area of a Semicircle
- Finding the Perimeter of a Semicircular Region
- Using a Scale

Exercise 3
- Finding Angle Measures
- Using the Percent Equation

ELL Support

Explain that the target shown in Exercise 1 represents a dart board. Ask if students are familiar with the game of darts and have them share their knowledge. Provide information as needed.

Using the Problem-Solving Plan

1. $11.\overline{1}\%$

2. about 15.42 ft; about 14.12 ft^2; Sample answer: $d = 6$ ft, $r = 3$ ft,
$P = \frac{1}{2}(6\pi) + 6 \approx 15.42$ ft,
$A = \frac{1}{2}\pi(3)^2 \approx 14.12$ ft^2

3. $54°$; Sample answer:
$\angle CAD = 0.2(180°) = 36°$,
$\angle DAE = 180° - (90° + 36°)$
$= 54°$

Performance Task

The *STEAM Video Performance Task* provides the opportunity for additional enrichment and greater depth of knowledge as students explore the mathematics of the chapter within a context tied to the chapter STEAM Video. The performance task and a detailed scoring rubric are provided at *BigIdeasMath.com*.

T-635

Laurie's Notes

Scaffolding Instruction

- The goal of this lesson is to help students become more comfortable with problem solving. These exercises combine concepts of geometric shapes and angles with prior skills from other chapters and courses. The solution for Exercise 1 is worked out below, to help you guide students through the problem-solving plan. Use the remaining class time to have students work on the other exercises.
- **Emerging:** The goal for these students is to feel comfortable with the problem-solving plan. Allow students to work in pairs to write the beginning steps of the problem-solving plan for Exercise 2. Keep in mind that some students may only be ready to do the first step.
- **Proficient:** Students may be able to work independently or in pairs to complete Exercises 2 and 3.
- Visit each pair to review their plan for each problem. Ask students to describe their plans.

▶ Using the Problem-Solving Plan

Exercise 1

⇨ **Understand the problem.** You are given the dimensions of a circular dart board. You are asked to find the theoretical probability of hitting the center circle.

⇨ **Make a plan.** Find the area of the center circle and the area of the entire dart board. To find the theoretical probability of scoring 100 points, divide the area of the center circle by the area of the entire dart board.

⇨ **Solve and check.** Use the plan to solve the problem. Then check your solution.

- Find the area of the center circle and the area of the entire dart board.

Center circle		Dart board
$A = \pi r^2$	Write formula for area.	$A = \pi r^2$
$= \pi \cdot 4^2$	Substitute for r.	$= \pi \cdot (4 + 4 + 4)^2$
$= 16\pi$ in.^{2}	Simplify.	$= 144\pi$ in.^{2}

So, the area of the center circle is 16π square inches and the area of the entire dart board is 144π square inches.

- Find the theoretical probability of scoring 100 points.

$$P(\text{scoring 100 points}) = \frac{\text{area of center circle}}{\text{area of dart board}}$$

$$= \frac{16\pi}{144\pi}$$

$$= \frac{1}{9}, 0.\overline{1}, \text{ or } 11.\overline{1}\%$$

So, the theoretical probability that a dart hitting the board scores 100 points is $11.\overline{1}\%$.

- **Check:** Use the theoretical probability and the area of the dart board to verify the area of the center circle.

$$A(\text{center circle}) \stackrel{?}{=} P(\text{scoring 100 points}) \cdot A(\text{dart board})$$

$$16\pi \stackrel{?}{=} \frac{1}{9} \cdot 144\pi$$

$$16\pi = 16\pi \checkmark$$

D Connecting Concepts

Using the Problem-Solving Plan

1. A dart is equally likely to hit any point on the board shown. Find the theoretical probability that a dart hitting the board scores 100 points.

   Understand the problem. You are given the dimensions of a circular dart board. You are asked to find the theoretical probability of hitting the center circle.

   Make a plan. Find the area of the center circle and the area of the entire dart board. To find the theoretical probability of scoring 100 points, divide the area of the center circle by the area of the entire dart board.

   Solve and check. Use the plan to solve the problem. Then check your solution.

2. A scale drawing of a window is shown. Find the perimeter and the area of the actual window. Justify your answer.

   1 cm : 2 ft

3. ∠CAD makes up 20% of a pair of supplementary angles. Find the measure of ∠DAE. Justify your answer.

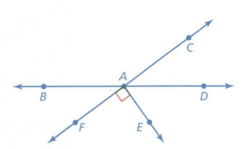

Performance Task

Finding the Area and Perimeter of a Track

At the beginning of the this chapter, you watched a STEAM video called "Track and Field". You are now ready to complete the performance task related to this video, available at *BigIdeasMath.com*. Be sure to use the problem-solving plan as you work through the performance task.

Connecting Concepts 635

D Chapter Review

 Go to *BigIdeasMath.com* to download blank graphic organizers.

▶ Review Vocabulary

Write the definition and give an example of each vocabulary term.

circle, *p. 600*
center, *p. 600*
radius, *p. 600*
diameter, *p. 600*
circumference, *p. 601*
pi, *p. 601*
semicircle, *p. 602*
composite figure, *p. 614*
adjacent angles, *p. 628*
complementary angles, *p. 628*
supplementary angles, *p. 628*
vertical angles, *p. 628*

▶ Graphic Organizers

You can use a **Four Square** to organize information about a concept. Each of the four squares can be a category, such as definition, vocabulary, example, non-example, words, algebra, table, numbers, visual, graph, or equation. Here is an example of a Four Square for *circumference*.

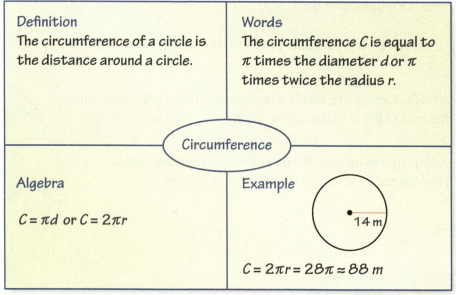

Choose and complete a graphic organizer to help you study each topic.

1. area of a circle
2. semicircle
3. composite figure
4. constructing triangles
5. constructing quadrilaterals
6. complementary angles
7. supplementary angles
8. vertical angles

"How do you like my **Four Square** on rubber duckies? Whenever I have my doggy bath, I insist that my ducky is with me."

Review Vocabulary

- As a review of the chapter vocabulary, have students revisit the vocabulary section in their *Student Journals* to fill in any missing definitions and record examples of each term.

Graphic Organizers

Sample answers:

1.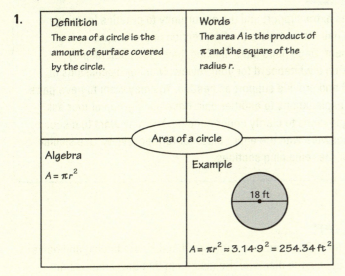

2.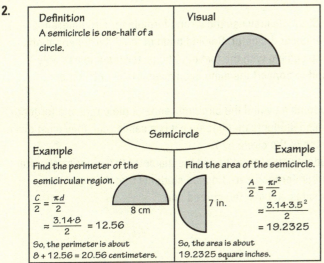

3–8. Answers at *BigIdeasMath.com*.

List of Organizers

Available at *BigIdeasMath.com*
Definition and Example Chart
Example and Non-Example Chart
Four Square
Information Frame
Summary Triangle

About this Organizer

A **Four Square** can be used to organize information about a concept. Students write the concept in the oval. Then students use each of the four squares surrounding the oval to represent a related category. Related categories may include: definition, vocabulary, example, non-example, words, algebra, table, numbers, visual, graph, or equation. Encourage students to use categories that will help them study the concept. Students can place their Four Squares on note cards to use as a quick study reference.

T-636

Chapter Self-Assessment

1. 2.5 cm
2. 50 mm
3. about 37.68 mm
4. about 4.71 ft
5. about 22 cm
6. about 15.42 in.; *Sample answer:*
   outside perimeter = $30 + \frac{1}{2}(30\pi)$
   ≈ 77.1,
   inside perimeter = $24 + \frac{1}{2}(24\pi)$
   ≈ 61.68,
   $77.1 - 61.68 = 15.42$
7. yes; *Sample answer:* The diameter of the cake is about 31.85 inches, so it will fit through the doorway.
8. about 7 m
9. *Sample answer:* You are seated at the very edge of a merry-go-round that has a diameter of 10 feet. How far do you travel in three full turns of the merry-go-round?; about 94.2 ft

Chapter Self-Assessment

The Success Criteria Self-Assessment chart can be found in the *Student Journal* or online at *BigIdeasMath.com*.

ELL Support

Allow students extra support and the opportunity to practice language by working in pairs to complete the first section of the Chapter Self-Assessment. Once pairs have finished, have each pair display their answers on a whiteboard for your review. Monitor discussions of Exercises 6–9 and provide support as needed. You may want to have pairs present their explanations to another pair. Have each group of four ask and answer questions to clarify understanding. You may want to discuss some of the answers with the entire class for further review. Use similar techniques for the remaining sections.

Common Errors

- **Exercises 1 and 2** Students may confuse what they are finding and halve the radius or double the diameter. Remind them that the radius is half the diameter.
- **Exercises 3–5** Students may use the wrong formula for circumference when given a radius or diameter. Remind them of the different equations. If students are struggling with the two equations, tell them to use only one equation and to convert the dimension given to the one in the chosen formula.
- **Exercise 6** Students may find the circumference of the circle and forget to divide by 2. Remind students that because it is a semicircle, they must divide the circumference of the circle by 2.
- **Exercise 6** Students may forget to add the diameter to the perimeter after they find the circumference part. Remind students that the perimeter includes all the sides, not just the curved part.

Chapter Self-Assessment

As you complete the exercises, use the scale below to rate your understanding of the success criteria in your journal.

1	2	3	4
I do not understand.	I can do it with help.	I can do it on my own.	I can teach someone else.

D.1 Circles and Circumference *(pp. 599–606)*

Learning Target: Find the circumference of a circle.

1. What is the radius of a circular lid with a diameter of 5 centimeters?

2. The radius of a circle is 25 millimeters. Find the diameter.

Find the circumference of the object. Use 3.14 or $\frac{22}{7}$ for π.

3. 6 mm

4. 1.5 ft

5. 7 cm

6. You are placing non-slip tape along the perimeter of the bottom of a semicircle-shaped doormat. How much tape will you save applying the tape to the perimeter of the inside semicircle of the doormat? Justify your answer.

30 in.

3 in.

7. You need to carry a circular cake through a 32-inch wide doorway without tilting it. The circumference of the cake is 100 inches. Will the cake fit through the doorway? Explain.

C = 44 m

8. Estimate the radius of the Big Ben clock face in London.

9. Describe and solve a real-life problem that involves finding the circumference of a circle.

D.2 Areas of Circles (pp. 607–612)

Learning Target: Find the area of a circle.

Find the area of the circle. Use 3.14 or $\frac{22}{7}$ for π.

10.

4 in.

11.

11 cm

12.

42 mm

13. A desktop is shaped like a semicircle with a diameter of 28 inches. What is the area of the desktop?

14. An ecologist is studying an algal bloom that has formed on the entire surface of a circular pond. What is the area of the surface of the pond covered by the algal bloom?

28 ft

15. A knitted pot holder is shaped like a circle. Its radius is 3.5 inches. What is its area?

D.3 Perimeters and Areas of Composite Figures (pp. 613–618)

Learning Target: Find perimeters and areas of composite figures.

Find the perimeter and the area of the figure.

16.
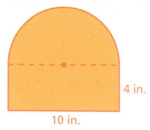
4 in.
10 in.

17.
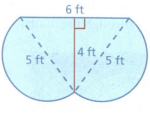
6 ft
5 ft   4 ft   5 ft

18. **GARDEN** You want to fence part of a yard to make a vegetable garden. How many feet of fencing do you need to surround the garden?

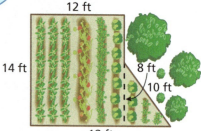
12 ft
14 ft
8 ft
10 ft
18 ft

Common Errors

- **Exercises 10–15** Students may write the incorrect units for the area. Remind students to carefully check the units and to square the units as well.
- **Exercises 12–14** Students may forget to divide the diameter by 2 to find the area. Remind students that they need the *radius* for the formula for the area of a circle.
- **Exercise 13** Students may forget to divide the area by 2. Remind students that they are finding the area of half of a circle, so the area is half the area of a whole circle.
- **Exercises 16–18** When finding the perimeter, students may include the dashed lines in their calculations. Remind them that the dashed lines are for reference and sometimes give information to find another length. Only the outside lengths are included in the perimeter.
- **Exercises 16–18** When finding the area, students may forget to include one of the areas of the composite figure or may count one area more than once. Tell students to separate the figure into several shapes. Draw and label each shape and then find the area of each. Finally, add the areas of each shape together for the area of the whole figure.

Chapter Self-Assessment

10. about 50.24 in.^{2}
11. about 379.94 cm^2
12. about 1386 mm^2
13. about 308 in.^{2}
14. about 615.44 ft^2
15. about 38.465 in.^{2}
16. about 33.7 in.; about 79.25 in.^{2}
17. about 21.7 ft; about 31.63 ft^2
18. 60 ft

Chapter Self-Assessment

19.

20. See Additional Answers.
21. not possible
22. *Sample answer:*

23. not possible
24. *Sample answer:* ∠VUW and ∠WUZ
25. *Sample answer:* ∠YUX and ∠XUZ
26. *Sample answer:* ∠YUZ and ∠ZUW
27. ∠YUX and ∠VUW
28. complementary; 21
29. vertical; 81
30. supplementary; 34
31. 1) Use vertical angles to find that the measure of ∠2 is 115°. 2) Use supplementary angles to find that the measure of ∠3 is 65°. Then use supplementary angles to find that the measure of ∠2 is 115°.
32. ∠XUZ = 50°, ∠ZUW = 90°, ∠WUV = 40°, ∠VUY = 140°

Common Errors

- **Exercises 19, 20, 22, and 23** Students may use the wrong set of angles on a protractor. Encourage students to decide which set to use by comparing the angle measure to 90°.
- **Exercises 25, 26, 28, and 30** Students may mix up the terms *complementary* and *supplementary*. Remind them of the definitions and use the alliteration that complementary angles are corners and supplementary angles are straight.
- **Exercises 28–30** Students may think that there is not enough information to determine the value of *x*. Ask them to think about the information given in each figure. For instance, Exercise 28 shows two angles making up a right angle. So, the sum of the two angle measures must be 90°. Students can use this information to set up and solve a simple equation to find the value of *x*.

Chapter Resources

Surface Level	Deep Level
Resources by Chapter • Extra Practice • Reteach • Puzzle Time Student Journal • Practice • Chapter Self-Assessment Differentiating the Lesson Tutorial Videos Skills Review Handbook Skills Trainer Game Library	Resources by Chapter • Enrichment and Extension Graphic Organizers Game Library
Transfer Level	
STEAM Video Dynamic Assessment System • Chapter Test	Assessment Book • Chapter Tests A and B • Alternative Assessment • STEAM Performance Task

D.4 Constructing Polygons (pp. 619–626)

Learning Target: Construct a polygon with given measures.

Draw a triangle with the given description, if possible.

19. a triangle with angle measures of 15°, 75°, and 90°

20. a triangle with a 3-inch side and a 4-inch side that meet at a 30° angle

21. a triangle with side lengths of 5 centimeters, 8 centimeters, and 2 centimeters

Draw a quadrilateral with the given angle measures, if possible.

22. 110°, 80°, 70°, 100°

23. 105°, 15°, 20°, 40°

D.5 Finding Unknown Angle Measures (pp. 627–634)

Learning Target: Use facts about angle relationships to find unknown angle measures.

Use the figure shown.

24. Name a pair of adjacent angles.

25. Name a pair of complementary angles.

26. Name a pair of supplementary angles.

27. Name a pair of vertical angles.

Classify the pair of angles. Then find the value of x.

28.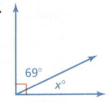

29.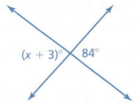

30.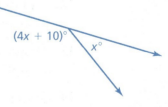

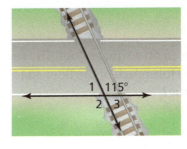

31. Describe two ways to find the measure of $\angle 2$.

32. Using the diagram from Exercises 24–27, find all the angle measures when $\angle XUY = 40°$.

Practice Test Item References

Practice Test Questions	Section to Review
1, 2, 3, 4, 14	D.2
5, 12, 15	D.3
6, 7, 8	D.4

Remind students to quickly look over the entire test before they start so that they can budget their time. This chapter contains many definitions that some students may find difficult to keep straight. Encourage them to jot down definitions on the back of the test before they start. Have them use the **Stop** and **Think** strategy before they write their answers.

Common Errors

- **Exercises 2 and 3** Students may use the wrong formula for circumference when given a radius or diameter. Remind them of the different equations. If students are struggling with the two equations, tell them to use only one equation and to convert the dimension given to the one in the chosen formula.
- **Exercises 2–5** Students may not use the correct units for the area. Remind students to carefully check the units and to square the units as well.
- **Exercise 3** Students may forget to divide the diameter by 2 to find the area of the circle. Remind students that they need the *radius* for the formula for the area of a circle.
- **Exercise 7** Students may find the perimeter of the semicircle by taking the circumference of the whole circle and dividing by 2. Remind students that because it is a semicircle, they must divide the circumference of the circle by 2.
- **Exercise 4** Students may forget to add the diameter to the perimeter after finding the perimeter of the semicircle. Remind students that the perimeter includes all the sides, not just the curved part.
- **Exercise 5** When finding the area, students may forget to include one of the areas of the composite figure or may count one area more than once. Tell students to separate the figure into several shapes. Draw and label each shape and then find the area of each. Finally, add the areas of each shape together for the area of the whole figure.
- **Exercises 9 and 10** Students may mix up the terms *complementary* and *supplementary*. Remind them of the definitions and use the alliteration that *complementary* angles *complete* a right angle.

8. a quadrilateral with angle measures of 90°, 110°, 40°, and 120°

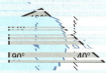
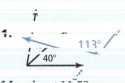

Test-Taking Strategies

Available at *BigIdeasMath.com*
After Answering Easy Questions, Relax
Answer Easy Questions First
Estimate the Answer
Read All Choices before Answering
Read Question before Answering
Solve Directly or Eliminate Choices
Solve Problem before Looking at Choices
Use Intelligent Guessing
Work Backwards

About this Strategy

When taking a timed test, it is often best to skim the test and answer the easy questions first. Read each question carefully and thoroughly. Be careful that you record your answer in the correct position on the answer sheet.

Cumulative Practice

1. C
2. 42
3. I
4. C

Item Analysis

1. **A.** The student does not convert to the same units (either 2 quarts to 8 cups or 5 cups to 1.25 quarts) and inverts one of the ratios.

   B. The student does not convert to the same units (either 2 quarts to 8 cups or 5 cups to 1.25 quarts).

   C. Correct answer

   D. The student uses the correct numbers but inverts one of the ratios.

2. **Gridded Response:** Correct answer: 42

   Common error: The student sets up the equation incorrectly. For instance, $2x + 1 + 85 = 180$ and finds $x = 47$.

3. **F.** The student writes an inequality that represents 5 less than the product of 7 and an unknown number is *less than* 42.

   G. On the left side of the inequality, the student writes an expression that represents the product of *n* and a number that is 5 less than 7.

   H. On the left side of the inequality, the student misinterprets the use of *less than* and reverses the order of the subtraction.

   I. Correct answer

4. **A.** The student does not square the radius.

   B. The student multiplies the radius by 2 instead of squaring it.

   C. Correct answer

   D. The student squares the diameter instead of the radius.

D Cumulative Practice

1. To make 6 servings of soup, you need 5 cups of chicken broth. You want to know how many servings you can make with 2 quarts of chicken broth. Which proportion should you use?

   A. $\dfrac{6}{5} = \dfrac{2}{x}$

   B. $\dfrac{6}{5} = \dfrac{x}{2}$

   C. $\dfrac{6}{5} = \dfrac{x}{8}$

   D. $\dfrac{5}{6} = \dfrac{x}{8}$

2. What is the value of x?

   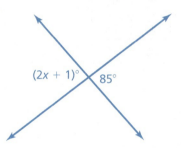

3. Your mathematics teacher described an inequality in words.

   > "5 less than the product of 7 and an unknown number is greater than 42."

   Which inequality matches your mathematics teacher's description?

   F. $7n - 5 < 42$

   G. $(7 - 5)n > 42$

   H. $5 - 7n > 42$

   I. $7n - 5 > 42$

4. What is the approximate area of the circle below? $\left(\text{Use } \dfrac{22}{7} \text{ for } \pi.\right)$

   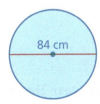

   A. 132 cm^2

   B. 264 cm^2

   C. 5544 cm^2

   D. $22{,}176 \text{ cm}^2$

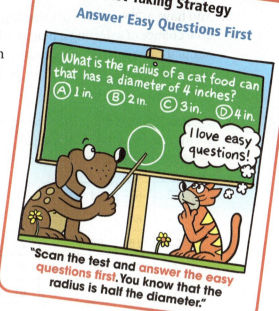

Test-Taking Strategy
Answer Easy Questions First

"Scan the test and answer the easy questions first. You know that the radius is half the diameter."

Cumulative Practice 641

5. You have a 50% chance of selecting a blue marble from Bag A and a 20% chance of selecting a blue marble from Bag B. Use the provided simulation to answer the question, "What is the estimated probability of selecting a blue marble from both bags?"

The digits 1 through 5 in the tens place represent selecting a blue marble from Bag A. The digits 1 and 2 in the ones place represent selecting a blue marble from Bag B.

52	66	73	68	75	28	35	47	48	02
16	68	49	03	77	35	92	78	06	06
58	18	89	39	24	80	32	41	77	21
32	40	96	59	86	01	12	00	94	73
40	71	28	61	01	24	37	25	03	25

F. 12%
G. 16%
H. 24%
I. 88%

6. Which proportion represents the problem?

"What number is 12% of 125?"

A. $\dfrac{n}{125} = \dfrac{12}{100}$

B. $\dfrac{12}{125} = \dfrac{n}{100}$

C. $\dfrac{125}{n} = \dfrac{12}{100}$

D. $\dfrac{12}{n} = \dfrac{125}{100}$

7. What is the approximate perimeter of the figure below? (Use 3.14 for π.)

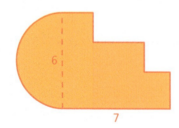

8. A savings account earns 2.5% simple interest per year. The principal is $850. What is the balance after 3 years?

F. $63.75
G. $871.25
H. $913.75
J. $7225

Item Analysis (continued)

5. **F.** Correct answer

   G. The student uses the digits 0 through 2 for Bag B instead of 1 and 2.

   H. The student uses the digits 0 through 5 for Bag A instead of 1 through 5 and the digits 0 through 2 for Bag B instead of 1 and 2.

   I. The student finds the probability of *not* selecting a blue marble from both bags.

6. **A.** Correct answer

   B. The student chooses a proportion that represents the problem "What percent of 125 is 12?"

   C. The student chooses a proportion that represents the problem "12% of what number is 125?"

   D. The student chooses a proportion that represents the problem "125% of what number is 12?"

7. **Gridded Response:** Correct answer: 29.42

   Common error: The student includes the circumference of the circle instead of just the circumference of the semicircle and gets 38.84.

8. **F.** The student finds the interest earned after 3 years instead of the balance.

   G. The student finds the balance after 1 year instead of 3 years.

   H. Correct answer

   I. The student uses 2.5 for r instead of 0.025.

Cumulative Practice

5. F
6. A
7. 29.42
8. H

T-642

Cumulative Practice

9. B

10. *Part A* about 942 ft²

    Part B about 134.2 ft

11. H

Item Analysis (continued)

9. **A.** The student switches the medians for the sample from Pond A and the sample from Pond B.

   B. Correct answer

   C. The student incorrectly thinks the measures of center are about the same for both samples.

   D. The student incorrectly thinks that the measures of variation are *not* about the same for both samples.

10. **4 points** The student's work and explanations demonstrate a thorough understanding of solving problems involving area and perimeter of composite figures. In Part A, the student correctly finds the area of the sprayed region to be approximately 942 square feet. In Part B, the student correctly finds the perimeter of the sprayed region to be approximately 134.2 feet. The student provides accurate work with clear and complete explanations.

    3 points The student's work and explanations demonstrate an essential but less than thorough understanding of solving problems involving area and perimeter of composite figures.

    2 points The student's work and explanations demonstrate a partial but limited understanding of solving problems involving area and perimeter of composite figures.

    1 point The student's work and explanations demonstrate a very limited understanding of solving problems involving area and perimeter of composite figures.

    0 points The student provides no response, a completely incorrect or incomprehensible response, or a response that demonstrates insufficient understanding of solving problems involving area and perimeter of composite figures.

11. **F.** The student subtracts 12 from -8 instead of adding.

    G. The student thinks $-8 + 12 = -4$ instead of 4.

    H. Correct answer

    I. The student incorrectly reads the inequality sign as *is greater than* instead of *is greater than or equal to*.

9. Two ponds each contain about 400 fish. The double box-and-whisker plot represents the weights of a random sample of 12 fish from each pond. Which statement about the measures of center and variation is true?

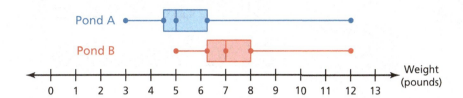

A. The variation in the samples is about the same, but the sample from Pond A has a greater median.

B. The variation in the samples is about the same, but the sample from Pond B has a greater median.

C. The measures of center and variation are about the same for both samples.

D. Neither the measures of center nor variation are the same for the samples.

10. A lawn sprinkler sprays water onto part of a circular region, as shown below.

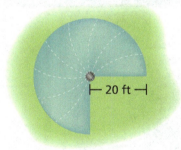

Part A What is the area, in square feet, of the region that the sprinkler sprays with water? Explain your reasoning. (Use 3.14 for π.)

Part B What is the perimeter, in feet, of the region that the sprinkler sprays with water? Explain your reasoning. (Use 3.14 for π.)

11. What is the least value of x for which $x - 12 \geq -8$ is true?

F. -20 **G.** -4

H. 4 **I.** 5

E Surface Area and Volume

- **E.1** Surface Areas of Prisms
- **E.2** Surface Areas of Cylinders
- **E.3** Surface Areas of Pyramids
- **E.4** Volumes of Prisms
- **E.5** Volumes of Pyramids
- **E.6** Cross Sections of Three-Dimensional Figures

Chapter Learning Target:
Understand surface area and volume.

Chapter Success Criteria:
- I can describe the surface area and volume of different shapes.
- I can use formulas to find surface areas and volumes of solids.
- I can solve real-life problems involving surface area and volume.
- I can describe cross sections of solids.

STEAM Video: "Paper Measurements"

Laurie's Notes

Chapter E Overview

This chapter is certainly one of my favorites! The geometric solids explored are shapes that students see in the world around them. I have a collection of solids that I have saved over the years, from package containers and party hats to mailing tubes and rubber balls. Nothing takes the place of students being able to hold and examine the solid. Looking at a two-dimensional picture of a three-dimensional object is just not the same.

Students have prior experiences with surface area and volume. They should be familiar with these two types of measurement, particularly for rectangular prisms. These measurements are now extended to include triangular prisms, cylinders, and pyramids.

To understand the surface area of a solid, students need to focus on the faces that make up the solid. One approach is to look at a *net* that can be folded to form the solid.

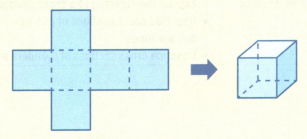

When students look at a pyramid, you want them to see one base and all of the triangular faces that form the lateral surface.

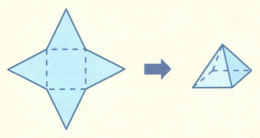

Nets help students reason that surface area is the area of the base(s) plus the areas of the lateral faces. In the lessons, the "formulas" are written in words and not as algebraic equations for most of the three-dimensional figures.

Volume is presented as a layering process, similar to how volume was introduced in previous courses. The height of a prism represents the number of congruent bases that have been stacked or layered. The volume of the prism is the area of the base times the height.

The chapter concludes with a lesson on cross sections of three-dimensional figures. Many students can relate to a knife or a wire slicing completely through a cake, a block of cheese, or a hard-boiled egg. What shape is the newly exposed region?

If you have not started collecting three-dimensional models, begin now. Next year you will be glad you did!

Suggested Pacing

Chapter Opener	1 Day
Section 1	1 Day
Section 2	1 Day
Section 3	1 Day
Section 4	1 Day
Section 5	1 Day
Section 6	1 Day
Connecting Concepts	1 Day
Chapter Review	1 Day
Chapter Test	1 Day
Total Chapter E	10 Days
Year-to-Date	52 Days

Chapter Learning Target

Understand surface area and volume.

Chapter Success Criteria

- Describe the surface area and volume of different shapes.
- Use formulas to find surface areas and volumes of solids.
- Solve real-life problems involving surface area and volume.
- Describe cross sections of solids.

Chapter E Learning Targets and Success Criteria

Section	Learning Target	Success Criteria
E.1 Surface Areas of Prisms	Find the surface area of a prism.	• Use a formula to find the surface area of a prism. • Find the lateral surface area of a prism.
E.2 Surface Areas of Cylinders	Find the surface area of a cylinder.	• Use a formula to find the surface area of a cylinder. • Find the lateral surface area of a cylinder.
E.3 Surface Areas of Pyramids	Find the surface area of a pyramid.	• Use a net to find the surface area of a regular pyramid. • Find the lateral surface area of a regular pyramid.
E.4 Volumes of Prisms	Find the volume of a prism.	• Use a formula to find the volume of a prism. • Use the formula for the volume of a prism to find a missing dimension.
E.5 Volumes of Pyramids	Find the volume of a pyramid.	• Use a formula to find the volume of a pyramid. • Use the volume of a pyramid to solve a real-life problem.
E.6 Cross Sections of Three-Dimensional Figures	Describe the cross sections of a solid.	• Explain the meaning of a cross section. • Describe cross sections of prisms and pyramids. • Describe cross sections of cylinders and cones.

Progressions

Through the Grades

Grade 6	Grade 7	Grade 8
• Find the areas of triangles, special quadrilaterals, and polygons. • Find the volumes of prisms with fractional edge lengths. • Use nets made up of rectangles and triangles to find surface areas.	• Describe the cross sections that result from slicing three-dimensional figures. • Solve problems involving the area and circumference of a circle. • Solve real-world and mathematical problems involving surface areas and volumes of objects composed of prisms, pyramids, and cylinders.	• Know and apply the formulas for the volumes of cones, cylinders, and spheres.

Through the Chapter

Standard	E.1	E.2	E.3	E.4	E.5	E.6
Describe the two-dimensional figures that result from slicing three-dimensional figures, as in plane sections of right rectangular prisms and right rectangular pyramids.						★
Know the formulas for the area and circumference of a circle and use them to solve problems; give an informal derivation of the relationship between the circumference and area of a circle.		■				
Solve real-world and mathematical problems involving area, volume, and surface area of two- and three-dimensional objects composed of triangles, quadrilaterals, polygons, cubes, and right prisms.	●		●	●	★	

Key

▲ = preparing ★ = complete
● = learning   ■ = extending

Laurie's Notes

STEAM Video

STEAM Video

1. 1 in.; 0.4 in.; 0.04 in.; 0.004 in.

2. *Sample answer:* Find the volume of the entire notepad and divide that volume by the number of pages in the notepad.

Before the Video
- To introduce the STEAM Video, read aloud the first paragraph of Paper Measurements and discuss the question with your students.
- ? "What other method can you use to measure the thickness of a piece of paper?"

During the Video
- The video shows Alex calculating the volume of a single sheet of paper.
- ? Pause the video at 1:00 and ask, "How does Alex calculate the volume of a single sheet of paper?" By finding the volume of a stack of papers and dividing by the number of pieces.
- Watch the remainder of the video.

After the Video
- ? Ask, "How did Alex and Enid calculate the diameter of a pin?" By filling a 1-inch line in a piece of clay with pin holes, counting the number of holes that fill 1 inch, and then dividing 1 inch by the number of pin holes.
- Have students work with a partner to answer Questions 1 and 2.
- As students discuss and answer the questions, they should begin to see a relationship between height and volume.

Performance Task

Sample answer: It may be hard to measure the dimensions of the object.

Performance Task

- Use this information to spark students' interest and promote thinking about real-life problems.
- ? Ask, "Why might it be helpful to use the volume of a container of objects to estimate the volume of one of the objects?"
- After completing the chapter, students will have gained the knowledge needed to complete "Volumes and Surface Areas of Small Objects."

Mathematical Practices

Students have opportunities to develop aspects of the mathematical practices throughout the chapter. Here are some examples.

1. **Make Sense of Problems and Persevere in Solving Them**
   E.3 Exercise 20, *p. 664*
2. **Reason Abstractly and Quantitatively**
   E.6 Exercise 27, *p. 682*
3. **Construct Viable Arguments and Critique the Reasoning of Others**
   E.4 Math Practice note, *p. 665*
4. **Model with Mathematics**
   E.5 Exercise 20, *p. 676*
5. **Use Appropriate Tools Strategically**
   E.4 Exercise 23, *p. 670*
6. **Attend to Precision**
   E.2 Math Practice note, *p. 653*
7. **Look for and Make Use of Structure**
   E.1 Math Practice note, *p. 647*
8. **Look for and Express Regularity in Repeated Reasoning**
   E.2 Exercise 21, *p. 658*

STEAM Video

Paper Measurements

The thickness of a single piece of paper cannot be precisely measured using a ruler. What other method can you use to measure the thickness of a piece of paper?

Watch the STEAM Video "Paper Measurements." Then answer the following questions.

1. A stack of 500 pieces of paper is 2 inches tall. How tall is a stack of 250 pieces? 100 pieces? 10 pieces? How thick is a single piece of paper?

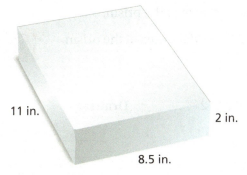

2. You have a circular notepad. How can you find the volume of one piece of paper in the notepad?

Performance Task

Volumes and Surface Areas of Small Objects

After completing this chapter, you will be able to use the concepts you learned to answer the questions in the *STEAM Video Performance Task*. You will be given the dimensions of a shipping box and the number of bouncy balls that fit in the box.

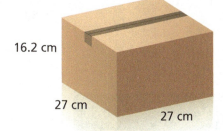

You will be asked to use the box to estimate the volume of each bouncy ball. Why might it be helpful to use the volume of a container of objects to estimate the volume of one of the objects?

645

Getting Ready for Chapter E

Chapter Exploration

1. Work with a partner. Perform each step for each of the given dimensions.

   - Use 24 one-inch cubes to form a rectangular prism that has the given dimensions.
   - Make a sketch of the prism.
   - Find the surface area of the prism.

   a. $4 \times 3 \times 2$ **Drawing**   **Surface Area**

      ▢ in.²

   b. $1 \times 1 \times 24$ **c.** $1 \times 2 \times 12$ **d.** $1 \times 3 \times 8$
   e. $1 \times 4 \times 6$ **f.** $2 \times 2 \times 6$ **g.** $2 \times 4 \times 3$

2. **MP REASONING** Work with a partner. If two blocks of ice have the same volume, the block with the greater surface area will melt faster. The blocks below have equal volumes. Which block will melt faster? Explain your reasoning.

Vocabulary

The following vocabulary terms are defined in this chapter. Think about what each term might mean and record your thoughts.

lateral surface area   slant height of a pyramid
regular pyramid   cross section

Laurie's Notes

Chapter Exploration

- Throughout this chapter, it is important for students to see, hold, and construct models of solids. In the exploration, they will use one-inch cubes to build various rectangular prisms. If one-inch cubes are not available, any cubes will work.
- In the previous course, students found surface areas of prisms using nets but they may need a quick review.
- **?** "What is surface area?" *the sum of the areas of all the faces of a solid*
- Have pairs complete Exercise 1 and then compare their answers with another pair. Discuss any discrepancies as a class.
- In Exercise 2, students should calculate the surface area of each block of ice. Because the volumes are the same, they know that the block of ice with the greater surface area will melt faster.

Vocabulary

- These terms represent some of the vocabulary that students will encounter in Chapter E. Discuss the terms as a class.
- Where have students heard the term *regular pyramid* outside of a math classroom? In what contexts? Students may not be able to write the actual definition, but they may write phrases associated with a *regular pyramid*.
- Allowing students to discuss these terms now will prepare them for understanding the terms as they are presented in the chapter.
- When students encounter a new definition, encourage them to write in their *Student Journals*. They will revisit these definitions during the Chapter Review.

ELL Support

Discuss the meaning of *surface area*. Examine each word. Remind students that in the previous chapter they learned the mathematical meaning of *area*—the amount of surface covered by a figure. Ask them to describe what they remember. Ask if students can identify a word they know in the word *surface*. Point out that a *face* is the outermost covering of the front of a person's head. *Surface* comes from the French language and means "outermost boundary."

Topics for Review

- Finding Areas of Special Quadrilaterals
- Finding Areas of Triangles
- Finding Volumes of Rectangular Prisms
- Three-Dimensional Figures
- Using Nets to Find Surface Areas

Chapter Exploration

1. a.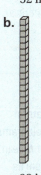
   52 in.^{2}

   b.
   98 in.^{2}

   c.
   76 in.^{2}

   d.
   70 in.^{2}

   e.
   68 in.^{2}

   f.
   56 in.^{2}

   g.
   52 in.^{2}

2. the block on the right; The block on the right has a surface area of 7 ft^2. The block on the left has a surface area of 6 ft^2.

T-646

Learning Target
Find the surface area of a prism.

Success Criteria
- Use a formula to find the surface area of a prism.
- Find the lateral surface area of a prism.

Warm Up
Cumulative, vocabulary, and prerequisite skills practice opportunities are available in the *Resources by Chapter* or at *BigIdeasMath.com*.

ELL Support
Remind students that the lateral faces of a prism are parallelograms. Explain that the meaning of *face* in mathematics is different from its meaning in everyday language. In everyday language, a face is the front of a person's head from the forehead to the chin. A face of a prism is a flat side of a prism.

Exploration 1
a. $S = 2wh + 2\ell h + 2\ell w$; The surface area of a rectangular prism is the sum of the areas of the faces of the prism.

b. *Sample answer:* $h = 3$ in., $w = 2$ in., $\ell = 5$ in.;

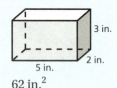

62 in.^{2}

Exploration 2
a. triangular prism; 48 units^2

b. *Sample answer:* Find the sum of the areas of the faces shown by the net.

Laurie's Notes

Check out the Dynamic Classroom.
BigIdeasMath.com

Preparing to Teach
- Students should know how to make a net for a prism and how to use the net to find the surface area of the prism. Now they will develop and use formulas to find the surface area of a prism.
- **Make Sense of Problems and Persevere in Solving Them:** Finding the surface area of a solid can be challenging when the faces are not all visible. Drawing a net allows students to see all of the faces of the solid.

Motivate
- Hold a prism, perhaps an empty box.
- ❓ "What is meant by the surface area of this box or rectangular prism?" Answers may vary, but listen for the areas of each side.
- ❓ "Each side of a prism is called a face. How many faces does this prism have?" 6
- ❓ "What does it mean when two figures are congruent?" They are the same size and shape. "Are any of the faces of this prism congruent? Explain." Yes, there are 3 pairs of congruent faces.
- "Why would I need to know the surface area of this prism?" Listen for the concept of making the box. Explain to students that when items are mass produced, someone needs to calculate the amount of material needed to produce the prism.
- Nets for different prisms are available online at *BigIdeasMath.com*.

Exploration 1
- **Teaching Tip:** Collect cardboard samples of prisms such as donut, pizza, and tissue boxes. These can be taken apart to demonstrate nets.
- Explain that any pair of opposite faces of a rectangular prism can be identified as the bases and the other four faces are the lateral faces.
- **Common Misconception:** The bases do not have to be on the top and bottom, although they are often identified that way.
- A net helps students see how to find the surface area of a prism.
- Encourage students to label each side length as h, w, or ℓ.
- **Look for and Make Use of Structure:** Have students discuss ways to write the formula. Here are a few.
  - $S = \ell h + wh + \ell h + wh + \ell w + \ell w$
  - $S = 2\ell h + 2wh + 2\ell w$
  - $S = 2(\ell h + wh + \ell w)$
- In part (b), students verify their formulas. Discuss their usability.

Exploration 2
- If students are having trouble visualizing the solid, have them copy the net, cut it out, and fold it. To save time, you could precut the nets before class.
- ❓ "What are the lateral faces of this triangular prism?" the 3 rectangles
- A prism is identified by the type of base it has, such as a triangular prism and a pentagonal prism. The lateral faces are all rectangles.
- In part (b), have students share their ideas with the class.

E.1 Surface Areas of Prisms

Learning Target: Find the surface area of a prism.

Success Criteria:
- I can use a formula to find the surface area of a prism.
- I can find the lateral surface area of a prism.

EXPLORATION 1

Writing a Formula for Surface Area

Work with a partner.

a. Use the diagrams to write a formula for the surface area of a rectangular prism. Explain your reasoning.

Math Practice

View as Components
Explain the meaning of each term in your formula.

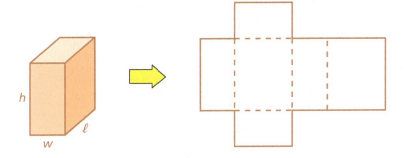

b. Choose dimensions for a rectangular prism. Then draw the prism and use your formula in part (a) to find the surface area.

EXPLORATION 2

Surface Areas of Prisms

Work with a partner.

a. Identify the solid represented by the net. Then find the surface area of the solid.

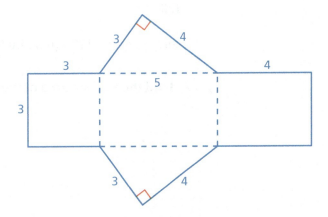

b. Describe a method for finding the surface area of any prism.

Section E.1   Surface Areas of Prisms   647

E.1 Lesson

Key Vocabulary
lateral surface area, p. 650

Key Idea

Surface Area of a Rectangular Prism

Words The surface area S of a rectangular prism is the sum of the areas of the bases and the lateral faces.

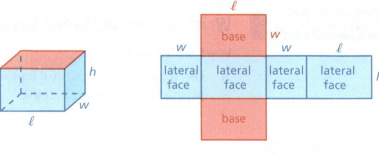

Algebra $S = 2\ell w + 2\ell h + 2wh$

↑ Areas of bases
↑↑ Areas of lateral faces

EXAMPLE 1   Finding the Surface Area of a Rectangular Prism

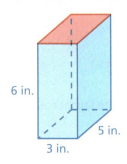

Find the surface area of the prism.

Draw a net.

$S = 2\ell w + 2\ell h + 2wh$

$= 2(3)(5) + 2(3)(6) + 2(5)(6)$

$= 30 + 36 + 60$

$= 126$

▸ The surface area is 126 square inches.

Try It   Find the surface area of the prism.

1.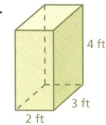

2.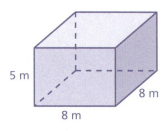

Laurie's Notes

Scaffolding Instruction

- In the exploration, students explored surface area using the nets of two prisms. Now they will use formulas to find the surface area and the **lateral surface area** of prisms.
- **Emerging:** Students may have trouble visualizing the net from a prism or the prism from a net. They will benefit from hands on experiences with nets and guided instruction for the examples.
- **Proficient:** Students understand how a prism can be separated into faces. They combine the areas of the faces to find the surface area. These students should review the Key Ideas and then proceed to the Self-Assessment exercises.

Key Idea

- Have a net available as a visual, whether it is a cardboard box or a rectangular prism made from snap-together polygon frames.
- Note the color-coding of the prism, net, and formula.
- **FYI:** Remind students that any two opposite faces can be called the bases. Once the bases are identified, the remaining 4 faces form the lateral portion.
- **?** "Can you explain why there are three parts to finding the surface area of a rectangular prism?" Students should recognize that there are 3 pairs of congruent faces.

EXAMPLE 1

- The challenge for students is not to get bogged down in symbols. Students need to remember that there are 3 pairs of congruent faces. They need to make sure that they calculate the area of each one of the 3 different faces, then double the answer to account for the pair.
- **Common Error:** When students multiply (2)(3)(5), they sometimes multiply $2 \times 3 \times 2 \times 5$, similar to using the Distributive Property. Remind them that multiplication is both commutative and associative, and they can multiply in order ($2 \times 3 \times 5$) or in a different order ($2 \times 5 \times 3$).
- **Teaching Tip:** Write the equation for surface area as:
S = bases + sides + (front and back). Students can follow the words and find the area of each pair without thinking about the variables.

Try It

- Students need to record their work neatly so they, and you, can look back and see what corrections are needed.
- **Think-Pair-Share:** Students should read each exercise independently and then work in pairs to find the surface areas. Have each pair compare their answers with another pair and discuss any discrepancies.

Scaffold instruction to support all students in their learning. Learning is individualized and you may want to group students differently as they move in and out of these levels with each skill and concept. Student self-assessment and feedback help guide your instructional decisions about how and when to layer support for all students to become proficient learners.

Extra Example 1

Find the surface area of a rectangular prism with a length of 6 yards, a width of 4 yards, and a height of 9 yards. 228 yd^2

ELL Support

After reviewing Example 1, have students work in pairs to practice language as they complete Try It Exercises 1 and 2. Have one student ask another, "What is the length? the width? the height? What is the formula? What is the surface area?" Have students alternate roles.

Beginner: State or write numbers and the formula.

Intermediate: Use phrases or simple sentences such as, "two feet."

Advanced: Use detailed sentences such as, "The length of the rectangular prism is two feet."

Try It

1. 52 ft^2
2. 288 m^2

Extra Example 2
Find the surface area of the prism.

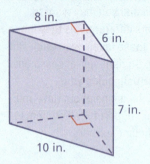

216 in.²

Try It

3. 150 m²

ELL Support

Allow students to work in pairs instead of independently. Then have two pairs form a group to check their work. Monitor discussions and provide support. You may want to review each group's answers with the class.

Self-Assessment
for Concepts & Skills

4. $2\ell w$ represents the areas of the bases. $2\ell h$ and $2wh$ represent the areas of the lateral faces.

5. Find the area of the bases of the prism; 12 cm²; 60 cm²

Laurie's Notes

Key Idea

- This is the general formula for a prism without variables. Most students are comfortable with this form.
- ❓ "How many faces are there that make up the bases?" 2
- ❓ "How many faces are there that make up the lateral faces?" It depends on how many edges the bases have.

EXAMPLE 2

- Note that the net is a visual reminder of each face whose area must be found. Color-coding the faces should help students keep track of their work.
- Encourage students to write the formula in words for each new problem: S = areas of bases + areas of lateral faces.
- Make sure students label their answers appropriately. Remind them that surface area is measured in square units.

Try It

- Give students sufficient time to complete their work before asking volunteers to share their work *and* sketch at the board.
- ❓ "If the triangular prism is rotated so that a rectangular face is on the bottom, will the surface area be the same?" yes "Will it still be a triangular prism? Explain." Yes, the bases are the two parallel, congruent faces, no matter how the prism is oriented.

Formative Assessment Tip

Point of Most Significance

This technique is the opposite of *Muddiest Point*. Students are asked to identify the most significant idea, learning, or concept they gained in the lesson. Students reflect on the lesson and identify the key example, problem, or point that contributed to their attainment of the learning target. It is important to know whether the lesson was effective or whether the lesson should be modified. Share with students what you learn from their reflections. Students will take reflections more seriously if they see that you value and use them.

✓ Self-Assessment for Concepts & Skills

- ⦿ Stop and ask students, "What was the *Point of Most Significance* in this lesson?"
- Students should complete the problems independently and then *Turn and Talk* with a neighbor to discuss any discrepancies.

The Success Criteria Self-Assessment chart can be found in the *Student Journal* or online at *BigIdeasMath.com*.

 **Key Idea**

Surface Area of a Prism
The surface area S of any prism is the sum of the areas of the bases and the lateral faces.

$$S = \text{areas of bases} + \text{areas of lateral faces}$$

EXAMPLE 2 **Finding the Surface Area of a Prism**

Find the surface area of the prism.

Draw a net.

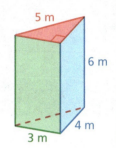

Area of a Base

Red base: $\frac{1}{2} \cdot 3 \cdot 4 = 6$

Areas of Lateral Faces

Green lateral face: $3 \cdot 6 = 18$
Purple lateral face: $5 \cdot 6 = 30$
Blue lateral face: $4 \cdot 6 = 24$

$S = \text{areas of bases} + \text{areas of lateral faces}$
$= 6 + 6 + 18 + 30 + 24 = 84$

There are two identical bases. Count the area twice.

▶ The surface area is 84 square meters.

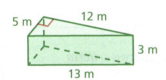

Try It

3. Find the surface area of the prism at the left.

 Self-Assessment for Concepts & Skills

Solve each exercise. Then rate your understanding of the success criteria in your journal.

4. **WRITING** Explain the meaning of each term in the formula for the surface area of a rectangular prism.

5. **DIFFERENT WORDS, SAME QUESTION** Which is different? Find "both" answers.

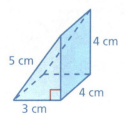

| Find the surface area of the prism. | Find the area of the bases of the prism. |
| Find the area of the net of the prism. | Find the sum of the areas of the bases and the lateral faces of the prism. |

Section E.1   Surface Areas of Prisms   649

The **lateral surface area** of a solid is the sum of the areas of each lateral face.

EXAMPLE 3 Modeling Real Life

The outsides of purple traps are coated with glue to catch emerald ash borers. You make your own trap in the shape of a rectangular prism with an open top and bottom. What is the surface area that you need to coat with glue?

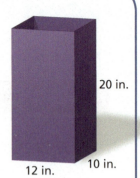

Use the formula for the surface area of a rectangular prism. To find the lateral surface area, do not include the areas of the bases in the formula.

$S = 2\ell h + 2wh$	Write the formula.
$= 2(12)(20) + 2(10)(20)$	Substitute.
$= 480 + 400$	Multiply.
$= 880$	Add.

▸ So, you need to coat 880 square inches with glue.

Self-Assessment for Problem Solving

Solve each exercise. Then rate your understanding of the success criteria in your journal.

6. You want to stain the lateral faces of the wooden chest shown. Find the area that you want to stain in *square inches*.

7. One can of frosting covers about 280 square inches. Is one can of frosting enough to frost the cake? Explain.

8. **DIG DEEPER!** Find the surface area of the bench shown. Justify your answer.

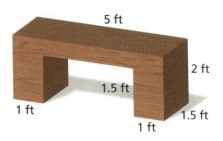

Laurie's Notes

EXAMPLE 3

- **FYI:** The emerald ash borer is an exotic beetle that was found in southeastern Michigan near Detroit in the summer of 2002. The adult beetles nibble on ash foliage but cause little damage. The larvae (the immature stage) feed on the inner bark of ash trees, disrupting the tree's ability to transport water and nutrients. The emerald ash borer probably arrived in the United States on solid wood packing material carried in cargo ships or airplanes originating in its native Asia. Since its discovery in Michigan, the emerald ash borer has killed millions of ash trees.
- Remind students that lateral faces are faces that are not bases.
- ? "How many faces does the trap have?" 4
- ? "How will you find the surface area of the trap?" Only find the area of the lateral faces.
- ? "How can you modify the surface area formula to find the lateral surface area?" Remove the area of the bases ($2\ell w$) from the surface area formula to make a formula for the lateral surface area, $S = 2\ell h + 2wh$.
- Work through the problem as shown.
- Encourage students to write the formula in words: S = areas of lateral faces.

✓ Self-Assessment for Problem Solving

- The goal for all students is to feel comfortable with the problem-solving plan. It is important for students to problem-solve in class, where they may receive support from you and their peers.
- Students should read through the problems independently and then make a plan for each. Examples:
  - In Exercise 6, students may plan to use the modified formula from Example 3 to find the lateral surface area.
  - In Exercise 7, students may plan to find the surface area and then subtract the area of one base because you do not frost the bottom of the cake.
  - In Exercise 8, students may break up the bench into several pieces and find the area of each, including the areas under the bench and legs.
- Students should discuss their plans with a partner before solving Exercises 6 and 7 independently. Exercise 8 should be done with a partner.

The Success Criteria Self-Assessment chart can be found in the *Student Journal* or online at *BigIdeasMath.com*.

Closure

- **Exit Ticket:**
  - Find how many different nets there are for a cube. Use standard grid paper or investigate at *illuminations.nctm.org*. There are 11.
  - ? "What is a simplified formula for the surface area of a cube?" $S = 6s^2$, where s is the length of a side of the cube.

Extra Example 3
In Example 3, the height of the trap is 30 inches. What is the surface area that you need to coat with glue? 1320 in.^{2}

Self-Assessment
for Problem Solving

6. 9216 in.^{2}

7. yes; Because you do not need to frost the bottom of the cake, you only need 249 square inches of frosting.

8. 36.5 ft^2; Top: $5(1.5) = 7.5$,
   Front: $2(1)(2) + 3(0.5) = 5.5$,
   Back: $2(1)(2) + 3(0.5) = 5.5$,
   Outside sides: $2(2)(1.5) = 6$,
   Inside sides: $2(1.5)(1.5) = 4.5$,
   Bottom:
   $2(1)(1.5) + 3(1.5) = 7.5$
   Surface area:
   $7.5 + 5.5 + 5.5 + 6 + 4.5 + 7.5$
   $= 36.5$

Learning Target
Find the surface area of a prism.

Success Criteria
- Use a formula to find the surface area of a prism.
- Find the lateral surface area of a prism.

Review & Refresh

1. supplementary; 146
2. complementary; 16
3. vertical; 49
4. about 1386 in.²
5. about 1017.36 mm²
6. about 226.87 m²

Concepts, Skills, & Problem Solving

7. triangular prism; 264 units²
8. rectangular prism; 62 units²
9. 324 m²
10. 294 yd²
11. 136 m²
12. 920 ft²
13. 49.2 yd²
14. 382.5 in.²

Assignment Guide and Concept Check

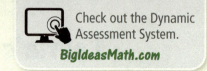

Scaffold assignments to support all students in their learning progression. The suggested assignments are a starting point. Continue to assign additional exercises and revisit with spaced practice to move every student toward proficiency.

Level	Assignment 1	Assignment 2
Emerging	2, 3, 5, 8, 9, 10, 11, 15	7, 12, 13, 14, 16, 18, 20
Proficient	2, 3, 5, 7, 9, 10, 11, 15	13, 14, 16, 17, 18, 19, 20
Advanced	2, 3, 5, 7, 10, 11, 13, 15	14, 16, 17, 19, 20, 21, 22

- Assignment 1 is for use after students complete the Self-Assessment for Concepts & Skills.
- Assignment 2 is for use after students complete the Self-Assessment for Problem Solving.
- The red exercises can be used as a concept check.

Review & Refresh Prior Skills

Exercises 1–3 Using Pairs of Angles
Exercises 4–6 Finding an Area of a Circle

 ## Common Errors

- **Exercises 9, 10, and 13** Students may find the area of only three of the faces instead of all six. Remind students that each face is paired with another. Show students the net of a rectangular solid to remind them of the six faces.
- **Exercises 11, 12, and 14** Students may try to use the formula for a rectangular prism to find the surface area of a triangular prism. Show them that this will not work by focusing on the area of the triangular base. For students who are struggling to identify all the faces, draw a net of the prism and tell them to label the length, width, and height of each part before finding the surface area.

E.1 Practice

 Go to BigIdeasMath.com to get HELP with solving the exercises.

▶ Review & Refresh

Classify the pair of angles. Then find the value of *x*.

1.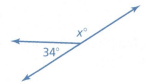
2.
3.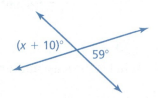

Find the area of a circle with the indicated dimensions. Use 3.14 or $\frac{22}{7}$ for π.

4. radius: 21 in.
5. diameter: 36 mm
6. radius: 8.5 m

▶ Concepts, Skills, & Problem Solving

SURFACE AREA OF A PRISM Identify the solid represented by the net. Then find the surface area of the solid. (See Explorations 1 & 2, p. 647.)

7.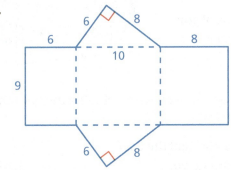
8.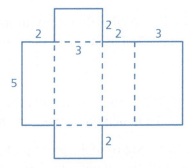

FINDING THE SURFACE AREA OF A PRISM Find the surface area of the prism.

9.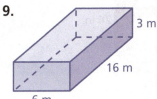
10.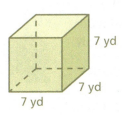
11.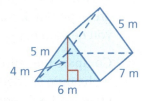

12.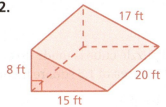
13.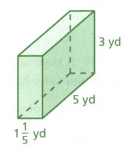
14.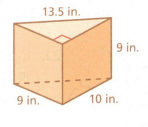

Section E.1 Surface Areas of Prisms 651

15. **YOU BE THE TEACHER** Your friend finds the surface area of the prism. Is your friend correct? Explain your reasoning.

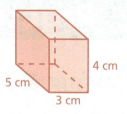

$$S = 2(5)(3) + 2(3)(4) + 2(5)(3)$$
$$= 30 + 24 + 30$$
$$= 84 \text{ cm}^2$$

16. **MODELING REAL LIFE** A cube-shaped satellite has side lengths of 10 centimeters. What is the least amount of aluminum needed to cover the satellite?

FINDING SURFACE AREA Find the surface area of the prism.

17.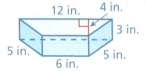

18.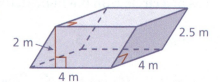

19. **OPEN-ENDED** Draw and label a rectangular prism that has a surface area of 158 square yards.

20. **DIG DEEPER!** A label that wraps around a box of golf balls covers 75% of its lateral surface area. What is the value of x?

21. **STRUCTURE** You are painting the prize pedestals shown (including the bottoms). You need 0.5 pint of paint to paint the red pedestal.

    a. The edge lengths of the green pedestal are one-half the edge lengths of the red pedestal. How much paint do you need to paint the green pedestal?

    b. The edge lengths of the blue pedestal are triple the edge lengths of the green pedestal. How much paint do you need to paint the blue pedestal?

    c. Compare the ratio of paint volumes to the ratio of edge lengths for the green and red pedestals. Repeat for the green and blue pedestals. What do you notice?

22. **NUMBER SENSE** A keychain-sized puzzle cube is made up of small cubes. Each small cube has a surface area of 1.5 square inches.

    a. What is the edge length of each small cube?

    b. What is the surface area of the entire puzzle cube?

Mini-Assessment

Find the surface area of the prism.

1.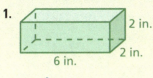

   56 in.²

2.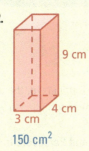

   150 cm²

3. Find the least amount of wrapping paper needed to cover the box.

   22 ft²

4. Find the least amount of fabric needed to make the tent.

   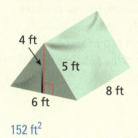

   152 ft²

Section Resources

Surface Level	Deep Level
Resources by Chapter • Extra Practice • Reteach • Puzzle Time Student Journal • Self-Assessment • Practice Differentiating the Lesson Tutorial Videos Skills Review Handbook Skills Trainer	Resources by Chapter • Enrichment and Extension Graphic Organizers Dynamic Assessment System • Section Practice

 Concepts, Skills, & Problem Solving

15. no; The area of the 3 × 5 face is used 4 times rather than just twice.

16. 600 cm²

17. 156 in.²

18. 68 m²

19. *Sample answer:*

    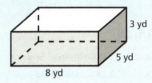

20. $x = 4$

21. a. 0.125 pint

    b. 1.125 pints

    c. red and green: The ratio of the paint volumes (red to green) is 4 : 1 and the ratio of the edge lengths is 2 : 1.

    green and blue: The ratio of the paint volumes (blue to green) is 9 : 1 and the ratio of the edge lengths is 3 : 1.

    The ratio of the paint volumes is the square of the ratio of the edge lengths.

22. a. 0.5 in.

    b. 13.5 in.²

Learning Target
Find the surface area of a cylinder.

Success Criteria
- Use a formula to find the surface area of a cylinder.
- Find the lateral surface area of a cylinder.

Warm Up
Cumulative, vocabulary, and prerequisite skills practice opportunities are available in the *Resources by Chapter* or at BigIdeasMath.com.

ELL Support
Students found the lateral surface area of a prism in the last section. Point out that in this lesson they will find the lateral surface area of a cylinder. Explain that the word *lateral* means "side." Spanish-speaking students may connect *lateral* to the phrase *al lado*, which means "to the side." Both are derived from the Latin word *latus*, meaning "side."

Exploration 1
a. See Additional Answers.

b. One dimension of the paper is the circumference of the can, and the other dimension of the paper is the height of the can.

c. $S = 2\pi rh + 2\pi r^2$

d. tuna can: radius ≈ 1.75 in., height ≈ 1.5 in., surface area ≈ 36 in.^{2};
tomato soup can: radius ≈ 1.5 in., height ≈ 4 in., surface area ≈ 52 in.^{2}

Laurie's Notes

Preparing to Teach
- Students should know the formulas for the area of a rectangle and the area of a circle. They will use these formulas to write a formula for the surface area of a cylinder.
- **Make Sense of Problems and Persevere in Solving Them:** Drawing, cutting, and measuring the components of a cylinder allow students to make sense of the formula for the surface area of a cylinder.

Motivate
- Use two different cans (cylinders), where the taller can has a lesser radius. A tuna can and a 6-ounce vegetable can work well.
- ❓ Hold both cans. "Which can requires more metal to make?" Answers will vary, depending on can sizes.
- Find two cans (cylinders) that have volumes in the ratio of 1 : 2 (e.g., 10 fl oz and 20 fl oz).
- ❓ "The larger can has twice the volume of the smaller can. Do you think the surface area is twice as much?" Answers may differ, but most students believe this is true. Return to this question at the end of the lesson.
- These questions focus attention on the surface areas of the cans, the need to consider their components, and how they were made.

Exploration 1
- Each pair of students will need scrap paper, tape, scissors, and a can. It is more interesting when the cans around the room are of different sizes.
- **Teaching Tip:** Recycle plastic bags and tape them to desks for trash disposal.
- Students wrap paper around the can to make the net for the lateral surface. This helps them relate the dimensions of the cylinder to the dimensions of the rectangle. Then trace around the bases to complete the net.
- **Discuss:** Students should describe the parts of a cylinder, how to find the area of each part, and how the dimensions of each part are related to the dimensions of the cylinder.
- ❓ "How can you find the length of the rectangle?" Find the circumference of a base. Give sufficient *Wait Time* before soliciting responses.
- **Make Sense of Problems and Persevere in Solving Them:** Making the cylinder and calculating its surface area help students to remember the process and understand the formula.
- When estimating the dimensions of the common cylinders, encourage students to use their hands to visualize the size of the cylinder.
- If time permits, set up stations in the room with a different cylinder at each. Provide rulers. In small groups, students move from one station to the next. Have a good variety of common cylinders: soup can, tuna can, AA battery, etc.
- ❓ "What dimensions did you measure for each cylinder?" Students will often say diameter and height.
- ❓ "Could the radius be measured? Explain." Yes, take half of the diameter to find the radius.
- **Extension:** Gather the results of the exploration and then find the mean for several of the cylinders.

E.2 Surface Areas of Cylinders

Learning Target: Find the surface area of a cylinder.

Success Criteria:
- I can use a formula to find the surface area of a cylinder.
- I can find the lateral surface area of a cylinder.

A *cylinder* is a solid that has two parallel, identical circular bases.

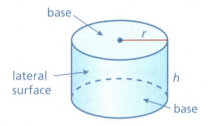

EXPLORATION 1
Finding the Surface Area of a Cylinder

Work with a partner.

a. Make a net for the can. Name each shape in the net.

b. How are the dimensions of the paper related to the dimensions of the can?

c. Write a formula that represents the surface area of a cylinder with a height of h and bases with a radius of r.

d. Estimate the dimensions of each can. Then use your formula in part (c) to estimate the surface area of each can.

Math Practice

Specify Units
What units did you use in your estimations in part (d)? What are the units for the surface areas of the cans?

E.2 Lesson

Key Idea

Surface Area of a Cylinder

Words The surface area S of a cylinder is the sum of the areas of the bases and the lateral surface.

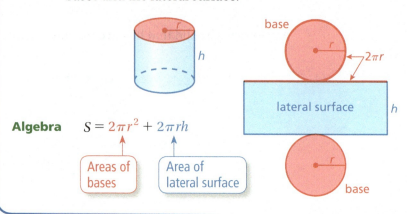

Algebra $S = 2\pi r^2 + 2\pi rh$

↑ Areas of bases   ↑ Area of lateral surface

Remember
Pi can be approximated as 3.14 or $\frac{22}{7}$.

EXAMPLE 1 — Finding the Surface Area of a Cylinder

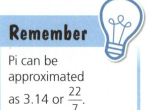

Find the surface area of the cylinder.

Draw a net.

$S = 2\pi r^2 + 2\pi rh$

$= 2\pi(4)^2 + 2\pi(4)(3)$

$= 32\pi + 24\pi$

$= 56\pi$

≈ 176

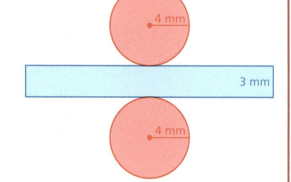

▶ The surface area is about 176 square millimeters.

Try It Find the surface area of the cylinder. Round your answer to the nearest tenth if necessary.

1.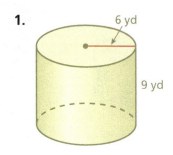

2.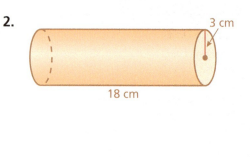

Laurie's Notes

Scaffolding Instruction

- Students discovered how to find the surface area of a cylinder by examining the net that makes up a cylinder. Now they will work with a formula for the surface area of a cylinder.
- **Emerging:** Students may understand the parts of the net for a cylinder but struggle to identify the dimensions. They will benefit from guided instruction for the Key Idea and examples.
- **Proficient:** Students can identify the dimensions of the net for a cylinder. They can find the surface area and the lateral surface area of a cylinder. These students should review the Key Idea and then proceed to the Self-Assessment exercises.

Scaffold instruction to support all students in their learning. Learning is individualized and you may want to group students differently as they move in and out of these levels with each skill and concept. Student self-assessment and feedback help guide your instructional decisions about how and when to layer support for all students to become proficient learners.

Key Idea

- ❓ "How are cylinders and rectangular prisms alike? different?" Both have 2 congruent bases and a lateral portion; Cylinders have circular bases, while rectangular prisms have rectangular bases.
- Refer to the diagram with the radius marked. Review the formulas for area and circumference of a circle.
- Write the formula in words first. Before writing the formula in symbols, ask direct questions to help students make the connection between the words and the symbols.
- ❓ "How do you find the area of the bases?" Find the area of one base, πr^2, and then multiply by 2.
- ❓ "How do you find the area of the lateral portion?" The dimensions of its rectangular net are the height and circumference of the cylinder, so the area of the lateral portion is $2\pi rh$.
- Write the formula in symbols and in words.

$$S \quad = \quad 2\pi r^2 \quad + \quad 2\pi rh$$
surface area = areas of bases + area of the lateral surface

EXAMPLE 1

- Write the formula first to model good problem-solving techniques.
- Notice that the values of the variables are substituted, with each term being left in terms of π.
- **Common Misconception:** Students are unsure of how to perform the multiplication with π in the middle of the term. Remind students that π is a number, a factor in this case, just like the other numbers. Because of the Commutative and Associative Properties, the whole numbers can be multiplied first. Then the two like terms, 32π and 24π, are combined. The last step is to substitute 3.14 for π.
- ❓ **Attend to Precision:** Review ≈. "What does this symbol mean? Why is it used?" approximately equal to; Because an estimate for π is used in the calculation.

Extra Example 1
Find the surface area of a cylinder with a radius of 3 inches and a height of 4 inches. about 132 in.^{2}

ELL Support

After reviewing Example 1, have students work in pairs to practice language as they complete Try It Exercises 1 and 2. Have one student ask another, "What is the height? the radius? the formula? the surface area?" Have students alternate roles.

Beginner: State or write numbers and the formula.

Intermediate: Use phrases or simple sentences such as, "nine yards."

Advanced: Use detailed sentences such as, "The height of the cylinder is nine yards."

Try It

- Have students work independently and then share their answers.

Try It
1. about 565.2 yd^2
2. about 395.6 cm^2

Extra Example 2
Find the lateral surface area of the cylinder.

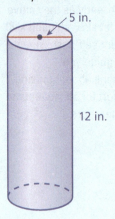

about 188.4 in.^{2}

Try It

3. about 75.4 cm^2
4. about 75.4 yd^2

Self-Assessment
for Concepts & Skills

5. $2\pi rh$; $2\pi r^2$
6. Use the given circumference to find the radius by solving $C = 2\pi r$ for r. Then use the formula for the surface area of a cylinder.
7. 150.7 in.^{2}
8. 25.1 cm^2

Laurie's Notes

EXAMPLE 2

❓ "What is the difference between the surface area and the lateral surface area of a cylinder?" The surface area includes the areas of the bases and the lateral surface area does not.

❓ "Who might need to know the lateral surface area?" Sample answer: Someone that makes soup can labels. If you have a can with a label, you could carefully peel it off to illustrate the lateral surface area.

- Work through the problem as shown.
- Notice that the answer is left in terms of π until the last step.
- Remind students that if they use the π key on their calculators, their answers may differ from those in the book. On standardized tests, students should always read the problem and/or formula sheet carefully to see which value of π they should use.
- Remind students to always label their answers. Lateral surface area is measured in square units.

Try It

- Give students sufficient time to complete their work before asking volunteers to share their work at the boards.

Formative Assessment Tip

Parking Lot
Give each student two sticky notes. Ask them to write something they learned on one note and something they still have a question about on the other. Write "Parking Lot" at the top of a large sheet of paper and draw a line down the middle of the paper. On one side write "Something I Learned" and on the other side write "Something I Have a Question About." Hang the paper near the door so students can place their sticky notes as they leave. Replace the paper for each class and review the notes to help direct your instruction for the next day.

✓ Self-Assessment for Concepts & Skills

- **Think-Pair-Share:** Students should read each exercise independently and then work in pairs to complete the exercises. Then have each pair present their answers to the class. Discuss any discrepancies.
- Use *Parking Lot* to assess students' understanding of the lesson.

ELL Support

Allow students to work in pairs. Have pairs display their answers for Exercises 5, 7, and 8 on whiteboards for your review. After pairs complete Exercise 6, discuss their answers as a class.

The Success Criteria Self-Assessment chart can be found in the *Student Journal* or online at *BigIdeasMath.com*.

EXAMPLE 2 Finding the Lateral Surface Area of a Cylinder

Find the lateral surface area of the cylinder.

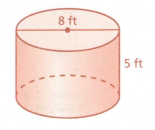

Use the formula for the surface area of a cylinder. To find the lateral surface area, do not include the areas of the circular bases in the formula.

The radius is $8 \div 2 = 4$ feet.

$$S = 2\pi rh \qquad \text{Write the formula.}$$
$$= 2\pi(4)(5) \qquad \text{Substitute 4 for } r \text{ and 5 for } h.$$
$$= 40\pi \qquad \text{Multiply.}$$
$$\approx 125.6 \qquad \text{Use 3.14 for } \pi.$$

▶ The lateral surface area is about 125.6 square feet.

Math Practice
Look for Structure
Explain why the area of the lateral face is the product of the height of the cylinder and the circumference of the base.

Try It Find the lateral surface area of the cylinder. Round your answer to the nearest tenth.

3.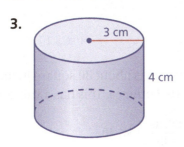

4.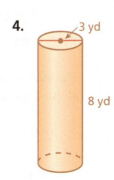

Self-Assessment for Concepts & Skills

Solve each exercise. Then rate your understanding of the success criteria in your journal.

5. **WRITING** Which part of the formula $S = 2\pi r^2 + 2\pi rh$ represents the lateral surface area of a cylinder? the areas of the bases?

6. **CRITICAL THINKING** You are given the height of a cylinder and the circumference of its base. Describe how to find the surface area of the cylinder.

7. **FINDING A SURFACE AREA** Find the surface area of the cylinder at the left. Round your answer to the nearest tenth.

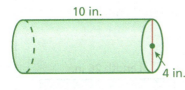

8. **FINDING A LATERAL SURFACE AREA** Find the lateral surface area of the cylinder at the right. Round your answer to the nearest tenth.

Section E.2 Surface Areas of Cylinders 655

EXAMPLE 3 Modeling Real Life

The iced tea can is made from a sheet of aluminum that weighs 0.01 ounce per square inch. You receive $0.40 per pound of aluminum that you recycle. How much do you earn for recycling 24 iced tea cans?

Understand the problem. You are given a unit rate in dollars per pound for recycled aluminum, the weight of one square inch of an aluminum can, and the dimensions of the can. You are asked to find how much you earn for recycling 24 cans.

Make a plan. Find the surface area of one can and use it to find the weight of 24 cans. Then use the unit rate given in dollars per pound to find the value of the cans.

Solve and check.

$S = 2\pi r^2 + 2\pi rh$ Write the formula.

$ = 2\pi(1.5)^2 + 2\pi(1.5)(7)$ Substitute 1.5 for r and 7 for h.

$ = 4.5\pi + 21\pi$ Simplify.

$ = 25.5\pi$ Add.

$ \approx 80$ Use 3.14 for π.

The surface area of one can is about 80 square inches. So, 24 cans weigh about $24(80)(0.01) = 19.2$ ounces. This has a value of

$$19.2 \text{ oz} \times \frac{1 \text{ lb}}{16 \text{ oz}} \times \frac{\$0.40}{1 \text{ lb}} = \$0.48.$$

▶ So, you earn about $0.48 for recycling 24 cans.

Check Reasonableness
19.2 ounces is greater than 16 ounces, or 1 pound, so the value should be greater than $0.40. Because $0.48 > $0.40, the answer is reasonable. ✓

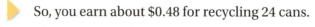

Self-Assessment for Problem Solving

Solve each exercise. Then rate your understanding of the success criteria in your journal.

9. You remove the lid of the can. What is the percent of change in the surface area of the can?

10. After burning half of a cylindrical candle, the surface area is 176 square inches. The radius of the candle is 2 inches. What was the original height of the candle?

11. **DIG DEEPER!** The area of the sheet of wrapping paper is equal to the lateral surface area of a cylindrical tube. The tube is 14 inches tall. What is the surface area of the tube, including the bases? Explain your reasoning.

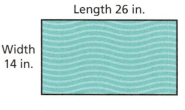

Length 26 in.
Width 14 in.

Laurie's Notes

EXAMPLE 3

- **Make Sense of Problems and Persevere in Solving Them:** Ask a volunteer to read the problem aloud. Give students time to think about the problem before asking, "What do you need to know to solve this problem?" the surface area of the can, how much each can weighs, how many ounces are in a pound
- Have students make a plan: find the surface area of the can, find the weight of the can (in pounds), and then multiply by $0.40 per pound.
- Work through the problem as shown. Pay careful attention to the last step, the unit analysis. Make sure students understand why they can "cancel" the units.

✓ Self-Assessment for Problem Solving

- Allow time in class for students to practice using the problem-solving plan. It is important for students to problem-solve in class, where they may receive support from you and their peers.
- Have students work independently to make a plan for each problem. They should include what they need to know and what they will do to solve the problem. Use *Popsicle Sticks* to select several students to share their plans for each problem. Students should solve the problems independently and then check their answers with a neighbor.
- ⦿ Ask students to use *Thumbs Up* to indicate their understanding of each success criterion.

The Success Criteria Self-Assessment chart can be found in the *Student Journal* or online at *BigIdeasMath.com*.

Closure

- Hold the two cans from the Motivate and ask:
  - ❓ "Which of the two cans requires more metal to make? Explain." Answers will vary, depending on can sizes.
  - ❓ "Which of the two cans requires more material to make the label? Explain." Answers will vary, depending on can sizes.

Extra Example 3

A lemonade can has a radius of 1.5 inches and a height of 9 inches. The can is made from a sheet of aluminum that weighs 0.02 ounce per square inch. You receive $0.35 per pound of aluminum that you recycle. How much do you earn for recycling 38 lemonade cans? about $1.65

Self-Assessment
for Problem Solving

9. about 25.8% decrease

10. about 24 in.

11. about 471.6 in.²; The circumference of the tube is 26 inches, so the radius is $\frac{13}{\pi}$ inches.

$$S = 2\pi\left(\frac{13}{\pi}\right)^2 + 2\pi\left(\frac{13}{\pi}\right)(14)$$
$$\approx 471.6$$

Learning Target

Find the surface area of a cylinder.

Success Criteria

- Use a formula to find the surface area of a cylinder.
- Find the lateral surface area of a cylinder.

T-656

Review & Refresh

1. 142 cm^2
2. 2520 ft^2
3. A

Concepts, Skills, & Problem Solving

4. about 82,896 mm^2
5. about 8195.4 in.^{2}
6. about 94.2 ft^2
7. about 31.4 m^2
8. about 527.5 ft^2
9. about 87.9 mm^2
10. about 489.8 ft^2
11. about 282.6 cm^2
12. about 376.8 ft^2
13. about 226.1 in.^{2}
14. about 87.9 m^2

Assignment Guide and Concept Check

Scaffold assignments to support all students in their learning progression. The suggested assignments are a starting point. Continue to assign additional exercises and revisit with spaced practice to move every student toward proficiency.

Level	Assignment 1	Assignment 2
Emerging	2, 3, 4, 6, 7, 8, 12, 13, 15	5, 9, 10, 11, 14, 16, 17, 20
Proficient	2, 3, 5, 9, 10, 11, 12, 13, 15	14, 17, 18, 19, 20
Advanced	2, 3, 5, 9, 10, 11, 12, 14, 15	17, 18, 19, 20, 21

- Assignment 1 is for use after students complete the Self-Assessment for Concepts & Skills.
- Assignment 2 is for use after students complete the Self-Assessment for Problem Solving.
- The red exercises can be used as a concept check.

Review & Refresh Prior Skills

Exercises 1 and 2 Finding the Surface Area of a Prism
Exercise 3 Writing Fractions as Decimals and Percents

Common Errors

- **Exercises 6–11** Students may add the area of only one base. Remind students of the net for a cylinder and that there are two circles as bases.
- **Exercises 6–11** Students may double the radius instead of squaring it. Remind students of the formula for the area of a circle and also the order of operations.
- **Exercises 11 and 14** Students may use the diameter instead of the radius. Remind students that the radius is in the formula, so they should find the radius before they find the surface area or lateral surface area.
- **Exercises 12–14** Students may multiply the height by the area of the circular base instead of the circumference. Review with students how the lateral surface is created to show that the length of the rectangle is the circumference of the circular bases.

E.2 Practice

Go to *BigIdeasMath.com* to get HELP with solving the exercises.

▶ Review & Refresh

Find the surface area of the prism.

1.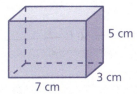

2.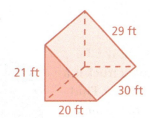

3. Which of the following is equivalent to 0.625?

   A. $\dfrac{5}{8}$ **B.** $\dfrac{625}{100}$ **C.** 0.625%   **D.** 6.25%

▶ Concepts, Skills, & Problem Solving

FINDING SURFACE AREA Find the surface area of the cylinder. (See Exploration 1, p. 653.)

4. a can with a radius of 60 millimeters and a height of 160 millimeters

5. a hay bale with a diameter of 30 inches and a height of 72 inches

FINDING SURFACE AREA Find the surface area of the cylinder. Round your answer to the nearest tenth if necessary.

6.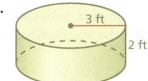

7.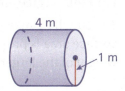

8.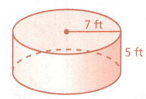

9.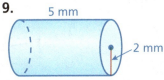

10.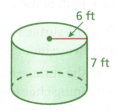

11.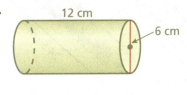

FINDING LATERAL SURFACE AREA Find the lateral surface area of the cylinder. Round your answer to the nearest tenth if necessary.

12.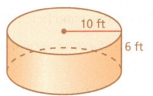

13.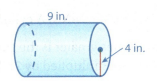

14.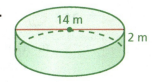

15. **YOU BE THE TEACHER** Your friend finds the surface area of the cylinder. Is your friend correct? Explain your reasoning.

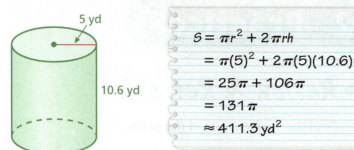

$$S = \pi r^2 + 2\pi rh$$
$$= \pi(5)^2 + 2\pi(5)(10.6)$$
$$= 25\pi + 106\pi$$
$$= 131\pi$$
$$\approx 411.3 \text{ yd}^2$$

16. **MODELING REAL LIFE** The tank of a tanker truck is a stainless steel cylinder. Find the surface area of the tank.

17. **MODELING REAL LIFE** The Petri dish shown has no lid. What is the surface area of the outside of the Petri dish?

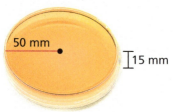

18. **REASONING** You have two 8.5-by-11-inch pieces of paper. You form the lateral surfaces of two different cylinders by taping together a pair of opposite sides on each piece of paper so that one cylinder has a height of 8.5 inches and the other has a height of 11 inches. Without calculating, compare the surface areas of the cylinders (including the bases). Explain.

19. **DIG DEEPER!** A *ganza* is a percussion instrument used in samba music.

   a. Find the surface area of each of the two labeled ganzas.

   b. The smaller ganza weighs 1.1 pounds. Assume that the surface area is proportional to the weight. What is the weight of the larger ganza?

20. **PROBLEM SOLVING** The wedge is one-eighth of the wheel of cheese.

   a. Find the surface area of the cheese before it is cut.

   b. Find the surface area of the remaining cheese after the wedge is removed. Did the surface area increase, decrease, or remain the same?

21. **REPEATED REASONING** A cylinder has radius r and height h.

   a. How many times greater is the surface area of a cylinder when both dimensions are multiplied by 2? 3? 5? 10?

   b. Describe the pattern in part (a). Write an expression for the surface area of the cylinder when both dimensions are multiplied by a number x.

Mini-Assessment

Find the surface area of the cylinder. Round your answer to the nearest tenth if necessary.

1.
   3 ft
   8 ft
   about 207.2 ft^2

2.
   2 in.
   6 in.
   about 44.0 in.^{2}

3. Find the surface area of the roll of paper towels.

   11 in.
   ⊢5 in.⊣
   about 212.0 in.^{2}

4. How much paper is used for the label on the can of tuna?

   2 in.
   1 in.
   about 12.6 in.^{2}

Section Resources

Surface Level	Deep Level
Resources by Chapter • Extra Practice • Reteach • Puzzle Time Student Journal • Self-Assessment • Practice Differentiating the Lesson Tutorial Videos Skills Review Handbook Skills Trainer	Resources by Chapter • Enrichment and Extension Graphic Organizers Dynamic Assessment System • Section Practice

Concepts, Skills, & Problem Solving

15. no; The area of only one base is added. The first term should have a factor of 2.

16. about 1356.48 ft^2

17. about 12,560 mm^2

18. The cylinder with a height of 8.5 inches has the greater surface area; The lateral surface areas of both cylinders are the same, but the bases of the cylinder with a height of 8.5 inches have a circumference of 11 inches, which is greater than the circumference of the bases of the other cylinder, 8.5 inches. Because the circumference is greater, the radius is greater, which means the area is greater.

19. **a.** about 129.1 cm^2, about 470.6 cm^2

    b. about 4.0 lb

20. **a.** about 75.36 in.^{2}

    b. about 71.94 in.^{2}; decreased

21. **a.** 4 times greater; 9 times greater; 25 times greater; 100 times greater

    b. When both dimensions are multiplied by a factor of x, the surface area increases by a factor of x^2;
    $x^2(2\pi r^2 + 2\pi rh)$

T-658

Learning Target
Find the surface area of a pyramid.

Success Criteria
- Use a net to find the surface area of a regular pyramid.
- Find the lateral surface area of a regular pyramid.

Warm Up
Cumulative, vocabulary, and prerequisite skills practice opportunities are available in the *Resources by Chapter* or at BigIdeasMath.com.

ELL Support
Ask students if they are familiar with the pyramids shown in the pictures or if they have seen pictures of other pyramid-shaped structures. Explain that the base of a pyramid is a polygon and the lateral faces come to a point (the vertex). If you have a model of a pyramid, point to each feature as you describe it. Review the pyramids in the diagrams at the top of the page.

Exploration 1

a. *Answer should include, but is not limited to:*

A scale model for a net of one of the pyramids with the model slant height and base length labeled and scale included or explained.

b. Cheops Pyramid: 85,560 m², Louvre Pyramid: 1960 m²; Find the area of a lateral face and multiply that by the number of lateral faces, 4.

c. *See Additional Answers.*

T-659

Laurie's Notes

Preparing to Teach
- Students should know how to find the area of a triangle and the general properties of squares and isosceles triangles.
- **Model with Mathematics:** Finding the surface area of a pyramid can be challenging when the faces are not all visible. Drawing a net for a scale model allows students to see all the faces of the pyramid.

Motivate
- Share information about the Great Pyramid of Egypt, also known as Cheops Pyramid.
- The Great Pyramid is the largest of the original *Seven Wonders of the World*. It was built in the 5th century B.C. and is estimated to have taken 100,000 men over 20 years to build it.
- The Great Pyramid is a square pyramid. It covers an area of 13 acres. The original height of the Great Pyramid was 485 feet, but due to erosion its height has declined to about 450 feet. Each side of the square base is 755.5 feet in length (about 2.5 football field lengths).
- The Great Pyramid consists of approximately 2.5 million blocks that weigh from 2 tons to over 70 tons. The stones are cut so precisely that a credit card cannot fit between them.

Exploration 1

- Discuss the vocabulary of pyramids and how they are named according to the base. Make a distinction between **slant height** and height.
- This exploration connects scale drawings with the study of pyramids.
- To ensure a variety, assign one pyramid to each pair of students and make sure about half of the class makes each pyramid.
- Students will need to decide on the scale they will use.
  Example: To make a scale model for the Cheops Pyramid, assume the scale selected is 1 cm = 20 m.

  $\dfrac{1\text{ cm}}{20\text{ m}} = \dfrac{x\text{ cm}}{230\text{ m}} \rightarrow x = 11.5$ $\dfrac{1\text{ cm}}{20\text{ m}} = \dfrac{x\text{ cm}}{186\text{ m}} \rightarrow x = 9.3$

- Students will use their eyesight and knowledge of squares and isosceles triangles to construct the square and four isosceles triangles.
- **Attend to Precision:** Have pairs discuss the scale they used and how they found the lateral surface area. Listen for how clearly they communicate the process. Multiply the area of one triangular face by 4.
- Have rulers, scissors, and tape available for the students to construct their pyramids. Making a pyramid from a net and finding the lateral surface area helps students remember the process and understand the formula. It is likely that students will draw nets that do not actually fold into a pyramid. This is okay. They are investigating the process of finding lateral surface area, so precise dimensions are not necessary.
- ? "How are prisms and pyramids similar? different?" The base(s) determines the name; Prisms have two bases and the lateral faces are rectangles. Pyramids have one base and the lateral faces are triangles.

E.3 Surface Areas of Pyramids

Learning Target: Find the surface area of a pyramid.

Success Criteria:
- I can use a net to find the surface area of a regular pyramid.
- I can find the lateral surface area of a regular pyramid.

Many well-known pyramids have square bases, however, the base of a pyramid can be any polygon.

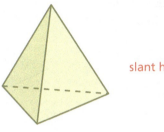
Triangular Base

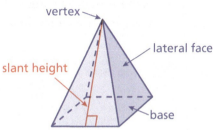
Square Base

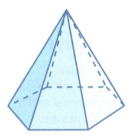
Hexagonal Base

EXPLORATION 1

Making a Scale Model

Work with a partner. Each pyramid below has a square base.

Cheops Pyramid in Egypt

Side ≈ 230 m, Slant height ≈ 186 m

Louvre Pyramid in Paris

Side ≈ 35 m, Slant height ≈ 28 m

Math Practice

Analyze Relationships

What is the relationship between the lateral surface area of your scale model and the lateral surface area of the real-life pyramid?

a. Draw a net for a scale model of one of the pyramids. Describe the scale factor.

b. Find the lateral surface area of the real-life pyramid that you chose in part (a). Explain how you found your answer.

c. Draw a net for a pyramid with a non-rectangular base and find its lateral surface area. Explain how you found your answer.

E.3 Lesson

Key Vocabulary
regular pyramid, *p. 660*
slant height, *p. 660*

A **regular pyramid** is a pyramid whose base is a regular polygon. The lateral faces are triangles. The height of each triangle is the **slant height** of the pyramid.

Key Idea

Surface Area of a Pyramid

The surface area S of a pyramid is the sum of the areas of the base and the lateral faces.

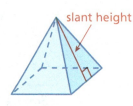
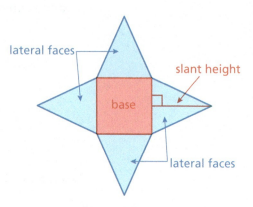

Remember
In a regular polygon, all the sides are identical and all the angles are identical.

S = area of base + areas of lateral faces

EXAMPLE 1 — Finding the Surface Area of a Square Pyramid

Find the surface area of the regular pyramid.

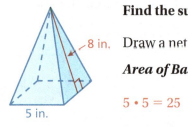

Draw a net.

Area of Base   **Area of a Lateral Face**

$5 \cdot 5 = 25$ $\dfrac{1}{2} \cdot 5 \cdot 8 = 20$

Find the sum of the areas of the base and the lateral faces.

S = area of base + areas of lateral faces
$= 25 + 20 + 20 + 20 + 20$
$= 105$

There are 4 identical lateral faces. Count the area 4 times.

▶ The surface area is 105 square inches.

Try It

1. What is the surface area of a square pyramid with a base side length of 9 centimeters and a slant height of 7 centimeters?

Laurie's Notes

Scaffolding Instruction

- In the exploration, students discovered how to find the lateral surface area of a pyramid by examining the net that makes up the pyramid. Now they will formalize that study by using a formula for the surface area of a pyramid.
- **Emerging:** Students may struggle with the terms height, slant height, surface area, and lateral surface area. They need guided instruction for the Key Idea and examples.
- **Proficient:** Students can visualize the shape of the base and the number of lateral faces of a pyramid. They can differentiate between surface area and lateral surface area and can find both. They should review the Key Idea and then proceed to the Self-Assessment exercises.

Scaffold instruction to support all students in their learning. Learning is individualized and you may want to group students differently as they move in and out of these levels with each skill and concept. Student self-assessment and feedback help guide your instructional decisions about how and when to layer support for all students to become proficient learners.

Key Idea

- Introduce the vocabulary: **regular pyramid**, regular polygon, **slant height**.
- ❓ "What information does the type of base give you about the lateral faces?" number of sides in the base = number of congruent isosceles triangles for the lateral surface area
- ❓ "If you know the length of each side of the base, what else do you know?" the length of the base of the triangular lateral faces
- Make sure students understand that the height of the pyramid is *not* the same thing as the heights of the triangular faces of the pyramid.

Extra Example 1

What is the surface area of a square pyramid with a base side length of 3 meters and a slant height of 5 meters? 39 m^2

EXAMPLE 1

- Draw the net and label the known information. This should remind students of the work they did making a scale model of a pyramid.
- Write the formula in words first to model good problem-solving techniques.
- ❓ Continue to ask questions as you find the total surface area: "How do you find the area of the base? How many lateral faces are there? What is the area of just one lateral face? How do you find the area of a triangle?"
- **Common Error:** In using the area formula for a triangle, the $\frac{1}{2}$ often produces a computational error. In this instance, students must multiply $\frac{1}{2} \times 5 \times 8$. Remind students that it is okay to change the order of the factors (Commutative Property). Rewriting the problem as $\frac{1}{2} \times 8 \times 5$ means that you can work with whole numbers: $\frac{1}{2} \times 8 \times 5 = 4 \times 5 = 20$.
- **Look for and Make Use of Structure:** Intuitive students may recognize that because there are 4 triangles, there is no need to multiply $\frac{1}{2} \times 5 \times 8$ because they can multiply $4 \times \frac{1}{2} \times 5 \times 8$ to find the lateral area.

ELL Support

After reviewing Example 1, have students work in groups to complete Try It Exercise 1. Have them consider the questions: What is the area of the base? What is the area of one lateral face? What formulas will you use? How many lateral faces are there? Expect students to perform according to their language levels.

Beginner: State numbers and write formulas.

Intermediate: Use simple sentences such as, "The area of the base is eighty-one square centimeters."

Advanced: Use detailed sentences such as, "To find the area of the base, you multiply the length and width of the base."

Try It

- Students should work independently on whiteboards.
- Encourage students to sketch a three-dimensional model of the pyramid and the net. Label the net with the known information.

Try It

1. 207 cm^2

T-660

Extra Example 2
Find the surface area of the regular pyramid.

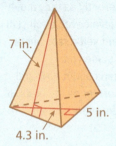

63.25 in.²

Try It

2. 105.6 ft²

Self-Assessment
for Concepts & Skills

3. no; The lateral faces of a pyramid are triangles.
4. 245 m²
5. 28 cm²
6. triangular pyramid; The other three are names for the pyramid.

Laurie's Notes

EXAMPLE 2

- Remind students of the definition of a regular pyramid. This is important because the base, as drawn, does not look like an equilateral triangle. This is the challenge of representing a three-dimensional figure on a flat two-dimensional sheet of paper.
- Drawing the net is an important step. It allows the key dimensions to be labeled in a way that can be seen.
- Encourage mental math when multiplying $\frac{1}{2} \times 10 \times 8.7$ and $\frac{1}{2} \times 10 \times 14$. Ask students to share their strategies with other students.

Try It

- Give students sufficient time to complete their work before asking volunteers to share their work at the board.

Formative Assessment Tip

Quick Write
This technique allows students to write about a process or concept in their own words. Give students 2–4 minutes to respond to a short writing prompt, or sentence stem, relating to the lesson. Then collect the responses and review the information. *Quick Write* not only provides you a quick assessment of your students' level of understanding, but it also helps students become more aware of their own learning.

Self-Assessment for Concepts & Skills

- Students should work independently before sharing answers with the class.
- **Quick Write:**
  - Prisms and pyramids are similar because_____. The base(s) determines the name.
  - Prisms and pyramids are different because _____. Prisms have two bases and pyramids have one base. The lateral faces of prisms are rectangles and the lateral faces of pyramids are triangles.

ELL Support

Have students work in pairs for extra support and to practice language. Have pairs answer Exercise 3 by using a thumbs up to answer *yes* and a thumbs down to answer *no*. Have pairs display their answers to Exercises 4 and 5 on whiteboards for your review. Discuss students' reasoning about Exercise 6 as a class.

The Success Criteria Self-Assessment chart can be found in the *Student Journal* or online at *BigIdeasMath.com*.

EXAMPLE 2 Finding the Surface Area of a Triangular Pyramid

Find the surface area of the regular pyramid.

Draw a net.

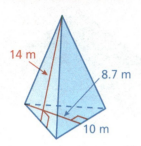

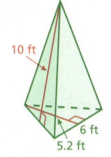

Area of Base

$\frac{1}{2} \cdot 10 \cdot 8.7 = 43.5$

Area of a Lateral Face

$\frac{1}{2} \cdot 10 \cdot 14 = 70$

Find the sum of the areas of the base and the lateral faces.

$S =$ area of base $+$ areas of lateral faces

$= 43.5 + 70 + 70 + 70$

$= 253.5$

There are 3 identical lateral faces. Count the area 3 times.

▶ The surface area is 253.5 square meters.

Try It

2. Find the surface area of the regular pyramid at the left.

Self-Assessment for Concepts & Skills

Solve each exercise. Then rate your understanding of the success criteria in your journal.

3. **VOCABULARY** Can a pyramid have rectangles as lateral faces? Explain.

FINDING THE SURFACE AREA OF A PYRAMID Find the surface area of the regular pyramid.

4.

5.

6. **WHICH ONE DOESN'T BELONG?** Which description of the solid does *not* belong with the other three? Explain your reasoning.

square pyramid   regular pyramid

rectangular pyramid   triangular pyramid

Section E.3   Surface Areas of Pyramids   661

EXAMPLE 3 Modeling Real Life

The roof is shaped like a square pyramid. One bundle of shingles covers 25 square feet. How many bundles should you buy to cover the roof?

You are given the dimensions of a roof that is shaped like a square pyramid. You are asked to find the number of bundles of shingles you should buy to cover the roof when each bundle covers 25 square feet.

The base of the roof does not need shingles. So, find the sum of the areas of the lateral faces of the pyramid. Then divide the area by 25 square feet to find the number of bundles needed to cover the roof.

Area of a Lateral Face

$$\frac{1}{2} \cdot 18 \cdot 15 = 135$$

There are four identical lateral faces. So, the lateral surface area is

$$135 + 135 + 135 + 135 = 540 \text{ square feet.}$$

Because one bundle of shingles covers 25 square feet, it will take $540 \div 25 = 21.6$ bundles to cover the roof.

▶ So, you should buy 22 bundles of shingles.

Check Reasonableness
20 bundles cover
$20 \times 25 = 500$ square feet
and 25 bundles cover
$25 \times 25 = 625$ square feet.
Your answer is reasonable because
$500 < 540 < 625$.

 Self-Assessment for Problem Solving

Solve each exercise. Then rate your understanding of the success criteria in your journal.

7. A building in the shape of a square pyramid is covered with solar panels. The building has a slant height of 12 feet and a base with side lengths of 15 feet. The solar panels cost $70 per square foot to install. How much does it cost to install enough solar panels to cover the entire surface of the building?

8. You use the glass pyramid shown to display rainbows on the walls of a room. The pyramid is regular and has a surface area of 105.35 square centimeters. Find the height of each triangular face. Justify your answer.

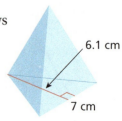

662 Chapter E Surface Area and Volume

Laurie's Notes

EXAMPLE 3

- Ask a volunteer to read the problem aloud. Then ask another volunteer to explain the problem. If necessary, have another student re-read the problem.
- "What do you need to find first?" the lateral surface area
- "How does the lateral surface area relate to the bundles of shingles needed?" The lateral surface area divided by the area each bundle covers gives the number of bundles needed to cover the roof.
- Have students compute the lateral surface area. Some students may need to draw the triangular lateral face first before performing the computation.
- **Reason Abstractly and Quantitatively:** "Suppose you compute the number of bundles needed on another roof and get an exact answer of 25.2. Is it okay to round down to 25 bundles? Explain." No, you need to round up to the next whole number, so you do not run short of shingles.
- Remind students to always label their answers.
- **FYI:** When shingles are placed on a roof, they need to overlap the shingles below. The coverage given per bundle takes into account the overlap.
- **Extension:** "Suppose a bundle of shingles sells for $34.75. What will the total cost be for the shingles?" $764.50

✓ Self-Assessment for Problem Solving

- Students may benefit from trying the exercises independently and then working with peers to refine their work. It is important to provide time in class for problem solving, so that students become comfortable with the problem-solving plan.
- **Neighbor Check:** Give students sufficient time to complete their work for each problem before sharing with a neighbor to discuss any discrepancies.

The Success Criteria Self-Assessment chart can be found in the *Student Journal* or online at *BigIdeasMath.com*.

Closure

- **Exit Ticket:** Sketch a net for a hexagonal pyramid and describe how to find the lateral surface area.

Find the area of one of the lateral faces and multiply by 6.

Extra Example 3
The slant height of the roof in Example 3 is 13 feet. One bundle of shingles covers 30 square feet. How many bundles of shingles should you buy to cover the roof? 16 bundles of shingles

Self-Assessment
for *Problem Solving*

7. $25,200

8. 8 cm; *Sample answer:*
$$105.35 = \frac{1}{2}(7)(6.1) + 3\left(\frac{1}{2} \cdot 7 \cdot h\right)$$
$$105.35 = 21.35 + 10.5h$$
$$84 = 10.5h$$
$$8 = h$$

Learning Target
Find the surface area of a pyramid.

Success Criteria
- Use a net to find the surface area of a regular pyramid.
- Find the lateral surface area of a regular pyramid.

Review & Refresh

1. about 244.9 ft²
2. about 345.4 m²
3. about 306.5 mm²
4. C

Concepts, Skills, & Problem Solving

5. 40 in.²
6. 178.3 mm²
7. 151.9 m²
8. 144 ft²
9. 64 cm²
10. 322.5 in.²
11. 170.1 yd²
12. 56.25 m²
13. 1240.4 mm²

Assignment Guide and Concept Check

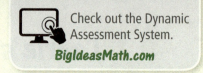

Scaffold assignments to support all students in their learning progression. The suggested assignments are a starting point. Continue to assign additional exercises and revisit with spaced practice to move every student toward proficiency.

Level	Assignment 1	Assignment 2
Emerging	3, 4, 5, 6, 7, 9, 11, 13	10, 12, 14, 16, 17, 21, 22
Proficient	3, 4, 5, 6, 7, 11, 12, 13, 16	14, 15, 17, 18, 19, 20, 21, 22, 23
Advanced	3, 4, 5, 6, 7, 11, 12, 13, 16	15, 17, 18, 19, 20, 21, 22, 23

- Assignment 1 is for use after students complete the Self-Assessment for Concepts & Skills.
- Assignment 2 is for use after students complete the Self-Assessment for Problem Solving.
- The red exercises can be used as a concept check.

Review & Refresh Prior Skills

Exercises 1–3 Finding Surface Area of a Cylinder
Exercise 4 Writing and Solving a Proportion

Common Errors

- **Exercises 8–13** Students may forget to include the area of the base when finding the surface area. Remind students that when asked to find the surface area, the base is included.
- **Exercises 8–13** Students may add the wrong number of lateral face areas to the area of the base. Examine several different pyramids with different bases and ask if they can find a relationship between the number of sides of the base and the number of lateral faces. (They are the same.) Remind students that the number of sides of the base determines how many triangles make up the lateral surface area.

E.3 Practice

Go to *BigIdeasMath.com* to get HELP with solving the exercises.

▶ Review & Refresh

Find the surface area of the cylinder. Round your answer to the nearest tenth.

1.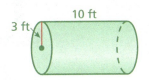
2.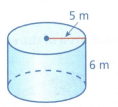
3.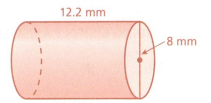

4. The ratio of the distance between bases on a professional baseball field to the distance between bases on a youth baseball field is 3 : 2. Bases on a professional baseball field are 90 feet apart. What is the distance between bases on a youth baseball field?

   A. 30 ft **B.** 45 ft **C.** 60 ft **D.** 135 ft

▶ Concepts, Skills, & Problem Solving

USING A NET Use the net to find the surface area of the regular pyramid. (See Exploration 1, p. 659.)

5.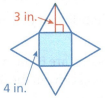
6.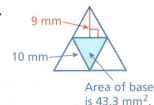
7.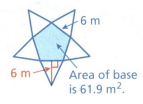

FINDING THE SURFACE AREA OF A PYRAMID Find the surface area of the regular pyramid.

8.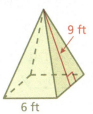
9.
10.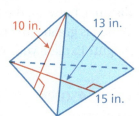
11.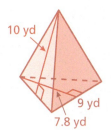
12.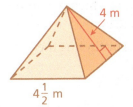
13.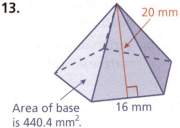

Section E.3 Surface Areas of Pyramids 663

14. **MODELING REAL LIFE** The base of the lampshade is a regular hexagon with side lengths of 8 inches. Estimate the amount of glass needed to make the lampshade.

15. **GEOMETRY** The surface area of a square pyramid is 85 square meters. The side length of the base is 5 meters. What is the slant height?

FINDING SURFACE AREA Find the surface area of the solid.

16. 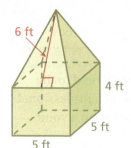   17. 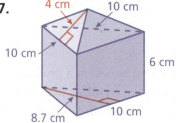   18.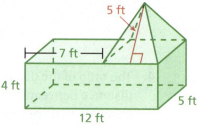

19. **GEOMETRY** A tetrahedron is a triangular pyramid with four faces that are identical equilateral triangles. The total lateral surface area of a tetrahedron is 93 square centimeters. Find the surface area of the tetrahedron.

20. **PROBLEM SOLVING** You are making an umbrella that is shaped like a regular octagonal pyramid.

    a. Estimate the amount of fabric that you need to make the umbrella.

    b. The fabric comes in rolls that are 60 inches wide. Draw a diagram of how you can cut the fabric from rolls that are 10 feet long.

    c. How much fabric is wasted?

21. **REASONING** The *height* of a pyramid is the perpendicular distance between the base and the top of the pyramid. Which is greater, the height of a pyramid or the slant height? Explain your reasoning.

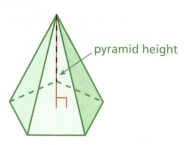

22. **REASONING** Both pyramids at the right have regular bases.

    a. Without calculating, determine which pyramid has the greater surface area. Explain.

    b. Verify your answer to part (a) by finding the surface area of each pyramid.

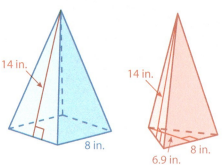

23. **CRITICAL THINKING** Is the total area of the lateral faces of a pyramid *greater than, less than,* or *equal to* the area of the base? Explain.

Common Errors

- **Exercise 14** Students may think that there is not enough information to solve the problem because it is not all labeled in the picture. Tell students to use the information in the word problem to finish labeling the picture. Also, ask students to identify how many lateral faces are part of the lamp before they find the area of one face.
- **Exercise 21** Students may not remember the definition for *perpendicular*. Remind them that perpendicular lines intersect to form a right angle.

Mini-Assessment

Find the surface area of the regular pyramid.

1.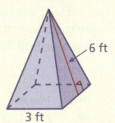
   20 cm^2

2.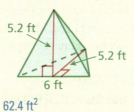
   45 ft^2

3.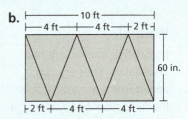
   62.4 ft^2

4. Find the surface area of the roof of the doll house.
   480 in.^{2}
   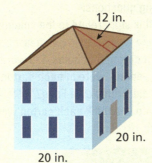

Section Resources

Surface Level	Deep Level
Resources by Chapter • Extra Practice • Reteach • Puzzle Time Student Journal • Self-Assessment • Practice Differentiating the Lesson Tutorial Videos Skills Review Handbook Skills Trainer	Resources by Chapter • Enrichment and Extension Graphic Organizers Dynamic Assessment System • Section Practice
Transfer Level	
Dynamic Assessment System • Mid-Chapter Quiz	Assessment Book • Mid-Chapter Quiz

Concepts, Skills, & Problem Solving

14. 240 in.^{2}
15. 6 m
16. 165 ft^2
17. 283.5 cm^2
18. 281 ft^2
19. 124 cm^2
20. a. 80 ft^2
    b.
    c. 20 ft^2
21. the slant height; The height is the distance between the top and the point on the base directly beneath it. The distance from the top to any other point on the base is greater than the height.
22. a. square pyramid; The square pyramid has a larger base. Each lateral face in both pyramids has the same area, and there are 4 in the square pyramid and only 3 in the triangular pyramid.
    b. square pyramid: 288 in.^{2}
       triangular pyramid: 195.6 in.^{2}
23. greater than; If it is less than or equal to, then the lateral face could not meet at a vertex to form a solid.

Learning Target
Find the volume of a prism.

Success Criteria
- Use a formula to find the volume of a prism.
- Use the formula for the volume of a prism to find a missing dimension.

Warm Up
Cumulative, vocabulary, and prerequisite skills practice opportunities are available in the *Resources by Chapter* or at *BigIdeasMath.com*.

ELL Support
Students may be familiar with the word *volume* as it is used in everyday language. Ask them to describe what they know, which may be a measure of sound. Explain that in math, volume is a measure of the amount of space that a three-dimensional figure occupies. It is measured using cubic units of measurement. Relate the word *cube* to the word *cubic*. For example, a prism with dimensions 2 feet, 3 feet, and 2 feet has a volume of 12 cubic feet. So, 12 cubes measuring 1 foot by 1 foot by 1 foot would fit inside it.

Exploration 1
a. See Additional Answers.
b. See Additional Answers.
c. $V = Bh$, where B is the area of the base and h is the height of the prism.

T-665

Laurie's Notes

Check out the Dynamic Classroom.
BigIdeasMath.com

Preparing to Teach
- Students should know how to find areas of two-dimensional figures, surface areas of three-dimensional figures, and volumes of rectangular prisms using $V = \ell wh$ or by counting unit cubes. Now they will use a formula to find volumes of prisms.
- **Look for and Express Regularity in Repeated Reasoning**: To develop a formula for the volume of a prism, students will consider repeated layers with the same base. Mathematically proficient students notice that each layer increases the volume by the number of units of the area of the base.

Motivate
- **True Story:** Baseball legend Ken Griffey Jr. owed teammate Josh Fogg some money and paid him back in pennies. Griffey stacked 60 cartons, each holding $25 worth of pennies, in Fogg's locker.
- Ask the following questions.
  - "How does this story relate to the volume of a prism?" The volume of the carton is being measured in pennies.
  - "How big is a carton that holds $25 worth of pennies?" Answers will vary.
  - "How many pennies were in each carton?" 2500
  - "How much did Griffey owe Fogg?" $1500
  - "How much do you think each carton weighed?" A $25 carton of pennies weighs about 16 pounds.

Exploration 1
- In part (a), students should see that the bottom layer has 6 cubes, the second layer has 6 cubes, the third layer has 6 cubes, and so on.
- If students are not thinking about layers (height), suggest that writing the volume of each prism would be helpful: 6, 12, 18, 24, 30.
- **Big Idea:** The area of the base (denoted B) is 6. The height (denoted h) is how many layers?
- In part (b), tell students that the sliced cubes are exactly half a cubic unit.
- **Make Sense of Problems and Persevere in Solving Them:** Students can memorize formulas and have little understanding of why the formula makes sense. It is important throughout this chapter that students see that the formulas are all similar. The volume is found by finding the area of the base (B) and then multiplying by the number of layers (h).
- **Common Misconception:** The height of a prism does not need to be the vertical measure. Demonstrate this by holding a rectangular prism (a tissue box is fine). Ask students to identify the base (a face of the prism) and the height (an edge). Chances are students will identify the (standard) bottom of the box as the base. Now, rotate the tissue box so that the base is vertical. Again ask students to identify the base and height. Students may stick with their first answers or switch to the "bottom face" as the base.
- Give students time to discuss the solids. If you have physical models, ask six volunteers to describe how to find the volume of the solid. Expect volunteers to point to the bases and the heights as they explain how to find the volumes.

E.4 Volumes of Prisms

Learning Target: Find the volume of a prism.

Success Criteria:
- I can use a formula to find the volume of a prism.
- I can use the formula for the volume of a prism to find a missing dimension.

EXPLORATION 1

Finding a Formula for Volume

Work with a partner.

a. In the figures shown, each cube has a volume of 1 cubic unit. Compare the volume V (in cubic units) of each rectangular prism to the area B (in square units) of its base. What do you notice?

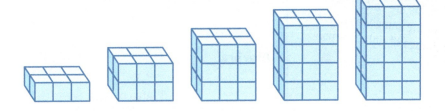

b. Repeat part (a) using the prisms below.

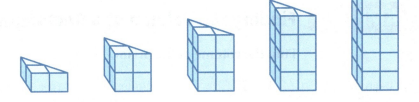

c. Use what you learned in parts (a) and (b) to write a formula that gives the volume of any prism.

Math Practice

Make Conjectures

How can you find the volume of the prism shown? Explain your reasoning.

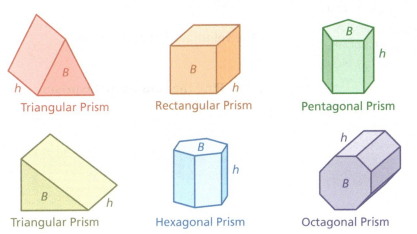

Triangular Prism

Rectangular Prism

Pentagonal Prism

Triangular Prism

Hexagonal Prism

Octagonal Prism

Section E.4 Volumes of Prisms 665

E.4 Lesson

The *volume* of a three-dimensional figure is a measure of the amount of space that it occupies. Volume is measured in cubic units.

 Key Idea

Volume of a Prism

Words The volume V of a prism is the product of the area of the base and the height of the prism.

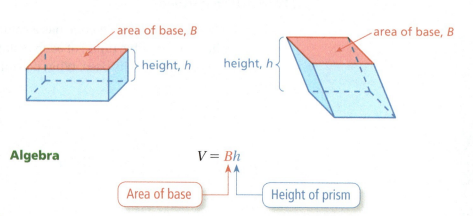

Algebra $V = Bh$

Area of base ↑ Height of prism

The slanted figure is called an oblique prism. Volumes of oblique prisms are calculated in the same way as volumes of right prisms.

EXAMPLE 1 Finding the Volume of a Rectangular Prism

Find the volume of the prism.

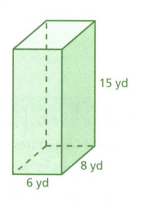

$V = Bh$	Write the formula for volume.	
$= 6(8) \cdot 15$	Substitute.	
$= 48 \cdot 15$	Simplify.	
$= 720$	Multiply.	

▶ The volume is 720 cubic yards.

The area of the base of a rectangular prism is the product of the length ℓ and the width w. You can use $V = \ell wh$ to find the volume of a rectangular prism.

Try It Find the volume of the prism.

1.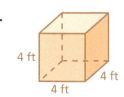

2.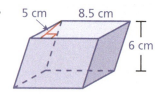

Laurie's Notes

Scaffolding Instruction

- Students explored how to find the volume of a prism. They will now solve problems using a formula for the volume of a prism.
- **Emerging:** Students may understand how to find the volume of a rectangular prism but struggle with finding the volumes of other prisms. They will benefit from guided instruction for the Key Idea and examples.
- **Proficient:** Students can find the volume of a prism, no matter the shape of the base. They should proceed to the Self-Assessment exercises.

> **Teaching Strategy**
>
> Ask students to use an index card for each solid from the chapter: prism, cylinder, and pyramid. On each card, have students draw the figure, a net for the figure, and write a sentence or two explaining how to find the surface area and/or volume of the figure. They should *not* write a formula.
>
> Often students just want to memorize a formula with little understanding as to how the formula was developed. This strategy helps them make sense of the formulas rather than just memorizing them.

Key Idea

- ❓ "What is a prism?" a three-dimensional solid with two congruent bases and lateral faces that are rectangles
- ❓ "What are cubic units? Give an example." Cubic units are cubes which fill a space completely without overlapping or leaving gaps. Cubic inches and cubic centimeters are common examples.
- Point out to students that the bases of the prisms are shaded red. The height will be perpendicular to the two congruent bases. The dotted lines are edges that would not be visible through the solid prism. If the bases are perpendicular to the faces, it is called a *right prism* (not slanted). If the prism is oblique (slanted), the bases are congruent but *not* perpendicular to the sides. In the case of an oblique prism, the height is still the perpendicular distance from one base to the other.
- **Teaching Strategy:** Have students summarize the information they know about three-dimensional figures. Students can add a volume explanation to their pyramid cards in the next section.

EXAMPLE 1

- Discuss the push-pin note with students.
- ❓ "Could the face measuring 8 yards by 15 yards be the base? Explain." Yes, then the height would be 6 yards.
- ❓ **Extension:** "What if the 6-yard edge had been labeled 18 feet, how would you find the volume?" Convert all 3 dimensions to yards or to feet before finding the volume.

Try It

- Students should solve the problems independently before checking with a neighbor.

Scaffold instruction to support all students in their learning. Learning is individualized and you may want to group students differently as they move in and out of these levels with each skill and concept. Student self-assessment and feedback help guide your instructional decisions about how and when to layer support for all students to become proficient learners.

Extra Example 1
Find the volume of a rectangular prism with a length of 2 meters, a width of 6 meters, and a height of 3 meters. 36 m^3

> **ELL Support**
>
> After reviewing Example 1, have students work in pairs to practice language as they complete Try It Exercises 1 and 2. Have one student ask another, "What is the area of the base? What is the height of the prism? What is the formula? What is the volume?" Have students alternate roles.
>
> **Beginner:** State or write numbers and equations.
>
> **Intermediate:** Use phrases or simple sentences such as, "sixteen square feet."
>
> **Advanced:** Use detailed sentences such as, "The area of the base of the cube is sixteen square feet."

Try It

1. 64 ft^3
2. 255 cm^3

Extra Example 2
Find the volume of the prism.

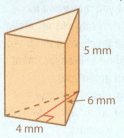

60 mm³

Try It

3. 270 m³
4. 2.25 m³

Self-Assessment
for Concepts & Skills

5. 168 in.³
6. 360 ft³
7. 480 yd³
8. 4925 mm³
9. *Sample answer:*

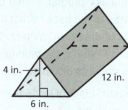

$V = Bh = \frac{1}{2}(6)(4) \cdot 12$

$= 144$ in.³

Laurie's Notes

EXAMPLE 2

- Ask a volunteer to describe the base of this prism. a triangle
- Students might think that the rectangle with dimensions of 5.5 inches and 4 inches is the base because of the orientation of the solid. Remind them that triangular prisms have triangular bases.
- ❓ "What property is used to simplify the area of the base?" Commutative Property of Multiplication
- Caution students to distinguish between the height of the base and the height of the prism.
- Remind students to always check their answers.
  - Did they answer what the problem asked?
  - Does the answer make sense?
  - Did they label the answer appropriately?

Try It

- **Popsicle Sticks:** Select students to share their work at the board.

✓ Self-Assessment for Concepts & Skills

- Ask students to use *Fist of Five* to indicate their understanding of finding the volume of a prism.
- Circulate while students work independently to solve these problems. When everyone is finished, select students that used correct methods to share their work at the board.

> **ELL Support**
>
> Allow students to work in pairs. Have them display their answers for Exercises 5–8 on whiteboards for your review. As they complete Exercise 9, circulate to review their drawings and provide support as needed.

The Success Criteria Self-Assessment chart can be found in the *Student Journal* or online at *BigIdeasMath.com*.

EXAMPLE 2 **Finding the Volume of a Triangular Prism**

Find the volume of the prism.

$V = Bh$ Write the formula for volume.

$= \frac{1}{2}(5.5)(2) \cdot 4$ Substitute.

$= 5.5 \cdot 4$ Simplify.

$= 22$ Multiply.

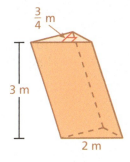

▸ The volume is 22 cubic inches.

Math Practice

Check Progress
How can you use a cube with edge lengths of 1 foot to check the reasonableness of the volume in Example 2?

Try It Find the volume of the prism.

3.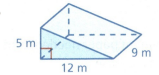

4.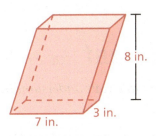

Self-Assessment for Concepts & Skills

Solve each exercise. Then rate your understanding of the success criteria in your journal.

FINDING THE VOLUME OF A PRISM Find the volume of the prism.

5.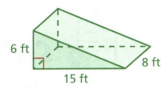

6.

7.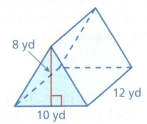

8.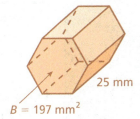
   $B = 197$ mm^2

9. **OPEN-ENDED** Draw and label a prism with a volume of 144 cubic inches. Justify your answer.

Section E.4 Volumes of Prisms 667

EXAMPLE 3 Modeling Real Life

Each popcorn bag shown holds exactly 96 cubic inches of popcorn. Which bag should a movie theater choose in order to use less paper when making popcorn bags?

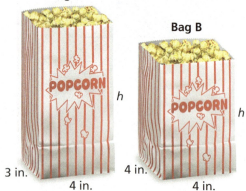

Bag A

Bag B

Use the formula for volume to find the height of each bag.

Bag A

$V = Bh$

$96 = 4(3)(h)$

$96 = 12h$

$8 = h$

Bag B

$V = Bh$

$96 = 4(4)(h)$

$96 = 16h$

$6 = h$

To determine the amount of paper needed, find the surface area of each bag. Do not include the top base.

Bag A

$S = \ell w + 2\ell h + 2wh$

$= 4(3) + 2(4)(8) + 2(3)(8)$

$= 12 + 64 + 48$

$= 124 \text{ in.}^2$

Bag B

$S = \ell w + 2\ell h + 2wh$

$= 4(4) + 2(4)(6) + 2(4)(6)$

$= 16 + 48 + 48$

$= 112 \text{ in.}^2$

▸ The surface area of Bag B is less than the surface area of Bag A. So, the movie theater should choose Bag B.

Self-Assessment for Problem Solving

Solve each exercise. Then rate your understanding of the success criteria in your journal.

10. **DIG DEEPER!** You visit an aquarium. One of the tanks at the aquarium holds 450 gallons of water. Draw a diagram to show one possible set of dimensions of the tank. Justify your answer. (1 gal = 231 in.^{3})

11. A stack of paper contains 400 sheets. The volume of the stack is 140.25 cubic inches. Each sheet of paper is identical, with a length of 11 inches and a width of 8.5 inches. Find the height of each sheet of paper. Justify your answer.

Laurie's Notes

EXAMPLE 3

- This example connects volume, surface area, and equations.
- Ask a student to read the problem aloud. Ask another student to interpret the problem. If necessary, have another student re-read the problem.
- **Make Sense of Problems and Persevere in Solving Them:** Ask probing questions to make sure that students understand the problem.
- ❓ "What type of measurement is 96 cubic inches?" volume
- ❓ "What will you need to find to answer the question?" the surface areas of both bags
- ❓ "How do you find the surface area of a prism?"
  S = areas of bases + areas of lateral faces
- ❓ "Is there something special you need to consider for this problem?" The tops of the bags are open, so only five of the six faces should be considered.
- Work through the solution as shown.
- Remind students to label their surface areas using square units and to answer the question.

✓ Self-Assessment for Problem Solving

- Encourage students to use a Four Square to complete these exercises. Until students become comfortable with the problem-solving plan, they may only be ready to complete the first square.
- **Think-Pair-Share:** Students should read each exercise independently and then work in pairs to complete the exercises. Then have each pair compare their answers with another pair and discuss any discrepancies.

The Success Criteria Self-Assessment chart can be found in the *Student Journal* or online at *BigIdeasMath.com*.

Closure

- **Exit Ticket:** Sketch a rectangular prism. Label the dimensions 4 centimeters, 6 centimeters, and 10 centimeters. Find the volume of the prism.

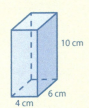

240 cm³

Extra Example 3

Each box shown holds exactly 120 cubic centimeters of packing peanuts. Which box should a shipping company choose in order to use less cardboard when making boxes?

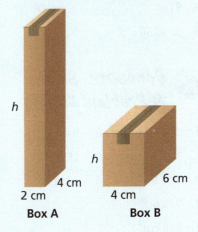

Box B

Self-Assessment for Problem Solving

10. *Sample answer:*

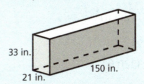

$V = (21 \text{ in.})(150 \text{ in.})(33 \text{ in.})$
$\left(\dfrac{1 \text{ gal}}{231 \text{ in.}^3}\right)$
$= 450 \text{ gal}$

11. 0.00375 in.; *Sample answer:*
$140.25 = 11(8.5)h \cdot 400$
$140.25 = 37,400h$
$0.00375 = h$

Learning Target

Find the volume of a prism.

Success Criteria

- Use a formula to find the volume of a prism.
- Use the formula for the volume of a prism to find a missing dimension.

Review & Refresh

1. 57 m²
2. 1290 mm²
3. 115.5 cm²
4. $90
5. $144
6. $240.50

Concepts, Skills, & Problem Solving

7. $V = 24$ units³; $B = 8$ units²
8. $V = 64$ units³; $B = 16$ units²
9. $V = 24$ units³; $B = 12$ units²
10. 729 in.³
11. 288 cm³
12. 238 m³
13. 210 yd³
14. 121.5 ft³
15. 420 mm³
16. 172.8 m³
17. 645 mm³
18. 3320 ft³

Assignment Guide and Concept Check

Scaffold assignments to support all students in their learning progression. The suggested assignments are a starting point. Continue to assign additional exercises and revisit with spaced practice to move every student toward proficiency.

Level	Assignment 1	Assignment 2
Emerging	1, 3, 5, 7, 10, 11, 12, 19	13, 15, 16, 17, 20, 21, 22, 27
Proficient	1, 3, 5, 8, 10, 12, 13, 14, 19	15, 16, 18, 20, 21, 22, 23, 24, 27
Advanced	1, 3, 5, 9, 12, 13, 15, 18, 19	21, 22, 23, 24, 25, 26, 27, 28

- Assignment 1 is for use after students complete the Self-Assessment for Concepts & Skills.
- Assignment 2 is for use after students complete the Self-Assessment for Problem Solving.
- The red exercises can be used as a concept check.

Review & Refresh Prior Skills

Exercises 1–3 Finding the Surface Area of a Pyramid
Exercises 4–6 Finding a Selling Price

Common Errors

- **Exercises 10–18** Students may write the units incorrectly, often writing square units instead of cubic units. Remind students that they are working in three dimensions, so the units are cubed. Give an example showing the formula for the base as three units multiplied together. For example, write the volume of Exercise 11 as $V = \frac{1}{2}(6 \text{ cm})(8 \text{ cm})(12 \text{ cm})$.

T-669

E.4 Practice

> Go to **BigIdeasMath.com** to get HELP with solving the exercises.

▶ Review & Refresh

Find the surface area of the regular pyramid.

1.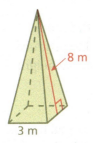

2.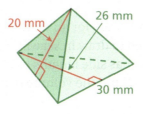

3.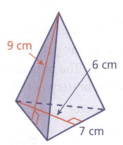

Find the selling price.

4. Cost to store: $75
   Markup: 20%

5. Cost to store: $90
   Markup: 60%

6. Cost to store: $130
   Markup: 85%

▶ Concepts, Skills, & Problem Solving

MP USING TOOLS In the figure, each cube has a volume of 1 cubic unit. Find the volume of the figure and the area of its base. *(See Exploration 1, p. 665.)*

7.

8.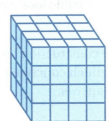

9.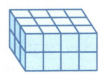

FINDING THE VOLUME OF A PRISM Find the volume of the prism.

10.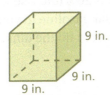

11.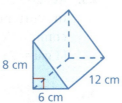

12.

13.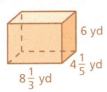

14.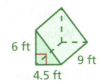

15.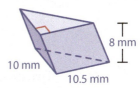

16.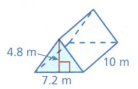

17.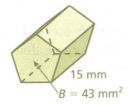

18.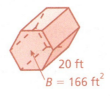

Section E.4 Volumes of Prisms 669

19. **YOU BE THE TEACHER** Your friend finds the volume of the triangular prism. Is your friend correct? Explain your reasoning.

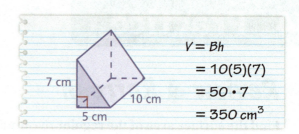

20. **MODELING REAL LIFE** A battery for an underwater drone is in the shape of a square prism. It is designed to draw in seawater that is then used to produce energy. The base of the battery has side lengths of 15 centimeters and the height of the battery is 10 centimeters. Find the volume of the battery.

21. **MODELING REAL LIFE** A cereal box has a volume of 225 cubic inches. The length of the base is 9 inches and the width of the base is 2.5 inches. What is the height of the box? Justify your answer.

22. **REASONING** Each locker is shaped like a rectangular prism. Which has more storage space? Explain.

23. **USING TOOLS** How many cubic inches are in 1 cubic foot? Use a sketch to explain your reasoning.

24. **PROBLEM SOLVING** A concrete construction block has the measurements shown. How much concrete is used to make the block? Justify your answer.

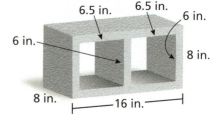

25. **RESEARCH** The gas tank is 20% full. Use the current price of regular gasoline in your community to find the cost to fill the tank. (1 gal = 231 in.^{3})

26. **DIG DEEPER!** Two liters of water are poured into an empty vase shaped like an octagonal prism. The base area is 100 square centimeters. What is the height of the water? (1 L = 1000 cm^3)

27. **LOGIC** Two prisms have the same volume. Do they *always*, *sometimes*, or *never* have the same surface area? Justify your answer.

28. **CRITICAL THINKING** How many times greater is the volume of a triangular prism when one of its dimensions is doubled? when all three dimensions are doubled?

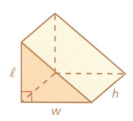

Mini-Assessment

Find the volume of the prism.

1.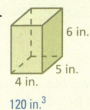
   120 in.³

2.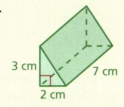
   21 cm³

3.
   27 m³

4. Find the volume of the fish tank.

   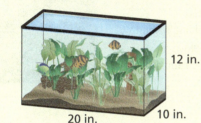

   2400 in.³

Section Resources

Surface Level	Deep Level
Resources by Chapter • Extra Practice • Reteach • Puzzle Time Student Journal • Self-Assessment • Practice Differentiating the Lesson Tutorial Videos Skills Review Handbook Skills Trainer	Resources by Chapter • Enrichment and Extension Graphic Organizers Dynamic Assessment System • Section Practice

Concepts, Skills, & Problem Solving

19. no; The area of the base is wrong.

20. 2250 cm³

21. 10 in.; Sample answer:
    $V = \ell \cdot w \cdot h$
    $225 = (9)(2.5)h$
    $225 = 22.5h$
    $10 = h$

22. the gym locker; It has a greater volume.

23. 1728 in.³

    $1 \times 1 \times 1 = 1$ ft³

    $12 \times 12 \times 12 = 1728$ in.³

24. 400 in.³; Sample answer:
    Volume of block
    = total volume − volume of
      2 rectangular holes
    = (8)(16)(8) − 2(8)(6.5)(6)
    = 1024 − 624
    = 400

25. Check students' work.

26. 20 cm

27. sometimes; The prisms in Example 3 have different surface areas but the same volume. Two prisms that are exactly the same will have the same surface area.

28. The volume is 2 times greater; The volume is 8 times greater.

Learning Target
Find the volume of a pyramid.

Success Criteria
- Use a formula to find the volume of a pyramid.
- Use the volume of a pyramid to solve a real-life problem.

Warm Up
Cumulative, vocabulary, and prerequisite skills practice opportunities are available in the *Resources by Chapter* or at BigIdeasMath.com.

ELL Support
Point out that in this and other lessons formulas are used to find mathematical calculations. Ask if students know other uses of the word *formula*. Possibilities include milk for babies, a category of racecar, or chemical symbols. In math, a formula is a rule that is expressed using mathematical symbols.

Exploration 1

a. *Sample answer:* The volume of the cube is 3 times larger than the volume of the pyramid.

b. $V = \frac{1}{3}Bh$, where B is the area of the base of the pyramid and h is the height of the pyramid.

c. Volume of prism = $2 \cdot 3 \cdot 5 = 30$

$V = \frac{1}{3}(3 \cdot 5)(2) = 10$

$V = \frac{1}{3}(2 \cdot 3)(5) = 10$

$V = \frac{1}{3}(2 \cdot 5)(3) = 10$

$10 + 10 + 10 = 30$

Check out the Dynamic Classroom.
BigIdeasMath.com

Laurie's Notes

Preparing to Teach
- Students should know how to perform operations on rational numbers. In the previous lesson, they learned how to find volumes of prisms. Now they will use their understanding of both concepts to find volumes of pyramids.
- **Reason Abstractly and Quantitatively:** In constructing physical models of a prism and a pyramid that have the same base area and height and then comparing their volumes, students make sense of the formula for the volume of a pyramid.

Motivate

- Show and discuss a picture of the Transamerica Pyramid building.
- It is the tallest building in San Francisco.
- The tapered design reduces the building's shadow to let more light reach the streets below.
- A San Francisco regulation limits the ratio of surface area to height for a building.

Exploration 1

- Students will need something to fill their prisms and pyramids. Rice or popcorn kernels work well. Sand will also work.
- **Teaching Tip:** Cover desks with newspaper to help with clean up.
- ❓ "How are the two shapes alike?" same base, same height "How are they different?" One is a pyramid and the other is a prism.
- ❓ "How do you think their volumes compare?" Most students guess that the prism has twice the volume of the pyramid.
- ❓ "How can you test your guess about the volumes?" If students have looked at the exploration, they will want to fill the pyramid.
- After the first pour, students should start to suspect that their guess might be off.
- After the second pour, students are pretty sure the relationship is 3 to 1.
- This hands-on experience of making and filling the prism will help students remember the factor of $\frac{1}{3}$. The formula should now make sense to them. The volume of a pyramid should be $\frac{1}{3}$ the volume of a prism with the same base and height as the pyramid.
- ❓ "What is a formula for the volume of a prism?" $V = Bh$
- ❓ "What is a formula for the volume of a pyramid?" $V = \frac{1}{3}Bh$
- For part (c), discuss with students how to follow the color-coding so that correct dimensions can be matched up.
- Have students complete part (c) and then share their ideas with the class.

E.5 Volumes of Pyramids

Learning Target: Find the volume of a pyramid.

Success Criteria:
- I can use a formula to find the volume of a pyramid.
- I can use the volume of a pyramid to solve a real-life problem.

EXPLORATION 1

Finding a Formula for the Volume of a Pyramid

Work with a partner. Draw the two nets on cardboard and cut them out. Fold and tape the nets to form an open cube and an open square pyramid. Both figures should have the same size square base and the same height.

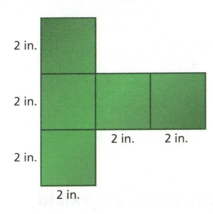
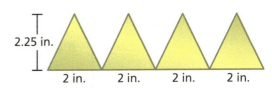

a. Compare the volumes of the figures. What do you notice?

b. Use your observations in part (a) to write a formula for the volume of a pyramid.

c. The rectangular prism below can be cut to form three pyramids. Use your formula in part (b) to show that the sum of the volumes of the three pyramids is equal to the volume of the prism.

Math Practice

Interpret a Solution

How do your calculations in part (c) help you verify that your formula is correct?

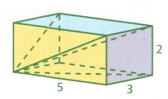

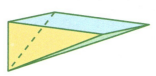
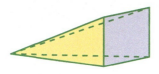
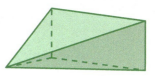

E.5 Lesson

Key Idea

Volume of a Pyramid

Words The volume V of a pyramid is one-third the product of the area of the base and the height of the pyramid.

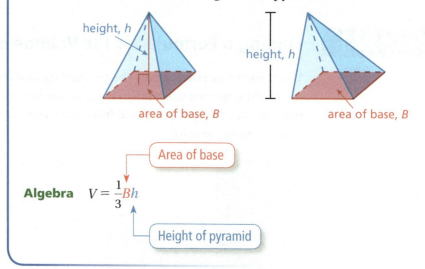

Algebra $V = \dfrac{1}{3}Bh$ — Area of base, Height of pyramid

Volumes of oblique pyramids are calculated the same way as volumes of right pyramids.

EXAMPLE 1 Finding the Volume of a Pyramid

Find the volume of the pyramid.

$V = \dfrac{1}{3}Bh$ Write the formula for volume.

$= \dfrac{1}{3}(48)(9)$ Substitute.

$= 144$ Multiply.

▸ The volume is 144 cubic millimeters.

Try It Find the volume of the pyramid.

1.   2.

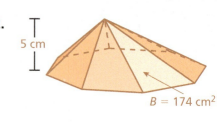

672 Chapter E Surface Area and Volume

Laurie's Notes

Scaffolding Instruction

- Students explored how to find the volume of a pyramid by comparing it to the volume of a prism with the same base and height. Now students will work with a formula to find the volumes of different pyramids.
- **Emerging:** Students may have noticed that it took three pyramids to fill a prism with the same base and height, but they may not understand how to find the volume of a pyramid. They may have difficulty visualizing the division of the prism into three parts. These students need guided instruction for the Key Idea and examples.
- **Proficient:** Students recognize the relationship between the volume of a pyramid and the volume of a prism. They should review the Key Idea before completing the Self-Assessment exercises.

Key Idea

- Write the formula in words and then in symbols.
- **?** "How will you find the area of the base?" It depends on what type of polygon the base is.
- Discuss the dotted lines and the shaded base. Pyramids are difficult to draw in two dimensions. Have students sketch a triangular pyramid and a square pyramid to practice. Remind students that the height of the pyramid is the perpendicular distance from the vertex to the base, not an edge length.

EXAMPLE 1

- Model good problem solving. Write the formula in words. Write the symbols underneath the words. Substitute the values for the symbols.
- **Common Error:** In using the volume formula, students often find $\frac{1}{3}$ of both B and h $\left(\frac{1}{3} \text{ of } 48 \text{ and } \frac{1}{3} \text{ of } 9\right)$ as though they are using the Distributive Property. Remind them that the Distributive Property is used when there is addition or subtraction involved. The correct steps for this problem are to multiply from left to right.
- **Attend to Precision:** Remind students to label their answers with cubic units.

Try It

- Students should solve the problems on whiteboards. Discuss any discrepancies as a class.
- **Teaching Strategy:** In Exercise 1, have students list what they need to know before finding the volume: formula for the volume of a pyramid, area of the base (pentagon), and the height of the pyramid.

Scaffold instruction to support all students in their learning. Learning is individualized and you may want to group students differently as they move in and out of these levels with each skill and concept. Student self-assessment and feedback help guide your instructional decisions about how and when to layer support for all students to become proficient learners.

Extra Example 1

Find the volume of a pentagonal pyramid with a base area of 24 square feet and a height of 8 feet. 64 ft^3

> **Teaching Strategy**
>
> As students begin to practice using a new skill or formula, encourage them to write a list of what they need to know to solve the problem.

> **ELL Support**
>
> After reviewing Example 1, have students work in pairs to practice language as they complete Try It Exercises 1 and 2. Have one student ask another, "What is the area of the base? What is the height? What is the formula? What is the volume?" Have students alternate roles.
>
> **Beginner:** State or write numbers and equations.
>
> **Intermediate:** Use phrases or simple sentences such as, "twenty-one square feet."
>
> **Advanced:** Use detailed sentences such as, "The area of the base of the pyramid is twenty-one square feet."

Try It

1. 42 ft^3
2. 290 cm^3

Extra Example 2

Find the volume of the pyramid.

a.

12 m³

b.

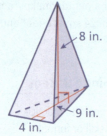

48 in.³

Try It

3. $186\frac{2}{3}$ in.³

4. 231 cm³

Self-Assessment
for Concepts & Skills

5. The volume of a pyramid is $\frac{1}{3}$ times the area of the base times the height. The volume of a prism is the area of the base times the height.

6. infinitely many; *Sample answer:* Because the height and volume are the same, the area of the base will also be the same. So, the base can be any shape as long as the area is the same.

7. 20 yd³

8. 48 cm³

Laurie's Notes

EXAMPLE 2

- "Describe the base of each pyramid." rectangular base; triangular base
- "How do you find the area of the base in part (b)?" $\frac{1}{2}(17.5)(6)$
- **FYI:** A statement like "one-half of the base times the height" will confuse students in part (b). Help students differentiate between the base of the triangle and the base of the pyramid. Typically, *B* represents the area of the base of a three-dimensional figure and *b* represents a base length.
- Students may need help in multiplying the fractions in each problem. They can apply the Commutative Property to get products of reciprocals in each problem. In part (a), $\frac{1}{3} \times 3 = 1$ and in part (b), $\frac{1}{3} \times \frac{1}{2} \times 6 = 1$.

Try It

- Students should work independently and then check their answers with a neighbor.
- **Teaching Strategy:** In Exercise 3, have students list what they need to know before finding the volume: formula for the volume of a pyramid, area of the base (rectangle), and the height of the pyramid.

✓ Self-Assessment for Concepts & Skills

- Students should complete these exercises independently.
- Take time to discuss Exercise 6 with students.
- **Thumbs Up:** Have students indicate their understanding of the first success criterion.

ELL Support

Have students work in pairs for extra support and to practice language as they work on Exercises 5 and 6. Then have two pairs discuss their answers and reach an agreement. Monitor discussions and provide support as needed. You may want to review each group's answers with the class. Have pairs display their answers for Exercises 7 and 8 on whiteboards for your review.

The Success Criteria Self-Assessment chart can be found in the *Student Journal* or online at *BigIdeasMath.com*.

EXAMPLE 2 **Finding the Volume of a Pyramid**

Find the volume of the pyramid.

a.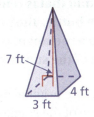

b.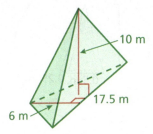

> The area of the base of a rectangular pyramid is the product of the length ℓ and the width w. You can use $V = \frac{1}{3}\ell wh$ to find the volume of a rectangular pyramid.

$V = \frac{1}{3}Bh$

$= \frac{1}{3}(4)(3)(7)$

$= 28$

▶ The volume is 28 cubic feet.

$V = \frac{1}{3}Bh$

$= \frac{1}{3}\left(\frac{1}{2}\right)(17.5)(6)(10)$

$= 175$

▶ The volume is 175 cubic meters.

Try It Find the volume of the pyramid.

3.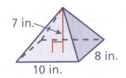

4.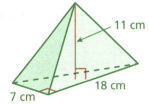

Self-Assessment for Concepts & Skills

Solve each exercise. Then rate your understanding of the success criteria in your journal.

5. **WRITING** How is the formula for the volume of a pyramid different from the formula for the volume of a prism?

6. **MP PROBLEM SOLVING** How many different pyramids can you draw with the same height and volume? Explain.

FINDING THE VOLUME OF A PYRAMID Find the volume of the pyramid.

7.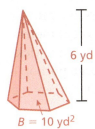

8.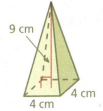

Section E.5 Volumes of Pyramids 673

EXAMPLE 3 Modeling Real Life

The diagram shows the portion of a rectangular pyramid that is removed to make a sunscreen bottle. The portion that is removed is also a rectangular pyramid. Find the unit cost of the sunscreen.

Find the volume of the original pyramid and subtract the volume of the smaller pyramid.

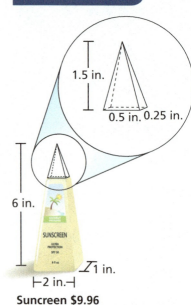

Suncreen $9.96

Original Pyramid

$$V = \frac{1}{3}Bh$$

$$= \frac{1}{3}(2)(1)(6)$$

$$= 4 \text{ in.}^3$$

Smaller Pyramid

$$V = \frac{1}{3}Bh$$

$$= \frac{1}{3}(0.5)(0.25)(1.5)$$

$$= 0.0625 \text{ in.}^3$$

The volume of sunscreen in the bottle is $4 - 0.0625 = 3.9375$ cubic inches. The bottle of sunscreen costs $9.96. Find the unit rate.

$9.96 per 3.9375 cubic inches: $\frac{9.96}{3.9375} \approx \$2.53$ per cubic inch.

▶ So, the unit cost of the sunscreen is about $2.53 per cubic inch.

Self-Assessment for Problem Solving

Solve each exercise. Then rate your understanding of the success criteria in your journal.

9. A resort features a square pyramid with a water slide. The length of the water slide is 90% of the height of the pyramid. The base of the pyramid has side lengths of 60 feet. The volume of the pyramid is 60,000 cubic feet. What is the length of the water slide?

10. **DIG DEEPER!** To make a candle, you use a mold to create the wax pyramid shown. You cut off the top 3 centimeters of the pyramid to make space for a wick. If the base area of the removed portion is 5.4 square centimeters, what percentage of the wax did you remove?

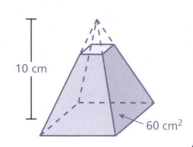

Laurie's Notes

EXAMPLE 3

- If you have any lotion or shampoo that is in a pyramidal bottle, use it as a model.
- Read the problem aloud.
- ❓ "What do you need to know to find the unit cost?" *the volume of the original pyramid and the volume of the removed pyramid*
- Make sure students understand what is meant by unit cost.
- Work through the volume computation for each bottle.
- **Reason Abstractly and Quantitatively:** Explain different approaches to multiplying the factors in the original pyramid: (1) multiply in order from left to right or (2) use the Commutative Property to multiply the whole numbers and then multiply by $\frac{1}{3}$.
- Complete the problem as shown. Remind students to always label their answers and to make sure they answer the question.
- **Check Reasonableness:** Students can estimate the unit cost using the volume of the original pyramid ($2.49 per cubic inch). Because a small portion of the original pyramid is removed, it makes sense that the unit cost is slightly greater than $2.49 per cubic inch.
- ❓ **Extension:** "Why is unit cost important?" *Sample answer:* It can help you determine which product or quantity is the better buy.
- **Model with Mathematics:** Suggest that students look for price labels on the shelves of a grocery store the next time they are there. Most labels contain unit prices. Encourage students to decide which box of laundry soap is the better buy. It is *not* always the largest quantity!

✓ Self-Assessment for Problem Solving

- The goal for all students is to feel comfortable with the problem-solving plan. It is important for students to problem-solve in class, where they may receive support from you and their peers.
- Before solving these problems, ask students to give examples of real-life situations that could involve volumes of pyramids.
- **Teaching Strategy:** For each problem, ask students to make a list of things they need to know and then make a plan for solving the problem.
- After making their lists and plans independently, students should work with a partner to discuss and solve each problem.
- ◉ **Thumbs Up:** Have students indicate their understanding of the second success criterion.

The Success Criteria Self-Assessment chart can be found in the *Student Journal* or online at *BigIdeasMath.com*.

Closure

- **Writing Prompt:** If you know the volume and the area of the base of a pyramid, how can you find the height of the pyramid?

Extra Example 3

The diagram shows the portion of a rectangular pyramid that is removed to make a lotion bottle. The portion that is removed is also a rectangular pyramid. Find the unit cost of the lotion.

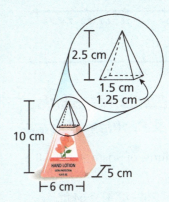

Lotion: $10.00

about $0.10 per cubic centimeter

Self-Assessment for Problem Solving

9. 45 ft
10. 2.7%

Learning Target

Find the volume of a pyramid.

Success Criteria

- Use a formula to find the volume of a pyramid.
- Use the volume of a pyramid to solve a real-life problem.

Review & Refresh

1. 189 ft^3
2. 60 cm^3
3. $r < -0.9$

4. $z \geq 1.8$

5. $h \leq 1.3$

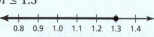 **Concepts, Skills, & Problem Solving**

6. Volume of prism $= 4 \cdot 6 \cdot 8$
   $= 192 \text{ ft}^3$

   $V = \frac{1}{3}(6 \cdot 8)(4) = 64 \text{ ft}^3$

   $V = \frac{1}{3}(4 \cdot 6)(8) = 64 \text{ ft}^3$

   $V = \frac{1}{3}(4 \cdot 8)(6) = 64 \text{ ft}^3$

   $64 + 64 + 64 = 192 \text{ ft}^3$

7. Volume of prism $= 6 \cdot 6 \cdot 6$
   $= 216 \text{ in.}^3$

   $V = \frac{1}{3}(6 \cdot 6)(6) = 72 \text{ in.}^3$

   $V = \frac{1}{3}(6 \cdot 6)(6) = 72 \text{ in.}^3$

   $V = \frac{1}{3}(6 \cdot 6)(6) = 72 \text{ in.}^3$

   $72 + 72 + 72 = 216 \text{ in.}^3$

8. $1\frac{1}{3} \text{ ft}^3$
9. $13\frac{1}{3} \text{ ft}^3$
10. 112 ft^3
11. 20 mm^3
12. $26\frac{2}{3} \text{ yd}^3$
13. 80 in.^3
14. 700 mm^3
15. 7 cm^3
16. 252 mm^3

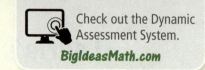

Check out the Dynamic Assessment System.
BigIdeasMath.com

Assignment Guide and Concept Check

Scaffold assignments to support all students in their learning progression. The suggested assignments are a starting point. Continue to assign additional exercises and revisit with spaced practice to move every student toward proficiency.

Level	Assignment 1	Assignment 2
Emerging	1, 2, 5, 6, 8, 9, 10, 11, 17	12, 15, 16, 18, 19, 20, 21, 22
Proficient	1, 2, 5, 7, 10, 11, 12, 17	14, 15, 16, 18, 19, 20, 21, 22
Advanced	1, 2, 5, 7, 10, 14, 16, 17	18, 19, 20, 21, 22, 23, 24

- Assignment 1 is for use after students complete the Self-Assessment for Concepts & Skills.
- Assignment 2 is for use after students complete the Self-Assessment for Problem Solving.
- The red exercises can be used as a concept check.

Review & Refresh Prior Skills

Exercises 1 and 2 Finding the Volume of a Prism
Exercises 3–5 Solving an Inequality

Common Errors

- **Exercises 8–16** Students may write the units incorrectly, often writing square units instead of cubic units. This is especially true when the area of the base is given. Remind students that the units are cubed because there are three dimensions.
- **Exercises 8–16** Students may forget to multiply by one of the measurements, especially when finding the area of the base. Encourage students to find the area of the base separately and then substitute it into the equation. Using colored pencils for each part can also assist students. Tell them to write the formula using different colors for the base and the height, as in the lesson. When they substitute values into the equation for volume, they will be able to clearly see that they have accounted for all of the dimensions.

E.5 Practice

? Go to *BigIdeasMath.com* to get HELP with solving the exercises.

▶ Review & Refresh

Find the volume of the prism.

1.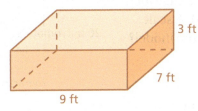

2.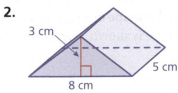

Solve the inequality. Graph the solution.

3. $r + 0.5 < -0.4$
4. $z - 2.4 \geq -0.6$
5. $h - 5 \leq -3.7$

▶ Concepts, Skills, & Problem Solving

VOLUMES OF PYRAMIDS The rectangular prism is cut to form three pyramids. Show that the sum of the volumes of the three pyramids is equal to the volume of the prism. *(See Exploration 1, p. 671.)*

6.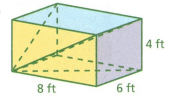

7.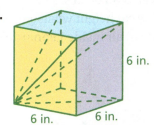

FINDING THE VOLUME OF A PYRAMID Find the volume of the pyramid.

8.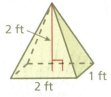

9.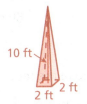

10.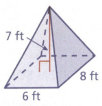

11.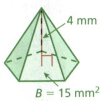

12.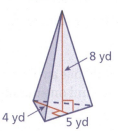

13.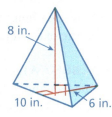

14.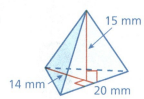

15.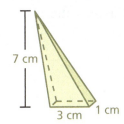

16.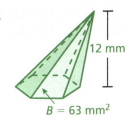

Section E.5   Volumes of Pyramids   675

17. **YOU BE THE TEACHER** Your friend finds the volume of the pyramid. Is your friend correct? Explain your reasoning.

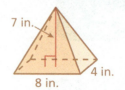

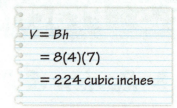

18. **MODELING REAL LIFE** A researcher develops a cage for a living cell in the shape of a square-based pyramid. A scale model of the cage is shown. What is the volume of the model?

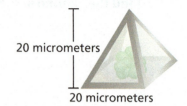

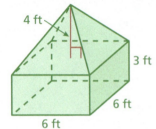

19. **FINDING VOLUME** Find the volume of the composite solid. Justify your answer.

20. **MODELING REAL LIFE** In 1483, Leonardo da Vinci designed a parachute. It is believed that this was the first parachute ever designed. In a notebook, he wrote, "If a man is provided with a length of gummed linen cloth with a length of 12 yards on each side and 12 yards high, he can jump from any great height whatsoever without injury." Find the volume of air inside Leonardo's parachute.

Not drawn to scale

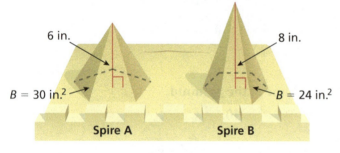

21. **MODELING REAL LIFE** Which sandcastle spire has a greater volume? How much more sand do you need to make the spire with the greater volume?

22. **PROBLEM SOLVING** Use the photo of the tepee.

   a. What is the shape of the base? How can you tell?

   b. The tepee's height is about 10 feet. Estimate the volume of the tepee.

23. **OPEN-ENDED** A rectangular pyramid has a volume of 40 cubic feet and a height of 6 feet. Find one possible set of dimensions of the base.

24. **REASONING** Do the two solids have the same volume? Explain.

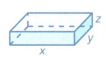 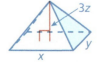

676   Chapter E   Surface Area and Volume

Mini-Assessment
Find the volume of the pyramid.

1.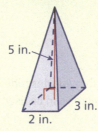
10 in.³

2.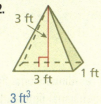
3 ft³

3.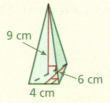
36 cm³

4. Find the volume of the paper weight.

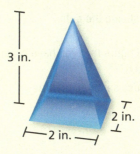

4 in.³

Section Resources

Surface Level	Deep Level
Resources by Chapter • Extra Practice • Reteach • Puzzle Time Student Journal • Self-Assessment • Practice Differentiating the Lesson Tutorial Videos Skills Review Handbook Skills Trainer	Resources by Chapter • Enrichment and Extension Graphic Organizers Dynamic Assessment System • Section Practice

 Concepts, Skills, & Problem Solving

17. no; Your friend forgot to multiply by $\frac{1}{3}$.

18. $2666\frac{2}{3}$ cubic micrometers

19. 156 ft³; *Sample answer:*
Total volume
$\quad$ = volume of rectangular prism
$\quad\quad$ + volume of rectangular pyramid
$\quad = 6 \cdot 6 \cdot 3 + \frac{1}{3}(6 \cdot 6) \cdot 4$
$\quad = 108 + 48$
$\quad = 156$

20. 576 yd³

21. Spire B; 4 in.³

22. **a.** dodecagon (12-sided polygon); There are 12 sticks.
    b. about 267 ft³

23. *Sample answer:* 5 ft by 4 ft

24. yes; Prism: $V = xyz$
Pyramid: $V = \frac{1}{3}(xy)(3z) = xyz$

T-676

Learning Target
Describe the cross sections of a solid.

Success Criteria
- Explain the meaning of a cross section.
- Describe cross sections of prisms and pyramids.
- Describe cross sections of cylinders and cones.

Warm Up
Cumulative, vocabulary, and prerequisite skills practice opportunities are available in the *Resources by Chapter* or at BigIdeasMath.com.

ELL Support
Discuss the meaning of a *cross section*. Ask students what they think of when they see the word *cross*. The symbol of a cross, a crossroad, or crossing a street may all come to mind. Support ideas by drawing simple visuals. Have students describe what they understand a *section* is—part of a whole. Explain that when one thing is cut into sections, the two-dimensional shapes formed at the ends of the cut are cross sections.

Exploration 1
a. rectangle

b. rectangle

c. triangle

d. yes; A slice can be made vertically through the bread from the top to the bottom near the corner at an angle.

e. See Additional Answers.

T-677

Laurie's Notes

Check out the Dynamic Classroom.
BigIdeasMath.com

Preparing to Teach
- Students have identified three-dimensional figures. Now they will describe cross sections of three-dimensional figures. Styrofoam figures can be used to demonstrate slicing the figures to create cross sections.
- **Construct Viable Arguments and Critique the Reasoning of Others:** Mathematically proficient students communicate their conclusions to others and justify their thinking. They relate finding cross sections of real-life objects to finding cross sections of three-dimensional solids.

Motivate
- Hold a cube in your hand. A clear one works best.
- Stretch a rubber band around the middle of the cube.
- ❓ "If I could slice through the cube where the rubber band is located, what shape would the perimeter of each end be?" a square
- Tell students that this is called a **cross section**.
- ❓ "How many different shapes could I create from slicing the cube?" Answers will vary.
- "Describe a cross section of a three-dimensional figure that you have created in real life." *Sample answer:* slicing a stick of butter
- Tell students that in this lesson they will study cross sections of three-dimensional figures.

Exploration 1
- It is helpful for students to see and hold models of solids when thinking about cross sections. You can stretch a rubber band around the model of a solid to help students visualize the shape of the cross section.
- **Use Appropriate Tools Strategically:** Students could cut Styrofoam rectangular prisms as described in the exploration. If knives are a safety concern, they could use floss or you could demonstrate each cross section. If Styrofoam solids are not available, clay or playdough works as well. If possible, give students several options and let them decide what to use.
- As students work through the exploration, have them discuss their ideas in pairs and then with the class. They should create or draw the rectangular prism and then slice or use dotted lines to represent each cut.
- Part (d) may be difficult for students to visualize. Build upon part (c) to show students how it is possible.
- Discuss the Math Practice note.

E.6 Cross Sections of Three-Dimensional Figures

Learning Target: Describe the cross sections of a solid.

Success Criteria:
- I can explain the meaning of a cross section.
- I can describe cross sections of prisms and pyramids.
- I can describe cross sections of cylinders and cones.

EXPLORATION 1

Describing Cross Sections

Work with a partner. A baker is thinking of different ways to slice zucchini bread that is in the shape of a rectangular prism. The shape that is formed by the cut is called a *cross section*.

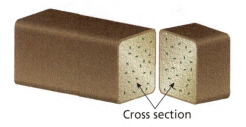
Cross section

a. What is the shape of the cross section when the baker slices the bread vertically, as shown above?

b. What is the shape of the cross section when the baker slices the bread horizontally?

c. What is the shape of the cross section when the baker slices off a corner of the bread?

Math Practice

Justify Conclusions

How can you use real-life objects to justify your conclusions in parts (d) and (e)?

d. Is it possible to obtain a cross section that is a trapezoid? Explain.

e. Name at least 3 cross sections that are possible to obtain from a rectangular pyramid. Explain your reasoning.

E.6 Lesson

Key Vocabulary
cross section, *p. 678*

Consider a plane "slicing" through a solid. The intersection of the plane and the solid is a two-dimensional shape called a **cross section**. For example, the diagram shows that the intersection of the plane and the rectangular prism is a rectangle.

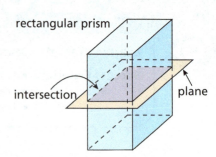

EXAMPLE 1   Describing Cross Sections of Prisms and Pyramids

Describe the intersection of the plane and the solid.

a.

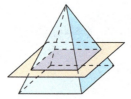

> The diagram shows the intersection of a plane and a rectangular pyramid. The intersection is a rectangle.

b.

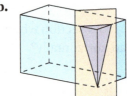

> The diagram shows the intersection of a plane and a rectangular prism. The intersection is a triangle.

Try It Describe the intersection of the plane and the solid.

1.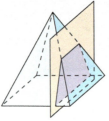

2.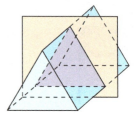

678   Chapter E   Surface Area and Volume

Laurie's Notes

Scaffolding Instruction
- Students explored cross sections of a rectangular prism. Now they will continue to describe cross sections of three-dimensional figures.
- **Emerging:** Students may struggle to visualize cross sections. The orientation of the figures may confuse them. They will benefit from guided instruction for the vocabulary and examples.
- **Proficient:** Students intuitively "see" and describe the shapes of cross sections. They should proceed to the Self-Assessment exercises.

Discuss
- Read the text at the top of the page aloud.
- Discuss the definition for a **cross section** and the parts of the diagram.
- Make sure students understand what a *plane* is and what is meant by "slicing."

EXAMPLE 1
- It is helpful for students to see and hold models of solids when thinking about how a plane intersects a solid. You can stretch a rubber band around the model of a solid to help students visualize the intersection of a plane with the solid.
- Technology that displays the animation of a plane cutting through a solid can also help students visualize the resulting cross section.
- Allow students to explain the slicing to each other.

Try It
- **Think-Pair-Share:** Students should review each diagram independently and then work in pairs to describe the intersections. Then have each pair compare their descriptions with another pair and discuss any discrepancies.

ELL Support
After demonstrating Example 1, have students work in groups to complete Try It Exercises 1 and 2. Monitor discussions and provide support as needed. Expect students to perform according to their language levels.

Beginner: Use a single word or a short phrase.

Intermediate: Use a detailed phrase or a simple sentence.

Advanced: Use a detailed sentence and help guide discussion.

Scaffold instruction to support all students in their learning. Learning is individualized and you may want to group students differently as they move in and out of these levels with each skill and concept. Student self-assessment and feedback help guide your instructional decisions about how and when to layer support for all students to become proficient learners.

Extra Example 1
Describe the intersection of the plane and the solid.

a.

a rectangle

b.

a square

Try It
1. trapezoid
2. triangle

T-678

Extra Example 2

Describe the intersection of the plane and the solid.

a.

a circle

b.

a circle

Try It

3. rectangle
4. circle

Self-Assessment
for Concepts & Skills

5. A cross section is a two-dimensional shape formed by the intersection of a plane and a solid.
6. rectangle
7. circle, oval, rectangle
8. circle; *Sample answer:* There is no way to get a curved cross section from a square prism.

Laurie's Notes

Discuss
- Read aloud the text at the top of the page.
- The word *polyhedron* is used. Although polyhedrons were introduced to students in the previous course, a quick review might be beneficial.
- ❓ "What is a polyhedron?" a solid whose faces are all polygons
- Describe the features of a cone. Structurally it is the same as a pyramid. There is one base and a lateral surface with one vertex not on the base.
- Remind students that prisms and pyramids are polyhedrons, but cylinders, cones, and spheres are not.

EXAMPLE 2
- You can investigate these cross sections for a cylinder and cone using a flashlight, overhead projector, or document camera to show two-dimensional projections of three-dimensional objects. For instance, hold a cylinder (a can) in different orientations to show different projections.
- Do the same for a cone (a party hat or a cone-shaped cup).
- A rubber band stretched around the solid will also reveal the perimeter or circumference of the cross section.
- Have students discuss the Math Practice note in pairs.

Try It
- The intersections are shaded and should be clear to students.
- **Extension:** Ask students to describe how the size of the cross section changes as the plane moves through the cylinder in Exercise 3.

✓ Self-Assessment for Concepts & Skills

- ⦿ **Quick Write:** To determine the shape of a cross section of a three-dimensional figure…
- **Neighbor Check:** Have students work independently and then have their neighbors check their work. Have students discuss any discrepancies.

ELL Support
Allow students to work in pairs instead of independently. Then have two pairs form a group to check their work. Monitor discussions and provide support. Have groups present their answers to the class. Encourage questions and discussion.

The Success Criteria Self-Assessment chart can be found in the *Student Journal* or online at *BigIdeasMath.com*.

Example 1 shows how a plane intersects a polyhedron. Now consider the intersection of a plane and a solid having a curved surface, such as a cylinder or cone. As shown, a *cone* is a solid that has one circular base and one vertex.

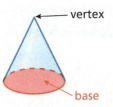

EXAMPLE 2 **Describing Cross Sections of Cylinders and Cones**

Describe the intersection of the plane and the solid.

a.
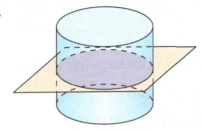

▸ The diagram shows the intersection of a plane and a cylinder. The intersection is a circle.

b.
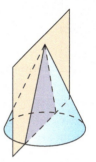

▸ The diagram shows the intersection of a plane and a cone. The intersection is a triangle.

Math Practice

Communicate Precisely

Can a cross section be three dimensional? Explain your reasoning.

Try It Describe the intersection of the plane and the solid.

3.
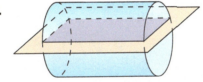

4.
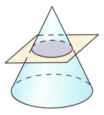

 Self-Assessment for Concepts & Skills

Solve each exercise. Then rate your understanding of the success criteria in your journal.

5. **VOCABULARY** What is a cross section?

6. **DESCRIBING CROSS SECTIONS** Describe the intersection of the plane and the solid at the left.

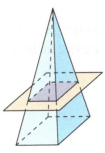

7. **MP REASONING** Name all possible cross sections of a cylinder.

8. **WHICH ONE DOESN'T BELONG?** You slice a square prism. Which cross section does *not* belong with the other three? Explain your reasoning.

Section E.6 Cross Sections of Three-Dimensional Figures

EXAMPLE 3 Modeling Real Life

An ice sculptor cuts the block of ice into 3 identical pieces. What is the percent of increase in the surface area of the ice?

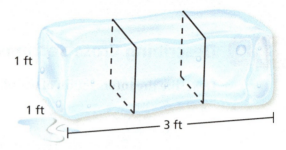

Find the surface area of the ice before it is cut.

$S = 2\ell w + 2\ell h + 2wh$	Write the formula.
$= 2(1)(1) + 2(1)(3) + 2(1)(3)$	Substitute 1 for ℓ, 1 for w, and 3 for h.
$= 2 + 6 + 6$	Simplify.
$= 14 \text{ ft}^2$	Add.

When the ice is cut, the cross sections are squares with side lengths of 1 foot. The ice is cut into three cubes, each with edge lengths of 1 foot. Find the total surface area of the three cubes.

Remember
The surface area S of a cube with an edge length of s is $S = 6s^2$.

$S = 3(6s^2)$
$= 3(6 \cdot 1^2)$
$= 3(6)$
$= 18 \text{ ft}^2$

▶ So, the percent of increase in the surface area of the ice is $\dfrac{18-14}{14} \approx 29\%$.

Self-Assessment for Problem Solving

Solve each exercise. Then rate your understanding of the success criteria in your journal.

9. A steel beam that is 12 meters long is cut into four equal parts. The cross sections are rectangles with side lengths of 1 meter and 2 meters.

   a. What is the perimeter of each cross section?
   b. What is the area of each cross section?
   c. What is the volume of the original beam?

10. **DIG DEEPER!** A lumberjack saws a cylindrical tree trunk at an angle. Is the cross section a circle? Explain your reasoning.

680   Chapter E   Surface Area and Volume

Laurie's Notes

EXAMPLE 3

- Ask a student to read the problem aloud. Ask another student to interpret the problem. If necessary, have another student re-read the problem.
- ❓ "What are you asked to find?" *the percent of increase in the surface area of the ice*
- Tell students that an ice sculptor would want to know this because ice melts faster when it has a greater surface area. The percent of increase in surface area of the ice could give the ice sculptor a gauge for how much faster it will melt.
- ❓ "What do you need to know to answer the question?" *the original surface area and the new surface area*
- ❓ "How do you find percent of increase?"

   If students cannot remember how to calculate percent of increase, have them look it up.
- Work through the problem as shown.

✓ Self-Assessment for Problem Solving

- Encourage students to use a Four Square to complete these exercises. Until students become comfortable with the problem-solving plan, they may only be ready to complete the first square.
- **Think-Pair-Share:** Students should read each exercise independently and then work in pairs to complete the exercises. Then have each pair compare their answers with another pair and discuss any discrepancies.

The Success Criteria Self-Assessment chart can be found in the *Student Journal* or online at *BigIdeasMath.com*.

Formative Assessment Tip

Write the Test

Give each student 2 index cards. Divide students into groups equal to the number of sections in the chapter. Assign each group a different section. Tell students that they are going to write the test! Have each member of the group write 2 test questions for the assigned section. Each question should be written on an index card with the solution worked out on the back. Have each student give his or her cards to two students in the group to evaluate the questions and solutions. When students are confident in their solutions, collect the cards. Select problems from the cards to create a chapter test.

Closure

- **Write the Test:** Divide students into six groups and assign each group a section to write test questions for.

Extra Example 3

A carpenter cuts the piece of wood into four identical pieces. What is the percent of increase in the surface area of the wood?

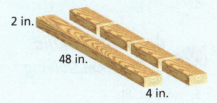

about 8%

Self-Assessment
for Problem Solving

9. a. 6 m
   b. 2 m^2
   c. 24 m^3

10. no; *Sample answer:* The distances from the center of the cross section to the edge of the tree trunk are not the same.

Learning Target

Describe the cross sections of a solid.

Success Criteria

- Explain the meaning of a cross section.
- Describe cross sections of prisms and pyramids.
- Describe cross sections of cylinders and cones.

T-680

Review & Refresh

1. $37\frac{1}{3}$ in.^{3}
2. $61\frac{1}{3}$ cm^3
3. $-5w - 12$
4. $4b + 14$

Concepts, Skills, & Problem Solving

5. not possible
6. possible
7. possible
8. possible
9. possible
10. not possible
11. rectangle
12. triangle
13. triangle
14. rectangle
15. circle
16. circle

Assignment Guide and Concept Check

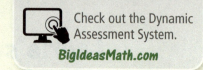

Scaffold assignments to support all students in their learning progression. The suggested assignments are a starting point. Continue to assign additional exercises and revisit with spaced practice to move every student toward proficiency.

Level	Assignment 1	Assignment 2
Emerging	1, 2, 4, 5, 6, 7, 8, 9, 10, 11, 12, 15, 17	13, 14, 16, 18, 19, 20, 21, 22, 25, 26
Proficient	1, 2, 4, 5, 6, 7, 8, 9, 10, 12, 14, 15, 16, 17	18, 19, 20, 21, 22, 23, 24, 25, 26
Advanced	1, 2, 4, 5, 6, 7, 8, 9, 10, 12, 14, 15, 16, 17	19, 20, 21, 22, 23, 24, 25, 26, 27

- Assignment 1 is for use after students complete the Self-Assessment for Concepts & Skills.
- Assignment 2 is for use after students complete the Self-Assessment for Problem Solving.
- The red exercises can be used as a concept check.

Review & Refresh Prior Skills

Exercises 1 and 2 Finding the Volume of a Pyramid
Exercises 3 and 4 Adding Linear Expressions

Common Errors

- **Exercises 11–16** Students may describe a three-dimensional figure that results from the intersection of the plane and the solid instead of the cross section. Remind students that a cross section is a two-dimensional shape.

E.6 Practice

Review & Refresh

Find the volume of the pyramid.

1.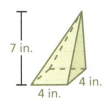

2.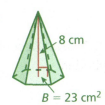

Find the sum.

3. $(w - 7) + (-6w - 5)$

4. $(8 - b) + (5b + 6)$

Concepts, Skills, & Problem Solving

DESCRIBING CROSS SECTIONS Determine whether it is possible to obtain the cross section from a cube. *(See Exploration 2, p. 677.)*

5. circle
6. square
7. equilateral triangle
8. pentagon
9. non-rectangular parallelogram
10. octagon

DESCRIBING CROSS SECTIONS OF PRISMS AND PYRAMIDS Describe the intersection of the plane and the solid.

11.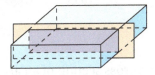

12.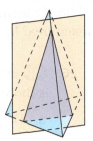

13.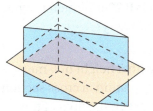

14.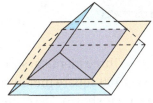

DESCRIBING CROSS SECTIONS OF CYLINDERS AND CONES Describe the intersection of the plane and the solid.

15.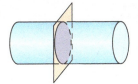

16.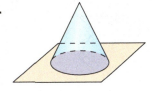

Section E.6 Cross Sections of Three-Dimensional Figures

DESCRIBING CROSS SECTIONS Describe the shape that is formed by the cut in the food.

17.

18.

19.

20. **DESCRIBING CROSS SECTIONS** Describe the intersection of the plane and the cylinder.

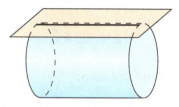

MP REASONING Determine whether the given intersection is possible. If so, draw the solid and the cross section.

21. The intersection of a plane and a cone is a rectangle.

22. The intersection of a plane and a square pyramid is a triangle.

23. **MP REASONING** A plane that intersects a prism is parallel to the bases of the prism. Describe the intersection of the plane and the prism.

24. **MP REASONING** Explain how a plane can be parallel to the base of a cone and intersect the cone at exactly one point.

25. **MP MODELING REAL LIFE** An artist plans to paint bricks.

    a. Find the surface area of the brick.

    b. The artist cuts along the length of the brick to form two bricks, each with a width of 2 inches. What is the percent of increase in the surface area? Justify your answer.

26. **MP MODELING REAL LIFE** A cross section of an artery is shown.

    a. Describe the cross section of the artery.

    b. The radius of the artery is 0.22 millimeter. What is the circumference of the artery?

27. **MP REASONING** Three identical square pyramids each with a height of h meters and a base area of 100 square meters are shown. For each pyramid, a cross section parallel to the base is shown. Describe the relationship between the area of the base and the area of any cross section parallel to the base.

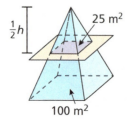
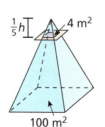
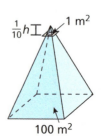

Common Errors

- **Exercises 17–19** Students may describe a three-dimensional figure instead of the cross section. Remind students that a cross section is a two-dimensional shape.

Mini-Assessment

Describe the intersection of the plane and the solid.

1.
   a triangle

2.
   a point

3. a rectangle

4. A cross section of a log is shown.

   a. Describe the cross section of the log.
      a circle
   b. What is the circumference of the log?
      about 47.1 in.

Section Resources

Surface Level	Deep Level
Resources by Chapter • Extra Practice • Reteach • Puzzle Time Student Journal • Self-Assessment • Practice Differentiating the Lesson Tutorial Videos Skills Review Handbook Skills Trainer	Resources by Chapter • Enrichment and Extension Graphic Organizers Dynamic Assessment System • Section Practice
Transfer Level	
Dynamic Assessment System • End-of-Chapter Quiz	Assessment Book • End-of-Chapter Quiz

Concepts, Skills, & Problem Solving

17. circle
18. rectangle
19. circle
20. line segment
21. not possible
22. possible; *Sample answer:*

23. The intersection is the shape of the base.
24. The intersection occurs at the vertex of the cone.
25. a. 164 in.²
    b. about 37%;
       Brick before cut:
       $S = 2(10 \cdot 4) + 2(10 \cdot 3) + 2(4 \cdot 3) = 164$ in.²
       Bricks after cut:
       $S = 2[2(10 \cdot 2) + 2(10 \cdot 3) + 2(2 \cdot 3)] = 224$ in.²
       $\frac{224 - 164}{164} = \frac{60}{164} \approx 0.37$ or 37%
26. a. circle
    b. about 1.38 mm
27. *Sample answer:* The area of a cross section is the square of the coefficient of h times the area of the base.

Skills Needed

Exercise 1
- Finding a Selling Price
- Finding the Volume of a Prism
- Using Conversion Factors

Exercise 2
- Converting Measures
- Finding the Volume of a Pyramid
- Writing and Solving an Equation

Exercise 3
- Finding Lateral Surface Area of a Cylinder
- Writing and Solving a Proportion

ELL Support

Many ELLs are more familiar with metric measurements than with U.S. standard measurements. Explain that pounds measure weight and cubic feet describe volume. You may want to review the relationships of some of these measurements, such as there are 16 ounces in a pound, there are 12 inches in 1 foot, and there are 3 feet in 1 yard.

Using the Problem-Solving Plan

1. $6.50

2. See Additional Answers.

3. 5 cm; The original lateral surface area is 63π cm^2, so $63\pi = 2\pi r(7)$, and $r = 4.5$ cm. The new lateral surface area is 45π cm^2, so $45\pi = 2\pi(4.5)h$, and $h = 5$ cm.

Performance Task

The *STEAM Video Performance Task* provides the opportunity for additional enrichment and greater depth of knowledge as students explore the mathematics of the chapter within a context tied to the chapter STEAM Video. The performance task and a detailed scoring rubric are provided at *BigIdeasMath.com*.

Laurie's Notes

Scaffolding Instruction

- The goal of this lesson is to help students become more comfortable with problem solving. These exercises combine finding surface areas and volumes of three-dimensional figures with prior skills from other chapters and courses. The solution for Exercise 1 is worked out below, to help you guide students through the problem-solving plan. Use the remaining class time to have students work on the other exercises.
- **Emerging:** The goal for these students is to feel comfortable with the problem-solving plan. Allow students to work in pairs to write the beginning steps of the problem-solving plan for Exercise 2. Keep in mind that some students may only be ready to do the first step.
- **Proficient:** Students may be able to work independently or in pairs to complete Exercises 2 and 3.
- Visit each pair to review their plan for each problem. Ask students to describe their plans.

▶ Using the Problem-Solving Plan

Exercise 1

▷ **Understand the problem.** You are given the dimensions of a container of popcorn kernels and the price that a store pays for the kernels. You also know the weight of one cubic foot of popcorn kernels. You are asked to find the selling price of the container when the markup is 30%.

▷ **Make a plan.** Use the volume of the container to find the weight of the kernels. Then use the weight of the kernels to find the cost to the store. Finally, use the percent markup to find the selling price of the container.

▷ **Solve and check.** Use the plan to solve the problem. Then check your solution.

- Use the volume of the container (in cubic feet) to find the weight of the kernels.

$$
\begin{aligned}
V &= Bh & &\text{Write the formula for volume.} \\
&= 4(4) \cdot 6 & &\text{Substitute.} \\
&= 16 \cdot 6 & &\text{Simplify.} \\
&= 96 & &\text{Multiply.}
\end{aligned}
$$

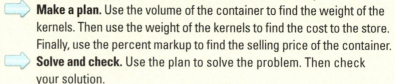

So, the kernels in the container weigh 2.5 pounds.

- Find the cost to the store.

$$\text{cost to store} = 2.5 \text{ lb} \times \frac{\$2}{1 \text{ lb}} = \$5$$

- Use the percent markup to find the selling price of the container.

$$
\begin{aligned}
a &= p\% \cdot w & &\text{Selling price} = \text{Cost to store} + \text{Markup} \\
a &= 0.30 \cdot 5 & &\phantom{\text{Selling price}} = \phantom{\text{Cost to store}} 5 + 1.5 \\
a &= 1.5 & &\phantom{\text{Selling price}} = 6.5
\end{aligned}
$$

So, the selling price of the container is $6.50.

- **Check:** Verify that the markup is 30%.

$$\text{percent markup} = \frac{6.5 - 5}{5} = \frac{1.5}{5} = 0.3, \text{ or } 30\% \checkmark$$

T-683

Connecting Concepts

▶ Using the Problem-Solving Plan

1. A store pays $2 per pound for popcorn kernels. One cubic foot of kernels weighs about 45 pounds. What is the selling price of the container shown when the markup is 30%?

Understand the problem. You are given the dimensions of a container of popcorn kernels and the price that a store pays for the kernels. You also know the weight of one cubic foot of popcorn kernels. You are asked to find the selling price of the container when the markup is 30%.

Make a plan. Use the volume of the container to find the weight of the kernels. Then use the weight of the kernels to find the cost to the store. Finally, use the percent markup to find the selling price of the container.

Solve and check. Use the plan to solve the problem. Then check your solution.

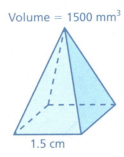

2. The pyramid shown has a square base. What is the height of the pyramid? Justify your answer.

3. A cylindrical can of soup has a height of 7 centimeters and a lateral surface area of 63π square centimeters. The can is redesigned to have a lateral surface area of 45π square centimeters without changing the radius of the can. What is the height of the new design? Justify your answer.

Performance Task

Volumes and Surface Areas of Small Objects

At the beginning of this chapter, you watched a STEAM Video called "Paper Measurements." You are now ready to complete the performance task related to this video, available at *BigIdeasMath.com*. Be sure to use the problem-solving plan as you work through the performance task.

E Chapter Review

Go to BigIdeasMath.com to download blank graphic organizers.

▶ Review Vocabulary

Write the definition and give an example of each vocabulary term.

lateral surface area, *p. 650*
regular pyramid, *p. 660*
slant height, *p. 660*
cross section, *p. 678*

▶ Graphic Organizers

You can use an **Information Frame** to help organize and remember a concept. Here is an example of an Information Frame for *Surface Areas of Rectangular Prisms*.

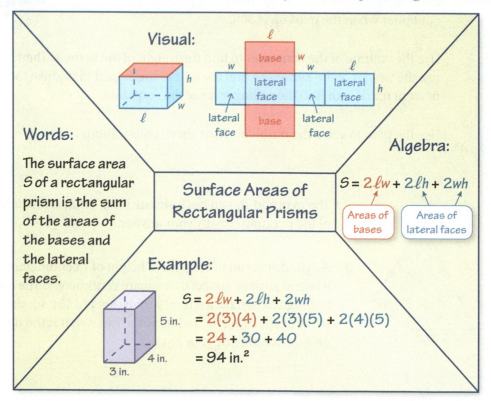

Choose and complete a graphic organizer to help you study the concept.

1. surface areas of prisms
2. surface areas of cylinders
3. surface areas of pyramids
4. volumes of prisms
5. volumes of pyramids
6. cross sections of three-dimensional figures

"I'm having trouble thinking of a good title for my **Information Frame**."

684 Chapter E   Surface Area and Volume

Review Vocabulary

- As a review of the chapter vocabulary, have students revisit the vocabulary section in their *Student Journals* to fill in any missing definitions and record examples of each term.

Graphic Organizers

Sample answers:

1.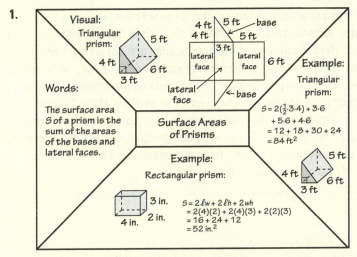

2.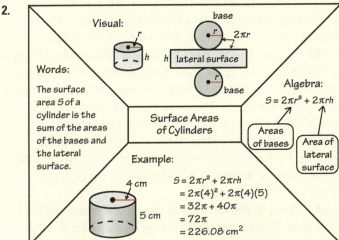

3.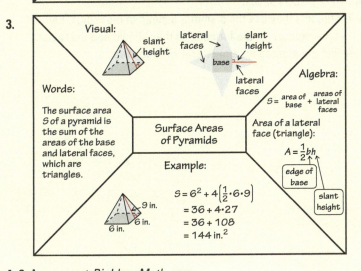

4–6. Answers at *BigIdeasMath.com*.

List of Organizers

Available at *BigIdeasMath.com*
Definition and Example Chart
Example and Non-Example Chart
Four Square
Information Frame
Summary Triangle

About this Organizer

An **Information Frame** can be used to help students organize and remember concepts. Students write the concept in the middle rectangle. Then students write related categories in the spaces around the rectangle. Related categories may include: words, numbers, algebra, example, definition, non-example, visual, procedure, details, or vocabulary. Students can place their Information Frames on note cards to use as a quick study reference.

Chapter Self-Assessment

1. 158 in.²
2. 400 cm²
3. 108 m²
4. yes; The surface area of the box is 4180 cm², and the area that the wrapping paper can cover is 4256 cm².
5. 25 in.²
6. about 169.6 yd²; about 113.0 yd²
7. about 34.2 cm²; about 30.1 cm²
8. about 100.48 cm²

Chapter Self-Assessment

The Success Criteria Self-Assessment chart can be found in the *Student Journal* or online at *BigIdeasMath.com*.

ELL Support

Allow students extra support and the chance to practice language by working in pairs to complete the first section of the Chapter Self-Assessment. Remind students to use square units of measurement when writing area answers. Monitor discussions and provide support. Once pairs are finished, have each pair display their answers on a whiteboard for your review. Adjust and use similar techniques for all sections of the Chapter Self-Assessment. As a comprehension check, have each pair present their explanations to another pair. Then have each group of four ask and answer questions to clarify understanding. You may want to discuss some of the answers with the entire class for further review.

Common Errors

- **Exercise 1** Students may find the area of only three of the faces instead of all six. Remind students that each face is paired with another. Show students the net of a rectangular solid to remind them of the six faces.
- **Exercises 2 and 3** Students may try to use the formula for a rectangular prism to find the surface area of a triangular prism. Show them that this will not work by focusing on the area of the triangular base. For students who are struggling to identify all the faces, draw a net of the prism and tell them to label the length, width, and height of each part before finding the surface area.
- **Exercises 6 and 7** Students may multiply the height by the area of the circular base instead of the circumference. Review with students how the lateral surface is created to show that the length of the rectangle is the circumference of the circular bases.
- **Exercises 6 and 7** When finding the surface area, students may add the area of only one base. Remind students of the net for a cylinder and that there are two circles as bases.
- **Exercise 7** Students may use the diameter instead of the radius. Remind students that the radius is in the formula, so they should find the radius before they find the surface area or lateral surface area.

Chapter Self-Assessment

As you complete the exercises, use the scale below to rate your understanding of the success criteria in your journal.

1	2	3	4
I do not understand.	I can do it with help.	I can do it on my own.	I can teach someone else.

E.1 Surface Areas of Prisms (pp. 647–652)

Learning Target: Find the surface area of a prism.

Find the surface area of the prism.

1.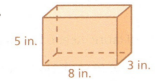
2.
3.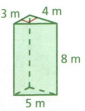

4. You want to wrap the box using a piece of wrapping paper that is 76 centimeters long by 56 centimeters wide. Do you have enough wrapping paper to wrap the box? Explain.

5. To finish a project, you need to paint the lateral surfaces of a cube with side length 2.5 inches. Find the area that you need to paint.

E.2 Surface Areas of Cylinders (pp. 653–658)

Learning Target: Find the surface area of a cylinder.

Find the surface area and lateral surface area of the cylinder. Round your answers to the nearest tenth.

6.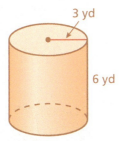
7.

8. The label covers the entire lateral surface area of the can. How much of the can is *not* covered by the label?

Chapter Review   685

E.3 Surface Areas of Pyramids (pp. 659–664)

Learning Target: Find the surface area of a pyramid.

Find the surface area of the regular pyramid.

9.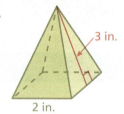

10.

11.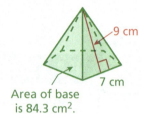

12. The tent is shaped like a square pyramid. There is no fabric covering the ground.

  a. Estimate the amount of fabric needed to make the tent.

  b. Fabric costs $5.25 per square yard. How much will it cost to make the tent?

E.4 Volumes of Prisms (pp. 665–670)

Learning Target: Find the volume of a prism.

Find the volume of the prism.

13.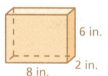

14.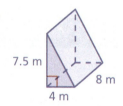

15.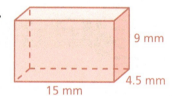

16.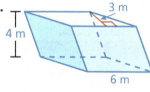

17.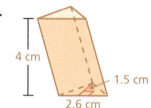

18.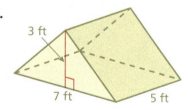

19. Two cereal boxes each hold exactly 192 cubic inches of cereal. Which box should a manufacturer choose to minimize the amount of cardboard needed to make the cereal boxes?

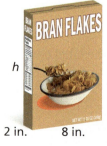

686 Chapter E Surface Area and Volume

Common Errors

- **Exercises 9–11** Students may forget to include the area of the base when finding the surface area. Remind students that when asked to find the surface area, the base is included.
- **Exercises 9–11** Students may add the wrong number of lateral face areas to the area of the base. Examine several different pyramids with different bases and ask if they can find a relationship between the number of sides of the base and the number of lateral faces. (They are the same.) Remind students that the number of sides of the base determines how many triangles make up the lateral surface area.
- **Exercises 13–18** Students may write the units incorrectly, often writing square units instead of cubic units. Remind students that they are working in three dimensions, so the units are cubed.

Chapter Self-Assessment

9. 16 in.^2
10. 147.6 m^2
11. 241.8 cm^2
12. **a.** 36 ft^2 or 4 yd^2
    b. $21
13. 96 in.^3
14. 120 m^3
15. 607.5 mm^3
16. 72 m^3
17. 7.8 cm^3
18. 52.5 ft^3
19. the box on the right

T-686

Chapter Self-Assessment

20. 850 ft^3

21. 2100 in.^{3}

22. 192 mm^3

23. a. 10,666.7 ft^3
    b. about 58,666.7 ft^3

24. a. 12.25 in.^{3}
    b. top: $2\frac{1}{3}$ in.^{3},
       bottom: $9\frac{11}{12}$ in.^{3}

25. rectangle

26. triangle

27.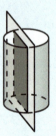

28.

29.

Common Errors

- **Exercises 20–24** Students may write the units incorrectly, often writing square units instead of cubic units. This is especially true when the area of the base is given. Remind students that the units are cubed because there are three dimensions.

- **Exercises 25 and 26** Students may describe a three-dimensional figure that results from the intersection of the plane and the solid instead of the cross section. Remind students that a cross section is a two-dimensional shape.

Chapter Resources

Surface Level	Deep Level
Resources by Chapter • Extra Practice • Reteach • Puzzle Time Student Journal • Practice • Chapter Self-Assessment Differentiating the Lesson Tutorial Videos Skills Review Handbook Skills Trainer Game Library	Resources by Chapter • Enrichment and Extension Graphic Organizers Game Library
Transfer Level	
STEAM Video Dynamic Assessment System • Chapter Test	Assessment Book • Chapter Tests A and B • Alternative Assessment • STEAM Performance Task

E.5 Volumes of Pyramids (pp. 671–676)

Learning Target: Find the volume of a pyramid.

Find the volume of the pyramid.

20.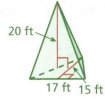
20 ft, 17 ft, 15 ft

21.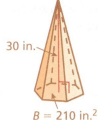
30 in., $B = 210$ in.²

22.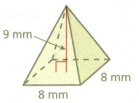
9 mm, 8 mm, 8 mm

20 ft, 30 ft, 40 ft, 40 ft

23. A pyramid-shaped hip roof is a good choice for a house in an area with many hurricanes.

   a. What is the volume of the roof to the nearest tenth of a foot?

   b. What is the volume of the entire house, including the roof?

24. A laboratory creates calcite crystals for use in the study of light. The crystal is made up of two pieces of calcite that form a square pyramid. The base length of the top piece is 2 inches.

   a. Find the volume of the entire pyramid.

   b. Find the volume of each piece of the pyramid.

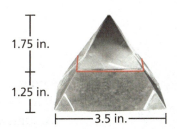
1.75 in., 1.25 in., 3.5 in.

E.6 Cross Sections of Three-Dimensional Figures (pp. 677–682)

Learning Target: Describe the cross sections of a solid.

Describe the intersection of the plane and the solid.

25.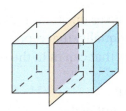

26.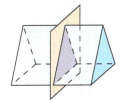

Sketch how a plane can intersect with a cylinder to form a cross section of the given shape.

27. rectangle

28. circle

29. line segment

Chapter Review 687

Practice Test

Find the surface area of the prism or regular pyramid.

1.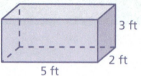
2.
3.

Find the surface area and lateral surface area of the cylinder. Round your answers to the nearest tenth.

4.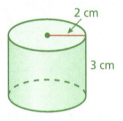
5.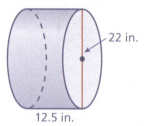

Find the volume of the solid.

6.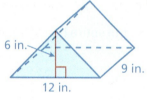
7.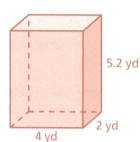
8.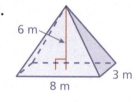

9. A quart of paint covers 80 square feet. How many quarts should you buy to paint the ramp with two coats? (Assume you will not paint the bottom of the ramp.)

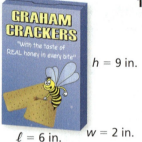

10. A manufacturer wants to double the volume of the graham cracker box. The manufacturer will either double the height or double the width.

    a. What is the volume of the new graham cracker box?

    b. Which option uses less cardboard? Justify your answer.

    c. A graham cracker takes up about 1.5 cubic inches of space. Write an inequality that represents the numbers of graham crackers that can fit in the new box.

11. The label on the can of soup covers about 354.2 square centimeters. What is the height of the can? Round your answer to the nearest whole number.

12. A lumberjack splits the cylindrical log from top to bottom with an ax, dividing it in half. Describe the shape that is formed by the cut.

Practice Test Item References

Practice Test Questions	Section to Review
1, 9, 10	E.1
4, 5, 11	E.2
2, 3	E.3
6, 7, 10	E.4
8	E.5
12	E.6

Test-Taking Strategies

Remind students to quickly look over the entire test before they start so that they can budget their time. This test is very visual and requires that students remember many terms. It might be helpful for them to jot down some of the terms on the back of the test before they start. Have them use the **Stop** and **Think** strategy before they write their answers.

Common Errors

- **Exercise 1** Students may find the area of only three of the faces instead of all six. Remind students that each face is paired with another. Show students the net of a rectangular solid to remind them of the six faces.
- **Exercises 4 and 5** Students may multiply the height by the area of the circular base instead of the circumference. Review with students how the lateral surface is created to show that the length of the rectangle is the circumference of the circular bases.
- **Exercises 4 and 5** When finding the surface area, students may add the area of only one base. Remind students of the net for a cylinder and that there are two circles as bases.
- **Exercise 5** Students may use the diameter instead of the radius. Remind students that the radius is in the formula, so they should find the radius before they find the surface area or lateral surface area.
- **Exercises 6–8** Students may write the units incorrectly, often writing square units instead of cubic units. Remind students that they are working in three dimensions, so the units are cubed.

Practice Test

1. 62 ft^2
2. 5 in.^2
3. 299.8 m^2
4. about 62.8 cm^2; about 37.7 cm^2
5. about 1623.4 in.^2; about 863.5 in.^2
6. 324 in.^3
7. 41.6 yd^3
8. 48 m^3
9. 13 quarts of paint
10. a. 216 in.^3
    b. doubling the width; When $h = 18$, $w = 2$, and $\ell = 6$, $S = 312 \text{ in.}^2$. When $h = 9$, $w = 4$, and $\ell = 6$, $S = 228 \text{ in.}^2$.
    c. $1.5x \leq 216$
11. 12 cm
12. rectangle

Test-Taking Strategies
Available at *BigIdeasMath.com*
After Answering Easy Questions, Relax
Answer Easy Questions First
Estimate the Answer
Read All Choices before Answering
Read Question before Answering
Solve Directly or Eliminate Choices
Solve Problem before Looking at Choices
Use Intelligent Guessing
Work Backwards

About this Strategy
When taking a multiple-choice test, be sure to read each question carefully and thoroughly. After skimming the test and answering the easy questions, stop for a few seconds, take a deep breath, and relax. Work through the remaining questions carefully, using your knowledge and test-taking strategies. Remember, you already completed many of the questions on the test!

Cumulative Practice
1. D
2. 152
3. G

Item Analysis
1. A. The student multiplies the length and height and adds the width.
   B. The student adds the areas of only three unique faces.
   C. The student multiplies the length, width, and height.
   D. Correct answer
2. **Gridded Response:** Correct answer: 152

   Common error: The student only finds the loss and gets 8.
3. F. The student finds how far the tip of the hour hand will travel in 1 hour instead of 2 hours.
   G. Correct answer
   H. The student does not multiply the radius by 2 to find the circumference and then uses the incorrect circumference to find how far the tip of the hour hand will travel in 12 hours.
   I. The student finds how far the tip of the hour hand will travel in 12 hours.

Cumulative Practice

1. A gift box and its dimensions are shown.

   What is the least amount of wrapping paper that you need to wrap the box?

   A. 20 in.² **B.** 56 in.²

   C. 64 in.² **D.** 112 in.²

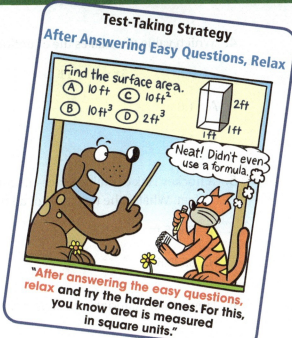

2. James is getting ready for wrestling season. As part of his preparation, he plans to lose 5% of his body weight. James currently weighs 160 pounds. How much will he weigh, in pounds, after he loses 5% of his weight?

3. How far will the tip of the hour hand of the clock travel in 2 hours? (Use $\frac{22}{7}$ for π.)

   F. 44 mm **G.** 88 mm

   H. 264 mm **I.** 528 mm

Cumulative Practice **689**

4. Which value of x makes the equation true?

$$5x - 3 = 11$$

   A. 1.6
   B. 2.8
   C. 40
   D. 70

5. A hockey rink contains 5 face-off circles. Each of these circles has a radius of 15 feet. What is the total area of all the face-off circles? (Use 3.14 for π.)

   F. 706.5 ft²
   G. 2826 ft²
   H. 3532.5 ft²
   I. 14,130 ft²

6. How much material is needed to make the popcorn container?

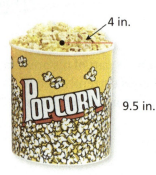

   A. 76π in.²
   B. 84π in.²
   C. 92π in.²
   D. 108π in.²

7. What is the surface area of the square pyramid?

   F. 24 in.²
   G. 96 in.²
   H. 132 in.²
   I. 228 in.²

Item Analysis (continued)

4. **A.** The student subtracts 3 from 11 instead of adding.
   B. Correct answer
   C. The student subtracts 3 from 11 instead of adding and then multiplies instead of dividing.
   D. The student multiplies instead of dividing.

5. **F.** The student finds the area of only one circle.
   G. The student uses the diameter of the circle instead of the radius, finding $\pi \cdot 30^2$ for the area and only finds the area of one circle.
   H. Correct answer
   I. The student uses the diameters of the circles instead of the radii, finding $\pi \cdot 30^2$ for the area each of the circles.

6. **A.** The student only calculates the lateral surface area.
   B. The student doubles the radius instead of squaring it when finding the area of the base.
   C. Correct answer
   D. The student includes the area of both bases instead of just one base.

7. **F.** The student finds the area of one lateral face.
   G. The student finds the lateral surface area.
   H. Correct answer
   I. The student forgets to multiply by $\frac{1}{2}$ when finding the area of each triangular lateral face.

Cumulative Practice

4. B
5. H
6. C
7. H

Cumulative Practice

8. 648
9. A
10. H
11. *Part A*

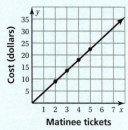

Part B 4.5; The cost of 1 movie ticket is $4.50.

Part C $36

Item Analysis (continued)

8. **Gridded Response:** Correct answer: 648

   Common error: The student does not read the entire question and finds the volume of the original rectangular prism, getting an answer of 24.

9. **A.** Correct answer
   B. The student solves $2x + 4 = 90$.
   C. The student subtracts 46 from 90.
   D. The student solves $2x + 4 + 46 = 180$.

10. **F.** The student does not realize that the sum of the angle measures of a triangle cannot be less than 180°.
    G. The student does not realize that the sum of the angle measures of a triangle cannot be greater than 180°.
    H. Correct answer
    I. The student does not realize that a triangle cannot have an angle with a measure of 0°.

11. **2 points** The student's work and explanations demonstrate a thorough understanding of graphing data points and finding the constant of proportionality. In Part A, the student correctly plots the points and graphs $y = 4.5x$, for $x \geq 0$. In Part B, the student correctly determines that the constant of proportionality is 4.5 and that it costs $4.50 per matinee ticket. In Part C, the student correctly determines that it costs $36 to buy 8 matinee tickets. The student provides clear and complete work and explanations.

    1 point The student's work and explanations demonstrate a partial but limited understanding of graphing data points and finding the constant of proportionality. The student provides some correct work and/or explanation.

    0 points The student provides no response, a completely incorrect or incomprehensible response, or a response that demonstrates insufficient understanding of graphing data points and finding the constant of proportionality.

8. A rectangular prism and its dimensions are shown.

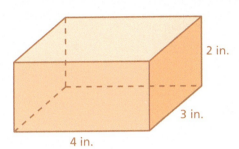

What is the volume, in cubic inches, of a rectangular prism whose dimensions are three times greater?

9. What is the value of x?

    A. 20
    B. 43
    C. 44
    D. 65

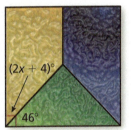

10. Which of the following are possible angle measures of a triangle?

    F. 60°, 50°, 20°
    G. 40°, 80°, 90°
    H. 30°, 60°, 90°
    I. 0°, 90°, 90°

11. The table shows the costs of buying matinee movie tickets.

Matinee Tickets, x	2	3	4	5
Cost, y	$9	$13.50	$18	$22.50

Part A Graph the data.

Part B Find and interpret the constant of proportionality for the graph of the line.

Part C How much does it cost to buy 8 matinee movie tickets?

Additional Answers

Chapter A

Section A.1
Exploration 1

a. *Sample answer:* Adding or subtracting the same number on both sides of the equation produces equivalent expressions; yes; Adding or subtracting any value on both sides of an equation produces equivalent expressions.

b. $x - 3 = -4$; *Sample answer:* Add three $+1$ tiles to each side; $x = -1$
$-5 = x + 2$; Add two -1 tiles to each side; $x = -7$
$x - 3 = 3$; Add three $+1$ tiles to each side; $x = 6$
$5 = x - 2$; Add two $+1$ tiles to each side; $x = 7$

Section A.2
Exploration 1

b. $8 = 4x$; Divide the eight $+1$ tiles into 4 equal groups; $x = 2$

$6x = -12$; Divide the twelve -1 tiles into 6 equal groups; $x = -2$

$-3x = -9$; Divide the nine -1 tiles into 3 equal groups, then add a $+$ variable and three $+1$ tiles to each side; $x = 3$

Section A.4
Self-Assessment for Problem Solving

11. $j \geq 2$

$p \geq 25$

$n \geq 10$

Sample answer: jog for 3 kilometers, perform 30 push-ups, perform 13 pull-ups

Section A.5
Self-Assessment for Problem Solving

13.

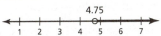

Sample answer: The volcanologist has 665 more feet to climb in 140 minutes.

Concepts, Skills, & Problem Solving

21. $z \geq 3.1$

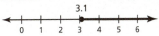

22. $-2.8 < d$

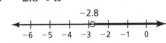

23. $-\dfrac{4}{5} > s$

24. $\dfrac{3}{4} \geq m$

25. $r < -0.9$

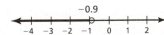

26. $h \leq -2.4$

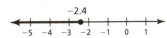

Section A.6
Exploration 1

c. When $a > 0$, divide both sides by a. When $a < 0$, divide both sides by a and reverse the inequality symbol.

Concepts, Skills, & Problem Solving

18. $x \leq -\dfrac{5}{12}$

19. $y \leq -3$

20. $b < 48.59$

Section A.7
Concepts, Skills, & Problem Solving

15. $g > -1$

Additional Answers A1

16. $w \leq 3$

17. $k \geq -18$

18. $d > -9$

19. $n < -0.6$

20. $c \geq -1.95$

Chapter B

Section B.1
Exploration 1
a. Spinner 1: more likely: 1, 5, 6, less likely: 2, 3, 4; The numbers 1, 5, and 6 have a greater area than the numbers 2, 3, and 4, so you are more likely to spin them.

On Spinner 2, all numbers have the same area, so you are equally likely to spin each number.

c. *Sample answer:* Use the area from the spinner that each number occupies and divide that area by the area of the entire spinner. Turning this decimal into a percent can be used to describe the likelihood of spinning each number.

Section B.2
Exploration 1
b. Answers will vary. The results for flipping the quarter should be close to equal numbers of heads and tails. The results for the thumbtack will vary.

c. Answers will vary. The prediction for the quarter should be close to 500, using the results from part (b). The prediction for the thumbtack should use the result from part (b) to find the number.

d. yes; The results of flipping a quarter tend to be 50% heads and 50% tails, so you can use a uniform probability model for flipping the quarter.

Section B.3
Exploration 1
e. The lock in part (c) is most difficult to guess because it has the greatest number of possible combinations compared to the other two locks.

Section B.4
Exploration 1
c. $\frac{13}{30}$, or $43.\overline{3}\%$; $\frac{1}{6}$, or $16.\overline{6}\%$; $\frac{5}{6}$, or $83.\overline{3}\%$; $\frac{7}{10}$, or 70%

d. *Sample answer:* Randomly generate 30 numbers from 0 to 9999. Let 0–5 represent made shots and 6–9 represent missed shots.

Try It
2. Answers will vary, but the theoretical probability is $\frac{343}{1000}$, 0.343, or 34.3%.

Self-Assessment for Concepts & Skills
3. Answers will vary, but the theoretical probability is $\frac{1}{625}$, 0.0016, or 0.16%.

4. Answers will vary, but the theoretical probability is $\frac{9}{50}$, 0.18, or 18%.

Chapter B Using the Problem-Solving Plan
3. $\frac{8}{25}$, or 32%; *Sample answer:* The table below represents the sample space of the problem.

×	−2	−1	0	1	2
−2	4	2	0	−2	−4
−1	2	1	0	−1	−2
0	0	0	0	0	0
1	−2	−1	0	1	2
2	−4	−2	0	2	4

Total outcomes = 25
Number of favorable outcomes = 8
$P(\text{product of titles selected} > 0) = \frac{8}{25}$

Chapter C

Section C.1
Exploration 1
c. *Sample answer:* The first sample is not random, but the second sample is random; no; In the first sample, students selected are more likely to choose band due to already being a band member. In the second sample, $\frac{1}{10}$ of the students in the random sample chose glee club, so the conclusion that 10% of the students in your school chose glee club is valid.

d. *Sample answer:* What percent of students in your school like math?; Sample every tenth student who enters the school on a given day.

Section C.3
Exploration 1
a. yes; *Sample answer:* The data set for female students completely overlaps the data set for male students.

yes; *Sample answer:* The data sets for male and female students partially overlap.

no; The oldest person in the 8 P.M. class is 40. The youngest person in the 10:00 A.M. class is 42.

Self-Assessment for Concepts & Skills
5. MAD of the second data set; *Sample answer:* When comparing two skewed distributions, use the median and the IQR.

Self-Assessment for Problem Solving
7. *Sample answer:*

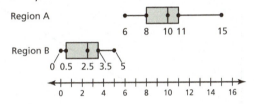

Section C.4
Exploration 1
a. male students: median = 2.5, IQR = 4
female students: median = 3, IQR = 4
The female students had a greater median homework time than the male students. The variation in the time spent on homework was the same for both male and female students.

d. female students spend more time on homework each week than male students; *Sample answer:* 75% of female students spend more than 3.5 hours on homework. Only 25% of male students spend more than 3.5 hours on homework.

e. *Sample answer:* If your sample size is too small, take multiple random samples so that you can compare two populations.

Chapter D
Chapter Exploration
1.

Sides	Large Perimeter	Diameter of Circle	Small Perimeter
6	120 mm	35 mm	108 mm
8	120 mm	35 mm	104 mm
10	110 mm	35 mm	110 mm

Large Perimeter / Diameter	Small Perimeter / Diameter	Average of Ratios
$\frac{24}{7}$	$\frac{108}{35}$	$\frac{114}{35} \approx 3.26$
$\frac{24}{7}$	$\frac{104}{37}$	$\frac{16}{5} = 3.2$
$\frac{22}{7}$	$\frac{22}{7}$	$\frac{22}{7} \approx 3.14$

Section D.1
Exploration 1
b. about 12.5 in.; *Sample answer:* The circumference of the circle was estimated to be a little over 3 times the length of the diameter.

Exploration 2
c. *Sample answer:* All students have the same ratio no matter what cylindrical object was used.

Section D.2
Concepts, Skills, & Problem Solving
25. circumference doubles and area quadruples; circumference triples and area is 9 times greater; double the radius: circumference = $2\pi(2r) = 4\pi r$,
$\frac{4\pi r}{2\pi r} = 2$ times larger, area = $\pi(2r)^2 = 4\pi r^2$,
$\frac{4\pi r^2}{\pi r^2} = 4$ times larger;

triple the radius: circumference = $2\pi(3r) = 6\pi r$,
$\frac{6\pi r}{2\pi r} = 3$ times larger, area = $\pi(3r)^2 = 9\pi r^2$,
$\frac{9\pi r^2}{\pi r^2} = 9$ times larger

Section D.4
Exploration 1

a. i.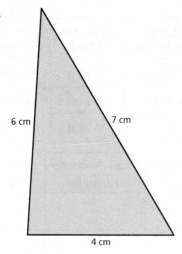
1 triangle

ii.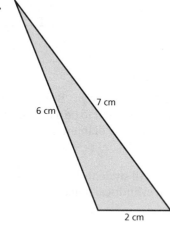
1 triangle

iii. none

iv. none

v. Sample answer:

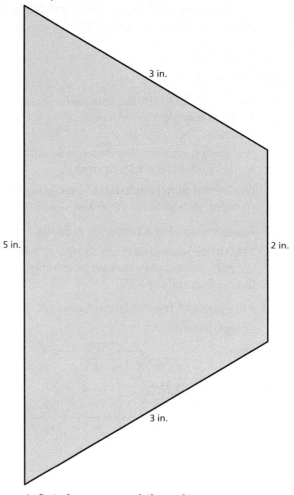

infinitely many quadrilaterals

vi. none

vii. Sample answer:

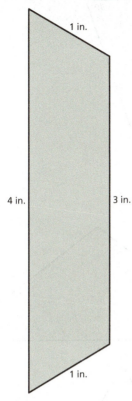

infinitely many quadrilaterals

viii.

infinitely many triangles

ix. none

x.

infinitely many triangles

xi. none   **xii.** none

xiii. Sample answer:

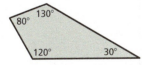

infinitely many quadrilaterals

xiv. Sample answer:

infinitely many quadrilaterals

b. when the sum of the angle measures is 180°; when the sum of the lengths of any two sides is greater than the length of the third side; Sample answer: All triangles that could be formed in part (a) follow these guidelines.

c. when the sum of the angle measures is 360°; when the sum of the lengths of any three sides is greater than the length of the fourth side; Sample answer: All quadrilaterals that could be formed in part (a) follow these guidelines.

Self-Assessment for Problem Solving

15. Sample answer:

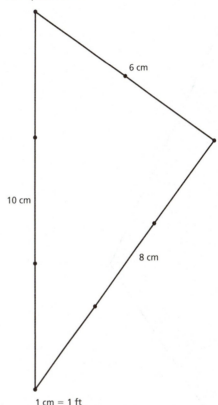

Concepts, Skills, & Problem Solving

8. Sample answer:

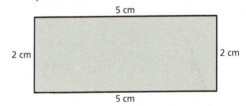

12.

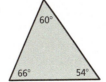

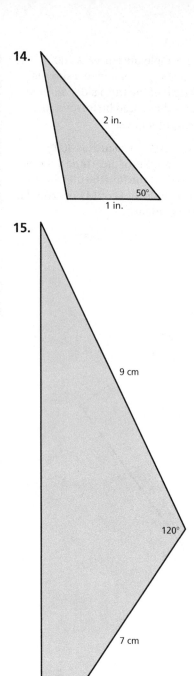
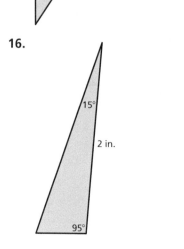
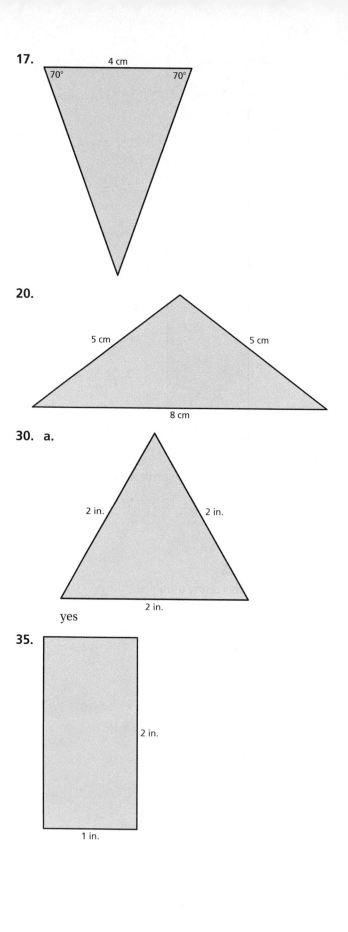

36.

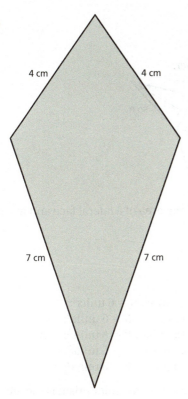

40. rhombus, square, parallelogram

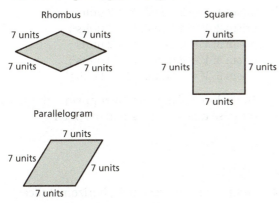

Section D.5
Exploration 1
a. ∠BAE and ∠BAC, ∠BAE and ∠EAD, ∠CAD and ∠BAC, ∠CAD and ∠EAD; *Sample answer:* All adjacent angles share a common side and have the same vertex.

c. $y = 155$; *Sample answer:* vertical angle to ∠BAC
$x = 25$; *Sample answer:* supplementary angle to ∠BAC
$z = 25$; *Sample answer:* Supplementary angle to ∠BAC

Review & Refresh
2.

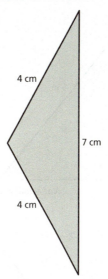

Concepts, Skills, & Problem Solving
6. ∠EAB and ∠BAC, ∠BAC and ∠CAD, ∠CAD and ∠DAE, ∠DAE and ∠EAB; *Sample answer:* All adjacent angles share a common side and have the same vertex.

7. ∠BAC and ∠EAD, ∠BAE and ∠CAD; *Sample answer:* All vertical angles are opposite angles formed by the intersection of two lines.

Chapter D Self-Assessment
20.

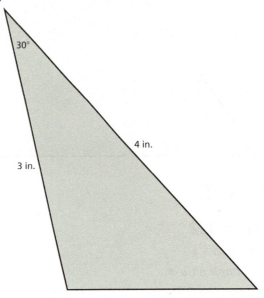

Additional Answers   **A7**

Chapter D Practice Test

6.

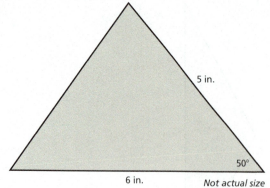

7.

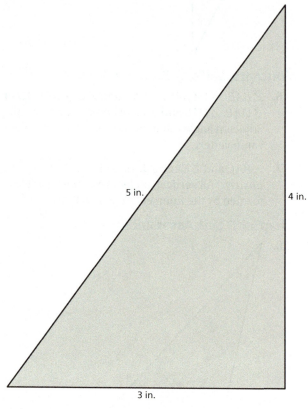

Chapter E

Section E.2
Exploration 1
a. *Sample answer:*

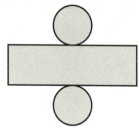

two circles and one rectangle

Section E.3
Exploration 1
c. *Sample answer:*

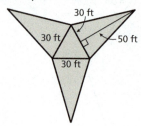

2250 ft^2; Find the area of a lateral face and multiply that by 3.

Section E.4
Exploration 1
a. prism 1: $V = 6$ units^3, $B = 6$ units^2;
prism 2: $V = 12$ units^3, $B = 6$ units^2;
prism 3: $V = 18$ units^3, $B = 6$ units^2;
prism 4: $V = 24$ units^3, $B = 6$ units^2;
prism 5: $V = 30$ units^3, $B = 6$ units^2;

The volume of the rectangular prism is the area of the base times the height of the prism.

b. prism 1: $V = 2$ units^3, $B = 2$ units^2;
prism 2: $V = 4$ units^3, $B = 2$ units^2;
prism 3: $V = 6$ units^3, $B = 2$ units^2;
prism 4: $V = 8$ units^3, $B = 2$ units^2;
prism 5: $V = 10$ units^3, $B = 2$ units^2;

The volume of the triangular prism is the area of the base times the height of the prism.

Section E.6
Exploration 1
e. *Sample answer:* rectangle, horizontal slice; triangle, vertical slice through top vertex; trapezoid, vertical slice not through top vertex; kite, diagonal slice through one of the bottom vertices; pentagon, diagonal slice through none of the vertices

Chapter E Using the Problem-Solving Plan
2. 20 mm or 2 cm;

$1.5 \text{ cm} = 15 \text{ mm}$

$V = \dfrac{1}{3}Bh$

$1500 = \dfrac{1}{3}(15 \cdot 15)h$

$1500 = 75h$

$20 = h$

English-Spanish Glossary

English | Spanish

A

adjacent angles *(p. 628)* Two angles that share a common side and have the same vertex

angle of rotation *(p. 56)* The number of degrees a figure rotates about a point

ángulos adyacentes *(p. 628)* Dos ángulos que tienen el vértice y un lado en común

ángulo de rotación *(p. 56)* El número de grados que gira una figura sobre un punto

B

base (of a power) *(p. 320)* The base of a power is the repeated factor.

biased sample *(p. 564)* A sample that is not representative of a population

base (de una potencia) *(p. 320)* La base de una potencia es el factor repetido.

muestra sesgada *(p. 564)* Una muestra que no es representiva de una población

C

center (of a circle) *(p. 600)* The point inside a circle that is the same distance from all points on the circle

center of dilation *(p. 70)* A point with respect to which a figure is dilated.

center of rotation *(p. 56)* The point about which a figure is rotated.

circle *(p. 600)* The set of all points in a plane that are the same distance from a point called the center

circumference *(p. 601)* The distance around a circle

complementary angles *(p. 628)* Two angles whose measures have a sum of 90°

composite figure *(p. 614)* A figure made up of triangles, squares, rectangles, and other two-dimensional figures

compound event *(p. 540)* A compound event consists of one or more events. The probability of a compound event is the quotient of the number of favorable outcomes and the number of possible outcomes.

centro (de un círculo) *(p. 600)* El punto dentro de un círculo que está a la misma distancia de todos los puntos en el círculo

centro de dilatación *(p. 70)* Un punto con respecto al cual se dilata una figura

centro de rotación *(p. 56)* El punto sobre del cualse rota una figura

círculo *(p. 600)* El conjunto de todos los puntos en un plano que están a la misma distancia de un punto llamado el centro

circunferencia *(p. 601)* La distancia alrededor de un círculo

ángulos complementarios *(p. 628)* Dos ángulos cuyas medidas tienen una suma de 90°

figura compuesta *(p. 614)* Una figura hecha de triángulos, cuadros, rectángulos, y otras figuras bidimensionales

evento compuesto *(p. 540)* Un evento compuesto consiste de uno o más eventos. La probabilidad de un evento compuesto es el cociente del número de resultados favorables y el número de resultados posibles.

cone *(p. 433)* A solid that has one circular base and one vertex

congruent angles *(p. 64)* Angles that have the same measure

congruent figures *(p. 64)* Figures that have the same size and the same shape

congruent sides *(p. 64)* Sides that have the same length

cross section *(p. 678)* The intersection of a plane and a solid

cube root *(p. 390)* A number that, when multiplied by itself, and then multiplied by itself again, equals a given number.

cono *(p. 433)* Un sólido que tiene una base circular y una vértice

ángulos congruentes *(p. 64)* Ángulos que miden lo mismo

figuras congruentes *(p. 64)* Figuras que tienen el mismo tamaño y la misma forma

lados congruentes *(p. 64)* Lados con la misma longitud

sección transversal *(p. 678)* La intersección de un plano y un sólido

raíz cúbica *(p. 390)* Un número que, al multiplicarse por sí mismo, y luego al multiplicarse de nuevo por sí mismo, es igual a un número dado

---

D

---

diameter *(p. 600)* The distance across a circle through the center

dilation *(p. 70)* A transformation in which a figure is made larger or smaller with respect to a fixed point called the center of dilation

diámetro *(p. 600)* La distancia a través de un círculo, pasando por el centro

dilatación *(p. 70)* Una transformación en la que una figura se hace más grande o más pequeña con respecto a un punto fijo llamado el centro de dilatación

---

E

---

equivalent equations *(p. 466)* Equations that have the same solutions

event *(p. 522)* A collection of one or more outcomes

experiment *(p. 522)* An investigation or a procedure that has varying results

experimental probability *(p. 530)* A probability based on repeated trials of an experiment

exponent *(p. 320)* The exponent of a power indicates the number of times a base is used as a factor.

exterior angles *(p. 105)* When two parallel lines are cut by a transversal, four exterior angles are formed on the outside of the parallel lines.

exterior angles of a polygon *(p. 112)* The angles adjacent to the interior angles when the sides of a polygon are extended

ecuaciones equivalentes *(p. 466)* Ecuaciones que tienen las mismas soluciones

evento *(p. 522)* Un grupo de una o más resultadas

experimento *(p. 522)* Una investigación o un método que tiene resultados variados

probabilidad experimenta *(p. 530)* Una probabilidad basada en ensayos repetidos de un experimento

exponente *(p. 320)* El exponente de una potencia indica cuantas veces una base es usada como un factor.

ángulos externos *(p. 105)* Cuando una transversal corta dos rectas paralelas, se forman cuatro ángulos externos por fuera de las rectas paralelas.

angulos exteriores de un polígono *(p. 112)* Los ángulos adyacentes a los ángulos interiores cuando los lados de una polígono están extendidos

F

favorable outcomes *(p. 522)* The outcomes of a specific event

function *(p. 277)* A relation that pairs each input with exactly one output

function rule *(p. 282)* An equation that describes the relationship between inputs (independent variable) and outputs (dependent variable)

Fundamental Counting Principle *(p. 538)* A way to find the total number of possible outcomes

resultados favorables *(p. 522)* Los resultados de un evento especifico

función *(p. 277)* Una relación que asocia cada entrada con una sola salida

regla de la función *(p. 282)* Una ecuación que describe la relación entre entradas (variable independiente) y salidas (variable dependiente)

Principio de conteo fundamental *(p. 538)* Un método para descubrir el número total de resultados posibles

G

graph of an inequality *(p. 486)* A graph that shows all the solutions of an inequality on a number line

gráfica de una desigualdad *(p. 486)* Una gráfica que muestra todas las soluciones de una desigualdad en una recta numérica

H

hemisphere *(p. 442)* One-half of a sphere

hypotenuse *(p. 382)* The side of a right triangle that is opposite the right angle

hemisferio *(p. 442)* La mitad de una esfera

hipotenusa *(p. 382)* El lado de un triángulo rectángulo opuesto al ángulo recto

I

image *(p. 44)* The new figure produced when a figure is transformed

indirect measurement *(p. 126)* Indirect measurement uses similar figures to find a missing measure when the measurement is difficult to find directly.

inequality *(p. 484)* A mathematical sentence that compares expressions; contains the symbols <, >, ≤, or ≥

input *(p. 276)* In a relation, inputs are values associated with outputs.

interior angles *(p. 105)* When two parallel lines are cut by a transversal, four interior angles are formed on the inside of the parallel lines.

interior angles of a polygon *(p. 112)* The angles inside a polygon

irrational number *(p. 402)* A number that cannot be written as the ratio of two integers

imagen *(p. 44)* La nueva figura producida cuando una figura esta transformada

medida indirecta *(p. 126)* Medida indirecta usa figuras similares para hallar una medida que falta cuando la medida es dificil de hallar directamente.

desigualdad *(p. 484)* Una oración matemática que compara las expresiones; contiene los símbolos <, >, ≤, or ≥

entrada *(p. 276)* En una relación, entradas son valores asociadas con salidas.

ángulos internos *(p. 105)* Cuando una transversal corta dos rectas paralelas, se forman cuatro ángulos internos dentro de las rectas paralelas.

ángulos interiores de un polígono *(p. 112)* Los ángulos que están dentro de un polígono

número irracional *(p. 402)* Un número que no puede escribirse como la razón de dos números enteros

English-Spanish Glossary

J

joint frequency *(p. 250)* Each entry in a two-way table

frecuencia conjunta *(p. 250)* Cada valor en una tabla de doble entrada

L

lateral surface area (of a prism) *(p. 650)* The sum of the areas of the lateral faces of a prism

área de superficie lateral (de un prisma) *(p. 650)* La suma de las áreas de las caras laterales de un prisma

legs *(p. 382)* The two sides of a right triangle that form the right angle

catetos *(p. 382)* Los dos lados de un triángulo rectángulo que forman el ángulo recto

line of best fit *(p. 245)* Out of all possible lines of fit, the line that best models a set of data

línea de mejor ajuste *(p. 245)* De todas las líneas de ajuste posibles, la línea que mejor modela un conjunto de datos

line of fit *(p. 244)* A line drawn on a scatter plot close to most of the data points; The line can be used to estimate data on a graph.

línea de ajuste *(p. 244)* Una línea dibujada en un diagrama de dispersión, cerca de la mayoría de los puntos de datos; La línea se puede usar para estimar datos en una gráfica.

line of reflection *(p. 50)* A line in which a transformed figure is reflected

línea de reflexión *(p. 50)* Una línea en donde una figura transformada está reflejada

linear equation *(p. 142)* An equation whose graph is a line

ecuación lineal *(p. 142)* Una ecuación cuya gráfica es una línea

linear function *(p. 290)* A function whose graph is a non-vertical line; A linear function has a constant rate of change.

función lineal *(p. 290)* Una función cuya gráfica es una línea no vertical; Una función lineal tiene una tasa de cambio constante.

literal equation *(p. 26)* An equation that has two or more variables

ecuación literal *(p. 26)* Una ecuación que tiene dos o más variables

M

mapping diagram *(p. 276)* A way to represent a relation

diagrama de función *(p. 276)* Una manera para representar una relación

marginal frequency *(p. 250)* The sums of the rows and columns in a two-way table

frecuencia marginal *(p. 250)* Las sumas de las hileras y columnas en una tabla de doble entrada

N

nonlinear function *(p. 296)* A function that does not have a constant rate of change; a function whose graph is not a line

función no lineal *(p. 296)* Una función que no tiene una tasa constante de cambio; una función cuya gráfica no es una línea

O

outcomes *(p. 522)* The possible results of an experiment

output *(p. 276)* In a relation, outputs are the values associated with inputs.

resultados *(p. 522)* Los resultados posibles de un experimento

salida *(p. 276)* En una relación, salidas son los valores asociadas con entradas.

P

perfect cube *(p. 390)* A number that can be written as the cube of an integer

perfect square *(p. 374)* A number with integers as its square roots

pi (π) *(p. 601)* The ratio of the circumference of a circle to its diameter

point-slope form *(p. 180)* A linear equation written in the form $y - y_1 = m(x - x_1)$; The graph of the equation is a line that passes through the point (x_1, y_1) and has the slope m.

population *(p. 563)* A population is an entire group of people or objects.

power *(p. 320)* A product of repeated factors

probability *(p. 523)* A measure of the likelihood, or chance, that an event will occur

Pythagorean Theorem *(p. 382)* In any right triangle, the sum of the squares of the lengths of the legs is equal to the square of the length of the hypotenuse: $a^2 + b^2 = c^2$.

cubo perfecto *(p. 390)* Un número que puede escribirse como el cubo de un entero

cuadrado perfecto *(p. 374)* Un número cuyas raíces cuadradas son números enteros

pi (π) *(p. 601)* La razón de la circunferencia de un círculo a su diámetro

forma punto-pendiente *(p. 180)* Una ecuación lineal escrita en la forma $y - y_1 = m(x - x_1)$; El grafico de la ecuación es una linea que pasa por el punto (x_1, y_1) y tiene la pendiente m.

población *(p. 563)* Una población es un grupo entero de personas u objetos.

potencia *(p. 320)* Un producto de factores repetidos

probabilidad *(p. 523)* Una medida de la probabilidad o posibilidad de que ocurrirá un evento

Teorema de Pitágoras *(p. 382)* En cualquier triángulo rectángulo, la suma de los largos de los catetos es igual al cuadrado del largo de la hipotenusa: $a^2 + b^2 = c^2$.

R

radical sign *(p. 374)* The symbol $\sqrt{}$ which is used to represent a square root

radicand *(p. 374)* The number under a radical sign

radius *(p. 600)* The distance from the center of a circle to any point on the circle

real numbers *(p. 402)* The set of all rational and irrational numbers

reflection *(p. 50)* A flip; a transformation in which a figure is reflected in a line called the line of reflection; A reflection creates a mirror image of the original figure.

símbolo radical *(p. 374)* El símbolo $\sqrt{}$ que es usado para representar una raíz cuadrada

radicando *(p. 374)* El número bajo un símbolo radical

radio *(p. 600)* La distancia desde el centro de un círculo hasta cualquier punto del círculo

números reales *(p. 402)* El conjunto de todos los números racionales e irracionales

reflexión *(p. 50)* Un reflejo; una tranformación en la que una figura se refleja en una línea llamada la línea de reflexión; Una reflexión crea un reflejo exacto de la figura original.

English-Spanish Glossary

regular polygon *(p. 120)* A polygon in which all the side are congruent, and all the interior angles are congruent

regular pyramid *(p. 660)* A pyramid whose base is a regular polygon

relation *(p. 276)* A pairing of inputs with outputs; can be represented by ordered pairs or a mapping diagram

relative frequency *(p. 524)* The fraction or percent of the time that an event occurs in an experiment

rigid motion *(p. 64)* A transformation that preserves length and angle measure

rise *(p. 148)* The change in y between any two points on a line

rotation *(p. 56)* A turn; a transformation in which a figure is rotated about a point

run *(p. 148)* The change in x between any two points on a line

polígono regular *(p. 120)* Un polígono en el que todos los lados son congruentes, y todos los ángulos interiores son congruentes

pirámide regular *(p. 660)* Una pirámide cuya base es un polígono regular

relación *(p. 276)* Una pareja de entradas con salidas; se puede representar por pares ordenados o un diagrama de funciones

frecuencia relativa *(p. 524)* La fracción o porcentaje de tiempo en que un evento ocurre en un experimento

movimiento rígido *(p. 64)* Una transformación que preserva la longitud y medida del ángulo

desplazamiento vertical *(p. 148)* El cambio en y entre dos puntos cualesquiera de una línea

rotación *(p. 56)* Una vuelta; una transformación en donde una figura se rota sobre de un punto

desplazamiento horizontal *(p. 148)* El cambio en x entre dos puntos cualesquiera de una línea

---

S

sample *(p. 563)* A part of a population

sample space *(p. 538)* The set of all possible outcomes of one or more events

scale factor (of a dilation) *(p. 70)* The value of the ratio of the side lengths of the image to the corresponding side lengths of the original figure

scatter plot *(p. 238)* A data display that shows the relationship between two data sets using ordered pairs in a coordinate plane

scientific notation *(p. 350)* A number is written in scientific notation when it is represented as the product of a factor and a power of 10. The factor must be greater than or equal to 1 and less than 10.

semicircle *(p. 602)* One-half of a circle

muestra *(p. 563)* Una parte de una población

espacio de muestra *(p. 538)* El conjunto de todas los resultados posibles de uno o más eventos

factor de escala (de una dilatación) *(p. 70)* El valor de la razón de las longitudes de los lados de la imagen a las longitudes de los lados correspondientes de la figura inicial

diagrama de dispersión *(p. 238)* Una presentación de datos que muestra la relación entre dos conjuntos de datos, usando pares ordenados en un plano de coordenadas

notación científica *(p. 350)* Un número está escrito en notación científica cuando se representa como el producto de un factor y una potencia de 10. El factor debe ser mayor o igual que 1 e inferior a 10.

semicírculo *(p. 602)* La mitad de un círculo

similar figures *(p. 78)* Figures that have the same shape but not necessarily the same size; Two figures are similar when corresponding side lengths are proportional and corresponding angles are congruent.

similar solids *(p. 446)* Two solids of the same type with equal ratios of corresponding linear measures

similarity transformation *(p. 78)* A dilation or a sequence of rigid motions and dilations

simulation *(p. 546)* An experiment that is designed to reproduce the conditions of a situation or process so that the simulated outcomes closely match the real-world outcomes

slant height (of a pyramid) *(p. 660)* The height of each lateral triangular face of a pyramid

slope *(p. 148)* The value of a ratio of the change in y (the rise) to the change in x (the run) between any two points on a line; Slope is a measure of the steepness of a line.

slope-intercept form *(p. 162)* A linear equation written in the form $y = mx + b$; The graph of the equation is a line that has a slope of m and a y-intercept of b.

solution of an inequality *(p. 484)* A value that makes an inequality true

solution of a linear equation *(p. 142)* An ordered pair (x, y) that makes an equation true

solution set *(p. 484)* The set of all solutions of an inequality

solution of a system of linear equations (in two variables) *(p. 200)* An ordered pair that is a solution of each equation in the system

figuras semejantes *(p. 78)* Figuras que tienen la misma forma pero no necesariamente el mismo tamaño; Dos figuras son semejantes cuando las longitudes de sus lados correspondientes son proporcionales y los ángulos correspondientes son congruentes.

sólidos similares *(p. 446)* Dos sólidos del mismo tipo con razones iguales de medidas lineales correspondientes

transformación de similitud *(p. 78)* Una dilatación o secuencia de movimientos rígidos y dilataciones

simulación *(p. 546)* Un experimento que es diseñado para reproducir las condiciones de una situación o proceso, de tal manera que los resultados posibles simulados coincidan en gran medida con los resultados del mundo real

apotema lateral (de una pirámide) *(p. 660)* La altura de cada cara lateral triangular de una pirámide

pendiente *(p. 148)* El valor de una razón entre el cambio en y (desplazamiento vertical) y el cambio en x (desplazamiento horizontal), entre dos puntos de una línea; Pediente es una medida de la inclinación de una línea.

forma intersección-pendiente *(p. 162)* Una ecuación lineal escrita en la forma $y = mx + b$; El grafico de la ecuación es una linea que tiene una pendiente de m y una intersección y de b.

solución de una desigualdad *(p. 484)* Un valor que hace una desigualdad verdadera

solución de una ecuación lineal *(p. 142)* Un par ordenado (x, y) que hace que una ecuación sea verdadera

conjunto solución *(p. 484)* El conjunto de todas las soluciones de una desigualdad

solución de un sistema de ecuaciones lineales (en dos variables) *(p. 200)* Un par ordenado que es una solución de cada ecuación en el sistema

sphere *(p. 439)* The set of all points in space that are the same distance from a point called the center

square root *(p. 374)* A number that, when multiplied by itself, equals a given number

standard form *(p. 168)* The standard form of a linear equation is $Ax + By = C$, where A and B are not both zero.

supplementary angles *(p. 628)* Two angles whose measures have a sum of 180°

system of linear equations *(p. 200)* A set of two or more linear equations in the same variables

esfera *(p. 439)* El conjunto de todos los pontos en el espacio que están a la misma distancia de un punto llamado centro

raíz cuadrada *(p. 374)* Un número que, multiplicado por sí mismo, es igual a un número dado

forma estándar *(p. 168)* La forma estándar de una ecuación lineal es $Ax + By = C$, donde A y B no son ambos cero.

ángulos suplementarios *(p. 628)* Dos ángulos cuyas medidas tienen una suma de 180°

sistema de ecuaciones lineales *(p. 200)* Un conjunto de dos o más ecuaciones lineales en las mismas variables

---
T
---

theorem *(p. 381)* A rule in mathematics

theoretical probability *(p. 530)* The quotient of the number of favorable outcomes and the number of possible outcomes when all possible outcomes are equally likely

transformation *(p. 44)* A change in the size, shape, position, or orientation of a figure

translation *(p. 44)* A slide; a transformation that shifts a figure horizontally and/or vertically, but does not change its size, shape, or orientation

transversal *(p. 104)* A line that intersects two or more lines

two-way table *(p. 250)* A frequency table that displays two categories of data collected from the same source

teorema *(p. 381)* Un enunciado que afirma una verdad demostrable

probabilidad teórica *(p. 530)* El cociente del número de resultados favorables y el número de posibles resultados cuando todos los resultados posibles son igualmente probables

transformación *(p. 44)* Un cambio en el tamaño, forma, posición u orientación de una figura

traslación *(p. 44)* Un deslice; una transformación que desplaza una figura horizontal y/o verticalmente, pero no cambia su tamaño, forma u orientación

transversal *(p. 104)* Una recta que interseca dos o más rectas

tabla de doble entrada *(p. 250)* Una tabla de frecuencia que muestra dos categorias de datos recogidos de la misma fuente

---
U
---

unbiased sample *(p. 564)* A sample that is representative of a population

muestra no sesgada *(p. 564)* Una muestra que es representativa de una población

---
V
---

vertical angles *(p. 628)* Opposite angles formed by the intersection of two lines

ángulos verticales *(p. 628)* Ángulos opuestos formados por la intersección de dos líneas

x-intercept *(p. 162)* The *x*-coordinate of the point where a line crosses the *x*-axis

intersección x *(p. 162)* La coordenada *x* del punto donde una línea cruza el eje *x*

y-intercept *(p. 162)* The *y*-coordinate of the point where a line crosses the *y*-axis

intersección y *(p. 162)* La coordenada *y* del punto donde una línea cruza el eje *y*

Index

A

Absolute value, of exponents, 351
Addition
    Distributive Property over (*See* Distributive Property)
    in scientific notation, 355, 356
    solving equations using, 465–470
    solving inequalities using, 489–494
Addition Property of Equality, solving equations with, 3, 4, 12, 18, 19, 465, 466, 478, 510
Addition Property of Inequality, solving inequalities with, 490, 504, 505
Adjacent angles, 627, 628, 629
Algebra tiles, 3, 465, 471, 477, 503
Alternate exterior angles, 105, 106
Alternate interior angles, 105, 106
Angle(s)
    adjacent, 627, 628, 629
    alternate exterior, 105, 106
    alternate interior, 105, 106
    complementary, 628, 629
    congruent, 64, 104, 105, 628
    corresponding, 104, 105
    drawing triangles using, 620
    exterior, 105
    identifying relationships of, 106
    interior, 105
    naming, 628
    pairs of, 629
    of polygons, 112, 117–122
    right (*See* Right angles)
    of rotation, 56
    of similar figures, 78
    of similar triangles, 124, 125
    supplementary, 105, 627, 628, 629
    transversals forming, 104, 105, 106, 111
    of triangles, 111–116, 124, 125
    using rules about, 627
    vertical, 105, 627, 628, 629
Angle measures
    constructing quadrilaterals using, 622
    constructing triangles using, 620
    drawing triangles from, 123
    finding unknown, 11, 104, 119, 627–634
    sum of
        in polygons, 118
        in triangle, 112

Approximation
    of cube roots, 403
    of irrational numbers, 403
    of numbers, 343
    of square roots, 401, 403
Areas. *See also* Surface areas
    of bases, 427, 428, 434, 649, 654, 660, 661, 666, 672
    of circles, 20, 377, 607–612, 616
    of composite figures, 613–618
    estimating, 614
    of lateral faces, 649, 660, 661
    of lateral surface, 650, 654, 655
    of rectangles, 616
    of semicircles, 615
    of similar figures, 84, 85
    of triangles, 615
Associative Property of Multiplication, 356
Axes, labeling, 295

B

Bar graphs, 256, 257
Bases (in exponential expressions)
    definition of, 319, 320
    dividing powers with same, 332
    multiplying powers with same, 326
    negative, 320
Bases (in geometry), areas of, 427, 428, 434, 649, 654, 660, 661, 666, 672
    in cylinder area formula, 654
    in prism volume formula, 666
    in pyramid volume formula, 672
    of pyramids, 659, 660, 661
    in surface area formula, 648, 649
Biased sample, 564, 565
Box-and-whisker plots, 256, 576, 578, 581, 582, 583, 584

C

Celsius, converting Fahrenheit to, 27
Center
    of circle, 600
    of dilation, 70
    of rotation, 56
    of sphere, 439
Challenge. *See* Dig Deeper
Change, rate of, 296
Chapter Exploration, *In every chapter. For example, see:* 2, 42, 102, 140, 198, 236, 274, 318, 372, 426

Chapter Practice, *In every chapter. For example, see:* 8–10, 47–48, 108–110, 145–146, 203–204, 241–242, 279–280, 323–324, 378–380, 431–432
Chapter Review, *In every chapter. For example, see:* 32–35, 90–95, 130–133, 186–191, 226–229, 264–267, 308–311, 362–365, 416–419, 454–457
Check Your Answer, *Throughout. For example, see:* 4, 46, 114, 164, 200, 252, 346, 356, 377
Choose Tools, *Throughout. For example, see:* 154, 255, 543
Circle(s), 599–606
    areas of, 20, 377, 607–612, 616
    circumference of (*See* Circumference)
    definition of, 600
    diameter of, 599, 600
    drawing, using compass for, 599
    radius of, 600
Circle graphs, 256
Circumference, 599–606
    definition of, 601
    exploring, 599
    finding, 601
    four square for, 636
Clockwise, rotating figure, 56, 57
Clusters, on scatter plots, 238
Common Error, *Throughout. For example, see:* T-47, 58, 64, 78, T-227, 326, 332, 345, T-372, 410
Commutative Property of Multiplication, 356
Comparison, of similar figures, 83, 84, 85
Compass, 599, 621
Complementary angles, 628, 629
Composite figures
    areas of, 613–618
    definition of, 614
    perimeters of, 613–618
Composite solids, 442
Compound events, 537–544
Conclusions, determining validity of, 565
Cones
    cross sections of, 679
    definition of, 433
    height of, 434
    radius of, 435

similar, 446, 448
volumes of, 433–438
Congruent angles
   formation of, 104, 105, 628
   in regular polygons, 120
   in similar triangles, 124, 125
Congruent figures, 63–68
   definition of, 64
   symbol of, 64
Congruent sides
   definition of, 64
   in regular polygons, 120
Connecting Concepts, *In every chapter. For example, see:* 31, 89, 129, 185, 225, 263, 307, 361, 415, 453
Converse
   meaning of, 409
   of Pythagorean Theorem, 409–414
Conversion, Fahrenheit to Celsius, 27
Coordinate plane. *See also* Graph(s); Origin; *x*-coordinates; *y*-coordinates
   congruent figures in, 63, 64, 65
   dilations in, 70–73
   drawing figures in, 43
   finding distances in, 384, 404, 411
   ordered pair in, 142
   reflections in, 49–52
   representing data in, 237
   rotations in, 55–59
   scatter plots in, 238–240
   similar figures in, 78, 79
   translations in, 44, 45
Correlation coefficient, 245
Corresponding angles
   in similar triangles, 125
   transversals forming, 104, 105
Counterclockwise, rotating figure, 57
Critical Thinking, *Throughout. For example, see:* 10, 54, 154, 166, 204, 242, 288, 327, 379, 432
Cross sections
   of cones, 679
   of cylinders, 679
   definition of, 677, 678
   describing, 677
   of prisms, 678
   of pyramids, 678
   of three-dimensional products, 677–682
Cube(s)
   finding edge lengths of, 389
   finding missing measures in, 17
Cube roots, 389–394
   approximating, 403
   definition of, 390

evaluating expressions with, 390
finding, 390
irrational numbers as, 402
of perfect cubes, 390
solving equations using, 391
symbol of, 390
Cubes, surface area of, 680
Cubing numbers, 390, 391
Cumulative Practice, *In every chapter. For example, see:* 37–39, 97–99, 135–137, 193–195, 231–233, 269–271, 313–315, 367–369, 421–423, 459–461
Cylinders
   cross sections of, 679
   definition of, 653
   finding height of, 428
   finding radius of, 428
   similar, 445, 446
   surface areas of, 653–658
   volumes of, 427–432, 454

D

Data. *See also* Relationships between data
   analyzing, 249
   displaying, 255–262
   distributions, comparing, 575
   estimating, 244
   representing by linear equation, 243
   representing by two-way tables, 250
   representing on scatter plots, 238
Decimal point, 350, 351
Decimals
   in equations, 466, 467, 472, 474
   in inequalities, 484, 491, 492, 496, 498, 499, 506
   numbers written as, 402
   repeating (*See* Repeating decimals)
   terminating (*See* Terminating decimals)
   writing probabilities as, 523
Definition and example chart, 186, 362, 588
Demand curve, 306
Dependent variable, 282
Diagrams
   interpreting, 275
   mapping, 276, 278, 284
Diameter
   in circumference formula, 601
   definition of, 599, 600

exploring, 599
finding, 600
Different Words, Same Question, *Throughout. For example, see:* 27, 58, 125, 181, 201, 284, 339, 384, 429
Differentiation, *see* Scaffolding Instruction
Dig Deeper, *Throughout. For example, see:* 7, 48, 110, 202, 242, 278, 322, 377, 430
Dilations, 69–76
   center of, 70
   definition of, 70
   meaning of word, 69
   scale factor of, 70
   types of, 71
Distances,
   finding, in coordinate plane, 384, 404, 411
Distributive Property
   performing operations in scientific notation with, 356
   solving equations with, 13, 18, 19, 181
   solving inequalities with, 505
   solving systems of linear equations with, 206
Division
   in scientific notation, 355, 356–357
   solving equations using, 471–476
   solving inequalities using, 495–502
Division Property of Equality, solving equations with, 3, 5, 12, 13, 18, 26, 471, 472, 478
Division Property of Inequality, solving inequalities with, 496, 497, 504, 505
Dot plots, 256, 577, 582
Drawings, *See* Scale drawings

E

Edge lengths, finding, 389
Elimination, solving systems of linear equations by, 211–218, 221
ELL Support, *In every lesson. For example, see:* T-2, T-51, T-105, T-140, T-198, T-257, T-281, T-326, T-383, T-426
Enlargement, 71
Equality
   Addition Property of, 465, 466, 478, 510
   Division Property of, 471, 472, 478

Multiplication Property of, 471, 472, 473, 478
Subtraction Property of, 465, 466, 478
Equations. *See also* Function rule
  equivalent, 466
  identifying functions from, 296
  with infinitely many solutions, 19
  information frame for solving, 32
  linear (*See* Linear equations)
  literal (*See* Literal equations)
  multi-step, solving, 11–16
  with no solution, 19
  rewriting, 25–30
  simple, solving, 3–10
  solving
    using addition and subtraction, 465–470
    using algebra tiles, 465, 471, 477
    using cube roots, 391
    using multiplication and division, 471–476
    using reciprocals, 473
    using square roots, 376
  two-step, solving, 477–482
  with variables, solving, 17–24, 26–27
  writing and solving, 20, 157, 467
Equilibrium point, 306
Equivalent equations, 466
Error Analysis. *See* You Be the Teacher
Estimation
  of data, 244
  of quantities, 343–348
Events
  compound, 537–544
  definition of, 522
Example and non-example chart, 130, 308
Exchange rate, 398
Experiment(s)
  conducting, 529
  definition of, 522
Experimental probability, 530, 531, 532, 546, 547
Explain your reasoning. *Throughout. For example, see:* 6, 81, 131, 182, 221, 267, 293, 343, 380, 426
Exponent(s), 319–324
  absolute value of, 351
  definition of, 319, 320
  negative, 337–342, 350, 351
  one as, 326
  and order of operations, 321

positive, 350, 351
  writing expressions using, 320
  zero, 337–342
Exponent notation, using, 319
Expressions
  with cube roots, 390
  with exponents
    evaluating, 320, 321, 338
    simplifying, 332, 333, 339
    writing, 320
  with square roots, 375
Exterior angles
  alternate, 105, 106
  definition of, 112
  formation of, 105
  of triangles, 111, 113

F

Factors
  repeated, 320
  in scientific notation, 350
Fahrenheit, converting to Celsius, 27
Favorable outcomes
  definition of, 522
  in theoretical probability, 530, 531
Figures
  congruent, 63–68
  dilating, 69–76
  dividing into triangles, 117
  finding length of, 383
  finding missing measures in, 17
  reflecting, 49–54
  rotating, 55–62
  rotational symmetry of, 61
  similar, 77–82
  sliding, 43, 44
  translating, 43–48, 90
  writing formulas for, 25
Fit, line of. *See* Line of fit
Flips. *See* Reflections
Formative Assessment Tips, *Throughout. For example, see:* T-5, T-57, T-106, T-151, T-201, T-229, T-292, T-333, T-384, T-436
Formulas
  definition of, 26
  finding, experimentally, 433, 439
  rewriting, 25–30
Four square, 226, 416, 552, 636
Fractions
  in equations, 466, 472, 473, 478
  in inequalities, 496, 498, 504
  writing, as decimals, 396
  writing probabilities as, 523
  writing repeating decimals as, 395, 397

Frequencies
  joint, 250, 252
  marginal, 250, 251
  relative, 524
Function(s), 275–280
  definition of, 277
  determining, 277
  evaluating, 282
  example and non-example chart for, 308
  as graphs, 283, 284, 289
  linear (*See* Linear functions)
  nonlinear (*See* Nonlinear functions)
  representations of, 281–288
  as tables, 283, 284
  writing, 289
Function rule
  definition of, 282
  writing, 282, 285
Fundamental Counting Principle, 538, 539

G

Gaps, on scatter plots, 238
General rule, 325, 331
Geometry software
  angles of triangles in, 111
  dilating polygons in, 69
  drawing polygons using, 619
  exploring lines in, 103
  similar triangles in, 123
Graph(s). *See also* Scatter plots
  analyzing, 302
  bar, 256, 257
  circle, 256
  creating, 141
  functions as, 283, 284, 289
  identifying functions from, 297
  of inequalities, 486, 504, 505
  interpreting, 301
  intersections of, as solutions of systems of linear equations, 200, 201
  line, 256, 257, 258
  of linear equations, 141–146
    in slope-intercept form, 161–166, 168
    in standard form, 167–172
  linear functions as, 290, 296, 297
  matching situations to, 301
  of proportional relationships, 155–160
  sketching, 303
  slope of (*See* Slopes of lines)
  in supply and demand model, 306

Index **A21**

of systems of linear equations, 199–204, 220, 221
using, 141, 155, 243, 281
Graphic organizers
definition and example chart, 186, 362, 588
example and non-example chart, 130, 308
four square, 226, 416, 552, 636
information frame, 32, 264, 684
summary triangle, 90, 454, 510
Graphing calculator, 199, 245, 246, 349
Grid, 613, 614

Height
of cones, 434, 446
of cylinders, 428, 446
of prisms, 427, 666
of pyramids, 383, 672
writing formula for, 25
Hemispheres, volumes of, 442
Hexagonal prisms, 427
Hexagons,
as bases of pyramids, 659
interior angle measures of, 120
Higher Order Thinking.
    See Dig Deeper
Histograms, 256, 257
Horizontal lines
graphing, 143, 175
slopes of, 149
Horizontal translation, 44
Hypotenuse, 382

Image. See also Figures
definition of, 44
naming, 44
Independent variable, 282
Indirect measurement, 123, 126
Inequality(ies)
Addition Property of, 490, 504, 505
definition of, 484
Division Property of, 496, 497, 504, 505
graphing, 486, 504, 505
Multiplication Property of, 496, 497, 498
solving, 484, 485
    using addition and subtraction, 489–494
    using algebra tiles, 503
    using multiplication and division, 495–502

Subtraction Property of, 490, 491
symbols of, 484, 497
two-step, solving, 503–508
understanding, 483
writing, 484, 489, 495
Information frame, 32, 264, 684
Input-output table, 283, 284, 285
Inputs, 275–278, 282, 283
Integers
as cube roots, 390
as real numbers, 402
as square roots, 374
Interior angles
alternate, 105, 106
definition of, 112
formation of, 105
of polygons, 117–119
of triangles, 111, 112
Interquartile range (IQR), 576, 582, 583, 584
Intersections of graphs, as solutions of systems of linear equations, 200, 201
Intersections of lines, 103–107
angle measures formed by, 104–106
exploring, 103
at right angles, 104
Irrational numbers, 401–408
approximating, 403
comparing, 403
definition of, 402
examples of, 402

Joint frequencies, 250, 252
Justify your answer, Throughout. For example, see: 7, 82, 116, 164, 225, 248, 294, 352, 408, 430

Lateral face
area of, 649, 660, 661
of pyramid, 659, 660
in surface area formula, 648, 649
Lateral surface area, 650, 654, 655
Learning Target, In every lesson. For example, see: 3, 43, 103, 199, 237, 275, 319, 373, 427
Legs, in right triangle, 382
Length, writing formula for, 25
Like terms, combining, before solving equations, 479
Likelihood
describing, 523
determining, 521

Line(s). See also Linear equations
horizontal
    graphing, 143, 175
    slopes of, 149
intersections of (See Intersections of lines)
parallel, 104–107
perpendicular, 104
of reflection, 50
slope of, 147–154
vertical, graphing, 143
Line graphs, 256, 257, 258
Line of best fit, 245, 246
Line of fit, 243–248
definition of, 244
finding, 244
Linear equations
definition and example chart for, 186
definition of, 142
graphing, 141–146
    in slope-intercept form, 161–166, 168
    in standard form, 167–172
representing data by, 243
representing proportional relationships with, 155–160
solutions of, 142
systems of (See Systems of linear equations)
writing
    in point-slope form, 179–184
    in slope-intercept form, 173–178
Linear functions, 289–294
definition of, 290
identifying, 296, 297
interpreting, 291
writing
    using graphs, 290
    using tables, 290
Linear regression, 245, 246
Linear systems. See Systems of linear equations
Literal equations
definition of, 26
formulas as, 26
solving, 26–27
Logic, Throughout. For example, see: 10, 62, 110, 140, 224, 330, 394, 444

MAD, 576, 577
Mapping diagrams, 276, 278, 284
Marginal frequencies, 250, 251

Mathematical Practices
  Make sense of problems and persevere in solving them, *Throughout. For example, see:* 11, 55, 88, 128, 205, 218, 288, 389
  Reason abstractly and quantitatively, *Throughout. For example, see:* 24, 68, 144, 160, 167, 223, 302, 357
  Construct viable arguments and critique the reasoning of others, *Throughout. For example, see:* 10, 29, 57, 147, 218, 249, 280, 345, 409, 444
  Model with mathematics, *Throughout. For example, see:* 23, 71, 141, 160, 210, 254, 275, 301, 388, 432
  Use appropriate tools strategically, *Throughout. For example, see:* 3, 43, 83, 154, 199, 255, 353, 407
  Attend to precision, *Throughout. For example, see:* 63, 85, 145, 237, 277, 295, 342, 388, 401
  Look for and make use of structure, *Throughout. For example, see:* 13, 54, 83, 117, 169, 219, 242, 348, 395, 414
  Look for and express regularity in repeated reasoning, *Throughout. For example, see:* 5, 25, 83, 117, 280, 331, 380, 445
Mean, 576, 577
Mean absolute deviation (MAD), 576, 577
Meaning of a Word, 69
Measurement, indirect, 123, 126
Median, 576, 582, 583, 584
Misleading data display, 258
Mixed numbers, writing, as decimals, 396
Model(s). *See* Scale models
Modeling Real Life, *In every lesson. For example, see:* 7, 46, 107, 144, 202, 240, 278, 322, 377, 430
Multiple Representations, *Throughout. For example, see:* 21, 45, 142, 156, 200, 202, 238, 257, 276, 283, 397
Multiplication
  Associative Property of, 356
  Commutative Property of, 356
  Distributive Property of (*See* Distributive Property)
  in scientific notation, 355, 356–357
  solving equations using, 471–476
  solving inequalities using, 495–502
Multiplication Property of Equality, solving equations with, 3, 5, 471, 472, 473, 478
Multiplication Property of Inequality, solving inequalities with, 496, 497, 498
Multi-step equations, solving, 11–16

N

Naming figures, 44
Natural numbers, as real numbers, 402
Negative linear relationship, 239, 244
Negative numbers
  as base, 320
  for correlation coefficient, 245
  as exponents, 337–342, 350, 351
  multiplying or dividing inequalities by, 497
  as slope of line, 148, 149
  square roots of, 374
  for translations in coordinate plane, 44
n-gon, 118
Nonlinear functions
  definition of, 296
  identifying, 296, 297
Nonlinear relationship, 239
Number(s)
  approximating, 343, 403
  classifying, 402
  cube roots of (*See* Cube roots)
  cubing, 390, 391
  decimals, 402
  estimating, 343–348
  irrational (*See* Irrational numbers)
  mixed, 396
  natural, 402
  negative (*See* Negative numbers)
  positive (*See* Positive numbers)
  rational (*See* Rational numbers)
  real
    classifying, 402
    definition of, 402
  rounding, 344, 345
  in scientific notation, 350
  square roots of (*See* Square roots)
  squaring (*See* Squaring numbers)
  in standard form, 351
  whole, 402
Number line, solutions of inequalities on, 486, 504, 505
Number Sense, *Throughout. For example, see:* 24, 76, 210, 247, 300, 336, 379

O

Oblique solids
  prisms, 666
  pyramids, 672
  volumes of, 428
Octagonal prisms, 427
One (1), as exponent, 326
Open-Ended, *Throughout. For example, see:* 6, 109, 128, 204, 242, 277, 327, 408
Order of operations, exponents and, 321
Ordered pairs. *See also* x-coordinates; y-coordinates
  definition of, 142
  finding slopes of lines from, 148, 149
  as functions, 283
  in input-output table, 283
  in point-slope form of equations, 180
  of relations, 276
  representing proportional relationships, 156
  on scatter plots, 238, 240
  as solutions of linear equations, 142, 144
  as solutions of systems of linear equations, 200, 201
Origin
  as center of dilation, 70
  graph of proportional relationship passing through, 156
  linear equations passing through, 162
Outcomes
  definition of, 522
  in experimental probability, 530, 532
  favorable, 522
  identifying, 522
  in sample space, 538, 539, 540
  simulating, 546, 547
  in theoretical probability, 530, 531
Outliers, on scatter plots, 238
Outputs, 275–278, 282, 283
Overlap of data distributions, 575, 577

P

Parallel lines, 104–107
   definition of, 104
   slopes of, 150
   transversals intersecting, 104, 105, 106, 111
Parallelograms
   congruent, 65
   writing formula for height of, 25
Patterns, 61, 242, 262, 324
Pentagonal prisms, 427
Percent(s), writing probabilities as, 523
Perfect cube, 390
Perfect square, 374
Performance Task, *In every chapter. For example, see:* 1, 41, 101, 139, 197, 235, 273, 317, 371, 425
Perimeters
   of composite figures, 613–618
   estimating, 614
   of semicircular region, 602
   of similar figures, 84
Perpendicular lines, 104
Pi (π), 402, 601, 608, 654
Pictographs, 256, 259
Plane, and cross sections, 678
Plots
   box-and-whisker, 576, 578, 581, 582, 583, 584
   dot, 577, 582
Point-slope form
   definition of, 180
   writing equations in, 179–184
Polygons
   angles of, 112, 117–122
   as bases of pyramids, 659
   constructing, 619–626
   definition of, 118
   dilating, 69
   drawing, using technology for, 619
   naming, 118
   regular, 120
Populations, 563–568, *See also* Sample(s)
   comparing, 575–580
      using random samples for, 581–586
   definition of, 563
   describing, using random samples for, 569–574
   estimating average of, 571
   using, 563
Positive linear relationship, 239, 240
Positive numbers
   as correlation coefficient, 245
   as exponents, 350, 351
   multiplying or dividing inequalities by, 496
   as slope of line, 148, 149
   square roots of, 374
   for translations in coordinate plane, 44
Powers
   definition and example chart for, 362
   definition of, 319, 320
   of powers, 326, 327
   of products, 326, 327
   products of, 325–330, 338, 339, 356, 357
   quotients of, 331–336, 338, 339, 357
   of ten, 343, 344, 345
      in scientific notation, 350
Practice Test, *In every chapter. For example, see:* 36, 96, 134, 192, 230, 268, 312, 366, 420, 458
Precision, *Throughout. For example, see:* 23, 24, 140, 145, 277, 330, 342, 380, 452
Prime symbols, 44
Prisms
   cross sections of, 678
   oblique, 666
   right, 666
   surface areas of, 647–652, 684
   volumes of, 427, 665–670
Probability, 521–528
   of compound event, 540
   definition of, 523
   describing likelihood using, 523
   experimental, 530, 531, 532, 546, 547
   four square for, 552
   relative frequency as measure of, 524
   theoretical, 530, 531
Problem Solving, *Throughout. For example, see:* 8, 48, 109, 146, 204, 242, 288, 330, 379, 432
Problem-Solving Plan, *In every chapter. For example, see:* 14, 46, 114, 164, 222, 246, 292, 346, 377, 442
Problem-Solving Strategies, 31
Products
   of powers, 326, 338, 339, 356, 357
   powers of, 326, 327
   of repeated factors, 320
   writing, using exponents, 320
Proportional relationships
   definition of, 156
   graphing, 155–160
Pyramids
   bases of, 659
   cross sections of, 678
   finding heights of, 383
   making scale model of, 659
   oblique, 672
   regular, 660
   right, 672
   similar, 445, 447
   slant height of, 659, 660
   surface areas of, 659–664
   volumes of, 671–676
Pythagoras, 381
Pythagorean Theorem, 381–388
   converse of, 409–414
   discovering, 381
   formula for, 382
   four square for, 416
   using, 382–384, 404
Pythagorean triple, 410

Q

Quadrilaterals, 622
Quantities
   describing relationships between, 275
   estimating, 343–348
   making sense of, 167, 349
Quotients, of powers, 331–336, 338, 339, 357

R

Radical sign, 374
Radicand, 374
Radius
   of circle, 377, 601, 608
   of cone, 435, 446
   of cylinder, 429, 446, 654
   definition of, 600
   finding, 600
   of sphere, 439, 440, 441
Random samples
   comparing, 582
   comparing populations using, 581–586
   describing populations using, 569–574
   using multiple, 581, 583
Ratio table, 155
Rational numbers, 395–400
   converting between different forms of, 395–397
   definition of, 396
   as real numbers, 402

Reading, *Throughout. For example, see:* 44, 64, 78, 118, 148
Real numbers
  classifying, 402
  definition of, 402
Real World. *See* Modeling Real Life
Reasonableness, checking for, 246, 292, 442, 525, 610, 616, 656, 662
Reasoning, *Throughout. For example, see:* 10, 48, 109, 153, 204, 280, 330, 380, 431
Rectangles
  area of, 616
  congruent, 65
  dilating, 71
  finding missing measures in, 17
  reflections of, 49
  rotating, 58
  similar, 83, 84
  writing formula for length of, 25
Rectangular prisms
  finding missing measures in, 17
  similar, 446
  surface area of, 647, 648, 684
  volume of, 427, 666
  writing formula for height of, 25
  writing formula for length of, 25
Rectangular pyramids, volume of, 673
Reduction, 71
Reflections, 49–54
  definition of, 50
  identifying, 50
  line of, 50
  as rigid motions, 64
Regular polygons, 120
Regular pyramid, 660
Relations, 275–280
  definition of, 276
  as functions, 277
  ordered pairs of, 276
Relationships between data
  analyzing, 275, 301
  describing
    between quantities, 275
    using graphs, 281, 301, 302, 303
    using table, 281
    using two-way table, 252
  finding, 237
  identifying, 239, 245
  proportional (*See* Proportional relationships)
  on scatter plots, 238–239, 244–245
  types of, 239
Relative frequency, 524

Remember, *Throughout. For example, see:* 4, 5, 26, 142, 174, 175, 282, 402, 428
Repeated Reasoning, *Throughout. For example, see:* 88, 117, 210, 280, 452
Repeating decimals
  definition of, 396
  writing, as fractions, 395, 397, 474
Response to Intervention, *Throughout. For example, see:* T-0B, T-60, T-129, T-138B, T-206, T-241, T-272B, T-341, T-415, T-424B
Review & Refresh, *In every lesson. For example, see:* 8, 47, 108, 145, 203, 241, 279, 323, 378, 431
Right angles
  lines intersecting at, 104
  in right triangles, 382
Right prism, 666
Right pyramids, 672
Right triangles. *See also* Pythagorean Theorem
  identifying, 410, 411
  sides of, 382
  using, 147
Rigid motions
  definition of, 64
  describing sequence of, 65
Rise, 148
Rotational symmetry, 61
Rotations, 55–62
  center of, 56
  clockwise, 56, 57
  counterclockwise, 57
  definition of, 56
  identifying, 56
  as rigid motions, 64
Rounding numbers, 344, 345
Ruler, 620, 623
Run, 148

S

Sample(s) 563–568
  biased, 564, 565
  definition of, 563
  definition and example chart for, 588
  random (*See* Random samples)
  unbiased, 564, 565
  using, 563
  variability in, 569
Sample space
  definition of, 538
  finding, 538, 539

Scaffolding Instruction, *In every lesson. For example, see:* T-4, T-64, T-112, T-174, T-225, T-244, T-276, T-344, T-390, T-453
Scale,
  in similar figures, 84
Scale drawings
  as dilations, 70
  similar figures as, 84
Scale factor
  of dilation, 70
  in scale drawings, 84
Scale models
  making, 659
Scatter plots, 237–242
  definition of, 238
  function of, 256
  information frame for, 264
  line of fit on, 243–248
  making, 238
Scientific notation, 349–354
  converting, to standard form, 351
  definition of, 350
  operations in, 355–360
  writing numbers in, 350
Self-Assessment for Concepts & Skills, *In every lesson. For example, see:* 6, 45, 106, 143, 201, 239, 277, 321, 376, 429
Self-Assessment for Problem Solving, *In every lesson. For example, see:* 7, 46, 107, 144, 202, 240, 278, 322, 377, 430
Semicircles
  area of, 615
  definition of, 602
Semicircular region, perimeter of, 602
Side(s)
  congruent, 64, 120
  drawing triangles using, 620, 621
  of pyramids, 659
Side lengths
  finding, 155, 373
  of right triangles, 382 (*See also* Pythagorean Theorem)
  of similar figures, 78
Similar figures, 77–82
  areas of, 84, 85
  comparing, 83, 84, 85
  definition of, 78
  describing, 79
  identifying, 78
  indirect measurement of, 126
  perimeters of, 84
  symbol of, 78

Index **A25**

Similar solids
- comparing, 445
- definition of, 446
- finding missing measures in, 446
- identifying, 446
- surface areas of, 447
- volumes of, 448

Similar triangles, 123–128
- angles of, 124, 125
- areas of, 84, 85
- drawing, 123
- formation of, 78
- identifying, 124, 125
- perimeters of, 84

Similarity statement, 78
Similarity transformation, 78
Simulations, 545–550
- definition of, 546
- using, 545

Slant height
- of cones, 446
- of pyramid, 659, 660

Sliding figures, 43, 44
Slope-intercept form, 296
- graphing linear equations in, 161–166, 168
- writing linear equations in, 173–178

Slopes of lines, 147–154
- definition of, 148
- finding, 148–149, 155, 174, 175
- formula for, 148
- interpreting, 156, 173
- in linear functions, 290, 291
- of lines of fit, 244
- in point-slope form of equations, 180, 181
- and proportional relationships, 156–158
- on scatter plot, 239, 240, 244
- in slope-intercept form, 162, 173–175

Solids
- comparing similar, 445
- composite, 442
- oblique, volumes of, 428

Solution set, 484
Spheres
- definition of, 439
- volumes of, 439–444

Square(s)
- as bases of pyramids, 659, 660
- finding missing measures in, 17
- finding side lengths of, 373
- rotating, 56

Square pyramid
- finding height of, 383

surface area of, 659, 660
volume of, 672, 673

Square roots, 373–380
- approximating, 401, 403
- definition of, 374
- evaluating expressions with, 375
- finding, 374–375
- irrational numbers as, 402
- of perfect squares, 374
- solving equations using, 376
- symbol of, 374

Squaring numbers
- finding square roots as inverse of, 375, 376
- in Pythagorean Theorem, 382

Standard form, graphing linear equations in, 167–172
STEAM Video, *In every chapter. For example, see:* 1, 41, 101, 139, 197, 235, 273, 317, 371, 425
Steepness of lines, 147, 148
Stem-and-leaf plots, 256
Structure, *Throughout. For example, see:* 9, 54, 122, 154, 169, 221, 262, 324, 388
Subscripts, 148
Substitution, solving systems of linear equations by, 205–210
Subtraction
- in scientific notation, 355, 356
- solving equations using, 465–470
- solving inequalities using, 489–494

Subtraction Property of Equality, solving equations with, 3, 4, 6, 12, 13, 18, 19, 20, 26, 465, 466, 478
Subtraction Property of Inequality, solving inequalities with, 490, 491
Success Criteria, *In every lesson. For example, see:* 3, 43, 103, 199, 237, 275, 319, 373, 427
Summary triangle, 90, 454, 510
Supplementary angles, 105, 627, 628, 629
Supply curve, 306
Surface areas, 445–452
- of cubes, 680
- of cylinders, 653–658
- lateral, 650, 654, 655
- of prisms, 647–652, 684
- of pyramids, 659–664
- of similar solids, 447
- writing formula for, 26, 647

Survey, 250, 251
Symbols
- of congruence, 64

- of cube root, 390
- inequality, 484, 497
- prime, 44
- of similarity, 78
- of square root, 374
- of triangle, 64

Symmetry, rotational, 61
Systems of linear equations
- definition of, 200
- solution of
  - definition of, 200
  - exploring, 219
- solving
  - algebraically, 205, 211
  - choosing method of, 214
  - by elimination, 211–218, 221
  - four square for, 226
  - by graphing, 199–204, 220, 221
  - with infinitely many solutions, 220, 221
  - with no solution, 220
  - with one solution, 220
  - by substitution, 205–210
- writing, 205

T

Tables
- advantages of using, 249
- describing relationships with, 281
- functions as, 283, 284
- identifying functions from, 296
- input-output, 283, 284, 285
- ratio, 155
- two-way (*See* Two-way tables)
- writing linear functions using, 290

Teaching Strategies, *Throughout. For example, see:* T-57, T-118, T-142, T-180, T-220, T-251, T-281, T-350, T-412, T-428
Temperature conversion, 27
Ten (10), powers of, 343, 344, 345, 350
Terminating decimals, 396, 397
Theoretical probability, 530, 531
Three-dimensional products, cross sections of, 677–682
Transformations. *See also* Dilations; Reflections; Rotations; Translations
- definition of, 44
- as rigid motions, 64
- similarity, 78, 79
- using more than one, 72

Translations
- in coordinate plane, 44, 45
- definition of, 44
- horizontal, 44

identifying, 44
as rigid motions, 64
summary triangle for, 90
vertical, 44
Transversals
angles formed by, 104, 105, 106, 111
definition of, 104
example and non-example chart for, 130
Trapezoids
dilating, 72
rotating, 57
translating, 72
Tree diagrams, 542
Triangle(s)
angles of, 111–116, 124, 125
area of, 615
as bases of pyramids, 659, 661
congruent, 63, 64
dilating, 70, 71, 73
dividing figures into, 117
drawing
using angle measures for, 620
using angles and sides for, 620
using side lengths for, 621
finding angle measures for, 11
reflections of, 50, 51
right (*See* Right triangles)
rotating, 55, 56
side lengths of, 155
similar (*See* Similar triangles)
sliding, 43
sum of interior angle measures of, 112
symbol of, 64
translating, 44, 45
writing formula for height of, 25
Triangular prisms, volume of, 427, 667
Triangular pyramids
surface area of, 659, 661
volume of, 673
Triple, Pythagorean, 410
Try It, *In every lesson. For example, see:* 4, 44, 104, 142, 200, 238, 276, 320, 374, 428
Two-step equations, solving, 12, 477–482
Two-step inequalities, solving, 503–508
Two-way tables, 249–254
definition of, 250
making, 251
reading, 250

Unbiased sample, 564, 565
Undefined slope, 149
Using Tools, *Throughout. For example, see:* 407, 670

Variables
dependent, 282
in formulas, 26
independent, 282
solving equations with, 17–24, 26–27
Verbal model, 285
Vertical angles, 105, 627, 628, 629
Vertical lines
graphing, 143
slopes of, 149
Vertical translation, 44
Volumes
of cones, 433–438
of cylinders, 427–432, 454
exploring, 427
finding, experimentally, 427
finding formula for, 665, 671
of prisms, 427, 665–670
of pyramids, 671–676
of similar solids, 448
of spheres, 439–444

Which One Doesn't Belong?, *Throughout. For example, see:* 6, 51, 106, 143, 214, 239, 297, 321, 404, 441
Whole numbers, as real numbers, 402
Writing, *Throughout. For example, see:* 6, 119, 169, 201, 261, 357, 380, 407, 411

x-coordinates
in dilations, 70, 71
in linear equations, 142–144
of ordered pair, 142
proportional to y, 156
in reflections, 50, 51
in rotations, 57
as run, 148
in scatter plots, 238–240
in slopes of lines, 148, 149
in translations, 44, 45

x-intercept
definition of, 162
graphing linear equations using, 169, 170

y-coordinates
in dilations, 70, 71
in linear equations, 142–144
of ordered pair, 142
proportional to x, 156
in reflections, 50, 51
as rise, 148
in rotations, 57
in scatter plots, 238–240
in slopes of lines, 148, 149
in translations, 44, 45
y-intercept
definition of, 162
graphing linear equations using, 169, 170
in linear functions, 290, 291
of lines of fit, 244
in slope-intercept form, 162, 173–175
You Be the Teacher, *Throughout. For example, see:* 9, 47, 108, 145, 203, 280, 323, 379, 451

Zero (0)
as exponent, 337–342
as slope, 149
square root of, 374

Credits

Chapter A

462 *top* zentilia/Shutterstock.com; *bottom* OnstOn/iStock/Getty Images Plus; **463** Georgethefourth/iStock/Getty Images Plus; **467** German-skydiver/iStock/Getty Images Plus; **470** ©iStockphoto.com/fotoVoyager; **476** *top* Alexander Mak/Shutterstock.com; *bottom* robertsrob/iStock/Getty Images Plus; **480** tolokonov/iStock/Getty Images Plus; **482** *top* zbruch/E+/Getty Images; *bottom* huePhotography/iStock/Getty Images Plus; **483** *top left* bitt24/Shutterstock.com; *top right* Amawasri/iStock/Getty Images Plus; *center left* mphillips007/E+/Getty Images; *bottom right* Creativ/iStock/Getty Images Plus; **486** gregepperson/iStock/Getty Images Plus; **488** Gregory James Van Raalte/Shutterstock.com; **492** ©iStockphoto.com/suriyasilsaksom; **494** *top* Khafizov Lvan Harisovich/Shutterstock.com; *bottom* Victoria_Novak/iStock/Getty Images Plus, Opka/iStock/Getty Images Plus; **499** *top* Ralph White/Corbis Documentary/Getty Images; *bottom* sweetmoments/E+/Getty Images; **500** LockStockBob/Shutterstock.com; **501** jacoblund/iStock/Getty Images Plus; **502** Jacek Chabraszewski/Shutterstock.com; **506** *top* GaryAlvis/E+/Getty Images; MaksTRV/iStock/Getty Images Plus; *bottom* graemenicholson/iStock/Getty Images Plus; **508** *top* ©Keddie. Image from BigStockPhoto.com; *bottom* GlobalP/iStock/Getty Images Plus; **509** OnstOn/iStock/Getty Images Plus; **511** urich84/iStock/Getty Images Plus; **514** ©iStockphoto.com/Jack Puccio

Chapter B

518 *top* zentilia/Shutterstock.com; *bottom* OnstOn/iStock/Getty Images Plus; **519** ©iStockphoto.com/ryasick; **520** ©iStockphoto.com/ryasick; **522** Sussenn/iStock/Getty Images Plus; **524** *top* Rattasak/iStock/Getty Images Plus, Oda_dao/iStock/Getty Images Plus, antoniotruzzi/iStock/Getty Images Plus; *bottom* Big Ideas Learning, LLC; **525** Roydee/E+/Getty Images; **527** 1550539/iStock/Getty Images Plus, Sussenn/iStock/Getty Images Plus; **528** RomoloTavani/iStock/Getty Images Plus; **529** *top* Meral Hydaverdi/Shutterstock.com; *bottom* Warren Goldswain/Shutterstock.com; **531** ©iStockphoto.com/Eric Ferguson; **532** marylooo/iStock/Getty Images Plus; **533** fatihhoca/E+/Getty Images; **534** gmnicholas/E+/Getty Images; **535** Juanmonino/iStock Unreleased/Getty Images; **536** Feng Yu/Shutterstock.com; **537** *top* FernandoMadeira/iStock/Getty Images Plus; *center* Krasyuk/iStock/Getty Images Plus; *bottom* Mark Aplet/Shutterstock.com; **538** the-lightwriter/iStock/Getty Images Plus; **539** Big Ideas Learning, LLC; **540** Rodrusoleg/iStock/Getty Images Plus; **541** *top* carlosalvarez/E+/Getty Images; *bottom* goir/iStock/Getty Images Plus; **543** Sussenn/iStock/Getty Images Plus; **544** *top left* basar17/iStock/Getty Images Plus; *top* ET-ARTWORKS/DigitalVision Vectors/Getty Images; *bottom* tele52/Shutterstock.com; **545** rbv/iStock/Getty Images Plus; **546** Dorottya_Mathe/iStock/Getty Images Plus; **548** ovro77/iStock/Getty Images Plus; **549** Kagenmi/iStock/Getty Images Plus; **550** *top* urbancow/E+/Getty Images; *bottom* IngaNielsen/iStock/Getty Images Plus; **551** *top* pioneer111/iStock/Getty Images Plus; *bottom* OnstOn/iStock/Getty Images Plus; **555** *top* asiseeit/iStock/Getty Images Plus; *bottom* monkeybusinessimages/iStock/Getty Images Plus

Chapter C

560 *top* zentilia/Shutterstock.com; *bottom* OnstOn/iStock/Getty Images Plus; **561** ©iStockphoto.com/Eric Isselée; **562** *a. left* ©iStockphoto.com/Shannon Keegan; *a. right* ©iStockphoto.com/Lorelyn Medina; *b. left* Joel Sartore/joelsartore.com; *b. right* Feng Yu/Shutterstock.com; *c. left* ©iStockphoto.com/kledge; *c. right* ©iStockphoto.com/spxChrome; *d.* ©iStockphoto.com/Alex Slobodkin; **563** 3bugsmom/iStock/Getty Images Plus; **564** sihuo0860371/iStock/Getty Images Plus; **566** macrovector/iStock/Getty Images Plus; **567** amwu/iStock/Getty Images Plus; **568** smontgom65/iStock Editorial/Getty Images Plus; **569** *top* DonNichols/E+/Getty Images; *bottom* BanksPhotos/iStock/Getty Images Plus; **570** RKaulitzki/iStock/Getty Images Plus; **572** zrfphoto/iStock/Getty Images Plus; **573** EVAfotografie/iStock/Getty Images Plus; **574** MariaBobrova/iStock/Getty Images Plus; **578** Aneese/iStock/Getty Images Plus; **579** EricFerguson/E+/Getty Images; **580** *top* Geerati/iStock/Getty Images Plus; *bottom* zhuzhu/iStock/Getty Images Plus; **584** ©iStockphoto.com/Rawpixel Ltd; **586** *right* rrocio/E+/Getty Images; *left* bdspn/iStock/Getty Images Plus; **587** OnstOn/iStock/Getty Images Plus; **589** DragonImages/iStock/Getty Images Plus; **591** funduck/iStock/Getty Images Plus; **595** Peter zijlstra/Shutterstock.com

Chapter D

596 *top* zentilia/Shutterstock.com; *bottom* OnstOn/iStock/Getty Images Plus; **597** peepo/E+/Getty Images; **599** *top* MichaelJay/iStock/Getty Images Plus; *bottom* urbancow/E+/Getty Images, johan10/iStock/Getty Images Plus, junce/iStock/Getty Images Plus; **603** *left* Mechanik/Shutterstock.com; *bottom right* mehmettorlak/E+/Getty Images; **604** *Exercise 6* ©iStockphoto.com/zentillia; *Exercise 7* Mr Doomits/Shutterstock.com; *Exercise 8* Nikolamirejovska/Shutterstock.com; *Exercise 9* ©iStockphoto.com/ALEAIMAGE; *Exercise 10* ©iStockphoto.com/iLexx; *Exercise 11* saicle/iStock/Getty Images Plus; *Exercise 12* boggy22/iStock/Getty Images Plus; *Exercise 13* wragg/iStock/Getty Images Plus; **605** *Exercise 17* akiyoko/iStock/Getty Images Plus; *Exercise 18* ZargonDesign/E+/Getty Images; *bottom* Inok/iStock/Getty Images Plus; **606** *left* ©iStockphoto.com/HultonArchive; *right* Dimedrol68/iStock/Getty Images Plus; **610** *top* trekandshoot/iStock/Getty Images Plus; *bottom* StockPhotoAstur/iStock/Getty Images Plus; **611** *Exercise 1* SergeBogomyako/iStock/Getty Images Plus; *Exercise 2* MileA/iStock/Getty Images Plus; *Exercise 7* ©iStockphoto.com/zentillia; *Exercise 8* boygovideo/iStock/Getty Images Plus; *Exercise 9* prmustafa/iStock/Getty Images Plus; *Exercise 10* ©iStockphoto.com/subjug; *Exercise 11* kulykt/iStock/Getty Images Plus; *Exercise 12* ©iStockphoto.com/7nuit; **618** ©iStockphoto.com/Scott Slattery; **623** asbe/iStock/Getty Images Plus; **624** Gino Santa Maria/Shutterstock.com; **626** Bliznetsov/E+/Getty Images; **633** mountainpix/Shutterstock.com; **634** ©iStockphoto.com/Jorgen Jacobsen; **635** OnstOn/iStock/Getty Images Plus; **637** *Exercise 3* ©iStockphoto.com/DivaNir4A; *Exercise 4* ©iStockphoto.com/Stacey Walker; *Exercise 5* JuSun/E+/Getty Images; *Exercise 6* simonkr/iStock/Getty Images Plus; *bottom* wrangel/iStock/Getty Images Plus; **638** StevenEllingson/iStock/Getty Images Plus; **640** Kalamazoo (Michigan) Public Library

Chapter E
644 *top* zentilia/Shutterstock.com; *bottom* OnstOn/iStock/Getty Images Plus; **645** tropper2000/iStock/Getty Images Plus; **646** ©iStockphoto.com/Remigiusz Załucki; **650** *left* Bob the Wikipedian/CC-BY-SA-3.0; *right* ©iStockphoto.com/Sherwin McGehee; **652** *top right* mihmihmal/iStock/Getty Images Plus; *center* kriangkrai_net/iStock/Getty Images Plus; *bottom left* ©iStockphoto.com/stevanovicigor; **656** Tsekhmister/iStock/Getty Images Plus; **658** *top* ©iStockphoto.com/Tomasz Pietryszek; *Exercise 17* 10174593_258/iStock/Getty Images Plus; *Exercise 19* Newcastle Drum Centre; *bottom* ©iStockphoto.com/scol22; **659** *left* ©iStockphoto.com/Luke Daniek; *right* vichie81/iStock Editorial/Getty Images Plus; **662** hxdyl/iStock/Getty Images Plus; **668** EuToch/iStock/Getty Images Plus; **674** Vladone/iStock/Getty Images Plus; **676** *top* ©iStockphoto.com/ranplett, Image © Courtesy of Museum of Science, Boston; *bottom* ©iStockphoto.com/Yails; **680** yocamon/iStock Editorial/Getty Images Plus; **682** *Exercise 17* ©iStockphoto.com/AlexStar; *Exercise 18* Knartz/Shutterstock.com; *Exercise 19* SOMMAI/Shutterstock.com; *Exercise 25* ©iStockphoto.com/Frank Wright; *bottom* 7activestudio/iStock/Getty Images Plus; **683** OnstOn/iStock/Getty Images Plus; **686** lucagal/iStock/Getty Images Plus; **687** Wimage72/iStock/Getty Images Plus; **688** Tevarak/iStock/Getty Images Plus; **690** ra-design/Shutterstock.com

Cartoon illustrations: Tyler Stout
Design Elements: ©iStockphoto.com/Gizmo; Valdis Torms; Juksy/iStock/Getty Images Plus

Mathematics Reference Sheet

Conversions

U.S. Customary
1 foot = 12 inches
1 yard = 3 feet
1 mile = 5280 feet
1 acre = 43,560 square feet
1 cup = 8 fluid ounces
1 pint = 2 cups
1 quart = 2 pints
1 gallon = 4 quarts
1 gallon = 231 cubic inches
1 pound = 16 ounces
1 ton = 2000 pounds
1 cubic foot ≈ 7.5 gallons

U.S. Customary to Metric
1 inch = 2.54 centimeters
1 foot ≈ 0.3 meter
1 mile ≈ 1.61 kilometers
1 quart ≈ 0.95 liter
1 gallon ≈ 3.79 liters
1 cup ≈ 237 milliliters
1 pound ≈ 0.45 kilogram
1 ounce ≈ 28.3 grams
1 gallon ≈ 3785 cubic centimeters

Time
1 minute = 60 seconds
1 hour = 60 minutes
1 hour = 3600 seconds
1 year = 52 weeks

Temperature
$$C = \frac{5}{9}(F - 32)$$
$$F = \frac{9}{5}C + 32$$

Metric
1 centimeter = 10 millimeters
1 meter = 100 centimeters
1 kilometer = 1000 meters
1 liter = 1000 milliliters
1 kiloliter = 1000 liters
1 milliliter = 1 cubic centimeter
1 liter = 1000 cubic centimeters
1 cubic millimeter = 0.001 milliliter
1 gram = 1000 milligrams
1 kilogram = 1000 grams

Metric to U.S. Customary
1 centimeter ≈ 0.39 inch
1 meter ≈ 3.28 feet
1 kilometer ≈ 0.62 mile
1 liter ≈ 1.06 quarts
1 liter ≈ 0.26 gallon
1 kilogram ≈ 2.2 pounds
1 gram ≈ 0.035 ounce
1 cubic meter ≈ 264 gallons

Number Properties

Commutative Properties of Addition and Multiplication
$a + b = b + a$
$a \cdot b = b \cdot a$

Associative Properties of Addition and Multiplication
$(a + b) + c = a + (b + c)$
$(a \cdot b) \cdot c = a \cdot (b \cdot c)$

Addition Property of Zero
$a + 0 = a$

Multiplication Properties of Zero and One
$a \cdot 0 = 0$
$a \cdot 1 = a$

Multiplicative Inverse Property
$n \cdot \frac{1}{n} = \frac{1}{n} \cdot n = 1, n \neq 0$

Distributive Property:
$a(b + c) = ab + ac$
$a(b - c) = ab - ac$

Properties of Equality

Addition Property of Equality
If $a = b$, then $a + c = b + c$.

Subtraction Property of Equality
If $a = b$, then $a - c = b - c$.

Multiplication Property of Equality
If $a = b$, then $a \cdot c = b \cdot c$.

Division Property of Equality
If $a = b$, then $a \div c = b \div c, c \neq 0$.

Squaring both sides of an equation
If $a = b$, then $a^2 = b^2$.

Cubing both sides of an equation
If $a = b$, then $a^3 = b^3$.

Properties of Inequality

Addition Property of Inequality
 If $a > b$, then $a + c > b + c$.

Subtraction Property of Inequality
 If $a > b$, then $a - c > b - c$.

Multiplication Property of Inequality
 If $a > b$ and c is positive, then $a \cdot c > b \cdot c$.
 If $a > b$ and c is negative, then $a \cdot c < b \cdot c$.

Division Property of Inequality
 If $a > b$ and c is positive, then $a \div c > b \div c$.
 If $a > b$ and c is negative, then $a \div c < b \div c$.

Properties of Exponents

Product of Powers Property: $a^m \cdot a^n = a^{m+n}$

Quotient of Powers Property: $\dfrac{a^m}{a^n} = a^{m-n}, a \neq 0$

Power of a Power Property: $(a^m)^n = a^{mn}$

Power of a Product Property: $(ab)^m = a^m b^m$

Zero Exponents: $a^0 = 1, a \neq 0$

Negative Exponents: $a^{-n} = \dfrac{1}{a^n}, a \neq 0$

Slope

$m = \dfrac{\text{rise}}{\text{run}}$

$= \dfrac{\text{change in } y}{\text{change in } x}$

$= \dfrac{y_2 - y_1}{x_2 - x_1}$

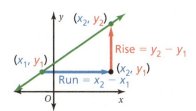

Pythagorean Theorem

$a^2 + b^2 = c^2$

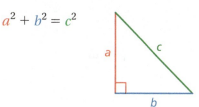

Converse of the Pythagorean Theorem

If the equation $a^2 + b^2 = c^2$ is true for the side lengths of a triangle, then the triangle is a right triangle.

Equations of Lines

Slope-intercept form
 $y = mx + b$

Standard form
 $Ax + By = C, A \neq 0, B \neq 0$

Point-slope form
 $y - y_1 = m(x - x_1)$

Angles of Polygons

Interior Angle Measures of a Triangle

$x + y + z = 180$

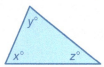

Interior Angle Measures of a Polygon

The sum S of the interior angle measures of a polygon with n sides is $S = (n - 2) \cdot 180°$.

Circumference and Area of a Circle

$C = \pi d$ or $C = 2\pi r$

$A = \pi r^2$

$\pi \approx \dfrac{22}{7}$, or 3.14

Surface Area

Prism

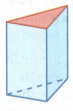

$S = 2\ell w + 2\ell h + 2wh$

S = areas of bases + areas of lateral faces

Pyramid

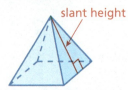

S = area of base + areas of lateral faces

Cylinder

$S = 2\pi r^2 + 2\pi rh$

Volume

Prism

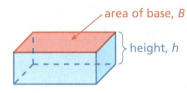
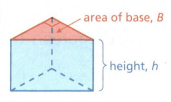

$V = Bh$

$V = Bh$

Pyramid

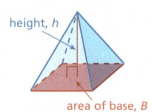

$V = \dfrac{1}{3}Bh$

Cylinder

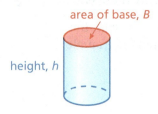

$V = Bh = \pi r^2 h$

Cone

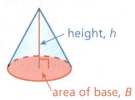

$V = \dfrac{1}{3}Bh = \dfrac{1}{3}\pi r^2 h$

Sphere

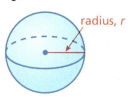

$V = \dfrac{4}{3}\pi r^3$

Simple Interest

Simple interest formula

$I = Prt$